3i

*fifty years
investing
in industry*

fifty years investing in industry

Richard Coopey
& Donald Clarke

Oxford   New York

OXFORD UNIVERSITY PRESS

1995

Oxford University Press, Walton Street, Oxford OX2 6DP

Oxford   New York
Athens   Auckland   Bangkok   Bombay
Calcutta   Cape Town   Dar es Salaam   Delhi
Florence   Hong Kong   Istanbul   Karachi
Kuala Lumpur   Madras   Madrid   Melbourne
Mexico City   Nairobi   Paris   Singapore
Taipei   Tokyo   Toronto

and associated companies in
Berlin Ibadan

Oxford is a trade mark of Oxford University Press

Published in the United States
by Oxford University Press Inc., New York

British Library Cataloguing in Publication Data
Data available

Library of Congress cataloguing in Publication Data
Data available

ISBN 0–19–828944–8

Designed by First Edition, London

Typeset by Create Publishing Services Ltd, Bath

Printed in Great Britain
on acid-free paper by The Bath Press, Avon

Acknowledgements

MANY PEOPLE HAVE BEEN generous with their time in helping to write the 3i history. Christabelle Biggs deserves special thanks for her enthusiastic contribution in compiling statistics, co-ordinating the project and advising on the text. The authors would also like to acknowledge the help and advice in steering the book towards completion received from Terry Gourvish, Director of the London School of Economics Business History Unit, David Kynaston, and from 3i, John Platt and Chris Woodward. Numerous 3i employees, past and present, and others provided valuable information and opinions. In particular we would like to thank Eric Barton, Alan Butt-Philip, Viscount Caldecote, Ted Cole, Sir John Cuckney, Mary Francis, Jon Foulds, Marc Gillespie, Frank Harber, Paul Hildesley, John Kirkpatrick, Philip MacKenzie–Ross, David Marlow, Alan Martin, Derek Millard, Roger Plant, Lord Richardson, Derek Sach, Lord Sherfield, Robert Smith, Richard Summers, Larry Tindale, Sir David Walker, Michael Wolff, and Peter Wreford.

Graham Bannock, Bret Feigh, Edwin Green, Janet Grenier, Les Hannah and Duncan Ross read parts of the manuscript and provided useful comments. The authors were also dependent on numerous archive collections and would particularly like to thank the Bank of England, the National Library of Scotland, the Bank of Scotland and Midland Bank for allowing access to material. A number of staff at 3i were also very helpful in compiling information, offering advice or typing manuscripts, including Elissa Armstrong, Carol Brennan, Gail Croston, Gillian Graystone, and Siobhan Heath.

The opinions expressed and conclusions drawn in this book are entirely those of the authors, and are not necessarily shared by 3i.

Contents

Introduction

THE STORY OF BRITISH INDUSTRY is one of continual tension between those who run it, those in the City who finance it, and those in government who try to influence it. All three have their own agenda and rarely, if ever, have they been able to agree on a common national purpose. This inherent conflict has led to many invidious comparisons with those apparently more successful countries—Germany, Japan, France among others—whose approach to economic management has arguably involved consensus rather than conflict, planning rather than pragmatism, and, underlying it all, a sense of national purpose.

The authors' objective in writing about 3i is to shed some light on a corner of the British industrial story which deserves to be better known and understood because though unfamiliar to many, the institution we describe has for fifty years been at the heart of British economic life. From that position it has been possible to observe and understand many of the difficulties which have bedevilled industry in its quest for support. Seeking always to make an acceptable return for its shareholders as a private sector institution, 3i has nevertheless carried out a function of national significance, intermediating between small- and medium-sized business, City and government. We believe our story shows that the sense of national purpose so visible elsewhere has been successfully demonstrated in the United Kingdom by 3i but, exceptionally, this mission has been accompanied by commercial success and thus without cost to either government or shareholders.

The institution, established initially as the Industrial and Commercial Finance Corporation and commonly known by its initials, has come a long way since its origins in the aftermath of the Second World War, although it has never lost sight of its original purpose—to serve the small- and medium-sized company sector by providing the long-term and permanent capital which larger companies were able to raise through the capital markets. In the fifty years since its formation it has provided investment capital to over 11,000 businesses, whilst in 1991 it was estimated that some 10 per cent of all manufacturing workers in Britain were employed by companies financed by 3i. Beyond the sheer number of investments its concentration on the long-term and, particularly, permanent funding of industry has answered the popular indictment of the financial sector's short-termism, its aversion to risk and its neglect of British industry in general and the small and medium sector in particular. 3i's portfolio is thus characterized by long-term investments, often equity-related and essentially permanent, a disproportionate number of them in the manufacturing sector, despite its general decline. Small- and medium-sized firms have featured prominently throughout its history, including many new and early stage businesses which have gone on to symbolize entrepreneurial success: Oxford Instruments in the scientific sector and Phileas Fogg (Derwent Valley Foods) in the consumer field are good examples, though few names are so familiar. Its presence among the major financial institutions is now well established and on its flotation in July 1994 3i ranked among the largest companies in Britain; but from an early date its operations have been regionally orientated and in addition to the branch network which spans Britain, the Group has expanding international operations in continental Europe.

How uncertain beginnings led to the successful, confident 3i of the 1990s is a story which reflects the efforts of key individuals, but it must also be set in the changing context of the financial and economic environment of postwar Britain. When it was founded, ICFC was envisaged as a belated response to the Macmillan Committee's report of 1931. The so-called Macmillan gap had by 1945 become a common expression, encompassing the persistent failure of the financial markets and banking system in Britain to provide long-term investment funds to smaller- and medium-sized companies. However, ICFC and its sister organization Finance Corporation for Industry (FCI) were only established after a great deal of debate among government officials and bankers about the nature, size and scope of any new initiative and indeed in some quarters even about the need for it. This debate continued during the Corporation's early years and under the stewardship of Lord Piercy and John Kinross the 1940s and 1950s were characterized by struggle, improvisation and a striking degree of financial entrepreneurship. But also during this period were forged the investment techniques, combining equity with loans whenever possible, and the industrial expertise which its founders saw as critical to ICFC's success.

The 1960s were years when ICFC grew steadily, constructing a national branch network in order to exploit regional opportunities. At the same time began the diversification into related areas and the move to independence in the financing of new investment. But it was a difficult passage, in the face of an economic environment which adversely affected both the size and the performance of its portfolio.

However, building on the base established by its founders, ICFC entered a phase of consolidation, as it moved into the 1970s, marked by a new degree of professionalism and training within the organization. The merger with FCI at this time, to become Finance for Industry (FFI), prefigured the more thoroughgoing changes of the 1980s but also enabled the turbulent 1970s to be weathered successfully, thanks not least to the long-term stability of its portfolio, largely insulated from the shocks of capital market instability, but also to increased fund-raising capacity, improved marketing, and the maintenance of high standards in the choice, negotiation, and monitoring of investments.

In the 1980s the axioms of 1945 were fundamentally challenged for the first time and policies aimed at fostering an 'enterprise culture' reshaped ownership patterns, encouraging the free play of market forces. In relaunching itself as Investors in Industry, formally abbreviated to 3i, the Group reacted to changes in the economy and the challenge of a new competitive financial environment, embodied in the nascent venture capital sector: in particular it pioneered and continued to lead the field in management buy-outs and later management buy-ins, seen by many as the epitome of entrepreneurial liberation. 3i was also at the centre of venture capital's personnel network, its comprehensive training programmes indirectly fuelling the expansion of new captive and independent funds. But again, as in previous decades, the 1980s were not easy and ended with a painful slimming down of the business as new foundations were laid for the flotation which finally took place in 1994.

The expansion of 3i's ownership brought about by its Stock Exchange flotation brings this unusual institution into yet another phase of development, prompting reflection on the changes which have occurred since 1945. Retrospection sheds light on many key issues in the history of British industrial investment in the post-war era: the role of the clearing banks, the Bank of England, and the City generally in responding to the needs of industry for external funding, the impact of venture capital, the significance of the small business sector in the economy and the problems it faced, all feature strongly in different periods of 3i's history. In writing its story over the past 50 years the authors have tried to illuminate these issues and give them sharper focus by approaching them from different points of view. Part One, written by Richard Coopey, represents an economic and social historian's perspective on the history of the Group, based on archival sources and oral accounts. The second part of the book, written by Donald Clarke, consists of a set of essays on aspects of 3i's business from the point of view of one who was closely involved, initially as a branch manager in the investment operation and then, for 23 years until he retired as Finance Director in 1991, in the strategic and financial direction of 3i, as well as in its external relations with government and the City. In juxtaposing these two approaches, we hope that the book will be accessible both to the general reader, interested in the history and the impact of this very important British institution, and to those, already familiar with 3i, who seek an insight into its inner dynamics.

We have also sought to illustrate this dual narrative in a number of ways which we believe are relevant to the understanding of an unusual institution. Despite its devotion to an ideal of service to the small- and medium-sized business, there has always been a healthy leavening of irreverence in 3i: a scorn for the leaden-footed interventionism of government, matched by scepticism about the good intentions of the City. The inclusion of a series of cartoons from the ever-popular 3i Calendar is intended not only to provide relief from the tedium of our argument but also to convey something of this iconoclastic tradition. The same purpose lies behind the reproduction of advertisements which over the years have attempted not only to declaim the serious purpose of 3i's investment activity but also to illustrate the genuine sympathy of its relations with the smaller end of industry.

Finally, but importantly, we have included a series of case studies illustrating particular aspects of 3i's investment method, aiming to give due weight to the relationship with its customers without distracting attention from the main narrative. By these varied means we hope to give readers some insight into a unique and very successful British institution and an appreciation of the pioneering spirit, sense of mission and long-term commitment to the small business sector which have characterized the first fifty years. For a pointer to the direction this remarkable institution will take as it enters its second half-century we are grateful to Ewen Macpherson, the present Chief Executive, who has provided the closing chapter.

September 1994   RICHARD COOPEY
                                                         DONALD CLARKE

Part One

A Historian's View

by Richard Coopey

Chapter 1

Identifying the Gap:
The Origins of 3i

THE RELATIONSHIP BETWEEN the finance sector and British industry has come
under a great deal of scrutiny during the twentieth century. As the British economy, pre-eminent in the nineteenth century, has been overtaken
by successive rivals, so questions about the role of the banks and
capital market in this relative decline have been repeatedly
posed. There are, to be sure, a range of other candidates for the
post of chief scapegoat—including a growing anti-industrial
culture, the costs of being the first industrial power, overseas
involvement and the legacy of empire, a history of adversarial
industrial relations, and a general demise of scientific and tech-
nical literacy. Nevertheless the City, which has become colloquial shorthand
for the financial system in Britain, remains one of the most prominent targets
for criticism.

Many of the broader explanations for problems in the British economy
can be encapsulated within a criticism of the functioning of the financial system
—a bias against industry and technology, and overseas priorities for investment, for example. There are other specific features generated by the peculiar
structure and functioning of the system which have also been highlighted,
however. Notable among these are accusations of short-termism, the failure of
investing institutions to forge close links with industry, the lack of funding
available to small- and medium-sized enterprises and a debilitating preoccupa-
tion with liquidity and security. These accusations apply in varying degrees to
the banks, other investment institutions, and the capital market.

3i owes its origins to these general criticisms. The findings of the
Macmillan Committee, in the depression years of the early 1930s, identified a
particular flaw in the system which denied small- and medium-sized firms
access to long-term capital. During the reconstruction phase at the end of the
Second World War these findings were to re-emerge; they were given a new

urgency as solutions were sought to the expected problems of transition to a peacetime economy, and as criticism of the finance system was reawakening. The respondents in this process—political parties, government departments, and the banks—all had a role in shaping 3i's predecessor institutions. In order to understand the way in which the Group has subsequently developed, and to assess its effectiveness in ameliorating the alleged shortcomings of the finance system, we must therefore begin in 1945.

Shaping ICFC

As Britain's economy faced the transition from wartime to peacetime activity, two completely new financial institutions were established. The Finance Corporation for Industry (FCI) was set up to provide capital in larger amounts to facilitate the rationalization of key sectors of British industry. The second institution, the Industrial and Commercial Finance Corporation (ICFC) was to provide 'credit' in the form of loans 'or the subscription of loan or share capital or otherwise', in amounts between £5,000 and £200,000, to smaller- and medium-sized enterprises. FCI was to be supported, principally in the form of debt, to a limit of £125 million by a large number of City institutions, mainly insurance funds. ICFC, on the other hand, was to be exclusively funded by the major clearing banks and the Bank of England, who collectively agreed to provide share and loan capital to £45 million.

From the moment that the establishment of these two institutions was announced by the Chancellor of the Exchequer, they were taken to be a direct, if belated, response to the Macmillan gap—a perceived failure by the banks and capital markets to supply long-term funds to key sectors of industry, and small- and medium-sized firms in particular. The gap was so called after the 1931 Report of the Committee on Finance and Industry, which had been chaired by Lord Macmillan. The establishment of ICFC was particularly closely linked to the Committee's recommendations.[1]

The nature of their announcement, and the circumstances surrounding the establishment of these two new institutions in 1945, meant that they were largely seen to be a government initiative. This is perhaps not surprising given that 1945 was a key moment in terms of state intervention in the economy. Keynesian demand management and a mixed economy were very much on the agenda at the end of the war, and the Labour government of Clement Attlee would soon embark on a radical programme of extending nationalization and constructing the welfare state. Yet ICFC and FCI were, in fact, firmly rooted in the private sector—at the time of their formation even the Bank of England had yet to be nationalized. Despite this, they were seen to be a response to a national economic need—a concerted response, by institutions which had been greatly criticized in the past, to a problem which was as much political as economic.

To understand precisely how this unity of action came about, and how the decisions over the ownership, structure, and market of ICFC and FCI were formulated we need to look carefully at the forces which were working to rebuild the post-war British economy, and how competing groups negotiated around the central tenets of intervention versus the free market. By understanding the processes which initially shaped FCI and in particular ICFC, since its influence was to prove considerably greater—the processes which determined their ownership and degree of autonomy—we will begin to shed light upon the subsequent history of the organization, and understand the fundamental characteristics of the group which was to emerge in the 1980s as 3i.

1945: Answers to the Problems of the 1930s

During the latter phases of the Second World War, as reconstruction and conversion to peacetime production began to be contemplated, many began to anticipate, and to fear, a return to the conditions of the 1930s. It was widely thought that the rearmament of the later 1930s had been largely instrumental in pulling the economy out of the worst depression so far experienced. It is not surprising, then, that the tentative solutions to the problems of the 1930s, untried in any real sense at the time, should come back into focus as reconstruction was planned. As the depression had deepened in the early 1930s, so debate had intensified over the causes of, and possible remedies for, protracted economic failure. This debate included the fundamental question of market forces versus some form of state intervention, and in this context attention began to be focused upon the working of the financial system in Britain.

The Committee on Finance and Industry was set up in November 1929, five months after the election of MacDonald's Labour government, to inquire into 'banking, finance and credit' in Britain. The Macmillan Committee, as it came to be known, was chaired by Lord Macmillan and included Reginald MacKenna, John Maynard Keynes, and Ernest Bevin. In spite of the wide-ranging remit of the committee and the breadth of its final report, it became principally remembered for its identification of the Macmillan gap—a chronic shortage of long-term investment capital for small- and medium-sized enterprises. No particular group of credit institutions was singled out as being responsible for this problem; the Committee chose instead to highlight the inability of smaller enterprises to go to the capital market. The expense of a public issue below £200,000 was deemed to be prohibitive in proportion to the capital raised. In addition there was no effective secondary market for such small issues.

The Macmillan Committee's solution to this problem was to recommend the formation of a company 'to devote itself particularly to these smaller industrial and commercial issues'. The proposed company would, in addition to its ordinary capital, issue preference share capital backed by the debentures or shares of the companies which it financed. Thus shares in the proposed company would enjoy a wide market based on a pooling of the risks involved in financing a large number of smaller enterprises. In this way the company would serve as an intermediary between small investors and small- and medium-sized industrial borrowers.[2]

Despite these recommendations, and subsequent publicity, it should be noted that the Macmillan Committee inquiry itself paid no particular attention to the question of the provision of finance for smaller firms. Little of the evidence presented to the Committee referred directly to this subject, the main exception being that of the National Chamber of Trade (NCT). In his testimony, Sir William Perring of the NCT criticized the centralization of British banking, pointing to the erosion of local managers' autonomy and the failure to exploit local knowledge.[3] The bulk of the Macmillan Committee's deliberations lay in a quite different direction, however. Much time was spent analysing international trade and the functioning of the gold standard. A great deal of emphasis was also placed on the need for rationalization in British industry, particularly in order to facilitate perceived economies of scale. In relation to this, British banks were unfavourably compared to those of many of the country's foreign competitors who were deemed to have much closer links with industry.[4] This is perhaps not surprising, given the nature of the crisis which the Committee was called upon to address. Nowhere in the report is the strategic importance of the small firm considered; indeed, it is by inference seen to be of no importance at all. The famous Macmillan gap is outlined in the very last paragraph (no. 404) of the report, with no specific reference to evidence collected, and it appears almost as an impressionistic afterthought.

Neither was there an immediate response to the findings of the Macmillan Committee. The most notable initiatives by the banking system of intervention to promote industrial rationalization in fact pre-date the Committee's report. The Bank of England had set up its Securities Management Trust (SMT) in November 1929 to co-ordinate its industrial investments. The Bankers Industrial Development Company (BIDC) had also been set up prior to the Committee's report. BIDC and SMT were both attempts to rationalize whole sectors, principally cotton and steel, using Bank of England funds in the case of SMT, and the funds of the Bank of England, the clearing banks, and other financial institutions in the case of BIDC.[5] Initiatives such as BIDC can be seen as an attempt, in the short term, to pre-empt recommendations for greater levels of what the Bank of England saw as 'political' intervention in directing investment. For example, the Governor of the Bank of England, Montagu Norman, in discussing BIDC 'feared that the government might step in to finance rationalisation and it seemed essential that means should be devised to avoid the need for their intervention'.[6] A similar dynamic, of 'great pressure from Downing Street', lay behind the proposal, in 1932 and again in 1934, to form an Industrial Mortgage Corporation (IMC).[7] In this initiative the Bank of England had one eye on the government and the other on the generally critical tone of popular opinion regarding the banks' role in the depression. Despite the exhortations of Norman that 'all banks should assist owing to the public criticism that has been levied against them in not assisting various industries', nothing came of the IMC proposals.[8]

These proposals, unlike the BIDC or SMT initiatives, would have had an impact on smaller- and medium-sized enterprises. Other institutions which were set up did favour this sector, although within a regional development framework. These included the Treasury Fund, the Nuffield Trust, and, perhaps the most important, the Special Areas Reconstruction Association (SARA). The latter organization was set up in 1935, capitalized by the City, insurance companies, and industrial companies in equal proportion. Again this was seen by the Bank of England as a pre-emptive move to offset greater government interference, and probably had only a marginal impact.[9]

There were two further institutions set up in the 1930s which claimed the parentage of the Macmillan Report. Credit For Industry (CFI) was set up by United Dominions Trust (UDT), itself 50 per cent owned by the Bank of England, to provide long-term loans of between £100 and £50,000, administered through UDT's national network. In appealing for the approval of the Bank of England UDT noted that: 'The company will specifically answer the requirements of the Macmillan Committee as laid down particularly in clause 404 . . . (and) will adequately answer any public or political criticism of the banking system.'[10] The second of these institutions, the Charterhouse Industrial Development Company (CID), was a subsidiary of Charterhouse Investment Trust. Shareholders included two of the clearing banks—Lloyds with 5 per cent and the Midland with 2 per cent—but Prudential Assurance had by far the largest shareholding.[11]

The rather chequered response to the Macmillan Committee does little to answer the question of the existence of a shortfall in the provision of long-term funds for small- and medium-sized firms. The Macmillan gap institutions, CFI and CID, were held by the Board of Trade at least, and later by the Bolton Committee inquiry into small firms, to have performed disappointingly throughout the 1930s, having little impact upon the overall demand for capital.[12] The clearing banks rejected the idea of a gap altogether, however, and continued to maintain that they provided adequate credit for small firms where levels of risk were not inappropriate. Indeed, the Board of Trade was later to note that during the 1930s the banks had done more for small business 'than is

11

commonly supposed'.[13] For the clearers the limited impact of CFI and CID were later to be held up as proof that no such gap existed.[14] Somewhat ironically, an indication of the banks' willingness to operate at this level can be gleaned from the complaint that the clearers frustrated CFI's business. It could do little to stop banks poaching its customers, being reliant on them for the provision of credit references only to find that 'many applicants have frequently been financed by the bankers after the proposals have been examined and vetted by CFI'.[15]

Recent work by Ross tends to support the clearing banks' own claims that, within their acceptable field of risk, they provided adequately for small- and medium-sized firms.[16] The problem was, and remains, that small firms often stand outside the parameters of what might be termed orthodox risk. Given that they are likely to be seeking funds for expansion, they are probably less able to cope with heavy initial debt burdens, a problem compounded by the fact that these frequently carry comparatively high interest rates in order to reflect lenders' perceptions of greater risk levels. In addition, many smaller firms have difficulty finding the required levels of security demanded.

Other sources of capital besides the clearing banks and specialist institutions were effectively closed off to smaller firms during the inter-war period. Investment trusts did little for this sector, whilst insurance companies and merchant banks had from the 1920s been investing in British industry, but only above a certain threshold.[17] Where such institutions did invest smaller amounts, say £5,000, they were reluctant to provide more than 5 per cent of the borrowing required. Thus a multiplier came into effect which disqualified firms seeking, in this example, less than £100,000 in total borrowing. The rise and increasing dominance of institutional lenders standing as intermediaries between savers and borrowers had replaced localized investors in small enterprises in a trend which complemented the centralization of banking and stock exchanges into the twentieth century. ICFC's future first Chairman, William Piercy, commented on this trend in the late 1930s, noting that although the upper threshold of the Macmillan gap had been reduced by increased activity in the new issue market, the gap still remained.[18]

The clearers sought to deny their role in this process and, given the endemic poverty of statistics and the counter-factual nature of the question, it remains unestablished whether or not the Macmillan gap was myth or reality in the 1930s. As Sir Otto Niemeyer, Deputy Governor of the Bank of England, was to note in 1944: 'Whether or not the Banks have in the past in fact filled the need, as they maintain . . . is an opinion hardly capable of proof'.[19] What is not in doubt, however, is that the impression was growing in some circles that there was a gap, as part of a wider critique that the clearing banks were somehow failing British industry in the 1930s. This must be set against a growing belief in a new political economy of intervention in finance and industry. The

Macmillan Report can be viewed as representative of this trend, being heavily influenced by Keynes's own presence on, and perhaps dominance of, the Committee. The response to calls for a rejection of the axioms of *laissez-faire* was limited in pre-war Britain—there was no attempt to emulate America's New Deal, for example. Yet the marginal initiatives such as BIDC and SARA arguably prepared the ground for later post-1945 measures when more interventionist ideas were to come into their own. The 1930s also set the scene for the Bank of England's pre-emptive strategies to head off government intervention by cajoling the private sector into measured responses, such as BIDC and SARA, which were to be repeated in 1945. The Bank of England was in fact destined to play a central role within a group of forces which determined the form which ICFC and FCI took in 1945.

Reconstruction and Small Firm Finance

Ideas which were gaining ground in the 1930s were forced onto the agenda during the war. Government intervention in industry had accelerated through the rearmament process and dominated all aspects of production during the war itself.[20] Early in the war, and intensifying from around 1942 onwards, serious consideration began to be given to post-war problems. Many saw this as an opportunity to consolidate the initiatives which had been made necessary by the exigencies of war, rather than attempt a return to business as usual, as had happened in 1918.

A Party Political Initiative?

The Labour Party, on the face of things, seems central to the story of ICFC. Attlee came to power in 1945, the year of ICFC's formation, pledged to undertake radical reforms of the economy including nationalization of the Bank of England and key industries, within a general policy framework aimed at maintaining full employment. The first Chairman of ICFC was William Piercy—created Lord Piercy by Attlee in November 1945. He had been the personal assistant to Attlee during the war, and a prominent member of XYZ, an advisory group of Labour sympathizers in the City.[21] ICFC was deemed from the beginning to have a 'distinct socialist aroma',[22] and the impression was formed in many minds, lasting well into the 1980s, that the Corporation was some form of quango.[23] It is surprising to find, therefore, that links between ICFC and Labour were at best indirect.

Labour's ideas on control of the economy had been the subject of vigorous debate throughout the 1930s, the key question being how a socialist government could control capitalism without replacing it as a system. Within this debate the financial institutions were often held to be particularly in need of

13

reform. Douglas Jay's comments in 1938 capture the flavour of what was by then a long-standing antagonism: 'Few in the City care whether it is socially desirable that this or that industry should be enabled to develop. Any such motive our financiers would regard as "political". Instead they stick to "business"—which means the attempt to outwit one's neighbour by cunning, luck, inside information, or the deliberate spreading of false rumours. Small wonder that scandals abound, savings are misinvested, and the small investor continually robbed.'[24]

Two elements of Labour's developing programme are of interest here—the proposal to set up a National Investment Board (NIB), and the proposal to nationalize the Bank of England and the clearing banks. The latter proposal became official policy in 1935, after discussions within the Party during the early 1930s which put 'control of the financial machine, of currency, banking and investment policy . . . in the forefront' of Labour's strategy to replace the 'chaotic muddle of private capitalism'.[25] The clearing banks were held to be particularly remiss in their failure to provide adequate support in depressed areas. This trenchant stance was short lived, however. By 1936 leading figures within the Party had doubts about direct control of the clearers. Hugh Dalton, for example, called nationalization 'bad politics, and at this stage unnecessary economics'.[26] By the time 'Labour's Immediate Programme' was published in 1937, bank nationalization proposals were limited to the Bank of England only. Subsequently nationalization of the clearers was never seriously considered.

Proposals to restrict nationalization within the financial sector solely to the Bank of England reflect a trend within Labour thinking away from ideas of micro-interventionism towards more general, indirect forms of control. The Bank of England, for example, was in a position to control general credit levels through the mechanism of the bank rate. Official Labour publications still posited wide-ranging powers; the 'Full Employment and Financial Policy' report of May 1944, for example, envisaged a Chancellor with statutory power 'to require any bank to lend him any sum he likes, for as long as he likes and on what terms he likes' to spend towards achieving full employment. Such vague proposals were more a reflection of the general imprecision of Labour's policy on financial machinery, however. In the decade before 1945 none of the Party's official publications contain any mention of the Macmillan gap or small-firm finance, or detailed outlines of the way financial institutions should function under socialist guidelines.

The major institutional proposal of the 1930s—the NIB—conforms to this pattern of generalization. Proposals began to emerge and form a consistent part of policy around 1935. The NIB was envisaged as an institution which would 'approve, and increasingly perhaps initiate, all important new capital issues'.[27] A NIB was advocated in the reconstruction policy section of 'Labour's Win the Peace Programme' in 1943 and in 'Let Us Win the Future', published in 1945. In that year Labour had a draft bill prepared to set up the NIB.[28] Behind the scenes, however, doubts were being expressed. Evan Durbin told Attlee in May 1944 that 'the time was scarcely ripe' for detailed plans 'since there is as yet no agreement on the desirability of creating a National Investment Board'.[29]

In the event the proposed NIB was not set up in 1945. Labour went instead for an immediate retention of wartime physical controls over man-power and materials. It had been pointed out that borrowing only accounted for a small proportion of total investment, perhaps as little as an eighth, the majority coming from retained profits and other internal funds. Physical con-trols such as those administered by the Board of Trade were seen, in the short term, as a more effective way of directing economic activity.[30] By the time these controls were dismantled, Labour had arguably abandoned direct intervention in favour of macro-economic management; and, as Tomlinson notes, this resulted in 'a displacement of the proposed role of the NIB onto fiscal policy'.[31]

It is tempting to see ICFC as a form of substitute for the stillborn NIB. Superficially there would seem to be a strong case for viewing the new Corporation as the result of lobbying by key Labour figures, operating within the Government machinery during the war. Dalton, Gaitskell, and Jay, for example, had all worked in the Board of Trade, where they pushed radical ideas against the conservatism of permanent officials.[32] The Board's influence in shaping ICFC may not have been very strong however, as we shall see below. Can a more direct case be made for the influence of the rather clandestine XYZ in the process, given that Piercy and James Lawrie, ICFC's first Chairman and General Manager respectively, were prominent and active members of this Labour Party think-tank?

In the early 1930s Dalton had formed a number of official committees within the Labour Party including the Finance and Trade Committee and the Reorganization of Industry Committee, but by 1932 some party advisers were still 'horrified by the Labour Party's ignorance of the City machinery and their complete lack of contacts with the banking world'.[33] The XYZ, founded in 1932, attracted figures such as Piercy who, in addition to being a socialist, was busy becoming a major financial figure.[34] The group surrounded itself in a shroud of secrecy from the beginning, keeping no minutes or permanent files, for example.

The influence of such think-tanks is always difficult to assess. If XYZ members discussed a proposed ICFC there are no records to substantiate this. It is perhaps easy to exaggerate the influence of XYZ, its covert nature arti-ficially enhancing its apparent importance. Certainly Dalton was not averse to mythologizing XYZ as his group of 'inside' City experts. He may have pre-ferred this to revealing the comparatively humble occupations of some of its participants, the majority of whom were accountants, statisticians, and financial journalists. Piercy was a substantial figure, but his involvement in ICFC seems to have begun after it was set up in 1945. Piercy's own XYZ files reveal that his contribution conformed to the group's involvement in quite detailed discussion along 'conventional' NIB lines.

That Piercy may have *operated* ICFC along lines compatible with Labour's policy goals is a different question, to which we shall return below. Here we must note that in a direct sense XYZ, in common with general 'official' Labour-party policy-makers, in fact had a very marginal influence on the formation of ICFC in 1945. Labour, as we have seen, had abandoned ideas of controlling the clearing banks by all but the most indirect means. Similarly, policy aimed at directing investment through an NIB had come to nothing. We are left, therefore, with the influence of Labour figures within the government machinery itself, particularly the Board of Trade, as perhaps the only direct participation in the formation of the Corporation.

State Intervention in the Finance of Industry

If Labour figures did have an influence within the Board of Trade this may have been in turn ineffective in contrast to the other major agents in the process, notably the Treasury, the Bank of England, and the clearing banks. ICFC's immediate genesis can be traced to the interplay of competing proposals between these organizations from 1943 onwards. Within Whitehall the precise origin occurs with the setting-up of the Committee on Post-War Employment (CPWE) in July 1943.[35] This committee was dominated by the Treasury's three representatives. They were not convinced that the time had come for direct governmental intervention in the economy; and thus when the Board of Trade, in common with the Economic Section of the War Cabinet, argued in favour of government participation in any post-war finance initiatives—either for the funding of new enterprises or to fund conversion from wartime activity—this was summarily rejected.

In putting forward proposals, the Board of Trade clearly accepted the reality of some form of Macmillan gap, citing the very high issue costs for any sum below £150,000, and a general shortage of provision below £200,000. Their recommended criteria for lending in this gap were fairly radical, implicitly rejecting the levels of security expected in 'normal' banking, and the Board went on to recommend lending based on people and experience. For them it was 'important that in this type of business the institution should pay at least as much attention to the personality of the applicant, his present trading methods and his prospect of success as to the pledging of collateral or past balance sheet statements'. This highly risky approach thus called for at least partial government underwriting, it was argued.[36] When this proposition proved untenable within the CPWE the Board of Trade proposed a compromise. They would support the formation of a 'private . . . Commercial

Corporation', but pressed for the right to see full details of all acceptances and rejections. In particular it was argued that it should be open to the Board to 'review the refusals'. The Board pictured itself picking winners among the 'enterprise and new blood' which commercial lending might not support, especially in areas where strategic technological advances might be funded, even at a commercial loss. In arguing this case the Board cited the case of interferometer development—uncommercial in the immediate sense, but a keystone technology for many other industrial processes.[37]

Though its proposals were rejected on numerous occasions as imposing a compromise on the commercial freedom of the proposed corporation, the Board of Trade pressed its case for participation throughout 1943 and 1944.[38] These ideas reached high places. In December 1944, when the Chancellor, Sir John Anderson, accepted the final proposals for ICFC, he notified the Governor of the Bank of England of his hope that the new institution would support 'new applicants whose past experience and record' would be adequate collateral, paraphrasing earlier Board of Trade proposals.[39] In addition, the Chancellor requested that 'every consideration' be given to applications from development areas. The Chancellor was, at this stage, only suggesting such preferential lending and was mindful of the sensitivity of this issue ('every consideration' had been changed in the Chancellor's memo from the original 'special attention'). The Board of Trade proposals may have had an indirect effect upon the way ICFC was to operate after 1945, but they were effectively squashed in favour of the commercial independence of the Corporation. In this the view of the Treasury prevailed, although it will be seen that this department of government also hoped to use ICFC indirectly to fulfil its own policy goals.

Whereas the Labour Party and the Board of Trade proposals were weakly put or marginalized, it is within a Treasury–Bank of England nexus that the real determinants of ICFC lie. While the CPWE was deliberating throughout 1943 and 1944, Treasury staff were in regular contact with officials at the Bank of England. The Bank had set up its own Committee on Post-War Domestic Finance (CPWDF) early in 1943 to consider the specific issue of setting up specialist post-war institutions. When the Whitehall CPWE issued its report, under the authorship of Sir Alan Barlow, the Joint Second Secretary to the Treasury, in January 1944, it bore the strong imprint of the Bank of England's recommendations. The expressed goal of the Treasury ran counter to that of the Bank, however, in that the former wanted the proposed institution to have 'close relations' with government. Sir Wilfred Eady, the other Second Secretary, had notified the Deputy Governor of the Bank of England just before the release of the Barlow Report that the two proposed new institutions should consider applications as much from the 'industrial side' as from the 'commercial side'. By this Eady meant that the proposed companies should operate within Treasury macro-economic goals of maintaining full employment. For FCI this meant a sectoral role in rationalizing specific sectors of industry. For ICFC it meant taking on the mantle of SARA and operating as much as possible in the 'development areas' where high levels of unemployment were expected to return after the war. It was suggested at one point that SARA staff should form the basis of the new company.[40] The apparent paradox in the Treasury's rejection of the Board of Trade suggestions for a policy orientated institution and simultaneous advocacy of an institution directly linked to regional policy can be explained in the way ICFC was envisaged to operate. It would not be constrained in terms of accepting business of a certain character or on uncommercial grounds; it would pick its own winners, but within areas broadly defined by the Treasury.

The Treasury recognized the delicate nature of negotiations at that stage and admitted that its 'association with ICFC cannot be an unveiled and open one as before with SARA'. Nevertheless, it viewed a close operating relationship as vital in order to tap City expertise. As Compton of the Treasury noted in June 1945, it 'will be so important to link us with ICFC, since God knows where we get the high grade staff from which we shall require if we don't'.[41] While the Treasury were making preparations to administer the Distribution of Industry Act in 1945 they were looking to ICFC to play the role of the 'standing investor to whom applicants can be referred and on whose judgement and integrity we can rely . . . the chosen instrument in the forthcoming new regime should clearly be the new ICFC'.[42] The Treasury recognized that ICFC's constitution would not formally include any obligation to give preference to development areas, but noted that 'it is launched under sufficiently public auspices to give us the right to rely on it'.[43] The Treasury saw an urgent need to incorporate ICFC 'for we cannot make any progress until its organization is in being and working arrangements have been made between our staff and ICFC's'. With this envisaged arrangement, the Treasury, in true generalist tradition,[44] could avoid the necessity of recruiting staff of what it saw as 'negotiating calibre'. 'We need not recruit staff who can judge business prospects for intending investors—such men are rare and cost a lot of money.'[45] Unlike the Board of Trade, which wanted to impose direct constraints on the private financial sector, the Treasury sought to use the available expertise, channelled into broad 'social' policy goals. That they were secretive in their dealings on this issue reflected the hostility to such plans among the clearing bankers whose capital was to fund the project.

Between the Treasury and the clearing bankers stood the Bank of England, the only participant which knew precisely what all the others were thinking, and in possession of its own agenda for ICFC. Fforde puts it succinctly in highlighting this episode as a case study 'of the way the Bank went about the business of overcoming reluctance in the City while calming a degree of over-enthusiasm in Whitehall'. [46]

The Origins of Paternal Control

The Bank of England began formally planning for the post-war period in March 1943 when it set up its Committee on Post-War Domestic Finance. Key figures in the Bank were unsure of the need for initiatives to extend to smaller firms, yet mindful of the political sensitivity of this issue. Senior Executive Sir Otto Niemeyer viewed the small-business community as 'Misfits . . . [who] have a political importance disproportionate to their real importance'. Similarly, Kenneth Peppiatt, the Bank's Chief Cashier referred to them as 'a small but noisy minority'. The CPWDF issued its first report in October 1943, proposing a single institution to cater for temporary finance for larger enterprises and long-term finance for smaller firms, with a nominal capital of £50 million.[47] The clearing banks were seen as the logical source for this capital 'given that events had enormously increased their assets' during the war.[48]

A copy of the CPWDF report went to the Treasury for discussion. That the Bank and the Treasury were in close contact on the issue during this period is exemplified in notes referring to a meeting between Eady of the Treasury and the Chairman and General Manager of the National Provincial (NP) in February 1944, when Eady 'more or less indicated unpleasant alternatives propounded by Whitehall, if the banks did not play'. Catterns, the Bank's Deputy Governor, noted that he 'knew that Eady was lunching at the NP and asked him to be careful'.[49] The Bank was effectively playing off the two sides against each other and acting as the broker between them. The Governor, Montagu Norman, wrote to Eady at the Treasury in December 1943, noting that 'any scheme is likely to be knocked about by the bankers as soon as they get the chance'. He wrote soon afterwards to Clarence Sadd of the Midland that the Bank's current proposals had 'the blessing of Whitehall and nothing short of it has . . . my purpose is to satisfy Whitehall: to keep them out of the Banking business and free of malevolence towards the Bankers—which at the moment are stakes worth playing for.'[50] To keep the clearing banks in line, some officials at the Bank of England went so far as to raise the spectre of public ownership: 'combination to finance the small man is something the Government (as advised by Whitehall) wants, and to give them what they want is surely less likely to lead to nationalization than to refuse them.'[51]

It is clear that the Bank saw it could not resist the initiatives from Whitehall, that something had to be done by the clearers, and whatever was done needed to be of sufficient scale and independence to satisfy public opinion. What the Bank did not want was the kind of intrusion proposed by the Board of Trade in directing investment towards chosen cases.[52] Still less did the Bank favour the Treasury's central aim, to link the new initiative to development-area policy, not least because this would frighten off the clearing banks. Catterns was explicit on this point: 'what does worry me is that if the Government are considering any announcement regarding special facilities for

'It all started years ago, down there by plant number one … when I found forty million pounds under a rock.'

so-called distressed areas and they were to couple this up with the bankers' scheme for small business the fat really would be in the fire.'[53] The best the Bank hoped for was that ICFC would provide a useful instrument to fend off what it saw as the depredations of Whitehall, at least in the short term. ICFC was never intended to become a permanent entity, merely a significant gesture to deal with one aspect of the immediate dislocation in economic activity expected after the cessation of hostilities. An indication of the Bank's somewhat duplicitous stance can be gleaned from the account of ICFC's formation given by John Kinross, one of the Company's founder employees and a central figure in its subsequent development. Kinross recalled that Niemeyer's 'wise and resolute intervention' was 'decisive' in establishing ICFC and keeping it going. Yet early in 1945 Niemeyer, in a private note, was less than resolute: 'As you know I don't believe in this body and hope (and expect) that they won't do much.'[54]

Nevertheless, the Bank had resolved that something had to be done—preferably something visible, in view of the perceived need for public appeal. Only some form of new institutional response would suffice, and this must be relatively independent of the clearers, though with their backing in the form of capital, and packaged for the general public so as to make it appear as if it was initiated voluntarily.[55]

ICFC's Reluctant Shareholders

By 1943 the 'big five' clearing banks, aware of the mounting criticism, had begun their own deliberations on possible initiatives for post-war finance for small firms. Some emerging suggestions were fairly elaborate. A paper was circulated at the Midland Bank, for example, advocating a 'special advances' corporation to pool risk involved in small to medium long-term lending. Each bank was to pass on high-risk proposals to this institution, which would also be funded by the Bank of England and the Treasury.[56] Some clearing-bank staff recognized that wartime had created unique problems of adjustment, particularly in terms of returning servicemen, but also that the experience of government intervention and control had significantly changed the ideological argument for supporting industry.[57] These were minority voices, however. There were vociferous detractors among the ranks of Chairmen and General Managers, who sought a return to business as usual, without the added burden of trying to operate outside the realm of 'traditional' business. This meant sticking to 'self-liquidating advances' and 'readily realizable securities'. Government-sponsored schemes would have them lending to 'the incompetent, the thriftless and the indolent, to say nothing of the unbusinesslike inventor, who are sadly apt to lose other people's money as well as their own'.[58] The idea that smaller firms which were inherently more risky should get preferential treatment in terms of rates on borrowing, effectively penalizing larger, well-established customers, also ran counter to banking logic. That the banks should provide capital for an independent company to lend money in this sector was clearly beyond the pale. The proposed scheme from the Bank of England was 'simply an attempt to placate political critics' to which the banks' response should be a firm negative—even if this meant 'some embarrassment on account of misunderstandings in political and other quarters'.[59]

There were some sections of opinion among the clearers which began to take a more pragmatic line, however, and by early 1944, following reports in the press that an initiative was definitely in the offing, voices were heard counselling some form of bank participation 'in order to satisfy public opinion and keep out non-banking advances from our balance sheet'.[60] Initially, the idea was presented to the Bank of England that each of the five major banks should set up its own subsidiary for small-firm finance. This was summarily rejected by the Bank as being inadequate, comprising 'five sheep wandering at random', none with any particular competence, and altogether lacking the publicity value of a single new institution.[61] The bankers capitulated and agreed to set up a committee of general managers to draft a blueprint for what was to become ICFC.[62]

The committee comprised A. W. Tuke (Barclays), R. A. Wilson (Lloyds), H. L. Rouse (Midland), Ernest Cornwall (National Provincial), and Charles Lidbury (Westminster). Lidbury placed himself in the vanguard of opposition to encroachment on the banks' traditional role, yet even he was forced to concede that the situation, what he termed 'the present political ferments', called for some response.[63] Even so, he continued to rail against what he considered to be an 'indirect levy on the resources of the commercial banks for the subsidising of commercial and industrial "adventures" in the interests of the "full employment" campaign . . . political losses will be borne by the banks'. Because he feared that it would not be possible to limit the activities of the proposed institution to those within the Macmillan gap, the banks must retain 'some *indirect* finger in the management'. Lidbury envisaged a bankers' advisory panel vetting all applications and ensuring that interest rates on lending did not fall below those charged to their own established customers.[64] Lidbury, as one of his contemporaries at the Bank of England later put it, 'at that time was the boss-cat of the clearing bank managers'[65] and, in this role, attempted to dominate the committee's deliberations.

However, there were others among the general managers who recognized the direction in which the tide was flowing and were less obstructive. Tuke of Barclays, for example, 'in spite of the discouraging result of appeasement in other fields' held that the banks should find the 'least objectionable' way to proceed. This meant that the banks must act independently since, in Tuke's mind, a government guarantee would mean a degree of government control. To offset more criticism of the banks, they should be 'as far as possible dissociated from the direction and management of (the company)' but 'some means of ensuring . . . effective control', not publicly visible, must be found. A central problem remained: that of securing the right calibre of management. Tuke could not imagine 'a man of capacity and assured position being prepared to link his fortunes with this new venture, the prospects of which are so extremely dubious'. Tuke's pragmatism stemmed partly from a belief that the Bank of England had gone over to the other side and was 'more nearly allied to the Government than to the clearing banks'.[66] He thus recommended that participation should be by the clearers alone. Tuke was not alone in his support. Wilson, of Lloyds, had written earlier of the need to recognize that wartime had brought about changes which would be permanent and that the banks ought to be 'willing to play'.[67]

Lidbury's response to these softer attitudes was unyielding. He refused to alter derogatory references to the State in the draft under preparation, and held to the view that the proposed corporation was entirely unnecessary.[68] The result was a proposal from the drafting committee which attempted to appease both camps. When this was presented to the Bank of England in May 1944 it provoked Montagu Norman's replacement as Governor, the recently appointed Lord Catto, to 'congratulate the drafter (or drafters); he has a sense of humour. First he has provided convincing evidence that a new institution is entirely unnecessary and then, after sleeping on that, he has clearly set out how it could be set up'.[69] This meeting proved to be the turning point. Catto framed the Bank's demands in lofty rhetoric, stating that he 'should like the great ideal to be attempted'. Fisher of Barclays restated the belief that the banks could do the job individually, but conceded that there might be a hidden advantage in supporting a new institution at one remove. 'If you have a separate company it does preserve the reputation of British Banking from the imputation that they are getting into a system of continental banking.'[70]

The Industrial and Commercial Finance Corporation

It only remained, after this meeting, to hammer out the final shape of ICFC, including the issues of the type of business to be undertaken by the new institution, Bank of England participation, nomination of directors, and levels and conditions attached to the subscription of loan and share capital. Tuke, of Barclays, urged that the proposed corporation 'contrary to our natural instincts as bankers' should subscribe for share capital wherever possible, in view of the fact that this was 'to some extent a philanthropic' proposition.[71] Debate also centred on the lower limit of operation. Tuke favoured no statutory restriction, whereas Lidbury, keen to obviate competition, wanted the threshold raised to £10,000.[72] The Scottish banks had argued throughout the process for their own separate institution, but in the event, following pressure from the Bank of England and Secretary of State for Scotland, they were prevailed upon to settle for a special Scottish Committee within ICFC.[73]

Debate continued over the role to be played by the Bank of England, and it was eventually agreed that it should provide a small percentage of capital. This did not reflect the scope of the Bank's continuing paternal influence, however, signalled at this stage by the right to appoint the Corporation's Chairman.[74] The final report of the drafting committee was ready in October 1944. The Bank and the clearers agreed to provide £15 million of share capital, £15 million of loan capital, and a pledge of another £15 million in loans dependent on certain conditions being met. This capital was to be drawn upon in instalments as needed and agreed by the shareholders. Unlike the Chairman, the rest of the Board were to be nominated by the major clearing banks. It only remained to choose a name for the new institution and, after the rejection of several unsuitable permutations, Industrial and Commercial Finance Corporation was agreed upon. The Bank of England Committee of Treasury agreed the proposals in November 1944, and ICFC was incorporated on 20 July 1945.

Guaranteeing the Autonomy of ICFC

Towards the end of the war a new spirit of planning and intervention to ensure full employment was emerging, partly as a result of the example of *dirigiste* wartime practice and partly because of a fear of a return to the depression of the 1930s. Within the general debate the financial system was of central importance. Yet general criticisms and proposals for wholesale replacement were not seriously advanced. Instead, the notion of market failure in the form of the Macmillan gap, whether of unsure provenance or not, held centre stage, and solutions to this particular problem, rather than structural reform, dominated policy formation.

As an amorphous consensus among government departments emerged around the Macmillan gap, a range of protagonists and antagonists of intervention made their case. It was precisely because of the conflicting interests of the various groups attempting to shape or frustrate new institutions during the reconstruction debates that ICFC was set up with enough independence to enable it to survive. What would appear to be the direct political dynamic behind the institution, notably plans formulated by the Labour Party since the mid-1930s, had in fact played a marginal role in its formation. Nevertheless, these plans had an important role in a negative sense, sustaining a general fear that greater intervention and control by government was on the way; and this eventually encouraged the banks to overcome their objections. That ICFC was not tied directly into the plans of the State, especially not those of the Board of Trade or the Treasury, was the result of the Bank of England's insistence on keeping the government at bay. Instead the Bank maintained that a private-sector institution, using the clearing banks' capital, could fulfil the role of providing finance for small firms in the difficult reconstruction period. However, because of the hostility expressed by the clearing banks to the fundamental principles of long-term industrial 'continental' banking, they in turn had to be compelled to participate, under threat of sterner action. This compulsion meant that ICFC had to be set up with enough freedom from interference by its own shareholders. The Bank of England was well aware of the continuing hostility among some of the bankers to the proposals, and that these banks envisaged that the Corporation would prove to be an ephemeral creation.

Most of the participants in the process, including the Bank of England, the Treasury, and the clearing banks, knew more clearly what they did not want than what they did. It was this indecision and mutual distrust which was to guarantee a significant degree of autonomy and protection for ICFC, creating a fortuitous space for the first Chairman of ICFC to mould the Corporation into a distinctive shape which was to form the basis of its longevity. ICFC would experience a difficult rite of passage in its early years as it struggled to establish a position in a largely untried field, against opposition and lack of support from some of the actors in the above process. With the protection of the Bank of England, however, and the flexibility allowed by its independence of ownership, the Corporation was to survive intact.

NOTES

[1] The public memorandum of the Committee of London Clearing Banks (CLCB) which outlined the form ICFC should take specifically detailed the findings of the Macmillan Committee, and subsequent accounts usually follow the same pattern. The Bolton Committee report of 1970 into small firms, for example, describes ICFC as 'a new institution specifically designed to fill the Macmillan gap'. *Report of the Committee of Inquiry on Small Firms*, Cmnd 4811 (1970), 154. A more recent account takes the same line, seeing ICFC as 'designed to close the Macmillan gap'; C. E. Heim, 'Limits to Intervention: The Bank of England and Industrial Diversification in the Depressed Areas', *Economic History Review*, 2nd ser. 37/4 (Nov. 1984), 534.

[2] *Report of the Committee on Finance and Industry* (hereafter *Macmillan Committee*), Cmnd 3897 (June 1931), para. 404, 173–4.

[3] *Minutes of Evidence taken before the Committee on Finance and Industry* (1931), ii. 72–5.

[4] *Macmillan Committee*, 377–96.

[5] S. Tolliday, *Business, Banking and Politics: The Case of British Steel, 1918–1939* (Cambridge, Mass., Harvard Univ. Press, 1987), 200–3; R. S. Sayers, *The Bank of England, 1891–1944*, i (Cambridge, Cambridge Univ. Press, 1976), 324–30; Heim, 'Limits to Intervention', 545–9; M. H. Best and J. Humphreys, 'The City and Industrial Decline', in B. Elbaum and W. Lazonic (eds.), *The Decline of the British Economy*, Oxford, Clarendon Press, 1987, 233–4.

[6] Bank of England, Minutes of Committee of Treasury, 23 Apr. 1931, Bank of England Archive (hereafter BE) G14/62. On the temporary nature of SMT and BIDC, see R. Harrod, *The Life of John Maynard Keynes* (Macmillan, 1951), 418–19.

[7] 'Industrial Mortgage Corporation', note by W. F. Tuke of a meeting of London clearing bankers at the Bank of England, 1 Feb. 1934, National Library of Scotland, Kinross Coll. (hereafter NLS) 8699/1.

[8] Ibid.

[9] Heim, 'Limits to Intervention'.

[10] J. Gibson Jarvie to Montagu Norman, 20 Mar. 1934, NLS 8699/1.

[11] 'Memorandum of the Committee of London Clearing Bankers Respecting a Projected Industrial and Commercial Finance Corporation Limited', 29 Mar. 1944, p. 3, NLS 8966/1; L. Dennett, *The Charterhouse Group 1925–1979: A History* (Gentry, 1979), 35–43.

[12] 'General Support of Trade', Board of Trade, Public Record Office (hereafter PRO CAB 87/63), Committee on Post-War Employment, (hereafter CPWE) minutes, 15 Oct. 1943. The Bolton Committee later noted that 'Those who were active in that market [in the 1930s] will admit, and some have done so to us, that it was not possible to meet more than a fraction of the potential demand for capital from small business.' *Report of the Committee of Inquiry on Small Firms* (hereafter Bolton Report), Cmnd 4811 (Nov. 1971), 154.

[13] CPWE minutes, 15 Oct. 1943, PRO CAB 87/63.

[14] 'Memorandum of the Committee of London Clearing Banks', 4. Unsigned memo, Committee of London Clearing Banks (hereafter CLCB), 29 Dec. 1943, NLS 8699/1.

[15] 'Finance for Small Business', undated memo by the Deputy Governor, BE SMT2/308. In a meeting at the Bank of England on 26 Apr. 1944 Gibson-Jarvie of CFI told Deputy-Governor Catterns that of potential investments '75 per cent had been snapped up by banks who were supposed to be supporting him, and this after CFI had agreed to find the money'.

[16] D. Ross, 'The Clearing Banks and Industry: New Perspectives on the Inter-War Years', in J. J. Van Helten and Y. Cassis (eds.), *Capitalism in a Mature Economy: Financial Institutions, Capital Exports and British Industry, 1870–1939* (Aldershot, Elgar, 1990); W. A. Thomas, *The Finance of British Industry 1918–76* (Methuen, 1978), 74–8.

[17] For investment trusts see Y. Cassis, 'The Emergence of a New Investment Institution: Investment Trusts in Britain, 1870–1939', in Van Helten and Cassis, *Capitalism in a Mature Economy*.

[18] W. Piercy, 'The Financing of Small Business', *British Management Review*, 3 (1938), 31–43.

[19] Otto Niemeyer, untitled memo, 10 May 1944, BE SMT2/308.

[20] M. M. Postan, *British War Production*, (HMSO, 1952); D. Thoms, *War, Industry and Society: The Midlands, 1939–45* (Routledge, 1990); C. Barnett, *The Audit of War* (Macmillan, 1986).

[21] E. Durbin, *New Jerusalems: The Labour Party and the Economics of Democratic Socialism* (Routledge & Kegan Paul, 1985), *passim*; B. Pimlott, *Hugh Dalton* (Macmillan, 1985), 223–4.

[22] *News Chronicle*, 14 May 1952.

[23] e.g. *Independent* recently referred to 'Government owned venture capital group 3i', *Independent*, 19 Mar. 1994.

[24] Douglas Jay, *The Nation's Wealth at the Nation's Service* (Labour Party Pamphlet, 1938), 6.

[25] 'Labour's Financial Policy', Labour Party, July 1935, 9; 'Nationalisation of the English Banking System: Policy No. 301', June 1935, Memo. London School of Economics, Piercy Coll. (hereafter Piercy) 8/74; 'Why the Banks Should be Nationlised', Labour Party, July 1936; 'Labour's Immediate Programme', Labour Party, Mar. 1937.

[26] Durbin, *New Jerusalems*, 246.

[27] Jay, *The Nation's Wealth*, 6.

[28] 'Draft Bill for NIB', 1935, Piercy 8/74.

[29] Evan Durbin to Clement Attlee, 'Capital Issues Control After the War', 25 May 1944, Piercy 8/74.

[30] J. C. R. Dow, *The Management of the British Economy 1945–60* (Cambridge, 1965); A. Cairncross, *Years of Recovery: British Economic Policy 1945–1951* (Cambridge, 1985); N. Rollings, 'The Reichstag Method of Government', in H. Mercer, N. Rollings, and J. Tomlinson (eds.), *Labour Governments and Private Enterprise: The Experience of 1945–51* (Edinburgh, 1992).

[31] J. Tomlinson, 'Attlee's Inheritance and the Financial System: Whatever Happened to the National Investment Board?', *Financial History Review*, Vol I (1994).

[32] L. Johnman, 'The Labour Party and Industrial Policy, 1940–45', in N. Tiratsoo (ed.), *The Attlee Years* (Pinter, 1991).

[33] Durbin, *New Jerusalems*, 82.

[34] Piercy was to have a distinguished career in the City. A member of the Stock Exchange, he pioneered the unit trust movement. See below, Ch. 2.

[35] Whitehall, CPWE, July 1943: Sir Richard Hopkins—Permanent Secretary to the Treasury; Sir Thomas Philips—Permanent Secretary to the Ministry of Labour; Sir Alfred Hurst—War Cabinet Secretary; Sir Alan Barlow—Joint Second Secretary to the Treasury; Sir Wilfred Eady—Joint Second Secretary to the Treasury; Sir Arnold Overton—Permanent Secretary to the Board of Trade; Prof. Lionel Robbins—Director, Economic Section, Office of the War Cabinet; William Gorell Barnes, D. Norman Chester—secretaries to CPWE.

[36] CWPE minutes, 9 Oct. 1943, PRO CAB 87/63.

[37] 'General Support of Trade', Board of Trade memo., 15 Oct. 1943. PRO CAB 87/63.

[38] 'Industrial Efficiency and Employment and the Support of Trade', Board of Trade memo to CPWE, 25 Nov. 1943; 'Finance for Small Businesses', Note of a meeting with Board of Trade officials, 30 June 1944; BE SMT2/308.

[39] Sir J. Anderson to Lord Catto, 8 Dec. 1944, BE SMT2/308.

[40] Sir Richard Hopkins to Lord Catto, 22 Dec. 1944, BE SMT2/308.

[41] E. G. Compton to E. H. D. Skinner, 16 June 1944, BE SMT2/301/1.

[42] E. G. Compton, 'Distribution of Industry Act, Section 4', 12 July 1945, 1–4, BE SMT2/308.

[43] Ibid.

[44] For a general discussion of specialism versus generalism see P. Hennessy, *Whitehall* (Secker & Warburg, 1989), *passim*.

[45] 'Distribution of Industry Act', 4.

[46] J. Fforde, *The Bank of England and Public Policy, 1941–58* (Cambridge, 1992), 705.

[47] 'Niemeyer report', 19 Oct. 1943, NLS 8699/1; J. Kinross and A. Butt-Philip, 'ICFC, 1945–1961', unpubl. MS., 3i (1985), 8–11.

[48] Ibid.

[49] O. Niemeyer to B. G. Catterns, 11 Feb. 1944, BE SMT2/308.

[50] Montagu Norman to Sir Wilfred Eady, 29 Dec. 1943; Norman to Clarence Sadd, 7 Jan. 1944; BE SMT2/308.

[51] Memo by E. H. D. Skinner, 13 Mar. 1944, BE SMT2/308. Skinner was a special adviser to Norman at the time. Fforde, *Bank of England*, 706.

[52] Fforde, *Bank of England*, 707–10.

[53] Catterns to Neimeyer, 16 May 1944, BE SMT2/308.

[54] Niemeyer to Skinner, BE SMT2/308/1. This note is undated but is in response to enquiries raised by Skinner early in 1945.

[55] Memo by Niemeyer, 13 Mar. 1944; Notes of a meeting between Sir William Goodenough and Catterns, 14 Mar. 1944; NLS 8699/1.

[56] W. F. Crick to C. T. A. Sadd, 'Special Advances', 2 Nov. 1943, Midland Bank Archive (hereafter Midland), 200/10.

[57] Letter from R. A. Wilson, Chief General Manager of Lloyds Bank, in R. Fear, *Post-War Industrial Reconstruction* (1944).

[58] Unsigned memo, 29 Dec. 1943, NLS 8699/1.

[59] Ibid.

[60] Barclays Bank, 'Finance for Industry After the War', Fisher memo, Jan. 31 1944, NLS 8699/1.

[61] Memo by Niemeyer, Jan. 31 1944, NLS 8699/1.

[62] Memo by C. Campbell, Chairman of CLCB, 15 Mar. 1944, NLS 8699/1.

[63] Sir Charles Lidbury to Rupert Beckett (Chairman of the Westminster Bank), 'Proposed Reconstruction Finance Corporation Limited', 14 Mar. 1944, NLS 8699/1.

[64] Ibid.

[65] E. D. H. Skinner, 'Notes on the Formation of ICFC', (Aug. 1973), 3i Archive (hereafter 3i).

[66] A. W. Tuke, 'Long Term Credit to Small Business', 21 Mar. 1944, NLS 8699/1.

[67] Tuke to Lidbury, 'Proposed industrial Finance Corporation Limited', 14 Apr. 1944, NLS 8699/1.

[68] Lidbury to Tuke, 17 Apr. 1944; Lidbury reiterated these feelings in a later letter to W. M. Fullerton of the Ulster Bank but urged that 'you must keep this private view to yourself as it is not one that is held in Government and Official circles', 1 May 1944, NLS 8699/1.

[69] Minutes of meeting of the CLCB at the Bank of England, 11 May 1944, 8699/1.

[70] Ibid.

[71] A. W. Tuke, 'Proposed Industrial Finance Corporation', 6 June 1944; Tuke to J. D. Blackbourne, 7 June 1944; Tuke to H. B. Meredith, 8 Feb. 1945; C. Lidbury, 'Notes for a Meeting of CEO', 27 June 1944; NLS 8699/1.

[72] Tuke to Lidbury, 24 July 1944, 8699/1.

[73] Director's Minutes, British Linen Bank, 30 May 1944; 6 June 1944; 27 June 1944; 4 July 1944; 11 July 1944; 18 July 1944; 10 Oct. 1944; 27 Dec. 1944; Bank of Scotland Archive.

[74] Memo of a meeting between Colin Campbell and Lord Catto, 1 Aug. 1944; Catto to Campbell, 2 Aug. 1944, NLS 8699/1.

Chapter 2

Bridging the Gap: 1945–1960

DESPITE THE OPPOSITION of certain of its own shareholders and the difficult economic circumstances in which it was set up, ICFC was to prosper steadily throughout the 1950s and into the 1960s. This was in large part due to the often innovatory methods developed by a small, highly motivated team under the leadership of William Piercy, ICFC's first Chairman. Piercy believed in being an executive chairman, and devoted considerable energies to the everyday business of building ICFC up to become what he fervently hoped would be a great and lasting institution.[1] In order to do this ICFC had to establish a *modus operandi* capable of identifying worthwhile enterprise and structuring financial packages accordingly, in addition to devising a system to monitor investments and provide follow-up support. This called for a departure from 'traditional' banking and finance practices in terms of using industrial as well as financial assessment criteria. If the Corporation was to fund business in the Macmillan gap this meant making a long-term commitment of funds, greatly increasing the need for an accurate assessment of risk, often with new and unproven enterprises. But Piercy's determination that ICFC should succeed meant, in his judgement,

that ICFC would also need to support its activities with business 'outside the gap', either as the opportunity presented itself, or by a planned strategy of diversification into other areas of finance. In the event ICFC operated inside and outside the Macmillan gap with considerable success.

The 'Hard Core' of ICFC Staff

William Piercy had worked his own way up through the City hierarchies without the aid of a privileged family background. He began work in the City office of Pharaoh Gane, a timber broker, at the age of 12. He studied at night and eventually, in 1910, became a full-time undergraduate at the London School of Economics, where he later taught economics.[2] During the First World War he worked in the Ministries of Munitions and Food and spent some time in the USA as a member of the Allied Provisions Export Commission. After the war he eventually returned to Pharaoh Gane as joint Managing Director and resumed teaching at the LSE on a part-time basis. In 1934 he became a partner in Capel, Cure & Terry, and a member of the Stock Exchange, where he was to play a key role in developing the nascent unit trust sector. During the Second World War he entered government service once again, working in the Ministries of Supply and Production and returning to the USA as head of the British Petroleum Mission. Later, by virtue of his socialist sympathies and membership of groups such as XYZ, he was to join Evan Durbin as joint personal assistant to Clement Attlee. He was created Baron Piercy of Burford in 1945 and appointed to the Court of the Bank of England in 1946.[3]

Piercy was an unusual combination of financier, largely self-made, and socialist intellectual. That he sent his children to Eton while studiously planning Labour Party economic and financial policy is perhaps not as incongruous as it first appears, when considering the antecedents of many prominent Labour figures at the time, including Hugh Dalton, Piercy's close friend and political mentor.[4] His appointment, supported by key figures in the Bank of England and the clearing banks, confirmed his position as a man the financial community thought they could trust, yet his social background and socialist affiliations meant that in some quarters he was never to be fully accepted. Piercy's political persuasions also contributed to a great deal of lasting confusion about the autonomy of ICFC.

ICFC opened for business in July 1945 and Piercy immediately began work assembling the team which was to run the Corporation during its formative years. One of the earliest appointments was that of James Lawrie, who became ICFC's first General Manager. Lawrie came from a conventional banking background, having been secretary and London manager of the National Bank of New Zealand, and in the early months at ICFC he continued to spend much of his time working for the bank, in whose building the first offices of the Corporation were situated. John Kinross was also an early recruit. In the 1920s Kinross had worked as manager of the issue department at Gresham Trust, under the wing of Sir Arthur Wheeler, and in 1934 had set up the Cheviot Trust, specializing in issues below what was then considered to be the viable threshold of £200,000.

Cheviot achieved this by the direct mailing of prospectuses to a list of active small investors which Kinross had compiled, thus eliminating normally prohibitive advertising costs. Kinross adopted this method in emulation of Wheeler, who had made (and was later to lose) a considerable fortune by operating outside the mechanisms of the Stock Exchange.[5] Cheviot proved to be a considerable success in its own limited field. It was, however, a very labour-intensive operation, most of which Kinross handled personally. He suffered a nervous breakdown in 1941, which he attributed to personal rather than business pressures; nevertheless, it forced him to give up the City, and soon afterwards he began a new life as a farmer. This

Man of the Month

It's a £45,000,000 Smile !

Lord Piercy, C.B.E.

Early publicity for ICFC and its Chairman. *Scope* magazine 1947.

proved to be only a temporary setback, and the irrepressible Kinross soon turned his farming interests into a successful enterprise.[6] His return to the City in 1945 came as the result of a letter which he wrote to the Bank of England, following the announcement of ICFC's formation, offering his services to the new corporation. Kinross had written a paper in 1938, which had been circulated at the Bank, pointing out the large number of sound firms, too small to mount even a Cheviot style issue, which would benefit from an organization able to provide capital from its own funds.[7] Kinross met Piercy and Lawrie in July and August 1945, and it was agreed that he would work on a part-time basis assessing the quality of applications. In the event Kinross worked full-time during the first and each subsequent week, becoming chief controller and later, in 1948, ICFC's general manager.

Kinross and Piercy thus began a partnership which was to become the nerve centre of the Corporation in its early years.[8] Both had an interest in smaller operations, outside the normal remit of the City, Piercy through his interests in the unit trust movement, Kinross in his small-issue dealings at Cheviot. Kinross was intensely interested in the minutiae of finance. So was Piercy, but to a lesser extent, being slightly wary of complex financial schemes.[9] Piercy's forte was to be found in more 'macro' perspectives, and he was keenly aware of the wider political and economic context in which ICFC was to operate. Kinross, however, had no time for ethereal economic or political matters, and it was thus that these two figures, 'quite unlike each other in qualities and style',[10] came to be two halves of a complementary partnership. Kinross was to view this double act in a self-deprecating way: 'I possessed none of Bill's intellectual qualities and he was the architect of our policy. He once said to me with a roguish twinkle in his eye "I make the policy, you make the money"'.[11]

In order to begin making money ICFC had to set up offices, recruit staff, and establish working practices to identify and fund sound business. This was no easy feat late in 1945, when post-war austerity was at its height. During its first winter ICFC managed in the temporary accommodation provided by the Bank of New Zealand, and it was not until January 1946 that the Corporation set up in its own premises at 7 Drapers Gardens. Most office essentials were in short supply, including furniture, floor-covering, stationery, typewriters, and telephones. Ted Cole, recruited as one of ICFC's industrial assessors, spent a large portion of his time during this period on the mundane tasks involved in equipping the office for business. Strings were pulled, government

Cases Committee in the 1940s. Left to right: Colin Kirkpatrick (Controller), James Lawrie (General Manager), William Piercy (Chairman), John Kinross (Chief Controller) and Julian Sorsbie (Controller).

connections used, and a few unconventional methods employed until eventually supplies were procured. An air of frugality remained with the Corporation during these formative years, which perhaps reached its epitome in the harsh winter of 1947 which saw the staff working cheek by jowl in overcoats and gloves as the heating system failed during frequent power cuts. The abstemious aura of the early years was only partly due to prevailing circumstance. Piercy and Kinross decried any seemingly unnecessary or ostentatious expense in running the business. Staff were, for example, encouraged to write a letter rather than telephone, and to take the bus rather than a taxi to meetings in London. It was to be many years before company cars were approved for those travelling further afield.[12]

During 1945 and 1946 what Kinross was later to call the 'hard core' of ICFC staff was assembled. There was no formal recruitment process. Following the example of Kinross and Lawrie people were normally introduced via personal connections.[13] New staff came from a variety of backgrounds—Julian Sorsbie, recruited as an investment controller, had previously been a stockbroker; G. S. 'Rocky' Stone was an accountant, a role he continued at ICFC; Nicholas Momtchiloff, a Bulgarian mathematician and banker, and a friend of Piercy, was recruited as an examiner, but soon established himself as head of ICFC's Economic Intelligence Unit; Guy Drummond came to the Corporation with a background in merchant banking, to become an examiner; Brian Tew, later to become a full-time academic, joined as an economist; Ted Cole, who became an assistant examiner, had previously worked as a valuer in a building society; Peter Wreford, recruited as a controllers' assistant, had worked briefly at a merchant bank. Others, including James Turner and Paul Hildesley, had no experience of finance whatsoever. Lack of formal training and experience did not deter Piercy in the least, since his strategy involved taking on staff when they were young and allowing them to gain experience of ICFC's methods on the job. This was a long-term employment commitment. Piercy thought it might take as long as ten years for staff to become proficient in the new field of industrial finance he was endeavouring to create, but this would still leave ten to fifteen years of further productive life for ICFC.[14] Perhaps as a result of this policy, many of the 'young Turks' recruited at the time recall a friendly, relaxed atmosphere at ICFC, in contrast to other City institutions, with most people on first-name terms.[15] When new people arrived they were simply 'educated in the culture—they sat at Nelly's elbow'.[16]

Filling the Macmillan Gap

As staff were assembled and offices furnished, ICFC began to get down to business. The obstacles facing the Corporation as it began to trade were a microcosm of the general difficulties facing British industry following the war, shortages and restrictions on such things as raw materials, factory space, and labour, which compounded the structural economic problems facing firms within the Macmillan gap. Many firms had to make the transition from war-production to production for civil markets. This meant finance was needed for capital investment to develop and install new product lines. Extra working capital was also necessary, since emergency government provisions had now been withdrawn.[17] Many firms had grown considerably on the strength of war production, and now sought finance to consolidate their position in peacetime. Whether or not they were able to do so ICFC was called upon to judge.

These specific considerations merely added to the perennial problems of finance for small firms and the viability of an organization devoted to investing in this sector. Kinross was personally convinced that there was a wealth of good business to be done, citing the many hundreds of applications he had been forced to reject at the Cheviot Trust.[18] If finance could be provided without the high cost of an issue (the advertising costs of which were alone estimated to run at between £8,000 and £10,000), and if the finance could be structured in such a way that a high debt burden could be avoided—possibly by equity participation—then, providing the lender was prepared to enter into a long-term commitment, the Macmillan gap might be partially closed. In many cases the central problem was that firms could not provide an established profit record, so good judgement on the part of the investor was crucial. In addition, the kind of expansion involved often entailed a high element of risk, since it meant investing in new, and often unproven, products and markets. This risk was all the more acute because money would be tied up over a long period. Yet another drawback was that there was little or no secondary market for any equity which ICFC might take. These factors were responsible for limiting the clearing banks' investment in small firms. As ICFC's first brochure notes: 'the responsibilities of the banks to their depositors impose upon them limitations as to the type of lending in which they may properly engage', i.e. loans must be recallable at short notice. Other sources of finance, notably the insurance companies and pension funds, which had steadily absorbed an increasing proportion of savings during the twentieth century, and might have considered taking a long-term position, were neither capable of assessing the prospects of small firms, nor interested in investing what they considered to be small amounts.[19]

ICFC did little to market itself actively in its early years. It published a rather unobtrusive little brochure for circulation among the clearing banks, and relied on *ad hoc* press articles, mentions in the *Board of Trade Journal* and the occasional talk given by Piercy to various Trade Associations.[20] This lack of advertising was partly due to inexperience, and the shareholding banks' antipathy to ICFC 'touting for business',[21] but it also reflected the adequate number of applications which the Corporation received during this period. ICFC did not yet have the administrative machinery to cope with more applications than were already to hand from a variety of sources, including the clearing banks, government departments, accountants, and solicitors.[22]

From the outset, ICFC's chosen method of assessment of the worthiness of applicants was based on a wide-ranging combination of perspectives. Given that the Corporation was expecting to take a higher degree of risk and not link loans as closely to security as did the banks, it had to have a good idea of prospects in addition to past performance. This entailed a closer technical investigation than traditional bankers were equipped to carry out,[23] which in practice meant building up an in-house capability, as there were considered to be few industrial consultants able to fulfil ICFC's needs at the time.[24] In addition, consultancies were often regionally based, whereas ICFC's own staff, as they travelled around Britain, could begin to build up a national overview.[25] ICFC's industrial staff and their non-financial appraisal marked the Corporation off as unique among the financial institutions[26] and frequently saved it from making unsound investments, staff with a technical background often being in closer touch with markets and being able to spot poor development strategies among applications.[27]

The strength of ICFC's technical expertise was necessitated by, and is reflected in, the high proportion of investments which the Corporation made

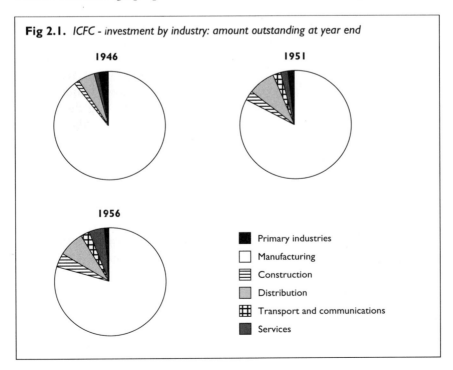

Fig 2.1. *ICFC - investment by industry: amount outstanding at year end*

1946

1951

1956

■ Primary industries
□ Manufacturing
☰ Construction
▨ Distribution
▦ Transport and communications
▨ Services

MANNOFF

'Don't be overly alarmed—this is just a negotiating stance.'

in manufacturing industry during these early years, as Figure 2.1 demonstrates. This was a trend which was to hold constant throughout the subsequent history of the group.

It nevertheless took a few years for the industrial department to get fully into its stride, and there remained a degree of tension between those with industrial expertise and their financial counterparts. Some of the latter group often remained convinced that a seemingly poor prospect from the technical point of view still held out the possibility of some return if the finance was structured accordingly.[28] Kinross was particularly worried by Sorsbie's advocacy of support for 'third-rate' business, which he thought could be made acceptable by applying 'a sufficiently ingenious financial scheme'.[29]

There were other methods of assessment used by ICFC beyond technical appraisal. The Corporation made use of credit reference agencies such as Moody's,[30] and also applied to the banks for information. In the latter case these were often of positive value, but there was always the possibility that the proposal would be taken over by the clearers in an attempt to restrict ICFC's business.[31] By 1947 the Corporation had also adopted the habit of sending its accountants to visit factories and examine the accounts *in situ*. A typical application might thus be scrutinized on a number of levels. The 1947 report on Triangle Products, for example, reveals that ICFC 'accountants have carried out a careful examination at the works, and in addition one of our engineers has revisited the factory. We also invited Mr. Frederick Fyleman, an industrial consultant (whom we propose to nominate as director) to make an independent investigation of the position'.[32]

One of the central features of the assessment process remained the 'personnel audit', whereby the personal qualities of the applicant and staff were scrutinized.[33] Individual impressions were an important part of the process by which ICFC assessed the quality of an application, and it could, on occasion, be a somewhat quixotic process. Michael Maurice, one of the Corporation's rather more flamboyant members of staff, who was in the habit of travelling to visit prospective customers in an open-top Rolls Royce, could reject an application on the basis that the managing director's socks were too colourful.[34] Ted Cole had a list of aversions including suede shoes, monogrammed shirts, and 'flashy' cars.[35] Such apparently irrational prejudices often masked a logical rejection based on the style of management which they were likely to reflect. If an applicant was found to be a local Justice of the Peace, for example, this would be taken as a negative sign that management was likely to be settled into a comfortable, but not too dynamic, pattern. Patriarchal management was also occasionally judged to be a problem. As Frank Harber recalled, 'You'd get a memo and it would start off "this is an old-established family company" and your heart would sink.'[36]

The obverse of this process was that many proposals were successful on the strength of personal appraisal. Early application files contain many recommendations to invest money on the basis of individual management qualities: 'This proposal is essentially a case of backing Mr. Hardman . . . he is well worth backing as he is a first-class man who knows the whole quarrying business from A to Z . . . undoubtedly a man of considerable substance . . . entirely a case of backing a man . . . much impressed by Lonsdale and Stephenson, the men who count in this business.'[37] That personal assessment was important in ICFC was a wider manifestation of the particular style of Kinross and Piercy in evaluating proposals. They often relied on a 'hunch' or a sense of instinct in deciding to do business.[38] This sense had to be particularly acute in cases where new businesses were being funded, a proportion in excess of 20 per cent of ICFC business over the first ten years of operation.[39]

Once applications were accepted ICFC attempted to keep its terms as competitive as possible, taking account of the cost of its own money. A general rate of 4.5 per cent was introduced in 1945, but 'particularly sound propositions', or larger loans in excess of £50,000, might be charged at 4 per cent. 'Troublesome cases', unsecured loans, and preference shares, on the other hand, carried higher rates, often 5 per cent. ICFC set its lower limit of operation at £5,000, lending below that level being judged to be 'uneconomic'. This was also in deference to the clearing banks, however, who remained wary of ICFC poaching what they considered to be their business.[40] Applicants were charged a negotiation fee, although this was to become the subject of widespread criticism, and would on occasion be waived. As in most things, ICFC was 'always willing to do a deal' on an individual basis, reducing rates, or offering a 'holiday' of one or two years on repayments.[41]

The structure of loans was also an important consideration for ICFC.

At the outset the Board considered a variety of loan and share-subscription options, deciding that equity participation would at times be the most satisfactory method, and debentures or mortgages the worst.[42] The latter, it was considered, would 'limit the client's development', whereas equity participation by ICFC would not impose a high debt burden during what was often a delicate phase of expansion. Equity had the added attraction for ICFC in that if enterprises were successful then the Corporation would share proportionally in that success. The reverse of this could be true, of course, such investments carrying a high degree of risk. Nevertheless, Kinross was particularly confident in ICFC's ability to pick winners, and considered the adoption of this strategy to be his 'most important contribution' to ICFC's operating methods.[43] The problem was that many owners of small firms were extremely reluctant to give up an equity stake in their company, and negotiations had to be handled with great care, with many firms continuing to prefer loans or preference shares.[44] ICFC was well aware of this dislike and would occasionally gain business by offering to take less equity than rival investors were insisting upon.[45]

The proportion of equity in ICFC's portfolio nevertheless grew steadily throughout the 1940s. The Corporation would occasionally be rewarded with a substantial gain, where a firm had grown considerably and decided to go public. An early investment of this type was George Godfrey and Partners, an aircraft engineering firm in which ICFC gradually built up a 40 per cent stake. When the company was floated in 1956 ICFC made a profit of over £1,250,000.[46] This presaged later, even more spectacular successes such as British Caledonian.[47] ICFC could afford to take an equity position in view of its long-term realization strategy. As Piercy put it, the Corporation relied on 'borrowers ploughing back profits into the business to enable us eventually to get out',[48] but there was to be no pressure exerted by ICFC to force companies to float or be sold off, and the Corporation's style of control and monitoring of its clients was to reflect this hands-off approach.

The decision-making process at ICFC during the 1940s and 1950s was a mixture of evolving bureaucracy and enlightened autocracy. Formal systems were put in place early to evaluate applications and a departmental structure was set up. Examiners, accountants, and controllers had their separate roles, and there were technical, legal, and economic intelligence departments all in place by 1948. Several committees met on a regular basis, including the Chairman's Committee, the Cases Committee, and the After-care Committee. The most important and durable of these was the Cases Committee, which usually comprised the Chairman, general manager, and chief controller, and met twice a week, from 1946 onwards, to consider applications.[49] This was a forum where the merits of an application were subjected to rigorous scrutiny, and controllers presenting cases for funding had to be on their mettle to steer prospective business through. In the early days both Piercy and Kinross were in the habit of reading the entire correspondence and reports of every case, but as this proved increasingly burdensome they began to share responsibility.[50] This led some controllers to attempt to schedule their appearance before the Committee to coincide with the chairmanship most likely to favour their particular application.[51] Many ICFC staff recall the 'ordeal' of the Cases Committee with a grudging affection. It could be a gruelling process, yet if a submission were successful, it could certainly result in a feeling of considerable achievement.

Once investments had been allocated a series of monitoring procedures was put in place. It was the Corporation's policy from the outset not to nominate ICFC staff as directors of client companies, thus avoiding the problems of dual loyalties.[52] ICFC did often insist on a range of conditions affecting the boards of companies, including reduced or fixed directors' fees, agreed distribution of profits, long-dated service agreements for key directors, and in some cases, life insurance on individual directors considered to be key figures in the running of the business.[53] The Corporation also nominated people not employed by ICFC to directorships in investee firms,[54] although this procedure was itself not without problems, as in the case of Pest Control in 1949, when the finance director whom ICFC had nominated went completely 'native' in supporting the firm against the Corporation.[55] Such problems with representation were to prove largely insoluble, given that ICFC had decided upon a policy of avoiding direct control over clients. As Piercy was to tell Stafford Cripps, the Corporation was continually faced with the difficulty of 'improving the efficiency of management while declining entrepreneurial functions ourselves'.[56]

The problem was indirectly reduced by a system of after-care which was to become an important feature of ICFC's organization. This function was coveted for a while by both technical and accounting staff, and involved the monitoring of monthly reports on sales, purchases, credit, and so on, with the object of reporting any disturbing trends to the After-care Committee. In this way ICFC investments forced firms to adopt good accounting practices in keeping accurate cost and budget records.[57] In some cases firms chose to borrow from ICFC precisely because this system was in place and was judged to be of material help.[58]

The Crisis Years

Despite these measures, designed to ensure the acquisition of sound business and continued supervision, ICFC ran into a severe crisis after two or three years' trading. This was due to a combination of circumstances. As it was finding its feet the Corporation's assessment methods were not yet fully developed, and early warning of potential problems was often missed.[59] Piercy also felt constrained to build up a substantial portfolio for ICFC and to invest up to the limits of share and loan capital made available by the shareholders as soon as was practically possible, in order to demonstrate to the shareholders that the Corporation was here to stay. Delays in the examining process and in completions of loans only served to intensify Piercy's sense of urgency.[60] The result was that ICFC began doing an increasing amount of business where, as Kinross put it, 'the risk factor was pretty high'.[61] This was perhaps the most inopportune moment to adopt such a strategy, since a number of problems began to emerge which were also 'thrown up by the nature of the times'.[62] An example was ICFC's considerable losses in the Minneapolis–Moline (England) company in 1949. This was a company formed to manufacture combine harvesters under licence from a company in the USA. Steel from the USA was unavailable at the time due to prevailing import controls, and the standard of British steel available was judged to require design modifications to the final product. Unfortunately the redesigned components failed, with disastrous consequences in what was a seasonal product market. The company collapsed and ICFC was forced to write off the whole of its original loan and £50,000 in rescue money—a total of £172,000.[63]

During 1947 and 1948 ICFC was at what Kinross later described as the 'low ebb' of its fortunes. The banks took ICFC's mounting bad-debt problem as a signal to begin what was to be an almost perennial campaign to withdraw or withhold funds from the Corporation. As more problems emerged Piercy was tempted to undertake even more risky business in an attempt to 'balance the books'.[64] He did what he could to disguise the true level of the problem in the Annual Reports, but even so, the figures remained unimpressive. In 1947 ICFC had a trading profit of £23,965 but had written off £140,000 in bad debts. In 1948 bad-debt provisions were £275,000, and 1949 continued the trend, with a provision of £340,000, bringing the total to date to over £600,000 out of advances and investments totalling £14,465,000.[65]

These failures prompted a range of responses from ICFC. In some early cases their long-term commitments were abandoned and they urged customers to sell up; in others the curtailment of new product lines was suggested in favour of a return to established production.[66] In 1947 a management team, known informally as the 'breakdown gang', was set up, headed by Michael Maurice, soon to be followed by a second team, to concentrate on attempting to sort out the growing list of ailing companies. The Corporation was also forced to call on the services of outside consultants to attend to some firms. These often gave poor results, however, reinforcing Piercy's determination to rely in future on in-house expertise.[67]

By 1950 the crisis was largely over, and Kinross was able to start the year in 'optimistic' mood.[68] The general economic climate had improved, ICFC's more considered investments were beginning to pay off, and many of the more risky clients had been shaken out. Piercy, Stone, Kinross, and Maurice, all of whom had spent a large proportion of their time on ailing firms, could now return to the business of looking for sound investments. In many ways it had been a valuable learning experience for the Corporation, and emphasis was henceforth placed on co-ordinating after-care more effectively in order to provide an early warning of potential problems.[69] There were further crises for ICFC, particularly in 1951 and 1955, when the banks, prompted by the prevailing credit squeeze, raised ICFC's borrowing costs and restricted its flow of capital, as described in Chapter 3. However, these were externally generated problems over which ICFC had little control, and not a reflection on the functioning of its own organization and methods; these had become established by the early 1950s and had begun to demonstrate that ICFC was well able to operate successfully.

Branching Out

Having established ICFC and weathered the storm of the late 1940s, Piercy began the 1950s with plans for expansion and diversification. Expansion took the form of a steadily growing portfolio, but also involved decentralizing the Corporation's operations by setting up a regional network. Piercy had expressed his intention to set up branch offices as a goal of long-term policy at the outset in 1945,[70] but it was not until June 1950 that the Board was formally asked to consider this issue. It had been noticed that ICFC had been receiving proportionately fewer applications from the Midlands region in particular, and it was suggested that this was partly attributable to a reluctance of businessmen to travel to London in search of finance.[71] Birmingham was thus chosen to be the location of ICFC's first branch office, with Ernest Ralph as the first branch manager, and the office was officially opened in October 1950.[72] The branch was to prove a great success, and business from the Midlands area grew steadily as a proportion of ICFC's total investment throughout the 1950s, rising from 15 per cent in 1951 to 24 per cent in 1961.[73]

The success of the Birmingham branch was due in part to the establishment of a network of local contacts. Accountants provided introductions, as did branch bank managers. Ralph soon began to receive invitations to dinner, 'formal and otherwise', from individuals and from accountants' and bankers' district societies. He also dined as the guest of the Birmingham Book Club; 'not irrelevant as they help to get one known'. He spread the gospel of ICFC among local brokers, solicitors, Chambers of Commerce, and Trade Associations. Contacts established in this way could result in business for the Corporation, but the process was also invaluable in providing informal references. One of Ralph's reports to head office outlines the operation of the local network at

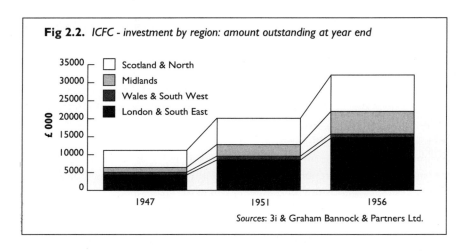

Fig 2.2. *ICFC - investment by region: amount outstanding at year end*

£000

35000
30000
25000
20000
15000
10000
5000
0

☐ Scotland & North
▨ Midlands
■ Wales & South West
■ London & South East

1947　　　　1951　　　　1956

Sources: 3i & Graham Bannock & Partners Ltd.

length, at times reading more like the narrative of a social anthropologist than an ICFC manager:

The business and professional communities are closely knit within themselves. A great many of the men here were at school together and were brought up within a few miles of each other. They know each other's strengths and weaknesses, and with due discrimination on our part are a source of useful and sometimes valuable information. However, in seeking information one has to bear in mind the close connections existing between the Catholic, Quaker and Unitarian families respectively. It would be easy to say the wrong thing or go to the wrong person.[74]

One example of the attempt by ICFC to foster these local-group connections was a low-interest loan to Bourneville Village Trust, set up by Cadbury, the prominent Quaker family.[75]

Further branch offices were opened following the success of Birmingham. The Manchester branch was opened in March 1952, but failed to match the level of business generated in the Midlands, partly due to the dominance in the region of the textile industry, which was now in steady decline, and the lesser number of small, independent enterprises in the area. Nevertheless an office was opened in Charlotte Square, Edinburgh in May 1953 and further branches were opened at Leicester and Leeds in 1955, and the London, Bristol, Glasgow and Cardiff branches were opened in 1960 and 1961. The local branches were to push for autonomy after they had found their feet, insisting on their own industrial advisers and independence in making decisions below a certain threshold. Larger business went to head office for approval.[76] In setting up this regional system, which was to be greatly expanded later into the 1960s, ICFC became the only major financial institution of its type to have a national presence. It is small wonder that some of the shareholder banks objected to this development; yet, as it was pointed out, ICFC was not expanding into the banking business, but rather spreading the geographic base of its long-term investment function. As Figure 2.2 shows, the regional pattern of investment by ICFC remained fairly constant from the late 1940s onwards, although there was a marked increase in the proportion of funds taken up by Midlands industry, reflecting the effect of the Birmingham office.

ICFC did begin to diversify its activities in the 1950s, not into banking, but notably into two other areas.[77] The first of these was the foray into the provision of mortgages for shipping. This had been discussed by the Board as early as June 1946, when a report by Edmund Thompson, the chairman of National Galvanisers, was considered. The proposal was rejected at the time as being outside the sphere of ICFC's proper activities, but was revived in December 1950, and the establishment of the Ship Mortgage Finance Company (SMFC) was announced to the public in March 1951. ICFC subscribed for £200,000 of the initial £1 million share capital, other shareholders including the Shipbuilding Conference, Hambros Bank, and several leading insurance companies, who each appointed directors.[78] SMFC was not intended to fund the construction of ships, but rather to provide post-launch finance, which it did with considerable success until government guarantees under the Shipbuilding Act in 1967 effectively put an end to the business.[79] SMFC could be said to be reasonably long-term business—it had a maximum limit of ten years on loans—but its major activity, funding tanker-charter companies serving the major oil companies like BP and Shell, was outside the usual ambit of ICFC activities.

Closer to ICFC's normal business was that which was undertaken by the Estate Duties Investment Trust, known by the acronym EDITH, set up in 1952. Such a company had first been suggested in 1950, and negotiations were undertaken during the following two years. The Trust was designed with the objective of meeting (or anticipating) the needs of predominantly family-owned companies faced with the loss of a major shareholder and the ensuing problem of estate duties. What was necessary in many cases was 'a reliable neutral holder' willing to take a share of the company. ICFC had devised a way of taking a holding—convertible preferred ordinary shares—which paid dividends to the Corporation whilst the other shareholders would eventually be compensated by an issue of equivalent tax-free bonus shares. This scheme was first devised in the case of the Lincoln Electric Company, and became known thereafter as 'doing a Lincoln'. EDITH was designed to expand what looked like being a profitable niche in the market.[80] There was, predictably, considerable opposition to the idea of EDITH from the clearing banks, as indeed there had been with the formation of SMFC. However, with the support of Barclay's General Manager, A. W. Tuke, it was eventually agreed that, providing ICFC limited its interest to £200,000, the company should be formed.[81] Finding the other institutional backers for EDITH was not as easy as first supposed, and initially only the Commercial Union could be persuaded to subscribe. A suggestion that ICFC should go it alone and provide the whole of the proposed £1,000,000 capital was quickly rebuffed by the clearing banks.[82] Piercy instead concentrated on the Prudential, maintaining that 'the Pru money bags are the key point'. They initially refused to participate, but eventually were won over and, with the other major insurance companies and various investment trusts following their lead, the formation of EDITH was publicly announced in March 1953.[83]

Initially operating under the managership of Julian Sorsbie, followed from 1955 onwards by Peter Wreford, EDITH was a considerable success, and in 1956 the Trust increased its capitalization to £2,000,000. Its business was much closer to the natural preserve of ICFC than was SMFC, EDITH taking equity in small, usually family-owned firms. Initially it operated in harmony with ICFC, but later on considerable friction was to develop between the two. Proposals were vetted by the established ICFC Cases Committee before being passed on to EDITH, and the Corporation was to be accused of diverting business from EDITH to its own portfolio.[84]

The business of EDITH dovetailed quite closely with the 'traditional' Macmillan gap activities which ICFC was originally expected to undertake, but other ventures undertaken by Piercy were markedly outside the gap. Piercy had stated early on that it 'would not be possible to lay down any general principles . . . precise policy would be determined by experience', and, despite the frequent opposition of the shareholder banks, the Corporation's articles of association were sufficiently ambiguous to allow him some considerable leeway.[85] Kinross attempted to rationalize these wider activities at the time: 'unless we were able to mix in a small amount of first-class business it was not possible to conduct a viable, long-term business based solely on the Macmillan gap style of case'.[86]

This wider activity took numerous forms. ICFC occasionally invested in large firms, including public companies whose shares were quoted on the Stock Exchange, or their subsidiaries.[87] The Corporation often exceeded its nominal £200,000 limit, as in the case of loans to Smith and Nephew, Jaeger, Baker Perkins, and Cementation for example,[88] all of which were very large and well-established companies. Wary of shareholders' objections, ICFC frequently attempted to disguise such activities, doing deals 'under the counter', as Kinross put it,[89] or investing in separate companies within the same group, as in the case of Solway Chemicals and Marchon in 1954.[90] In other cases large loans could be syndicated with other City institutions, and during the 1950s many £200,000-plus deals were shared with insurance companies, including the Prudential, the Pearl, Legal and General, and the Commercial Union, as well as, on occasion, with the merchant banks (some of whom were also shareholders in EDITH). Barclays was not above taking a share, with ICFC, in some larger investments, as in the case of John Baker and Bessemer, where the bank provided £300,000 of a £500,000 loan.[91] ICFC also joined the Treasury in funding some very large projects through their joint ventures with Development Areas Treasury Advisory Committee (DATAC).[92] The Corporation also gradually acquired a portfolio of quoted investments from the late 1940s onwards, again outside the definition of the Macmillan gap. The performance of these investments fluctuated over the years, but by 1961 they had a value of over £7.5 million.[93] In spite of these occasional forays into larger investments, the majority of ICFC business remained inside the gap, and, as Figure 2.3 shows, most investments were well below the upper limits specified.

ICFC was also accused of straying from its 'authorized' activities when it began a limited involvement in the new issue business. The first foray into this area was in the case of Viscose Developments. In 1947 the Corporation agreed to lend this company £135,000 and to underwrite a planned share issue for a further £129,000. The money was to fund 50 per cent of the cost of setting up a new factory in Swansea, the other 50 per cent coming from Viscose's French parent company.[94] The controversial part of this deal was ICFC's underwriting agreement, carried out for a fee of only 1 per cent, at a time when the usual charge would be 2.5 per cent plus a fee. This drew protests from the established issuing houses and the row spilled over into the public domain. Questions were asked in Parliament,[95] and the press began to examine ICFC's

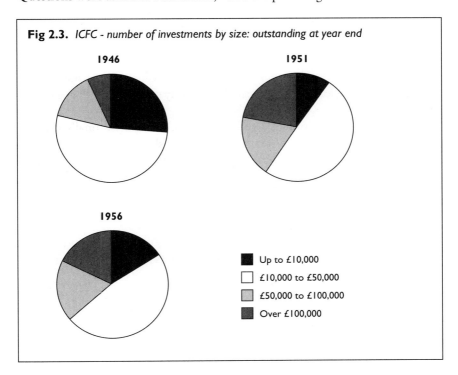

Fig 2.3. *ICFC - number of investments by size: outstanding at year end*

1946 1951

1956

■ Up to £10,000
□ £10,000 to £50,000
▨ £50,000 to £100,000
■ Over £100,000

recent business. In addition to the Viscose issue, the Corporation had recently subscribed for £172,000-worth of shares in the National Gas and Oil Engine Company as part of an attempt to beat off a takeover bid by Associated British Engineering.[96] *The Times* noted that 'the subscription of new shares in a £1,000,000 company and an underwriting transaction each come rather near to morally forbidden ground'.[97] Others were more lenient. The *Financial Times* noted that it was inevitable that sooner or later ICFC would come into conflict with existing City institutions if it was not to become a 'waste-paper basket' for the business these had rejected.[98] Piercy received visits from delegations of the Issuing Houses Association, but the best he would offer was that ICFC would limit the level of its underwriting and would not 'undertake the floating of private companies as a business in itself'.[99] Throughout the 1950s the Corporation continued to conduct a 'substantial' underwriting business, involving firms such as Murphy Radio and Marley Tile. At the same time the prevailing rate for issues fell to around 1.25 per cent. Kinross, who for a long time had complained of the high cost of underwriting, saw ICFC's intervention as a contributory factor in this fall.[100]

ICFC's relationship with other City institutions was generally good. Piercy had a particularly close relationship with Sir Charles Hambro, and ICFC carried out numerous joint operations with Hambros Bank, including large investments up to £800,000.[101] The Corporation also conducted joint business with Samuel, Lazard Bros., and Warburg.[102] ICFC also occasionally received proposals from other specialists in the field, notably Charterhouse, although these were seldom taken up as it was felt that the business on offer usually only involved 'difficult cases'.[103] There had been some disdain for ICFC among traditional City institutions in the early years, and the Corporation was originally regarded as consisting of 'enthusiastic amateurs'.[104] The merchant banks soon came to recognize that ICFC's appraisal mechanisms had begun to be effective, however, and in some cases paid the Corporation the compliment of offering better terms to companies who could show they had a positive assessment from ICFC.[105]

The Piercy–Kinross Style

The business that ICFC did 'outside the gap' was a reflection of both Piercy's opportunistic style and his determination to establish ICFC as a major City institution by expanding operations as widely as possible. His hands-on technique and direct control made this strategy possible, but only after he had consolidated his position at the head of the Corporation. From the beginning Piercy attempted to maximize his independence from control by the Board. In 1945 it was established that the Chairman, General Manager, and one other

IT'S LONELY AT THE TOP

director should have authority to approve loans up to £50,000, for example.[106] However, within the management of ICFC there was a certain amount of friction at the outset. Differences between Piercy and General Manager James Lawrie had developed into a serious rift by 1947. Lawrie had been used to working under more traditional, less interventionist chairmen, and resented Piercy's intrusion into the everyday running of the Corporation. In addition, Lawrie's more conventional banking background was perhaps less suited to the environment which Piercy was endeavouring to create. Despite their personal friendship, stemming from their mutual involvement in the XYZ (see Chapter 1), rivalry between the two extended to territorial claims over office space, and began to split the Corporation into two camps, those loyal to Piercy and those loyal to Lawrie.[107] By early 1948 relations had deteriorated to the point where the two men were no longer speaking to each other, and soon after this, partly in protest at the appointment of a deputy general manager with authority over after-care, Lawrie resigned to take up a post with the newly formed Film Finance Corporation.[108]

Lawrie's departure cleared the field for Piercy and his ensuing partnership with Kinross, enabling him to operate as freely as the shareholders would allow, even if this involved occasionally sailing a little close to the wind. Sometimes this adventurous method of working could go wrong, and ICFC would be left facing substantial losses, as in the case of Wood Bros. in 1953, when ICFC was involved in a complex scheme to finance a textile firm, and having invested over £400,000 was forced to take over an almost worthless business to avoid a total loss.[109] Kinross was candid about the way ICFC operated under his partnership with Piercy: 'both Bill and I enjoyed playing (business) poker with people who were not trustworthy. It was our form of sport . . . one had to know when to call it a day and one had to be absolutely ruthless at times . . . If Bill and

I had not been pretty opportunistic characters I doubt whether ICFC would have lasted more than 5 or 7 years at most. Later we could "afford" to raise our standards and did so.'[110]

The Piercy–Kinross alliance fostered work practices which were generally informal as long as work was being done. The two had adjoining offices, with a communicating door, and were constantly in conference.[111] Enthusiasm for work was one of the qualities which bound the two together. Piercy would be up late on Saturday night reading company reports, and JBK, as Kinross was generally referred to, regularly spent Sunday afternoons at home scanning financial journals and reports.[112] Even at the annual office party the two could be found in a corner talking shop.[113] An impression of this zeal for work can be gleaned from one of Kinross's diary entries in the winter of 1950: 'Some fog this a.m. and anxious in case this makes me late for the office. Especially on Monday when I'm always anxious to get there.'[114] Even serious injury could not stall the Kinross work ethic, as he was to demonstrate while recovering from an accident in the Middlesex Hospital, where he promptly turned his ward into 'ICFC's West End office'.[115] The rest of the staff at ICFC were expected to follow this pattern and many recall putting in very long hours during the early years.[116]

This Piercy–Kinross regime of intensive personal control was only feasible while ICFC was growing, and the volume of applications remained manageable. Initially both men simply read everything pertaining to each case—reports, correspondence, monthly returns. As early as 1949, however, they began to realize that a degree of delegation would be necessary.[117] By the mid-1950s there was mutual recognition that in order to ensure the longevity

John Kinross at the office!

of ICFC a permanent managerial pattern would have to be fashioned. Kinross had always been more of a financial technician than a manager and he knew that 'the time had come for a different style of (highly professional) management'.[118] Piercy concurred that between them they must set about 'so organizing ICFC that it shall be there for good and not in any respect a personal *tour de force*. That was all right for creating it: now we want to make sure it is permanently knit into the financial structure.'[119]

Major changes were to be delayed, however, until the end of the decade. With the coming of the 'new deal' in 1959, when the banks finally allowed the Corporation to go to the market for money and opened the door for a considerable expansion of ICFC's business, the transition could be delayed no longer. If Piercy was determined that ICFC was to continue to grow, and the 'new deal' meant that the transition could take place, then crucial decisions about the future operating structure of ICFC had now to be made.

A Solid Foundation

ICFC had established both its independence and its presence in the market due to a combination of factors. As we have seen in the previous chapter, the combination of forces involved in its foundation had in some measure ensured its autonomy. The Treasury and Bank of England had combined to ensure that an institution was set up to deal with the perceived Macmillan gap, which was expected to widen in the turmoil of post-war reconstruction. Their primary goal was that the Government should as far as possible be kept from attempting to intervene directly in financial investment. The Bank of England also saw that the clearers could be pushed, by this same threat of government intervention, and by virtue of mounting popular criticism, to use some of their high level of liquidity in funding the new venture. The banks' reaction was a mixture of antipathy and pragmatism; but eventually agreement was reached that if something was to be done then an independent organization would be appropriate, if only to avoid the impression that they were involved in 'continental' universal banking. There remained elements among the clearers whose intention was to carry on the campaign to limit the effectiveness of the nascent ICFC; and it was therefore imperative that the Corporation be set up with enough autonomy, when allied to the continuing patronage of the Bank of England, to ensure its ability to survive.

Despite the popular misconception, the link between ICFC and government was always indirect at most. Although the Corporation was a child of 1945, a moment of heightened intervention, it was not strongly guided by government policy. After a series of initial joint ventures with the Treasury and DATAC, many of which proved unsatisfactory, contact with government faded. Piercy had sought to use his political influence, particularly with Dalton, to obtain business, but more importantly to add to the support which ICFC needed to stave off the depredations of the clearers. It may not be coincidental that some of the banks renewed their attempts to undermine the Corporation in 1951, the year of Labour's fall from office. But political support had never been crucial to the Corporation's survival, and as with the resignation of Dalton in 1947, the change of government had little, if any, effect upon the strength of ICFC.

However, this balance of forces among the various factions involved in the setting up of ICFC is only half the picture. Within the space that had been guaranteed to the Corporation, individuals like Piercy and Kinross managed to craft an organization capable of operating in a very difficult sector of the market. They also used their own considerable skills in investment strategy to build ICFC up to a point where it could enter a new phase of independence. The 1940s and early 1950s had not only been a struggle against hostile shareholders, as we shall see in the following chapter, but also against the roller-coaster of the economic environment. These difficult early years had ensured that ICFC had developed a resilience to short-term setbacks and an operating method which could accommodate the unorthodox; but also, most importantly, they had established that long-term provision of capital to small- and medium-sized firms, based on thorough industrial and financial appraisal, was not only a viable, but also a mutually beneficial enterprise.

NOTES

[1] Piercy had published an article in 1938 discussing the need for some form of institutional mediation in the Macmillan gap: 'The Financing of Small Businesses', *British Management Review*, 3 (1938).

[2] Piercy was proud to recall that he was asked to teach at the LSE before actually graduating.

[3] *Investors Chronicle*, 10 Oct. 1958; Royal Statistical Society, 130/2 (1967), 274–6; *The Times* 9 June 1965; J. B. Kinross and A. Butt-Philip, *ICFC 1945–1961*, unpubl. MS, 3i Archive (hereafter 3i), 52–3.

[4] B. Pimlott, *Hugh Dalton* (Macmillan 1985), *passim*.

[5] Wheeler's own direct mailing list at one time included over half a million small investors. L. Dennett, *The Charterhouse Group* (1979), 16–7; Kinross, *Fifty Years in the City: Financing Small Business* (John Murray, 1982), 36–68.

[6] J. B. Kinross, *50 Years in the City*, 69–115.

[7] Kinross *ICFC*, 61.

[8] Paul Hildesley, interviewed by Richard Coopey, 4 Mar. 1992.

[9] Frank Harber, interviewed by Richard Coopey, 28 Feb. 1992.

[10] Lord Richardson, interviewed by Richard Coopey, 8 Oct. 1992.

[11] Kinross, *ICFC*, 297.

[12] Kinross, *ICFC*, 62, 67, 85, 118; Ted Cole, interviewed by T. Gourvish; Frank Harber, interview.

[13] Harber, interview.

[14] 'Man of the Month 47', *Scope* (Feb. 1947), 45.

[15] Harber, interview.

[16] Ibid.; Kinross, *ICFC*, 232.

[17] Sir Eric Faulkner, interviewed by Terry Gourvish, 13 Dec. 1991; Kinross, *ICFC*, 80.

[18] Kinross, *ICFC*, 60–1.

[19] Piercy, 1956; Hannah.

[20] Kinross, *ICFC*, 59, 92, 205.

[21] Kinross, *ICFC*, 225.

[22] Kinross, *ICFC*, 138.

[23] 'Industrial and Commercial Finance Corporation', Midland Bank memo, 9 Mar. 1951, Midland Bank Archive (hereafter Midland) 200/10.

[24] Harber, interview; Kinross, *ICFC*, 57.

[25] Harber, interview.

[26] *Financial Times*, 15 May 1951.

[27] Kinross, *ICFC*, 195.

[28] Ted Cole, interview.

[29] Kinross, *ICFC*, 136.

[30] Kinross Application Files, 3i, *passim*.
[31] Kinross Applications File SA(47)20, 3i; for a discussion of the clearing banks' attempts to encroach on ICFC business see below, Ch. 3.
[32] Kinross Applications File, SA(47)15, 3i.
[33] Minutes of the meeting of the Committee of the Board on liaison with customers. 5 Nov. 1946, 3i.
[34] Kinross, *ICFC*, 83.
[35] Harber, interview.
[36] Ibid.
[37] SA(47)21; Druce and Co., Application, 1947; SA(47)13; 3i. Birmingham and Blackstone Construction Co., Piercy Coll. LSE (hereafter Piercy), 217.
[38] Lord Jenkins, in conversation with Richard Coopey, 13 Oct. 1992; Kinross, *ICFC*, 136.
[39] ICFC, *Annual Report*, Chairman's Statement, 1956.
[40] ICFC, Minutes, 4 Sept. 1945.
[41] 'Industrial and Commercial Finance Corporation', Midland Bank memo, 9 Mar. 1951; ICFC Minutes, 2 Apr. 1946; Kinross, *ICFC*, 70, 77.
[42] ICFC, Board Minutes, 2 Oct. 1945, 3i.
[43] Kinross, *ICFC*, 297.
[44] 'Comments on the Comparison of Two Years Operations', 28 Jan. 1948, Box K, 3i; *Annual Report*, Chairman's Statement, 1957, 11.
[45] SA(47)13, 3i.
[46] Kinross, *ICFC*, 97, 213, 223.
[47] See BCal Case Study.
[48] Piercy to Sir Wilfred Eady, 28 Oct. 1945, Piercy 9/180.
[49] For a discussion of the functioning of the Cases Committee, and its role in structuring the policy of ICFC, see below, Ch. 11.
[50] Kinross, *ICFC*, 104, 133–6.
[51] Harber, interview.
[52] ICFC, Board Minutes, 5 Mar. 1946.
[53] ICFC, Board Minutes, 30 July 1946; 24 Sept. 1946; 7 Jan. 1947; 4 Mar. 1947; SA(47)10, 3i.
[54] SA(47)5, 3i.
[55] Kinross, *ICFC*, 290–1.
[56] Piercy to Cripps, 31 Dec. 1947, Piercy 9/180.
[57] Kinross, *ICFC*, 122–3.
[58] SA(47)13, East Anglia Chemical Company, 3i.
[59] Hildesley, interview.
[60] 'Copy of Minute, General Manager to Chairman', 8 Oct. 1947, National Library of Scotland (hereafter NLS) 8699/3; Piercy to Kinross, 9 Aug. 1947, NLS 8699/4.
[61] Kinross, *ICFC*, 77.
[62] Piercy, 'Introductory Review', 1951, 8699/3, 3.
[63] Kinross, *ICFC*, 199.
[64] Kinross, *ICFC*, 77, 144, 137. Piercy to Kinross, 22 Apr. 1947, NLS 8699/6.
[65] 'Industrial and Commercial Finance Corporation Ltd.', Nov. 1947, NLS 8699/1; ICFC Board Minutes, 5 Oct. 1948, 2 Nov. 1948; Kinross, *ICFC*, 211; ICFC *Annual Report and Accounts* 1947, 1948, 1949, 1950.
[66] Minutes of a meeting of the board on liaison with customers, 7 Jan. 1947, 3i.
[67] Piercy, 'Introductory Review', 4.
[68] Kinross, *Diaries*, 1 Jan. 1950. NLS 8699/36.
[69] M. Maurice, memo, 3 Jan. 1951; Piercy, 'Introductory Review'.
[70] ICFC, Board Minutes, 4 Sept. 1945, 3i.
[71] Kinross, *ICFC*, 215.
[72] ICFC, Chairman's Statement, Annual Report 1951.
[73] *Annual Reports*, 1951, 1961.
[74] E. Ralph, 'Birmingham Office', 6 Feb. 1951, NLS 8699/3.

[75] Kinross, *ICFC*, 229.
[76] Harber, interview.
[77] For a general discussion of the impact of diversification on the group, see below, Ch. 12.
[78] Kinross, *ICFC*, 96, 158, 218.
[79] Larry Tindale, interviewed by Richard Coopey, 31 Mar.1992.
[80] Kinross, 'Lincoln Electric', June 1984, NLS 8699/14; SA(52)93 3i.
[81] 'A Note By Lord Piercy on a Project for an Estate Duties Investment Trust Company', 1952; A. Tuke to Piercy, 31 July 1952; CLCB Minutes, 31 July 1952; NLS 8699/14.
[82] Tuke, Chairman's note to CLCB, 'Estate Duties Investment Trust Company', 11 Dec. 1952, NLS 8699/14.
[83] Piercy to Kinross, 9 Aug. 1952; Lord Blackford to Kinross, 26 Feb. 1972, NLS 8699/4.
[84] Kinross, *Diaries, 1950*, annotations by Kinross, 1984, NLS 8699/36.
[85] Minutes of a meeting between representatives of ICFC and the FBI, 28 Oct. 1945, Modern Records Centre, Warwick.
[86] Kinross, *ICFC*, 224–5.
[87] As early as 1947 these included The National Gas and Oil Engine Company, British Drug Houses, Viscose Development, Waite and Sons, and John Baker and Bessemer. G. S. Stone to Piercy, 9 Apr. 1947, Piercy 9/108; P372, P383, P362, SA(47)2, 3, 5, 3i.
[88] Kinross, *ICFC*, 224–5; SA(48)117, SA(49)1, 3i.
[89] Kinross, *Diaries, 1950*, annotations. NLS 8699/36.
[90] Piercy to Kinross, 7 Apr. 1954, NLS 8699/6.
[91] P336, SA(47)6, 3i.
[92] See below, Ch. 3.
[93] *Annual Reports*, 1949–51.
[94] P372 SA(47)2, 3i.
[95] Kinross, *ICFC*, 112–16.
[96] Kinross, *ICFC*, 105–8; P383 SA(47)4, 3i.
[97] *The Times*, 2 Apr. 1947.
[98] *Financial Times*, 3 Apr. 1947.
[99] Kinross, *ICFC*, 116; *The Times*, 20 Mar. 1948.
[100] Kinross, *ICFC*, 116.
[101] Kinross, *Diaries*, 11–13 Jan. 1950.
[102] Siegmund Warburg was particularly impressed with Kinross and later attempted to recruit him onto the board at the bank. Kinross memo, 22 Nov. 1966, NLS 8699/3; Kinross, *ICFC*, 140–1.
[103] ICFC Board Minutes, 6 Aug. 1948. Kinross, 'ICFC'.
[104] Hildesley, interview.
[105] Derek Millard, interviewed by Richard Coopey.
[106] ICFC Board Minutes, 4 Sept. 1945.
[107] Ted Cole, interview.
[108] Kinross, *ICFC*, 130–1; Piercy, 'Introductory Review', 2.
[109] J. Kinross, 'The Braunsberg Saga', chs. 14 and 15, MS. 3i.
[110] Kinross, *Diaries, 1950*, 1984 annotations, 5–6.
[111] Mary Francis, interviewed by Richard Coopey. 24 March 1992
[112] Lord Richardson, interview 8 October 1992; Kinross, *Diaries, passim.*
[113] Kinross, *ICFC*, 214.
[114] Kinross, *Diaries*, 9 Jan. 1950. A subsequent entry on Feb. 22 recalls: 'During the latter part of the afternoon I actually had some time on my hands—goodness knows when this last occurred.'
[115] Kinross, *ICFC*, 283.
[116] Harber, Millard, interviews.
[117] Piercy to Kinross 9 Feb. 1949, NLS 8699/3.
[118] Kinross, ICFC, 284.
[119] Piercy to Kinross, 4 Apr. 1954, NLS 8699/6.

Chapter 3

Establishing Independence

THE PUBLIC ANNOUNCEMENT in January 1945 of the formation of ICFC and FCI was generally greeted with praise, tinged with some apprehension. The *Daily Telegraph* hailed it as an 'encouraging and forward-looking development'. *The Times* also welcomed the initiatives but expressed 'anxiety lest the new organizations should either bolster up uneconomic industrial concerns or developments or should compete, possibly on a privileged basis, with existing financial channels'.[1] Others recognized that the immediate post-war period would usher in unusual times, calling for 'unusual risks' to be taken on behalf of British industry.[2] At the heart of these comments lies the notion of competition versus intervention and, as we saw in the first chapter, the various actors in the process of setting up ICFC and FCI each had their own ideas, in this respect, about the optimal functioning of the finance system and whether the new institutions should be state-directed, independent, or even non-existent. As the institutions became a reality, the debate over their functioning was by no means brought to a close, but rather, in some senses, was seriously engaged for the first time. During the 1940s and 1950s each of the participants in the process which had shaped ICFC and FCI, notably the Bank of England, the clearing banks, the Treasury, and to a limited extent the Board of Trade and the Labour Party, sought to a greater or lesser degree to ensure that the Corporation behaved according to their particular plan. ICFC in turn was to respond in a variety of ways which, after a period of considerable struggle, were eventually to ensure the Corporation's autonomy and subsequent growth.

Shareholder Control or Independence?

The first board meeting was held at the Bank of England on 24 July 1945, four days after the incorporation of ICFC. The Corporation opened for business on

That's very sweet, Mr. Sefton, but you still don't have enough money in your account to cover this cheque.

27 July at offices rented from the National Bank of New Zealand at 8 Moorgate, incidentally, on the same day it became clear that Labour would form the first post-war government. The Bank of England nominated William Piercy to be Chairman of the Corporation.[3] Other Board members were Edward De Stein, a merchant banker nominated by the Westminster Bank; W. H. Frazer, Chairman of the National Bank of Scotland, nominated by Lloyds Bank; Lord Dudley Gordon, Chairman of Hadfields; J. E. Hall, nominated by Barclays Bank; the Earl of Limerick, a director of the London Life Association and Chairman of Parnell Aircraft; G.K. Mason (later Lord Blackford), a director of, and nominated by, the Midland Bank; Hugh Roberts, ex-Chairman of Fisher and Hallow, an industrialist who was considered for the Chairmanship of ICFC but nominated for a directorship instead by Lord Catto, the Governor of the Bank of England; and finally Colin Skinner, a director of the Lancashire Cotton Corporation.

The loyalty of this Board to Piercy and ICFC was to prove an important factor into the 1950s as a volatile relationship between the Corporation and its shareholders developed. All of the directors had varying degrees of interest in the clearing banks,[4] but with one notable exception the Board could usually be relied upon to rally to the support of Piercy. The exception, Edward De Stein, the Westminster's representative, had only grudgingly accepted the appointment, believing the new Corporation to have little prospect of success. In the event his tenure was short-lived. After only fifteen months in office, in November 1946, De Stein felt compelled to resign in protest at what he considered to be ICFC's trespass on the natural preserve of the merchant banks.[5]

Piercy's success in strongly asserting his independence at the head of ICFC, and his insistence on the kind of role he had begun to fashion for the Corporation, was reflected in the fact that the rest of the Board did not support De Stein when he stood down. This stance was in marked contrast to the attitude of key figures at some of the shareholder banks, however. The problematic relationship between ICFC and its shareholders was to prove to be one of the greatest difficulties which the Corporation would face in becoming established.

Clipping the Wings of ICFC

If the shareholders hostile to ICFC could not rely on the Board to restrict or curtail the activities of the Corporation, they could look to other methods. The conditions under which the Corporation was set up meant that it was solely reliant upon the clearing banks for the provision of capital, at least until it could generate an income stream of its own. ICFC was also partially dependent upon the clearers' goodwill in forwarding business and providing credit references. Both these aspects of dependence were to be used by some of the clearers in their campaign to frustrate the progress of ICFC.

Moves by some of the clearing banks to offset the impact of ICFC had begun in earnest early in 1945, following the public announcement of its formation. The National Provincial, for example, circulated a memo to all branches stating that, although the new company had been set up to deal with the extraordinary circumstances of reconstruction, the bank itself would continue to provide all necessary finance, especially that required by small traders, and that any enquiries which seemed to fall into the ambit of ICFC should be sent direct to the bank's own headquarters.[6] Barclays circulated a similar memo, admitting there might be cases where long-term finance might be appropriate and the services of ICFC necessary, but generally reaffirming the bank's own commitment to small firms and insisting all applications be channelled to head office in order to keep track of ICFC activity.[7] Bank head offices also noted that ICFC was not expected to operate as a bank. The location of accounts would therefore be unaffected, and ICFC money would not be used to repay overdraft facilities.[8]

It had been initially envisaged that the banks would work in concert with ICFC, each bank appointing a liaison officer to deal with the Corporation, circulate its publicity, and forward a steady supply of enquiries deemed to be outside the province of the normal banking business. These hopes began to founder at an early date. At the Westminster, for example, Charles Lidbury continued the trenchant opposition he had mounted during the wartime debates. In response to a letter which James Lawrie had sent to the Liaison Officers, accompanying the first issue of ICFC's publicity brochure, Lidbury wrote that in fact none of these brochures was wanted, that there was 'no place' for ICFC, and the idea of circulating information about the corporation to local managers should be rejected.[9]

In spite of such opposition a limited number of introductions did begin to arrive at ICFC, forwarded by the clearers. Piercy was still optimistic in late 1945 that a 'regular flow' would eventually result, but rather paradoxically told his Board that the banks were 'holding their hands to give the immature organization some time to develop'.[10] An analysis of ICFC's investment up to February 1946, by which time it had lent over £1.5 million, shows that the banks had introduced 35 per cent of ICFC's agreed loans by number, 24 per cent by value. Barclays alone accounted for half of this total in number, but tended to forward smaller applications only. The Westminster's meagre offerings resulted in only one agreed loan, for £5,000—the lower limit of ICFC activity.[11]

An analysis of total introductions refused or accepted reflects even more impressively in favour of Barclays, who supplied over 80 per cent of the enquiries forwarded by banks. However, in this case, volume of introductions is probably a misleading measurement, since it was noted that some banks had a tendency to forward 'third-rate business' which they themselves had shunned. ICFC's own analysis showed that a high proportion of rejected applicants subsequently failed to secure funding from any source.[12] To make matters worse the banks had liberalized their own criteria for accepting business. Piercy had cause to complain to Lord Catto at the Bank of England that the banks were, by late 1945, 'prepared to accept any business which, in the broadest lines, is reasonably sound, irrespective of whether it is a lock-up, or for how long or indefinite a period it may be so'.[13]

The banks' widening of their sphere of operations in order to encroach on ICFC's territory was only part of the problem. Some banks actively sought to take business away from ICFC, after the Corporation had spent time evaluating prospective cases. ICFC's initial method of assessment necessitated applying to the banks for credit references for prospective customers, and the Corporation's application forms called for permission to do this. Once terms were agreed, the practice was to notify liaison officers at the bank in question to inform them of business being transacted. This meant that the banks were privy to information about ICFC's applicants and, in many early cases, they could step in and offer arrangements on equal or better terms. ICFC's very first approved case, a loan to the London printers Williams-Cook, was subsequently lost in this way. Kinross later recalled one particularly ominous case in late 1945 when a £50,000, 10-year loan was offered to Novello and Co., the music publishers. When Lidbury was informed of the case he immediately stepped in and offered to lend the money without investigation. This provoked an angry confrontation with ICFC's Lawrie, but with little effect on Lidbury's attitude.[14] Such activities mirrored those which had been the cause of complaints made by ICFC's erstwhile predecessor, Credit for Industry, in the 1930s.

Through the 1940s and into the 1950s this pattern of behaviour began to settle down. Some of the banks periodically complained about ICFC's limited publicity, which stated that 'existing facilities provided by the Banking Institutions and Stock Exchange are not readily and easily available'.[15] Banks also continued to insist on a central monitoring of ICFC activity by head offices.[16] For its part, ICFC modified its already rather limited publicity in line with some of the complaints received. The Corporation also adopted a more cautious approach to contacting the banks for credit references, reflecting the fact that some of the banks were to remain intransigent. As Ted Cole recalled, one of the shareholders was inclined to 'put the skids under us whenever they could'.[17] It would be a mistake, however, to view all the banks as universally hostile to ICFC, or to view relationships as difficult across the board.

It had been argued that ICFC's provision of funds should be complementary to services provided by the banks. The former would provide long-term 'lock-up' capital for buildings, plant, and machinery, for example, while the banks could continue to finance trade credit, stock, work in progress, and so on. Increased turnover, it was argued, would boost overdraft requirements to the benefit of bankers. It was ICFC's avowed policy not to provide funds to replace overdrafts, and the Corporation's minutes show cases where funds requested 'to pay out the bank' had been refused.[18] Statistics assembled on a sample of eighty-nine ICFC companies in 1951 supported the argument that a loan from ICFC boosted business for the banks. Overdraft facilities in these cases had risen from £1,900,000 to £2,890,000.[19] Banks could also be reassured in that ICFC's security on loans ranked partially behind that of the banks themselves. This was achieved by a sandwich arrangement, developed by James Lawrie, whereby the banks retained a charge on the customers' floating assets, and ICFC took a charge on the fixed assets and used part of their money for share capital.[20]

Despite these arrangements, most of the banks continued to be wary of ICFC, seeing its activities as potentially competitive rather than complementary. There was strong opposition from some quarters to the Corporation's ambition to set up a branch system. This was seen as a step towards active competition, rather than the bank's preferred role for ICFC as a form of "lender of last resort". The issue of ICFC expanding into the regions evidently worried the Committee of London Clearing Bankers (CLCB). A memo declared that: 'The impression given . . . is that the Corporation has reached a stage of contemplating an active search for business, as distinct from the more passive stage of holding itself available to meet the requirements falling within the range of the "Macmillan gap".'[21]

At a local level, bank branches may have adopted a more conciliatory stance. The insistence of central control of the monitoring of the Corporation's activities probably reflected a distancing between the attitude of banks' headquarters and those of their branch managers, who in many cases were more easily persuaded to co-operate with ICFC. Bankers in the locality could see real benefits in attracting ICFC money for their customers, and many became reluctant to pass information on to their own headquarters, for fear of losing control of accounts.[22] At an early stage ICFC recognized the value of forging local links between the branches of the clearing banks and its own regional network.[23]

Distrust of ICFC was not universal; for example, the headquarters staff at Barclays remained the most friendly, taking a pragmatic approach in their dealings with the Corporation. ICFC did some joint business with Barclays, for example, in cases where the required loans exceeded ICFC's nominal £200,000 limit.[24] Barclays' general attitude to ICFC was supportive, seeing the relationship as potentially mutually beneficial.[25] John Kinross frequently lunched with the Barclays' general managers. In 1950, for example, Kinross noted that Cecil

Your mother called to remind you she owns controlling interest of this company . . .

Ellerton of Barclays' was a 'very nice man I'd say, and wholly friendly to us'.[26] When A. W. Tuke was General Manager at Barclays he also proved to be one of the key supporters of ICFC.[27] In addition, the Corporation found support among its minor shareholders, which included Martins, the District, and Glyn Mills.[28]

The Midland Bank also rallied supporters. Lord Blackford, Deputy Chairman of the Midland and one of ICFC's directors, was to become a 'stabilizing influence' in the conflicts which were to develop between ICFC and its shareholders.[29] Clarence Sadd, too, General Manager at the Midland during the Corporation's formative years, formed a close relationship with Piercy. The two regularly exchanged books by authors such as Carlyle and Huxley, and Sadd kept Piercy informed of the Midland's activities in the small-firm sector.[30] Sadd's support for Piercy stemmed in part from their mutual socialist affiliation. Sadd, professing to having been 'an untamed radical all my life', was an ardent admirer of Attlee and spoke in glowing terms of the prospects for the Labour administration. He wrote that 'Mr Attlee's personality and character is just what we want for our peace recovery' and found great pleasure in saying so to his banking colleagues, 'to their undisguised surprise, even consternation'.[31] It may well be that Sadd was 'working assiduously' to promote his relationship with government ministers and saw Piercy as a useful contact in this respect; he frequently raised issues which he asked Piercy to bring to the attention of Cripps and Attlee.[32]

Notwithstanding the support of Sadd and Tuke, ICFC still faced a difficult time with the clearing banks. The Committee of London Clearing Banks and its Chief Executive Officers (CEO) committee, provided the forum where concerted opposition was to develop. ICFC's relationship with the CLCB varied periodically, often fluctuating in line with a change of chairman, but it fared worse with the CEO committee. As Kinross noted, this committee 'always contained so many men hostile to ICFC that the influence of its current chairman was pretty limited'.[33] It was from these committees that a series of challenges to ICFC was to emerge.

The first major confrontation was in 1948. In the first two years of trading, due to a combination of inexperience and anxiety to build its portfolio, ICFC had lent money to customers who represented a greater risk than it was perhaps prudent to take. The Corporation's monitoring procedures were also not fully developed, and the uncertain post-war environment added difficulties for many firms. The result was that from 1947 onwards ICFC began to accumulate an unacceptably large number of bad debts. These were particularly visible in ICFC's accounts since the income from other business, notably long-term loans and equity holdings, had not begun to accrue in the short term. Piercy attempted to keep bad-debt provisions as low as possible in the Company Reports, but as Kinross noted, by September 1948, 'troubles were emerging all over the place . . . we were operating too near to the edge of the financial precipice'.[34]

The crisis at ICFC was made worse by the appointment in 1948 of Lord Linlithgow as Chairman of the CLCB. This, Piercy noted, 'was to herald a painful period of relations' between ICFC and its shareholders.[35] From early 1948 onwards Linlithgow made repeated calls for a report from ICFC giving full disclosure of information about companies which were failing, and full details of ICFC's operations. Lack of detailed information had previously been railed at by the clearers, who complained that it was 'not possible to more than second-guess the average lending of the Corporation'.[36] Now Linlithgow attempted to use the bad-debt position of ICFC to force the issue. Piercy's immediate response was to offer a 'special report', although he also insisted on mentioning the incident to the Governor of the Bank of England.[37] The report was duly presented as a supplement to the published ICFC figures, but was deemed to be inadequate.[38]

The report did produce a temporary lull in hostilities, but in 1949 Linlithgow returned to the offensive and again demanded full information. Piercy responded that the banks would not want details of bad debts circulated among their rivals and besides, such action would result in 'my directors taking the huff'.[39] This tactic reflected Piercy's confidence in the support of his own Board, but served only to elicit a burst of indignation from Linlithgow: 'Lord Piercy takes an entirely distorted view of "his" Board. It is "our" Board appointed to represent our interests. If any director feels he is unable to do that he should resign . . . I feel this to be a very poor reply and only emphasises the necessity for firm action now.'[40] Although some of the bankers advocated caution in pressing this matter, lest it simply worsen relations, others agreed with Linlithgow that each ICFC director's loyalty should be to the shareholders.[41]

Linlithgow reiterated, at regular intervals, his calls for full disclosure, but was forced to concede by the end of 1950 that such requests were unlikely to bear fruit, since Piercy, it seemed, commanded 'one hundred per cent attachment of his board and practically one hundred per cent secrecy'.[42] More important than this, however, was the fact that Piercy could call on one other very powerful ally, the Bank of England. When Lord Catto was the Bank's Governor, he poured cold water on the idea that ICFC should provide more information to the banks and when, in the early 1950s, they attempted to restrict the level of capital available to ICFC, linked to this demand, he stepped in again.

The banks seemed to be committed to provide up to £45 million to ICFC in share and loan capital. The Corporation's Articles of Association stipulated that the shareholders would provide up to £15 million in share capital, matched by a further £15 million in loans, subject to a majority approval. A further £15 million of loan capital could be made available on the approval of

The Frizzell Group

3i's INVESTMENT IN FRIZZELL is a good example of its willingness to accept long-term involvement. The business was started in 1920 as an insurance broker with associated underwriting syndicates at Lloyd's. The founder, T. Norman Frizzell was still chairman of the company which had net assets of £175,000 when ICFC was approached, in 1954, to buy a bonus issue of preference capital for the provision of estate duty. ICFC made an initial investment of £40,000 and retained its holding throughout the next forty years as Frizzell expanded steadily under the control of family members.

In 1975, after an abortive attempt at flotation ICFC and EDITH jointly were invited in their capital market substitution role to purchase a further substantial holding. As the chairman expresses it in his letter to shareholders, this was intended to 'enable all members, if they so wish, to realize part of their holding in the company without the control or direction of the company's affairs being greatly affected'.

In the later 1970s and early 1980s further rounds of capital were provided as Frizzell consolidated its position, specializing in insurance for 'affinity groups' such as the Caravan Club, National Trust, and Civil Service Motoring Association, and moving into banking services. By the 1990s the company had over half a million customers and a staff of 1,450. 3i's equity interest grew eventually to 40.8 per cent, at a cost of nearly £4.4 million. In 1992 when the American firm of Marsh and McLennan, the world's largest insurance brokers and a specialist in affinity group business in the USA, put in an offer for the financial services section of the company, 3i sold all of its holding for over £40 million. An equity partner in Frizzell for 38 years, 3i continues as shareholder, alongside the Frizzell family, in the broking business which has retained its independence as 'First City Insurance Brokers', providing specialist products for insurance intermediaries, insurance for professional firms, and reinsurance.

75 per cent of the shareholders. The total of £45 million in capital which was potentially available to ICFC was thus a conditional undertaking, at least in the eyes of some of the shareholders. Publicity surrounding ICFC had given the impression that the money was freely available to Piercy, much to the chagrin of some of the clearers. Articles such as the one in *Scope* in 1947 with a picture of Piercy captioned 'It's a £45,000,000 smile!' and commenting that Piercy 'still has some £44,000,000 to give away' did little to calm the situation.[43] By 1949 some of the shareholders were re-examining ICFC's Articles, looking for loopholes. They concluded that the £45 million was merely a 'notional' figure and

that the 'obligation' of the banks could vary with circumstances.[44] It was argued that ICFC's refusal to comply with requests for information had already weakened this obligation, as had its high proportion of bad debts. In addition, the clearers were to become uneasy about ICFC apparently operating outside its remit, by doing non-Macmillan gap business.

This situation came to a head in 1951 when the first of the post-war credit squeezes hit the clearing banks. The government, moving to curb inflation, raised the bank rate above 2 per cent, signalling the end of the period of cheap money which had prevailed since the early 1930s.[45] By March 1952 the rate had doubled to 4 per cent. The government also called for a restriction on the provision of credit, and the Capital Issues Committee (CIC) was later to reduce the lower limit on loans needing its approval, from £50,000 down to £10,000. There followed a period of continual wrangling between ICFC and the clearers over both the supply of capital and the rate of interest which the Corporation was to be charged on it. The ratio of share capital to loan capital which ICFC took up also became a focal point of the argument, since share capital carried no interest, whereas loan capital did. It therefore seemed to benefit ICFC to take as much share capital as possible, more so in the early years since the question of dividend payments remained in abeyance.

The argument over the ratio of share to loan capital continued throughout the early 1950s. Linlithgow repeatedly urged Piercy to take a higher ratio of loan capital, and Piercy, in a calculated response, took this as an invitation to simply increase ICFC's overall borrowing.[46] The balance between loan and share capital was to have been pegged at a ratio of 2 : 1, limiting the amount of loan capital at any one time to a figure twice that of share capital. In 1951 ICFC backed down and agreed to a change in its Articles which would permit loans to be in proportion to the 'nominal amount of issued capital' rather than actual paid-up capital. This produced a new limit of £30 million on loans.[47] In fact, Piercy was not averse to taking up loan capital, since he had begun to plan for the day when ICFC could go to the market to raise funds; and he considered the Corporation to be more attractive to prospective investors if it retained a higher level of uncalled share capital.[48] With the exception of a brief period in 1953 when Piercy was persuaded to take more share capital, ICFC's borrowings continued to rise disproportionately. By 1958 £25 million of loan capital had been taken up, compared to £7.5 million of share capital.[49]

With the increase in the level of loan capital taken up by ICFC came an intensification of the general problem of interest rates payable. In 1947 ICFC had been paying 2 per cent. This was increased by stages after 1951 and in March 1952 a general agreement fixed the rate on all outstanding loans at 0.5 per cent over that of the bank rate. This created real problems for ICFC, since they had no way of passing on this increase on money already advanced as long-term loans at fixed interest rates. Although it was agreed to limit the rise in interest to a maximum of 3 per cent on loan capital taken up before 1952, ICFC's expected profit margins were severely squeezed.[50] Piercy complained vociferously that the nationalized industries continued to enjoy funding at a lower rate, guaranteed by the Treasury, but ICFC was forced to bear increased costs.[51] The Corporation had no choice but to continue to offer fixed-interest long-term loans. This created real problems, as by 1956 some 92 per cent of ICFC money was lent at fixed rates and it was receiving only 4.4 per cent net interest on post-1952 money. The Corporation was by then actually paying 6 per cent on this money.[52]

ICFC did stay in profit during this period, thanks partly to income from equity gains where its investee companies had gone to the market. Nevertheless this was an extremely difficult time for the Corporation. The level of new business which ICFC could do was severely restricted, and a second credit squeeze in the mid-1950s again caused the banks to restrict the provision of capital.[53] The banks were reluctant to provide their own funds to what they saw as a rival institution, while they themselves were restricted, and by 1956 the banks actually began to ask for repayment of some of the loan capital outstanding. These requests were beaten off by Piercy, but an overall reduction in the flow of loan capital from the banks was unavoidable. This resulted in a period of 'enforced inactivity' from late 1956 onwards, when ICFC was forced to turn away a large amount of sound business.[54]

Piercy's New Deal

Throughout this period of credit restriction the Bank of England had proved the final arbiter. In the 1950 squeeze the banks had put forward the argument that ICFC was operating outside its Macmillan gap remit by lending sums over £200,000, becoming involved in syndicated business for larger amounts, acting as an issuing house, and lending money to larger, often publicly quoted, companies. Further developments, including the establishment of the Estate Duties Investment Trust and the Ship Mortgage Finance Corporation, added fuel to the argument that ICFC was expanding beyond the original intentions of its founders.[55] There were also complaints that these latter activities had been undertaken without formal consultation between ICFC and the banks. Also, the banks noted that the idea of ICFC was tolerable in 1945, given their high level of liquidity at the time, but that this had changed radically by the 1950s. The banks maintained that, with these developments, they were no longer 'morally obligated' to support ICFC, and suggested that the Bank of England alone should take responsibility for providing ICFC with funds. This seemed particularly appropriate as the Bank had been nationalized since 1946.[56]

The Bank of England's response to the clearing banks' resolution to 'take whatever steps are necessary to limit their commitment to ICFC' was to resort to the old threat of government intervention. In keeping with the prevalent policy of the 1950s the Bank resorted to reasoned persuasion rather than formal mechanisms of control.[57] The banks were reminded that ICFC was set up in order to avoid such involvement, and that it had 'filled a useful job in that it has made it much easier for the Bank of England to resist action by the government from time to time'.[58] The Governor, Lord Catto, thought at the time that ICFC 'had done well and had proved there was a gap to be filled'.[59] The Bank took Piercy's side as far as possible, and continued to point out that the clearing banks were 'morally bound' to support ICFC.[60]

Piercy had nurtured the support of the Bank of England. He had, for example, been careful to keep the Bank informed of all ICFC activities, such as the proposal for EDITH, in advance of consulting the CLCB.[61] He also put his own side of the case to the Governor, complaining of the 'bankers' clamp' he found himself in. Despite the support of the Bank, however, the experience of the early 1950s convinced Piercy that he needed a greater degree of freedom and security, and it hardened his resolve to break free from the straitjacket created by being solely reliant on the banks for capital. ICFC's own earnings were growing to a point where 57 per cent of the investments made in 1953 were funded from repayments, realizations and retained profits.[62] This still left ICFC vulnerable, however, as the 1955–6 period was to show, and pointed to a rate of growth which was insufficient for Piercy's ambitions.

Piercy had first mentioned the idea of a 'new deal' for ICFC at the start of the 1950s, whereby the Corporation would be free to borrow money from other sources beside the clearing banks. Tentative suggestions were quickly rebuffed by Linlithgow in 1950, and Piercy dropped the subject.[63] He raised the issue again in 1953, however, but, somewhat ironically, on this occasion the banks refused to consider it because the temporary lull in the credit squeeze meant they were under less pressure themselves.[64] Some of the bankers, such as Tuke, did consider the suggestion seriously, however, and thought it a possibility that ICFC had reached the limits of the banks' commitment.[65] Piercy pursued the plan, insisting on the payment by ICFC of a dividend and arguing that a good dividend record would improve the prospects of attracting funds.

With the problems of 1955: when the supply of funds from the clearers was curtailed, Piercy again began to press for more independence, stating that the banks should pay up without question or allow ICFC to go to the market for money. Again this was rejected. The following year, however, saw a change at the CLCB, when David Robarts became Chairman and Sir Oliver Franks became Deputy. By 1958 the attitude of the CLCB had changed to the point where ICFC's suggestion of independence was being seriously considered. Piercy himself was slightly surprised: 'What has thawed them, I can't imagine, except that two decent men like Robarts and Franks feel as bad as we do about this cat and mouse business . . . if we can get this done right, it may mean open water for us.'[66] Coincidentally, R. G. Thornton of Barclays and A. D. Chesterton of the Westminster, both of whom Kinross took to be 'reasonable men', occupied the chair of the CEO committee between 1955 and 1959.

Discussions began in earnest in late 1958, and it was agreed soon after that ICFC should issue debenture stock to rank ahead of its bank loans in priority. The first debenture, for £10,000,000, was issued in July 1959, and, after a period of mild apprehension at the slow call for prospectuses, was entirely successful, being substantially oversubscribed.[67] Part of the money was used to repay a portion of the loans outstanding to the clearers, and an undertaking was given by ICFC that further issues would progressively reduce the balance of loans from the banks, to the point at which their interest would be solely share capital.

The boost to ICFC in financial terms—with approximately £6 million of new capital to invest—was judged to be a new dawn. It did not simply mean that ICFC, previously 'perennially short of money', could now begin to fund the considerable amount of business which it had been forced to turn away. It also meant that, with a fixed rate of interest on ICFC's long-term borrowing, the Corporation could now balance its borrowing with the long-term lending it undertook; and it was also taken by Piercy to herald a new era of freedom. Immediately he began to anticipate 'spreading our wings a little', possibly doing 'some good underwriting'. He also initiated a move into the hire purchase business.[68] With no formal limit on the amount of capital ICFC could raise on the market, the Corporation would now become largely its own master in terms of the kind of business it did. The 'new deal' was to be accompanied by a shake-up in the Board of ICFC. Since the banks had also relinquished the right to appoint directors, Piercy took the opportunity to effect a 'transformation to a younger board'. Beyond this, he began to look to the managerial expertise within ICFC 'with a view to professionalising its organization'.[69]

Throughout the period 1945–59 the banks had used both indirect and direct means to limit the activities of ICFC. They had not proved to be the hoped-for conduit through which business could flow; indeed, they had frequently intervened to take business away from ICFC. They had attempted, with varying success, to restrict the availability of funds to ICFC, or to price those funds too high to enable the Corporation to compete effectively. With the support of a minority of friendly bankers, however, and the continued patronage of the Bank of England, ICFC had survived this, its most perilous period, emerging at the start of the 1960s as an established and now reasonably independent institution.

Before going on to consider other influences on ICFC's progress, it is worth highlighting one particular aspect of the ICFC–shareholder relationship, that between the Corporation and the Scottish banks. From the outset, they had been hostile to the idea of a single ICFC, based in London, and had only reluctantly agreed to participate on condition that a separate Scottish Committee would be set up within the Corporation. In the event this committee proved to be a limited success. The Scottish banks themselves aggressively intervened to compete with ICFC, and by 1951 Kinross was referring to Scotland as 'a dead loss'. 'There is so much prejudice and the attitude of the Scottish banks is such that I doubt if this will ever prove a lucrative field for our business.'[70] The Scottish banks, it has been suggested, were adept at spotting the potential of some smaller firms, leaving only 'the most difficult type of ordinary business' for ICFC.[71] Whether due to the skill of the Scottish banks or the lack of effectiveness of ICFC's Scottish Committee, the fact remained that Scotland continued to attract a proportionately low level of funds from ICFC, and this compounded the animosity among the Scottish shareholder banks. In 1947 only 4.9 per cent of ICFC business was done in Scotland. This, the Scottish banks pointed out, was a net loss to the country since they contributed 10.86 per cent of ICFC's capital. By 1953 business transacted had only risen to 5.8 per cent, and it was not until 1966, twenty-one years after ICFC's foundation, that investment in Scotland reached more than 10 per cent of ICFC business.[72]

Industrial Policy versus the Market

If, by the beginning of the 1960s, ICFC had successfully freed itself from the influence of the clearing banks, how did it fare with other parties which had been interested in its establishment between 1943 and 1945? Government departments were prominent among these, particularly the Treasury, which had helped to shape the Corporation, and to a lesser extent the Board of Trade. This is an interesting relationship to explore, not least in view of the lasting, and mistaken, impression among many observers that ICFC was some form of government-funded institution.

There was, of course, no formal connection between the activities of ICFC and government policy. The Macmillan Committee report had noted that financial policies 'must not be imposed so as to thwart the energies of enterprise',[73] and ICFC was to be nominally free to be as enterprising as it wished. In response to questions raised by Aneurin Bevan about the possible control of ICFC, when its formation was officially announced, the Chancellor, Sir John Anderson, had to admit that both ICFC and FCI were to act independently of the government. Anderson merely stated that it was 'intended that the Corporations should keep in touch with the government so that the government may be fully aware of what was being done'.[74] The official stance of ICFC reciprocated this non-involvement. One of the earliest minutes notes that 'The Corporation is primarily concerned with only the soundness and attractiveness or otherwise of proposals from the business point of view, and considerations of national and general economic policy did not fall within the Company's province.'[75]

The matter was sealed officially in 1947, when controversy arose over ICFC's role in purchasing a large block of shares in the National Gas and Oil Engine Company. Under prompting from a disgruntled competitor, Conservative MP, E. H. Keeling, asked Labour Chancellor Hugh Dalton if he would see to it that ICFC did no further business outside its remit of providing finance for small businesses. Dalton replied that the purchase in question had been sanctioned by the Treasury. When pressed on the matter of ICFC being limited to the provision of funds to small businesses Dalton replied that he would 'reserve the right to change any arrangements that may then have been made'.[76] This somewhat hasty remark brought widespread press comment and further questions in the Commons. Government replies were, in line with all statements concerning ICFC, rather vague and non-committal, but the official line remained that ICFC was free to act as it wished while keeping in close contact with the government. There was contact between the government and ICFC and an unofficial relationship did develop between the Corporation, and the Treasury in particular. Whatever the intentions of the government were in 1945, however, this relationship was destined to develop along lines which largely suited Piercy and ICFC.

Treasury patronage came in useful almost immediately for ICFC at a very mundane level. The department used its influence to ensure that ICFC was supplied with basic office requirements in 1945. Office furniture, telephones, even newspapers were all subject to various restrictions in the immediate post-war period, but supplies were procured by ICFC, occasionally by rather devious means. Extra telephones were obtained, for example, by a pre-arranged charade whereby when a senior Treasury official made a visit to Piercy the meeting was constantly interrupted by staff using the solitary 'phone in the Chairman's office.[77]

The services of other government departments were used by ICFC in the more serious business of evaluating potential customers and gaining official reaction to investment proposals. Each government department appointed a liaison officer to deal with ICFC enquiries, and ICFC frequently sought the recommendations of officials in the Ministry of Supply and the Ministry of Works. The Ministry of Works' national and regional experts often accompanied ICFC representatives on trips to assess potential investments. In the brick industry, for example, the Ministry of Works co-operated with ICFC in an attempt to establish a major new brick producer.[78] In return ICFC often seemed to be sympathetic to general government policy where appropriate.

The Corporation was sensitive to the government's export drive in the late 1940s, for example, and was occasionally prepared to fund a more speculative venture on the basis that it was involved in the export business.[79]

Piercy continued to link ICFC's activities with government policy as long as it seemed to be mutually beneficial. One noticeable connection was with the Treasury's 'development area' policies, aimed at fostering regionally based industries which had suffered disproportionately since the 1930s. Piercy met with officials from the Development Areas Treasury Advisory Committee—set up under the Distribution of Industry Act, soon after ICFC was founded—to discuss areas of possible co-operation.[80] Piercy also suggested that ICFC join with the Treasury in the joint funding of selected companies, the Treasury offering lower interest rates than ICFC.

Treasury officials were nervous about the suggested ranking of security on these loans, but Piercy's suggestions were supported by his ally, Sir Wilfred Eady.[81] Eady had been one of the principal actors behind the formation of ICFC, and was to continue his involvement through a close association with Piercy throughout the Corporation's early years. Piercy called on Eady for support on a number of further occasions, seeking more information on government policy and backing for proposals that ICFC should specialize in specific sectors of industry (pursuing a policy of nationalization on a smaller scale than that undertaken by FCI).[82]

Some joint projects were undertaken by ICFC and DATAC, including finance for Marchon Products, a subsidiary of Solway Chemicals in which DATAC had a major interest. This investment yielded a substantial profit for

Table 3.1. Investment in Development Areas; £000 (Year ending September or March)

	Sept. 1947 Amount approved	%	Sept. 1948 Amount approved	%	Sept. 1949 Amount approved	%	March 1950 [a] Amount approved	%	March 1951 Outstanding	%	March 1952 Outstanding	%	March 1953 Outstanding	%
Scotland	321.5	20.2	371.0	20.2	521.0	21.7	567.2	16.9	518.9	19.2	645.1	21.3	666.8	18.8
North-east	939.1	58.9	909.6	49.5	918.5	38.2	990.6	29.5	n.a.	n.a.	n.a.	n.a.	n.a.	n.a.
North-west	160.0	10.0	245.0	13.3	522.0	21.7	522.0	15.5	n.a.	n.a.	n.a.	n.a.	n.a.	n.a.
Northern	n.a.	n.a.	n.a.	n.a.	n.a.	n.a.	n.a.	n.a.	730.6	27.0	681.3	22.5	762.6	21.5
West Cumberland	n.a.	n.a.	n.a.	n.a.	n.a.	n.a.	n.a.	n.a.	413.3	15.3	442.1	14.6	598.3	16.9
South Lancashire	n.a.	n.a.	n.a.	n.a.	n.a.	n.a.	300.0	8.9	219.1	8.1	262.0	8.7	358.3	10.1
Merseyside	n.a.	n.a.	n.a.	n.a.	n.a.	n.a.	385.0	11.5	293.0	10.8	311.0	10.3	437.0	12.3
Wales	173.0	10.9	312.6	17.0	442.6	18.4	592.6	17.7	531.7	19.6	684.7	22.6	716.0	20.2
TOTAL IN DEV. AREAS	1,593.6		1,838.2		2,404.1		3,357.4		2,706.6		3,026.2		3,539.0	

a) NB some double counting with year to Sept. 1949

ICFC in the mid-1950s.[83] In addition, ICFC's overall development area investment coincided with Treasury goals. This varied from year to year, but in 1946, for example, showed that a relatively high level of business was done in these areas at 24 per cent of the total.[84] This in part reflected Piercy's own strategy of investing in areas where firms could gain a comparative advantage. He noted, for example, that construction firms in development areas will be provided for in areas of material shortage.[85]

Despite Piercy's efforts to conform to policy goals, there were early indications that his overtures to the Treasury were not entirely successful and that 'rather a one-way relationship' was developing.[86] Piercy continued to press the Treasury to do joint business with ICFC and to use his contacts to obtain approvals for loans from the Capital Issues Committee.[87] ICFC had initially hoped that its dealings would be exempt from scrutiny by the CIC, since the money it was advancing had already been 'issued' to it by the clearers.[88] But it was forced to submit all transactions exceeding the £50,000 limit operating in the 1940s, and not infrequently these were rejected, particularly those cases involving the finance of companies wholly or partly owned by foreign firms.[89]

By 1947 it was becoming clear that any lasting close links with DATAC, or special consideration from the CIC, were unlikely. In the case of DATAC doubts were beginning to be expressed by Piercy about its efficiency. By 1948, however, Eady began to call for 'closer and more confidential' links between ICFC and DATAC, since the latter had 'done very little'.[90] Eady proposed that ICFC should act as an investigative arm of DATAC, following up proposals and assessing their potential, and acting as a monitor for the progress of any loans

March 1954 Outstanding	%	March 1955 Outstanding	%	March 1956 Outstanding	%	March 1957 Outstanding	%	March 1958 Outstanding	%	March 1959 Outstanding	%	March 1960 Outstanding	%
695.2	18.8	851.2	22.4	1101.1	31.4	1115.3	33.0	1244.6	36.4	1325.3	38.2	1556.4	40.7
n.a.	n.a.	n.a.	n.a.	n.a.	n.a.	n.a.	n.a.	n.a.	n.a.	n.a.	n.a.	n.a.	n.a.
n.a.	n.a.	n.a.	n.a.	n.a.	n.a.	n.a.	n.a.	n.a.	n.a.	n.a.	n.a.	n.a.	n.a.
796.4	21.5	836.2	22.0	756.7	21.6	653.3	19.4	545.4	16.0	464.3	13.4	482.7	12.6
688.6	18.6	639.9	16.9	169.0	4.8	100.0	3.0	90.0	2.6	75.0	2.2	70.0	1.8
385.0	10.4	345.3	9.1	323.8	9.2	363.0	10.8	340.5	10.0	390.5	11.2	324.2	8.5
459.5	12.4	482.7	12.7	524.5	15.0	529.7	15.7	551.5	16.1	582.0	16.8	621.0	16.2
671.4	18.2	641.0	16.9	629.4	18.0	614.3	18.2	645.3	18.9	635.6	18.3	772.2	20.2
3,696.1		3,796.3		3,504.5		3,375.6		3,417.3		3,472.7		3,826.5	

made.[91] These proposals were reaffirmed in a meeting at the Treasury in October 1948 attended by both Kinross and Piercy. The move stemmed partly from disappointment in the progress of DATAC and partly from a similar disappointment in the work done at ICFC's sister organization, FCI. Linking ICFC to DATAC, and perhaps raising ICFC's lending limits to £400,000, would enable it to undertake significant industry-wide rationalization through investment policy—a strategy Piercy had been interested in for some time.[92]

Despite general agreement between Piercy and Eady on the benefits of linking ICFC and DATAC, the suggestion was never formally taken up. Piercy continued to send information and proposals to the Treasury, some of which were successful, prompting him to occasionally attempt to elicit special favours for some of these joint ventures.[93] By late 1950 there were only three of these cases on the ICFC books, however,[94] and relations had deteriorated significantly. ICFC had experienced difficulties with government departments generally, particularly with their lack of co-ordination. The Corporation ran into problems in the construction industry, for example, where they found the controls of labour, materials, and licences to be haphazard, so much so that in 1948 ICFC was forced to withdraw temporarily from investing in this sector altogether.[95] Piercy had also begun to have doubts about the soundness of some of the proposals which the Treasury were offering to ICFC, and felt that the Corporation was being asked to fund projects which had failed to attract support elsewhere in the City.[96] It had never been Piercy's intention that ICFC should become a lender of last resort, a fate which seemed to have befallen FCI, yet the quality of business on offer from the Treasury seemed to be leading the Corporation this way. Worse than this, in the event of failure, the Treasury were, in Piercy's opinion, over-zealous in recovering their money, accelerating problems for the firm in question.

By 1951 the relationship had completely broken down. In January Piercy met Lord Balfour of the CLCB, who recorded that 'there have been cases where the Treasury have put up money on a debenture and, subsequently, after the failure of the business, have proved themselves ruthless and grasping partners. Lord Piercy firmly intends never to do business with them jointly again.'[97] There was also a rather embarrassing incident which arose when ICFC's examination department consulted Whitehall over a particular case, only to find that information passed on had been used to the detriment of the company in question by 'persecuting bureaucrats'.[98] ICFC continued to inform the Treasury of important changes in its operations, for example the decision to establish EDITH in 1955, but links were never to be formally re-established, and throughout the 1950s the only influence wielded by this section of government was the negative sanction administered through the CIC.

ICFC contact with other departments also tailed off, as the

Corporation found its feet, and discovered it could do without the often ponderous help and advice it received from government.[99] In March 1952 in was announced that the Corporation would administer the Fuel Efficiency Loans Scheme for the Ministry of Fuel and Power. This merely involved vetting the creditworthiness of applicants and administering loans, however, for which ICFC received a modest fee.[100] Real co-operation with other important departments affecting ICFC, particularly the Board of Trade, was never fully established. The Board of Trade had strongly advocated close government control of the Corporation during the wartime debates. Once ICFC was set up in the private sector, however, the Board of Trade withdrew from involvement altogether, since the view was held by some in the department that officials talking to ICFC were liable under the Official Secrets Act.[101] At the end of 1948 Piercy had approached the Board of Trade, seeking a more positive relationship than had so far developed, and a committee was set up to consider how closer relations might be implemented.[102] Doubts were again expressed about what kind of help the Board of Trade could fairly give to ICFC, with some committee members maintaining that information should be limited to that available in the published economic surveys. It was noted that Piercy wanted general information to help plan an industry-wide investment strategy, and it was generally agreed that, since such information was already passed on an informal basis to FCI, then a similar arrangement should be made available to ICFC. Beyond this rather vague undertaking, however, no real co-operation developed between the two bodies.[103]

Political Alliances

This decline in close contact between ICFC and the government can be viewed as a general reluctance or failure on the part of the various departments involved to tie ICFC in to a national economic strategy. But it can also be interpreted in terms of political allegiances. The Corporation's contacts with government were at their strongest during the early part of the Attlee administration, particularly while Hugh Dalton was Chancellor. Piercy's background as one of Attlee's personal assistants, his continued membership, along with Lawrie, of the XYZ, and his ennoblement by the Labour administration in 1945, led many to the seemingly obvious conclusion that ICFC was simply an indirect means for carrying out Labour Party policy. During the controversy over the issue of National Gas and Oil Engine shares, for example, *Branch Banking* was moved to complain that 'the whole of ICFC is under the thumb of a Socialist Chairman assisted by a number of convinced Socialists on his staff'.[104]

Piercy enjoyed a close relationship with Hugh Dalton and undoubtedly sought to use this to the advantage of ICFC. The two men had been friends since their years together at the London School of Economics before the First World War, and had built up a mutual regard over the intervening years. Piercy was a prominent figure in the XYZ, which Dalton tended to view as his personal City advisory group.[105] Dalton also attempted to get Piercy appointed as Governor of the Bank of England in 1946. While he was Chancellor their relationship was as close as ever in personal as well as professional terms. Dalton was a frequent visitor to Piercy's house in the Cotswolds and the two took annual holidays together in the Cairngorms where they inevitably discussed the prospects for ICFC.[106] For example, Piercy wrote to Kinross from Aviemore, in the summer of 1946: 'The Chancellor is due the coming weekend. It will certainly be an opportunity to discuss perspectives—and I am quite sure we must eventually take on the complete function of a finance house . . . I mean us to emerge as a great institution and I am still sure we shall do it.'[107] The following week Piercy wrote with satisfaction that he had 'sold the Chancellor' on the idea that ICFC should extend its activities into the issuing business, and that the two had agreed some cases which needed the support of DATAC. Piercy also tried to steer Dalton towards general policies which would favour ICFC's growth strategy.[108]

Dalton was undoubtedly of help to Piercy and ICFC while he remained as Chancellor. This was not destined to last, however, as Dalton was forced to resign in 1947. Piercy made contact with Dalton's successor, Stafford Cripps, but there could be no repeat of the intimate relationship which Piercy had enjoyed with Dalton. Only a few cursory enquiries, ultimately proving impractical, emanated from the new Chancellor. Piercy experienced a similar lack of overt interest when Gaitskell in turn became Chancellor.[109] This may, in part, be attributable to the Labour Party's general abandonment of using directed investment as a key factor in economic policy in favour of a general Keynesian demand-management strategy.[110] Piercy continued, however, to foster the support of prominent Labour figures, inviting many of them to ICFC headquarters.[111] He also continued for a time to work within XYZ, formulating general strategy. One suggestion which came from this group envisaged the establishment of a National Investment Council to co-ordinate the control of investment, combining the activities of FCI, ICFC, and the CIC.[112]

It is likely, however, that Piercy began to realize that he might make ICFC a hostage to fortune by identifying the Corporation too closely with the Labour Party. With Dalton no longer in a position of power Piercy's trump card was no longer playable. There is evidence that, as an alternative strategy, he began to curry favour with the Bank of England, whose support was crucial to ICFC's survival, by being seen as one who could be relied upon to 'torpedo' what the Bank considered to be the 'half-baked suggestions' being advocated by Piercy's XYZ colleagues.[113]

Independence: Pragmatism, Strategy or Stewardship?

Throughout the 1940s and 1950s ICFC had to struggle against active opposition or developing indifference among those who might have helped more effectively to get the Corporation established. The failure of government departments in this respect was due to a lack of strategic vision in failing to link the regulatory role of the CIC and the proactive role of DATAC to the activities of ICFC. There is no doubt that Piercy wanted a broader role for ICFC initially, at least partly in order to build up the business of the Corporation. There was a further reason for links with government, however: personal support from figures such as Dalton and Eady, although it may have been of marginal value in the provision of business or smoothing the flow of some of ICFC's loans, was nevertheless important as part of the marshalling of general 'political' backing to ward off the continued depredations of ICFC's principal antagonist, its own shareholders. Independence from government was, in the end, a pragmatic choice for ICFC. Independence from the banks was a different issue.

It is difficult to overestimate the level of animosity which developed between ICFC and some of the clearing banks. An indication can be gleaned from the fact that when the Corporation held a dinner to celebrate its tenth anniversary in 1955, all the shareholders declined to send a representative.[114] The banks' opposition to ICFC can be seen to range from general ideological antipathy, often at a personal level, to a lack of understanding of the nature of the business in which ICFC was attempting to become involved. At the personal level Piercy in particular was distrusted by many of the bankers, partly as a result of his political allegiances and partly because he seemed to be able to muster undue influence within the Bank of England. An indication of the level of personal distrust occurred in 1951 when Kinross was approached by one of the bank general managers with an offer of the Chairmanship of ICFC if the banks could oust Piercy 'who was . . . neither liked or trusted by himself or his colleagues'.[115] It is tempting to link this distrust solely to Piercy's socialism, Attlee supporters like Sadd being among a distinct minority among the bankers of the time. Yet Piercy had managed to keep a foot in both camps—the City and Labour—for a number of years,[116] achieving considerable success and becoming widely respected among his peers in the financial world.

A more credible explanation may be that many of the bankers considered Piercy to be 'devious', as Kinross had noted that he could be on occasion.[117] Piercy was an experienced Whitehall operator, thanks to his government service during both wars, and he attempted to capitalize on this in addition to maximizing his political connections during ICFC's early years.

However, the roots of animosity may have gone beyond this. The banks never fully understood the nature of, or felt comfortable with, the kind of business which ICFC was undertaking. Piercy and Kinross had the ability to assess industrial prospects; their knack of identifying sound financial deals and the close involvement with firms in what was a difficult sector—the Macmillan gap—left some bankers feeling a sense of disdain mixed with inferiority. ICFC was created to provide a source of long-term investment. This called for a wide-ranging assessment of potential at the outset—of management quality, and industrial processes and markets, in addition to purely 'financial' criteria. Bankers' 'conventional training', their familiarity with dealing on the basis of overdrafts, recallable on demand, rather than locking up capital over an extended period, left them unprepared to make the considered judgements that such a strategy demanded. It may have seemed to some of the shareholders that Piercy was simply 'cleverer' than they were.[118]

It is difficult to assess with any accuracy to what extent full support from the clearing banks, whether by making capital more freely available or by working to the original intention and providing introductions to investments deemed to be outside the remit of 'normal' banking, would have boosted the fortunes of the Corporation. If this had been the case ICFC would certainly have been spared the need to operate at the margins of risk described by Kinross. There seems little doubt that a fully funded ICFC, using the investment strategies forged in the 1950s, would have made an even greater impact on the Macmillan gap.

Despite the negative attitude of some of the shareholders, whether driven by personal animosity or by an aversion to becoming involved in 'political' or 'continental' banking, ICFC survived its most difficult formative years; and following the 'new deal' of 1959, it went on to become self-financing and fully independent. The Bank of England's role in protecting and nurturing ICFC throughout this period was particularly important, and certainly saved it from extinction. It had been the Bank which had engineered the Corporation at the outset and, under duress, had persuaded the clearers to participate. Similarly the Bank, using the same arguments about avoiding further government intervention in the financial sector, had staved off the intermittent attempts by the clearers to relinquish their obligation to support the Corporation. The eventual success of ICFC in compiling a profitable portfolio, based on the Piercy and Kinross methods, guaranteed the Corporation's longevity, but without the guardianship of the Bank of England this would certainly not have been enough.

NOTES

[1] *Daily Telegraph*, 24 Jan. 1945; *The Times*, 24 Jan. 1945, see also *Financial Times*, 24 Jan. 1945.
[2] *News Chronicle*, 24 Jan. 1945.
[3] Bank of England, Committee of Treasury Minutes, 8 Nov. 1944; F. C. Ellerton to Tuke, 7 June 1945, NLS 8699/1.

[4] ICFC Minutes, 24 July 1945.

[5] J. B. Kinross and A. Butt-Philip, *ICFC 1945–1961*, unpublished MS. 1985, 56, 78 (hereafter Kinross, *ICFC*).

[6] 'Post-War Finance for Industry', Circular No. 1945/1, 7 Feb. 1945, National Provincial Bank Ltd. National Westminster Bank Archive (hereafter NatWest).

[7] 'Finance Corporation for Industry Ltd., Industrial and Commercial Finance Corporation Ltd.', Barclays Bank Ltd., Head Office Circular No. 9630, 9 Feb. 1945, Barclays Bank Archive.

[8] Ibid.; 'ICFC', Circular to Managers of the Branches, Midland Bank Ltd., 13 Nov. 1945, Midland Bank Archive (hereafter Midland).

[9] J. H. Lawrie to Liaison Officers appointed by the Member Banks, 26 Oct. 1945, NatWest 7522.

[10] ICFC Minutes, 4 Sept. 1945.

[11] Kinross, *ICFC*, 91.

[12] Kinross, *ICFC*, 81; 'P's Rejected During 1946', 3i Archive (hereafter 3i), Box K.

[13] Piercy to Lord Catto, 12 Oct. 1945, National Library of Scotland, Kinross Collection (hereafter NLS) 8699/2.

[14] Kinross, *ICFC*, 74–6.

[15] W. Hadwick to J. H. Lawrie, 29 Jan. 1947, Natwest 7522; London Clearing Banks, Chief Executive Officers Committee Minutes, 16 Sept. 1954, 21 Sept. 1954, Midland.

[16] Unsigned memo, 26 Jan. 1955, Midland 200/10.

[17] Ted Cole, interviewed by Terry Gourvish, 12 July 1991.

[18] ICFC Minutes, 2 Oct. 1945.

[19] Circular letter from C. F. Cobbold to Governors of Central Banks in the Empire, 21 Nov. 1951, Bank of England Archive (hereafter B.E.) G14/54.

[20] Kinross, *ICFC*, 71.

[21] CLCB Memo, 26 July 1950, 4, Midland.

[22] Derek Millard, interviewed by Richard Coopey, 16 Mar. 1992.

[23] E. V. Ralph, 'Decentralisation', Memo, 28 Jan. 1951, 3, NLS 8699/3.

[24] See e.g. John Baker and Bessemer Ltd., 7 Jan. 1947, 3i SA(47)6.

[25] 'Industrial and Commercial Finance Corporation Ltd.', Barclays Bank Memo, Chairman's copy, 6 Nov. 1946, copy in NLS 8699/1.

[26] J. B. Kinross, *Diaries*, 3 May 1950, NLS 8699/36; Mary Francis, interviewed by Richard Coopey, 24 Mar. 1992.

[27] Kinross, *ICFC*, 92, 142; retirement speech, L. Tindale; Cole, interview, 12 July 1991.

[28] Kinross, *ICFC*, 142; Paul Hildesley interviewed by Richard Coopey, 4 Mar. 1992.

[29] Kinross, *ICFC*, 54.

[30] C. Sadd to W. Piercy, 12 Dec. 1945, 23 Dec. 1947, Piercy Collection, LSE (hereafter Piercy) 9/162.

[31] Sadd to Piercy, 17 Dec. 1945, 24 Nov. 1945, 23 Dec. 1945; Piercy 9/162.

[32] Sadd to Piercy, 12 Dec. 1945, 23 Jan. 1946, 24 July 1946, 3 Nov. 1947; Piercy to Sadd, 23 Oct. 1947, Piercy 9/162, Kinross, *ICFC*, 92.

[33] Kinross, *ICFC*, 192.

[34] Kinross, *ICFC*, 137.

[35] W. Piercy, 'Discussion with Shareholding Banks (Committee of London Clearing Bankers) in 1948 with regard to a Suggested Report', NLS 8699/2.

[36] 'Note prepared for Sir Charles Lidbury', 3 Nov. 1947, NatWest 7522.

[37] CEO Minutes, 11 June 1948; CLCB Minutes, 1 July 1948, copies in NLS 8699/1.

[38] 'Industrial and Commercial Finance Corporation', memo by Lord Piercy; 'Comments on

the ICFC Statistical Summary', Midland Bank Intelligence Department, 2 June 1950, Midland 200/10.

[39] Piercy to Linlithgow, 21 Dec. 1949, CLCB Minutes, Midland.

[40] Linlithgow's notes on Piercy to Linlithgow, 21 Dec. 1949.

[41] Crick to Rouse, 28 Dec. 1949; Rouse to Linlithgow, 29 Dec. 1949.

[42] CLCB Minutes, 7 Mar. 1930, 15 Mar. 1950, 27 Mar. 1950, 22 May 1950, 18 Dec. 1950.

[43] 'It's a £45,000,000 Smile. Lord Piercy: Man of the Month', *Scope*, 1947; 'Capital Obligations of Member Banks', L. C. Mather, 11 Nov. 1949, Midland.

[44] 'Industrial and Commercial Finance Corporation Ltd.', L. C. Mather, Midland Bank Legal Department, 21 Oct. 1949, Midland; CLCB memo, 26 July 1950.

[45] J. C. R. Dow, *The Management of the British Economy 1945–60* (Cambridge University Press, 1965), 253.

[46] CLCB minutes, 7 Aug. 1947, 8 June 1950; Linlithgow to Piercy, 15 Mar. 1950, 30 Mar. 1950; Piercy to Linlithgow, 27 Mar. 1950, 3 Apr. 1950; Midland 200/10.

[47] CLCB minutes, 4 Oct. 1951.

[48] A. W. Tuke, memo to CLCB, 2 Dec. 1953, Midland 200/10.

[49] Kinross, *ICFC*, 176, 186, CLCB minutes, 15 Apr. 1953.

[50] CLCB minutes, 2 Aug. 1951, 7 Feb. 1952, 20 Mar. 1952, 10 Apr. 1952, 6 June 1962; Kinross, *ICFC* 164.

[51] Piercy, 'Talk with Sir Wilfred Eady', 14 Mar. 1951, Piercy 9/180, CLCB minutes, 15 Apr. 1953.

[52] Kinross, *ICFC*, 171, 181.

[53] D. Ross, 'British Monetary Policy and the Banking System in the 1950s' *Business and Economic History*, Vol 21 1992.

[54] Kinross, *ICFC*, 175–7; ICFC, *Annual Reports*; Chairman's statement 1956, 10, 1957, 9–11; CLCB Minutes, 3 Nov. 1955.

[55] Report of a meeting between the representatives of the CLCB at the Bank of England, 18 Dec. 1950, Midland. See also Ch. 2 above.

[56] CLCB Minutes, 26 July 1950, Kinross, *ICFC*, 171–2, 224–5.

[57] For an account of the control of bank advances during this period see W. A. Thomas, *The Finance of British Industry 1918–76* (Methuen, 1978), 184–99.

[58] Report of a meeting between the representatives of the CLCB at the Bank of England, 18 Dec. 1950, Midland.

[59] Kinross, *Diaries*, 12 Jan. 1950.

[60] CLCB Minutes, 7 Dec. 1950.

[61] Kinross, *ICFC*, 242.

[62] 'Sources of Funds Required for Investment', Piercy to Tuke, 19 Nov. 1953, Midland 200/10.

[63] Kinross, *Diaries*, 24 Feb. 1950, 7 Mar. 1950.

[64] Kinross, *Diaries*, 22 Jan. 1953; ICFC Annual Report, 1958, 11.

[65] CLCB Minutes, 3 Dec. 1953, 7 Jan. 1954, 4 Feb. 1954.

[66] Piercy to Kinross, 8 Nov. 1958, NLS 8699/6.

[67] Kinross, *ICFC*, 280–1.

[68] Piercy to Kinross, 20 July 1959, NLS 8699/6.

[69] Kinross, *ICFC*, 284.

[70] Kinross, 'Scotland', memo, late 1951, 2, NLS 8699/3.

[71] Philip McKenzie-Ross interviewed by Richard Coopey, 23 April 1992; J. B. Kinross, 'Visit to Scotland', 14 Dec. 1950, NLS 8699/3.

[72] Kinross, *ICFC*, 127–8, 242.

[73] Macmillan Report, 5.

[74] *The Times*, 24 Jan. 1945; Hansard, 2 Mar. 1945, Cols. 1686–1785.

[75] ICFC Minutes, 4 Sept. 1945.

[76] Kinross, *ICFC*, 107–8.

[77] Ted Cole, interview.

[78] ICFC Minutes, 3 Sept. 1946; Ted Cole, interview; 223, 3i.

[79] 3i, SA/47/10, 8; 'Report from Intelligence Department', Midland Bank, 30 Nov. 1949, Midland.

[80] ICFC Minutes, 4 Dec. 1945; Piercy to A. E. Shillito, 19 Dec. 1945, Piercy 9/180. For an account of Eady's involvement in the formation of ICFC see Ch. 1 above.

[81] 'DATAC: Co-operation between the Corporation and the Treasury', 3 Dec. 1945, Piercy 9/180.

[82] Piercy, 'Talk with Sir W. Eady', 7 Jan. 1946; Piercy to Eady, 4 Nov. 1947, Piercy 9/180.

[83] Kinross, *ICFC*, 202–3.

[84] MO 40; Table of Approvals, July 1946, Box K, 31.

[85] MO 4; Pratchett & Co. SA(47)20, 3i.

[86] Piercy, 'Talk with Sir W. Eady', 7 Jan. 1946, Piercy 9/180.

[87] Piercy to Kinross, 7 Dec. 1946, NLS 8699/6.

[88] ICFC Minutes, 4 Sept. 1945, 8 Jan. 1946.

[89] P. F. G. Hildesley to Piercy, 'Approved Cases Withdrawn or Rejected', Box K, 3i; Piercy to Eady, 24 May 1946; Eady to Piercy, 31 May 1946, Piercy 9/180.

[90] Notes on a talk with Sir Wilfred Eady, 5 July 1948.

[91] Piercy, 'Talk with Sir Wilfred Eady', 7 Jan. 1946; 'DATAC: Note on a Talk at the Treasury', 19 Oct. 1948, Piercy 9/180.

[92] Piercy to Eady, 12 Dec. 1949; 21 Jan. 1949; 26 June 1950, Piercy 9/180.

[93] Piercy to Eady, 12 Dec. 1949; 21 Jan. 1949; 26 June 1950, Piercy 9/180.

[94] These comprised Cambrian Tools of Whitehaven, Ming Ware of Dundee, and Smart and Brown of Spennymore. Piercy to Douglas Jay, 1 Nov. 1950. Piercy 9/108.

[95] P. W. A. Simmonds to Kinross, 30 Jan. 1948, Box K, 3i; Ted Cole, interview.

[96] Piercy to Kinross, 11 Oct. 1949, NLS 8699/6.

[97] CLCB memo, 25 Jan. 1951, NLS 8699/2.

[98] C. S. B. Attlee to Piercy, 'Government Liaison', 11 Dec. 1952, Piercy 9/180.

[99] Ibid.

[100] ICFC, *Annual Report*, 1956, 12.

[101] Ibid.

[102] 'The Finance Corporation for Industry and the Industrial and Commercial Finance Corporation', 5 Jan. 1949; 'Note of a Meeting to Consider Relations Between the Board of Trade and FCI and ICFC', 6 Jan. 1949, Public Record Office (hereafter PRO), BT64/2994.

[103] 'Relations Between the Board of Trade and the Industrial Finance Corporations', 18 Jan. 1949; Tippett to Hughes, 5 Mar. 1949, PRO BT64/2994.

[104] Quoted in Kinross, *ICFC*, 108.

[105] See above, Ch. 1.

[106] Dalton, *Diaries*, xxxiii, 28 July 1945; 1 Sept. 1946, BLPES.

[107] Piercy to Kinross, 9 Aug. 1946, NLS 8699/6.

[108] Piercy to Kinross, 24 Aug. 1946, NLS 8699/6.

[109] Kinross, *Diaries*, 15 May 1950; Kinross, *ICFC*, 127.

[110] J. Tomlinson, 'Attlee's Inheritance and the Financial System: Whatever Happened to the National Investment Board', *Financial History Review*, 1 (1994).

[111] Kinross, *Diary*, 2 Feb. 1951, 1984 annotation; NLS 8699/36.

[112] XYZ, 'Suggested Reforms in Financial Machinery', Oct. 1948, Piercy 5/117.

[113] 'National Investment Council', 15 Oct. 1947, BE G1/247 1396/2.
[114] Tenth Anniversary Dinner—5 July 1955, NLS 8699/3.
[115] Kinross, *ICFC*, 224.
[116] R. Jenkins, *A Life at the Centre* (Pan, 1992), 59–61.
[117] Kinross, *ICFC*, 297.
[118] Lord Richardson, interviewed by Richard Coopey, 8 Oct. 1992.

Chapter 4

Developing the Network: The 1960s

THE BEGINNING OF THE 1960s was marked by important changes for ICFC, setting the scene for a decade of steady expansion. The year 1959 had seen a new degree of freedom from the periodic restrictions which the shareholder banks had placed upon the Corporation's supply of capital. This had been taken as an opportunity by Piercy and Kinross to look for ways to set ICFC on a secure, permanent footing as an important financial institution. One of the most important tasks in this respect was selecting staff capable of safeguarding ICFC's position, and simultaneously building the kind of organizational structure which would ensure continued expansion beyond that which could be supervised by the kind of personal intervention and control which had typified the Piercy–Kinross years. Comparisons with other organizations are difficult in that ICFC's methods and field of operations differ significantly from banks and other institutional investment funds. Table 4.1 gives an impression of the scale of ICFC, however, set against the leading merchant banks of the period.

Professionalizing the Organization

Gordon Richardson, future Governor of the Bank of England, had been recruited in 1955 with a view to eventual succession, but by 1957 there seemed to be no sign of Piercy relinquishing control, and Richardson left to take up a position with Schroders, the merchant bank.[1] This loss spurred Piercy and Kinross to reconsider the leadership succession. In 1958 they approached a young chartered accountant named Larry Tindale who was then working for McClelland Moores. Kinross and Tindale had regular meetings from the summer of 1958 onwards, and in May 1959, at a lunch with the senior partners at McClelland Moores, Piercy, Kinross, and Tindale agreed that the latter should join ICFC in October 1959, on the understanding that he would take

Table 4.1. Total assets, ICFC and some Merchant Banks (£ million)

	1945	1955	1959	1962	1967	1973
ICFC	—	29	36	48	99	217
J. Henry Schroder/Schroder Wagg	5	24	28	68	174	397
Schroders Limited	—	—	—	137	293	706
Baring Brothers	24	30	33	53	93	222
Hambros Bank	38	85	108	129	270	1,226
Morgan Grenfell	11	23	24	39	125	281
S. G. Warburg	—	—	13	29	84	329

Note: Year ends vary.

Sources: ICFC Accounts, *Schroders: Merchants and Bankers* (Richard Roberts, The Macmillan Press Ltd., 1992)

over the General Manager's job from Kinross two years later. Tindale duly joined as Assistant General Manager in October to replace Rocky Stone, who had resigned during the summer. This recruitment of outside talent clearly being groomed for the top was not without difficulties. Other senior staff at ICFC, upon hearing of Tindale's expected arrival, began to protest very strongly to Kinross. Youth and inexperience were the main criticisms levelled at the proposed newcomer, although there was also a general aversion to the idea of recruiting from outside. The fact that Tindale's appointment was seen by some as 'deflationary to the morale of some of the senior staff' was doubtless a reflection of the intimate group atmosphere which Piercy and Kinross had endeavoured to build up at the Corporation, and which naturally generated a resentment of interlopers from beyond the 'family' (Piercy had also recently recruited Stanley Blackstone from outside as Chief Industrial Adviser). In the event, despite threatened resignations, tempers were calmed and Tindale duly took up his post.[2] The lesson was a salutary one for Piercy and Kinross, however, who agreed that they had done enough 'speculating' for the time being, and that the next senior appointment should come from within. Kinross accepted the situation, although he felt compelled to inform Piercy, in characteristic fashion, that while ICFC staff had an abundance of intelligence, experience, reliability, and loyalty, 'our difficulty (as I see it) is that we lack anyone with the necessary steel in his backbone'.[3]

Piercy was prepared to compromise on the original plan, perhaps in deference to the feelings expressed by his senior staff, or perhaps preferring a strategy of 'divide and rule', as Tindale later put it.[4] Thus, when Kinross did step down in 1961, ICFC appointed two Joint General Managers. In addition to Tindale, Piercy appointed Arthur English, who was due to retire in three years. Kinross took a seat on the board in August 1961. These changes in senior management coincided with arrangements to move to new premises. By 1960

ICFC was 'coming out of the seams' at Drapers Gardens and a long lease was subsequently acquired on a modern building in Copthall Avenue, soon to be named Piercy House.

The move was completed in January 1963, but changes at the top were still in an interim phase. With English due to retire, Tindale was clearly in a position to assume general control; but Piercy, who had been used to operating in a hands-on way, in close conjunction with Kinross, found it more difficult than he had anticipated to let go the reins. Piercy was due to retire in the following year, but meanwhile he kept up his routine of involvement in all decision making, 'interfering' in all Tindale's reorganization plans. Tindale recalled the strain of 1963: 'One of the worst years I ever had in my life was the year in which he knew he'd got to go'.[5] Fortunately he could afford to offer a robust defence to Piercy's attempted incursions. This supported Kinross's advocacy of outsiders who would not be intimidated by the imposing figure of a Chairman who had, after all, been the guiding light since the Corporation's foundation. Tindale, confident of his value elsewhere, could afford to forego too much deference: 'I knew perfectly well I could always go back to my accounting firm . . . other people, who might have committed their whole career to ICFC, were a little more chary about upsetting Piercy.'[6]

Despite this reluctance, Piercy duly retired as Chairman in July 1964. He came to recognize that the symbiotic way in which he and Kinross had worked from the early years would be difficult to replicate, and had become increasingly inappropriate for a large financial institution. Thus when Piercy approached Lord Sherfield to take over the Chairmanship, he did so in the knowledge that a new and fundamentally different partnership would be necessary at the Corporation. Sherfield came from a non-financial background. As Sir Roger Makins he had been a diplomat and a civil servant, notably as ambassador in Washington and Joint Permanent Secretary at the Treasury. Like a true generalist he had then been called in to head the Atomic Energy Authority (AEA) until retiring at 60 in 1964. The AEA encompassed both nuclear power and weapons programmes comprising the largest, most advanced scientific and technological research, development, and production facilities in Britain at that time.

Piercy recognized in Sherfield a man who could look after the environmental welfare of ICFC, and mix freely, on equal terms, with the Corporation's shareholders. Many of the chairmen and deputy chairmen of the clearing banks belonged to what Sherfield called the 'circuit'. Sherfield readily admitted that his strength was not to be found in the kind of specialized control which had characterized Piercy's Chairmanship. 'I had quite a lot of experience at foreign economic policy but . . . no experience of domestic finance and I was not versed at all really in the technicalities of finance and banking.'[7] The intricacies of finance, like those of atomic physics, could be left to the expert.

Sherfield was also unused to dealing with the relatively small-scale operations which were at the core of ICFC activity. As Tindale was to comment, 'At the Treasury they never let him see anything under £30 million . . . he never understood how a company that wanted to borrow £200,000 worked.'[8] But this was precisely how Tindale wanted things. For him Sherfield was a 'marvellous' chairman from a managing director's point of view. Sherfield proved to be an astute provider—'tell him what needed doing, and he would get it done'.[9]

Piercy and Kinross had thus passed on control of ICFC to an altogether different kind of leadership, typified by an enabling Chairman and highly professional General Manager. Kinross, as a director, was content to give advice if it was sought, but otherwise stayed in the background.[10] Piercy at last relinquished control in July 1964, and Tindale became sole General Manager in the following September. Piercy continued to be fully occupied with his many other interests outside ICFC. He also remained as Chairman of both EDITH and Ship Mortgage Finance, and stayed on the Board of ICFC until the annual general meeting on 5 July 1966, when he finally retired at the age of 80. Two days later in Stockholm, while at a meeting of the Kuwait International Committee, the 'architect of the Corporation's fortunes', Lord Piercy of Burford, died.[11]

New Leadership, New Directions

Tindale quickly instituted a range of reforms affecting ICFC's staff and organization. Salaries were improved and perks enhanced. Lunches at the canteen were soon to be provided free of charge—this remains an attraction for staff at 3i right up to the present day. Employment policy became focused on graduate recruitment and professional qualifications. Tindale himself saw the value of continued academic activity, albeit of the American variety, and enrolled on Harvard Business School's Advanced Management Programme in the autumn of 1966, to be followed in turn by most of ICFC's senior staff.

The central aim in these and other measures was to enthuse an organization which Tindale considered to have 'run into the sand'. 'I had to get it rolling and the obvious way, in management terms, was to give some authority down the line; get people out selling and not sitting around protecting their own backsides.'[12] Decision-making at ICFC had become too centralized, and too focused on a limited number of head-office staff in London. In order to correct this imbalance more responsibilities were to be given to all levels of senior management at head office, the Cases Committee was to be shaken up, and most importantly, branch managers were to be given a much greater degree of autonomy.[13]

'He's young . . . I don't like that in a man.'

ICFC's branch network had been steadily growing since the early 1950s, and was one of the key factors in ICFC's success in attracting customers from the regions. Local knowledge of markets and products, allied to a personal identification with the local 'ICFC man', gave ICFC a crucial advantage over other financial institutions. At the time the clearing banks, ICFC's only rival in terms of a national network, had been increasingly centralizing their own decision-making, and moving away from providing term loans to smaller, regionally based firms.[14] Tindale recognized this opportunity, and immediately began a programme of extending ICFC's branch network. In 1960 and 1961 new branches had been opened in Cardiff, Bristol, and Glasgow but there had been no further expansion until Tindale became General Manager. In 1965 two new branches were opened, one for London and surrounding areas, the other, located in Newcastle, serving Durham, Cumberland, and the North Riding. The Reading branch was opened the following year, followed in 1968 by branches at Liverpool and Wolverhampton. By 1972 further branches had been added, including those at Nottingham, Sheffield, and Southampton, with a new London branch in the West End bringing the total to nineteen. The branches which had opened throughout the 1960s served to maintain the general spread of investments throughout Britain, but with a decrease in the overall proportion going to London and the South-East (see Fig. 4.1).

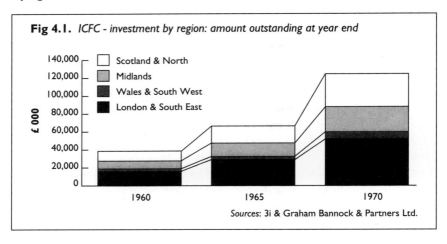

Fig 4.1. *ICFC - investment by region: amount outstanding at year end*

□ Scotland & North
▨ Midlands
■ Wales & South West
■ London & South East

£ 000

140,000
120,000
100,000
80,000
60,000
40,000
20,000
0

1960   1965   1970

Sources: 3i & Graham Bannock & Partners Ltd.

Tindale was determined that the new branches should be insulated from too much interference by head office, and he made it a point 'to see that the committee structures did not frustrate what they were trying to do'. The branch structure also served to foster a spirit of competition among ICFC staff, and there existed a 'friendly rivalry' between many of the regional offices.[15] More importantly, however, the branch network was also to prove a testing ground for ICFC staff, later to make the transition to head office. Jon Foulds, for example, who would later take on the role of Chief Executive, began his career at the Manchester branch in 1959, taking over as manager in 1963.

The 1960s also saw a continuation of the trend towards diversification in ICFC activity.[16] Like Piercy, Tindale was alert to any development in the economic environment which might provide an opportunity for ICFC, and two particular initiatives—Technical Development Capital (TDC) and Industrial Mergers Ltd—stand out as children of the times. The first of these, TDC, reflected ICFC's belief in the growing importance of technological development in British industry. From the early 1960s fears of a widening 'technology gap' had been expressed from many quarters, often pointing to the failure of British industry to capitalize on indigenous research. Technology had been given a very high profile by the Labour Party in the run-up to the 1964 General Election, when Harold Wilson had made his famous speech calling for a revitalized manufacturing sector 'forged in the white heat of the scientific revolution'.[17] Following Labour's election victory in 1964, increased government activity through existing bodies like the National Research Development Corporation (NRDC) and the new Ministry of Technology, encouraged ICFC to become involved in this sector, as did the obvious and growing importance of high-technology industries such as computers, electronics, and aerospace. In some ways this interest flowed naturally from the Corporation's continuing emphasis on investment in the manufacturing sector, although throughout the 1960s investments in other sectors had grown proportionally, notably in services and distribution (see Fig. 4.2).

TDC had been formed in 1962, partly in response to recommendations in the Radcliffe Report of 1959, which had outlined the need for selective investment to finance the development and production stage of new technologies.[18] The company, which was the brainchild of Sir John Benn, Chairman of UK Provident, started with a capital of £2 million, subscribed by the insurance companies and other institutions. ICFC had been involved from the beginning, taking a 5 per cent stake in TDC and providing the company with office accommodation. Kinross was drafted in as a director, to sit on TDC's cases committee, with Edward Hawthorne, an engineer and full-time director, under the chairmanship of Benn. The company, hailed as an 'inventors' charter', attracted a good deal of attention, not least among individuals wishing to find capital to back their private projects, and the staff at ICFC began to notice a steady stream of callers to the head office, 'carrying brown paper parcels'.[19]

It is in the nature of funding new technologies that assessment of likely success is difficult when compared to established processes and known markets. Three months passed before any investments were made, and progress there-

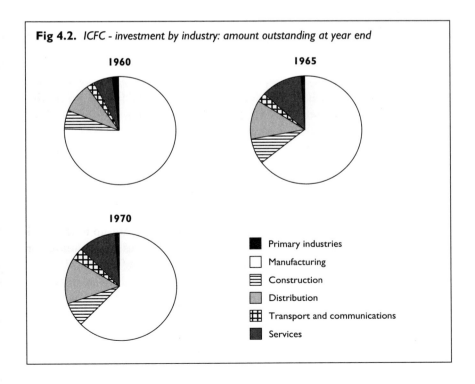

Fig 4.2. *ICFC - investment by industry: amount outstanding at year end*

1960

1965

1970

■ Primary industries
□ Manufacturing
☰ Construction
▨ Distribution
▦ Transport and communications
■ Services

after was slow.[20] Kinross and Benn began to disagree over investment policy, the former advising caution: 'The fact is that if we were to finance a number of worthwhile and even notable innovations but without any profit to ourselves we should sooner or later fail . . . In this materialistic and rather ruthless world in which we now live we ourselves shall get nowhere unless we are successful.'[21] Kinross regarded Benn as an 'idealist', prepared to back projects from an almost altruistic point of view.[22] Benn in turn told Kinross that having 'worked like a black' to start TDC, and having adequate capital to allocate, he was 'rather chagrined' to find some of the projects he favoured being turned down.[23] Kinross continued to work for TDC, but by the spring of 1965 relations had become too strained and he stepped down, to be replaced by Sir Hugh Weeks, who was already on the Board of ICFC.[24]

TDC's performance failed to impress, and in June 1966 it was decided that ICFC should make an offer for the whole company. This was accepted by the shareholders, who were happy to cut their losses, and TDC was given a new lease of life under the full guidance of ICFC. Sherfield remained convinced that the small- and medium-sized firm sector would accelerate its investment in more sophisticated production technologies which were becoming available in the mid-1960s. The company laid out its aim, which was to ensure that 'no worthwhile technical development fails to be exploited in this country merely through lack of financial backing at the commercial stage'.[25] During the 1960s many looked to the USA to provide an exemplar of successful commercial exploitation of high-technology based research and development. TDC board members were duly dispatched to the Massachusetts Institute of Technology to study 'the most celebrated example' of institutional promotion of advanced technology spin-off. In the first year of ICFC's ownership TDC increased its activities significantly, including two large investments in advanced machine-tool projects.[26] The following year, seeking to emulate MIT's methods, representatives from TDC held discussions with most of the universities in Britain, resulting in a programme of funding to enable the development of selected prototypes at Cambridge, and a jointly commissioned survey, with the NRDC, at Imperial College, to evaluate development projects with commercial potential.

The level of TDC's investment activity continued to grow at a steady, if relatively modest, level throughout the rest of the 1960s, and the number of failures was less than expected. Returns were not spectacular, but it was recognized that 'most of TDC's customers have still a long haul ahead of them'. By 1970 the company had invested over £6 million in a total of more than 100 companies, but it was still held to be prudent to make substantial provisions against losses. Investment levels began to fall significantly during the early 1970s, reflecting both problems with the economy in general, and the end of the romance with technology in particular. The TDC experience, in common with the many government technology initiatives of the 1960s, had demon-strated the problems inherent in investing in what was, by its nature, a very volatile sector of industrial activity. Advanced technology projects were costly and carried a very high level of risk, calling for specialized knowledge of processes and markets and for a long-term commitment on the part of the investor. TDC as part of ICFC, with its industrial department and its tradition of long-termism, was better-placed than most financial institutions to evaluate potential investments, yet in this very particular sphere, it too had to admit more risk than that to which it was accustomed. The nascent venture capital industry in the USA had begun to emerge during the 1950s, but even there the 'long haul' was the norm, and very few predicted the spectacular returns which would be experienced in the 1970s and 1980s.[27] The problems inherent in investing in high-technology start-ups were to re-emerge for ICFC at a later date, as we will see in Chapter 7.

The other notable feature of the 1960s was an increasing level of con-centration among firms as a wave of mergers began to sweep Britain.[28] This trend was encouraged by the Labour government's intervention after 1966 in the form of the Industrial Reorganisation Corporation (IRC).[29] Large organ-izations, typified by the American multinational corporation, were held to be the most efficient economic units.[30] Studies have since noted that many of the mergers which took place around this time did little to increase efficiency, plant size often being unaffected within new groupings. Nevertheless it was widely believed at the time that efficiencies would in fact result.[31]

It would seem that such a trend went completely against the traditional areas in which ICFC was developing its strength, the finance of small- and medium-sized firms; but it was against this background that ICFC set up Industrial Mergers Ltd in January 1967. This move reflected the fact that a number of ICFC's customers were caught up in the merger wave, but it was more to do with seizing the opportunity at hand to profit from this trend. Industrial Mergers had a wide remit. This ranged from advice to ICFC cus-tomers, seeking non-customers to join with ICFC customers, and promoting mergers between non-customers. Fees were between 0.5 per cent and 3 per cent of the transaction value, and the company had its own capital available to put into deals where appropriate. Kinross was to be the first Chairman, Weeks and Tindale directors, and Eric Izod the first manager.

Industrial Mergers got off to a good start, with over 1,000 enquiries in the first few months of operation. There was soon found to be an imbalance within these enquiries, however, with potential buyers outnumbering sellers by around four to one. Most approaches came from firms in the engineering indus-try, traditionally a strong sector of ICFC operations, but the Corporation also looked for merger opportunities in the textile industry, another strong sector for ICFC in certain regions and considered to offer opportunities to gain from

Oxford Instruments

OXFORD INSTRUMENTS IS A CLASSIC STORY of a garden shed start-up which has grown into a world-class high technology company. The shed belonged to Martin Wood, a research engineer at the Clarendon Laboratory in Oxford during the 1950s, who began a small business custom-manufacturing very powerful electromagnets. The technological breakthrough came in 1961 when developments in the USA led to the availability of new superconducting alloys, making it possible to generate powerful magnetic fields at low cost, thus opening up a potentially large market. However, superconducting materials would only function at low temperatures, so a parallel development in the production of cooling vessels or 'cryostats' was also necessary.

By 1967 Wood's growing business was being compared to the Route 128 companies surrounding Boston in the USA and had won a Queen's Award to industry. However, this growth brought with it administrative and financial problems. Although Martin Wood and his wife, Audrey, the finance director and very much partner in the enterprise, had correctly foreseen the growth of demand for the new magnets, technical difficulties with new generations of superconducting materials, which were often not revealed until the equipment was actually in use, led to product liability claims seriously affecting profitability. As the company grew, scientific and engineering staff were recruited fairly easily, many 'spun off' from the Atomic Energy Research Establishment at Harwell. Managerial expertise was a different question, however, and the considerable entrepreneurial skills of the Woods were soon in need of support or replacement by professionals and organizational changes. Financially, the company needed an external source of capital, not least to placate the local bank, which was beginning to express serious misgivings.

The possibility of some form of takeover by one of Oxford Instruments' major suppliers (Air Products supplied liquid helium coolant and ICI superconductor materials) was explored in 1967 but rejected in favour of an injection of capital by ICFC. Although Oxford Instruments had been approached by ICFC earlier in the 1960s the company was sufficiently capitalized at that time. However an agreement was rapidly reached under which ICFC took 20 per cent of the equity while injecting £90,000 of loan capital. Subsequently a close working relationship with David Ellis, the ICFC branch office manager in Reading, developed through a continuing period of difficulty which saw two further rounds of financing.

In the early 1970s Oxford Instruments finally turned the corner. Its new-found profitability allowed the company to diversify, partly through the acquisition of the BOC Superconducting Magnet Systems Division and Newport Instruments, and to expand into the medical electronics field. One of its most notable successes in the 1970s was the introduction of nuclear magnetic resonance (NMR) applications, now used in body scanners. During this crucial period ICFC had provided more than just financial help. Both Audrey and Martin Wood had earlier attended an ICFC management training course, which Martin acknowledges as a turning point for the company. In making its investment, ICFC had recognized the value of the Woods in entrepreneurial terms, but the Company also saw the need for help in extending the overall managerial competence of the firm, improving budgeting and tightening financial controls. This was achieved with the help of ICFC's Management Advisory Service. The Company was also instrumental in finding a new managing director. The job called for a demanding blend of technical and managerial qualities and with the decision to appoint Barrie Marson, one of two people short-listed by ICFC, 'a new, more professional era began'.

In 1983, when Oxford Instruments was floated on the Stock Exchange, it had grown into a company with 1,100 staff worldwide and a turnover approaching £50 million. 3i realized £4.3 million from its investment in 1983 but has maintained its position as long-term equity investor, retaining a 6.3 per cent stake in the company, which now has an annual turnover in excess of £100 million. Martin Wood has remained active in the company and in the local economy, supporting start-ups through his own private initiative, the Oxford Trust.

the consolidation of production and marketing. Firms gave a number of reasons for seeking mergers, including diversification, the pooling of research and development resources, and the general rationalization of production, marketing, and sales capacities. The sellers were often firms interested in securing management succession. These could be either younger management teams seeking a rapid route to expansion, or owners interested in teaming up with larger, quoted companies in order to obtain a market for their holdings.[32] In the first year of operation the company was involved in thirty-three mergers, most notably the takeover of KMT by Thorn Electrical Industries.

Subsequent years saw a steady growth in the number of deals in which Industrial Mergers was involved. These rose from 62 in 1968 to 119 in 1972, when the company committed nearly £12 million of its own capital in support. There were problems, however, and many mergers were considered to be proposed without sufficient attention to the long-term health of the merged businesses, simply in order to realize short-term gains. Although the number of mergers arranged by the Corporation continued to grow, it did not reach the potential which Tindale had envisaged. He was later to state that ICFC's plans in this sphere were 'destroyed by the IRC', but it is probably more accurate to say that the merger movement itself ran out of steam in the early 1970s. Like

the dash for technological growth, the 'big is beautiful' movement proved to be elusive as a panacea for the ills of the British economy. Sherfield had recognized this at an early stage, noting in 1965 that 'while the trend toward merger and integration is in principle a healthy one, this is a matter on which generalizations are apt to be misleading'.[33] In fact ICFC's pattern of investments by size during the 1960s remained fairly constant, as Figure 4.3 demonstrates.

Another source of new business which attracted ICFC in the mid-1960s was hire purchase and leasing. This started in 1964, as sale and lease-back became an increasingly widespread activity, with many firms taking advantage of the tax regime which favoured leasing rather than ownership.[34] By mid-1965, after one year of operation in this sector, ICFC and its subsidiaries had placed over £1.25 million worth of contracts. Two years later, agreements had reached the rate of over 200 a year.[35] Leasing was seen by Tindale both as an opportunity to cash in on what was a growing and very lucrative new sector of the market, and as a complement to ICFC's normal lending activity.[36] This was true in the first instance, although in one particular area—the leasing of property—it was to lead the Corporation into new and problematic terrain.

The provision of finance by ICFC through the purchase and lease-back of freehold and leasehold property began in earnest towards the end of the

1960s. ICFC had always been prepared to undertake first-class property mortgages, but competition from specialist institutions had meant that this remained a 'sideline' in the 1950s.[37] Piercy had been against becoming too involved in property deals, seeing them as overly complex, but Tindale saw this as another opportunity for ICFC,[38] and by the early 1970s the Corporation was negotiating over £2 million worth of contracts annually. This activity was originally seen as a back-door route to obtaining some form of equity stake in companies which were reluctant to give a formal share of the business to ICFC.[39] Following the election of the Conservative government under Heath in 1970, and the subsequent relaxation of tax restriction on capital transfers, the property market began the first of a series of booms in 1971, and it became clear that ICFC was in a good position to exploit the rising trend in prices. Thus in 1972 Anglia Commercial Properties became a subsidiary, 70 per cent being owned by ICFC and 30 per cent by Royal Insurance. Anglia was primarily intended to develop small industrial estates, but was soon to expand beyond this narrow remit. The property side of ICFC business was to expand and diversify far beyond the original intentions of Tindale when acquiring Anglia Properties, and was to prove a difficult diversification in future years.[40]

The other significant diversion of the early 1970s, which was also to prove problematic in the long term, was the move to expand the consultancy

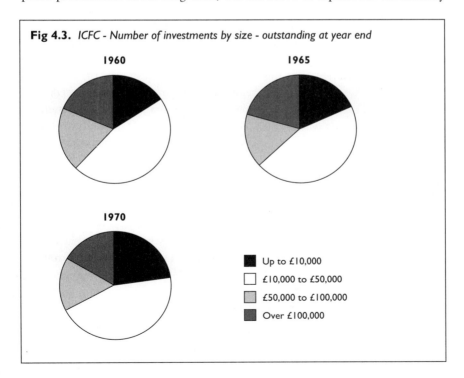

Fig 4.3. *ICFC - Number of investments by size - outstanding at year end*

1960

1965

1970

■ Up to £10,000

□ £10,000 to £50,000

▨ £50,000 to £100,000

■ Over £100,000

activities of ICFC. In May 1970 ICFC's own newly created Management Consultancy Division was expanded by merging with the National Union of Manufacturers' Advisory Service (NUMAS), which was bought in. Later in the same year the Management Studies Centre, which had previously operated as an associated company, became a wholly owned subsidiary.[41] ICFC also moved into the expanding computer services industry when Capital Cities Computer Services, CRC Information Systems, and Assets Computer Services were acquired in 1970, to provide bureau and real-time facilities. The following year ITF Training and International Data Highways were added.[42] By 1971 these aspects of ICFC activity had risen to such prominence that the Annual Report of that year noted that 'the principal activity of the Corporation is that of providing capital, financial advice and computer bureau and other services to small- and medium-sized companies'.[43] The volume of business which these new additions generated remained disappointing, however, and failed to pick up. A series of 'difficult' years was reported, partly blamed upon the depressed industrial environment.[44]

During the 1960s and early 1970s ICFC's earlier 'diversifications', Estate Duties Investment Trust and Ship Mortgage Finance Company, continued to form an important part of ICFC activity. EDITH made 'steady, if sedate, progress', obtaining a Stock Exchange listing in August 1962.[45] Kinross, who became a director of EDITH in 1967, eventually replaced Sherfield as Chairman in 1973, with Roger Plant as manager. ICFC's 26 per cent stake in EDITH was increased to 41 per cent in 1974, when, in order to beat new takeover rules which were imminent,[46] Kinross set up a rapid, and overpriced, rights issue for EDITH. The high price was set deliberately, in order that the issue would fail, leaving ICFC to take the total amount. This increase in ICFC's stake in EDITH reflected the large amount of time spent on EDITH business by ICFC staff, especially at branch level.[47]

SMFC, in which ICFC had a 30 per cent holding, ran up against a potentially disastrous problem in 1967 when the government introduced a guaranteed loan scheme aimed at promoting shipbuilding in UK yards. This was part of the general rationalization programme outlined in the Shipbuilding Industry Act, aimed at concentrating and revitalizing the industry.[48] SMFC's mortgage business suffered accordingly, reaching a low ebb by 1972.[49] The company had turned gamekeeper in the interim, however, and was the official agent for the government scheme, administering loans for a fee.[50] Meanwhile SMFC became a wholly owned subsidiary of ICFC in January 1970 and, in a change of strategy, began to concentrate on post-delivery finance. Through two subsidiaries, the Nile Steamship Company and the Falkland Steamship Company, SMFC became one of the pioneers of bare-boat chartering. In 1970, for example, delivery was taken of three new vessels, and there were contracts for the delivery of four more, to be chartered to 'responsible' shipowners.[51]

Another feature of the Tindale years was the increased emphasis placed on publicity. ICFC did little in the way of advertising throughout the 1950s, initially in deference to the banks' objections to 'touting for business' and because there was adequate business for the growing Corporation to handle arriving through existing channels of information. There had been some talk of wider advertising, in the mid-1950s, Piercy being enthusiastic enough to compose his own 'snappy' adverts. 'Machine Tools' was one example:

> Do you know what machine tools can do for you?
> Why not get yourself one or two?
> Money? That's easy: Apply to ICFC.[52]

In addition a market research officer had been appointed as early as 1950, in the Economic Intelligence Department,[53] but publicity and marketing continued to have a relatively low profile at ICFC, business arriving through the connections within informal networks, particularly at branch level.

When Tindale joined the Corporation in 1959 publicity was being left to the chairman's secretary. Lack of advertising was seen at the time as a general failure within the financial sector. The Radcliffe Committee, for example, had pointed to the 'information gap' which existed between providers of finance and small firms.[54] An additional spur came in the early 1960s, when competition increased as the clearing banks began to offer term loans to small enterprises.[55] An extensive marketing campaign was opened up, run by Peter Gummer, to reinforce the efforts of the branches. ICFC began to study all the available marketing indicators and began advertising extensively. Early campaigns were to set the pattern for much of ICFC's and 3i's advertising in stressing the continued independence of customers. ICFC also emphasized its role as an intermediary in the banking system, pointing to the fact that it never closed during credit squeezes.[56]

During the 1960s Tindale also took ICFC on the road. Piercy had often addressed audiences arranged by various Trade Associations, and ICFC had booked space intermittently at exhibitions.[57] At the end of 1964, however, this activity was greatly expanded through a series of regional conferences which ICFC set up. Widely publicized through institutions like the National Association of British Manufacturers and the British Institute of Management, the conferences took for their theme the general problems of growth for small- and medium-sized firms. Tindale and Weeks headed what became known as the 'Flying Circus' of touring ICFC speakers, giving an increasingly popular series of talks at venues throughout the country.[58]

Throughout the years of Tindale's leadership the core of ICFC's business remained the supply of finance to small- and medium-sized firms. The Corporation's performance in this sector had been commented upon to the effect that if there was a Macmillan gap, then ICFC had gone a considerable

Laura Ashley plc

IT WAS IN 1953 THAT Bernard and Laura Ashley started the business which has become a household name, printing tea towels and scarves to their own design. With the aid of a continuous textile printing machine designed by Bernard Ashley they expanded into supplying furnishing and dress fabrics, mainly to department stores.

The growing business was moved to Wales and in 1966, when sales had reached £1,000 a week, Laura Ashley began designing her first dresses. In 1968, encouraged by the prospects for growth in this field, they took the significant step of opening their first shop in South Kensington and moving into direct retailing of their own manufactured products to Laura Ashley's distinctive designs.

By the end of 1980, the Group owned seventy-five shops worldwide and sales had exceeded £74 million; but in the early 1980s the pace of growth accelerated further and by October 1985 the number of shops exceeded 200. Annual turnover also trebled during this period to £40 million and by the time of flotation the following year the company was able to report sales of £96 million and profit before tax of £14 million. Market capitalization at the issue price was £220 million.

3i's first investment in Laura Ashley, a £14,000 loan, was made in 1966 when sales were £30,000 and profit before tax £4,000. The loan carried the right to convert £1,500 into 15 per cent of the equity. Several further small advances were made in the early days to fund expansion and 3i was involved in the recruitment of a Finance Director, John James, who subsequently became Managing Director, and, together with Sir Bernard Ashley, was a driving force of the business for many years.

3i declined to help with the major move into the manufacture and retailing of dresses to Laura Ashley's designs, although it was subsequently recognized that this was the turning point in the Group's fortunes. It was an expensive decision because it resulted in the equity option being effectively diluted to under 4 per cent. In the reorganization which preceded flotation 3i's holding in a subsidiary was transferred to the parent company where it represented 1.8 per cent of the group equity. Even at this level, however, 3i was amply rewarded for its early support with a market value of shares in excess of £3 million. A proportion of the holding was made available to the market, pro rata to the contribution of other shareholders, and the remainder was sold in 1987.

way towards closing it.[59] The Radcliffe Committee, reporting in 1959, was satisfied that the gap had been closed, although it did make a series of recommendations. The most important of these were that the joint stock banks should begin to offer term loans as an alternative to overdrafts, and that the ICFC upper limit should be revised to reflect the change in real monetary values. The committee also recommended the setting-up of a corporation to facilitate the commercial exploitation of technical innovation.[60] All these points were partially responded to. The clearers began to offer term loans to smaller firms in the early 1960s; Technical Development Capital addressed the needs of finance for innovations, albeit in a limited way; and ICFC's effective operating limits, which had been informally raised throughout the 1950s, were formally increased to £300,000 (£500,000 in the case of further applications). With no call for any major new institutional initiative in small- and medium-sized firm finance, ICFC could be satisfied that they were adequately fulfilling their intended role.[61]

In the mid-1960s the role of the smaller company in the economy was again beginning to attract attention, but this was the period when the gospel of economies of scale was being widely preached, and Sherfield reported that the 'official attitudes appeared rather ambivalent and doubt remains as to whether small- and medium-sized companies are regarded as important for the economy'.[62] By the late 1960s, however, the problem of the small firm sector had attracted sufficient attention to merit the setting-up of an official inquiry, chaired by J. E. Bolton. The Bolton Report, published in 1971, while conceding that ICFC was 'by far the most important institutional provider of long-term capital to small firms', nevertheless pointed to persistent problems. Small firms had an increasing need for new capital, yet ceilings remained on bank lending, and the Stock Exchange continued to be out of reach on a cost basis, as well as providing no secondary market for small issues. In short, the Bolton Committee found that 'the "Macmillan gap", first defined in 1931, still exists'.[63] The difference between Bolton and Macmillan, however, was that the former took into account a considerable body of evidence in support of its conclusions, presented by financial institutions, trade associations, government departments, and individual firms. A survey conducted by the CBI, for example, showed that nearly 50 per cent of small firms saw lack of external finance as a major problem. Bolton also again noted the 'information gap' between small firms and financial institutions which Radcliffe had pointed out, and a general level of 'dislike and distrust' on the part of owners and managers of small enterprises.[64]

Despite the problems highlighted by Bolton, the 1960s were reasonably successful years for ICFC, and there seemed to be no apparent lack of new enterprises in which ICFC could invest.[65] In 1964, following a record year of new business, the Corporation's cumulative gross investment since its foundation exceeded £100 million. Outstanding financial facilities which had been extended to customers, after provision for bad and doubtful debts, stood at over £50 million.[66] ICFC's share of the existing market remained modest. In 1965, for example, the Company's net investment was £9 million against a total of bank advances in the industrial sector of over £300 million, and new issues on the financial market of over £275 million.[67] Efforts were made to increase the proportion of lending to smaller firms within ICFC's range of interest and there was a trend, as Figure 4.3 shows, towards a greater number of investments in this sector.

Investment in this area reflected the Corporation's policy, but also fluctuated in line with levels of bank lending since, when banks periodically cut back on levels of credit, they tended to give priority to larger firms.[68]

ICFC's method of financing the small- and medium-sized enterprise changed little during the 1960s, building on the strength of the system put in place by Piercy and Kinross. One of the first things which struck Tindale when he first took up his position with the Corporation was the very high level of skill in financing small businesses.[69] He did 'shake up' the examinations department, which carried out the first stage in the vetting procedure of new business before handing it on to the investment controllers.[70] Tindale also tried to instil a greater sense of independence among branch managers. He was aware that presenting prospective business to the Cases Committee was often seen as a formidable process by many branch managers, and that negotiating with this Committee was a much bigger job than actually negotiating with the customer. This process could have its drawbacks, however, since affirmation by this centralized process depleted individual responsibility. Tindale later noted that he had to work hard to persuade branch managers 'that it was their job and their judgement—they must not shelter behind the Cases Committee'.[71] The industrial department, staffed predominantly by people with direct experience of industry, often ex-line managers, continued to be an important foundation in assessing new business. There were also staff in this department with a background in accounting, but the key element, for Tindale, was that industrial department staff had no formal experience in banking. This department was the one element which really marked ICFC off from the ordinary run of banking, and gave a crucial advantage in assessing levels of risk.

ICFC could compensate for taking higher levels of risk in the small firm sector either by pricing its loans higher, or by taking equity and a resulting direct share in profits and growth. Loans were carefully limited so that firms should not be overstretched: in a continuation of policies established in the early years, total borrowing was never allowed to exceed total shareholders' funds and new finance was limited to a proportional lower level.[72] Equity participation also served to lower the risk by reducing the debt burden on customers. The trouble with equity was, as noted by the Bolton Committee, that

An example of an ICFC advertisement from the early 1980s showing landmarks in the Company's growth.

the small firm sector was, and remains, distrustful of financial institutions. 'The whole question of getting equity was a major problem . . . in those days when you went in and started talking about equity you had to be prepared to be thrown out, almost by the scruff of your neck.'[73] Above all ICFC had to continue to take a flexible, and, at times, catholic approach to the structure of the finance which it was prepared to offer. Kinross continued to evangelize about the need for flexibility and innovation. 'I am constantly preaching to controllers . . . that they should not be mesmerised by the printed word, but must always adapt.'[74]

Table 4.2. *New investments and those made to existing customers, 1959-1968—number of investments (year ending March)*

	1959	1960	1961	1962	1963	1964	1965	1966	1967	1968
New cases	71	131	174	161	131	199	122	191	241	189
Existing customers	73	112	80	89	111	123	131	149	186	169

Despite common misgivings among the small-firm community about financial institutions, ICFC frequently succeeded in fostering a congenial relationship. This was often due to the way in which the Corporation kept in 'friendly, if arm's-length' contact with customers.[75] Long-term commitment also served to keep many firms with ICFC, and, by the 1960s, a pattern had begun to emerge of repeat business and very long-term involvements. W. Edwards and Company, for example, was one of ICFC's earliest customers, having first taken out a loan in 1946. When, as Edwards High Vacuum, the firm became part of British Oxygen in 1968, this ended twenty-two years of continuous support by ICFC.[76] As Table 4.2 shows, throughout the 1960s repeat business sometimes accounted for a high proportion of loans and equity.[77] In 1970 £18 million out of a total advanced of £35 million went to existing customers.

Long-termism and continuing commitment could create problems for the Corporation in terms of planning investments. The open-ended arrangements which ICFC had with many customers, particularly that the Corporation was prepared to hold on to its equity until companies were floated or sold at the customer's discretion, could cause difficulties in this respect. In 1960, for example, ICFC's balance sheet became unusually liquid following a series of takeovers and flotations and consequent repayments. This was in addition to the increased capital which ICFC had raised in 1959 in its first debenture. The

'Catherine, have everyone stop whatever they're doing.'

problem of short-term liquidity was a new problem for ICFC in many ways, since capital from the shareholders had previously been taken in smaller increments. This problem was solved by the expedient of placing short-term loans with large corporations or public institutions.[78]

Outside the core business of long-term finance to small- and medium-sized firms ICFC continued to do such non-Macmillan gap business as seemed appropriate. In this sense Tindale continued the Piercy tradition, ensuring that the message went out that ICFC would consider any business as an adjunct to its small-firm lending.[79] The Company continued to hold a substantial portfolio of quoted shares, although these were reduced in the mid-1960s in order to finance more conventional business. Profits on this portfolio looked impressive in the balance sheet, but there were significant realization problems caused by the size of investment, undertakings given by ICFC, and by unfavourable market conditions.[80] The Corporation also continued and expanded its issuing business into the 1960s. Following the eventual success of the British Belting and Asbestos issue in 1961,[81] an increasing number of issues was undertaken. This business came to a temporary halt in 1964 when the market 'boiled over a little', but subsequently continued at a steady pace, into the late 1960s.[82]

ICFC's somewhat difficult relationship with its shareholders became considerably less tense into the 1960s, by which time Piercy, with the help of sympathetic figures such as Robarts and Franks, had established a sound, permanent financial structure for the Corporation. It is significant that the banks were well represented at the Corporation's 21st anniversary celebrations in 1966, in contrast to their earlier boycott.[83] There remained a legacy of suspicion among some of the clearers, however, as Tindale later noted: 'I don't know that we ever actually scotched the feelings between the clearing banks and ourselves.'[84] Resentment centred on the fact that ICFC was seen as a competitor, especially as the banks began to move into term loans during the 1960s. Sherfield diagnosed a case of 'schizophrenia' over issues such as branch expansion. The banks 'could never make up their mind whether ICFC was an investment which should be encouraged to expand, or a competitor who should be throttled'.[85] Occasionally resentment took a tangible form, as when the National Commercial Bank, which had begun operations in leasing and industrial hire purchase, raised such a fuss that ICFC was forced to limit its planned activities in this sphere. This was an exception, but an important one, as Tindale later noted: 'This was the only time we really backed away from pressure—otherwise we might have had a very big finance business.'[86] When credit restrictions were lifted and banks did move into term loans they had the potential to affect ICFC seriously. In 1960, for example, Piercy maintained that banks took £2 million of ICFC business with which the Corporation had already made contact.[87] Similar pressure was exerted in 1965 when the banks renewed their interest in term loans, forcing ICFC to concentrate further on unsecured loans and more equity-based deals.[88] Nevertheless, as an investment ICFC continued to do well for the clearing banks. It paid a dividend of 6 per cent throughout the early 1960s, rising incrementally after 1968, and reaching 9 per cent by 1972. The Corporation also distributed £2.5 million to shareholders in the form of extra shares in 1964.[89]

ICFC's ability to raise funds on the capital market was one of the key developments of the 1960s. In severing its total dependence on the clearing banks for finance, the Corporation had come closer to the institution sketched out by the Macmillan Committee. In 1959 a £10 million debenture issue was launched, Hoare & Co. acting as underwriters and Glyn Mills handling the applications.[90] The issue was a success, with 241 institutional investors taking £8.7 million and 972 'other holders' taking £1.3 million. Further issues followed; £6 million in April 1961, £4 million in December 1961, £10 million in 1964, £15 million in 1966 and £10 million in 1969. These issues proved very popular—the Prudential took the whole of the £10 million issued in 1964. The 1966 issue was more than four times oversubscribed, with applications totalling over £66 million.[91]

Despite the freedom to go to the market for funds, ICFC had continued sporadically to call on the clearers for share capital. These calls reached the limits of the ratio of share to loan capital at £40 million in 1968, however.[92] Further problems arose in the following year as rising interest rates forced ICFC to look for short- and medium-term rather than long-term money, and in November of that year a total of £9.5 million was raised by the issue of three unsecured loan stocks of two, three, and five years, aimed at private investors. These went to over 7,750 subscribers, two-thirds of which held £1,000 worth or less. During the following two years, owing to persistently high interest rates, the Corporation continued to resort to medium-term borrowing, including tap issues of the earlier 1969 loan stocks. In 1972 ICFC received a boost to its capital from an unexpected source. In 1970 the Corporation had entered into an agreement with the Union Jack Services Club to develop their site at Waterloo Road. Two years later, when it was decided to sell the lease on Piercy House by public tender, a very gratifying offer of £15.3 million was received for premises which were on the books at £2.25 million.[93]

The Limits of Government Influence

One of the key features which marked ICFC out from other financial institutions was the general sense of mission which went with specializing in the provision of finance for the small- and medium-sized firm sector. Staff at ICFC still point with pride to the Corporation's role in fulfilling a national purpose by aiding a key sector of the economy. Little wonder, then, that the Corporation continued to be mistakenly interpreted as a form of quango. ICFC did indeed fulfil a national purpose, yet unlike larger institutions overseas, such as the Kreditanstalt für Wiederaufbau (KfW) in Germany or the Credit National (CN) in France, ICFC operated in the private sector, without any subsidy or formal government connection.[94] As we have seen, ICFC followed the contours of government policy in investing in Technical Development Capital and promoting industrial mergers, but it did this independently, and with an opportunistic eye to doing good business.

There were occasionally 'suggestions' from government that ICFC might follow a certain course, concentrating investment in firms in the export sector, for example, to ease balance of payment difficulties. These requests, which came from both Conservative and Labour governments via the Bank of England, were noted at ICFC, but no discernible change in investment patterns resulted. Where investment activity did increase in line with government policy, as in the case of investment in Scotland between 1964 and 1969, this was the result of the knock-on effect of government funds reviving general economic activity in the region.[95] There were direct links between government institutions and initiatives and ICFC. TDC entered into joint ventures with the National Research Development Corporation for example, and Ship Mortgage Finance administered the government's loan guarantee scheme for the shipbuilding industry. In doing this ICFC was simply carrying on a tradition, established earlier, of benign co-operation where no financial disadvantage would result.

ICFC staff were sometimes called upon to advise government, as in the case of the Bolton Committee, which contained a number of ICFC staff, past and present, including Tindale and Brian Tew. In common with other financial institutions some members of ICFC staff crossed the boundary into the government sector. Michael Knight, Tindale's personal assistant, went to the Industrial Reorganisation Corporation in 1968, and in 1971 Tindale himself went on secondment to the Industrial Development Executive of the Department of Trade and Industry (DTI). He was joined at the DTI the following year by Rocky Stone. For Tindale the brief spell in government service was a salutary experience, and gave an insight into the difficulties of trying to direct investment from within a large bureaucracy. It also confirmed the imperative to keep ICFC as independent as possible. Tindale came away, 'more determined than ever . . . to keep away from government funding'.[96] Direct government involvement in ICFC may have seemed a remote prospect, given the lack of formal links since the Corporation's foundation. There was a moment, however, in the early 1970s, when serious consideration was given to bringing ICFC into the public sector. This came about as part of a major restructuring operation, promoted by Sherfield, with the aim of linking ICFC with the Finance Corporation for Industry and possibly the IRC. The attempt failed, for reasons outlined in the following chapter, but a merger of ICFC and FCI did eventually result, with profound ramifications for ICFC.

NOTES

[1] R. Roberts, *Schroders* (Macmillan, 1992).
[2] Maurice O'Connell to Kinross, 2 June 1959; Arthur English to Kinross, 4 June 1959; Paul Hildesley to Kinross, 5 June 1959; Geoffrey Scarlett to Kinross, 11 June 1959; NLS 8699/3.
[3] Kinross to Piercy, 16 July 1959, NLS 8699/3.
[4] Tindale, interviewed by R. Coopey, 17 Mar. 1992.
[5] Ibid.
[6] Ibid.
[7] Lord Sherfield, interviewed by R. Coopey, 31 Mar. 1992.
[8] Tindale, interview.
[9] Ibid.
[10] Mary Francis, interviewed by R. Coopey, 24 Mar. 1992.
[11] ICFC, *Annual Reports*, 5 July 1966, 12; 4 July 1967, 12.
[12] Tindale, interview.
[13] ICFC, *Annual Report*, 1964, 7.
[14] F. Carnevali, 'Finance in the Regions: The Case of England after 1945' in Y. Cassis, G. Feldman, and Ulf Olssen (eds.), *The Evolution of Financial Institutions and Markets in 20th Century Europe* (Aldershot, Scholar Press, 1995).
[15] Alan Gould Martin, interviewed by R. Coopey, 11 Sept. 1992.
[16] For a full discussion of the origins and effects of diversification see below, Ch. 12.
[17] R. Coopey, S. Fielding, and N. Tiratsoo, *The Wilson Governments* (Pinter, 1992); N. Vig, *Science and Technology in British Politics* (Oxford, Pergamon, 1968).
[18] *Report of the Committee on the Working of the Monetary System*, (Radcliffe Report) Cmnd 827.
[19] Peter Wreford, interviewed by R. Coopey, 12 May 1992.
[20] J. B. Kinross, *50 Years in the City*, 194–6.
[21] Kinross to Sir John Benn, 7 May 1962, NLS 8699/3.
[22] J. B. Kinross, op cit.
[23] Benn to Kinross, 10 May 1962, NLS 8966/19.
[24] Weeks had been a director of ICFC since 1960.
[25] ICFC, *Annual Reports*, 1965, 16; 1967, 12.
[26] ICFC, *Annual Report*, 1967.
[27] For an account of the early venture capital industry in the USA, see W. D. Bygrave and J. A. Timmons, *Venture Capital at the Crossroads* (Boston, Harvard Business School Press, 1992), 10–21.
[28] J. Scouller, 'The United Kingdom Merger Boom in Perspective', *National Westminster Bank Review* (May 1987).
[29] The IRC was controlled by a group of industrialists including Charles Villiers and Frank Kearton, who had access to a budget of £150 million to be used to promote the rationalization, by achieving economies of scale, of chosen sectors of British industry. It had a hand in the consolidation of the ball-bearing, scientific instrument, and computer industries. Although it participated in comparatively few of the 3,000+ mergers taking place between 1966 and 1970, IRC gave considerable publicity to the merger movement. See S. Young and A. V. Lowe, *Intervention in the Mixed Economy*, 1974.

[30] Coopey, *Wilson Governments*.

[31] IRC, Cmnd 2889, Jim Tomlinson, 27–30.

[32] ICFC, *Annual Report*, 1967, 16.

[33] ICFC, *Annual Report*, 1966, Chairman's Statement, 15.

[34] Ted Cole, interviewed by T. Gourvish, 12 July 1992.

[35] ICFC, *Annual Reports*, 1965, 1967.

[36] Tindale, interview.

[37] B. Tew, 'ICFC Revisited', *Economica* (Aug. 1955). Tew was an early recruit to ICFC who subsequently went on to pursue an academic career.

[38] Frank Harber, interviewed by R. Coopey, 28 Feb. 1992.

[39] ICFC, *Annual Reports*, 1970, 1971, 1972; Tindale, interview.

[40] Tindale, interview; Harber, interview.

[41] ICFC, *Annual Report*, 1971.

[42] ICFC, *Annual Reports*, 1970, 1971, 1972.

[43] ICFC, *Annual Report*, 1971.

[44] ICFC, *Annual Reports*, 1970, 1971, 1972, 1973.

[45] ICFC Annual Report, 1963; Tindale, interview; Roger Plant, interviewed by R. Coopey, 2 June 1992.

[46] Under these new rules ICFC would have been forced to bid for the whole capital once 30 per cent had been reached. Kinross would have liked to do this but at that time ICFC 'hadn't the resources'. 'Estate Duties Investment Trust. Offer for Subscription', Kinross annotations, June 1984 NLS 8699/14.

[47] Kinross, *Fifty Years in the City*, 216–17.

[48] *Report of the Shipbuilding Inquiry Committee* (Geddes Report) (March, 1965), Cmnd 2937; *The Economist* 10 May 1969, 56; *Financial Times* 24 Jan. 1969.

[49] Loans were administered under Section 7 of the Shipbuilding Industry Act.

[50] ICFC, *Annual Reports*, 1969, 1970, 1971.

[51] ICFC, *Annual Reports*, 1969, 1970, 1971; Tindale, interview.

[52] Piercy to Kinross, 13 May 1954, NLS 8699/6.

[53] 'Introductory Review', (1951) 5, NLS 8699/3.

[54] Bolton Report, 155.

[55] Tindale, interview.

[56] Tindale, interview.

[57] ICFC Board minutes, 28 July 1959.

[58] Kinross, *ICFC*, 290, ICFC *Annual Reports*, 1965, 1966, 1968.

[59] *New Scientist*, 19 June 1958.

[60] *Report of the Committee on the Working of the Monetary System* (Radcliffe Report), Cmnd 827.

[61] ICFC, *Annual Report*, 1960, 11.

[62] ICFC, *Annual Report*, 1967, 16.

[63] Bolton Report, op. cit. 151.

[64] Bolton, Report, op.cit. 155–6.

[65] ICFC, *Annual Report*, 1961, 11.

[66] ICFC, *Annual Report*, 1964, 12.

[67] ICFC, *Annual Report*, 1965, 16.

[68] ICFC, *Annual Report*, 1966, 14.

[69] Tindale, interview.

[70] Derek Millard, interviewed by R. Coopey, 16 Mar. 1992.

[71] Tindale, interview; Harber, interview.

[72] Millard, interview; Kinross, *ICFC*, 70.

[73] Tindale, interview.

[74] J. B. Kinross to B. L. Mann, 17 Apr. 1973, NLS 8699/12.

[75] ICFC, *Annual Report*, 1964.

[76] Kinross, *ICFC*, 70.

[77] The relative upsurge in new business following 1961 reflects the effect of ICFC's increase in capital following the Corporation's freedom to raise capital on the market. See below Ch. 10. The figures quoted exclude new business in plant purchase and leasing, which became a major activity after 1967.

[78] e.g. ICFC lent £1 million for 2 years to the LCC, and £500,000 for 2 years to Thorn Electrical Industries in 1959. ICFC Board Minutes, 28 July 1959, 6 Oct. 1959. ICFC Annual Report, 1960, 10.

[79] Roger Plant, interviewed by R. Coopey, 2 June 1992.

[80] ICFC, *Annual Reports*, 1966, 1967, 1968.

[81] During this issue the bank handling subscriptions overstated the response, which led Kinross to give an erroneous public statement to the effect that the issue had been oversubscribed, when in fact there was a shortfall in applications. This was rectified by some deft buying in by ICFC. See Kinross, *Fifty Years in the City*.

[82] Issues included John E. Sturge (1961), Evans Golden Produce (1962), Copperad (1963), Vic Hallam (1963), KMT Holdings (1966), Norwest Construction (1966), Northern Dairies (1966), and Howard Tenens (1966).

[83] Piercy to Robarts, 15 June 1964, NLS 8699/2.

[84] Tindale, interview.

[85] Lord Sherfield, interviewed by R. Coopey, 31 Mar. 1992.

[86] Tindale, interview.

[87] ICFC, *Annual Report*, 1960.

[88] Tindale, interview.

[89] ICFC, *Annual Reports*, 1961–73.

[90] ICFC Board Minutes, 7 July 1959, 28 July 1959; *Annual Reports*, 1960–67.

[91] ICFC, *Annual Report*, 1966, 14; Minutes of KFC Allotment Committee, 4 Mar. 1964, 3i.

[92] ICFC's freedom after 1959 to call on the general capital market for funds was to have important ramifications. For a full discussion see below, Ch. 11.

[93] ICFC, *Annual Reports*, 1970–72.

[94] For a comparative analysis of ICFC, KfW, and CN see Yao-su Hu, 'Industrial Banking and Special Credit Institutions: A Comparative Study', *Policy Studies Institute*, 632 (Oct. 1984).

[95] ICFC, *Annual Report*, 1969, 21.

[96] Tindale, interview.

Chapter 5

Finance For Industry: The 1970s

FINANCE CORPORATION FOR INDUSTRY was the sister organization to ICFC, set up in May 1945 with a nominal capital of £25 million and the ability to borrow a further £100 million. Share capital was subscribed by the insurance companies (40 per cent), investment trust companies (30 per cent), and by the Bank of England (30 per cent).[1] The Corporation was to provide temporary or long-term finance in larger amounts than those advanced by ICFC, and aimed at rationalizing and restructuring specific sectors of industry and providing capital for post-war re-equipment. In many ways FCI was seen as operating as a replacement for the Banker's Industrial Development Company which the Bank of England had set up in the 1930s.[2] The Board of Directors encompassed a wide range of experience, including three businessmen, two accountants, a trade unionist, a scientist, and an ex-civil servant.[3] FCI was also to operate with the help of an Industrial Advisory Panel of trade unionists, economists, and industrialists.

It was originally envisaged that FCI would focus its attention on the basic industries, notably coal, transport, steel, and textiles. However, nationalization after 1945 obviated the need for large concentrations of FCI finance in coal and transport, and the textile industry remained fragmented, not calling for finance on the scale which FCI was set up to provide.[4] Of the original targets, this left just the steel industry. Other industrial sectors, such as engineering and chemicals, featured large firms and remained in the private sector, but many of these ended the war with an unusually high level of liquid resources, certainly enough to purchase what plant and equipment was available at the time.[5] FCI was similar to ICFC in that it was intended to operate at a profit, albeit a marginal one. However, two further operating criteria marked it off as a radically different institution. These were, first, that 'any project invested in must be of importance to the national economy', and secondly, that 'required finance could not be found elsewhere'.[6] Thus, in effect, FCI was set up as the

"WELL, I'M SORRY THEY FEEL THAT WAY. BUT THEN WHAT THE HELL FUN IS A TAKEOVER IF IT'S NOT A HOSTILE TAKEOVER?"

lender of last resort driven by politically determined investment decisions, a potentially disastrous situation from a purely commercial point of view. This situation left FCI subject to the vagaries of shifting political trends and was made worse by occasionally quixotic government policies. This was apparent not only in terms of nationalization, which removed much of FCI's *raison d'être*, but also in specific cases. For example, in 1947 FCI made a loan of £210,000 to a company which the Corporation 'had been invited to assist on the grounds of its high national importance' only to find the company going into receivership after the withdrawal of a crucial government contract, with the result that FCI incurred a substantial loss.[7]

It was to the steel industry that a large proportion of FCI funds went in the first instance, setting a trend which was to dominate most of its history until it was merged with ICFC in 1973. The most important early intervention in this industry came in 1948, when FCI invested £35 million to finance the Steel Company of Wales's scheme aimed at modernizing the tin-plate and sheet-steel industries in South Wales. By 1950 this and other loan undertakings to the steel industry totalled over £53 million out of FCI's total commitment of £67 million. When the industry was nationalized in 1951, therefore, and these loans were repaid, FCI was left high and dry with a relatively small portfolio. The very close relationship which had developed between FCI and the steel industry was evidenced by the fact that in 1953 two directors, Sir John Morrison and Sir Archibald Forbes, resigned from the Board to take up appointments as Chairmen of the Iron and Steel Holding and Realization Agency and the Iron and Steel Board respectively.[8] Other major loans were made by FCI, notably to Petrochemicals Ltd., F. Perkins, the diesel engine manufacturer, and the oil company Ultramar, but steel continued to dominate the portfolio.

Investments in the steel industry were not very profitable by the time they had been repaid by the government—but they did not prove to be loss-making. Other investments did, however. The year 1954 was a particularly bad one; with assets now totalling only £22 million, FCI was forced to write off over £2.6 million. The Company returned to profit the following year and began to pay a dividend—in practice quite a small amount, since the paid-up capital was relatively modest. This proved to be only a temporary respite, however, and continued difficulties came to a head in 1958 when the FCI had to be rescued by the intervention of the Bank of England. The manager of FCI, G. S. Nelson, wrote to the Bank at the time, pointing out that the clearing banks, which were providing the Company loan capital, were in fact taking virtually no risk, since loans were either covered by government guarantees or by FCI's uncalled capital (only £500,000 of the £25 million share capital had been issued up to this point). By March 1958, however, the guaranteed loans to the steel industry had all been repaid, and unsecured loans exceeded uncalled capital by £6 million. Nelson called for the banks to assume part of the risk by subscribing share capital, as they had done in the case of ICFC.[9] Following a series of meetings between the then Chairman of FCI, Lord Weeks, and Lord Cobbold, the Governor of the Bank of England, an alternative solution was arrived at. The Bank of England agreed to advance £5 million free of interest and a further £5 million on certain conditions. It also undertook to provide a further £5 million should this prove necessary. The agreement became known as the 'umbrella of £15 million'. The shareholders were only informed of the first £5-million part of this arrangement, and Kinross later noted that 'it is clear that the whole operation was far from easy to carry through, and obviously caused embarrassment within the Bank'.[10] The loan was to prove something of an albatross, and repayment proved very difficult. Sir Humphrey Mynors, who became Chairman of FCI in 1964, was later to state his irritation at this continuing obligation: 'The Bank of England's £5 million loan in advance of calls irks me. It is a constant reminder of a last-ditch rescue operation without which we would probably not have survived.'[11]

The size of FCI's portfolio remained modest. In 1959 there were no new agreements to add to the fifteen which were on the books. This low level of activity partly reflected the depression in the steel industry, still the focus of FCI activity, but also reflected the low rate of deal flow which characterized the Company—only 41 cases had been handled to this date since 1945. A deviation came in 1964, when a short-term loan of over £30 million was arranged with Cunard for the building of a new liner, the QE2.[12] The following year FCI saw a massive upsurge in activity, lending to the full limit of its capacity with over £42 million of further advances. In what was now time-honoured style, the steel industry was the recipient of these loans, as FCI intervened in its role as lender of last resort. Re-nationalization of the steel industry was mooted and the financial markets were understandably reluctant to invest in this sector. Steel companies were 'compelled by the prevailing political uncertainty to turn to the Corporation for the resources they need'. When re-nationalization eventually came in July 1967, of the £99 million FCI loans outstanding, £56 million were to steel companies. As in the early 1950s, when the government repaid these loans over the next two years, FCI's portfolio was drastically reduced. In the late 1960s and early 1970s lending began to accelerate again, this time to companies outside the steel industry, particularly among those investing in productive capacity to replace imports. Ever mindful of 'the public interest', rates on these loans continued in the FCI tradition of minimized margins.[13]

The record of FCI up to the early 1970s provoked considerable criticism. *The Director* magazine had noted in 1951 that the Company, left high and dry with the steel industry, had to deal with quite a different 'gap' to that identified by Macmillan, notably 'the period between the Labour Party's announcement of steel nationalization and the eventual carrying out of that decision'.[14] That this situation was to repeat itself in the 1960s added an element of near farce to the Company's history. This enforced narrow specialization, at least until the late 1960s, had caused consternation among the initial supporters of FCI. Piercy, in conversations with Treasury officials as early as 1948, reported that there was 'bitter disappointment' with the performance of the Company.[15] FCI should perhaps have shaken off this role before the 1970s, but the literal interpretation of its function as a politically responsive lender of last resort, not seeking to make anything but the barest profit, reduced any incentive to change. As the Chairman, Lord Bruce noted, on the occasion of his retirement after ten years in office, his was 'a task I suggest few would envy'.[16] Kinross was disparaging in his later comments on FCI, asserting that he could 'never remember meeting with anyone who got any positive action out of our sister company'.[17] He also suggested that FCI could and should have contemplated changing the rules, as he maintained that ICFC had done, and sought to develop a profitable institution by competing for viable business, ending their role as lender of last resort and matching risk with some equity involvement.[18] As it turned out, if Charles Lidbury had been wrong in his forebodings about

ICFC in 1944, he had been nearer the mark in comments about the proposed FCI when noting that it was 'likely lending will be arranged with an eye to political ends rather than safety and real business'.[19]

The Rt Hon Lord Sherfield GCB GCMG Chairman 1964–74

This situation was to be radically changed in 1973 when FCI was brought together with ICFC. The merger had first been seriously contemplated in 1969 when Sherfield approached the Governor of the Bank of England, Sir Leslie O'Brien. He explained ICFC's increasing difficulty in meeting its funding requirement, which had necessitated going to the short-term market in 1969, and that 'our eyes had caught the resources of FCI'. Sherfield also noted that a link-up would result in an increased shareholding in ICFC by the Bank of England, which he would regard as an advantage. The Governor was interested in this scheme, noting that, while ICFC had established a viable long-term role for itself— FCI, following the nationalization of steel, was now at a loose end.[20] The proposed link-up could be seen as symptomatic of ICFC's own susceptibility to the contemporary 'merger mania', but it made good sense in terms of access to resources, and in terms of freeing ICFC from the formal constraints of operating below a given limit, which, for example, had recently restrained the Corporation in its merger business.[21]

Upon receiving the tentative approval of the Bank of England, Sherfield approached Sir Humphrey Mynors, the Chairman of FCI, suggesting the setting-up of a holding company to encompass their two Corporations. Mynors was understandably lukewarm towards the idea and, while he recognized that a link with ICFC would substantially increase FCI's management resources, he preferred to retain the latter's independence. To this end he was in fact pursuing the idea of emulating ICFC by encouraging the banks to buy out his insurance and investment trust shareholders.[22] Mynors later reported to Sherfield that he had met with CLCB members, Robarts and Sir Archibald Forbes (then Chairman of the Midland). They informed him that the Committee had rejected this idea. In fact, it later transpired that the banks were in favour of winding up FCI altogether.[23] Things had by now reached something of an impasse, Mynors' only suggestion being that ICFC should manage

FCI on some form of consultancy basis. Sherfield saw this as unacceptable and reported as much to Mynors and the Bank of England. He could now only see a way forward if the latter took control of negotiations.[24]

In the meantime another player had entered the field in the form of the Industrial Reorganisation Corporation (IRC), the government-funded corporation which had been set up to rationalize sectors of the British economy by promoting mergers. ICFC's ambitions for its merger business had led to suggestions that these two organizations should link up in some way, perhaps doing syndicated business. In May 1969 Sherfield met Charles Villiers of the IRC for general discussions, but at this time no firm proposals were forthcoming. It was observed, however, that the IRC, with its very high political profile, was unlikely to survive in its present form if there was a change of government, although this did not stop suggestions that the IRC should take over both FCI and ICFC.[25] Negotiations between ICFC, IRC, and FCI had thus come to nothing, principally because at this time the Bank of England had been reluctant to step in and force the issue, and the clearing banks, especially Forbes at the Midland, had been vociferously against any reorganization.[26] It was clear at this time, however, that there was a great deal of uncertainty over the future of two organizations—the IRC and FCI—and a desire for substantial change on behalf of the third, ICFC, and that a lull in negotiations could only be temporary.

The following year the election of the Heath government proved to be the catalyst which restarted discussions. The imminent demise of the IRC was predicted, since it had always been seen by Tories as an agent of 'back-door nationalization' and had few friends in the new government in its present form.[27] Sherfield judged that the 'moment has come':

With the change in government and the question mark over the IRC's future, there may emerge the need for the creation in the private sector of a body capable of discharging some of the IRC functions in the rationalisation of industry. ICFC/FCI would, I believe, be able to discharge this function, as the two Corporations together should be able to command the financial resources and provide the management.[28]

When Sherfield approached the Governor at the Bank of England, however, he was surprised to learn that it had been agreed some months previously, at a meeting between the Bank, representatives of the clearers, and Sir Humphrey Mynors, that FCI should be wound up. Sherfield told the Governor of his intentions, given that the IRC would not last much longer, but agreed to 'walk warily' in view of the political sensitivity of the situation.[29] Sherfield next went to Sir Richard Clarke, Permanent Secretary at the Ministry of Technology,[30] explaining that he had come 'on a fishing expedition in relation to IRC'. Clarke agreed that there would indeed be an IRC role to be performed, perhaps in the private sector, if the IRC itself were axed, and he noted that ICFC's management expertise would be very useful since the IRC experience had shown that 'changing the management was often as important as injecting money'.[31] Clarke went on to enquire whether ICFC would be prepared to accept government money in order to carry this out. This suggestion was going too far for Sherfield, who replied in the negative. Sherfield noted that ICFC had been at great pains to deny the notion, still commonly held, that they were some form of government agency, and that acceptance of government money would undo this. He did not rule out the idea that FCI might take government money as a separate corporation within a group comprising ICFC and FCI under a holding company arrangement. In his resistance to government funds Sherfield was not representative of all at ICFC, however, and he later noted that 'some of my colleagues were, I found, rather more favourably disposed to getting their hands on government money than I was'.[32]

Sherfield next approached Eric Faulkner, knighted in 1974, the acting Chairman of the CLCB during Forbes's temporary absence, who confirmed that the banks were indeed in favour of winding up FCI and noted that 'his colleagues were tired of pulling government chestnuts out of the fire'.[33] He was also cautious about Sherfield's IRC proposals, warning that the banks might not want to have any part in a 'quasi-IRC' organization in the private sector. Faulkner advised Sherfield to put his case to other bankers, which he duly did, notably recruiting the support of Robarts, ICFC's erstwhile supporter, who agreed that the wind-up of FCI was a rather defeatist proposal and promised to promote Sherfield's plan.

Throughout these negotiations Sherfield maintained that the ICFC/FCI merger stood on its own merits, irrespective of the fate of the IRC. The main sticking point with the merger, from the banks' point of view, remained the issue of buying out the existing shareholders—the insurance companies and investment trusts. Forbes put the case that the banks regarded the uncalled capital as security for overdraft and loan facilities committed by them, and were reluctant to let the existing shareholders off the hook.[34]

As the future of the IRC began to look more and more uncertain, overtures began to arrive with increasing urgency from its Chairman, Sir Joseph Lockwood, and Charles Villiers, during July and August 1970. Villiers in particular was full of ideas for a link-up of IRC, FCI, and ICFC, with an interchange of staff and a mixture of government and private capital. By now, however, it was probably apparent to Sherfield that the IRC was a dead duck, and there was no need for ICFC to become part of a rescue operation. If the IRC went out of business, which was looking increasingly likely, this would only strengthen the case for an amalgamation between ICFC and FCI to perform some of the IRC's vestigial functions, albeit in the private sector.[35] In distancing himself from the IRC Sherfield made a prudent choice, as the corporation was indeed closed down in 1970. The ICFC/FCI link-up also went into abeyance, however, largely due to the continuing hostility of the clearers. The time had come to lie low for a while.[36]

Sherfield, who was committed to a merger of FCI and ICFC, had successfully placed this idea on the agenda, however, and when the Chairmanship of the CLCB was handed over to Eric Faulkner in 1973 the proposals were pressed again with renewed vigour. With the continued support of O'Brien at the Bank of England, the time had finally come for the merger to go ahead. Negotiations were reopened in the summer of 1973, the main sticking point being the apportionment of shareholder participation between the Bank of England and the clearers.

Finance For Industry

When agreement was finally reached in November 1973, ICFC and FCI both became subsidiaries of a newly created holding company, Finance for Industry (FFI) which acquired the whole of the issued share capital of FCI for cash, and the shares of ICFC in exchange for its own shares. The Bank of England subscribed for additional shares in FFI, raising its shareholding from 3 to 15 per cent, and total shareholders' funds were increased from £40 million to £73.3 million. The clearers initially resisted this increase, which brought the Bank's shareholding closer into line with their own, but only succeeded in delaying the merger.[37]

The FFI Group was born early in a decade which featured an extremely turbulent economic environment. The British economy as a whole began to experience severe problems throughout the 1970s, and the decade is characterized by a loss of political and economic direction. For the Conservative Party it was the decade which began with the election of Edward Heath, bringing the promise of a modernizing, dynamic Toryism, but which was lost in U-turns, confrontational industrial relations legislation, the three-day week, and electoral defeat in 1974. For Labour the decade began in opposition, following the demise of the hopes of the Wilson years. The return to power in 1974 was beset by rising inflation and unemployment, recourse to the IMF, and an inability to control the union movement resulting in the so-called 'winter of discontent'. The decade ended in the election of Margaret Thatcher in 1979, determined to purge the Tory Party of 'wet' politics, paving the way for the introduction of a radical redirection of economic and social policies. The consequence for Labour was a split in the party in 1981, which produced the breakaway Social Democratic Party, and internecine disputes over policy, which combined to precipitate the subsequent long years in opposition.

Against this background of transitory politics FFI continued along a path characterized by both stability and change. The 1970s was also a period

Group organisation

FFI

Finance for Industry Limited
policy making and fund raising to meet the needs
of its two principal operating subsidiaries.

ICFC

Industrial and Commercial Finance
Corporation Limited
long term finance for the smaller business
in amounts ranging from £5000 to £1m or more.

FCI

Finance Corporation for Industry Limited
medium term loans at fixed or fluctuating rates in
amounts ranging from £1 million to £25 million.

when various government initiatives threatened to compete with FFI's business, and when deregulation of certain aspects of the banking industry fostered competition from the clearers. Competition and Credit Control was followed by years of boom in equities and property, and the subsequent property slump, secondary banking crisis, and Stock Exchange collapse. The Group's business could hardly remain unaffected by these fluctuations, which periodically reduced business, limited profits, and influenced fund raising.

Running the Group: A New Phase of Expansion

In 1974 Sherfield stepped down and Lord Seebohm was appointed as the Group Chairman. 'Freddie' Seebohm was the first Chairman to have a background in banking, and was seen by the clearers as their inside man, particularly at a time when ICFC began to experience some difficulties.[38] If it was the shareholders' hope that Seebohm would undertake such a role it probably proved to be in vain. Later, in 1977, when Sir Eric Faulkner was appointed as Seebohm's deputy, he too felt he had been appointed as 'a sort of watchdog', but on this occasion to watch Seebohm![39] To ICFC insiders Seebohm was an excellent choice as Chairman, having been on the Board for five years and having a good understanding of ICFC's business philosophy. On Seebohm's appointment in

113

1974, Larry Tindale returned from the DTI to take up the Deputy Chairmanship, with Paul Hildesley continuing as Group General Manager.[40]

FFI was to be responsible for general policy within the Group, for contacts with government departments and EEC organizations, and for raising Group finance. ICFC was to continue in its role of providing medium- and long-term funds for smaller enterprises, while FCI was to provide finance in larger amounts. Thus Group activity was no longer nominally tied to the Macmillan gap, but was instead held to be 'to provide medium- and long-term funds for the growth of British industry'.[41] In line with the increased involvement of the Bank of England a series of regular meetings was instigated at the Bank. At the first of these it was formally noted that FCI should not swamp ICFC and starve it of resources within the Group. It was also affirmed that ICFC operating methods, in particular the provision of a mixture of loan and equity finance, should be adopted by FCI, and that the latter, in a tacit deprecation of its previous operating strategy, should avoid becoming involved in the finance of 'lame ducks'.[42] In practice, however, FCI was to continue as a loan-based business, although no longer acting as a lender of last resort. It was also envisaged that the Group would continue to pursue a balanced investment programme, financing equity holdings from shareholders' funds and retained profits and loans with matching debt.[43]

The debate continues over the causes of economic turmoil during the 1970s. These range from the immediate and global, notably the oil-price shock, to long-term structural problems, delayed in their appearance by the full-employment policies pursued by post-war governments. FFI was to be affected in a number of interrelated ways. Existing customers began to experience difficulties during economic downturns and investment opportunities fluctuated, leading to periodic reductions in the number of applications. The instability in interest rates, reflecting increasingly high inflation, also made for an extremely volatile environment for long-term finance. As Seebohm noted in 1979, the previous year's swing in the Minimum Lending Rate by nearly 7.5 per cent had made 'financial planning for both lenders and borrowers something of a nightmare'.[44] ICFC had instigated a system of forward corporate planning on a five-yearly basis in 1968, and the 1973 plan was still seen as an 'indispensable part of management'[45] taking into account projected changes in competition, government policies, electoral changes, European developments, and so on, using available forecasts from institutions such as National Institute of Economic and Social Research (NIESR) and the universities. There were also plans to initiate a computer modelling process. By 1976, however, the value of 'professional' forecasts, given the turbulent state of the economy, was in serious doubt. FFI noted that 'any businessman is as qualified as the forecasting institutes to decide which scenario he considers most likely'.[46] However, despite these difficulties, and periodic downturns in performance, the FFI Group as a whole was to recover from its problems in the early 1970s and consolidate its position throughout the rest of the decade.

Under the umbrella of FFI, each component of the Group continued to operate in a fairly autonomous fashion. ICFC began to experience a downturn in activity around 1974 and investments in that year, at only £23.7 million, were in sharp contrast to the previous years' run of steady annual increases. The following year was no better, reflecting what Seebohm saw as the 'most severe recession in this country since the 1930s',[47] and the Corporation was forced to record its first yearly loss, some £19.9 million, since the very early years of its existence. ICFC was soon back into profit, but investment continued at a low rate into 1976, and the level of its 'unused capacity' began to cause serious concern.[48] In response to these problems ICFC put increasing effort into marketing, embarked on internal cost-cutting exercises, raised its upper limit on investments to £2 million, and relaxed its requirements in relation to equity.[49]

After the retirement of Paul Hildesley, Jon Foulds became Group General Manager in July 1977, and lending policy was liberalized. The following year, ICFC saw a significant increase in activity as investment levels doubled. The Corporation maintained this improvement throughout 1978 and the following year again nearly doubled the level of its investments. In the five years from 1977 onwards ICFC experienced one of the largest expansions of its portfolio in its history. The number of approved applications rose from 518 in 1977–8 to 1040 in 1981–2, and the level of funds invested annually began regularly to exceed £100 million. Reflecting this growth in activity, the total number of customers on the ICFC books rose from 2,200 in 1978 to 3,800 in 1982.[50] Much of this increase in investment went to smaller enterprises.

A considerable proportion of ICFC business continued to be calls from existing customers, although the number of new businesses applying to the Corporation also showed a steady increase throughout the latter 1970s. In 1979, for example, of 920 approved applications 618 were from firms which had not previously approached ICFC for support.[51] The average level of investment began to increase, rising from £97,000 in 1978 to £105,000 in 1981, but in real terms the average size of investment had fallen by over 50 per cent between 1975 and 1981.[52] A continuing high proportion of investment went to firms requiring smaller amounts. Of the approved applications in 1981–2, for example, 48 per cent were for amounts between £5,000 and £50,000.[53] Of these smaller firms the majority continued to require growth capital. Start-ups were important to ICFC and TDC, however, and in the ten years to 1977 they had provided capital for 277 start-up or green-field developments. With the expansion in ICFC activity after 1977, investment in new companies—classified by the Corporation as those having traded for three years or less—showed a steady increase, rising to a total of 440 in 1981–2.[54] Start-ups continued to be a problem, however, even for ICFC's increasingly sophisticated assessment and mon-

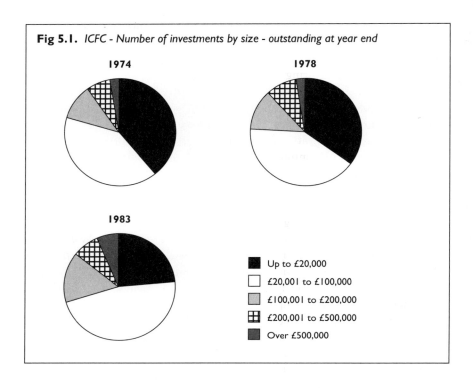

Fig 5.1. *ICFC - Number of investments by size - outstanding at year end*

1974

1978

1983

■ Up to £20,000
□ £20,001 to £100,000
▨ £100,001 to £200,000
⊞ £200,001 to £500,000
■ Over £500,000

itoring procedures. These companies often required not only a high ratio of equity finance, constituting a greater risk, but also a greater degree of liaison and advisory support. This created difficulties for ICFC, whose administration was geared to a hands-off approach once the initial investment had been made.[55]

One increasingly important component of the rising level of activity towards the end of the 1970s was the funding of management buy-outs (MBOs). It has to be noted that MBOs were a feature of ICFC activity predating the 'enterprise culture' of the 1980s, and they began to increase rapidly from 1978 onwards. By the beginning of the 1980s ICFC had already funded over 200 MBOs in total, sometimes providing up to 90 per cent of the finance involved. MBOs and, later, management buy-ins (MBIs) and buy-in management buy-outs (BIMBOs)[56] were to become an increasingly important feature of ICFC, and later 3i activity; indeed, as we shall see in subsequent chapters, the Group was to become the leading UK supporter of MBOs in the 1980s. MBOs initially proved to be very safe risks, certainly in contrast to start-ups and high-technology investments, for example. Nevertheless, as more institutions competed to provide funding, and gearing levels were bid up, problems did begin to emerge, as new management teams took on very high debt-repayment burdens.

FFI's other divisions had a somewhat chequered experience from 1973 onwards. Technical Development Capital continued to struggle, and its fortunes were at a low ebb during this period. It was thought that more publicity, boosted by the establishment of TDC's Innovation Award, might improve the company's prospects;[57] but by 1976 there had been no significant improvement. It was noted by Seebohm that TDC's business seemed to be 'an often expensive exercise where attempts to identify and pull out the plums more often than not result in painfully burnt fingers'.[58] By 1978 investment was still below £1 million annually, and despite hopes inspired by a brief resurgence in the number of applications in 1979, TDC ended the decade 'rather disappointingly', with investment levelling out yet again although there were some promising investments coming onto the books, notably a US firm setting up in Britain to manufacture large-scale integrated circuits, and a British bio-technology company. At the beginning of the 1980s TDC began to narrow its focus, concentrating on information technology, bio-technology, and robotics, but there were by now a growing number of specialist funds beginning to operate in these areas, in an attempt to emulate some of the spectacular venture capital gains which had featured in the United States in the 1970s.[59]

TDC's limited impact must be placed in context. It is in the nature of investment in high-technology that greater risks need to be taken by investors, compensated for by the possibility of high returns from a minority of companies in the portfolio. TDC could be judged to have been unlucky in that no 'shooting stars' appeared among its investments.[60] An apt comparison might be made with its government-sector counterpart, the National Research Development Corporation, which owed almost all of its limited success to a single pharmaceutical investment which came up trumps, while other initiatives, including attempts to foster the development of the computer industry in Britain, proved less than successful.[61]

TDC should not be portrayed as a total failure. It was, indeed, a moderate success in financial terms. It also fulfilled an additional role to the benefit of FFI. TDC was judged to be useful in gaining continued approval in political circles by showing that the Group was operating in areas deemed to be of national economic importance. This was Tindale's view, later supported by Foulds,[62] although the latter also maintained a 'hidden agenda' designed to limit TDC to its original brief and not to encroach on what might be seen as ICFC's business. Rivalry between different companies within the FFI Group had occurred in the past, most notably between EDITH and ICFC, whose overlapping fields of interest, given ICFC's administrative involvement and pursuit of equity investments, had led to serious confrontations.[63] In the case of TDC no comparable rivalry developed, however, with ICFC continuing its emphasis on investments in the manufacturing sector. It must be noted, however, that there was, during the mid-1970s, an increasing proportion of service-sector companies on the Corporation's books (see Fig. 5.2).

Among other FFI Group interests there was a greater degree of success. Ship Mortgage Finance business, as noted in the previous chapter, had been largely superseded by government-guaranteed loans under the 1967 Shipbuilding Act. This 'Home Credit Scheme' was continued under the Industry Act of 1972, and SMFC was recruited to investigate the creditworthiness of applicants, act as agent in negotiations, and advise the department on monitoring procedures on behalf of the DTI. To offset the loss of mortgage business ICFC had acquired and expanded the activities of other shipping-related companies and entered the bare-boat chartering business. In 1975 these operations were consolidated as FFI acquired the whole of Falkland Shipowners Ltd., renaming it Finance for Shipping (FFS). FFS then in turn bought SMFC and the Nile Steamship Company, thus consolidating FFI's marine division. FFS continued to expand steadily, despite recessionary tendencies within the industry, until the mid-1980s, administering the government scheme, providing post-delivery finance, and bare-boat chartering its own ships. However, this latter part of the business came to an end when free depreciation of ships was discontinued in the 1985 budget.

Other activities of FFI continued to expand including leasing and hire purchase, consultancy, and property investment. Leasing continued its steady

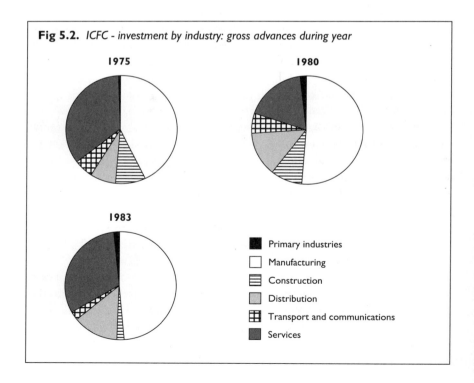

Fig 5.2. *ICFC - investment by industry: gross advances during year*

1975

1980

1983

■ Primary industries

□ Manufacturing

⊟ Construction

▨ Distribution

⊞ Transport and communications

▩ Services

progress from 1973 onwards and was held to be an area of great potential.[64] Hamilton Leasing, which had been founded in 1962, with ICFC as one of the original shareholders, was bought in 1974 to expand the activities of the Group into the office-equipment and medical-and-dental sectors. ICFC took over Hamilton partly because the company was in trouble, hoping to turn it around. Hamilton had some very troublesome leasing agreements on its books, including a substantial deal with Alfred Herbert, the ailing machine-tool firm, soon to be rescued by the government.[65] In the event Hamilton was put onto a sound footing and sold off to Lloyds and Scottish in 1981. A more ambitious project came with the acquisition of Highland Leasing in 1977. This company specialized in leasing in the agricultural sector, where ICFC had done very little business. The hoped-for breakthrough proved elusive, however, and Highland never lived up to expectations, being sold to Mercantile Credit in 1980. Throughout the 1970s it was recognized that ICFC's terms for leasing were not really any better than those of its competitors. Its advantage lay in the captive market of its own portfolio and the publicity and marketing of its national branch network.[66] New initiatives such as Hamilton were labour-intensive however, calling for activity beyond this existing structure; and ultimately they proved difficult to sustain. Nonetheless, ICFC-style industrial leasing continued to be an important component of FFI activity, and by 1980 over £100 million of contracts were being negotiated annually.[67]

Other FFI Group activities had a chequered experience during the difficult economic circumstances of the 1970s. Consultancy business continued to be troublesome and remained at a low ebb from 1973 onwards.[68] For both ICFC–NUMAS, which concentrated on data processing and production-related consultancy, and for ICFC Training, which continued its long-established group-training schemes for apprentices in small firms,[69] the 1970s were very difficult indeed. It was proving an arduous task to persuade the small- and medium-sized firm sector that training was important enough to warrant the payment of substantial fees. In addition ICFC–NUMAS and ICFC Training found it difficult to recruit and keep adequate staff.[70] In 1978 ICFC–NUMAS launched its 'Understanding Industry' project, designed to bring schools and industry closer together. But the following years saw continuing difficulties for what became ICFC Training and Management Consultants and subsequently ICFC Consultants. The situation was made even worse by the onset of recession in 1981 when a very sharp fall in demand led to the discontinuation of two training services.[71]

FFI property interests also ran into problems following the end of the boom years of the early 1970s. In 1974–5, for example, Anglia Commercial Properties was compelled to make £15 million of provisions. Its portfolio included some very speculative purchases, occasionally in anticipation of planning permission, in line with the general rush for property from 1971 onwards.

Bond Helicopters Ltd

BOND WAS FOUNDED IN 1961 by David Bond, the father of the present Chief Executive, Stephen Bond. In the mid-1960s the business was sold to Fisons, where David Bond became Chief Aviation manager of the crop spraying division. In 1968, aware of the potential market for helicopter services, he arranged to buy back the helicopters and restart his own business, continuing to provide Fisons with a seasonal flying service, but expanding the scope of the work to encompass activities such as power line patrols and underslung load lifting.

3i entered the scene in 1970, providing a £25,000 loan with an option to convert into 18.5% of the equity, which enabled the company to buy Fisons' agricultural crop-spraying division. Two years later came the company's first and most important change of direction; with the development of North Sea oil and gas the opportunity arose to establish a helicopter service for the new fields with 3i providing the capital to acquire the necessary twin-engined helicopters. Rapid expansion of the business required further injections by 3i throughout the mid-1970s: in the first five years of the offshore operation, £800,000 was provided for helicopter and equipment purchases.

The scale of operations continued to increase in the 1980s, 3i being asked to provide a further £4.8 million for new helicopters and modifications. In the mid-1980s, the oil industry slump had a serious effect on the company's cash flow which was eased when 3i led a debt rescheduling. In the 1990s, as the company continues to flourish, further capital expenditure and latterly the purchase of Lloyd Helicopters of Australia have been financed by loans totalling £13 million.

The company's growth record is well illustrated by comparing the 1993 performance with that of 1970 when 3i first became involved:

	1970 £	1993 £
Turnover	137,000	80 million
Profit before tax	10,000	8 million
Net Assets	38,000	25 million

In 1994, the merger of Bond Helicopters with Helikopter Service of Norway created the world's largest civil helicopter operating group, Brokers'.

"GOOD IDEA. LET'S MERGE AND BE BIG."

The lengthy and complex task of realizing these investments, involving 'patient and often frustrating' negotiations with local councils, was to take up about half of the property division's time for the rest of the 1970s.[72] From 1976 onwards the Group's property activities were divided between Anglia, ICFC Properties, and ICFC Developments. The latter companies continued to invest in and develop smaller industrial properties, notably factories and warehouses, a concentration which increased towards the end of the decade. In 1979–80, for example, 55 per cent of developments were under 5,000 square feet, and by 1981 this had risen to 80 per cent. In focusing on this area FFI were again filling a gap left by other institutional investors. Insurance companies and pension funds in particular were unwilling to invest in industrial properties of less than 10,000 sq. ft.[73] Sale and lease-back of property was frequently seen by FFI as a substitute for equity in smaller companies, as a way of establishing a long-term relationship with firms who were otherwise reluctant to accept equity participation.[74]

Outside the small firm sector ICFC continued its corporate finance and merger-broking activities, which were consolidated into ICFC Corporate Finance in 1977. ICFC continued to be a member of the Issuing Houses Association, occasionally sponsoring new companies to the Stock Exchange, many of which were ICFC customers. ICFC Corporate Finance also continued to sponsor rights issues for listed companies, and, in the tradition of Kinross, pushed down costs wherever possible, 'much to the chagrin of some lawyers and accountants'.[75] In the field of portfolio management ICFC also managed two listed investment trusts, London Atlantic Investment Trust

(LAIT) and North British Canadian Investment Trust (NBC); its fund managers also provided investment management services to a number of pension funds and assisted the Post Office Pension Fund in establishing a specialized portfolio of small-company investments.

While ICFC itself and its related companies experienced a range of fortunes following the formation of FFI, the other important component in the Group, FCI, saw its activities profoundly redirected. As we saw earlier, FCI had become tied to a very narrow range of investments, at marginal rates of return, for most of its pre-FFI existence. Under its new ownership the Company began to re-orientate both its areas of lending and its methods. Appraisal methods in particular were to be improved, with more stress on industrial and personal appraisal. It was noted, however, that the simple transfer of ICFC methods in this respect would be difficult, since policy in larger firms tended to be made by many people, unlike smaller firms where key individuals were of central importance.[76] FCI did not abandon its old customer base entirely, continuing to provide finance for established customers such as Alcan for example, but it began an active search for new industries in which to become involved. One of the earliest of these was the burgeoning North Sea oil industry, where FCI financed drilling ships and maintenance companies.[77] An informal upper limit of £15 million was set on loans, although this was occasionally exceeded. These loans were often unsecured, since larger companies were 'accustomed' to this type of borrowing, and FCI, competing as it was with other sources of borrowing including British and American banks and the capital markets, felt constrained to conform.[78]

After a tentative start, with only £3 million loaned in 1973, investments rose sharply. In 1975 £134 million was invested, and there were negotiations in progress for a further £304 million. These ranged across a number of industrial sectors and included large advances to Beecham, British Aluminium, Distillers, GKN, and Pilkington.[79] By 1977 a total of £241 million had been invested in forty companies, nearly half of which was unsecured lending. This figure would undoubtedly have been larger had not interest rates begun to climb, resulting in the curtailment of many larger investment programmes. In the following year business continued to ebb, with more investment plans moth-balled and a growing reliance among larger firms on cash flow. In an attempt to counter this trend FCI began to offer extended variable-rate loans of up to fifteen years, in replacement of the previous ten-year limit.[80] What FCI wanted, however, was a return to an environment which would favour long-term fixed-rate lending, but this did not seem an immediate prospect in the late 1970s. With interest rates continuing at high levels and a ready availability of bank finance at increasingly competitive floating rates, companies, many of which were now highly liquid, continued to shun long-term agreements. Indeed, some began to repay FCI loans early, a situation reminiscent of the company's pre-FFI days.[81]

To counter this trend FCI introduced an innovatory 'drop lock' loan in 1979. This loan offered a variable rate which was switchable to a fixed rate once interest rates had fallen to a level pre-selected by the borrower. Despite this innovation, however, competition remained intense, and FCI was compelled to become increasingly medium term in its lending. In an attempt to reorientate its activities the Company began to seek

The Rt Hon Lord Seebohm Chairman 1974–79

more equity-style investment in its sector, and with the onset of recession in 1981 began to look for a role in the capital restructuring of recession-hit firms. Investments continued at a relatively modest level, however, which was a contributory factor in the decision later that year to drop the name FCI altogether, all large company business henceforth going under the name of FFI.

The £1 Billion Fund

The absorption of FCI was to enable a renaissance of larger-scale investment activity under the guise of 3i City Office as the 1980s progressed, as discussed in Chapter 8, but the Chairman noted at the time of its official demise that FCI 'had never been able to shake off the mantle of lender of last resort which it had acquired in its early years'.[82] It is true that FCI had brought this image with it when the initial merger took place in 1973, although during the early years of the FFI Group it had gone a long way towards perpetuating the notion by involvement in one of the most remarkable developments in industrial finance during the 1970s—the £1 billion fund.

The story of this fund began soon after the formation of FFI. Many commentators began to call for some form of intervention to improve the general flow of investment into British industry which, by late 1974, was experiencing problems due to the drying-up of the long-term fixed-interest market and the collapse of the equity market. FFI began to be proposed as a possible institutional mechanism to channel funds into industry on some form of guaranteed basis. Philip Chappell of Morgan Grenfell, wrote to *The Times* in September suggesting an increase in the funds available to FFI, in line with those of Credit National in France or Kreditanstalt für Wiederaufbau in Germany, both of which were between fifteen and thirty times larger than FFI in its current form.[83] At the same time, Harold Lever, Chancellor of the Duchy of Lancaster in Wilson's recently re-elected Labour administration, began to propose that the government should channel £1,000 million into industry either through the clearing banks or through a newly created medium-term credit bank.[84] The following month Seebohm and the Governor of the Bank of England, Gordon Richardson, met with other senior staff at the Bank, where the figure of £1,000 million was discussed, and it was revealed that the Bank had been in continuous discussion with the Treasury over the issue.[85] Seebohm saw it as a possibility that FFI would get this money, and went to the Bank prepared to plead the case, noting that if such an amount were to be raised in the short term it would be necessary to tap the considerable resources of the insurance companies and pension funds. Others feared that direct involvement by the banks would 'lead to the disintegration of orthodox balance-sheet principles' by adversely affecting their overall liquidity structure, especially in the wake of pressures created by the recent secondary bank recycling operations.[86]

The 'Lever Bank' captured headlines throughout October and November 1974, and many began to see immediate parallels with the previous Labour government initiative, the Industrial Reorganisation Corporation.[87] Speculation was rife, and reports began to appear that Sir Frederick Catherwood had been chosen to head the new institution. Catherwood, Chairman of the British Institute of Management, was apparently the choice of Denis Healey, the Chancellor of the Exchequer. This was significant in that Catherwood opposed the more interventionist policies advocated by Tony Benn, the Secretary of State for Industry.[88] Reaction from the Left to the Lever proposals was swift. The scheme was seen as a deliberate attempt to pre-empt the proposed National Enterprise Board (NEB), and to subvert the principle that government-sponsored investment should be linked to a share in control of companies and a general trend towards social objectives and employment policy. Clive Jenkins saw the proposed institution as merely representing a 'retreat into the old client–customer relationships'.[89]

Despite this criticism, the idea of a £1,000 million fund gathered support and was formally announced by Healey in mid-November, firmly linked to FFI. Some supporters, such as ex-IRC chairman Charles Villiers, were very enthusiastic, seeing FFI becoming a proactive institution, providing finance, trouble-shooting, and being selective in investment to favour export industries.[90] Others, including the Bank of England, which was again standing behind a major re-orientation of the Group, certainly did not envisage that FFI, in its newly expanded role, would go this far, but rather the arrangement was seen as an 'ingenious and attractive compromise', minimizing government intervention and simultaneously orchestrating bank and institutional funds.[91]

Cavaghan & Gray Ltd

3i's CONNECTION WITH CAVAGHAN & GRAY dates back to 1957 when EDITH bought shares for estate duty purposes. Turnover at that time was £15 million per annum and profit before tax £150,000. Since then development capital has been provided on many occasions, bringing 3i's total investment in 1994 to £8.6 million in the form of equity, preference shares and loans.

At the time of EDITH's investment the company was engaged in pig slaughtering and bacon production. Since then, under continuous family ownership and three successive generations of management, combining experienced family members and professionals from the industry, the business has steadily expanded, moving away from commodity slaughtering and into a range of prepared food dishes, yoghurt manufacture, and fish processing.

The company has enjoyed a close relationship with their principal customer Marks & Spencer. This has been especially evident in the area of product development, with staff from both companies working in collaboration on new products.

Turnover is now in excess of £90 million and profitability has been maintained by an aggressive capital expenditure-led strategy and continuous fine-tuning of production facilities, aided by heavy investment in information systems.

3i's long-term connection with Cavaghan & Gray has continued to be active, nearly 40 years after EDITH's first involvement, with the financing in 1992 of the company's largest acquisition to date, Emille Tissot, a manufacturer of frozen, ready-made meals.

Arrangements were still not finalized, however, and it was unclear what precise mechanisms for raising the necessary funds would be put in place. Nevertheless, in reports redolent of those publicizing Piercy in 1945, Tindale was singled out as a 'Santa with £1 Billion'.[92] Some of the insurance companies and pension funds were understandably alarmed and resentful of the very low margins they could expect on money in support of the scheme, only fractionally above gilt-edged securities. Some of the banks were also sceptical about the ability of FFI to take on 'this mammoth role'.[93] Lever was also a little sceptical about the diversion of his idea to FFI, which he was reported to regard as 'a sleepy, third-rate organization'.[94] Elsewhere expectations ran high that FFI was set to become one of the most powerful lending institutions in Europe.[95]

In spite of the burst of publicity which followed the official announcement, and the debates it sparked off,[96] the shareholders of FFI were at first reticent, Hildesley reporting 'a deafening silence' from that quarter.[97] FFI took the initiative, however, and began to put concrete form to the proposals, including methods and cost of raising money, terms of loans, margins for FFI, and risk-taking policy. It was expected that the Group would issue loan stocks in FFI's name, and balance risk by purchasing convertible preference shares if possible. Although all the publicity had referred to the provision of medium-term finance, FFI looked for longer-term loans, up to ten years if possible, noting that the clearers 'still think 7 years is long term'.[98] Loans were likely to be directed towards favoured sectors including manufacturing and construction, foreign currency earners, and possibly the small firm sector. It was widely emphasized that wherever the loans went they would not be to finance 'lame ducks', nor should they be to fund existing bank borrowing. The Bank of England was keen to see an upper limit of £50 million on loans, although Tindale was wary of such a large amount since the effect of one failure would be disastrous. In the event FFI acquiesced and accepted the Bank's suggestion.[99] To permit an early start to lending, the clearing banks and the Bank of England agreed to subscribe £85 million of new capital and provide increased short-term facilities. Institutions were to provide the balance by subscribing to loan stock issues, and to accommodate this, borrowing powers were to be increased from four to seven times capital and reserves. The banks agreed to this on the 'assurance given to them by the Bank of England that institutional funding is available'.[100]

FFI foresaw no great difficulty in adjusting FCI to its larger task. Existing staff were expected to be well able to cope, augmented by help from ICFC and possible secondments from the merchant banks or the DTI. At board level it was suggested that there might be additions, particularly from the Trades Union movement, Len Murray's name being mentioned.[101] Nothing came of these suggestions, but an FCI Loans Committee was established which included Seebohm, Tindale, Hildesley, and two nominees from the CLCB.[102] Harold Lever soon contacted FFI with a view to getting to know the organization which had eventually taken on the mantle of the 'Lever Bank', but also, Hildesley thought, to offer political 'help in dealing with any troubles we might be encountering with the banks or institutions'.[103] This was probably unnecessary, given the long history of political guardianship afforded to the Group by the Bank of England.

The official announcement of the terms offered was made in January 1975. Loans were to be either fixed or floating and up to ten years in duration, floating-rate loans being calculated at 2.25 per cent over the London Interbank Offered Rate (LIBOR). It was stressed that funds would only be available on a commercially viable basis.[104] However, the liquidity crisis which had sparked calls for the 'Lever Bank' in 1974 was to prove short-lived. 'In early 1976 it was apparent that the anticipated liquidity crisis which had led to the suddenly enlarged role for FCI had evaporated.'[105] FFI had only needed to call upon an extra £25 million of share capital, and there was no follow-up to the initial £75 million loan-stock issue, which had itself proved difficult to place.[106] Unlike the expansion of ICFC in the late 1970s, FCI continued to struggle to maintain lending levels after the initial expansion in 1975.

Although the 'Lever Bank' episode was short-lived and had only a minor impact, it is a very interesting example of the way in which FFI interacted with political ideas and government during the 1970s. In many ways the development is reminiscent of the circumstances surrounding the establishment of FCI and ICFC in 1945. The Bank of England in particular can be seen to be taking a central role in establishing an organizational capacity to offset more direct intervention by government, and to ensure the primacy of the market over government-selective intervention linked to employment policy. As in 1945, if the City could be seen to be taking the initiative this would avoid the need for government funds, which, certainly in Seebohm's view, simply added to inflationary pressure in the economy, 'the most demoralizing thing I know. It could destroy the country'.[107] Seebohm maintained that investment should be demand-led, by demonstrably worthy projects. Reacting to Tony Benn's continued call, in 1975, for the large institutions to divert half their funds towards nationalized industries, Seebohm was unequivocal: 'I believe this is a most dangerous philosophy . . . To say there is too little investment and blame the financiers is to have the thing the wrong way round.' Seebohm was dismayed that the case for the City was not being put more effectively against the wave of criticism which emerged in the mid-1970s:

Proposals for the coercion of industrial investment, compelling firms to invest out of blocked profits or forcing private savings unwillingly into directions chosen by the planners, disregard the obvious liquidity of financial institutions and the remarkable resilience of the capital market . . . The most disturbing aspect of all is the lack of effective arguments to counter these distorted views.[108]

It was during this period that Sir Eric Faulkner helped to establish the City Communications Organisation as a device to 'answer the political attacks that were constantly being mounted on the City, particularly from the Labour benches'.[109]

The limited initiative of the £1 billion fund did enough to persuade critics that the City was capable of acting under its own volition to assuage the investment problems in industry and close the 'Lever gap'. The establishment of the National Enterprise Board in 1975, with the aim of injecting government finance in return for a stake in industry, also helped take the pressure off the City by reducing the call for alternative investment funds. The idea of the 'Lever Bank' resurfaced briefly in 1977 when the Labour Party 1972 Industry Group proposed the establishment of a British Industrial Development

Commission based on FFI with an injection of government money to guarantee lending of up to £2,500 million,[110] but the time for this idea had passed.

The intrusions of government schemes with which FFI had to deal was a natural adjunct to the operations of FCI, given its traditional role. ICFC did not have this tradition, yet had managed to foster the idea that it too had a sense of national purpose as outlined in the 1973 Corporate Plan:

> The corporation has been able to reconcile the social purpose of serving the whole small business sector with the commercial purpose of making an acceptable return for its shareholders.[111]

ICFC had successfully combined the role of making money with the role of serving the country in the small firm sector, under the 'paternal' eye of the Bank of England.[112] The Bank had never had any formal mechanism for monitoring the progress of ICFC. With the formation of FFI, however, they instigated a regular series of six-monthly meetings beginning in June 1974. These discussed the business of the Group in some detail, although the Bank's request for details of applications to FCI was rejected on the grounds of sensitivity.[113]

'On Wall Street today, news of lower interest rates sent the stock market up, but then the expectation that these rates would be inflationary sent the market down, until the realization that lower rates might stimulate the sluggish economy pushed the market up, before it ultimately went down on fears that an overheated economy would lead to a reimposition of higher interest rates.'

It had always been intended that ICFC should remain the core of FFI business, and that the merger with FCI had the advantage of increasing the Group's facilities at the cost of occasional political depredations.[114] There was an indirect cost, however, in that many potential customers continued to labour under the misapprehension that FFI and ICFC were financed and controlled directly by government. ICFC's own operations had partly contributed to this misunderstanding.[115] The administration of the shipping loans by FFS, for example, and later involvement in the Small Firms Loan Guarantee Scheme in 1981, did little to dispel the myth. The same could be said of ICFC's involvement in European schemes which included administering loans under an agreement with the European Investment Bank (EIB) in development areas, and for the European Coal and Steel Community (ECSC) in areas affected by closures in the coal and steel industries.[116] Having the Bank of England as a major shareholder was another factor. The persistent misunderstanding was frequently noted and held to be a serious impediment since many firms were wary of giving information on their activities to the government.[117] As the Chairman was to note in 1981, 'many people still think we are some kind of quango or even government department'.[118] As we shall see in the next chapter, this identity problem was only to be comprehensively addressed when FFI restructured its image to become 3i.

Throughout the 1970s FFI's relationship with its shareholders remained fairly stable, and with the exception of the troubled year of 1974–5, the Group paid a steady dividend. There was, however, a rising level of competition throughout the decade, as regulatory and strategic changes led to an increase in the number of medium- and long-term loans which the clearing banks were prepared to offer, especially following the introduction of Competition and Credit Control in 1971.[119] ICFC had historically benefited from the various quantitative credit controls which had been placed on the clearing banks and other finance houses, being itself only subject to imprecise qualitative controls via the Bank of England.[120] At first ICFC was not unduly worried by the prospect of increased competition. This had always existed to some extent from the clearers, merchant banks, and insurance companies. ICFC felt assured that whatever the resources other institutions could bring to the market they would have difficulty, in the short-term, in acquiring the staff or experience necessary to assess effectively and administer long-term business in the small- and medium-sized firm sector.[121] What was worrying for ICFC was that the clearers might take over some of the merchant banks, thus importing assessment skills to rival the Corporation, tied to the resource base and national network which the clearing banks had in place.[122] The clearers did form term-lending subsidiaries, including County Bank at National Westminster, Midland Bank Finance Corporation, and Barclays Bank (London and International).[123] Interestingly, there was no attempt by these institutions to match borrowing with lending, ICFC estimating that only 1 per cent of advances were funded by longer-term loan capital. Instead it was thought that the banks had adopted the rather precarious practice of borrowing short and lending long.[124]

By 1978 Seebohm was reporting 'competition on all fronts', especially from the clearers, who 'have steadily . . . moved quite a long way into our traditional fields of investment'. The following year it was estimated that nearly half of the loans offered by ICFC were to companies who eventually chose to borrow from banking-related competition.[125] Nevertheless, ICFC was still confident of its position, even as, in the early 1980s, competition for equity capital in the small- and medium-sized firm sector began to mount. The Corporation remained convinced that their rivals lacked the technical resources of ICFC.[126] The banks had no comparable in-house staff with industrial experience or investigating accountants. They were, instead, frequently reliant upon the advice of consultancies, which incurred extra costs, and could often be non-committal.[127] Thus secured lending, rather than more risky unsecured loans or equity investment remained a priority with the banks.[128] ICFC also continued to maintain that, in contrast to its new rivals, its purpose lay in long-term growth rather than short-term profit.

The 1970s had been an important decade for what had now become FFI. In a testing economic climate the ICFC base of the business had continued to expand its activities, despite a period of difficulty around 1974. The merger with FCI, which had created a group structure, had shown less positive direction. A role in succeeding the IRC had failed to emerge, and the £1,000 million fund had, as expected, proved to be an ephemeral initiative. Other diversified activities within the Group also failed to fit within a cohesive overall strategy. In effect, despite the change in the Group structure, it tended to be business as usual at ICFC, leading to accusations of aloofness and élitism from some of the other, still disparate, components of FFI. This situation could only be temporary, however, and as the Group entered the 1980s, fundamental changes in organization and identity were to reshape both the Group and its image.

NOTES

[1] The Prudential Assurance Co. was the largest shareholder after the Bank of England, with nearly 10 per cent, the next largest being the Pearl Assurance Company with 2.95 per cent. There were a total of 204 shareholders most holding a relatively small amount of shares.

[2] 'Memorandum to the Committee to Review the Functioning of the Financial Institutions: History and Business of Finance for Industry', FFI (May 1977), 28; S. Tolliday, 'Steel Rationalisation Policies, 1918–1950', in B. Elbaum and W. Lazonick, *The Decline of the British Economy* (Clarendon Press, Oxford, 1987), 94–100.

[3] Lord Hyndley was the first chairman; other directors were Professor C. D. Ellis, Thomas Frazer, Sir John Morrison, Sir A. Jeremy Raisman, Sir Robert J. Sinclair, J. Ivan Spens, Lt.-Gen. Sir Ronald M. Weeks, and Lord Westwood.

[4] 'Has the Macmillan Gap Been Closed?' *The Director*, 2/5 (Feb. 1951), 48.

[5] 'Industrial and Commercial Finance Corporation and Finance Corporation for Industry', Bank of England, G14/184.

[6] FCI, *Annual Report and Accounts*, Chairman's Statement, 1957, 5.

[7] FCI, *Annual Report and Accounts*, 1948.

[8] Ibid., 1951, 1952, 1953.

[9] 'FCI Capital Structure: Suggested Basis for Revision', G. S. Nelson, 5 May 1958, NLS 8699/3.

[10] J. B. Kinross, 'FCI and the Bank of England: The Crisis of 1958', 18 Feb. 1980, NLS 8699/3.

[11] Sir H. Mynors, memo, 24 Jan. 1972, quoted in Kinross, 'FCI and the Bank of England'.

[12] F. E. Hyde, *Cunard and the North Atlantic: 1840–1973* (Macmillan, 1975), 304.

[13] FCI, *Annual Report and Accounts*, 1965–73.

[14] 'Has the Macmillan Gap Been Closed?', 48.

[15] Piercy, 'Talk With Sir W. Eady', 7 Jan. 1946. Piercy 9/180.

[16] FCI, *Annual Report and Accounts*, 1957, 11.

[17] Piercy, 'Talk With Sir Wilfred Eady', 19 Aug. 1948: Kinross, *Diaries*, 9 Jan. 1950 and 1984 annotations.

[18] Kinross, 'FCI and the Bank of England', 2.

[19] Lidbury comments upon 'Projected National Industrial Finance Corporation', memo, 11 Dec. 1944, 4, NatWest 4285.

[20] Sherfield to Tindale, 16 Jan. 1969, NLS 8699/5.

[21] 'Notes on Various Interests in Proposed Merger', 24 Feb. 1969; 'Proposed Amalgamation of FCI and ICFC', 24 Feb. 1969; NLS 8699/8.

[22] 'FCI–ICFC', 25 Feb. 1969; 'FCI', 6 Mar. 1969; NLS 8699/5.

[23] Mynors to Sherfield, 26 Apr. 1969, NLS 8699/5.

[24] 'FCI–ICFC', 22 May 1969; 23 May 1969; NLS 8699/5.

[25] 'FCI–ICFC. Note for the Record', 9 May 1969; 20 May 1969; 30 July 1969, NLS 8699/8.

[26] Sherfield to Mynors, 10 July 1970, NLS 8699/8; Kinross, *Fifty Years in the City*, 218–19.

[27] 'Proposal to Acquire FCI', 7 July 1970; Mynors to Sherfield, 10 July 1970, NLS 8966/5; Mintech refs. to IRC.

[28] Sherfield to Mynors, 10 July 1970, NLS 8699/5.

[29] 'Note for the Record: FCI/ICFC', 12 July 1970, NLS 8699/5.

[30] By 1970 the Ministry of Technology had responsibility for the IRC in its capacity as a 'Ministry of Industry', having absorbed the functions of the Department of Economic Affairs, The Board of Trade, and the Ministry of Fuel and Power, and accrued wide responsibilities for industrial policy and defence procurement. See Coopey, *The Wilson Governments*.

[31] 'Note for the Record: ICFC/FCI', 14 July 1970, NLS 8699/5.

[32] 'Note for the Record: FCI/ICFC', 21 July 1970.

[33] 'ICFC/FCI: Note for the Record', 14 July 1970.

[34] Sherfield, 'ICFC/FCI', 27 July 1970, NLS 8699/5.

[35] Sherfield, 'Confidential Note for the Record', 3 Aug.1970; 11 Aug. 1970; 24 Aug. 1970, NLS 8699/5.

[36] Sherfield, 'FCI/ICFC', 24 Aug. 1970, NLS 8699/5.

[37] The 60,000 shares in FFI were held as follows: Bank of England, 9,011,736; Bank of Scotland, 1,870,022; Barclays Bank, 11,314,459; Lloyds Bank, 8,220,791; Midland Bank, 9,708,264; National Westminster Bank, 13,795,912; Clydesdale Bank, 1,107,692; Royal Bank of Scotland, 2,750,637; Williams and Glyn's Bank, 1,801,187; Coutts and Co., 419,210.

[38] Sir Eric Faulkner, interviewed by T. Gourvish, 13 Dec. 1991: Jon Foulds, interviewed by R. Coopey, 1 Dec. 1992.

[39] Faulkner, interview.

[40] Tindale's absence at the DTI had not made him a stranger at ICFC. He had continued to attend the Executive Committee Meetings, for example, throughout his secondment. Ivan Momtchiloff, interviewed by R. Coopey, 20 Jan. 1993.

[41] FFI, *Annual Report and Accounts*, 1974.

[42] FFI Bank of England Meeting, 27 July 1974, Report, 3i B35.

[43] Ibid.

[44] FFI, *Annual Report and Accounts*, 1979, 3.

[45] ICFC *Corporate Plan 1973–78*, Mar. 1973, 5.

[46] FFI, 'Group Position Paper', Apr. 1976, 3i B37.

[47] FFI, *Annual Report and Accounts*, 1976, 4.

[48] FFI, *Annual Report and Accounts*, 1977, 4.

[49] L. N. G. Olsen, *The FFI Group: Into the Eighties* (Oct. 1978).

[50] ICFC, *Annual Report and Accounts*, 1978–82.

[51] ICFC, *Annual Report and Accounts*, 1980, 5.

[52] Olsen, *FFI Group: Into the Eighties*, 8.

[53] This compares with a figure of 58 per cent 5 years previously, although overall levels of investment must be adjusted to take inflation into account. ICFC *Annual Report and Accounts*, 1977–82.

[54] ICFC investments in new companies (the first figure for each year represents companies with 3 years' trading, the second figure represents completely new businesses): 1978/9— 112, 64; 1979/80—309, 146; 1980/1—417, 216; 1981/2—440, 305. (FFI, *Annual Report and Accounts*, 1977–82.)

[55] Momtchiloff, interview.

[56] MBIs occur when management teams, sometimes following an unsuccessful MBO bid, buy their way into an enterprise with which they were not previously connected. BIMBOs, as the name suggests, are buy-outs carried out by a combination of existing and external management teams. See below, Ch. 7.

[57] ICFC Bi-Monthly Management Meeting, Minutes 26 July 1973, 3i CC5.

[58] FFI, *Annual Report*, 1976, 5.

[59] W. D. Bygrave and J. A. Timmons, *Venture Capital at the Crossroads* (Harvard Business School Press, 1992), 95–123; FFI *Annual Report*, 1981.

[60] Momtchiloff, interview.

[61] J. Hendry, *Innovating for Failure: Government Policy and the Early British Computer Industry* (MIT, 1989).

[62] Momtchiloff, interview; Foulds, interview.

[63] Roger Plant, interviewed by R. Coopey, 2 June 1992, Hildesley, interview.

[64] FFI Bi-Monthly Management Meetings, Minutes 31 July 1973.

[65] FFI Bank of England Meeting, 27 July 1974, 3i B35.

[66] Olsen, *FFI Group: Into the Eighties*, 13–14.

[67] FFI, *Annual Report*, 1979, 1980, 1981.

[68] FFI Bi-Monthly Management Meeting, Minutes 27 Nov. 1973.

[69] ICFC Training had been established in 1953. It used part- time retired staff, known as group engineers, and full-time regionally based training officers, and it co-ordinated and managed group apprentice schemes for firms in the engineering sector.

[70] FFI Bi-Monthly Management Meetings, Minutes 29 May 1974; 25 Sept. 1974.

[71] FFI, *Annual Report and Accounts*, 1978–82.

[72] Olsen, *FFI Group: Into the Eighties*, 15–16; Momtchiloff, interview.

[73] FFI, *Annual Report and Accounts*, 1980, 1981; *FFI Group Into the Eighties*, 15.

[74] Foulds, interview.

[75] Roger Plant, interviewed by R. Coopey, 2 June 1992.

[76] FFI, 'Investigation of FCI Applications', 22 Feb. 1974.

[77] Bank of England Meeting, Report, 27 July 1974, 3i B35.

[78] FFI, *Annual Report and Accounts*, 1977.

⁷⁹ FCI, 'Details of Major Approvals and Industrial Breakdown', 27 June 1975, 3i.FCI.79.

⁸⁰ FFI, *Annual Report and Accounts*, 1978.

⁸¹ FFI, *Annual Report and Accounts*, 1979.

⁸² FFI, *Annual Report and Accounts*, 1982, 7.

⁸³ 'One Possible Solution to the Liquidity Dilemma', *The Times*, 22 Sept. 1974.

⁸⁴ *The Sunday Times*, 15 Sept. 1974.

⁸⁵ Seebohm to D. R. Clarke, Memorandum of Meeting at the Bank of England, 15 Oct. 1974; *Investors Chronicle*, 18 Oct. 1974, 238.

⁸⁶ Ibid.; Seebohm to Clarke, 14 Oct. 1974.

⁸⁷ 'The Lever Principle', *Observer*, 27 Oct. 1974; 'Give Lever's Bank a Fair Chance', *The Times*, 28 Oct. 1974; 'Lever of Last Resort', *The Times*, 29 Oct. 1974.

⁸⁸ *Observer*, 27 Oct. 1974.

⁸⁹ *The Times*, 29 Nov. 1974, 13 Nov. 1974, 15 Nov. 1974; *Guardian*, 30 Oct. 1974.

⁹⁰ *Financial Times*, 15 Nov. 1974.

⁹¹ *Financial Times*, 13 Nov. 1974.

⁹² *Sunday Times*, 17 Nov. 1974.

⁹³ 'Life-raft for Both City and Industry', *Observer*, 17 Nov. 1974.

⁹⁴ Ibid.

⁹⁵ *The Economist*, 16 Nov. 1974.

⁹⁶ T. Benn, *Against the Tide: Diaries 1973–76* (Hutchinson, 1989), 302.

⁹⁷ 'FFI £1bn', memo, 18 Nov. 1974, 3i.

⁹⁸ Ibid.

⁹⁹ 'Note of a Meeting at the Bank of England', 19 Nov. 1974; 'Proposed Guidelines for the Investment of £1bn of Additional Resources', 26 Nov. 1974.

¹⁰⁰ J. Prideaux (Chairman of the CLCB) to Seebohm, 9 Jan. 1975.

¹⁰¹ Ibid.

¹⁰² Seebohm to Sir J. Prideaux, 28 Nov. 1974; Foulds, interview.

¹⁰³ 'Note of a Meeting at Piercy House', 21 Nov. 1974.

¹⁰⁴ 'Rates and Guidelines for FFI's £1bn Fund', 14 Jan. 1975.

¹⁰⁵ Olsen, *FFI Group: Into the 1980s*, 20.

¹⁰⁶ See below, Ch. 11.

¹⁰⁷ *The Bristol Evening Post*, 29 Apr. 1974.

¹⁰⁸ FFI, *Annual Report and Accounts*, 1976, 4.

¹⁰⁹ Faulkner, interview.

¹¹⁰ The 1972 Industry Group, *Industry Investment and Finance* (June 1977), 16–18.

¹¹¹ ICFC, 'Corporate Plan 1973–78', 3.

¹¹² Momtchiloff, interview; Faulkner, interview.

¹¹³ 'Notes of a Meeting Held at the Bank of England', 27 June 1974, 3i B35.

¹¹⁴ Tindale, interview; Millard, interview.

¹¹⁵ Momtchiloff, interview.

¹¹⁶ FFI, *Annual Report and Accounts*, 1973–81; Bi-Monthly Management Meetings, Minutes 31 July 1973, 25 Sept. 1973.

¹¹⁷ 'Loan Administration in FCI', 7 Jan. 1975.

¹¹⁸ FFI, *Annual Report and Accounts*, 1981.

¹¹⁹ Sir David Walker, interviewed by R. Coopey, 11 Nov. 1992.

¹²⁰ ICFC *Corporate Plan* 1973, 6; J. R. Winton, *Lloyds Bank 1918–1969* (Oxford University Press, 1982) 145–7; F. Capie and M. Collins, *Have the Banks Failed British Industry?* (Institute of Economic Affairs, 1992), 60–9; D. M. Ross, 'British Monetary Policy and the Banking System in the 1950s' in *Business and Economic History* (1992), Second Series, vol. 21.

[121] ICFC, *Corporate Plan* 1973, 4.

[122] ICFC, *Corporate Plan* 1973, 8.

[123] ICFC, 'Banks as a Source of Medium and Long-Term Finance', Oct. 1973.

[124] 'Banks as a Source of Medium and Long-Term Finance'.

[125] ICFC, *Annual Report and Accounts*, 1975, 1978, 1979.

[126] ICFC, *Annual Report and Accounts*, 1981.

[127] Plant, interview.

[128] D. Marlow, interviewed by R. Coopey, 6 Jan. 1993.

Chapter 6

Remaking the Image

AS WE SHALL SEE in the following chapters, the 1980s presented 3i with a range of challenges, arising from enhanced competition and a radically expanding market-place, and from a need to rethink fundamentally questions of ownership and control. Viewed from a long-term perspective, the Company's reaction to these developments, in particular the changes in competition, is quite remarkable. By the start of the 1980s, under the general banner of FFI, the Company had grown into a somewhat labyrinthine collection of subsidiaries and associated companies, in a planetary system rather elliptically centred on ICFC. It could perhaps be expected that by this stage in the life-cycle of a group such as FFI, the ability to react and adapt would be limited. Broadly speaking, the early phase of establishment—the 'heroic' years of Piercy and Kinross— had led on to the successful transitionary phase instigated by Tindale and Sherfield, whereby professional, organizational reforms and expansion had ensured FFI a solid niche in the financial community. It might be reasonable to assume that in this life-cycle the Company had now entered a mature phase, assured of a degree of prestige among its peers and a steady flow of business commensurate with the consolidation and maintenance of its position. What happened instead, however, confounds the above schema. The Company in fact regenerated itself, taking on a striking new identity, restructuring and rationalizing its activities and radically altering its corporate philosophy. As a result it consistently achieved record levels of both new- and traditional- style investments. If 3i, as the Company was to become from 1983 onwards, is viewed in some circles as a relatively conservative institution, it is only against the background of the extreme turbulence of the 1980s. Seen against the backdrop of its own history, however, 3i in the 1980s can be seen to embark on a renaissance, driven from within, which enabled it not merely to cope with the challenges of a changing economic environment, but to lead the way in many developments of the period.

This renaissance was prefigured by changes in the leadership of the Group. In 1979 Lord Caldecote took over the Chairmanship of FFI from Lord Seebohm, and Jon Foulds became overall Group General Manager. This year

"THIS IS GREAT. I DIDN'T KNOW YOU KNEW ANYTHING ABOUT MARKETING."

saw the beginnings of consolidation of Group activities away from the old divisions which constituted FFI, ICFC, FCI, and FFS, each with a separate management structure, towards a General Management team with specified responsibilities. The first team headed by Foulds—soon to be collectively known as the 'gang of five'—comprised Don Clarke (finance), David Marlow (ICFC), Ivan Momtchiloff (property, shipping, and consultancy, and from 1981, Technical Development Capital) and Nigel Olsen (leasing, and from 1981, corporate finance, shipping, and FCI Head Office Division—subsequently City Office).

Caldecote's appointment marked yet another change in terms of the background of Group chairmen. Piercy had been active in finance, Sherfield in diplomacy and the civil service, and Seebohm in banking. Caldecote came with a broad experience in engineering, although immediately prior to taking over at FFI he had been chairman of Legal and General. For him the move to FFI, with its strong tradition of investment in the manufacturing sector, represented an exciting contrast to the rather stuffy world of insurance.[1]

The elevation of Jon Foulds to the post of Group General Manager represented the continued triumph of the insider from ICFC. Foulds had joined the company in September 1959, at the age of 26. He had briefly run the family textile business of Thos. Foulds and Son at the behest of elderly relatives, but, in the face of increasing foreign competition, he was led to recommend the liquidation of the firm. Foulds, who had studied for technical qualifi-cations fit for a career in the textile industry, brought no formal, finance-related qualifications with him to ICFC; but, in common with many contemporaries, he learnt quickly on the job: '3i was, in the early days, my university as well as my workplace. There were a lot of people there who were more intelligent, better educated, and more skilful financially than I was, and I learned prodi-giously from them.'[2] Foulds's career reveals a steady progression through the hierarchy of the Group, beginning in the examinations department, moving on to the regional offices in Birmingham and later Manchester where, after only three years at ICFC, he became branch manager. Returning to head office, he took responsibility for FCI in the 1970s, successfully revitalizing the Group's interest in larger investments.[3] Foulds's emergence at the head of FFI repre-sented a key transition, and the end of the Tindale era. The latter had remained very influential through his role as Deputy Chairman, but now Foulds would need to emerge from beneath Tindale's shadow and begin to assert his own authority.[4] This would prove difficult, especially given Foulds's background as an insider, in common with other members of the 'gang of five' who were all bred in ICFC culture, and it led to expectations that the Group would continue on a path of steady growth through what were by now tried and trusted meth-ods. Foulds, however, was to opt for radical change.

The Genesis of 3i

He was later to be candid about the limitations of the new team: 'We did not know very much about management, with one exception, and had to learn as we went along, probably doing some things rather badly.'[5] Foulds's style was to turn these limitations to advantage, however, by instigating a fundamental rethink about the way in which the Group operated. Noted for a strong and aggressive style of leadership (which was, on occasion, to make for a somewhat acerbic relationship with 3i shareholders)[6] Foulds determined that, in the increasingly competitive and changing environment of the 1980s, not only would the somewhat disparate activities of the Group be better unified under a rationalized structure, but also its whole identity, viewed externally and inter-nally, should be remade. This meant that the management style, the structure of the Group, the forging of a 'Group identity', and the external image and impact of FFI all became the focus of attention.

Caldecote came to share Foulds's conviction, becoming convinced that, as a group, FFI, despite considerable expertise in all its different activities, was 'not much greater than the sum of its parts'; and in a staff conference at Gleneagles in 1981 he outlined the intention to instigate a programme of change.[7] Suggestions aimed at resolving the confusion engendered by all the different names and activities which constituted the Group began to circulate in the summer of 1981. At first these were limited to bringing everything under the banner of FFI and adopting a divisional structure for various activities— FFI /FCI Division, FFI Leasing and so on. At the outset the idea of dropping the initials ICFC, or giving them secondary prominence behind FFI, drew an unfavourable reaction, a portent of serious problems which were to emerge later.[8]

The idea of building a cohesive group structure around a new corporate identity was reinforced by the collaboration of John Hunt of the London Business School, who was Plowden Professor of Human Relations. A course undertaken by the LBS, in 1979, for ICFC area managers had seemed to point to dissatisfaction with perceived management skills. Hunt suggested that prior to the next conference of area managers a survey of staff should be undertaken and the results fed back. Momtchiloff and Marlow were enthusiastic about the idea, Foulds less so. Nevertheless he agreed to the exercise. The results revealed that the decision-making and analysis processes in ICFC were not a problem, but organization and communication were poor. This came as some-thing of a shock. 'Since ICFC was a division which was generally assumed to have a very high morale and motivation these findings made potential results in other divisions a sobering prospect and raised questions about the whole FFI business. The General Managers could not avoid the conclusion that all was not well. The post-Tindale era was struggling for direction, the "Top Team" was seen to be uncohesive and uncertain.'[9] Hunt advised Foulds to contemplate carefully his thoughts on management and his ambitions for the Group. Foulds had previously intimated a preference for a cellular, locally autonomous struc-ture which somehow needed to be reconciled with the belief in a centralized management team.[10] Foulds, now converted to the idea of eliciting the atti-tudes of staff, agreed with the LBS that a further, comprehensive survey of the entire FFI workforce was imperative. Results confirmed the earlier findings. Technical competence was good, but management of staff and overall Group cohesiveness and identity were below the norms established by surveys of other organizations.[11]

As a result of these surveys Foulds was encouraged by Hunt to encapsu-late his vision, style, and philosophy in such a way that it might be generally communicated. These ideas were to form the core of a weekend conference for senior management, during which participants would be introduced to behav-ioural-science concepts about organizations, and in this context consider future direction for the FFI Group.[12] Human-relations theory and its deriva-tives had a long history by the 1980s, originating in Britain and the USA in the early years of the twentieth century. Its dominant characteristic was the notion that complex organizations tended to obscure common goals and that indivi-dual workers ran the risk of becoming alienated, and not attuned to the overall purpose and aims of the institution, and that they thus perform to sub-optimal levels. Recognizing the powerful tendency towards social interaction at work, human-relations based schemes which saw a resurgence in the 1980s, such as Employee Involvement, Quality Circles, and Quality of Working Life, sought to harness this tendency through the promotion of team structures, open communications, and rationalized hierarchies. (It was no coincidence that these schemes echoed popular perceptions of the dominant operational features of the newly transcendent Japanese economy.) The central idea which crystallized during FFI's October 1981 conference at Gleneagles reflected these ideas, recommending that the Group should be reconstructed on a divisional basis and unified under a single title, both to circumvent the development of internal parochialism which had built up within different components of the Group, and to appear externally as a unified entity, and thus greatly facilitate future marketing initiatives. As Olsen put it, 'We urgently need to "Think Group" '.[13]

To facilitate this process Hunt was brought in as a consultant, and a two-year process of team building and counselling was set in train. The General Management team began a series of quarterly 'away-day' weekends, and regular fortnightly meetings were instituted for a wider Group of twenty-five managers. Senior management was brought under scrutiny, and in at least one case persuaded to move on. Perhaps the major difficulty came with the rationalization of the personnel department. The Group had, in effect, two separate personnel departments, with ICFC retaining its own separate responsibility. With the sale of Hamilton Leasing in 1982 and the consequent reduction of staff, Foulds saw an opportunity to unify the personnel function for the whole Group. John Stewart, in charge of non-ICFC Group personnel, who had been given increasing responsibility by Foulds for human resource policy, had begun, from 1981 onward, to take key people out of ICFC Personnel to work on some of the new programmes being implemented. When the proposal was eventually put forward to merge the personnel functions, against the wishes of David Marlow, the existing ICFC personnel manager, on whom Marlow had come to rely very heavily, found the position intolerable and resigned. Stewart himself resigned soon afterwards to return to the IMF in Washington, consultants at the LBS noting that 'he was aware that his relationship with the team was now coloured by collective guilt'.[14] The General Management had, during this episode, been forced to make uncharacteristically confrontational decisions, for them a difficult and painful process. LBS observers saw this as a moment of great significance, however: 'The embarrassment experienced by the top team, over this dispute, appeared to make the members more determined to succeed; there was no going back'.[15]

The general changes to the structure of the Group evolved over a period of two years, emerging in 1983 in a newly divisionalized form. A revised committee structure was also proposed, designed to facilitate inter-divisional communication, although importantly, as the LBS noted, this 'also placed power in the hands of Jon Foulds and his team, rather than Larry Tindale'.[16]

The second major objective to emerge in this process was a new and cohesive identity for the Group, and serious consideration began to be given to the tangible form which this should take. Initial thoughts that Finance for Industry should be adopted as a name were soon under critical scrutiny. It was noted that there had not been extensive expenditure in promoting FFI, in contrast to ICFC which had continued to dominate advertising budgets, and so a complete change of Group name would not incur a waste of previous promotional resources. There was not even an FFI Group brochure at this time.[17] The exception to this general lack of awareness was among the institutions from whom FFI raised funds, where the name was well-known in view of the Group's exemplary credit standing. Outside this specialized sector there was either confusion over, or little awareness of, the relationship of Group components and their function. Among MPs interviewed by MORI, for example, half thought ICFC owned FFI and the other half the opposite.[18] 'Finance' was therefore thought, by Foulds and others, to be dispensable, a view strengthened by the feeling that the word retained governmental connotations, an idea no doubt boosted in the early 1970s through the involvement of FFI with the short-lived 'Lever bank' proposals. 'Finance' was also thought to denote short-termism, and in some parts of the United States, where the Group was seeking to expand its operations, the name would be considered misleading unless it offered a banking service, which it did not intend to do.[19]

An alternative strategy would be to rename everything under the ICFC banner. As things stood this name was well-known in its own right, but it was felt that it was too closely associated with the small company sector, and that it did not reflect the range of activities which the Group undertook. As with FFI, however, there remained the strong general feeling, revealed by commissioned surveys, that ICFC was strongly associated with government, reflecting its origins and the fact that the Bank of England remained a major shareholder.[20] Besides, Foulds felt that ICFC was a cumbersome title with 'a very low mnemonic value'. He preferred a third alternative—an entirely new 'brand name' designed to demonstrate the unique features of the Group.[21]

The alternatives—FFI, ICFC, or a brand new name—were set out by Foulds in a memo to the Chairman, which was later circulated to the senior management in December 1981. The response was varied, but included a significant degree of partisanship for the existing titles. Some gainsaid the negative image of Finance for Industry, if anything preferring the full title to proposals to adopt the abbreviation FFI. Clarke, who had put a great deal of effort into successfully establishing FFI in the international finance markets, thought this name had a very potent identification that should be aggressively promoted, with ICFC disappearing after a transitional phase.[22] Momtchiloff

MORI

MARKET & OPINION RESEARCH INTERNATIONAL (MORI) was first brought into contact with 3i in 1973 when Peter Gummer, founder of the public relations consultancy Shandwick, but at that time still 3i's PR manager, commissioned Bob Worcester, MORI's owner, to undertake a survey of customer satisfaction. A working partnership developed, and throughout the past 20 years MORI has undertaken many major studies among the group's staff and customers, MPs, the press and industry leaders, in line with the increasing importance attached by 3i to monitoring opinions both among its own staff and externally.

In 1985 Worcester and his deputy, Roger Stubbs, decided to realize some of their equity in MORI. However, since the company was very much their own creation and selling out might mean a loss of identity as well as independence, options were limited. A number of approaches came from others in the communications business, mainly advertising and PR companies, but these were rejected by Worcester who feared that MORI's reputation for objectivity might be compromised. He considered going public but was not happy with the approach of the City; amongst other things, he balked in particular at the underpricing of his shares.

3i's Neil Cross had written to Worcester to wish him well when it was first announced that MORI was considering going public. When Cross and Worcester met a few months later, negotiations were speedily and successfully concluded, 3i becoming a 25 per cent shareholder. One of the crucial factors persuading Worcester to go with 3i was the survey which MORI had carried out for Cross among the Group's customers. He recalled the high percentage of respondents who were satisfied with their relations with 3i, and who stressed that 3i did not interfere in their activities but worked instead in a supportive way. Worcester has since observed many times that MORI has operated without any pressure from its equity partner and retains its independence. He has on several occasions recommended others to link up with 3i, and describes himself as a '3i booster', as well as a shareholder!

was in broad agreement and considered FFI to be an 'excellent' name, insisting that ICFC, with its close smaller company identification, should be jettisoned as soon as practicable. Momtchiloff was aware of the gravity of such a move, but insisted nevertheless that 'the halfway house (of keeping FFI and ICFC) is only an option if it is accepted as a temporary step until we are ready to do it properly without the patient dying of shock'.[23]

Others were considerably less sanguine about the threatened demise of ICFC, at the hands of FFI or any other name. Marlow, for example, was convinced that, while there was a general problem arising from the spread of the Group's activities, any difficulties with retaining the name ICFC would be 'considerably outweighed' by the extent to which the Corporation was known.[24] This view was supported by Shandwick, the Group's public-relations consultants, who averred that a unified branding under FFI was essential, but so was the retention of ICFC 'to maintain visibility in a highly competitive market'—a visibility which had been developed over many years of publicity.[25] The Chairman, kept informed of the debate, also inclined towards retaining ICFC at least in the interim, as a prominent division within FFI, primarily for internal reasons relating to the morale of the staff, given 'the current good spirit in ICFC and a feeling that they are doing a nationally important job as well as making some money'.[26] This inherent loyalty which was inspired by ICFC stood in stark contrast to feelings about FCI, which it was universally accepted should be quietly dropped, since it was still generally stigmatized as a 'lender of last resort'.[27] FCI was indeed allowed to lapse in the reorganization marking the final demise of ICFC's sister organization which had followed such a divergent path since 1945.

The general consensus, which had emerged through the process of consultation with the twenty-five strong senior management group, was that there was a need for unity under a single title, probably FFI, with a divisional structure as cohesively organized as possible and with the retention, for some unspecified transitionary period, of ICFC.[28] In January 1982 Peter Gummer of Shandwick began the search for a design company to carry out the change. Wally Olins of the Wolff Olins partnership, which had recently handled image changes for Renault and Bovis, soon emerged as a front runner, with a clear empathy for the changes needed, and his company was duly appointed to undertake a major study of the possible routes to a new identity.[29] Foulds chose this moment formally to take personal charge of the project.[30]

Wolff Olins undertook a survey of the Group throughout the summer of 1982, examining the ways in which it was perceived, and how this tied in with present and possible future functions. This confirmed many of the shortcomings which had led to the call for a new identity. Externally, many people, including potential customers, opinion leaders, and competitors, had a poor understanding of the totality of the Group, its ownership or size. Internally there was little Group feeling, with staff rarely viewing career paths as being within the Group. Wolff Olins detected a feeling of élitism within ICFC which tended to view other Group activities as peripheral, a feeling fostered in part by the geographical dispersal of ICFC offices. Overall the Group did not have any 'added value'.[31] By the time the survey was undertaken it was also apparent that the increasing competition which was to characterize the mid-1980s was under way, reinforcing the urgent need for distinctive marketing of the Group.[32] Key messages were identified in terms of the innovative way the Group made investments, its unique character, and its potentially global outlook. The new Group identity had somehow to convey the qualities of the Group, but Finance for Industry, Finance for Industry Group, and FFI were all judged to be inadequate, being variously non-descriptive, governmental, pejorative, or confusing.[33]

Foulds and Olins began to think about variations on the keyword 'investment', perhaps used as investment, investors, or investing in industry, the primary characteristic of which was the obvious abbreviation to iii—3i. From the outset they began to see 3i, and not the longer title of Investors in Industry, as the new brand name. Abstract names had plenty of precedents: Red Cross, Blue Circle, and Penguin, for example, and there were notable mnemonics which stood as legal entities and easily remembered brands, such as 3M and P&O.[34] 3i was short, unique, would represent no problems on the international stage, and the initial 'i' could be used in ingenious ways for promotions: imaginative, innovative, inventive, insight, and so on.[35] This rather radical departure had one major drawback: being an entirely new name it would necessitate a very heavy and costly promotion both internally and externally. Foulds was committed to a new look, however, and was determined to push for 3i, in spite of the caution urged by others. As Michael Wolff later recalled: 'Jon was the accelerator, others were the brake pedal.'[36] Foulds was to need considerable resolve during the autumn of 1982 as the proposals were unveiled to a wider critical audience.

The first major obstacle to overcome was the Board of FFI.[37] Wally Olins made a presentation of the new image in November 1982, which, partly due to its forceful nature and radical stylistic content, was greeted with a less-than-enthusiastic response in some quarters.[38] Among the non-executive directors, Sir Donald Barron, Chairman at that time of the Midland Bank, thought that there might be confusion between the various components of the Group, but that ICFC carried a strong image. If there was a need for change, focus on one of the existing names would suffice. The Foulds–Olins solution would not do, being 'gimmicky and not altogether suitable in style'.[39] John Eccles was also unsure, being unconvinced of the need to drop the word 'Finance'. Other non-executive directors were still wavering when Caldecote intervened to quell dissent, first by toning down the impact of Olins's presentation, stressing that ideas on the pictorial presentation of 3i were still only tentative suggestions, and secondly, by reaffirming support for the general principle of bold changes: 'I was myself at first put off by the gimmicky aspect of the 3i proposal, but after further thought I have become more and more convinced that this is the best alternative which could make a valuable impact both inside and outside the Group.'[40] Sir George Kenyon of Williams and Glyn's, the other bank representative on the Board, accepted 'Investors in Industry', but continued to be uncertain about the 'gimmicky . . . "three small i's" idea'.[41] In spite of these reservations, by the time the Board met again in January 1983 Foulds's campaign of persuasion had worn down the opposition and the decision was carried through.[42] Backing was also gained soon after from the chairmen of the shareholding banks, albeit somewhat grudgingly. Robin Leigh-Pemberton, then Chairman of the Committee of London Clearing Banks, reported that among his fellow bank chairmen, none were 'terribly impressed' by the new name, but that the new converts, Barron and Kenyon, had proved to be ample advocates and thus the shareholders would not resist the proposal.[43] The Bank of England felt it could give only 'tentative support', registering no attraction for the name or its acronym.[44]

It had been a considerable struggle to win enough converts, albeit some not very zealous ones, to the name 'Investors in Industry', and the more extreme '3i'. Internal dissent was still evident; Clarke, for example, went on the record to register his strong opposition to the dropping of FFI after the November Board meeting,[45] on the grounds of its possible damage to the Group's position in the international bond markets and, as would become evident later, the pro-ICFC lobby would prove to be tenacious in their defence of their old title. The first hurdle had been successfully negotiated, however, in securing majority Board support, including the blessing of the external directors and shareholders. Caldecote, himself initially worried that the changes were too revolutionary and might do damage to the Group, ascribed the victory to Foulds's undoubted enthusiasm, noting that the latter had 'implemented it all with great skill and considerable determination and courage'.[46] There now began the really difficult work of establishing a practical organizational structure, designing the new image, and implementing a programme of transition.

A Style for the 1980s

The new Group structure, which was finalized throughout the spring and summer of 1983, was to be a simplified organization based on divisional lines. This would dismantle some of the rather labyrinthine and complex agency arrangements which were the result of the way in which the Group had grown and had in the past had to meet certain criteria, such as the regulations of the Banking Act. It would also mean an end to the separate corporate identities, each with a discrete life and loyalty of its own, that Foulds was later to refer to as a series of 'separate baronies'.[47] The Group's UK assets, currently held by FFI (UK Finance) would be transferred to Investors in Industry, which would have five operating divisions: Head Office, Property, Shipping and Energy, Ventures, and ICFC. ICFC was, after all, to be kept for the time being, although its full title would be dropped and only the initials retained, echoing the example of IBM.[48] The advisory and fee-earning activities were to remain as separate limited companies. The reasons for this were varied: consultancy employed staff on separate terms and conditions, the advisory services needed a separate status to establish their independence from the investment arms of the Group, and portfolio management needed to adhere to the rules governing unit trust management, which it was hoped to enter. The overseas companies were separately incorporated in their countries of residence. The title of 'divisional director' was to be introduced for senior managers in order to align them more closely with their peers in rival firms which were rapidly becoming a problem in terms of competition for staff, but also to encourage a feeling that they represented the whole Group rather than individual fiefdoms.[49] Divisional Committees and Policy and Planning Committees were set up to monitor progress and make policy decisions.

Wolff Olins spent this period formalizing a new corporate style centred on the new identity. Investors in Industry was intended from the outset to be merely a descriptive phrase rather than a company title. The initials, or rather their numeric representation as 3i, was to form the immediate logo and eventual company name. Michael Wolff became more actively involved in the design process for the logo which was seen as crucial in conveying, if not a detailed message about the activity of the group, then the essence of its creativity and uniqueness. In the search for an image which would contrast with the 'double-headed eagles and intertwined letters' typical of other financial institutions a number of alternatives were explored, ranging from Japanese-style calligraphy to a highly decorated lettering, reminiscent of Kit Williams's popular *Masquerade*, complete with squirrels, nuts, and golden eggs. Eventually the watercolour artist, Philip Sutton with whom Wolff had worked on a previous project, was commissioned to paint a series of pictures, from which the logo was later developed.[50]

The result, the softly shaded watercolour logo with the representation of an eye replacing the dot over the 'i', was indeed, in style and concept, as radical a departure from the norms of company identity in the financial sector as could be envisioned at the time. Wolff, who conceived the eye pun while photocopying some of the original designs, wanted to go even further and drop the stalk of the 'i' altogether. This was seen as going too far at the time but remains, for Wolff at least, the final goal of the project.[51] The Sutton logo drew immediate criticism from a number of quarters on stylistic and functional grounds. Apart from the expected conservative reaction generally, the eye was seen by some to have 'nasty 1984-ish overtones'. On a practical level, the subtle colour shading was difficult and expensive to reproduce for publicity purposes, and lost virtually all its effect when shown in black and white.[52] Nevertheless Foulds

The 3i logo: from Chrysalis to Butterfly

Here are just a few of the many roughs that Philip Sutton produced en route to arriving at the 3i logo as it is today. They clearly illustrate (in chronological order) that it's far from simple to produce something 'simple'.
Logos are made not born!

To start with, classical images of the human face . . .

. . . the eye begins to dominate . . . . . . and the face disappears to be replaced with the figure 3

. . . and then it appears in the now familiar colours.

remained enthusiastic about the image it portrayed, which comprised original-ity together with a softness and humour which characterized the Group's more human approach to business, in contrast to the typical harder-edged symbolism which reflected attributes of the rest of the world of finance.[53]

The steering committee which was set up, comprising 3i, Shandwick, and Wolff Olins staff, to oversee the programme of conversion to 3i, worked

146

throughout the early summer of 1983 towards the official launch date. 'D-Day' was set for 1 July, when government officials, MPs, customers and contacts were to be informed, individually by letter, of the changes and their purpose. Subsequent press conferences and national advertising were to begin the process of building a general awareness of 3i, for which purpose a total budget of over £2.8 million had been allocated for the first year of operation. For internal purposes a roadshow was set up in June to explain the practical ramifications, and a video was produced as part of a new general communications plan.[54]

Initial reactions to the name-change were somewhat ambivalent. The press were slow in attuning themselves to the new style, and frequently failed to grasp the range of products and services being offered by the Group.[55] Internally the shorthand version of the title, 3i, was rapidly adopted in many parts of the Group, however, so much so that the official transition to using this as the lead name in public communications was brought forward, Investors in Industry being used only for explanatory purposes and as the legal name of the Group.[56] There was one remaining and fundamental problem however—the staunch loyalty which was still felt in many quarters to ICFC.

Foulds was mindful of this loyalty and the resistance which was to be expected to any suggestion of discontinuance. Although there were the expected problems inherent in retaining both names he was conciliatory: 'There is no doubt about the historical value in the ICFC name and we must not abandon it, at least until we have something of equal weight to put in its place'.[57] Nevertheless it was clear that the resistance to dropping ICFC was unlikely to abate of its own accord. This resistance, it was noted, was greater at higher levels in the ICFC hierarchy. Senior ICFC staff remained antipathetic to the 3i name, expressing the feeling that 'ICFC really means something', millions of pounds had been invested in it, and a change would risk 'a huge loss of momentum'.[58] ICFC staff at junior levels, in contrast, seemed to be enthusiastic about 3i and did not appear to share this overt sense of loyalty. In addition there was a growing resentment among other components of the Group about the special treatment meted out to ICFC, which was still seemingly being allowed to stand apart from the other divisions, perpetuating the élitism which many had felt in the past. Many among the non-ICFC divisions thought that an opportunity for complete change had been missed in the July launch, when ICFC should have been dropped entirely.[59]

By the end of 1983 this corporate schizophrenia had become a serious problem. A debilitating emotional climate had developed as many key ICFC staff began to think they had been presented with a *fait accompli*.[60] A second general attitude survey conducted in November showed that inter-divisional co-operation was still very poor, despite the efforts of the previous three years. Serious proposals were still being put forward to promote the autonomy of

ICFC, including the idea that the Corporation should become reformed as ICFC Ltd. and operate as an independent subsidiary, acting as an agent for 3i. It was also noted that public opportunities to stress the ICFC/3i relationship were being missed, as in the case of an ICFC promotional display at that time in Scotland.[61] In reaction Wolff Olins and Shandwick, mindful of this divisiveness, both began pushing for an early date for the full transition to 3i.[62] ICFC was to survive this onslaught, however, and in December, following a meeting of senior management at Leeds Castle, Foulds restated the dual identity policy, though he stressed that ICFC should always be promoted as 'Part of 3i' or in conjunction with the 3i symbol. The reprieve for ICFC in 1984 could prove only temporary, however.[63]

Throughout 1984, in the wake of the second attitude survey, there were repeated calls for a general continuation of the need to foster '3i-ness' as a whole, to avoid continued external confusion.[64] The growing competition in the jobs market was also creating added pressure to ensure Group loyalty, through remuneration packages, as discussed in the following chapter, but also through encouraging a feeling of identity within the Group.[65] In September a policy paper recommending the scrapping of ICFC was circulated in preparation for another meeting of senior management at Leeds Castle in November. This time the pro-3i lobby carried the day, and the decision was finally made to phase out the ICFC name.[66] It was stressed to staff that the decision did not mean any lessening of the Group's commitment to the small- and medium-sized firm sector and that the rapidity of the decision merely reflected the unexpectedly rapid popularity of the 3i name. ICFC as a separate entity was formally scheduled to be dropped in March 1985, a few months before its 40th anniversary, when ICFC area offices would henceforth be known collectively as 3i Regions and area managers would become local directors.[67] At the same time all divisional titles were to be dropped and separate activities within the Group simply identified with the prefix 3i.

The demise of ICFC as an independent entity was clearly an unwelcome development for many of its staff. The lack of cohesion and purpose which had been identified in the FFI Group had never applied very strongly to ICFC. Some observers mistook the loyalty and sense of exclusivity at ICFC for élitism, but it was perhaps more accurately portrayed as a reflection of the sense of mission, imparted from the early days onwards, which enabled ICFC staff to combine commercial activity with the wider goal of investing in a sector considered to be of national economic importance. It was also symptomatic of the longevity of employment of some of the staff, particularly the 'ICFC men' at the top, and the way in which many had been aware of, and indeed taken part in, the process of building up the Company from its precarious beginnings. Staff at the top of ICFC had, in the end, to accept change and concede that the time had come for the Group identity, reflecting a moment when a broader

3i Chairmen (*from left to right*) Lord Sherfield 1964–74, Sir John Cuckney 1987–93, Lord Caldecote 1979–87. Portraits of Lord Piercy 1945–64 (*right*) and Lord Seebohm 1974–79 (*left*).

focus of activity, at home and overseas, was imperative. Even so, the change was to be something of a wrench and, long after the renaming, staff still commonly referred to 'the Corporation' in conversations about work.[68]

A Marketing-led Organization

Coincidental with the demise of ICFC was the shift of emphasis towards marketing 3i effectively. Previously the marketing of the components of the Group had been undertaken in a rather *ad hoc* fashion. Research which had been carried out into the size and characteristics of the market or into customer attitudes had been done by different people for different purposes.[69] National advertising, in the press and on television, had been effective in promoting a general awareness of ICFC. The 'nose' advert in 1972, for example, had promoted a significant upsurge in business, but overall the results had not been spectacular.[70] The principal method of marketing the Corporation had traditionally been through the branch network, however, and with the absorption of ICFC within the Group the time now seemed apposite to establish a centralized and specialist marketing department. Again there was 'tremendous resistance' to the appropriation of this function, notably from the regional offices; nevertheless, Foulds was again determined to press ahead.[71]

149

Contrasting styles: 3i'snew logo gracing Charlotte Square, Edinburgh

Foulds became convinced that 3i should proceed through the 1980s as a 'marketing-led' rather than 'sales-led' organization.[72] In order to achieve this Chris Woodward was recruited from Uniroyal to lead the newly established marketing department. What Woodward found on his arrival at 3i, in 1986, was an organization which was good at developing and running products, with a strong 'deal' orientation, but which was in general very reactive. Typically ICFC would convey the message to lawyers, accountants and other intermediaries, 'this is who we are, this is what we do . . . when you've got something for us, bring it to us'.[73] There was little analysis of what the competition was up to, and this was a crucial period in terms of the encroachment of other institutions on 3i's potential business. Other venture capital firms were already establishing a lead in the targeting of specific market sectors, such as management buy-ins.

One of the fundamental reasons behind the move to 3i had been the need to present a cohesive and memorable image to its market. The concentration on the radical nature of the name and logo had obscured more fundamental issues, however, in what Woodward was later to describe as a 'triumph of style over strategy'.[74] Woodward needed to convince 3i management of the importance of marketing—both in terms of publicizing the Group, and also in terms of tracking competition, identifying key segments, listening to market needs (current and anticipated), redesigning products to fit these needs, and setting performance targets and monitoring procedures. In order to do this the marketing department would need to be afforded prominent status within the Group, but more than this, the culture of the organization would need to change to embrace the marketing imperative.

One of the key changes, led by the new department, was the implementation of direct-marketing campaigns. Direct-response advertising was used, for example, in the very successful 'Break-out' campaign. The popularity of the MBO and latterly the MBI had begun as a market-driven phenomenon, created by factors including corporate restructuring and taxation changes in the early 1980s. The 'Break-out' campaign actively sought to encourage the idea of change and entrepreneurial initiative. Targeting the middle-aged executive whose options seemed to be limited within his or her existing company, this campaign fostered the idea of 'breaking out' through a management start-up, buy-out or buy-in. The MBI Programme was set up in 1987, seeking further to promote what was becoming a fast-growing phenomenon from the mid-1980s onwards. 3i received over 1,000 applications for this programme, including very senior executives from major companies in the UK, and these were eventually whittled down to 200. Within four years over 60 per cent of this initial group were running their own company. A mobile presentation entitled 'The Enterprise Roadshow' was also set up in June 1987, to promote 3i at strategic sites in new factory and warehousing developments. In addition the Group began to reinforce and popularize ideas of entrepreneurialism through the widely distributed QED, the Quarterly Enterprise Digest, which contained a blend of articles by leading commentators and political figures including Lord Young, Norman Lamont, Tom Peters, and Peter Drucker.

The image presented by 3i was now seen to be crucial in generating a universally recognized brand name, essential in raising market awareness. In the finance sector this was seen to be essential given the difficulty in branding individual products. It was decided that 3i could best achieve higher awareness through a continued emphasis on artistic creativity, reinforcing the impression that the Company was itself creative and imaginative in its financial products. As the 3i mission statement was to emphasize, 'A clear understanding of 3i's leadership role will be an integral part of the advertising, not simply in arithmetical market share terms, but as an innovative and creative company in the vanguard of important economic and social trends.'[75]

Throughout the 1980s 3i had continued its long-standing advertising relationship with DDB Needham, and in the mid-decade it had featured some colourful, award-winning advertisements by Jeff Fisher.[76] These advertisements were more figurative than illustrative, however, and it was increasingly felt that, while awareness of 3i continued to rise, understanding of the Group's activity remained poor. In 1988, coincidentally with the formal adoption of 3i as the Group name, the Group appointed Howell Henry Chaldecott Lury (HHCL) to design an advertising campaign featuring more bullish, challenging copy, promoting the idea of 3i as a catalyst. The 3i Sutton watercolour was replaced at this point with the more striking 'Matisse' logo, which was seen to reflect confidence and leadership. In 1990, in another change of agency, J. Walter Thompson were commissioned to produce a series of advertisements designed to state precisely what 3i had to offer in terms of an understanding of the Group's products and an emphasis on the long-term, partnership elements in its relationship with investees. One of these was subsequently featured by the Newspaper Publishers Association in a nationwide press campaign as an exemplary newspaper advertisement. Evidence indicated that 3i's general advertising, public relations, mail shots, and press coverage during the latter half of the 1980s were increasingly successful in promoting a more precise understanding of what it had to offer. From 1985 onwards the Group commissioned an independent research organization to conduct a 'spontaneous awareness' survey, which showed a rise from 8 per cent in 1985 to around 60 per cent in the early 1990s, surpassing that of the clearing banks in its sector.[77]

Part of this increasing awareness reflects the fact that, from 1987 onwards, 3i had also moved into art sponsorship. The first major initiative in this field was an 'Images of London' exhibition at the Barbican in 1987, aimed at a City audience and featuring a wide collection of artists. In 1990 3i sponsored the British Art Show, marking a move into contemporary art sponsorship and reflecting more accurately the Company's design philosophy. Sir John

We put our money on both.

Once upon a time there were two men of business.

Mr. Tortoise had a small firm which was very sure and very steady. Not a fast mover, you would have said of him, but he knew exactly where he and his company were going.

Mr. Hare had a small company, too. And fast and furious was its pace.

For him it seemed, making a million overnight was slow progress.

There was, however, one thing that Mr. Tortoise and Mr. Hare had in common.

They both needed capital.

"I have lots of exciting ideas," cried Mr. Hare. "You can't lose if your money's with me."

Mr. Tortoise looked thoughtful, as he always did at times like this. "I've spent years building up my business," he said. "But I need money for expansion."

"Gentlemen," we said, "since you've both shown a good use for the money you need, we see no reason why we can't help the pair of you."

Mr. Hare and Mr. Tortoise went away very happy indeed.

We hadn't demanded seats on their boards. Or insisted on a majority shareholding.

They were free to go their own way. To run their businesses at their own speed.

"Of course," we pointed out, "we'll be around to offer advice when you need it.

But isn't that what friends are for?"

Industrial and Commercial Finance Corporation Limited.

Please contact your local office, listed under Finance Companies in Yellow Pages.

Head Office: Piercy House, 7 Copthall Avenue, London EC2R 5DD. **ICFC**

Early 1970s advertisement for ICFC

DDB Needham

The boss's wife has everything. Except the boss.

Clocking on and off is strictly for the employees.

When you're the boss of a small business there are never enough hours in the day. Even when you include half the night.

Doing the work of the Finance, Marketing, Export, Personnel, Production and Managing Directors all on your own is,

of course, bound to keep you pretty busy.

But there are limits to what one man can do and what one woman can put up with.

We know because we've helped thousands of bosses over the last 30 years.

To run more profitable, more efficient and less time-consuming businesses.

Our help consists of friendly advice and somewhere between £5,000 and £1 million on a long-term basis.

If that sounds like the kind of help you could use, give us a ring.

Industrial and Commercial Finance Corporation Limited. **ICFC**

Money isn't all we have to offer.

INDUSTRIAL AND COMMERCIAL FINANCE CORPORATION LIMITED. ABERDEEN, BIRMINGHAM, BRIGHTON, BRISTOL, CAMBRIDGE, CARDIFF, EDINBURGH, GLASGOW, LEEDS, LEICESTER, LIVERPOOL, LONDON, MANCHESTER, NEWCASTLE, NOTTINGHAM, READING, SHEFFIELD, SOUTHAMPTON. (HEAD OFFICE 01 928 8040.)

1970s advertisement for ICFC

DDB Needham

1980s advertisement for 3i

DDB Needham

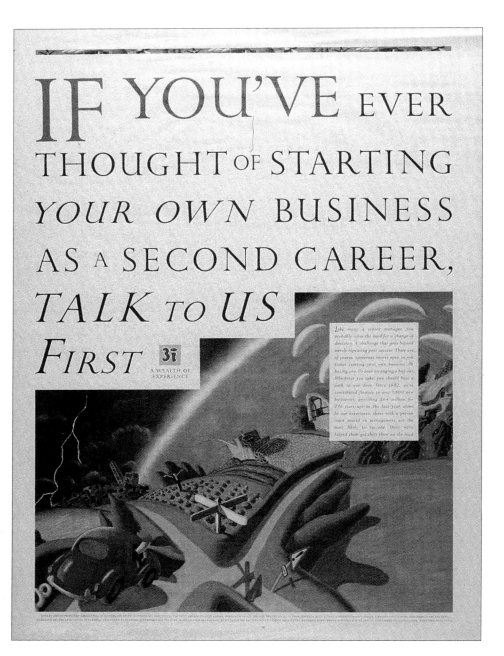

Late 1980s advertisement for 3i

J. Walter Thompson

If they ever decide to make something of themselves, we're the first people they should call on.

Who knows?
Ambition may well bring Steptoe & Son to our door one day.
Looking for capital for expansion, perhaps. Or money to back a new idea.
Whatever it is, you may be sure our door will be open.
As it has been to thousands of smaller businessmen over the past 25 years.
(Some have needed as little as £5,000. Others have had a good use for half-a-million.)

Hard cash isn't the only thing we've contributed, either.
Over the years, we've met hundreds of the problems businessmen like you are faced with.
We may not have had all the answers, but we've been able to come up with good advice.
Of course, that's not to say the business doesn't stay guided by you.
We won't want a controlling slice of your shares.
Nor will we expect you to go public if you don't want to.

Even if your business is rubbish, it's your business.
And we want it to stay that way.

Industrial and Commercial Finance Corporation Limited.
Please contact your local office, listed under Finance Companies in Yellow Pages.
Head Office: Piercy House, 7 Copthall Avenue, London EC2R 7DD. **ICFC**

Early 1970s advertisement for ICFC
DDB Needham

Front page of Financial Times Supplement, June 1991

J. Walter Thompson

Late 1980s advertisement for 3i

J. Walter Thompson

Cuckney elaborated the linkages: 'Innovation, be it in art or industry, is a theme close to 3i. Like industry, art must take paths that lead in new directions.'[78] This philosophy was also evident in 3i's decision in 1987 to commission or acquire works of contemporary art for the Group's own use. Works by British artists including Eduardo Paolozzi, Bridget Riley, John Hoyland, John Hubbard, Gwyther Irwin, and Gillian Ayres were successively used to give a striking impact to 3i Reports and promotional materials. 3i had also begun to produce its annual calendar in the mid-1980s featuring cartoons, most of which take an irreverent view of the City and industry, which became very popular indeed.

In addition to these measures aimed at widely promoting the image and awareness of 3i, the Group also began to pursue a strategy designed to secure a prominent position as a spokesman for the development capital industry. Commissioned surveys were undertaken on major trends in the economy, including the Bannock reports on management buy-outs, and enterprise in the 1980s and 1990s, and, in conjunction with the Centre for Management Buy-Out Research at Nottingham University, studies into MBOs in Europe. Initiatives also included the Enterprise Barometer, a regular confidence-tracking survey among 3i customers. This survey has subsequently established itself as a key indicator, used by a number of organizations involved in economic forecasting, including the Treasury. A similar European Enterprise Index was set up in conjunction with Cranfield School of Management. 3i staff continued to be called upon to provide evidence and testimony before various government select committees.

The 1980s and early 1990s had seen the remaking of what had been a disparate group of companies into the single entity, 3i. The project had been very much led by Jon Foulds, but with strong support from his chairman, Lord Caldecote. Change had begun with the recognition that the Group of companies under FFI was disunited and that staff lacked a Group-wide feeling of direction and purpose. What began as an exercise in restructuring the Group and its identity to meet these shortcomings built up a considerable momentum, boosted by increased competition in the economy and by growing ambitions for the scale and scope of investment activities. The dual strategy of reorganizing the Group and creating an entirely new identity meant a shift in the centre of gravity away from the old ICFC-dominated structure, towards a new locus of power. It was a difficult process. The symbolic debate over the new name obscured deeper misgivings in many quarters. The new name became such a key issue, however, that it almost became an end in itself, resulting in a neglect of more tangible benefits to the new unity—a distinctive marketing strategy and a functional reorganization to create a cohesive structure. The latter 1980s were years when this shortcoming was recognized and addressed, and in an increasingly high-profile sector of the economy 3i was recognized as the prominent player.

NOTES

1. Viscount Caldecote, interviewed by R. Coopey, 18 Mar. 1992.
2. *Independent on Sunday*, 25 Oct. 1992.
3. Paul Hildesley, interviewed by R. Coopey, 4 Mar. 1992.
4. Prof. John Hunt, interviewed by R. Coopey, 16 Aug. 1993.
5. *3i News* (Autumn 1992), 10–11.
6. Sir David Walker, interviewed by R. Coopey, 11 Nov. 1992.
7. 'Group Identity. First Progress Report from the Steering Committee', 16 Mar. 1983.
8. H. J. Foulds, untitled memo, 5 June 1981, 3i J. Foulds Board Papers (hereafter JFBP); L. N. G. Olsen to Foulds, memo, 10 June 1981, 3i JFBP.
9. S. Brown and J. W. Hunt, *3i Case Study* (London Business School, 1984), 10.
10. J. W. Hunt to Foulds, 22 Oct. 1981, 3i JFBP.
11. Ibid. 11–14.
12. Hunt to Foulds, 7 Oct. 1981; Hunt, 'Top Management Briefing: FFI Ltd.', Oct. 1981, 3i JFBP.
13. L. N. G. Olsen to Foulds, memo, 'Divisional Objectives', 29 Oct. 1980; H. J. Foulds, 'The Corporate Identity of Finance for Industry', 27 Oct. 1981, 3i JFBP.
14. LBS Case Study 30; John Hunt, interviewed by Richard Coopey, 16 Aug. 1993.
15. Ibid.
16. LBS Case Study II, 19.
17. Ibid.
18. Chairman's address, FFI Pensioners Association, Annual General Meeting minutes, 17 May 1983.
19. Foulds to Caldecote, 'The Corporate Identity of Finance for Industry', 27 Oct. 1981, 3i JFBP; Jon Foulds, interviewed by R. Coopey, 1 Dec. 1992.
20. 'ICFC Image Survey', MORI, 1976, p. iv.
21. Ibid.
22. D. R. Clarke to Foulds, 'Group Structure', 10 Nov. 1981, 3i JFBP; Clarke to Foulds, 'Name Change', 29 Nov. 1982, 3i JFBP.
23. I. N. Momtchiloff, 'Corporate Identity', 13 Nov. 1981.
24. D. E. Marlow, 'Group Structure', 16 Nov. 1981, 3i JFBP. David Marlow, interviewed by R. Coopey, 6 Jan. 1993.
25. T. R. Sermon to Foulds, 'The Corporate Identity of Finance for Industry', 18 Nov. 1981, 3i JFBP.
26. Caldecote to Foulds, 'The Corporate Identity of FFI', 4 Jan. 1982, 3i JFBP.
27. Olsen, 'Corporate Identity and Structure', 10 Oct. 1981, 3i JFBP; Momtchiloff, 'Corporate Identity', 13 Nov. 1981, 3i JFBP; Olsen, 'FCI/Special Deals Unit', 11 Dec. 1981, 3i JFBP; Foulds, interview.
28. Olsen to Foulds, 'Corporate Identity and Organisation', 6 Jan. 1982, JFBP.
29. P. Gummer to Foulds, 13 Jan. 1982, 3i JFBP.
30. Foulds, memo to General Management, 'FFI Corporate Identity Programme', 8 Apr. 1982, 3i JFBP.
31. 'Finance for Industry: A New Identity', Wolff Olins, Sept. 1982, 3.
32. 'Finance for Industry', 5.
33. FFI had one rather unfortunate previous usage, among servicemen in the war, where it was used to denote 'Free from Infection'.
34. Wolff Olins, 'Finance for Industry: A New Identity', 20.
35. Ibid.; Michael Wolff, interviewed by R. Coopey, 12 July 1993; Ivan Momtchiloff, interviewed by R. Coopey, 20 Jan. 1993.

[36] Michael Wolff, interview.

[37] The non-executive directors of the Board at this time were D. V. Atterton, Sir Donald Barron of the Midland, J. D. Eccles, Sir George Keynon of Williams and Glyns, W. J. Mackenzie, P. E. Moody, and G. S. Stone. The rest of the Board comprised Caldecote (Chairman), Tindale (Deputy Chairman), Foulds, Clarke, Marlow, Momtchiloff, and Olsen. (This is FFI (UK Finance)).

[38] Foulds, interview.

[39] D. Barron to Caldecote, 26 Nov. 1982, 3i JFBP.

[40] Caldecote to the FFI Board, 'Corporate Identity', 30 Nov. 1982, 3i JFBP.

[41] Sir George Kenyon to Foulds, 14 Dec. 1982, 3i JFBP.

[42] Foulds to Caldecote, 'Corporate Identity', 9 Dec. 1982; P. E. Moody to Foulds, 20 Dec. 1982; G. Kenyon to Foulds, 14 Dec. 1982; Foulds to FFI General Managers, 'Group Identity and Structure', 24 Dec. 1982, 3i JFBP.

[43] R. Leigh-Pemberton to Caldecote, 8 Feb. 1983, 3i JFBP.

[44] Foulds to Caldecote, 'The Group Name', 25 Jan. 1983, 3i JFBP. C. McMahon to Caldecote, 7 Feb. 1983, 3i JFBP.

[45] Clarke to Foulds, 'Name Change'.

[46] Caldecote, interview.

[47] Foulds, interview.

[48] Wolff Olins, 'A New Identity', 24.

[49] Foulds to General Management, 'FFI Identity', 1 Dec. 1982; FFI, memo from the Group General Manager, 'Group Structure', 30 Mar. 1983, 3i BM(83)3. The title 'divisional director' did not mean director in the Companies Act sense.

[50] Foulds, interview; Wolff, interview; 'An Eyecatching Answer to an Identity Crisis', *Financial Times*, 5 Dec. 1983; Olsen to Foulds, 27 July 1983, 3i JFBP.

[51] Wolff, interview.

[52] *The Financial Times*, 5 Dec. 1983; 'Corporate Identity', 25 Nov. 1983, 3i JFBP.

[53] Foulds, interview.

[54] Group Identity Steering Committee, Progress Reports; Identity Steering Group, Minutes. 'Working as a Group', memo (83) 11, 5 Feb. 1983; J. D. Driver to Olsen, 'Group Promotion Budget 1983/4', 25 Feb. 1983. For more senior staff a conference at Gleneagles was set up, where it was suggested that a song entitled 'Three Little Eyes' should be sung to the tune of 'Three Little Words', accompanied by the Pasadena Roof Orchestra:
'3 little eyes.
What's all this talk about 3 little eyes?
I know that
ever since we've had this intrusion
our minds are filled with absolute confusion.
3 little eyes.
We must all practice saying
these are our "3 wee eyes".'

[55] L. N. G. Olsen, '3i Project', 9 Sept. 1983, OM (83) 71, 3i.

[56] P. Gummer to Foulds, 'Investors in Industry—Name Change' 14 Sept. 1983; Foulds, 'The Relationship Between 3i and ICFC', 20 Oct. 1983; 3i JFBP.

[57] Foulds, 'The Relationship Between 3i and ICFC'.

[58] M. Wolff and W. Olins to Foulds, 7 Nov. 1983, 3i JFBP.

[59] Wolff and Olins 7 Nov. 1983; P. Stone, 'Corporate Identity', 25 Nov. 1983, 3i JFBP.

[60] P. C. Brown to Olsen and Marlow, 'The 3i and ICFC Names Working Together', 6 Feb. 1984.

[61] R. M. Drummond to Marlow, 'ICFC and 3i—the Names', 1 Dec. 1983; LBS Case Study, 32–3.

[62] Wolff and Olins, 7 Nov. 1983; Gummer to Foulds, 14 Sept. 1983.

[63] Foulds, 'Policy Statement on the Promotion of the Company's Business Through the 3i and ICFC Names', 7 Dec. 1983.

[64] S. Palmer, 'Corporate Identity Programme', 12 Mar. 1984; '3i Corporate Identity Programme', undated memo, 3i JFBP.

[65] In 1983 there had been an exodus of 20 per cent of staff from the financial stream at the level of controller or above.

[66] 'An Identity Policy', 25 Sept. 1984; Foulds, 'Corporate Identity', 6 Nov. 1984; Lord Caldecote to 3i Board, 8 Nov. 1984.

[67] Marlow, '3i Trading Names', 22 Nov. 1984; Foulds, 'Corporate Identity and Organisation', 11 Feb. 1985; 3i JFBP.

[68] Derek Sach, interviewed by Richard Coopey, 22 June 1993.

[69] A. L. Sell, 'ICFC's Selling Methods', Sept. 1968; I. N. Momtchiloff, 'Marketing Discussion Paper', 15 July 1974; Clarke Papers, 3i.

[70] Minutes, Bi-Monthly Management Meeting, 30 Jan. 1973, 31 July 1973.

[71] K. Stevenson and J. Hunt, 'Investors in Industry', LBS Case Study Pt. C, 1989, 42.

[72] Foulds, interview.

[73] C. Woodward, marketing presentation at LBS, 1985.

[74] Chris Woodward, interviewed by Richard Coopey, 5 Aug. 1993.

[75] '3i Advertising Mission Statement', Nov. 1989.

[76] In 1988 3i's 'Mountain' ad won the silver award for the best business advertisement in the Campaign Press Advertising Awards. The 'Sunbeam' and 'Crossroads' awards won awards for the best use of typography.

[77] The survey, conducted annually among a sample of 250 chief executives or finance directors of companies with a turnover of £2 million or above asked, in a direct way, which institutions they would consider in seeking finance. 3i results were: 1985: 8%; 1986: 8%; 1987: 17%; 1988: 28%; 1989: 49%; 1990: 61%; 1991: 41%; 1992: 58%. The 1992 survey figures for 3i's competitors included County NatWest 11%, Candover 5%, Kleinwort 5%, Midland Montagu 4%, Barclays Development Capital 3%, Citicorp 3%, Electra 3%, CINVEN 1%, Lloyds Development Capital 1%, and Charterhouse 1%. The High Street Banks' scores in 1992 were: Barclays 54%, NatWest 52%, Lloyds 45% and Midland 41%.

[78] 'The British Art Show 1990', South Bank Centre, London, 10. 3i has also sponsored events at the Royal Academy of Music and over the years has taken up associate sponsorships at The Royal Academy of Art, Regent's Park Open Air Theatre, the Royal Opera House, and the Young Vic.

Chapter 7

Competition, Expansion, and the Enterprise Culture

The 1980s Economy

THE 1980S WAS A DECADE of great change, for both the Group, which was to be renamed under the unifying title of 3i, and its environment. The post-war consensus on economic policy, however tenuous, finally broke down as successive Conservative governments embarked on a growing number of reforms aimed at enhancing market forces and regenerating an 'enterprise culture'. Many of these reforms directly affected the activities of 3i, creating new investment opportunities and generating an entirely new wave of competition. In this new and often turbulent atmosphere, 3i was to become increasingly influential, gaining prominence as a market leader and proving to be a central source of personnel. The Group was also to come under great pressure to adapt. The swings between recession and recovery in the British economy directly affected both 3i and its customers, creating cycles of expansion and retrenchment. In addition to generating these market opportunities and pressures, the decade also saw the fundamental ownership and operating rubric of 3i called into question, as the shareholding banks debated the idea of selling their interest by floating the Company. The ramifications of a publicly quoted 3i—ironically, a return to the original Macmillan recommendations—were to spark a continuing debate over the essential nature of 3i's business.

Viewed as a whole, the 1980s can be seen to encompass a recessionary beginning, selective sectoral and regionally-based recovery and boom faltering into a second, more persistent and widespread recession towards the closing years of the decade. The post-war consensus on the reduction of unemployment as the primary aim of policy was replaced after 1979 by a concentration on the reduction of inflation. The Conservative governments led by Margaret Thatcher were persuaded that the potentially adverse social consequences of rising unemployment had to be borne in an attempt to correct what they interpreted as a long-run, structural build-up of inefficiencies in the British economy. Throughout the decade, a spectrum of methods ranging from monetary to interest rate control was used in turn to achieve this aim, while policies aimed at enhancing entrepreneurialism and market forces included a restructuring of the tax system and a series of privatizations of the nationalized industries designed to broaden the base of ownership and implement a system of 'popular capitalism'. The labour market was confronted with the continual relative reduction of state unemployment support and new legal limits on the power of trade unions.

The results of these policies were profound. Initially rates of business failure and unemployment reached levels not experienced since the depths of the 1930s depression. Whole sectors of the economy, particularly manufacturing industry, experienced severe shocks reflected in the eclipse of some regional economies, notably those based in the older, traditionally industrial areas of the North-East, North-West, Wales and, in contrast to the 1930s, parts of the Midlands. The long-term effect of this 'shake-out' of British industry remains a keenly contested issue. GDP did not recover to 1979 levels until the mid-1980s, while manufacturing output failed to recover fully, reflecting a shift in the balance of economic activity towards the service sector. Debate continues about the most appropriate macro-economic indicators to reveal the health of the economy during the 1980s. A more vigorous debate, particularly pertinent to 3i, surrounds the less-tangible, avowed goal of government policy—the reconstruction of an enterprise culture in Britain.

3i's own commissioned study, *Britain in the 1980s: Enterprise Reborn?*, pointed to the obverse of a high business-failure rate—a high rate of new-business formation—especially in the more dynamic small- and medium-sized enterprise sector. This was allied to a reduction in size, and increased efficiency of existing businesses. In spite of obvious difficulties in the first half of the 1980s the report concluded that there had indeed been a tentative change in cultural attitudes and that 'enterprise has been reborn and will not easily be extinguished again'.[1] 3i, it was argued, seemed uniquely placed to aid and benefit from changes in economic activity and, indeed, was judged by many observers to be at the centre of a newly emerging financial sector, generally termed venture capital, which was held to parallel and enable the new spirit of enterprise. However, 3i's experience in the 1980s and its relationship to the nascent venture capital movement involve, in reality, a range of contrasts and similarities, points of contact and divergence.

Despite the 'welcome resurgence of entrepreneurial activity in the UK' the early 1980s saw an increasing number of failures among the 3i portfolio

'Hi there, vendee, this is vendor'.

companies: from 47 in 1979–80 to 153 in 1981–2, with provisions against losses rising in the latter year to over £86 million.[2] Returns from investments were more than sufficient to cover these reverses, although a falling number of applications did begin to give cause for concern by 1983. The following year saw a turnaround, with record profit levels in current price terms. The number of investments in 3i's portfolio continued to grow into the mid-1980s and by 1986 the company held equity in over 2,400 companies, around 2,300 of which were unquoted.[3] The peak in stock-market activity, which ran into late 1987, boosted 3i's realizations as an increasing number of companies began to seek quotations in order to take advantage of buoyant equity markets. 3i was able to make 'heavy but orderly sales' of existing equity holdings, and when the sale of British Caledonian (an investment held for over twenty years and at one time written off by 3i) coincided with this increase in selling the result was an unusually high volume of capital flowing in, £227 million in total. When the crash came in October 1987 the value of 3i's remaining portfolio began a roller-coaster ride as it fell from an estimated £1.2 billion to a low of around £800 million, rising on recovery to £985 million.[4] The crash had a relatively marginal effect on 3i's activities, however, and investment levels were rapidly re-established. Sir John Cuckney, Chairman of 3i at the time, was ambivalent about the cause and effect of the crash 'which owner-managers we back tend to see as a City phenomenon, unconnected with the real world'.[5] 3i investment in the two years following the crash continued the upward trend of the 1980s, totalling over £1.1 billion, a sum which, at current prices, represented around a quarter of all ICFC investment since 1945. In 1990 this trend continued with another record level of investment.[6]

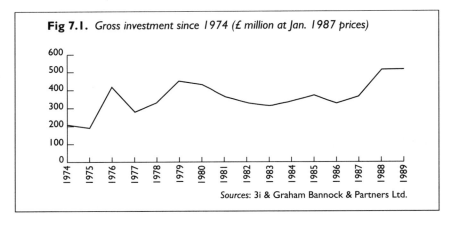

Fig 7.1. *Gross investment since 1974 (£ million at Jan. 1987 prices)*

Sources: 3i & Graham Bannock & Partners Ltd.

The Rise of Venture Capital in the UK

This escalation in activity by 3i during the 1980s was in parallel with the rise of what many came to view as a new investment industry in Britain—venture capital. The Group's relationship with this industry is complex and multi-faceted.[7] Competition, particularly from the banks, in 3i's sphere of activity had been steadily increasing since the 1970s following the changes in Competition and Credit Control in 1971. By the early 1980s, however, this rivalry had taken on new forms and a large number of new institutions began to emerge. Lord Caldecote, 3i's Chairman in 1983, reported that, there had never been a greater variety of finance available or more sources competing to provide it.

The nature and origins of the venture capital industry are difficult to delineate with any precision. As early as 1971 the Bolton Committee Report, for example, referred to the 'emergence of a number of venture capital companies specializing in small firms'.[8] Many accounts see venture capital as an import from the USA, where from the 1950s onwards specialist investors in selected high-growth industries, most notably computers and electronics, had achieved spectacular returns when companies such as Apple and Digital Equipment Corporation (DEC) went public.[9] There are a number of definitions of venture capital, but most encompass some element of permanent or long-term capital provision, usually in the form of equity, for unquoted or smaller quoted companies, usually newly formed and often in what are generally referred to as 'high-technology' or high-growth fields. It can be differentiated from other forms of investment in terms of reward. The greater risk inherent in equity finance is offset by the possibility of an eventual capital gain, rather than interest income or dividend yield. Venture capitalists, by virtue of the inherently higher risks involved in equity participation, are themselves seen to be a new entrepreneurial class of investor. Another feature often quoted to differentiate the venture capitalist organizations from other types of investor is the claim that these new institutions add value to investments by a more hands-on approach, enhancing managerial, product, and market efficiencies.

The new institutions deemed to conform to the above rather general parameters emerged in Britain from a number of different sources, and in fact operated in a variety of ways. An initial distinction between the various institutions collectively defined as venture capitalists lies in their ownership and source of funds to invest. A principal divide emerges here between the 'captives'—subsidiaries of other institutions such as banks and pension or insurance funds—and 'independents'; although other, more exact classifications abound. The industry journal *Venture Economics*, for example, classifies institutions as captive, independent, affiliated, or public-sector, whereas the British Venture Capital Association (BVCA), the industry's emergent representative body founded in 1983, utilizes a more exacting typology.[10] Notable among this variety of institutions expanded or formed in the late 1970s and early 1980s are the clearing bank subsidiaries, including County NatWest Ventures, Barclays Development Capital, Lloyds Development Capital, and Midland Montagu Ventures; Prudential Venture Managers, Legal and General Ventures, and CIN Ventures from the insurance and pension-fund sector; merchant bank subsidiaries such as Schroder Ventures and Morgan Grenfell Development Capital; stockbroker-backed Phildrew Ventures; and a number of independent funds including Electra, Candover, Apax, and ECI. At one end of the spectrum the 'captives' such as the clearing bank subsidiaries, had access to an internal source of funds, whereas the 'independents' needed to attract funds from a diverse range of external sources, predominantly pension funds, insurance companies, fund management groups, foreign institutions, private individuals,

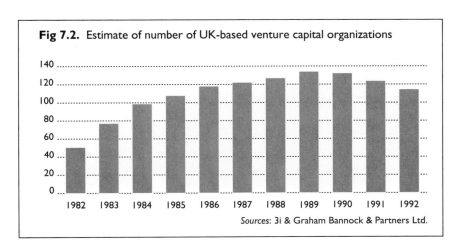

Fig 7.2. Estimate of number of UK-based venture capital organizations

Sources: 3i & Graham Bannock & Partners Ltd.

and trusts. 3i remained difficult tò classify under any of the above ownership terms. It was ostensibly a clearing bank related institution, yet it operated predominantly as an independent in fund-raising terms, although not raising capital from the aforementioned sources and not constrained to demonstrate performance in the same terms as the independents.[11]

The number of venture capital institutions operating in the 1980s, given definitional imprecisions and, as we shall see below, the actual type of investments made, is difficult to estimate. One fairly precise guide can be taken from the membership figures of the BVCA, the association established in 1983 to represent, collect, and disseminate information and organize training programmes for its members. The sector numbered only an estimated 30 institutions in 1980, yet by 1990 the BVCA could boast of a membership in excess of 120. The level of funds raised and invested by these institutions presents a more graphic picture of rapid growth. The amount invested by venture capital organizations excluding 3i in 1981 was around £200 million. By 1989 this had reached an annual peak of over £1.6 billion invested in over 1,500 companies, 86 per cent of which were in the UK. Independent venture capital institutions (excluding 3i and clearing bank subsidiaries) showed spectacular growth in the level of funds attracted for investment, raising £1.7 billion in 1989 alone.[12] This growth is even more marked when international comparisons are drawn. Direct comparisons are difficult to make given variations in classification but Britain's venture capital industry was, by the end of the 1980s, by far the largest in Europe.[13]

There are a number of contributory factors which explain the growth of

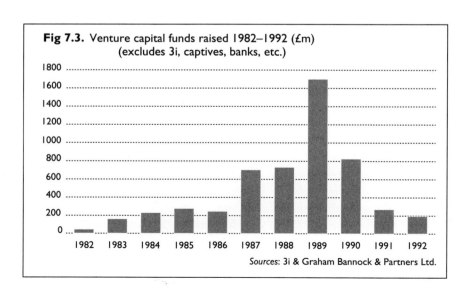

Fig 7.3. Venture capital funds raised 1982–1992 (£m)
(excludes 3i, captives, banks, etc.)

Sources: 3i & Graham Bannock & Partners Ltd.

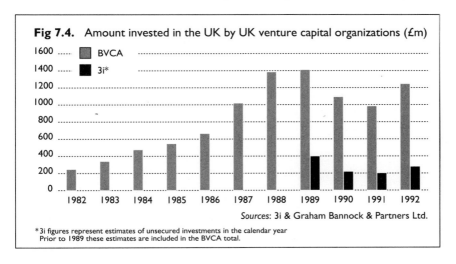

Fig 7.4. Amount invested in the UK by UK venture capital organizations (£m)

Sources: 3i & Graham Bannock & Partners Ltd.

*3i figures represent estimates of unsecured investments in the calendar year
Prior to 1989 these estimates are included in the BVCA total.

the venture capital industry in Britain during the 1980s. Government policy
and changes in the financial markets afford a partial explanation. The breaking
up of public sector industries provided a few early opportunities, bus companies and shipyards being notable examples. The government also established
the Business Start-Up Scheme, later remodelled as the Business Expansion
Scheme (BES), which allowed individuals to obtain tax relief on investments up
to £40,000 in unquoted equity for a minimum period of five years. Collective
funds were soon set up to manage these investments, which despite government intentions gravitated towards property investment, particularly in hotels.
The government also set up the small firms Loan Guarantee Scheme in May
1981 initially guaranteeing 70 per cent of loans up to £100,000.[14] 3i was to make
177 advances under this scheme during the first year of operation.[15] Another
stimulus to the activity of venture capital firms came when capital market
thresholds were significantly reduced with the introduction of the Unlisted
Securities Market (USM) in November 1981. Conditions of entry to the USM
were considerably less complicated and cheaper than a listing on the Stock
Exchange, and by 1985 the USM comprised over 330 companies worth a total
in excess of £3.5bn.[16] This had the effect of creating a market for shares which
would previously have presented difficulties in liquidity terms, and thus considerably enhanced the opportunities for smaller companies to float successfully. The USM also provided venture capital funds with an earlier exit and
increased their ability to realize successful investments. Thirty of the companies on 3i's books joined the USM during its first five years of operation.[17]

Restructuring of economic activity, particularly of the type witnessed
during the early 1980s, established an environment in which venture capital
could thrive. Gordon Murray has pointed to the contra-cyclical nature of ven-

'I make no apologies for my wealth, Dan . . . I pay people to do that.'

ture capital, seizing investment opportunities during both recessionary and recovery periods.[18] It is perhaps better described as multi-cyclical, since any period favouring corporate restructuring or regeneration presents opportunities for venture capital investment. The recession of the early 1980s, for example, saw a wave of business failures or retrenchment as many large companies began to hive off difficult or unprofitable subsidiaries. This provided the opportunity for a growing number of management buy-outs and buy-ins from parent companies or the receiver. Later, in the 1980s, corporate acquisition waves and the trend in some industries to revert to core activity provided similar opportunities, as unwanted subsidiaries were hived off. The creation of new industries where technological barriers to entry were periodically lowered, favouring smaller, skill-intensive operations (information-technology and biotechnology companies are the notable examples), also generated the opportunity for a new level of high-risk, equity-based investment in start-up companies.

The venture capital phenomenon can thus be partly explained by market opportunity generated by government policy and the economic turbulence of the 1980s. It was also an industry which was driven from within, however, by a new form of entrepreneurial investor, actively seeking investment opportunities but also playing an important part in generating the market in which it operated. More will be said below about 3i's central role in influencing, and often providing the staff involved in the expansion of this industry. Also of crucial importance were the new forms of investment developed to meet the needs of firms, especially in the small- and medium-sized sector, in the 1980s. These ranged from historical products such as the straightforward secured loan, through mezzanine finance, a tier of debt ranking between senior bank debt and equity, to pure equity involvement. The risk levels in many investments were quite considerable. Indeed as competition grew in the mid-1980s more highly geared investment became prevalent.[19] Investments were also directed at firms in a number of different phases of development, ranging from start-up and early-stage capital to development capital.

Empowering Managers: The Growth of the Buy-Out

Towards the end of the 1980s, however, an increasing amount of venture capital investment, and activity at 3i, went towards what was to become the *leitmotif* of the industry, management buy-outs and later on management buy-ins. The economic restructuring described above provided a number of opportunities for management teams to assume ownership of the firms in which they worked. These teams were motivated by a number of factors. Changes in the tax structure, and the chance to realize their 'sweat equity'—a calculation of the worth of individual managers' experience and expertise—were important incentives. Many managers foresaw that what were perceived as burdensome subsidiaries by larger companies could in fact be converted into successful operations when rationalized, relieved of head-office costs, more tightly focused, and guided by staff with a greater level of motivation by virtue of a direct interest in the progress of the firm. In the case of MBOs and MBIs involving established family firms, many of the new management teams were held to be more comfortable with complex and often fairly onerous financial packages which, while promising substantial gains, also introduced a new element of personal risk.

3i was the pioneer of MBOs in Britain, financing an increasing number of this type of ownership change in the 1970s. From a typical financing of four

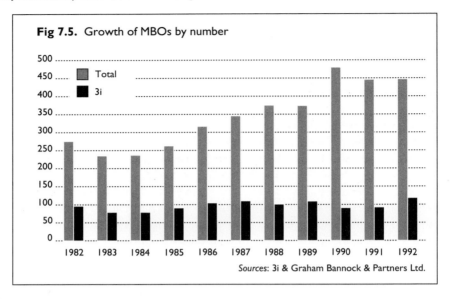

Fig 7.5. Growth of MBOs by number

Sources: 3i & Graham Bannock & Partners Ltd.

or five each year this became the fastest-growing sector of activity in 1978, when 20 MBOs were backed, rising to 49 the following year. By 1981 a total of over 200 MBOs had been financed by the Company. These early buy-outs originated in several ways, including an overseas or UK parent disposing of a UK division, companies going into receivership, or the selling of an interest by private company shareholders. Early examples include a £6.8 million buy-out of Truflo, the West Midland turbine component manufacturing company, sold by Rockwell International on its acquisition of parent company Wilmot Breedon; Panache Upholstery, a buy-out partially funded by the redundancy payments of the staff following receivership; and Decorettes, a small transfer manufacturing subsidiary sold off by Birmingham group Newman Tonks. Typically 3i provided between 80 per cent and 90 per cent of the funds required by subscribing for a minority stake in the shareholding and the provision of loan capital. In the case of Decorettes, for example, the management put up £100,000 and 3i (ICFC) supplied £500,000, the directors retaining control of 75 per cent of the equity while 3i held the remaining 25 per cent.[20] During this early phase competition was limited partly by the complexities involved in setting up an MBO. The 1948 Companies Act made it illegal for companies to purchase, or to provide assistance for the purchase of, their own shares and made it difficult for the lending institution to secure advances against the assets of the company being bought out. To set up an MBO thus required a rather baroque set of procedures involving hive down and liquidation schemes, referred to at 3i as 'doing a section 54', so-called after the relevant section of the Act, which served to discourage others from entering the field.[21]

The onset of recession, the growing publicity afforded to buy-outs, taxation incentives, and changes in the 1981 Companies Act which 'deskilled' the process of organizing MBOs[22] led to an increasing level of new entrants into the MBO business as the 1980s progressed. As Figure 7.5 shows, the overall number of MBOs held steady at around 300 per year from 1982 onwards. Then, as recovery was consolidated in some sectors of the economy, a steady rise began, from 1985 to the peak year of 1990 when over 465 MBOs took place.[23] This period also saw a considerable rise in the number of management buy-ins, a process identical to MBOs but involving a buy-out by a team of managers from outside the enterprise, often teams which had originally attempted an unsuccessful MBO. (Buy-outs by a combination of internal and external managers emerged later in the 1980s under the acronym BIMBO—buy-in management buy-out). Figure 7.6 shows the growing number of MBIs after 1985, again reaching a peak in 1989. In that year 147 MBIs totalling £3,599 million were completed, compared with only 5 to the value of £11 million in 1981.[24]

By 1989 MBOs and MBIs, 65 per cent of which were in the manufacturing sector, accounted for over 22 per cent, by value, of the total transfers of business in Britain.[25] A notable trend in the buy-out market from the mid-decade onwards was the increasing size of transactions. A list of all the buy-outs worth in excess of £150 million—twenty-seven in all—includes only one pre-1985 entry, all the rest taking place between 1985 and 1990.[26] This includes some very large deals including Reedpack, MFI/Hygena, Magnet, and the Lawson Mardon Group, all of which exceeded £500 million at 1992 prices.[27] The average size of MBIs also rose during this period, though the figures are somewhat distorted by the very large Isosceles buy-in of the Gateway super-

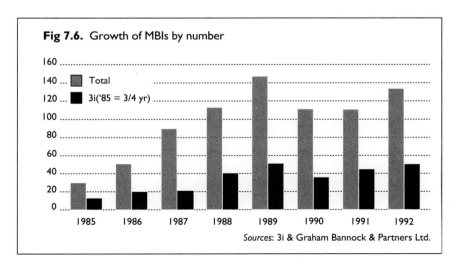

Fig 7.6. Growth of MBIs by number

■ Total
■ 3i('85 = 3/4 yr)

1985 1986 1987 1988 1989 1990 1991 1992

Sources: 3i & Graham Bannock & Partners Ltd.

167

market chain in 1989, worth a total of £2.4 billion. This rise in values was partly the result of increasing competition, including that from trade buyers, one effect of which was that gearing levels began to rise significantly. Though not reaching the scale involved in some of the more notorious leveraged buy-outs in the USA, deals in the UK involving ratios of 5 : 1 debt to equity were not uncommon by 1989, and some were higher, sometimes involving no equity at all. Larger deal size was also facilitated by the increasing resort to syndication among investors. The process of setting up a larger buy-out would typically involve an initial approach to various venture capital firms, perhaps through an intermediary such as one of the major accounting firms. Tenders submitted—a 'beauty parade'—would result in the choice of a lead investor, who would subsequently look for syndicate partners, frequently investors involved in the initial tendering process. 3i, through its City Office, was the most prolific deal leader of the 1980s, being lead investor in 35 £10-million-plus investments between 1981 and 1991, ahead of its nearest rivals, Candover Investments, Charterhouse Development Capital, Citicorp and County NatWest.[28] However, the average value of deals led by 3i, at £32 million, was significantly less than that of some other competitors, reflecting the fact that, towards the end of the 1980s, 3i withdrew from the larger end of the buy-out market.[29] The Company continued to dominate the market in smaller- and medium-sized investments, however, and the backing in 1990 of the MBO at Holden and

'Corporate raiders, sir—one, maybe two companies away.'

Brooke, a Manchester manufacturer of hydraulic pumps, represented 3i's one thousandth MBO. It was estimated that by 1991 the Company had funded over one third of all UK MBOs.

The MBO and MBI were, as noted above, very much symbolic of the venture capital industry in general and its meteoric rise in activity during the late 1980s. The subsequent decline in the early 1990s has led to many reappraisals by both practitioners and commentators. Lord Caldecote had sounded an early note of caution in 1982: 'Management buy-outs are not just financial engineering: a thorough understanding of the underlying business is necessary before entering into financial arrangements which by their nature create high initial gearing levels and where management often has no experience of operating independently.'[30] The trend towards increasingly large deals also led to accusations that one of the industry's positive benefits, the provision of start-up and growth capital to smaller companies, was being forgotten. The *Financial Times*, for example, commented at the end of 1985 that the 'venture capital industry is being drawn increasingly into an area which has more to do with corporate finance than with fostering the development of small businesses'.[31] Problems came to a head in the early 1990s when some of the more ambitious large-scale buy-outs began to run into trouble, either collapsing completely or calling for large levels of refinancing, due to a combination of over-gearing, rising interest rates, and the onset of recession which together limited growth in trading profits and prevented early asset-realization necessary for a reduction in debt burdens. Troublesome buy-outs like Lowndes Queensway and the MBI at Isosceles, which had been very highly geared at 11 : 1, led to a fall-off in the number of larger deals.[32] There was a simultaneous restriction of gearing levels which, typically, fell back to a ratio of 1 : 1 by 1992, as the banks placed more conservative limits on the level of finance they were prepared to provide. 3i itself was not immune from problems at the larger end of the market, being eventually forced to write off some £28 million in mezzanine debt and £45 million of equity in Isosceles, for example.[33]

Expected realization values also had to be revised as the capital markets began to take a less favourable view of larger flotations. In addition the Unlisted Securities Market, despite early optimism, was proving less attractive than expected. With the exception of a brief revival in 1988 the number of companies joining the USM declined steadily, and a report by the Stock Exchange in 1992 recommended the closure of what was now 'widely regarded as a dying market'.[34] Although larger, potentially troublesome MBOs were still successfully floated, MFI for example in 1992, the inflated expectations of returns which had been typical between 1987 and 1989 often failed to materialize. Problems subsequently emerged with both the supply and demand for venture capital funds. The very large amounts raised in 1989 failed to be replicated in following years as institutional suppliers of funds to the independent sector of

Domino Printing Sciences

DOMINO PRINTING SCIENCES FIRST CAME to the attention of 3i when it won the TDC Innovator Award in 1978. The company, which was less than a year old at the time, was founded by Graeme Minto, who had worked throughout the 1970s on ink-jet printing development at Cambridge Consultants Limited, under a programme funded by ICI. Initially financed by a loan from CCL and a second mortgage on his home, Minto secured licences from ICI and CCL to concentrate on smaller applications for the technology, a method of printing using electrostatic deflection of micro-droplets of ink. Ink-jet printing has numerous advantages over other methods, principally speed and the ability to print on irregular or delicate surfaces, making it ideal for use in the packaging industry and for business machines.

Domino approached TDC for funding in 1979. Impressed with the speed with which Minto had established Domino as a production company TDC were prepared to overlook his lack of business experience, and agreed to fund the company with a secured loan of £92,500 and £7,500 subscription for cumulative convertible participating preferred ordinary shares, representing just over a quarter of the equity. TDC also stipulated the appointment of a non-executive director to provide experienced commercial advice. Further rounds of support were supplied by TDC during the early 1980s including guaranteeing bank overdrafts, refinancing the purchase of a larger office, and funding production facilities.

The firm experienced early difficulties in realizing the true potential of its products, partly due to a poor marketing strategy and resistance of some potential customers to a new, non-traditional technology. No sales were made in the first year, and at one point the company, with its relatively high gearing, was technically insolvent. Nevertheless 3i continued its support, the level of liaison remaining very high, particularly during this troublesome period. Information supplied by Domino included monthly management accounts, marketing reports, analyses of sales leads and monthly R&D spending monitored against cash-flow. 3i's involvement was to become, according to Minto, 'crucial to the firm's change in fortunes' and the initial problems were eventually overcome. Domino subsequently grew to become one of the archetypal success stories of the 'Cambridge phenomenon' in the 1980s. When the company was floated in 1985 the issue was 43 times over-subscribed and 3i's shareholding was valued at some £6.5 million in a market capitalization of £26 million.

Expanding overseas into the US market, Europe, and the Far-East, the company has grown to become the world leader in ink-jet technology, particularly active in the bar-code printing industry. 3i remains a shareholder in the 1990s, in a company now capitalized at over £100 million.

the venture capital industry began to question the level of return which could be expected.[35] The capacity of the British economy to supply enough companies with sufficient growth potential to justify investment also came into question.[36] Many venture capital institutions continued to hold high levels of uninvested funds, particularly after 1989, the peak year of fund-raising. In general, doubts began to be expressed over whether or not the industry had generally oversold itself in the mid-1980s, particularly to institutional investors.[37] Captive funds in their turn, which did not view venture capital as their core activity, began to withdraw from the market.

By the early 1990s, recession notwithstanding, it seemed to many that the high hopes for venture capitalism as the engine of enterprise in a revitalized British economy had been premature. In its caricatured form the industry had promised many things: to empower entrepreneurs in start-up and high-growth areas, especially new technology fields; to release a new stratum of owner-managers from moribund enterprises in nationalized or declining private-sector companies; and perhaps most importantly, by acting as intermediaries, to channel money from the very large institutional investors, via venture capital funds, into long-term, equity-based, small- and medium-sized investments—a potential solution to the lingering Macmillan gap. It was this latter relationship, of acting as a conduit for institutional investors, which was to prove one of the advantages but also one of the impediments of venture capital. Independent funds and, in similar ways, captives were constrained by the need to demonstrate performance. As Murray has noted, the institutional suppliers of funds are the primary *customer* of these venture capital funds.[38] In the early years expectations based on the US experience, and one or two British successes with very high rates of return, proved enough to convince capital suppliers that venture capital was a worthwhile investment. Pressure began to build to demonstrate performance, however, such as at least to outperform gilts or the FTSE index. Such expectations were unfortunately not conducive to long-term investment. A tendency thus developed within the industry to favour comparatively low-risk and large-scale MBOs, with the probability of an early float or trade sale, usually within three to five years, at the expense of higher-risk and longer-term start-ups or high-technology investments.[39] Ronald Cohen, Chairman of Apax Partners, summed up this trend: 'Towards the middle of the decade there was a general shift away from business risk. This was partly the result of burnt fingers from start-up investments in the early 1980s but also because of a move towards the quicker returns to be made from backing MBOs and exiting in a rising market.'[40] The accusation of short-termism and opportunism has certainly tarnished the overall reputation of the venture capital industry—now disparagingly referred to in some quarters as 'vulture capitalism'—and undermined the notion that its closer investor–customer relationship added any significant value. In many deals the notion of managerial

171

intervention simply extended to the right to replace managerial staff in the event that the investment ran into difficulties. Another indictment is that the tendency towards higher gearing meant that venture capital did less than was expected towards filling the 'equity gap' which was still held to be prevalent in Britain.[41]

3i and the Venture Capital Community

3i's relationship with the venture capital industry during the 1980s was at best ambivalent. The Company was, from the beginning, bracketed with this new form of investment institution, usually reported in the press as '3i—Britain's leading venture capitalist'. This would perhaps have been less of a problem if the venture capital industry had conformed to expectations, funding long-term, equity-based, start-up, and development-capital investments. 3i, for its part, did continue to fund a relatively high proportion of new enterprises, involving commensurate levels of risk. Sir John Cuckney, 3i Chairman from 1987, was unequivocal on this point. 'What impresses me is the readiness [at 3i] to take a risk, particularly with start-ups. The list of failures is almost a roll of

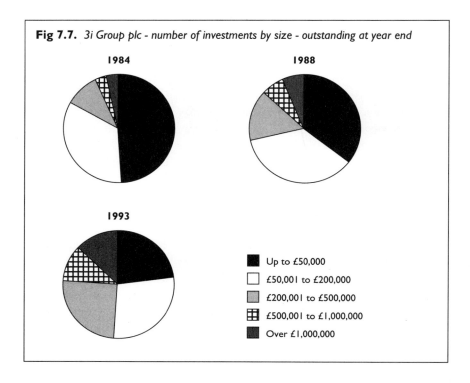

Fig 7.7. *3i Group plc - number of investments by size - outstanding at year end*

1984

1988

1993

■ Up to £50,000

□ £50,001 to £200,000

▨ £200,001 to £500,000

⊞ £500,001 to £1,000,000

■ Over £1,000,000

honour, in that you've got to take those risks if you are to succeed.'[42] Also, a relatively high proportion of the 3i portfolio continued to be composed of small- and medium-sized firms, again demonstrating one of the positive attributes initially expected of the venture capital industry as Fig.7.7 shows. The 3i policy on the gearing structure of lending and equity was relatively conservative compared to that of its nascent rivals, avoiding where possible unrealistic debt burdens. One of the key determinants in 3i's contrasting approach was its immunity from the kind of pressures to demonstrate performance in the short-term which shaped much of the activity of many other venture capital firms in the later 1980s. 3i could invest in enterprises for genuine growth purposes, and also tended to maintain its focus on the manufacturing sector (see Fig. 7.8).

Many critics of venture capital bemoan the fact that too much investment in reality went for simple restructuring, transfer of ownership, and generation of fees for intermediaries in the process.[43] It is still unclear, for example, whether many of the MBOs funded in the 1980s were transformed into more dynamic and efficient enterprises. A study by the Centre for Management Buy-Out Research at Nottingham University tentatively demonstrated that, following a period of enhanced efficiency in the first three years of operation,

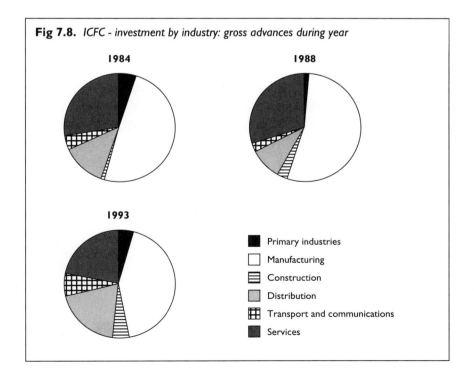

Fig 7.8. *ICFC - investment by industry: gross advances during year*

1984   1988

1993

■ Primary industries
□ Manufacturing
☰ Construction
▨ Distribution
▥ Transport and communications
■ Services

performance tended to fall away in subsequent years.[44] Bannock's survey, using a larger sample of 3i companies, was more positive, demonstrating that 3i's own MBOs consistently outperformed the non-MBO companies in its portfolio.[45] Another general criticism levelled at venture capital, certainly in contrast to 3i, was that it did not adequately cover the regions.[46] Some institutions, such as County NatWest and Murray Johnstone, did have a regional presence, but none could match the depth of coverage provided by 3i's specialist branch network system (see Fig. 7.9).

As the venture capital industry moves through into the 1990s and into maturity, questions remain as to whether it will be revealed to be a permanent and valuable addition to the financial structure, and go some way towards addressing problems such as the 'equity gap', or whether it will prove to be an ephemeral and opportunistic feature of the 1980s, unable to sustain its dynamism or continue to attract funds and identify opportunities into the 1990s, becoming instead a small sector of specialist funds operating in selected niches in the market. There is a degree of irony in the fact that 3i, from its very inception as ICFC, had invested in ways which conformed very closely to the ideals attributed to venture capital and yet felt reluctant to become too closely identified with the industry, in view of the way in which it was perceived actually to operate. By the end of the 1980s 3i had dropped the phrase 'venture capital' from its corporate vocabulary altogether, preferring 'investment capital' instead. Even so, as the venture capital industry matures into the 1990s there are signs that 3i will be less concerned to distance itself from the rest of the

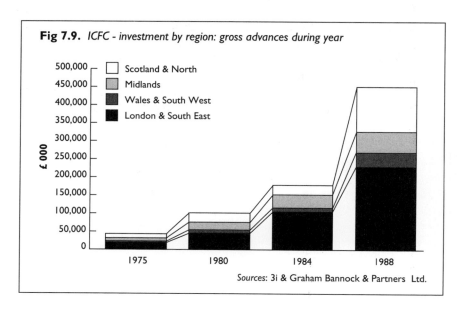

Fig 7.9. *ICFC - investment by region: gross advances during year*

Sources: 3i & Graham Bannock & Partners Ltd.

industry and that a form of *rapprochement* is taking place. In 1992, for example, 3i joined other venture capital firms in forming the City Group for Smaller Companies which, operating under the acronym CISCO, is intended to lobby in favour of smaller quoted companies in the wake of the USM closure.[47] Another indicator is 3i's changing involvement with the BVCA, which was initially very reserved. In 1993 Brian Larcombe, 3i's finance and planning director, was elected Deputy Chairman of the Association, and became Chairman in 1994.[48]

3i is inextricably linked with the venture capital industry in another, more informal, but very important way. Many of the people involved in setting up new funds, or recruited into the expanding institutions in the 1980s, had 3i origins. The rapid expansion of the industry naturally made for a very volatile labour market. 3i's dominant position in this market, allied to the company's tradition of training which was without peer in the finance community, made it 'the first place every headhunter would look'.[49] An early concentration on graduate recruitment, pioneered during Tindale's programme of professionalization of ICFC and carried on through the 1970s,[50] had combined with a commitment to an ongoing training programme of a quality which few, if any, rival institutions could afford to match.[51] When merged with the experience gained on the job in finding and constructing investments this had resulted in 3i becoming popularly known as 'the university of venture capital'. In short, 3i had generated 'a new kind of investment banker', and in its rapid expansion in the early 1980s the industry was bound to view the Company as 'a natural source of talent'.[52]

There were positive aspects to this development. At the very least it provided a general acknowledgement of the high quality of staff at 3i. As Lord Caldecote later recalled: 'We would have been pretty disappointed if they weren't pinched.'[53] It also meant the establishment of a network of contacts throughout the industry centring on 3i. Don Clarke highlighted at least two benefits in this: 'They were trained by us and they know the business . . . they aren't lousing up the market with stupid offers. Besides, they tend to bring us into deals and vice versa.'[54] These positive aspects were undoubtedly outweighed by the negatives, however. With staff turnover approaching 30 per cent in some years the exodus represented a serious drain on 3i's resources, since effective replacement could not be achieved in the short term. 3i staff are notoriously loyal to what has for a long time been viewed as a prestigious and worthwhile Company to work for, given its combination of commercial and national goals. They were nevertheless being lured away by a package which often included increased responsibility and remuneration linked to the performance of investments. 3i had never adopted a system of carried interest, a reflection of the similar policy of not permitting 3i personnel to sit on the boards of investee companies for fear of a conflict of interest.

Isosceles plc

IF THE £100 MILLION REALIZED on the sale of British Caledonian was 3i's largest-ever profit, the commitment of a similar amount to Isosceles was 3i's largest-ever investment and the £72 million provided against its residual holding also its largest potential loss.

Although it was the largest single investor in small buy-outs, 3i was also an active leader in larger buy-outs during the 1980s. Isosceles was, however, different. It was the vehicle put together by S. G. Warburg and underwritten by a venture capital consortium, including 3i, to mount a contested management buy-in ultimately totalling £2.1 billion for the Dee Corporation, owners of the underperforming Gateway supermarket chain. The heavy initial gearing was structured on the assumption that unwanted parts of the group could be sold off quickly and profitably and the proceeds used to reduce debt. However, these plans were delayed by the intervention of a competitive bid and by the recession which made disposals and a trading recovery more difficult. Despite initial strong trading, Gateway's competitive position deteriorated and successive capital restructurings became necessary, diluting the position of the initial investors.

3i could tolerate the loss of its staff at this rate for only so long, and in 1984 Foulds formulated a scheme to link remuneration to the general performance of the portfolio. In order to set up such a scheme, however, the support of the shareholders was necessary. At the time the clearing banks were themselves experiencing similar problems. Newly acquired subsidiaries were operating outside the traditional banking norms. As Sir David Walker recalls: 'All the clearing banks were having great problems of how to remunerate all these high-flying investment-banker types with conventional remuneration.'[55] Staff in the mainstream of the bank's business were naturally concerned that other sectors of the business were apparently being treated in a more favourable light. 3i's request thus met with a very lukewarm response from the shareholders.[56] Nevertheless Foulds's views prevailed, and a series of reforms was introduced establishing a bonus scheme and share option package, which saw over 60 per cent of staff becoming shareholders in the Company during the first year of operation.[57] Profit-share awards were to be based on revenue growth and, to a lesser extent, the unrealized value growth of 3i's investments. These new performance-related schemes operated within the preservation of an important principle however. Individual reward was still not directly linked, as in some rival institutions, to individual investment performance. Increases in remuneration were firmly fixed to the effectiveness of the whole portfolio.

3i Ventures

There was to be one exception to this general rule, and it coincided with the closest brush with venture capital which the Group was to have. Technical Development Capital, which had been established in the 1960s to invest in advanced technology companies[58] was revitalized in 1980 when it became the Ventures Division, later renamed 3i Ventures when the Group reorganizations took place in 1983. In its regenerated form 3i Ventures was set to expand 3i investment in high technology substantially, notably in start-ups and high-growth companies in microelectronics, computers, telecommunications, biosciences, and industrial automation, using its own funds and syndicated capital.

In doing so the division was to adopt a 'venture capital' *modus operandi*. 3i Ventures was to be run by staff with engineering and scientific expertise and was to be headed by a 'technologist/venture capitalist', Geoff Taylor. Taylor had been recruited in California in 1980, although he was in fact a British citizen 'who had gone to work there during a period of very high personal taxation in the UK'.[59] Early investments totalling £3 million were made within a few months in computer disk drives, biotechnology, photo-typesetting, and computer-based security systems. Such investments were to be run in a hands-on way, with direct participation by 3i staff on the boards of investee companies. Another significant difference was the decision to allow staff in 3i Ventures to have a carried interest in any investments which the division made. This linking of personal remuneration to the performance of investments, typical in other venture capital companies, went against the traditional practice of the Group and was, from the outset, a cause of considerable friction. 3i Ventures was also to have a wider, international remit, setting up offices in California and Massachusetts. It was hoped that high-technology investments in the USA, with direct involvement by 3i, would result in technology transfers back to the UK. LSI Logic was seen to be a good example of this trend, which carried positive commercial benefits for 3i 'while speeding up the process of industrial evolution in the country'.[60]

The first office in Boston was set up partly to take advantage of the environment surrounding the 'Route 128' high-technology companies in the area. It was also chosen because of the minimal time difference, East Coast culture, and the diversity of business in the region.[61] The pull of the West Coast, however, with its thriving local technological community, led to the establishment in 1984 of offices in Newport Beach and, later, Menlo Park in Northern

California, a region fast becoming a Mecca for information technologies, biotechnologies, and advanced health-care technology.[62]

3i Ventures was initially quite successful. Two early investments in Rodime, a company manufacturing computer disk drives, and LSI Logic, brought considerable gains at an early stage, and as the 3i Group was restructuring in the mid-1980s, and looking for a new corporate identity and new markets, it seemed possible that this new focus might come to dominate the activity of the whole Group.[63] However, the initial large gains were not replicated in the short term, and, as with TDC before it, the new Group had to be prepared for a lengthy wait before investments would show adequate returns. In addition, it proved more difficult than envisaged to identify worthwhile investments in the USA where the venture capital industry was considerably larger and more competitive.

Given the lack of tangible success, those elements within the 3i Group which had been alienated by what they saw as the cavalier style of 3i Ventures became more vociferous in their criticism of the division. Besides the different operational culture which existed at Ventures[64] there was also a significant degree of animosity between the division and some of the long-standing regional offices, such as Reading and Cambridge, which had built up their own portfolio of high-technology investments. This criticism carried increasing force given a growing disillusionment within the British finance community generally about the effectiveness of venture capital and its methods, which were now seen to be falling well short of their promised performance.[65] In this atmosphere 3i Ventures, which was itself unable to maintain its early promise, began to come under increasing pressure; and when, towards the end of the 1980s, 3i moved to rationalize its Group activity and adopted a policy of returning to its 'core' business and expansion into Europe, 3i Ventures was effectively closed down. No new investments were to be made, existing investments being transferred to a jointly owned management company.

The case of 3i Ventures in the 1980s demonstrates a different set of impediments to that which had slowed the progress of TDC. In this case there were no overtly 'political' origins to be resisted, as had been the cause of disagreements between Kinross and Sir John Benn, for example, as discussed in Chapter 4, and the methods used involved direct participation by 3i staff, themselves experts in technology rather than finance. In addition, 3i Ventures used the same long-term equity-based investment methods which had proved successful since ICFC's inception. The division failed to have a lasting impact for different reasons, however. Ventures aroused some animosity within the 3i Group precisely because of the closer links which were established between 3i Ventures staff and the client companies, in particular because of the practice of carried interest, which was common in the venture capital industry generally but resisted in the mainstream of British banking. At least one member of the

Group's staff combined a critique of technology investment with the move to the new investment industry: 'it was TDC which started the rot towards venture capitalism.'[66]

3i Ventures was an initiative encouraged by the apparent success of the venture capital industry in Britain in the 1980s. When the expectations of that industry proved to have been seemingly oversold in the later 1980s, 3i Ventures became vulnerable. The initial success of the two investments which came with Taylor set the scene for high expectations of 3i Ventures. Other 'shooting stars' proved elusive in the short term, and although the performance of the rest of the portfolio proved adequate, the case for special operating procedures, outside Group traditions, could not be sustained. Furthermore, the expansion into the USA had never been popular with 3i's shareholders including the Bank of England, which began to worry about the level of British capital which might be committed overseas, arguably compromising 3i's traditional *raison d'être*.[67] The decision was made in 1991 to limit further investment in the USA. The Group would continue with any necessary follow-on finance to the forty investments already made, while start-up and early-stage investments were transferred to Aspen Venture Partners, a venture-management company established in 1992, in which 3i was the sole general partner.

Other technology-based initiatives continued within the Group following the demise of 3i Ventures. 3i joined forces with Trinity Capital in 1993 to manage a proportion of the Ventures investments and finance information-technology based companies. The Group continued to finance start-up companies in science parks, notably through the Cambridge office. Another high-technology initiative was the joint venture set up with Imperial College, in 1984, to help capitalize on research and development undertaken in the university sector. Research Exploitation (RE) was set up in the wake of changes which broke the monopoly which the British Technology Group held over access to this work. RE, run by Charles DesForges, undertook technology audits at fifty-eight universities and higher-education institutes and supplied development finance to selected projects to develop them to patentable standards, prior to seeking licensing agreements with larger companies. RE had originally been a joint operation with the Research Corporation in the USA, but after four years 3i began running the company on its own. In a further reorganization in 1992 RE was merged with Impel, jointly owned by 3i and Imperial College.

Conclusions

3i as a Group underwent significant change during the 1980s, partly as a result of internally driven policy changes and partly because of changes in its competitive environment. The rise of the venture capital industry, stimulated in part by 3i's influence on products and staff, represented the greatest challenge. The Group was to benefit from the expansion of the market that this engendered, but also, because of a tradition and culture which had grown over the previous decades, 3i was to avoid many of the problems which beset the industry in the later years of the decade. Difficulties were encountered when the Group became involved in more adventurous MBOs, such as Isosceles for example, and the foray into an unrestricted venture capital method in the case of 3i Ventures was an uncomfortable experience. This was not the norm, however, and 3i as a Group, with its methods of raising and investing funds, and general outlook of long-termism, maintained its distinctive characteristics, and was ultimately strengthened by them throughout this very turbulent decade.

NOTES

[1] G. Bannock, *Britain in the 1980s: Enterprise Reborn?* (3i, 1987), 17.

[2] ICFC, *Annual Reports*, 1980, 1981, 1982.

[3] 3i, *Annual Reports*, 1983–86.

[4] 3i, *Annual Reports*, 1987, 5; 1988, 6.

[5] 3i, *Annual Report*, 1988, 6.

[6] 3i, *Annual Reports*, 1988, 6; 1989; 1990, 7.

[7] For a discussion of 3i's difficulties in reconciling its own form of investment capital with the new forms of financial engineering, see Ch. 10.

[8] Bolton Report, 155.

[9] W. D. Bygrave and J. A. Timmons, *Venture Capital at the Crossroads* (Harvard Business School Press, 1992), 1–30.

[10] The BVCA typology comprises: Clearing-Bank-related; Institution-backed; Captive/semi captive (incl. merchant banks); Independents; Business Expansion Scheme funds; Corporate/Academic/others; and Semi-state bodies (incl. local government). G. Murray, *Change and Maturity in the UK Venture Capital Industry* (Warwick University, 1991), 10–11.

[11] See below, Ch. 11.

[12] Figures from 3i; Murray, *Change and Maturity*, 1; BVCA reports. The figure for 1989 is inclusive of 3i investment.

[13] EVCA, *Venture Capital in Europe: Its Role and Development* (Venture Capital Policy Paper, 1993). Venture Capital invested per capita, 1990 (the first figure following each entry represents £m, the second figure represents £ per cap.): UK – 1,400, 25; Netherlands – 169, 12; France – 588, 11; Germany – 392, 5; Italy – 152, 3; Spain – 61, 2. (*KPMG/European Venture Capital Yearbook 1991.*)

[14] This was increased in 1993 to 85 per cent of £250,000.

[15] FFI, *Annual Report*, 1982.

[16] *Financial Times*, 3 Dec. 1985. The USM was followed by similar initiatives in Europe, including the Deuxième Marché, formed by the Paris Bourse in 1983, and the Dutch Parallelmarkt in 1984.

[17] 3i, *Annual Report*, 1987, 9.

[18] Murray, *Change and Maturity*, 17.

[19] *Financial Times*, 15 Oct. 1991.

[20] 'Notes for the Prime Minister's Office on ICFC', 29 Dec. 1980, 3i.

[21] D. Sach, interviewed by R. Coopey, 22 June 1993; R. Smith, 'Changes in the Buyout Market', *Acquisitions Monthly* (Feb. 1993), 44.

[22] Smith, 'Changes', 44.

[23] Centre for Management Buy-Out Research at Nottingham University (CMBOR), 1990.

[24] Ibid.

[25] G. Bannock, *The Economic Impact of Management Buy-outs* (3i, 1990), 6.

[26] At constant 1992 prices. CMBOR Annual Review, 1992, 15.

[27] Ibid.

[28] 'Capitalists and Their Ventures', *Accountancy* (Oct. 1992), 51.

[29] The average deal size over the same period led by Charterhouse was £130m, for Cinven £103m, and for Electra £112. Ibid.

[30] 3i, *Annual Report*, 1982, 5.

[31] *Financial Times*, 3 Dec. 1985.

[32] Smith, 'Changes'.

[33] *The Financial Times*, 12 Dec. 1992, 8. 3i Annual Report and Accounts, 1993.

[34] *Daily Telegraph*, 22 Dec. 1992.

[35] 'Investors are Calling the Tune', *Investors Chronicle*, 9 (Oct. 1992); 'Competition Intensifies in Venture Capital', *Ibid.*, 4 (Oct. 1991).

[36] 'Growth Companies—Are There Enough to go Round?' *UK Venture Capital Journal* (Sept. 1992), 22–7.

[37] Murray, *Change and Maturity*, pp. ii, 52.

[38] Murray, *Change and Maturity*, 24–5.

[39] The average investment length for an MBO sold in 1989 was 3.25 years. Murray, *Change and Maturity*, 46, 54. By this year trade sales had come to predominate as the form of exit. Bannock estimates that between 1985 and 1989 211 MBOs were sold to trade buyers, 143 were floated, 32 went into receivership. Bannock, *The Economic Impact of MBOs*, 8.

[40] R. Cohen, 'Venture Capital is Crucial to Recovery', *Observer*, 18 Oct. 1992.

[41] G. Bannock, *Venture Capital and the Equity Gap* (National Westminster Bank, 1992).

[42] *Institutional Investor* (Feb. 1989), 3.

[43] Murray, *Change and Maturity*, 46.

[44] Ibid.

[45] Bannock, *Management Buy-outs*, 22–3.

[46] C. Mason, 'Venture Capital in the United Kingdom: A Geographical Perspective', *National Westminster Bank Quarterly Review* (May 1987), 47–59.

[47] *Daily Telegraph*, 22 Feb. 1993.

[48] *Financial Times*, 10 June 1993.

[49] J. Foulds, interviewed by R. Coopey, 1 Dec. 1992.

[50] In 1976, for example, staff at ICFC included 92 graduates, 20 with MBAs—representing 27 per cent of the total number of employees. ICFC, *Annual Report*, 1977.

[51] Robert Smith, interviewed by R. Coopey, 24 June 1993.

[52] A. Butt-Philip, interviewed by R. Coopey, 6 Dec. 1991: 3i, *Annual Report*, 1983, 6.

[53] Lord Caldecote, interviewed by R. Coopey, 18 Mar. 1992.

[54] *Institutional Investor* (Feb. 1989), 3; Robert Smith, interview.

[55] Sir David Walker, interviewed by R. Coopey, 11 Nov. 1992.

[56] Caldecote, interview; Sir David Walker, interview.

[57] 3i, *Annual Report*, 1984, 9; 1985, 7.

[58] See above, Ch. 4.

[59] 'Notes for the Prime Minister's Office on ICFC', 29 Dec. 1980, 3i.

[60] Neil Cross, interview; Jon Foulds, ex-Chief Executive of 3i, interviewed by author; Chairman's Statement, 3i, *Annual Report*, 1984.

[61] Jon Foulds, interview.

[62] Ivan Momtchiloff, interview.

[63] Neil Cross, Executive Director of 3i, interviewed by author; Ivan Momtchiloff, Chairman of 3i Ventures USA, interviewed by author.

[64] See Ch. 15 below.

[65] 'Investors are Calling the Tune', *Investors Chronicle*, 9 Oct. 1992; 'Competition Intensifies in Venture Capital', *Ibid.*, 4 Oct. 1991; 'Growth Companies—Are There Enough to go Round?' *UK Venture Capital Journal* (Sept. 1992), 22–7; G. Murray, *Change and Maturity*, pp. ii, 52.

[66] Roger Plant, interviewed by author.

[67] Lord Caldecote, interview: Sir David Walker, interview; D. Sach, interview.

Chapter 8

Back to the Core: The Flotation Imperative

Back to the Core

THE LATER 1970S AND 1980S had seen great changes in the scale and characteristics of many of the operations within 3i. The competitive environment had changed dramatically in some respects, with increased intervention from the banks and venture capital industry. 3i had led the way in many of the changes in the market, such as MBOs, and had responded to others. The increasing scale of operations throughout this period can be seen from Figures 8.1–8.3 below. There was an search for a Group identity had reflected this growth and diversity, or had been made imperative by it. Yet in some respects the expansion of 3i into new fields and activities had proved difficult and unsatisfactory. In addition, towards the end of the 1980s problems within the economy generally forced a reappraisal of the fundamental nature of the Group's activities.

We have seen, in the previous chapter, how difficulties had been encountered with various aspects of the venture capital market, notably the problems with some of the larger MBOs and the incompatibility of 3i Ventures with the rest of the group. Against accusations of conservatism from some quarters of the venture capital industry 3i could point out that it had been largely successful in avoiding the painful results of some of the more excessive deals undertaken, and that the underlying strength of its portfolio provided a cushion against the possibility of recession. Nevertheless, the later 1980s were a period of some retrenchment, and an opportunity to rethink the fundamental strategy of the Group. With this rethinking came the realization that 3i's basic strength lay in its 'core' activity, and while there was a need to remain open to changes in products and markets, it was this core upon which 3i should concentrate.

Within this process of re-evaluation two areas in particular were to be subject to reduced activity. The first of these, property, had grown in a rather *ad*

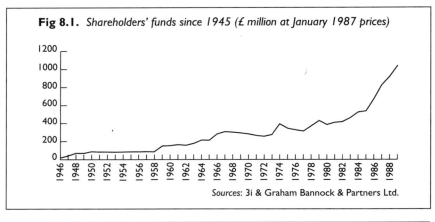

Fig 8.1. *Shareholders' funds since 1945 (£ million at January 1987 prices)*

Sources: 3i & Graham Bannock & Partners Ltd.

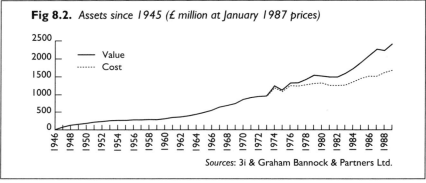

Fig 8.2. *Assets since 1945 (£ million at January 1987 prices)*

Sources: 3i & Graham Bannock & Partners Ltd.

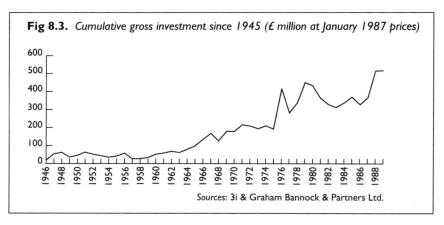

Fig 8.3. *Cumulative gross investment since 1945 (£ million at January 1987 prices)*

Sources: 3i & Graham Bannock & Partners Ltd.

hoc way since the earlier developments of the 1970s. Initially expanded from the acquisition of Anglia Commercial Property, the property division had gone through something of a renaissance in the mid-1980s. Headed by Peter Willcock, the division expanded its activities in what was at this time a buoyant market. However, as this market began to stagnate and decline in the second half of the decade, it was decided to curtail the extent of 3i's involvement. A major proportion of the property portfolio was sold in 1987 and the division was reduced, by 1989, to a small property team to 'maintain an investment presence' rather than invest directly in the market, or hold property purely as an investment.[1] The decision to pull out of the property market reflected a number of factors besides the downturn in market values. It had always been a rather peripheral activity within the Group as a whole, and when during the boom years the division had rapidly expanded its investment levels, it had begun to encroach upon the more established areas of Group activity. In addition, property investment carried its own operational, and perhaps speculative, culture which was at odds with the long-term traditions within 3i.[2] As with 3i Ventures, these could be overlooked during peak years, but as performance faded comparatively, non-core activities became increasingly vulnerable. An additional problem for the property division was its poor fit within the Group's overall strategy in terms of the appeal to attain investment company status as a preliminary to flotation, as we will see in Chapter 14.

A second area to be cut back during the later 1980s was that of consultancy. At one time ICFC-NUMAS had been the sixth largest firm of management consultants in the UK, offering advisory services, investigations, and project management on business, financial, and human-resource issues. These activities were seen to be very time-consuming, however, and a change in policy designed to utilize local accountancy firms' consultancy expertise led to a reappraisal.[3] It was decided in 1989 that 3i Consultant's future role would be to focus on strategic assignments relating to 3i's existing investment business. For this purpose the division became absorbed as part of the Group's regions division. As with property, consultancy had never attained recognition as a mainstream Group operation, and it seemed to those involved that this had, since the early 1970s, been something of a 'Cinderella' activity. When the trend towards core business emerged consultancy, was unable to justify its separate existence.[4]

Reorganization of the Group and retrenchment of some activities combined with general problems of recession in the later 1980s to put pressure on the staffing levels within 3i, and for the first time in its history the Group was forced to make a significant reduction in the number of its employees. During 1991 and 1992 staff numbers were reduced by over a third to less than 600. Cuts affected all levels of staff, from senior management down. Part of the reduction reflected the unusually rapid expansion of activity in the previous period, which had seen recruitment levels rise at above-average rates. Although those involved at the time had thought the 'good times would go on forever'[5] it was clear to 3i's Chief Executive that, in terms of the number of deals to be expected, 'the froth of the late eighties boom has been blown away by reces-

Waterstone's

DURING THE 1980S THE CHAIN of retail stores established by Tim Waterstone revolutionized bookselling in Britain. ICFC backed this business at the outset, when it was little more than an untried idea, and continued to provide finance, jointly with other investors, throughout a series of expansions. The key to success in this case was Waterstone himself, who had gained experience working in publishing and distribution for W. H. Smith, and had been influenced by a period spent in the USA when involved in expanding Smith's operations there.

Waterstone approached ICFC in December 1981 with a plan to launch a book-retailing business. Partly emulating the successful US chains, Waterstone planned to combine supermarket sales techniques with wide-range bookselling. He also wanted to keep late opening hours, sell discounted 'top of the market' lines wherever possible, and establish a mail-order business. ICFC recognized Waterstone's originality and experience and put together a package involving a subscription for ordinary shares and a loan under the Government's Small Firms Loan Guarantee Scheme. The first of what was to become a rapidly expanding chain of London book shops was opened in Old Brompton Road in September 1982. Before the end of the year this was followed by a branch in Southampton Row and another next to the famous Foyle's, in Charing Cross Road. Within three years the company had annual sales of over £7 million and the beginnings of a national chain. By 1989, sales were in excess of £40 million, and Waterstone's was amongst the leading booksellers in the UK.

Waterstone's rapid growth created stresses requiring rationalizations and further capital injections during the later 1980s. 3i played a continuing part in this process, advising and providing additional loan and equity capital. Tim Waterstone remained pleased with his relationship with 3i: 'They're great stuff at dealing with companies, achieving a balance between interfering and benignly standing back and watching. They've got a very amicable professional act. And they let managers manage.'

sion'.[6] Market demand fell to levels approximating to those of the early 1980s, with the number of proposals averaging about 100 per month, compared to a figure in 1990 of around 150. During this peak year 3i had made 916 investments. In 1991 and 1992 the figure fell to 663 and 714 respectively, which were now thought to be typical levels of activity.[7] Some reductions in support-service staff also reflected investments made by the Group in new computerized information systems. Rationalization also involved the sale to British Gas in 1991 of the major office development which 3i had built at Homer Road, Solihull, to house support staff in 1985.[8] Meanwhile 3i staff from Solihull moved to more modest accommodation at Trinity Park, near Birmingham International Airport, promising greater access to motorway, rail, and international links. Head office remained at the Waterloo Road buildings, which had been developed by the Group in the early 1970s.

Cut-backs eventually extended into the operational branch network, and late in 1992 several area offices were closed or rationalized. Following an earlier closure at Exeter, branches at Brighton, Guildford, and Milton Keynes were closed, and the two Yorkshire offices at Hull and Sheffield were consolidated into the Leeds office. As with the move to Trinity Park, part of the branch-closure programme was dictated by changing transport networks. Notwithstanding these arguments, and the imperatives of reduced activity, the closures drew criticism in some quarters. The *Daily Telegraph*, frequently a trenchant critic of policy at 3i, bemoaned the cut-backs, noting that if reductions were necessary then the branches were the last place they should occur.[9] Others agreed, that 3i was in danger of becoming 'top-heavy', and that cuts, both at head office and branch level, were necessary.[10] In rebuttal of criticisms Chief Executive Ewen Macpherson could point to the fact that 3i still retained an extensive network of seventeen area offices, several times greater than its nearest competitor, and an essential part of the continuing business generation of the Group.[11]

Cuts in staff were also related to efficiency measures within the Group designed to improve communications and reduce bureaucracy. An efficiency audit had begun in 1989 when Bain and Co. had been commissioned to undertake a fifteen-month survey of the quality of 3i customer service and internal effectiveness. Bain conducted a series of interviews and opinion polls within the Group which pinpointed the need for improved internal communications. In response, a series of task forces was established to draw up proposals for improving the situation.[12] In addition a specialized human-resources committee, headed by Macpherson, was also set up to deal with organizational structure, career management, and key appointments.[13] A later report by John Hunt of the London Business School also singled out internal communication which, relative to rival financial institutions, was judged to score 'a double minus'.[14] In response, in early 1993 a series of reforms was initiated to synchronize and speed up information flows, particularly from management meetings, and to re-establish managerial gatherings outside 3i. These were similar to the earlier 'Group of 25' meetings but in a modified, more representative form comprising bi-annual meetings of a conference group of one hundred senior members of staff.

3i in Europe

While the later 1980s had seen the running down of some of the non-core activities and the rationalization of the Group structure, other areas which had developed over the decade remained in place. Although overseas expansion in the USA had been curtailed, investment through subsidiaries in Europe continued and expanded. This was partly a result of the different strategy adopted by branches which were established on the Continent, and partly due to differing market opportunities.

The Group's European connections had begun earlier, in the 1970s, with a series of general initiatives channelling investment into Britain. In 1973 ICFC signed an agreement with the European Investment Bank to make loans at favourable rates 'for productive investment in development areas'.[15] Later, in 1977, ICFC also began to act as a conduit for European Coal and Steel Community funds which were lent at low rates to create employment in areas affected by closures in these industries. Amounts lent under this scheme grew in subsequent years from £20 million in 1979 to over £46 million in 1982, by which time it was estimated that over 9,000 jobs had been created as a result of funded schemes.[16] A further European connection had been initiated in November 1973 when the newly merged FFI became a member and UK representative of 'Le Club', a group of European long-term credit institutions which sought joint, trans-national financing operations. Representatives of the participants were to meet regularly to discuss financial and legal questions of common interest.[17] The Club never had a major impact on the business of the Group and was seen by some as 'an organization searching for something to do'. Nevertheless it provided FFI with some useful contacts in Europe.[18]

Group initiatives related to making 3i's own investments in Europe, also started in the early 1970s following Britain's membership of the EEC. ICFC's original articles forbade overseas activity, but had been changed at Tindale's request to allow the expansion of the Corporation's interests in the Channel Islands. Proposals emerged in 1973 to establish representation in Brussels and to recruit European employees to be trained in the UK with a view to establishing branches on the Continent in the near future. An overseas division was established to help customers acquire links within the EEC, and the issues and mergers department began providing advice on European expansion.[19] Despite these initiatives, expansion was slow, and the proposed opening of branches was to be delayed until the 1980s. This was partly due to difficulties with exchange controls and also reflected the fact that the Group had adequate business opportunities in the UK.[20]

The situation changed during the 1980s with increased competition and the more expansive strategy which came with the corporate change to 3i. Increased determination to expand overseas was one of the considerations

behind the choice of the new name, since 3i was seen as an internationally recognizable symbol. The Boston office in the USA, opened in 1982, was the first major step in this new phase, but it was rapidly followed in January 1983 by the opening of the first European branch in Paris. A German office was opened in Frankfurt in 1986, later followed by an Italian office in Milan, and a Spanish office in Madrid in 1990. By this time two further French offices had been opened in Strasbourg and Lyon, following the traditional pattern of 3i business in ensuring a regional presence. A series of further links within Europe was built up through the creation of partnerships and investment in venture capital companies, including Gilde Venture Fund in the Netherlands and Inter-Risco in Portugal.

The French portfolio was developed successfully, making 25 investments in the first three years of operation and predicting over 100 investments after ten years of operation. By the end of the decade they were on schedule to meet this prediction, having made 70 investments at cost of £25 million, with a value of twice that amount. Authorized capital was increased from £50 to £100 million in 1989.[21] Most of the early investments took place in the pharmaceutical, textile, distribution, and industrial equipment sectors and were in development or growth capital areas rather than more risky start-ups. There were also comparatively few MBOs, thought to be discouraged by tax policy, although later these did begin to feature more prominently, representing 20 per cent of the portfolio by 1992. By this time 3i was estimated to have an over-all market share of around 5 per cent.

3i's German office expanded steadily, although the market proved diffi-cult to penetrate in some key areas. Awareness, among corporate executives, of the MBO/MBI concept was judged to be poor, yet thought to offer great potential, especially among the medium-range companies—the Mittelstand—which are a very strong component of the post-war German economic success story. 3i staff became aware of a gathering 'succession crisis', whereby estab-lished firms which had been built up by owner-managers now faced problems of transfer of ownership.[22] Polls undertaken indicated that the dominant con-cern among many of these owners was not maximizing realizations but rather ensuring a continuity of commitment to the local economy. This in turn pre-sented an opportunity to a long-term investor or equity partner, a course of action preferred by owners wary of selling out to larger corporations from out-side the region.[23] Set against this potential was the fact that the German eco-nomic environment was geared to comparatively lower rates of return for investors. The majority of 3i business in Germany, at over 80 per cent by 1992, was in support of the growing MBO/MBI market within a spread of industries including printing, light engineering, and building.[24]

3i's other non-USA interests continued during the 1980s including a joint venture with ANZ Grindlays in India and a wholly owned subsidiary, 3i Australia. The latter was supplemented by 3i's involvement in Business Loans and Equity Capital (BLEC), a joint venture with Westpac and AMP, which operates five offices in Australia and New Zealand. Another important joint venture was established in July 1990 when 3i signed an agreement with the Industrial Bank of Japan in Tokyo. By mid-1992 this had made over sixty investments in small- and medium-sized Japanese firms.

Despite this continuing global presence, some of which had been built up over a number of years, 3i's overseas strategy gravitated towards Europe. Foulds had at one point considered a widely spread global strategy to be an integral part of the Group's forward planning, although he admitted that some activities outside France, Germany, and the USA were somewhat speculative and might be considered as peripheral.[25] The negative experience in the USA and the general trend towards a return to core activities further sharpened the focus of this strategy, however. Continuing and strengthened interest in Europe took a different form to that undertaken by 3i Ventures in the USA, and saw the Group sticking to its last in promoting what had, by the end of the 1980s, become traditional activities, notably equity-based investments and the MBO/MBI sector. The European market was regarded as one of the most potentially lucrative, with opportunities enhanced by the wave of market reforms on the agenda after 1992.[26] Certainly in areas such as MBOs there remained a disparity between Britain and the rest of the Continent, pointing to the prospect of a significant expansion of investment opportunities.[27]

3i in the City

During the 1980s the 3i Group significantly expanded its presence as a large-scale City investor. In some ways, this led on from the merger between ICFC and FCI, which had freed the Group from the nominal constraints of the Macmillan gap, but it also reflected the opportunities which arose in the immediate economic environment. Since the merger in the early 1970s FCI had remained a separate entity within the Group, continuing a larger-scale loan-based business administered by a small group of staff. Renamed as 3i City Office, and headed by Ewen Macpherson, however, it began a series of innovative investment strategies which marked a new phase in the Group's development.

Economic difficulties in the early 1980s provided the opportunity for City Office to become involved in recovery finance, aiding the restructuring of fundamentally viable companies which were experiencing problems. Refinancing packages were put together in association with merchant banks, including Rothschild and Morgan Grenfell, with 3i acting as 'cornerstone' investor. In the case of Aurora, for example, its Special Steels division had experienced a severe downturn in its market and created balance-sheet problems which threatened the whole company. 3i took the view that the rest of the Aurora Group was sound, and partially underwrote a rights issue in 1983, following which the group returned to profit. Recovery investments were also undertaken at Weir Group, Benjamin Priest, Newman Industries, BSR International, and Dunlop, for example.

Pressure from competition in the loan market led the City Office to develop new loan-based products, extending the trend begun with drop-lock loans in the 1970s. As with recovery finance, developments were frequently driven by the exigencies of the market, as in the case of Deep Discounted Securities (DDS) following the budget of 1984. DDS loans incurred no interest payments during maturity, and therefore enabled borrowers to gain substantial cash-flow benefits. The first DDS was issued to William Collins within one week of the Finance Bill in August 1984. Loan business also included loans to Alcan to fund the purchase of British Aluminium and a joint scheme with Cadbury Schweppes to acquire a North American subsidiary.

Importantly, the City Office also moved beyond loan-based investments and, in some ways, began to mirror traditional ICFC investment practice in seeking equity. This was to be on a larger scale, however, and often

LDV Limited

PREVIOUSLY KNOWN AS FREIGHT ROVER, this business was merged with Daf in 1987. Although it has always been profitable it was forced into receivership when its Dutch parent collapsed early in 1993. Daf's local management quickly prepared a proposal for a management buy-out which was accepted by the receivers and within a few weeks 3i had agreed to underwrite the equity requirement. Time was of the essence in preserving the business intact and the purchase was completed only two months after the receivers were called in. Of the £6.5 million equity investment, 3i syndicated £2.5 million leaving it with an investment of £4 million, representing 27.7 per cent of the equity but with the bulk in the form of preference shares. Management and employees were allocated shares and options representing 55 per cent of the company.

The company continued to trade profitably after the acquisition, exceeding the forecasts prepared for the MBO in both turnover and profit. In its first 8-month accounting period it reported sales of £80 million and profit before tax of £8.6 million, both well in advance of forecast. Most significantly, the cash position has been materially strengthened allowing plans to enhance the product range to be accelerated and significant capital expenditure within the plant to be undertaken.

As a result of this buy-out a potential closure has been averted and a profitable part of the UK motor industry now employing over 1,200 people has been preserved.

involved underwriting or syndicating deals with other major City institutions. City Office was involved in some of the larger MBOs of the mid-1980s, including Westbury, Mecca Leisure Group, VSEL, and Swan Hunter. The syndications unit within of City Office, headed by Brian Larcombe, had a pioneering role in developing the market for this type of larger MBO, and 3i's comprehensive information memoranda broke new ground in formalizing what had generally become a rather haphazard information system. As Rupert Wiles recalled, 3i's memoranda began to be treated 'like a prospectus' by other City institutions.[28] Between 1980 and 1985 City Office was the lead investor in over sixty deals.

In developing a new range of activities, City Office began to generate its own brand image among the finance community. This was not based on a single product, however, as the division tended to adapt rapidly to opportunities generated by the market, some of which had a relatively short cycle. Recovery finance, buy-outs, DDS loans, and mezzanine finance were all examples of this trend. This path, though diverging from the activities traditionally associated with FCI, in some ways converged with ICFC traditions. Many of the early diversifications at ICFC, as we have seen, were driven by a degree of opportunism. Also, a greater flexibility in terms of finance packages, most notably equity involvement, mirrored ICFC methods.

A separate City Office, however, developing its own persona, was eventually seen to be working against Group cohesion into the late 1980s. In addition to a developing rivalry between the City Office and the regional offices, qualms began to be expressed about the exposure which came with some of the larger deals which were being done. Convergence between the methods of City Office and ICFC traditions had finally broken the dichotomy which kept ICFC and FCI apart during the 1970s. This meant that when the logic of City Office continuing as separate entity was called into question, as it was during the phase of returning 3i to its core, a decision to consolidate its functions throughout the Group was easily arrived at. City Office functions were dispersed through the Group into the regions, leaving only a large company unit at head office.

Flotation

One of the most important developments at 3i in the 1980s was undoubtedly the return of the fundamental question of its ownership. The banks had increasingly come to see 3i in a competitive light as they themselves had moved more into term-loan business from the 1970s onwards. With establishment of their own venture capital subsidiaries in the 1980s this feeling became more acute and 3i began to look like 'trade diversion rather than trade creation'.[29] This feeling had existed in various degrees since the foundation of ICFC in 1945, of course, but had become more intense due to contemporary developments. In addition, circumstances had changed in two significant ways in the 1980s, placing the possibility of the banks relinquishing their ownership of the company firmly on the agenda.[30] First, some of the banks had experienced problems generally and were in need of the capital which a sale of 3i would generate. Tighter capital requirements by the Bank of England had placed increased pressures on the clearing banks in the mid-1980s, adding to the greater difficulties resulting from the over-exposure in various foreign investments. These included the difficulties which had emerged in the less-developed countries in servicing their debts, calling for extensive rescheduling and write-downs. The Midland were under particular pressure, having also been weakened by losses connected with Crocker National Bank in California.[31]

The second change came from within the Bank of England itself, which had traditionally acted as a guardian, but had increasingly seen its relationship with 3i as compromising its independent, regulatory role. The Bank began to acquiesce on the ownership question and contemplated relinquishing its own holding, which, since the increase which came with the formation of FFI, had remained at just over 15 per cent. (See Table 8.1.)

Table 8.1. *Shareholders 1982 (% holdings)*	
Bank of England	15.02
Bank of Scotland	3.12
Barclays Bank	18.86
Lloyds Bank	13.70
Midland Bank Group	18.03
Royal Bank of Scotland Group	7.58
NatWest Bank Group	23.69

The decision to restructure the ownership of 3i was bound to promote controversy and once the idea had been put forward, initially by the Midland, real problems of lack of unanimity followed. The Company's Articles of Association required that the consent of all the shareholders be given before any one shareholder could sell their interest, and various suggestions and tentative offers which emerged provoked varying degrees of dissent.[32] Initially there was a reluctance on the part of some banks to agree to a flotation and thus strengthen the balance sheet of a rival bank in difficulties. Later NatWest upset negotiations, exploding a 'land mine' by letting it be known that, contrary to being sellers of 3i, they were interested in buying the whole Group.[33] The other banks firmly rejected this proposal, being reluctant to see 3i under the control of one rival, particularly since many of the companies on 3i's portfolio held accounts with banks other than NatWest. The banks also discouraged approaches from non-banking institutions interested in a complete or partial takeover, including Citicorp and the Prudential.[34] Despite these difficulties a degree of unanimity was eventually reached, and in February 1985 the shareholders asked Morgan Grenfell to advise them on the disposal of part or the whole of their shareholdings 'in a manner that would endeavour to maintain the position and character of 3i as a provider of long-term finance to UK industry and commerce'. The following September a formal set of proposals was submitted by the Board of 3i to change the basis of ownership.[35]

Throughout this process the role of the Bank of England was one of central importance. As the unofficial protector of ICFC the Bank had exercised its control in a gentle but firm way, in conformity with the traditional unofficial influence which it exercised over the clearers in more general matters, before the more formal regulations which came into force in 1981.[36] We have seen in previous chapters how, from the process of formation onwards, the Bank of

England had acted as the guardian of ICFC. This was no less the case in the early 1980s when the Bank had, as Sir David Walker saw it, 'kept a moderately tight rein' on the clearers:

On the whole the Bank of England's instinct was to keep the shareholders together and not allow them to rock the boat. In return the Bank thought that 3i should be ready, and on occasion it was ready, when the need arose, and where the Bank of England said 'this is a case where we think you ought to be ready *pro bono publico* to go a little bit further in the scale of cost pricing the terms of your support . . . than you might have done on a purely commercial basis'. We thought there was a sort of *quid pro quo* about that.[37]

Tensions had developed in the 1980s which made this mutually beneficial, 'paternal'[38] relationship untenable to a certain degree, however. The formal establishment of the Bank of England as the regulator of the banking system had created a conflict of interest, given its role as both regulator and shareholder of 3i which was authorized as a bank. At the same time, somewhat paradoxically, although formally their regulator, there was also a growing tendency within the Bank of England to intervene less in the business of the banks, in line with the more *laissez-faire* government policies of the 1980s.[39] Taking this into account the Bank decided that, although it was not the prime mover in the case, it would be prepared to sell its share of 3i in support of a sale by the clearers. It did this with a certain degree of resignation. Clearing bank ownership, always a troublesome concept, was perhaps an idea which was finally past its time. As Sir David Walker later put it, 'It's a bad formula. It may have been a good formula in the 1950s, but it's a bad formula now'.[40] The Bank now limited its intervention merely to expressing a hope that whatever the outcome of the ownership question, 3i should maintain its long-term stance in the unquoted sector.[41]

The proposal for flotation put forward by 3i's Board in September 1985 recognized the immediate importance of approaching the Inland Revenue, following the unequivocal opinion of 3i's counsel, in order to get the Company recognized and taxed as an investment company, rather than, as it was taxed then, as a trading company. This process is described in detail in Chapter 14. The then current taxation status, an anomaly from the outset given the nature of ICFC's business, had made little difference historically; but the possibility of flotation transformed the situation. If 3i were to be floated it was deemed most appropriate that it should be as an investment trust, but the necessary prior conversion into an investment company could give rise to a very large tax payment. Flotation as an investment trust would avoid this and, it was hoped, would have the further benefit of affording some relief from the immediate pressures of the stock market. Investment trust status had become the major objective of the Board of 3i in response to the prospective loss of their traditional ownership which, despite its occasionally turbulent nature, had afforded the Company a degree of protection from the pressures for short-term performance. These concerns were outlined in the proposal under the heading 'Preservation of 3i's Special Role' which included a succinct plea on behalf of a continuation of its long-term role:

We could not easily accept a situation in which market pressures forced us to abandon or severely modify these long-term policies in order to meet short-term income demands. It would be possible greatly to increase the short-term returns but only at the expense of cutting out new investments in high-risk areas where short-term income is not available and by forcing the realization of immature investments. Many of our customers welcome 3i as a shareholder because it is able to identify with their own needs and to accept a partnership role over a long period. In our view it would have been impossible to build such a large and valuable portfolio if we had not been able to give these assurances and had not the established reputation which now exists.[42]

Another, more problematic scenario than short-term market pressure was also envisaged at 3i—-the possibility of control by a single shareholder and dismemberment in order to maximize an immediate return, coupled with the probable running-down of the active investment business. Numerous safeguards could be built in to the flotation to prevent this, but these would have the effect of depressing the share price, and thus would involve a commitment on behalf of the present shareholders to preserving the long-term future of 3i by forgoing an immediate higher return. 3i proposed an approach to the Stock Exchange Investment Protection Committee to explore the possibility of a

restriction on shareholdings to a 15 per cent maximum, similar to that in the Jaguar sale, to be in force for the first five years following the sale, and also for a golden share to be held by the Bank of England. Alternatively the same effect could be obtained if the clearing banks retained a substantial proportion of their shares.[43] This was the solution preferred by 3i and ultimately the one chosen by its shareholders. The report which Morgan Grenfell had submitted to the clearing banks had explored numerous general possibilities including a private placing, sale to one institution, and breaking up the various parts of the Company for separate sale. In response 3i reiterated its preferred solution, the one finally chosen: flotation as an investment trust following the settlement of the Company's tax status.[44]

The initial proposal was, as it turned out, rather optimistic in terms of the time this process was envisaged to take, estimating that, Inland Revenue permitting, a listing would be obtained in mid-July 1986. This schedule was designed to take account of the calendar of government privatizations then planned and to be as far in advance of a prospective general election as possible.[45] In the event of recalcitrance by the Inland Revenue it was recognized that the process of pursuing the case with the Special Commissioners and, if necessary through the Court, would substantially delay the flotation. Buoyed by Counsel's opinion, 3i was hopeful that an early flotation would take place and, for good measure, pressed for the opportunity to raise up to £100 million additional capital in the issue.[46]

These hopes of an early flotation were short lived. Negotiations between the clearing banks and 3i went on for around three months at the end of 1986, with Warburgs being brought in as advisers to the process. These negotiations were well advanced by February 1987 when the problem of valuation arose, as it was destined to do a number of times in the future. On this occasion some of the clearers thought that 3i was being valued too cheaply in the light of recent sales of the Clydesdale and Yorkshire banks and the sale of Morgan Grenfell to Deutsche Bank, and thus the issue of a private sale to a single institution was again raised.[47] This came to nothing, but it had served to delay proceedings yet again, and it was not until the following year that the Inland Revenue was finally formally approached. They immediately raised objections to the change of tax status for 3i. After considering a series of rather convoluted definitions and precedents for what might be termed trade and what might be termed investment, an initial judgement was passed. 'Inevitably when one is considering questions of fact and degree and one is looking at a wide spectrum, there will be a substantial grey area in the middle. On the evidence at present before us we think that 3i's [*sic*] falls well on the trading side of that spectrum.'[48] In contrast, 3i saw the issue as black and white, and the lengthy process of appeal was duly set in train.[49]

With delays in getting started, the considerable time-lag before the successful conclusion of the tax case in 3i's favour, and a missed opportunity to sell while the market was at its peak, it was not until 1991 that plans for the flotation of 3i were finally deemed ready to be unveiled and the market was judged to be favourable. There was also general speculation that the clearers were keen to float in advance of a possible Labour victory in the summer of 1992 raising the old spectre of nationalization.[50] Barings were appointed to manage the flotation and were expected to take a lead underwriting role. They were joined by Cazenove in the following November. The official announcement of an impending float was made in October 1991—over six years after the initial proposal. 'Impact day' was not finalized but was expected to be as soon as practicable in the spring of 1992, when the price of shares would finally be announced. It was expected that the flotation would be worth around £1.2 billion. At least two of the clearing banks, Barclays and NatWest, announced their intention to remain as long-term shareholders, but as expected, the Bank of England, in view of its supervisory responsibilities under the Banking Act of 1987, decided that direct involvement was no longer appropriate and that it would sell its entire holding, which now stood at 14.67 per cent. 3i was at pains to stress, both in communications to the press and in a letter circulated to all investee companies, that flotation would not affect its role as a long-term investor. In the end, this particular exercise was called off in the face of deteriorating market conditions in early 1992 in the run up to the General Election which took place in April.

3i in the 1980s

From the early 1980s, profound changes had taken place both within 3i and throughout its environment. Against the background of radical economic restructuring in Britain the organization had remade its image and internal organization under the new name, and had greatly expanded its activities and its sphere of operation. A distance had opened up between 3i and the old ICFC, unwelcome in some quarters, hailed in others, as the new 3i had seemingly regenerated itself, embracing the new enterprise culture. Such was the rapidity of change in the 1980s, however, that relative to parallel developments in the financial community, in particular the rise of the venture capital industry, 3i still demonstrated a powerful traditionalism.

The 1980s were years when fundamental questions of ownership and entrepreneurial empowerment were pushed to the top of the political and economic agenda. As we have seen, this had important repercussions on 3i's business, creating the opportunity to expand the pioneering work which had been undertaken in MBO and, later, MBI support. Within a turbulent atmosphere 3i had, unlike some nascent rivals, been able to retain a grasp of basic tenets—the

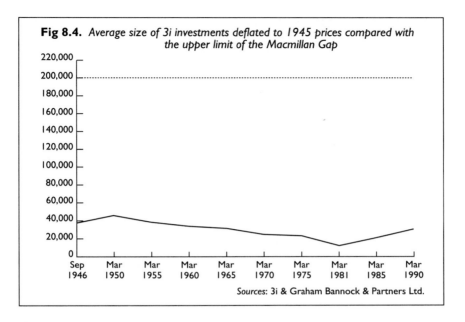

Fig 8.4. *Average size of 3i investments deflated to 1945 prices compared with the upper limit of the Macmillan Gap*

Sources: 3i & Graham Bannock & Partners Ltd.

need for long-term commitment on the part of the investor, a readiness to fund more risky start-up and development projects, and a firm commitment to the small- and medium-sized firm sector. It was a matter of perspective whether or not this was viewed as overbearing conservatism or underlying strength.

The questions of ownership and empowerment which had changed 3i's market-place had been brought to bear on the organization itself with the decision by the clearing banks to sell a substantial proportion of their interest. This process had a number of dynamics ranging from inter-bank rivalry and capital shortages to perceived conflicts in competitive operations. The delay in flotation brought its own difficulties, but the effect of the proposed change in ownership again raised questions of tradition versus change. What would be the effect of pressures from the market on a publicly quoted 3i, finally cut off from the benign paternalism of the Bank of England and, some feared, constrained to demonstrate profits in the short term? Unease ranged from the specific concerns of the customer base to the wider concerns of those people, including past chairmen, with an eye to the broader role of 3i in a national context. If the Company had, as many agreed, demonstrated an ability to combine commercial astuteness with a national economic imperative by successfully operating within the Macmillan gap, it was by no means clear that the gap was yet closed.

Conclusions

If the Macmillan gap remained, 3i had at least played an important part in attempting to fill it. The gap had, from the beginning, been a notional figure in terms of its exact limits. Macmillan put the upper threshold at around £200,000, and this was eventually enshrined in ICFC's early operating parameters. Piercy, writing in the later 1930s, had placed it lower, at around half this figure.[51] The question of definition was imprecise to begin with and has been constantly shifting historically. Changes in the strategy of competing sectors of the banking industry and capital market have raised and lowered this threshold many times. The rise of venture capital investors and the short-lived Unlisted Securities Market are more recent examples. Bearing this caveat in mind, if we do accept the larger of these two figures as signalling an area where difficulty in raising funds might be found, how has 3i performed historically? Figure 8.1 shows ICFC and 3i average investment size deflated to 1945 values against a constant Macmillan gap. It is interesting to note the general stability of the average size of investment and also that this average is well below the limit. Even during the later years of 3i, when larger-scale investments were undertaken, the average remains fairly constant.

We have seen that ICFC and 3i remained only informally linked to national economic imperatives, including the closing of the Macmillan gap. In the light of the criticisms aimed at the finance sector—that it has failed to support British manufacturing industry in particular—we have seen how the tradition of investing in this sector has been a feature of the Group's operations since the earliest years. While it is true that the proportion of investments in manufacturing industry has declined marginally over the years, when set against the general sectoral pattern of the post-war economy, 3i's involvement remains committed. As Table 8.2 shows, in 1990 the manufacturing sector in national terms has been reduced to less than 10 per cent, whereas 3i investments in manufacturing continue at over 50 per cent.

3i's continuing commitment to provide equity-related funding has also remained a constant feature throughout its history. Although, from the early years onwards, equity has proved difficult to obtain, and the problems of liq-

Table 8.2. *Distribution of 3i portfolio compared with number of UK businesses registered for VAT in 1990*

	3i	%	Vat registrations	%
Agriculture	56	1.4	175,000	10.2
Manufacturing & Extraction	2,090	50.7	158,900	9.3
Construction	113	2.7	270,200	15.8
Distribution, Hotels, & Catering	817	19.8	597,500	35.0
Transport & Communication	165	4.0	73,600	4.3
Services	885	21.4	433,900	25.4
	4,126		1,709,100	

uidity have persisted due to the lack of a secondary market, 3i has consistently attempted to structure investments to include some equity component where appropriate. In doing so it has acted to replace a market in smaller share issues by providing an institutional substitute. The long-term nature and spread of the 3i portfolio has meant that short-term realization pressures have been largely obviated. In an interesting postscript, as ownership of 3i becomes spread more widely and its own shares become marketable, the Group will finally take up the intermediary role in the capital market which Macmillan originally envisaged.

While the 3i Group has continued to provide long-term equity-related funding to the small- and medium-sized firm sector, much of it to manufacturing industry, it has also historically been adaptable or opportunist in seeking investments. This has at least partly been driven by necessity, from competition or from self-preservation. Lord Piercy began this tradition in order to support his determination that ICFC should survive during its difficult early years, and successive leaders have adapted and reshaped the Group in order to meet the needs of their own environment. The Group has featured a creative tension between traditionalism, exemplified in the culture which grew to surround ICFC, and change, notably in the frenetic atmosphere of the 1980s. It is this duality of tradition and adaptablity which has served to make 3i such a distinctive organization.

NOTES

[1] Chairman's Statement, *3i Annual Report*, 1988; D. S. Sach 'Property Investment', memo, 23 Nov. 1989, 3i.

[2] For an interpretation of this conflict of cultures see below, Ch. 12.

[3] D. Marlow, interviewed by R. Coopey. See also Ch. 12 below.

[4] G. M. J. Richardson, 'Corporate Identity and Reorganisation', 12 Feb. 1985, 3i.

[5] Robert Smith, interviewed by R. Coopey.

[6] E. Macpherson, 'Organisation Change', 1 Oct. 1992, 3i.

[7] Ibid.

[8] In 1992 the property was sold to Pearl Assurance.

[9] 'City Comment: Doors Closing as 3i Trims Sails', *Daily Telegraph*, 26 Nov. 1992.

[10] 'Jobs Go as 3i Shuts Five Offices', *Financial Times*, 2 Oct. 1992; F. Harber, interviewed by R. Coopey.

[11] Macpherson, 'Organisation Change'; Paul Whitney of CIN notes that the branch network is a crucial, if expensive, feature of 3i's operation, which competing venture capital funds cannot realistically hope to emulate. P. Whitney, interviewed by R. Coopey.

[12] D. Marlow, 'Consultancy Review of Working Methods', 19 Oct. 1989, 3i; id., 'Efficiency Improvement Programme', 11 May 1990, 3i.

[13] E. Macpherson, 'Human Resources', 3 Mar. 1992, 3i.

[14] 'Ewen Macpherson's After Dinner Speech at Creaton', 11 Feb. 1993, 3i.

[15] Bi-Monthly Management Meetings, Minutes, 31 July 1973, 25 Sept. 1973, 3i, B33.

[16] FFI, *Annual Reports*, 1980, 1981, 1982.

[17] Original members of the Club were: Credit National, France; Finance for Industry, UK; Finansiersingsinstituttet, Denmark; The Industrial Credit Company, Ireland; Istituto

Mobiliare Italiano, Italy; Kreditanstalt für Wiederaufbau, Federal Republic of Germany; and Société Nationale de Credit a l'Industrie, Belgium.

[18] D. Millard, interviewed by R. Coopey. For a discussion of the Club, and the operating methods of its members, see below, Ch. 15.

[19] ICFC, '1973 Corporate Plan', *passim*; Bi-Monthly Management Meetings, Minutes, 31 July 1973, 3i.

[20] J. Foulds, interviewed by R. Coopey.

[21] 3i International Update, 22 Nov. 1989.

[22] Andrew Richards, interviewed by R. Coopey. A similar succession problem has been found to exist in Italy, paralleled by the concerns over local control of the economy. Jonathan Bliss, interviewed by R. Coopey.

[23] Loan business, tied to equity in the traditions of 3i, is difficult in Germany, being hampered by corporate law which prevents lenders from taking a shareholding.

[24] Andrew Richards, interviewed by R. Coopey. For a discussion of the overall problems associated with investment in Germany see below, Ch. 15.

[25] LBS Meeting, 1988.

[26] 'Venture Capital in Europe: Its Role and Development', EVCA Venture Capital Policy Paper, 1993.

[27] G. Bannock *Attitudes to Breaking Out In Europe*, 3i, 1990; B. Chiplin, J. Coyne, and M. Wright, *Management Buy-outs: The Prospects in Continental Europe* (1989).

[28] Rupert Wiles, interviewed by R. Coopey, 18 May 1994.

[29] Sir David Walker, interviewed by R. Coopey, 11 Nov 1992.

[30] The suggestion that the banks dispose of their interest in 3i had been rejuvenated by the company itself in the late 1970s, but was then firmly rejected by the shareholders. Sir Eric Faulkner, interviewed by T. Gourvish, 13 Dec. 1991.

[31] *Financial Times*, 14 Oct. 1991, 2; Sir John Cuckney, interview.

[32] Cuckney, interview.

[33] Sir David Walker, interview.

[34] Ibid.

[35] 'Proposals on the Future Ownership of Investors in Industry Group PLC (3i)', 13 Sept. 1985, 3i.

[36] Informal controls are taken to mean interest rate control, limits on hire purchase lending, call for special deposits, and ceilings placed on lending.

[37] Sir David Walker, interview.

[38] Sir Eric Faulkner, interview.

[39] Lord Caldecote, interview.

[40] Sir David Walker, interview.

[41] Robin Leigh-Pemberton, quoted in *Financial Times*, 14 Aug. 1985, 10.

[42] 'Proposals on Future Ownership', 4.

[43] Ibid., 6, 10, App. II.

[44] Ibid., 8.

[45] Ibid., 1, 9.

[46] Ibid.

[47] Sir John Cuckney, interview.

[48] E. McGivern to D. R. Clarke, 28 Apr. 1988, 3i.

[49] See below, Ch. 14.

[50] *Evening Standard*, 4 Oct. 1991. Concern over this issue had arisen within 3i before the election of 1987, when a campaign was mounted better to inform targeted politicians in the Labour Party of the nature of 3i and its business, in the hope that this would avoid political predations.

[51] W. Piercy, 'The Financing of Small Businesses', *British Management Review*, 3 (1938), 35.

Part Two

An Insider's View

Eight Essays on Aspects of 3i

by Donald Clarke

Chapter 9

Inventing the Wheel: 3i as Innovator

A Unique Institution

BY COMMON CONSENT 3i is unique. It is not like a bank, or a typical venture capital company, nor does it resemble a finance company, although it has characteristics in common with all of these. Even the US rating agencies, for whom classification is all important, agreed, when they first attempted to rate it in 1980, that 3i was unique. Indeed when one of them returned a few years later to review the rating they said it was by then 'even more unique'.

This uniqueness has caused continual headaches, particularly for those concerned with regulating the financial system. All was well until the 1979 Banking Act became law, because 3i fell informally under the aegis of the Bank of England which recognized the oddities and understood the differences. For example, we operated in the inter-bank market but were not a bank. Did our borrowings and lendings therefore affect the money-supply numbers? Clearly the long-term borrowing and lending did not, but the short-term activity seemed to straddle the dividing line between the monetary sector and the rest. We carried on doing what suited us and kept the Bank informed.

But with the passing of the Banking Act something had to happen. 3i took deposits for liquidity purposes and could not continue to do so without a licence, either for banking or for deposit-taking. It did not meet all the requirements to be a bank; it did not, for example, offer current accounts, and we were unwilling to join the licensed deposit-takers which we feared might be regarded as inferior to the banks in credit terms. There was, however, a section of the Act enabling institutions which did not fully conform with the definition of a bank to be given specialized banking status. We thought that would suit 3i admirably and might avoid the stigma of licensed deposit-taking status; so we applied for recognition as a specialized bank.

The Bank of England unfortunately disagreed, while fully understanding the reasons for our concern. They accepted that 3i's credit standing was a great deal better than some of the institutions which were fully qualified as banks, and agreed that it seemed invidious to relegate us to the second division, but the specialized bank category was to be reserved for discount houses and 3i could hardly qualify as one of those. So licensed deposit taker it had to be, among the hire purchase companies, although the Bank did agree to the unusual step of stating publicly that licensed deposit-taking status did not of itself imply inferior credit standing. It was only a difference of kind, and in practice that distinction proved to be no disadvantage to our money market business.

Another anomaly was 3i's position under the Financial Services Act of 1987. This caught anyone involved in investment activity, and was intended for the protection of members of the public from unscrupulous operators seeking to part them from their savings, of which there had been a number of notorious examples. It could not be denied that 3i was in the business of investment and so it was required to register with one of the self-regulating bodies which represented the different areas of activity within the financial services field. But where did 3i fit? Yet again it was the odd man out. The sloppy, or perhaps excessively comprehensive, drafting of the Act meant that 3i was caught even though its business involved investing money with the public, not taking money from them. There are no self-regulating bodies for investors who need protection from themselves, so 3i had to come under the wing of the Securities and Investments Board, the watchdog body established by the Act.

These examples serve to illustrate the anomalous position 3i occupies in the financial system. Its unusual nature is derived from a combination of characteristics, none of them unique in themselves but together making up a body which fits no formal definitions. It provides loans but is not a bank; it makes equity investment in private companies but is not a typical venture capital company; it is a long-term investor but it takes overnight deposits; it accepts some responsibility for the whole small-business sector but each investment is on purely commercial terms.

Because nothing quite like 3i has ever existed there is no set of standards for assessing the kind of risks it takes; there are no investment products we can take down from the shelf; there is no universally applicable accounting system which gives a true and fair view of its business. There are no standards of liability and asset management, no comparable yardsticks for the returns its shareholders may expect, no analogues by which to judge 3i's creditworthiness, as the rating agents found.

So it is not boasting to say that 3i is a particularly innovative institution, with a record of original thinking in all aspects of its life which has continued throughout its history. Without innovation ICFC could not have got off the ground and the business could never have grown. The need for inventiveness has strongly influenced both recruitment policy and day-to-day management methods. We took on staff with original minds, gave them great freedom of action and encouraged them to take advantage of 3i's special opportunities and find solutions to its problems.

The Need for Innovation: Investment Products

The Cases Committee system was designed to reconcile these dedicated solutions to individual customer needs with our own income and capital requirements, and to ensure that the necessary innovation provided a proper balance of risk and reward. It fostered this process by requiring investment executives, then known as controllers, in the field to produce their own solutions to customers' financing needs and to test them for relevance and commercial value against the combined experience and judgement of the senior management sitting in committee. Where ideas found favour they could be disseminated throughout the Company by means of Cases Committee minutes, supplemented by the informal commentary of its secretary. They could then be adopted as standard practice but were also available for development and variation to meet changing situations. An example is the management buy-out. We lay no claim to originality with the concept, but we did find the solution to particular UK legal and tax problems which before 1979 made them almost impossible to accomplish.[1]

So it was a major achievement by the staff, including the tax and legal departments, to solve these problems and enable 3i to start up seriously in the business of management buy-outs, fostering in the process a whole new industry. But the MBO did not take long to spawn its own offspring, the management buy-in. Whereas the MBO was designed for existing management to become owners of their own businesses, the MBI catered for companies with inadequate management or which offered an opportunity for completely new management teams. This variant of the MBO was more difficult and riskier, needing a proactive approach from 3i, but at a time when the MBO market was becoming saturated with competitors from the venture capital industry the MBI provided a welcome source of business and one which was much more difficult to copy. For not only were we always looking for new ways of meeting customer needs, but also increasingly in the 1980s we needed new ideas which could not be easily copied—for example, because they needed expensive databases or costly backing—and which the volume of 3i's investments could justify.

ICFC at its formation was a highly specialized organization concentrating entirely on finding ways of providing capital in loan and share forms to companies which might have widely differing needs, so all the ingenuity of its investment staff was concentrated on this one requirement. The main problem was to reconcile the needs of its customers for appropriate kinds of capital, at the lowest cost, with its own need for a stream of income to meet its overheads, service its debt, and pay dividends to its own shareholders. The stream must flow continuously for ICFC's own credibility—and creditworthiness—to be maintained during the long and often indefinite period of the investment. It was all the more important in those early days to establish and maintain a stream of income because there was no means of unlocking the capital and reinvesting it. The clearing bank shareholders had to be convinced that further tranches of their loan and share commitment were justified by the results.

As far as possible, therefore, the income stream should be contractual, or, if it was not, then failure to pay should have some penalty attached to it. For a long-term investor with ICFC's passive approach, income was more impor-

TROUBLE

tant than influence and in the equity field there could be a trade-off between dividends and voting power.

Loan contracts relate only to the lending of money, payment of interest on it, and the repayment of capital. They do not incorporate any rights to own or control the business except in a default situation. However, in many cases the risks involved in lending cannot be fully compensated by an interest margin alone. It was apparent to its founding fathers that they must be prepared to go beyond the limits of available security if ICFC were not to be merely an extension of its shareholders' banking business. So the first innovation in 3i's history was to look beyond available security and to accept the risks inherent in unsecured lending. But in doing so there must be the prospect of a reward which would provide adequate compensation for that extra risk. It would be possible in theory simply to increase the interest rate in order to compensate for additional risk, but such solutions are counter-productive. The additional cost burden which the higher interest rate imposes itself increases the risk of failure and thus the lender's own exposure. The Loan Guarantee Scheme brought in by the Thatcher government in the early 1980s was an extraordinary illustration of the fallacy that extreme capital risks can be insured against by adding a premium to the interest rate. Money at risk is equity, whatever it may be called. We lobbied strongly against the introduction of loan guarantees: it made no sense for a small company which was already in debt to the limit of its bankers' willingness to lend, to be encouraged further into debt at a cost enhanced by the risk premium. This inevitably increased rather than reduced the risk of failure, but the ultimate nonsense was that it was not the borrowers who were protected, but the lenders. A more ridiculous scheme could hardly be imagined, but we were assured that the government were insisting on doing something for small business and this was the least awful of the options!

The easiest way of compensating for extra risk without adding to the interest burden on the company was by taking the right for some part of the loan to be converted into equity. Although this was never a popular mechanism it allowed the lender to defer a judgement about the potential of the company and in the meantime to maintain the all-important stream of income. But, although the interest rate could be kept at normal levels, there remained a prudential limit on the amount of debt a company could expect to service from its cash-flow. The ideal mechanism for meeting a company's need for capital without straining its capacity to meet interest payments was the combination of a loan, secured as far as possible on property, and share subscription making up the balance of the capital requirement. This allowed the customer to raise the full amount of capital he needed—it was not restricted only to the amount which could be borrowed on a fully secured basis. If the package was structured correctly the company would have a loan obligation which could be serviced without strain from its cash flow, combined with additional share capital which did not have to be repaid, and, on which dividends had to be paid only when sufficient profits were available. The new share capital and long-term loan capital not only allowed the company to acquire long-term income-generating assets but provided underpinning for its trade and finance creditors. With this combination of loan and equity ICFC also had what it wanted—a secured loan with a reasonably secure income flow and a stake in the business to compensate for the risks inherent in subscribing capital which could not be repaid.

Lord Piercy and his colleagues were willing to provide this additional, more risky capital if it was justified by the company's needs and prospects, but on terms which recognized the risk involved. If at the same time the package provided limited the customer's obligations to a level he could comfortably meet, then the chances of his success would be improved and ICFC would be properly rewarded.

ICFC's first and greatest achievement was thus the package of loan and equity. The capital needed by a company for its expansion might be provided only by way of secured loan or, in other cases, pure equity subscription; but between these extremes it was possible to subscribe whatever combination of loan and equity was appropriate for the company and gave ICFC an acceptable return. Unlike the bankers who set it up, the founders of ICFC were able to contemplate with equanimity the possible loss of some part of their investment, because it was in equity form and the risk of loss was therefore properly compensated by the possibility of gain from a rise in its value. ICFC could not, however, provide capital to all applicants: there were inevitably situations where the risks were too great to be matched by any acceptable proportion of the equity. The implication of accepting risks which took ICFC's share of the equity beyond 50 per cent was that the company would have to be taken over and managed by ICFC. This was out of the question not only because neither the skills nor the resources were available, but particularly because it would have breached a fundamental tenet of ICFC's philosophy, to back only those managements who were judged capable of running their own businesses successfully. ICFC was after all in business to preserve the independence of owner-managers, not to deprive them of it.

This combination of loan and share capital in packages which preserved independence, enhanced growth prospects and gave ICFC a proper return was the foundation of its business in 1945 and has remained its staple diet ever since. On this base were built a number of ingenious variations designed to meet the complex and very different needs of individual companies. It was apparent from the beginning that there was no single package solution to corporate capital requirements. Companies' existing capital structures varied widely, from those which were cash-rich with a strong capital base, to those which were over-borrowed and had inadequate capital to support further expansion. It was therefore possible for two companies with a similar capital requirement to be offered quite different packages. The well capitalized company with a strong cash-flow from its existing business might support and service a major expansion simply by borrowing. At the other extreme, the heavily borrowed company, whose cash flow was fully taken up with servicing existing debt, could only embark safely on further expansion by taking on new capital and reducing its dependence on borrowing.

Such packages therefore had to be tailor-made for individual companies, and many devices were invented by ICFC in its early days to meet the varying needs of customers and reconcile them with its own needs for income, security, and compensation for risk. The solutions were complicated by the basic fact that share capital represents not only a source of funds for the operation of the business but also a means of control, incorporating ownership rights as well as the right to income and capital. This integration of ownership and capital represented the most difficult obstacle to ICFC's acceptance not only as provider of capital but also as a shareholder and non-interventionist co-owner. It was to the resolution of this conflict that most ingenuity was applied in the early days. It was not until the 1970s that similar problems of differentiating loan products began to arise.

One early mechanism for separating ownership and capital was the preference share, which had long been common in the quoted market, and its adoption provided a useful device ensuring an adequate income for ICFC without affecting control of the customer's business. Preference shares carry rights to income and capital which rank ahead of those attaching to ordinary shares, allowing ICFC to receive a fixed annual dividend, but without conveying voting rights. Preference shares could be perpetual or redeemable on a fixed date, so they could either be permanent capital or the equivalent of long-term debt. Their disadvantage for ICFC was that they ranked behind all forms of debt and therefore carried not much less risk than the equity capital, but they had no residual rights to share in either income or capital. However, for many years they were useful in providing a strong income stream without watering down the ownership of the investee company. They were thus most effective in those cases where owners of well-established companies needed to make provision for estate duty without sacrificing ownership or floating their company's equity on the stock market. A combination of preference and ordinary shares maximized the capital taken out for a given share in the equity and at the same time improved ICFC's running income. But if earnings began to decline, preference shares became exposed and in times of economic recession heavy provisions were made. Those which were irredeemable had to be written down to values which reflected the higher dividend yields of recent years and redeemable preference shares were generally written off.

These potential disadvantages of preference capital were perceived early on and variants were devised to improve its defensive qualities. One such

Prontaprint

IN 1988, 3i ESTABLISHED ITS Management buy-in Programme—conducting a national advertising campaign in order to establish a register of potential management buy-in candidates. This was intended to find and then prepare selected managers for buy-ins, and also to foster a network of contacts in order to put management teams together. By 1994 this register had over 200 participants who had attended evening and weekend training and information-based seminars given by 3i.

One example of the success of this programme is the Prontaprint Group. In September 1992, 3i led a public-to-private management buy-in/buy-out of Continuous Stationery Plc contributing some £2 million to the purchase cost of £11.7 million, and taking 27 per cent of the equity. The new Chairman of Prontaprint was Richard Raworth, drawn from the 3i Management buy-in Programme. Prontaprint Group has three distinct businesses—a network of some 270 quick print and business service franchises under the Prontaprint name, a business form printer, Carwin Continuous, and Fairfield Graphics, a company specializing in thermal and ink-jet papers for digital imaging systems. In the first two years of private ownership Prontaprint comfortably exceeded its original sales and profits plan, at the same time repaying £3.2 million of its £5.2 million senior debt well ahead of schedule. Raworth puts this success down to the independence of being a newly private company—'it is the single-minded concentration of the executives on the core business without the "quoted company" distractions that has made this performance possible.'

was to give preference shares a limited participation in profits, allowing ICFC to share in the growth of corporate income even though they still had no rights to residual capital growth. A participating preference share carried a minimum fixed dividend and the right to additional amounts if the company's profit exceeded a predetermined level. This was a valuable bonus for ICFC, going some way to meet its need for a growing income stream, and it allowed rather higher prices to be paid for the shares, but of course it had limited value as an equity substitute in times of declining profits. Preference shares could also carry cumulative rights so that dividends not paid in unprofitable years were accumulated for payment when profits were restored. This too had value for both ICFC and the customer, but the experience of actually receiving deferred dividends once the profits slide had begun was not good.

The real breakthrough was the invention of the Convertible Preferred Ordinary Share, the CPO, commonly known within ICFC as 'Lincolns',[2] with variants including dividend accumulation and profit participation, which, as the name suggests, gave ICFC everything it could ask for. It carried both a preferential minimum dividend and preferential repayment rights, plus participation and accumulation if appropriate, together with the right to convert into ordinary shares in certain circumstances—usually on a sale of the company or flotation. Such rights were heavily loaded in favour of the outside investor and the shares would have been unmarketable without a particularly ingenious compensatory device. When the CPOs were converted to ordinary shares, usually at the point of flotation, the other shareholders received compensation in the form of a bonus issue of ordinary shares for the income they had foregone. The difference between their dividend income and that received by ICFC while it held the preferred ordinary shares was calculated, and this amount was credited to the ordinary shareholders in the form of a bonus issue of ordinary shares, which ICFC then purchased for cash. The ordinary shareholders, who would not normally have wanted to receive dividends, thus received a lump sum instead. ICFC got what it wanted in the form of dividends throughout the life of its shareholding, together with a capital gain on ultimate realization in compensation for the risk inherent in being locked in. The majority shareholders had the use of the capital subscribed or purchased by ICFC, plus income on ultimate realization pro rata to that received by ICFC, but in capital form.

In the loan field the staple product for many years was the long-term fixed-interest loan which mirrored the only available form of long-term debt available to larger companies. Mortgage debentures had been long established in the stock market—the first investment trusts, formed in the 1860s and 1870s, had as their prime function the purchase of debenture stocks. It was normal for the stock to be secured by fixed charges on the company's property— the only form of asset likely to retain its value as security over the very long time-scales needed to match the obligations of the life assurance companies.

The floating charge was a useful supplement to the fixed charge, allowing security to be extended from specified fixed assets to all a company's assets. The charge given by the company did not crystallize, and thus immobilize the assets until an event of default, and so the company was able to deal freely with its assets, subject to limitations on the amount of future borrowing, and to absolute constraints on the granting of prior charges. It was normal for a company's bankers to be the only loan creditor and to hold both fixed and floating charges over the company's assets. For ICFC to take security it was necessary for the shareholding banks to allow a prior charge to be granted on the company's fixed assets, while the bank retained its first charge on the current assets. ICFC then took a second charge behind the bank on the current assets and the bank accepted a second charge on the fixed assets behind ICFC. This arrangement, known as a 'sandwich' debenture, was essential if ICFC was to be able to do lending business at all. It was accepted by the banks at the outset and, despite the growth in competition between the banks themselves and between them and ICFC, the arrangement has remained unchallenged throughout. The banks have always reserved the right to compete with 3i on its own ground but they have never attempted to undo the 'sandwich' mechanism, which proved very workable in practice and allowed the interests of the banks and ICFC to be reconciled without unduly hampering the management of the customer company. Natural though such an arrangement seems, it appears to be almost unique in the world, the concept of the floating charge being unknown in many countries.

The investment products so far described, while innovative at the time of their introduction, quickly became standard techniques for providing loan and share capital and have survived more or less intact. But as economic conditions varied, so the needs of the smaller companies, and in particular the ambitions of their owners, changed. The dawning of the Thatcher era in 1979 gave rise to a more entrepreneurial attitude generally, as the profit motive became acceptable and the tax system allowed a higher proportion of profits to be retained. The dynastic family business also became a less significant part of the small-company scene as professional managers who had grown up with the large companies began to see that small was beautiful. The prospect of capital gains seemed to be a powerful motivator, encouraging middle managers to take on personal risks of a kind they would not previously have considered. As a result of this freeing of the entrepreneurial spirit a new breed of owner-manager began to appear, a professionally trained manager with high-level business experience, whose only problem was lack of capital.

In the late 1970s ICFC adopted the management buy-out, which had been developed in the United States. The idea of employee management taking over the business they were running had not taken off in the United Kingdom, partly because business was subject to the boom-and-bust consequences of inconsistent economic management, but also because the security of life in the large corporation was not worth abandoning for the risks of ownership when the rewards were taxed at ridiculous rates. Once the serious legal and tax obstacles to the MBO had been conquered it became an ideal vehicle for the new breed of entrepreneur. By providing the greater part of the capital and accepting a minority of the ownership 3i was able to facilitate their purchase of the division or subsidiary they managed. With parent companies looking to liquidate underperforming or incompatible parts of their business, local managements had an opportunity to become their own masters. In addition to solving the technical problems, 3i staff had to balance 3i's needs for income and compensation for risk with the existing owners' needs for a financial deal they could justify to shareholders and the management team's need to acquire assets at a price which would not involve excessive amounts of debt and put too heavy a burden on initial income flows.

The management buy-in was ambitious and perhaps even more ingenious, meeting as it did a new need for complete management teams to be brought in and installed in companies which lacked adequate management. This was more difficult to copy because it required a proactive approach, identifying companies in need of new management and putting together teams of experienced managers to go in and run them. The higher risks inherent in this kind of financing made it more difficult to do well but, having been attacked in its own MBO market, 3i's response was to find a less vulnerable variant.

The common feature in all these ways of investing capital in private companies is that they were all designed to meet a market need, particularly the requirement to leave owners in control of their businesses even though the bulk of their capital needs might be provided by 3i.

Innovation in Accounting

In accounting practice also, an area of activity not generally known for innovation—imaginative engineering perhaps, but not wholly new accounting practices—3i had its own unique methods. For many years the Annual Accounts were prepared on the standard basis appropriate for a trading company, reflecting the company's tax treatment but completely ignoring the value of its equity portfolio. For creditworthiness purposes a system which required assets to be written down but not up, and once written down never to be reinstated, was very suitable. Loan creditors of 3i could be sure that the asset base against which they were lending was rock-solid. There might be hidden surpluses, but there were no hidden deficiencies. This cautious policy, though admirable in establishing a strong balance sheet, was a constant source of concern to the auditors, Ernst & Young; successive senior partners have commented on this worry. 'Once a provision always a provision' became a watchword in the company: although the Inland Revenue might disallow a provision against an investment if the company concerned subsequently recovered, 3i would not reinstate the original cost but would regard the written-down value as the new base from which the investment's performance could be judged.

This policy was thought necessary because of the illiquid nature of our unquoted equity assets, and its worth was proved once and for all in the financial crisis of 1974–5. Before this the provisions charged in the accounts had not been matched by actual failures; as the provision fund grew, so the failures charged against it should have grown. But although individual provisions were always accepted as necessary, actual loss experience did not match that expected. It was a strange phenomenon that, with a portfolio the size of ICFC's, actual failures never reached the level of provisions despite the fact that failure was thought equally likely in all cases; the problem was to decide in advance which of the possible failures would actually happen. In 1973 the auditors prevailed on the Board to release some £3 million of the £10 million total provisions into profit on the grounds that it was no longer realistic and constituted a hidden reserve. Within two years the recession and its accompanying stock- and property-market collapse had forced the new FFI into making provisions of £20 million to show the only loss since 1946 and wipe out the greater part of its reserves. Included in those provisions was one of nearly £5 million to write off the recent investment in British Caledonian. It was carried thereafter at nil until its final disposal to British Airways produced cash proceeds of £100 million. At various times in the intervening period a range of values might have been attached to British Caledonian, but none would have been realistic by comparison with that final sale price. So, bearing in mind that the main purpose of the accounts was to demonstrate the company's creditworthiness and proof against any externally imposed shocks, we could see no justification for any carrying value other than nil.

For other purposes, of course, this was a hopelessly unrealistic method of accounting. ICFC was established to subscribe for all forms of corporate capital and its performance needed to be measured not only in terms of the income it earned by way of interest, dividends, and capital gains, but also by taking into account the growth in value of its equity portfolio. Under our conservative accounting methods losses and provisions were charged off against revenue and capital profits, but portfolio values were ignored.

For many years no account was taken of the growth in value of either unquoted or quoted investments, although those which were quoted could be easily valued, and all capital gains were brought into profit only when realized. EDITH, although a quoted investment trust, steadfastly refused to put a value on its unquoted portfolio on the grounds that there was no realistic way of doing so. We tended to agree, and when ICFC was forced by the 1967 Companies Act to give some information about the performance of its investments we stuck to the letter of the Act's requirements, obfuscating the whole question by giving aggregate details of ICFC's share in the profits, dividends, and retentions of those companies where we had equity investments but only based on their last filed accounts, which could be years out of date.

By avoiding valuations on the justifiable grounds that they would be too subjective, we undoubtedly produced an unrealistic performance record. This had long been recognized within the Company. The accounting standard on inflation which appeared at the end of the 1970s provided an unexpected opportunity to do something about it. The standard, in fact, was intended to apply to industrial companies, many of which had gone bankrupt in the high inflation period of the 1970s even while publishing nominal accounting profits. Those who were able to report profits only by including unrealized stock appreciation were understandably reluctant to publish real losses by taking out the inflation element, but ICFC had long before adopted the aim of attempting to invest the whole of our shareholders' funds in equity assets, that is, investments whose growth in value might offer some protection against an inflationary depreciation of the banks' own investment in 3i. By the end of the 1970s that objective had been achieved but normal accounting methods could not demonstrate its value.

The accounting standard on inflation specifically exempted 'investment entities' (a curious expression apparently invented for the purpose and not defined anywhere in the standard) and the auditors agreed that FFI could be regarded as such. We thought the exemption strange because it seemed at least as appropriate for an investment business as for any other. We assumed the Accounting Standards Committee had been unable to work out how to do it. For us the standard presented an opportunity to give shareholders a real, as opposed to a nominal, view of the Company's performance. The fact that we were exempted from strict compliance with a standard which was widely thought to be unrealistic allowed us to create our own version of inflation-adjusted accounts, which could truly take account of the effect of rising prices on a company which was essentially long-term in nature and needed to protect its locked-in shareholders from the ravages of inflation. This was one of the occasions when uniqueness worked to our advantage. The banks themselves, of course, had no such long-term assets, and their own shareholders were almost wholly unprotected against the depreciation of their capital.

In 1980 a set of accounts was produced which was innovative in form and revolutionary in its implications for FFI. In addition to the normal historic cost accounts, a balance sheet was prepared which included inflation adjustments to the cost of all those assets which were non-contractual in nature, principally equity shares and properties. Those which were contractual—mainly loans—repayable in fixed amounts and thus subject to depreciation for inflation were offset against the matching borrowings which were, of course, also subject to inflationary reductions in value. To the extent that there was a mismatch, either excess shareholders' funds would be financing loan assets and therefore unprotected against inflation, or loan liabilities would be financing equity assets and providing shareholders with additional protection against inflation but creating a gearing effect.

For the first time, and for this purpose only, values were attributed to equity assets. To avoid charges of subjectivity the values were arrived at by applying a simple multiple derived from quoted price-earnings ratios to investee companies' earnings. This formulaic method also allowed reasonable year-on-year comparisons to be made, even though it might not provide accurate absolute values in any particular year. By comparing the value thus arrived at with the historic cost increased by the RPI over the investment's life, it was possible to see to what extent value growth had exceeded or fallen short of inflation.

We were tempted to bring into the inflation-adjusted balance sheet the full value of investments, even where this exceeded the inflation-adjusted cost; but we were not concerned at that point with producing a fully valued balance sheet. The purpose of this exercise was specifically to determine the extent of the protection provided by equity and property assets against the erosion of shareholders' funds by inflation. The balance sheet so produced indicated realistically the degree of protection shareholders' funds had received by virtue of 3i's long term policies and its deliberate matching of contractual and non-contractual assets and liabilities. This balance sheet, more than any before or since, demonstrated 3i's true strength and resilience, showing that the growth in value of the equity and property assets had indeed outpaced inflation and so preserved the real value of shareholders' funds. Concern with balance-sheet strength has been a consistent feature of successive 3i managements, a policy which has seen it through all the vicissitudes of the UK economy, limiting its need to call on shareholders for new capital.[3]

The inflation-adjusted accounts were not the last or the most significant of the accounting innovations which 3i introduced. They were followed in 1986, when the accounting standard was abandoned, by the introduction of a full valuation of assets and its incorporation in a supplementary balance sheet. Its introduction, albeit as an informal addition to the 'legal' accounts, was encouraged by the rapid growth in values in recent years, by the very substantial realization profits which were arising and distorting the overall profit record, and by pressure from shareholders who were increasingly dissatisfied with what they saw as an inadequate return on their investment. The introduction of a second balance sheet in addition to, rather than in substitution for, the historic cost record was itself controversial, in particular as shareholder and press interest in the accounts grew but with a long-drawn-out battle in prospect between 3i and the Inland Revenue over the principal subsidiary's tax treatment, the management were disinclined to make any substantive changes in the legal accounts. It was also felt that several years' experience in the production of these accounts was necessary before they could be presented as a credible alternative to the historic cost accounts. There were also Companies Act problems in abandoning the historic cost accounts. We could only become an investment company for Companies Act purposes if we changed the Articles to prohibit distribution of capital profits, and only then could we bring in assets at value rather than cost. With our shareholders not unanimous on flotation and the possibility that they might demand a special dividend we thought such a move would be premature. The retention of the historic cost accounts was

Celebrating 3i's 1,000th Management buy-out—Sir John Cuckney (Chairman of 3i) with Bob Symms of Holden and Brooke, an old established manufacturer of hydraulic pumps.

therefore seen as being necessary for an interim period and it was only in 1991 that the historic cost and supplementary accounts were merged in an effort to produce figures which could more easily be compared with those published by investment trusts.

One of the subsidiary objects of the supplementary accounts was to establish 3i's valuation method as an industry standard which it could use in the event of flotation and would have to be followed by others holding similar port-folios. It also helped within 3i to focus management attention on the concept of 'total return'. This in 3i's case comprised the aggregate of net income from investments, realized capital profits, and the change in value of the remaining portfolio over the accounting year. By adding these three elements together we arrived at the amount by which the shareholders' interest in the business had increased over a year. This could be added to the dividend to show the total return. It is an extremely rigorous measurement technique because the return is effectively compounded. The total growth in shareholders' interest in each year is shown as a percentage of the opening capital for that year.

The method used for valuation became institutionalized, so that values

Tibbett & Britten Ltd

THIS COMPANY WAS BOUGHT in 1984 from its joint owners, Unilever and Van Gend en Loos, in an archetypal management buy-out. The management team raised £300,000 of the £5.3 million purchase price and took 75 per cent of the equity. The bank provided a loan of £3.5 million and 3i the remaining £1.5 million by loan, preference capital and equity representing the remaining 25 per cent of the capital. The buy-out took over 12 months to negotiate.

The company specializes in the collection, transport, and delivery of clothing to retailers, with Marks & Spencer as a major customer. From £27 million in 1983 turnover has risen to over £360 million ten years later and a pre-tax loss in 1983 has been transformed into a profit of £24 million, with operations in ten countries.

Tibbett & Britten has expanded consistently by organic growth and in recent years, by acquisition, by acquiring Lowfield Distribution in 1989 and Silcock Express in 1992 to facilitate its diversification.

Capitalized at £32 million on flotation in 1986 after two rights issues the company currently has a market value approaching £350 million and 3i retains a share stake in the company.

could be given subjective adjustment by those best qualified to make them—the line managers—within a rigid formulaic structure which ensured year-on-year consistency. The proof of valuation accuracy could never be absolute because investee companies' own fortunes could fluctuate wildly, but an important test was available in the treatment of reserves. We decided that a capital reserve should be created to receive all realized capital surpluses on the sale of investments and against which both realized and unrealized losses could be charged. A separate revaluation reserve was established which could be used only to record changes in the value of investments from year to year. It would rise if net values increased and fall if they fell. By showing separately the amount added to capital reserve, representing the actual profit realized on the sale of investments, and the amount deducted from revaluation reserve by the removal of those same investments at the previous year's valuation, we showed the world at large whether actual realized profits exceeded previous valuations, and thus whether our valuations had been optimistic or pessimistic. Over the whole period of the supplementary accounts the addition to capital reserve substantially exceeded the deduction from revaluation reserve, indicating under-valuation—at least in those cases where investments had been sold.

This difference provided great comfort to the management of 3i in demonstrating the consistently conservative valuation methods used from year to year. Inevitably, however, it created its own problems for shareholders attempting to arrive at a value for their own investments. To what extent could the excesses of realization proceeds over previous values be taken to imply undervaluations in the unrealized residue of the portfolio? The management view was that the balance of the portfolio was worth no more and no less than the figure at which it was valued in the year-end accounts. It was impossible to estimate convincingly what excess over that value a willing buyer might pay some time in the future. In the meantime they were unsaleable.[4]

In a situation where there were no analogues we not only had to invent our own accounting methods but had to justify them to the ever-widening con-stituency of interested parties—shareholders, auditors, rating agencies, invest-ment analysts, press, regulatory bodies, and not least, loan creditors. It was for the benefit of our bond and loan stock holders that 3i's Accounts in recent years also contained tables showing the extent to which the maturity of its borrow-ings was matched by that of its loan and other contractual assets. Tables were prepared projecting the lifetime maturities of both borrowing and lending which demonstrated consistently an excess of fixed interest loans being repaid over our obligations to repay 3i's own fixed interest debt and, on the variable rate side, an overall balance of maturities. These tables became more complex as we entered into swap arrangements to convert fixed-rate borrowing to vari-able, but they remained valuable and comforting statements to us and, I believe, at least some of our loan creditors. We were amused by the scepticism expressed by one senior New York banker. He could not believe we were not hiding a major mismatch somewhere; it was not done among the banks to reveal such sensitive information. For their part our own shareholders seemed to find the concept of matching assets and liabilities almost impossible to grasp; they were constantly asking for information about our interest-rate exposure and could not appreciate that there was none—a ten-year loan to a customer was financed by a ten-year borrowing, so we lived on the margin between what we paid and what we could persuade the customer to pay.[5]

Innovation as a Way of Life

If 3i was *forced* to be innovative in investment products and accounting meth-ods, it *chose* to be so in its marketing, although its problems in this field also stemmed from its unusual character. Making a virtue of necessity, its advertis-ing and public relations generally strove to emphasize its uniqueness and difference from other organizations. By 1983 it had become clear that the many millions spent on advertising and public relations over the years had had only a very limited impact. This was judged to be because FFI, as it was at that time called, was too anonymous in both name and function. ICFC itself was well-known in its market, but FFI had spread into related businesses, in each of which it had become a substantial player, and the overall perception of the whole business was confused. Its objectives were not clearly set out and the purpose of each part and its relationship to the whole was generally unknown. In addition, some widely believed misapprehensions were acting against the Company's interests. It was thought in some quarters that FFI was a government body and separate from ICFC, which was in the private sector. Others thought ICFC was the government body. It was not generally known that FFI was a highly commercial organization with a wide spread of interests.

So much of the innovative, witty, and widely admired advertising which had won ICFC awards—the first whole-page advertisement by a financial organization, the first in colour—had not achieved its main objective. At the same time competition was growing, from the shareholders themselves as well as from newly established funds, many set up by ex-FFI staff. The transformation of the corporate image by a redefinition of objectives, a new name, a striking and distinctive logo to replace the anonymous 'FFI', and the employment of graphic artists to design advertisements and brochures were all bold and innovatory and did much to bring the business to the centre of the financial stage.

By the time the FFI name was abandoned and the new, aggressive marketing stance adopted, the Company was already 38 years old. It was remarkable that sclerosis had not set in and that the same people who had been brought up in the old ICFC of the 1960s and 1970s were able to relaunch as 3i, Investors in Industry, with great success. The increased visibility, greater understanding of what 3i did, and the enormous growth in investment output which followed, were all achieved in spite of and to some extent because of, an extraordinary increase in competitive pressure which we chose to meet head-on. Many ingenious ideas flowed from its rebirth, in which all the old virtues were rediscovered and promoted, from the invention of the MBI to the 3i calendar, much sought-after and a source of Monday-morning cheer to a wide range of well-wishers.

There are many more examples of the imaginative and creative ideas which went to make 3i a great innovator in its field. They were not limited to the asset side of the business but, as Chapter 10 shows, the lack of any funding precedents forced us to adopt many imaginative devices for marketing 3i's debt. I hope these will illustrate the commitment to new ideas and new ways of doing things which saw it through the hazardous early years and which became a constant source of renewal, ultimately allowing a venerable and, in some eyes, stuffy institution to meet and overcome the fierce competition of the 1980s, while enjoying dynamic growth, producing record results and yet maintaining the basic principles on which it had been founded.

It was the chief source of pleasure in working for 3i that original thinking was encouraged and conformity discouraged. In the field there was a continuous search for new investment ideas to meet particular customer needs. At the strategy level we were proud of the Group's responsiveness, although it caused some dismay to staff to be told that we had no strategy other than opportunistic reaction to market changes—or gap-filling—and surprise to the shareholders when trying to decide what to do with their shareholdings.

For my part it was difficult to imagine a less exciting prospect in 1968 than the position of Company Secretary. It compared badly with the freedom and creativity of life in a provincial branch office, but the reality was quite different. There was even more freedom: to develop new ways of administering the business and of raising the funds which were its lifeblood—two of the many untypical functions which had fallen by default to the Company Secretary. When Larry Tindale suggested there were some improvements to be made in ICFC's management information I was not aware that the annual budget presented to the Board consisted of a single sheet of paper containing a forecast of gross investment and a detailed list of expense items. That gave plenty of scope for innovation.

The need to be continually devising new ways of doing things was quite tiring, and we undoubtedly reinvented the wheel more than once in seeking proprietary solutions, but it kept the organization vigorous, open minded and responsive, even into late middle age when many businesses might have gone into terminal decline.

NOTES

[1] See Ch. 7, p. 166.
[2] See Ch. 2, p. 43.
[3] See Appendix II for an example of an inflation adjusted balance sheet.
[4] See Appendix II for an example of the supplementary balance sheet.
[5] See Appendix II for an example of the matching tables.

Chapter 10

Investment Capital for British Industry: A Failure of Demand or Supply?

The Debate

ALTHOUGH THE FORMATION OF ICFC was a specific response to repeated complaints that the City in general, and the clearing banks in particular, had starved British industry and especially small business, of essential capital,[1] the same accusations have been repeated at intervals throughout 3i's life. It became a serious political issue in the mid-1970s with the election of the second Wilson government, and again as recently as the 1992 election, when a major plank of Labour's manifesto was the need for more investment, to be addressed by the formation of a National Investment Bank. The functions and investment criteria of this bank, as described in Labour's policy document, were indistinguishable from those of 3i laid down for ICFC in 1945 and from which it has never deviated.

It is as though nothing has happened over the intervening 50 years in the field of industrial investment, but 3i's experience during that period must surely be relevant to the debate. It has stood in the market continuously, offering capital for industrial investment, initially to smaller companies only but since the acquisition of FCI in 1973 to companies of all sizes, and as this chapter attempts to demonstrate it has almost always had ample funds to meet demand.

For the first 22 years of ICFC's existence the conditions imposed by the shareholders limited its access to funds and the uses to which they could be put.[2] The capital which was provided could in any case have been used by the banks themselves for industrial lending, which makes it difficult to argue that ICFC was bringing additional resources to bear. But once the last of the shareholders' loans had been capitalized and ICFC was set free to find its own sources of money, effectively from 1968 onwards, it became a genuine intermediary between the capital markets and industry. This unique position has provided a useful vantage point for observing the ebb and flow of demand for capital and the extent to which it could be met.

3i has always been demand-led, attempting to meet all justifiable requests for long-term and permanent capital and then financing its commitments by raising money wherever it can. In practice, new investment has normally outstripped the return flow of capital and income from earlier investments, and the portfolio has thus grown continuously. As a result, in almost every year since 1968 it has been necessary to find new funds from external sources in order to fill the gap between cash flowing out and that coming in. The success of these continuous efforts to find money should throw useful light on the question of whether British industry was ever genuinely starved of funds for profitable new investment.

Left To Our Own Devices

It had been the shareholders' agreement to external funding in 1959 which gave ICFC its first taste of freedom and an opportunity to test its independence. The banks were unwilling as always to give guarantees, but by this stage ICFC's balance sheet with £36 million of long-term income-producing assets was strong enough in its own right to provide acceptable security for a matching loan. It was thus possible to issue £10 million of $6\frac{1}{4}$ per cent Debenture Stock with a twenty-five-year maturity, secured by a floating charge on ICFC's assets. This first-ever issue was subscribed by the kind of institutions, principally life insurance companies, which subscribed for the publicly quoted loan stocks of larger companies and for gilt-edged stock. Because it was a long-term stock, and secured by a floating charge, its conditions placed tight restrictions on ICFC's ability to issue further stock ranking equally or ahead of it. Total borrowings secured in this way could not exceed one and a half times the company's capital and reserves and, with all available assets being charged in support of this borrowing, raising less well-secured or unsecured funds was virtually impossible. The amount which could be borrowed on such terms had implied limitations, because ICFC's reserves were not increasing rapidly and the only way to make room for a substantial amount of further debenture issues would be by raising new capital. Nevertheless this market provided an adequate source of funds for some ten years, as the shareholders' own loans were either repaid or converted into permanent capital.

As the banks' grip on funding was progressively relaxed, a series of 20- to 25-year debentures was issued, which proved fully acceptable to the institutions they were aimed at. Indeed the second issue of £10 million in 1960 was taken up in its entirety by the Prudential. However, by 1968, when I became Secretary of ICFC and responsible for its fundraising, some £60 million worth of debenture stock had been issued, and the amount outstanding was coming close to the limit of 1.5 times capital and reserves. In 1969 after one further issue of this kind of stock we found ourselves up against the ceiling. This was a critical point in ICFC's history; the shareholders' original responsibility to provide new capital had been fulfilled and they were unwilling to provide more, although they had no objection to our seeking new sources of debt. The Chairman, Lord Sherfield, in his Annual Statement for 1969 thought it necessary to sound a warning about the funding problems. Without referring directly to the shareholders' unwillingness to help, he commented: 'if ICFC is to continue to meet the demand for investment from the companies it serves it will need some assurance that the necessary resources will be there'.

First Efforts to Fill the Funding Gap

Larry Tindale's arrival ten years earlier had coincided with the new freedom to look elsewhere for funds. From the beginning he was concerned with the need to find new sources of money to supplement the commitment of the banks during a period when demand was being stimulated by rapid expansion in the branch network and an active marketing policy. There was no knowing what the resulting calls on ICFC's resources might be, but it was crucial that, whatever they were, the funds should be available to meet them. Although ICFC had coped successfully throughout the 1960s, by 1970 there was no obvious alternative source of supply.

The solution Larry produced for the dilemma was typically innovative. He suggested we should forget secured lending which was now closed to us, and borrow unsecured. Only companies with the very strongest credit standing were at that time able to borrow for long periods without offering security, whilst the concept of 'negative pledges' was relatively unknown. The negative pledge stood the idea of secured borrowing on its head. Instead of all borrowing having to be secured, which meant that growing numbers of loan creditors had to share a pool of security which was never likely to grow as rapidly as the total debt, it would all be unsecured. The same assets would be available in a winding up, but all lenders would rank equally in sharing it out rather than ranking in a predetermined order of priority. The main condition was that the company would undertake not to grant security—the negative pledge—to anyone without offering it to the other unsecured lenders.

The debenture stocks with their very long maturity dates had actually been designed to meet the needs of investors rather than those of ICFC's customers who normally repaid by annual instalments: the lending term was rarely more than 15 years and the initial capital would be outstanding on average for only about half that period. This meant in practice that the funds raised by the 25 year debenture issues were reinvested two or three times during their lives, and as luck would have it the long history of rising interest rates allowed ICFC to relend the same money at rising rates during the currency of the issues. This endowment from the debenture stocks was a source of valuable income in the 1970s and early 1980s when capital profits were hard to come by.

The risk of borrowing for periods which were longer than the term of ICFC's lending was apparent, but until 1969 there was no choice. The only appropriate source of funds for ICFC was the insurance companies, which were seeking to match their own very long-term commitments under life-assurance policies. Whilst they had a continuous appetite for 25-year money they had no, or few, shorter-term liabilities. Therefore if we were to issue loan stocks of a much shorter maturity, we should be taking a considerable risk of failure. We were aware that there was no large pool of medium-term money in the domestic capital market to which we were restricted, but there might be enough demand to satisfy ICFC's requirements, at that time in the low tens of millions. It was also likely that the lack of security would be less important for borrowings of up to ten years than for the more normal 25-year stocks.

Another novelty was the decision not to have the new issues underwritten. The cost would have been prohibitive because it had to be absorbed over only a few years. For medium-term issues to make economic sense we should simply have to take whatever was offered and not worry if it fell short of the amount we asked for. On the other hand, the after-market could be seriously affected if we were left with a large amount of unsold stock; the price at which the stock could be sold in the secondary market might fall, leaving investors with capital losses and a reduced appetite for the further issues we wanted to make. The risks were apparent, but the solution was calculated to minimize them. The plan was to issue three loan stocks of differing maturities, offered together but separately available so that subscribers could offer for one, two, or all three. The maturities, which were three, five, and seven years, were chosen for specific reasons. We did not really need three-year money, but because it was so short it might attract speculative interest and, if it was priced cheaply, it would probably be over-subscribed and so make the issue look like a success. But the pricing needed to make it attractive would at the same time make it expensive for ICFC; so the solution was to limit the amount to only £2.5 million, thus creating a kind of loss-leader.

The maturity we really wanted was five years, so £5 million of this was offered at a price which was appropriately above the comparable yield on government stock. The seven-year money was not so attractive and was accordingly priced less enticingly. In any case institutions might not be very interested in such a maturity. But there was another novel idea behind the creation of a seven-year stock. Once the initial issues had been made there should be no reason why further tranches of the same stocks could not be issued through a 'tap' mechanism similar to the one operated by the Bank of England in issuing government stock. After an initial gilt-edged issue has been made by public offer, further amounts of the same stock are sold into the market to meet demand. This would be less expensive and very useful for ICFC because it would create a flow of incoming money more nearly matching the outflow. New issues would still be necessary from time to time, but the tap mechanism would allow us to pick up interim demand at going market rates. Thus the five-year stock could be sold in further tranches to meet demand as it arose and when, with the passage of time, it became too short to be of value, the seven-year stock, by then having six or perhaps five years to go, would be brought into action as the main tap stock.

If all this was successful we should have established a new, though small, market in medium-dated stocks and a 'tap' mechanism for selling further amounts directly to investors between issues. It might not produce any long-term solutions but it would enable us to keep the supply of money ahead of growing demand.

It was a great relief that all this came to pass precisely as we had hoped, because we could see no alternative sources of money. Hoare Govett, who had been brokers to all the debenture issues, were a great help in marketing these new, unfamiliar, medium-dated stocks to the investment institutions. We also had valuable co-operation from the Stock Exchange, which made the necessary adjustments to its procedures to allow quotation of the tap issues on a 'when-issued' basis: quotation would be granted in advance to a tranche of stock conditionally on its sale into the market.

The issues were launched at the end of 1969, by way of a public offer for sale, without underwriting, the three stocks all carrying an interest rate of 10 per cent, 'A' being for £2.5 million of three-year term, 'B' for £5 million of five-year term, and 'C' for £5 million of seven-year term. The prices at which they were offered were adjusted to achieve our objectives for each—over-subscription for 'A', full subscription for 'B' and under-subscription for 'C'. The outcome was as hoped for the 'A' stock: £12.5 million was offered, the fivefold over-subscription giving the whole issue some of the glamour which attends a successful equity issue; it had rarely been seen before in the staid fixed-interest market. We were relieved, in view of this response, that the issue was restricted to £2.5 million and the cost of the underpricing contained. Offers for the five-year stock, which was targeted more seriously and had been priced accurately, totalled almost exactly the £5 million we wanted. The seven-year stock, which had been deliberately over-priced, only brought in subscriptions for £2 million, leaving £3 million unissued and thus available for the tap.

The over-subscription for the 'A' stock produced considerable publicity and market interest and we felt that we had managed to open up a new market in corporate medium-dated loan stock, which might prove to be a useful source of funds, but, most importantly, which had established ICFC's credit as a borrower without security. Thereafter issues were always made without offering security, and a few years later all documentation was standardized so that further issues of debt were on the same basic terms with regard to negative pledges and conditions. The main problem with negative pledges is that breach of an unusual condition, even though present in only one trust deed, could trigger a chain reaction throughout the whole of the unsecured debt issues, putting them all at call—with catastrophic results. So we sought to get a limited number of absolutely standard conditions attaching to all unsecured debt, and refused, except in the most unusual circumstances, to accept any variations.

Resource Management in the Turbulent 1970s

These successful issues allowed us to enter the 1970s reasonably confident that ICFC could meet normal demand, although Lord Sherfield again felt it necessary to warn about the resource problem in his 1970 report: there was no way of knowing how much this new market was capable of providing.

It was about this time that the Bank of England issued its 'Competition and Credit Control' policy, in the context of a dash for growth, later known as the Barber boom, which effectively removed all constraints on the banks after two decades of control. The result was a credit explosion, which incidentally played its part in limiting ICFC's growth. The banks, which were previously unable to compete with ICFC and had even been content to see hardcore overdrafts funded with ICFC capital, soon began offering medium-term loans in large quantities at rates which were linked to their short-term money costs.

As a result of the easing of credit, interest rates fell to their lowest levels since the end of the war, sparking off the infamous property boom which was to end with the secondary banking crisis of 1973–4. All this hyperactivity affected ICFC in a number of ways. Casting around as we always were for new sources of money, we found ourselves presented with an unusual opportunity to raise a large amount of cash and at the same time increase the capital base without involving the shareholders.

ICFC's office in Copthall Avenue, known as Piercy House, had been occupied since its completion in 1963 under a 42-year lease. It was no architectural masterpiece, but with its distinctive gold trims it was known familiarly as the 'Gilt-edged building'. It was to be a very apt title, for in 1971 the owners of the head lease agreed to sell it for £2.3 million, thus allowing ICFC to 'marry' the two leases.

The negotiation to agree the terms of the original lease in 1963, which John Kinross undertook personally, has entered 3i folklore as one of the cleverest that even he ever did. Incensed by the high starting rent which was demanded, he had been able to agree, almost as an afterthought to the negotiations, that it should remain fixed at its initial £2.50 per square foot for 21 years. Few would have foreseen in 1963 the dramatic rise in City rents which was to follow. By 1971 they had increased fourfold; and, as it was still fourteen years to the first rent review, the lease had acquired significant value and we leapt at the opportunity which then presented itself to merge the headlease with the underlease, creating an asset of even greater value. It was the view of the Board that ICFC could not afford the luxury of owning a valuable City property when all the capital at our disposal was needed for investment purposes. The boom was by now in full swing–short-term interest rates had fallen below 3 per cent and demand for first-class investment property was strong, so it was decided to put the lease up for sale and to plan a move out of the City.

We were advised by our agents, Hillier Parker, that in such a feverish market we should ask for sealed tenders in the hope of flushing out a buyer who really wanted the property and was prepared to pay up for it. The lease was valued at about £7 million and, indeed, most of the tenders were at about this level; but we were astonished to find one which offered £15.3 million, showing a yield of less than 3 per cent. We thought ICFC's Board would have little difficulty in agreeing to such an offer, and sent a formal acceptance round by hand within an hour of opening the tenders. This remarkable coup, due almost entirely to the advice of the agents, added at a stroke some 50 per cent to ICFC's reserves, as well as providing enough investment funds to last for most of the next year.

The boom continued, however, and long-term rates began to fall below the levels they had reached in the late 1960s, so in 1972 a 25-year unsecured loan stock was launched, tightly priced to yield $8\frac{7}{8}$ per cent, which was approximately $\frac{3}{4}$ per cent or 75 basis points above that of a comparable gilt-edged stock. This was another 'fingers-crossed' exercise, because ICFC's ability to borrow unsecured for such a long period was untested. However, Hoare Govett managed an institutional placing of £15 million without obvious difficulty, and we began to feel that with the new capital provided by the property sale, this loan stock in the bag, and the 'tap' stocks working, we were getting on top of the funding problem.

The Nightmare Years: 1973–7

The boom did not last much longer, and the 1972 loan stock was to be ICFC's and 3i's last such 25-year issue. Out of the economic chaos which ensued, exacerbated by the oil price explosion of 1973 and the subsequent world-wide inflation, came a new financial order. The 1970s were to become a nightmare period for the financial system. Our own circumstances also changed radically with the acquisition of FCI in 1973, leading to wholly new funding needs and the development of different techniques.

In financial markets the period after 1973 is characterized by increasingly innovative devices created by imaginative banks and issuing houses to meet the corporate sector's need for capital. It can be argued that the unstable conditions into which the inflation of the mid-1970s plunged all the major economies, far from making life difficult for business, simply prompted more ingenious ways of surviving and prospering. We ourselves were forced, as this chapter demonstrates, into ever more complex financial schemes to maintain the inflow of funds at a competitive price. Seen from the position which I occupied this process carried undoubted benefits for 3i in providing access to hitherto untapped sources of funds; but it was difficult to believe that the costs involved in devising and marketing these new financial products were entirely absorbed in productivity gains by the financial system. Although the increase in financial uncertainty was undoubtedly accompanied by what might be termed 'certainty-substitutes'in the form of options, swaps, and interest-rate caps, among many, they all carried a cost to the end-user, resulting in profits to the financial institutions for carrying the extra risk. Thus, whilst the effectiveness of the financial system was, if anything, increased, it was at a price which in a more stable system would not have to be paid.

The beginning of this new financial instability can be traced to the early 1970s. By late 1973 the United Kingdom had entered a period of economic turmoil, characterized by high and fluctuating domestic inflation which reached 26 per cent by 1976. At the same time the government's finances were getting in a mess; deficit financing on a large scale pushed up the borrowing requirement to unheard-of levels and with it the level of interest rates. By late 1976 gilt-edged yields had risen to 16 per cent and ICFC's lending rate was commensurately higher. It was understandable that the corporate sector was unwilling to commit itself for long periods to interest rates of 18 to 20 per cent, and long-term financing virtually dried up; instead companies turned to the banks which had become awash with deposits. The enormous increase in money flowing into the treasuries of the Middle Eastern oil producers could not be digested by their own economies, so the bulk of the proceeds was deposited with the Western banks, mainly on a short-term basis. The market which the banks created in London to receive and place these deposits, initially denominated entirely in dollars, was known as the eurodollar market. The going interest rate among the borrowing banks became known as the London Interbank Offered Rate or LIBOR.

Vast amounts of money were swilling about the banking system looking for a home, and the banks took the opportunity to invent a new product, the variable-rate term loan, in order to make use of their massively increased short-term deposits. For UK borrowers the variable-rate loan was a substitute for the debenture market and for the banks a means of achieving better margins on hard-core overdraft facilities. They formalized this lending by fixing repayment over a term of years, while retaining their right to call the money at any time so that they were not technically unmatched against their deposit liabilities. The interest rate on the lending was revised periodically—usually three- or six-monthly—and could therefore be related to the banks' own costs of three- or six-month money.

Loans to corporate customers were thus established at LIBOR plus some margin to allow for the individual credit risk, the rate varying periodically with changes in the LIBOR rate. The history of this market is well known; the huge dollar loans to both corporations and governments, many of which, as interest rates rose again in the early eighties, went into default. The rest of the 1980s were spent unravelling the mess.

This new lending device, which suited the banks well as a means of stretching their lending margins without compromising their balance-sheet matching, was a bastard invention. It was illegitimate in the sense that it was rarely appropriate for borrowers, whose main need was certainty, and had none of the desirable characteristics of the corporate bond market which, with the rise of inflation, had effectively disappeared. The certainty which that market had provided—the known money cost over a long period and the fixed repayment dates—was of great importance to companies working in an increasingly uncertain world. But it was one of the corrosive effects of inflation that they were driven into short-term expedients at the expense of long-term planning.

The variable-rate bank loan which became established in the 1970s, and is now the standard financial tool of the corporate sector, must take some responsibility for the severity of the two recessions experienced by the UK in the early and late 1980s. The effect of a variable interest rate is to increase money costs when liquidity falls, putting an increasing cost burden on corporate cash flow just at the time when it is most vulnerable. There have been a number of times in the last twenty years when fixed-rate funding in place of bank borrowing has been possible; but very little of it had been done until the arrival of the swap era in the mid-1980s. The argument of the nervous finance director is that he cannot justify to his Board borrowing for twenty years at 12 per cent to repay money from his bank which may currently be costing only 10 per cent.

In 1974, when all this was beginning, ICFC had just swallowed its contemporary, FCI. Although its existing investment portfolio was small, FCI provided an opportunity to increase significantly the scale of the new FFI's operations by opening up the whole corporate market and eliminating the ceil-

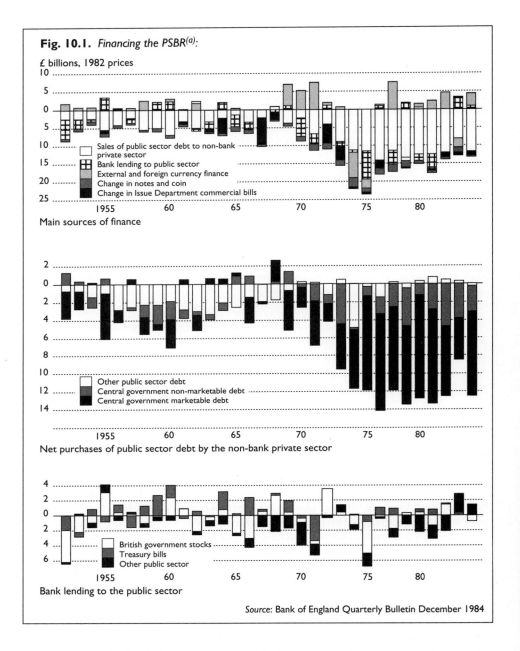

Fig. 10.1. *Financing the PSBR*[a]:

£ billions, 1982 prices

Sales of public sector debt to non-bank private sector
Bank lending to public sector
External and foreign currency finance
Change in notes and coin
Change in Issue Department commercial bills

Main sources of finance

Other public sector debt
Central government non-marketable debt
Central government marketable debt

Net purchases of public sector debt by the non-bank private sector

British government stocks
Treasury bills
Other public sector

Bank lending to the public sector

Source: Bank of England Quarterly Bulletin December 1984

ing on individual investments which had restricted ICFC's growth. Average annual funding needs had barely reached £20 million in the past, but with individual loans likely to be as large as £50 million we should need access to funds on a quite different scale. One of the attractions of acquiring FCI had been that it brought with it a dowry of £45 million in the form of a credit line, provided by the same banks who were ICFC's shareholders, which had been used to finance variable-rate term loans to its large corporate customers. ICFC had no such facility but we had, in the early 1970s, begun to develop our own treasury operation in order to borrow in the short-term markets. This was started by an informal agreement with a discount house, Smith, St Aubyn, of a £500,000 short-term credit line. The commitment was made by Jeremy Smith, at lunch one day, in red pencil on the back of an envelope. We were impressed by the casual way such a large commitment could be made, but were put in no doubt that it was serious on receipt, within twenty-four hours, of a fee note. From this small beginning we began to build up a collection of informal credit lines with banks, discount houses, and merchant banks.

It was apparent that the availability of FCI's existing facility from the shareholders could become a valuable supplement to the money-market operations which were increasingly used to bridge the major funding issues. We should normally be able to treat the short-term money covered by the standby facility as medium-term, because if the short-term market collapsed, leaving us unable to borrow, we should call down the bank facility to redeem outstanding deposits. This allowed us to defer long-term funding when market conditions were difficult and to wait for moments of strong demand when we should be able to strike a fine price, so it gave us real flexibility in the timing of new debt issues. It was to become even more useful when we finally accepted the inevitable and went into variable-rate lending to meet the growing bank competition.

The year 1974 was a traumatic one for FFI as for others. A new Labour government had come in, committed to raising taxes and spending its way out of unemployment, which had by then passed the politically sensitive million mark. The tax increases went nothing like far enough to defray the cost of its spending programme and it was apparent to us that we were going to have serious competition from the government as a major borrower in the fixed-interest market, in the face of which it was by no means clear how we could fund any real demand from the small- and large company sectors in combination.

The extent of the government's intervention in the capital markets and the effectiveness of the 'crowding out' which it caused are well illustrated by a chart published by the Bank of England in its Quarterly Bulletin of December 1984 (see Fig 10.1). In the last few years of the 1960s the Labour Chancellor, Roy Jenkins, had balanced the books and even generated a small surplus in the public sector's finances. In the 1970s, however, we were faced with rapidly accelerating demands on the gilt-edged market with a total of £50 billion borrowed in the decade as a whole, of which over £30 billion was raised in the last four years. It is a tribute to the efficiency of that market, and particularly the Bank of England's fundraising skills, that it was possible to raise such enormous amounts with so little damage to the financial system.

Of course such vast amounts of funding could not be done entirely without cost, and we began to observe from 1974 onwards a process of market management which was compared unkindly with the military tactics of the legendary Duke of York. Interest rates were raised progressively to the point where sufficient funding had been achieved and then rapidly lowered. The borrowing needs of the public sector were unpredictable and the market frequently out-guessed the government, holding back on gilt purchases in the expectation that more funding would be needed than forecast and that interest rates would have to be raised further in order to fund the extra amounts. For the Bank of England it must have been a trying time as funding needs went out of control and they were forced to issue more and more stock at increasing rates rather than being able to close down and wait for rates to fall.

For us in FFI this was a fascinating, if dispiriting, process and one which affected our own funding plans directly. We could obviously not compete when government issues were in full flood and chose to wait for the interludes when the appetites of both borrower and lenders had been temporarily sated. In those periods interest rates generally fell back, sometimes substantially, and we were able to avoid the peaks by either anticipating the Duke of York's next march up the interest-rate hill or waiting until he had marched down again.

For this purpose the availability of short-term bridging funds was essential, and we needed to build up the money-market operation. This in turn required an increase in the standby facility which the banks had agreed to continue on the same basis as for FCI.

FFI's Involvement in the City versus Industry Debate

The changed political climate of 1974 brought with it a particularly hostile attack on the City, accused, as always, of letting down British industry by preferring to finance 'candy-floss industries' and speculating in property. There was no doubt in the City about the seriousness of the threat; intervention in the financial system was being advocated strongly in order to divert funds into industry where, it was confidently believed, new investment would lead to more jobs. FFI, with its virtuous record of providing industrial capital, though not on an interventionist basis, was unwillingly caught up in the crossfire as the Bank of England sought to counter the black propaganda by providing evidence of the City's capacity to meet the need.

It is ironic that the main siphon of funds away from the corporate sector at this critical time was the government itself, rather than the property speculators or the 'candy-floss' financiers. Indeed ICFC, and therefore its customers, had benefited directly from £15 million worth of property 'speculation' by the sale of Piercy House and redeployment of the proceeds in industrial investment.

In one respect the Bank's proposal for a £1 billion fund[3] to boost the size of FFI's operations was of value to us. We had no experience of raising the really large sums of money which would be necessary if we were to fund large-scale industrial projects through FCI. There was a credibility problem in moving from total borrowings of £20 to £30 million a year, raised from the limited pool of funds available in the corporate loan stock market, to issues of £50 million or more which could now be necesssary. So we welcomed the new proposals despite the politically charged atmosphere in which they were published and the evident dislike among the City institutions of having their arms twisted. We were to pay a heavy price over the next few years for the unpopularity this caused, but it did show that large amounts of money could be raised.

It was clear to us from City gossip that despite the political success in diverting the government's attention from the need to intervene directly, the actual arrangements caused great anger. Although it was directed mainly at the Bank of England, FFI was inevitably affected and we were unhappy to be seen as some kind of tool of government—a misconception we had struggled for nearly thirty years to correct. Direction of investment was a concept greatly feared in the City and the obligation to support FFI was seen by many as the thin end of the wedge. It was well known and respected, but its shares were not quoted and any benefit arising from what was assumed would be subsidized lending would land in its shareholders' pockets. We gained the impression that it would have been less unpopular if the institutions had been equity investors in FFI. But the possibility of a public quotation for its shares was not to arise for another decade.

We did not think it wise to take immediate advantage of the new arrangements, for it seemed that the very announcement of the £1 billion fund had the hoped-for effect of muting the calls for intervention. In any case, to launch immediately into a funding operation would invite a hostile reception and the suspicion that FFI was in trouble. As it turned out a need emerged quite soon for which the new facilities were well suited; the growing industrial recession of 1974, following the property crash and the fringe bank crisis, led to a stock-market collapse. By the end of 1974 the market had dropped to its lowest level in years, leaving many corporate stocks standing below par and making new equity issues impossible. At the same time rising interest rates, exacerbated by the government's demands on the gilt market, made borrowing at fixed rates prohibitively expensive.

The collapse of the stock and property markets had a direct impact on FFI's balance sheet. At September 1974 it was necessary to make half-year provisions of some £20 million against the property portfolio and major unquoted equity investments. With the stock-market collapse, the surpluses on the portfolio of quoted shares (which were not brought into the balance sheet) were also nearly wiped out, falling by £35 million to only £1 million in the six months to September. We were thankful for the cushion provided by the sale of Piercy House barely two years previously, but FFI's capital and reserves were seriously reduced as we announced the only loss in our history, apart from the £26,000 loss reported at the end of ICFC's first year. It is worth recording, however, that not all the provisions we thought necessary in 1974–5 were eventually required: one such was almost £5 million to write off the investment in British Caledonian, most of it made only a year earlier. Fifteen years later it was to realize £100 million.

Cautious as our provisions had been, we felt it necessary to replenish the capital base before asking the reluctant institutions to implement their undertaking, and we called down £25 million of the £85 million share capital committed by the shareholders. It was clear that this was not exactly what the Bank of England had been thinking of when it set up the £1 billion fund, but we felt there was no choice and our shareholders dutifully paid up. This was the only time we felt it necessary to call on them and the rest of their commitment was eventually allowed to lapse. Since that time the only new capital they have provided has been £4 million to fund an investment in Equity Capital for Industry—which they asked FFI to make—and £15 million arising from the payment of a special dividend.

This capital-raising restored the capital base and made possible the first public issue of debt under the Governor's arrangements with an offer for sale in early 1975 of £75 million—a huge amount by our own previous standards. Apart from its sheer size, this issue had a number of unusual features. The Bank of England thought it would like to try its hand as an issuing house, which it had previously only done for government. We were quite pleased: a prospectus headed 'Bank of England Offers for Sale' sounded impressive. Having agreed that, the Bank thought the issue ought to be sold in the gilt-edged market rather than the corporate loan-stock market. We could understand why they wanted to do it in this way but we had our doubts about how it would be received. We had already had trouble with the local authorities, which at that time were issuing long-dated stocks in the gilt market on terms which we thought unnecessarily extravagant. We had been used to selling issues in the debenture market with an interest coupon which exceeded that on gilts by not more than 75 basis points (0.75 per cent) but the Greater London Council (GLC), no less, was selling its own bonds in the gilt-edged market at 125 basis points (1.25 per cent) over gilt-edged. This put an effective floor on our money cost, well above what we thought commercial: we should have to lend on to our customers at a minimum of 3 per cent over the gilt, and we had serious doubts about whether we could make such levels hold. It was all the more galling because one of the main arguments for the £1 billion fund was that it would allow FFI to borrow more cheaply. In the event the issue was priced very close to the yield on the GLC stock, which made it clearly unpopular. The arm-twisting, however, produced the desired effect in getting the issue more or less fully subscribed, and we had our £75 million. For all its unpopularity and the consequent effects on our money costs, it did achieve the breakthrough into large-scale funding which we needed. As expected, however, the tight pricing and the arm-twisting had a disastrous effect on the secondary market. The price of the FFI stock quickly fell as disgruntled institutions dumped their allocations on the market until the yield differential against the gilt had doubled and the *Financial Times* unkindly published a small chart in the Lex column, without comment, showing its adverse movement against gilts and the GLC stock. I framed the chart and it still holds a treasured position among my memorabilia (see Fig. 10.2).

So for all its achievements the issue was disastrous for FFI's reputation as a borrower and, with a secondary market yield higher than our own lending rate, it was impossible to go back to the market for some time. We felt that it could have been differently managed, with a smaller amount offered but at a much better price and without the aftermath. However, the combination of the capital issue and the loan stock, together with a slow recovery in the stock market, gave us the necessary resources for the expansion of FCI to begin without starving ICFC.

The rise in inflation, the collapse of sterling, and the rapidly growing public-sector deficit led to a humiliating invitation to the International Monetary Fund to help sort out Britain's financial mess. After their arrival in 1976 the capital markets took on a much healthier tone. We had been surprised to discover that we were able to continue selling the 'tap' stocks into the debenture market at the same sort of level of 50 to 75 basis points over the gilt as previously, despite the fact that the £75 million stock was languishing in the gilt market on a far higher yield. It said much about the inefficiencies within the

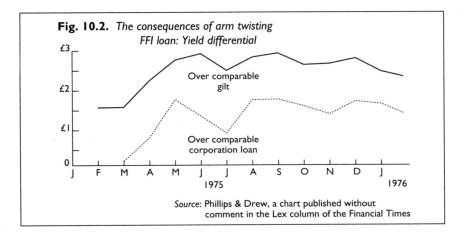

Fig. 10.2. *The consequences of arm twisting*
FFI loan: Yield differential

Over comparable gilt

Over comparable corporation loan

J F M A M J J A S O N D J
    1975   1976

Source: Phillips & Drew, a chart published without comment in the Lex column of the Financial Times

239

Stock Market at that time that institutions' corporate fixed-interest departments were buying ICFC stock at the same time as their gilt departments were selling the FFI stock on a much higher yield. It was apparent that we should not be able to issue more large amounts of the new stock economically until its yield was brought down, so we started using the proceeds of cheaper sales in the debenture market to buy in the more expensive £75 million stock for cancellation. In the process we had a double benefit; paying 0.75 per cent over the gilt in order to redeem at over 2 per cent gave us an income profit, and because we were buying in at well below the issue price and cancelling the stock, we were making a capital gain which, as it turned out, was not taxable. These were valuable financial benefits, but the main object was to take out unwilling holders of the stock and so tighten up its market yield.

As the IMF's medicine began to work, principally by reducing the government's own borrowing requirement, the combination of a general market improvement with the enhanced perception of the £75 million stock gave us another opportunity. We decided to make a further issue, of £50 million this time, on similar terms to the previous one but priced so attractively that it would be irresistible. We were able to take advantage of renewed demand in the gilt market as the government's funding needs were reduced and so felt it necessary to pay only 25 basis points ($\frac{1}{4}$ per cent) more than we might otherwise have to for a successful issue. This time the response was different: £1.5 billion was offered for our £50 million stock—a 30 times over-subscription. We felt fully justified because there could be no accusations of arm-twisting this time, and we were able to use the proceeds to continue mopping up the unpopular first issue until it ceased to be a drag on the market.

By 1977 all these efforts had restored FFI's position in the domestic fixed-interest market, but that £50 million issue was to be our last, except for some small loan-stock issues, because a new and much more attractive market was opening up.

The International Capital Market

The IMF's intervention had an even more significant effect for us than the reduction of government borrowing, interest rates, and inflation which followed, dramatic though these were. For the first time sterling-denominated assets began to interest foreign investors. We had eyed the growing eurobond market with envy: it had been developed for investors to acquire assets in currencies other than their own, thus adding to the return generated by the asset in its own currency a potential gain on the purchase and sale of the currency. The possibility of loss on currency devaluations made investors particularly careful about which currencies they would invest in, and for some years the US dollar was the dominant currency, desired by investors all over the world. The German mark and the Swiss franc were also desirable currencies because of their long and stable history, but sterling with its ever-present devaluation risk was seen as purely speculative and not a suitable medium for long-term investments. To the extent that these were bought by foreigners they had to be very liquid and easily sold. Gilt-edged stocks were uniquely qualified for this purpose, except that another requirement of the international investors, other than governments, was anonymity. They would not buy bonds which required their ownership to be registered, so all eurobonds had to be in bearer form with coupons conveying the right to periodic interest payments. Furthermore, the interest had to be paid gross, without any local withholding tax to be reclaimed through the tax system.

In combination these investor requirements made it difficult for UK borrowers to approach the eurobond market; borrowing from foreigners also required Exchange Control consent. But it was, and remains, a vast market based in London, bringing together borrowers and lenders from a variety of countries in contracts denominated in a wide range of currencies. Its very size and efficiency, together with the currency element, allowed tight pricing and yields which were often below those of the domestic market in the same currency. Until 1977 FFI was effectively barred from the eurobond market because sterling issues were regarded as too risky. Other currencies were of no use to us because FFI's customers were in general too small to operate across boundaries and few of them had sufficient foreign income flows to justify taking the serious risk of loss on currency exchanges. In the early 1970s a number of large British companies had borrowed in foreign currencies, particularly the Swiss franc, attracted by their low nominal interest rates and ignoring the potential for sterling devaluation which the interest differential implied. As the pound fell, so the sterling value of the currency liability increased, in some cases leading to breach of borrowing covenants.

Although we had felt unable to try out the eurobond market in foreign currencies, we had for some time been hoping for a market in sterling eurobonds to open up, when in late 1977 it appeared quite suddenly. Confidence in British economic management was improved by the government's acceptance of the IMF's discipline and the consequent improvement in the financial position of the UK, bank base rates falling from 15 per cent to 7 per cent, inflation from 26 per cent to 6 per cent, and government bond yields from 16 per cent to 10 per cent—all in the space of a year. It was ironic that the spending cuts which produced this transformation had been far greater than those intended by the government, resulting in an undershoot of several £'s billion in the borrowing requirement. The upward trend in government spending was resumed as soon as this mistake was discovered, thus contributing to the renewed rise in interest rates, the next inflation burst at the end of the 1970s, and the consequent recession.

But for the moment the market in sterling eurobonds was open. We noticed that the European Coal and Steel Community had made a successful issue in sterling at a yield below that on UK Government bonds—an indication that further sterling appreciation was confidently expected by foreign investors. ECSC, of course, was a supranational authority with the full faith and credit of the EC Governments behind it. FFI was a small, unknown UK corporate, but we thought it worth a try. Hoare Govett, who had been such a successful promoter of ICFC and FFI in the domestic market, were unable to operate in the eurobond market, and we had to find an international merchant bank who could lead-manage an issue for us. The fact that we chose Warburgs was due simply to the fact that they were the only UK investment bank visible in the bond-management league tables at that time; but they were to remain our dedicated and remarkably effective lead managers for many years. They had been involved from the beginning in the eurobond markets and had a successful record with foreign issues, so there was no need for chauvinism on our part; and the Bank of England, whom we consulted on this as on many such matters, fully supported our choice.

Warburgs leapt at the chance of bringing a UK company with FFI's pedigree to the international market. Its asset strength was of some value; but undeniably its ownership, particularly the Bank of England participation, was the key factor, even though there was no question of a shareholder guarantee. The sterling market was small, but there was enough demand to launch a £20 million ten-year issue at a full one percentage point *below* the yield on a comparable British government stock. There was no question that it was the currency play which allowed such a low yield, but it caused some pain in the Bank of England and great delight in FFI.

Warburgs put together a management group of extraordinary power and prestige, which we stuck to as far as we could, though one or two dropped out in the early stages for their own good reasons. Our own shareholders at that time had no significant presence in the eurobond markets, but we felt they should all be offered the opportunity to join the management group. The Bank of England naturally declined, but the others came in as a distinct group of co-managers, lending support to the prospectus. That trailblazing issue was the first of many, although we could never wholly rely on the sterling market: it came and went with the strength and weakness of the currency. But gradually FFI's name became known in international investor circles; not many knew what it did, but its pedigree was well understood and its credit was regarded as undoubted. For this we need to thank Warburgs for the remarkable skill with which they handled the FFI name. In addition, their own position as dealers in the secondary market for sterling eurobonds allowed them to assess the quan-

All these securities having been sold, this announcement appears as a matter of record only.

Finance for Industry Limited
(Incorporated in England under the Companies Acts 1948 to 1967)

£20,000,000

9¾ per cent. Sterling/U.S. dollar payable Bonds 1987

S. G. Warburg & Co. Ltd.

Salomon Brothers International
Limited

Swiss Bank Corporation (Overseas)
Limited

Westdeutsche Landesbank Girozentrale

Barclays Bank International
Limited

Lloyds Bank International
Limited

Midland Bank Group

National Westminster Bank Group

The Royal Bank of Scotland
Limited

Algemene Bank Nederland N.V.	A. E. Ames & Co. Limited	Amex Bank Limited	Amsterdam-Rotterdam Bank N.V.
Arnhold and S. Bleichroeder, Inc.	Bache Halsey Stuart Shields Incorporated	Banca Commerciale Italiana	Banca Nazionale del Lavoro
Bank of America International Limited	Bank Julius Baer International Limited	Bank Gutzwiller, Kurz, Bungener (Overseas) Limited	Bank Leu International Ltd.
Bank Mees & Hope NV	Bank of Scotland	The Bank of Tokyo (Holland) N.V.	Banque Bruxelles Lambert S.A.

Banque Française du Commerce Extérieur   Banque de l'Indochine et de Suez   Banque Internationale à Luxembourg S.A.

Banque Louis-Dreyfus   Banque Nationale de Paris   Banque de Neuflize, Schlumberger, Mallet   Banque de Paris et des Pays-Bas

Banque Populaire Suisse SA Luxembourg   Banque de l'Union Européenne   Banque Worms   Barclays Köl & Co. N.V.

Baring Brothers & Co., Limited   Bayerische Landesbank Girozentrale   Bayerische Vereinsbank   Joh. Berenberg, Gossler & Co.   Bergen Bank

Berliner Bank Aktiengesellschaft   Berliner Handels- und Frankfurter Bank   Blyth Eastman Dillon & Co. International Limited   Caisse des Dépôts et Consignations

James Capel & Co.   Centrale Rabobank   Chase Manhattan Limited   Citicorp International Group   Clydesdale Bank Limited

Commerzbank Aktiengesellschaft   Compagnie de Banque et d'Investissements (Underwriters) S.A.   Compagnie Monégasque de Banque   Continental Illinois Limited

Crédit Commercial de France   Crédit Industriel d'Alsace et de Lorraine   Crédit Lyonnais   Credit Suisse White Weld Limited

Creditanstalt-Bankverein   Credito Italiano (Underwriters) S.A.   Daiwa Europe N.V.   Den Danske Bank af 1871 Aktieselskab   Den norske Creditbank

Deutsche Bank Aktiengesellschaft   Deutsche Girozentrale —Deutsche Kommunalbank—   DG BANK Deutsche Genossenschaftsbank   Dillon, Read Overseas Corporation   Dominion Securities

Dresdner Bank Aktiengesellschaft   Drexel Burnham Lambert Incorporated   Effectenbank-Warburg   Eurocapital S.A.   Euromobiliare S.p.A.

European Banking Company Limited   First Boston (Europe) Limited   Robert Fleming & Co. Limited   Fuji International Finance Limited   Gefina International Ltd.

Genossenschaftliche Zentralbank AG Vienna   Girozentrale und Bank der österreichischen Sparkassen Aktiengesellschaft   Goldman Sachs International Corp.

Groupement des Banquiers Privés Genevois   Hambros Bank Limited   Handelsbank N.W. (Overseas) Limited   Hill Samuel & Co. Limited

Hoare Govett Ltd.   E. F. Hutton & Co. N.V.   IBJ International Limited   Istituto Bancario San Paolo di Torino

Jardine Fleming & Company Limited   Kidder, Peabody International Limited   Kleinwort, Benson Limited   Kredietbank N.V.

Kredietbank S.A. Luxembourgeoise   Kuhn, Loeb & Co. International   Lazard Brothers & Co., Limited   Lazard Frères et Cie

Lehman Brothers International Limited   London & Continental Bankers Limited   McLeod, Young, Weir International Limited   Manufacturers Hanover Limited

Merrill Lynch International & Co.   L. Messel & Co.   Samuel Montagu & Co. Limited   Morgan Grenfell & Co. Limited

Morgan Stanley International   Nederlandsche Middenstandsbank N.V.   Nesbitt, Thomson Limited   The Nikko Securities Co., (Europe) Ltd.

Nomura Europe N.V.   Norddeutsche Landesbank Girozentrale   Nordic Bank Limited   Sal. Oppenheim jr. & Cie.   Orion Bank Limited

Österreichische Länderbank   Phillips & Drew   Pierson, Heldring & Pierson N.V.   PKbanken   Postipankki   Privatbanken Aktieselskab

Rea Brothers Limited   Rothschild Bank AG   N. M. Rothschild & Sons Limited   J. Henry Schroder Wagg & Co.   Skandinaviska Enskilda Banken

Smith Barney, Harris Upham & Co. Incorporated   Société Bancaire Barclays (Suisse) S.A.   Société Générale   Société Générale de Banque S.A.

Société Séquanaise de Banque   Sparbankernas Bank   Strauss, Turnbull & Co.   Svenska Handelsbanken

Union Bank of Switzerland (Securities) Limited   Vereins- und Westbank Aktiengesellschaft   J. Vontobel & Co.   M. M. Warburg-Brinckmann, Wirtz & Co.

Warburg Paribas Becker Incorporated   Williams, Glyn & Co.   Dean Witter International   Wood Gundy Limited   Yamaichi International (Europe) Limited

The First Bond Issue Tombstone

tity of demand and the price at which it could be met with great precision, and thus bring us to market only when demand was known to be strong and at a price which would attract the right level of interest.

Variable Rate Funding

Valuable as this new source of funds was, it did not meet the whole need, because FCI was beginning to make large-scale loans at variable rates of interest. The bond markets only provided money at fixed rates, so a matching source was needed to fund this growing demand. Our money-market operation had started in the early 1970s as a mechanism for raising bridging finance more flexibly and economically than normal banking finance. By borrowing in the short-term markets alongside banks, local authorities, and large public companies, we were able to keep our money cost down to LIBOR and below, whereas if we had borrowed from banks as a non-bank ourselves, we should have paid something over LIBOR plus commitment fees for maintenance of a credit line. We were unwilling to pay for formal bank lines, and relied on having continuous access to the market through the money brokers. In this connection the creation of a £400 million standby facility as part of the £1 billion fund brought real benefits. It was also cheap to maintain: the commitment fee was only five basis points although any funds drawn down would be prohibitively expensive, starting at 1.25 per cent and rising to 1.5 per cent over LIBOR. We therefore used the facility purely as back-up for our short term borrowings.

Although FCI was lending predominantly at variable rates, ICFC turned its face against this form of lending until the early 1980s. We believed that our small business customers should take as much of their debt at fixed rates as possible, but the competition from the banks in offering loans, with the interest rate linked to LIBOR and varying every three or six months, threatened to undermine the lending side of ICFC's investment business. Lending at floating rates only began after we had decided that we could justifiably use the standby facilities to convert short-term borrowing into economically priced medium-term obligations. If the short-term market were to dry up we should be able to replace those funds with medium-term money drawn down from the shareholders. Without this facility we could not have entered the variable-rate loan market because there was at that time no source of medium-term funds other than the banks themselves. If we borrowed from them we should have been in the same position as our customers and would have been unable to take an adequate additional margin for the risk. As it was our money-market borrowing was very competitive and the treasury team developed great skill in holding down the cost.

As a matter of principle we always borrowed more than we actually needed for lending purposes, and the surplus was redeposited in the market. This gave us a number of advantages, of which the most important was that the market, when asked for a quote, never knew whether we were borrowing or lending, so had to quote both bid and offered prices. Any deficiency on the Group's cash balance for a particular day could be made up either by borrowing or by calling in deposits. The disadvantage was that in putting out money we had borrowed we were accepting some credit risk; and we made it a rigid rule that our treasury could only place money with a list of reputable institutions which had been approved by the Group Board. It would have been unacceptable our treasury dealers to have any discretion on lending in the amounts involved, which could be several million pounds, when amounts as small as £50,000 were going through the elaborate vetting procedures we had set up for the normal investment business. The treasury therefore operated on the basis of taking no credit risks and not attempting to make a profit. They were expected only to minimize the cost of money by skilful dealing. This seemed to work well and we had no problems of uncovered exposures or speculative dealing in the esoteric money-market instruments which were developed during the 1980s.

Although it worked well in practice, the money-market activity was not entirely satisfactory because it relied heavily on the standby facility. The shareholders insisted on renewing it annually, so it could be withdrawn at any review point, and if drawn down it would not have covered the full term of our variable-rate lending. This was another reason for our unwillingness to let ICFC meet the banks' competition head on. We still had no economical source of medium-term debt which would have matched exactly the variable-rate loans we were making.

As FFI's lending grew, the short-term borrowing which funded it rose closer to the limit effectively imposed by the £400 million available under the standby facility. One way of easing the problem was to establish a new line, this time in dollars, which at a push could be converted to sterling, through the New York Commercial Paper market.

This was a mixed blessing: the American financial system was subject to the exceedingly complex legislation aimed at separating banking from other financial activities. We had to go through protracted legal processes and a credit rating which made it barely worth the effort for the $150 million of 90-day deposit receipts it allowed us to issue. But it had some value in making us go through the rating process with the two principal agencies, Moody's and Standard and Poors. The strength of the shareholder backing, including, of course, the Bank of England, the asset position, and the standby facility helped to persuade both of the agencies to give FFI their prime ratings, A1+ and P1 respectively. These only applied to short-term debt, and were nothing like as rigorous as the long-term ratings, but they provided a benchmark view of FFI's credit at a time in the early 1980s when we needed to establish its undoubted quality. The dollars we borrowed through these issues of commercial paper, which are simply deposit receipts sold at a discount by non-banks, could really only be redeposited. So although they contributed to the amount of back-up resources available they were of marginal value.

The Opening of the Swap Market

Once again we were wondering whether we should be able to meet the growing demand for investment capital, this time in the form of variable-rate loans, when suddenly at the end of 1981 we found the means of raising medium-term variable-rate money which had eluded us for so long. We were approached by one of the major American banks with a device they claimed to have invented and had called an interest-rate swap. It was not a particularly complicated concept, but was difficult to put into place because it involved finding two companies, one needing fixed-rate funds and the other variable-rate, plus a bank able and willing to mediate between them. The company wanting variable-rate debt would borrow fixed-rate money and the company wanting fixed-rate debt would arrange a variable-rate credit with its bankers. Each would then enter into a similar contract with the intermediary bank. Under the back-to-back contracts the fixed-rate borrower would assume the variable-rate borrower's interest liability and vice versa.

In our case we would use our first-class credit standing to raise fixed-rate debt and the company on the other side would arrange a variable-rate bank credit of the same maturity and amount. In principle bank money should be relatively cheaper than bonds because of the close relationship involved and the banks' knowledge and understanding of their customers' business. It would then be possible for our advantageous borrowing costs in the bond market to be translated into a particularly attractive LIBOR-related rate. The other, less creditworthy, borrower would pay the intermediary bank a higher fixed rate than we were contracted to pay on our bond issue.

The theory put to me seemed to meet our needs perfectly. FFI had substantial borrowing power in the bond markets at rates only a few basis points above the yield on UK government stocks, but we had no source of medium-term variable-rate debt—other than the banks themselves. The possibility of being able to acquire such debt at sub-LIBOR rates was enticing. Unfortunately, because the idea was new and the bank which had invented the idea wanted to retain copyright for as long as possible, it was necessary for them to find a partner among their own global portfolio who could do the other side of the transaction. After six months impatiently waiting for them to deliver, we decided it was reasonable to ask Warburgs what they could do with this idea, which by then had become widely known, and within a few weeks a transaction had been put together. It involved a US corporation, Amfac, whose credit rating was inadequate to admit them to the long-term bond market, but who had access to ample bank lines. The complication was that they wanted dollars and we wanted sterling, but Warburgs were not daunted by this problem. They found an American bank able and willing to take on the Amfac credit on the one hand and FFI's on the other in dollars, and fixed up a swap of FFI's dollar obligations into sterling at a rate which showed us a sub-LIBOR cost.

To raise the necessary dollars we made a seven-year $50 million bond issue at 15.25 per cent fixed, and swapped the interest coupon with Wells Fargo Bank. The capital repayment obligation of $50 million in seven years' time was swapped simultaneously for an equivalent sterling obligation, and we received sterling at the same rate. So, by what seemed like sleight of hand, we had what we wanted, sterling at a very low margin over LIBOR for seven years, and the only additional exposure was the possibility that an AA-rated American Bank might not meet its obligation during and after seven years.

This was a monumental achievement on the part of Warburgs; it set the pattern for hundreds of billions' worth of cross-currency interest swaps for the next decade, and was not only proclaimed deal of the year in its category, but at the end of the 1980s, a prolific period for financial innovation, was included in *International Financial Review*'s 'notable market firsts' of the decade. It also set FFI on the road to floating-rate funding with a succession of foreign-currency issues in US dollars, Ecu, Swiss francs, French francs, Deutsche Marks, and Japanese yen which were all swapped into floating-rate sterling at below or slightly above LIBOR. This additional source of funding had the particular advantage that it gave us access to new investor groups in the other currencies and kept our powder dry for fixed-interest issues in the still shallow sterling eurobond market.

Over the four years to 1986 we entered into some twenty swaps of various kinds, involving capital sums of about £400 million, in addition to the fixed-interest sterling issues which we continued to make. During this period swaps ceased to be tailor-made, one-off arrangements between two parties brought together for the purpose, and became a commodity, traded between banks.

Internally Generated Funds

Despite the success of these innovative borrowing techniques it was fortunate that over the same period the Group, now calling itself Investors in Industry and subsequently 3i, was generating a strong cash-flow from its own operations, because new investment was also reaching record levels. The fact that the shareholders were considering reducing their holdings in 3i, first mooted in 1984, became public knowledge in 1986 and thereafter seriously affected our fund-raising ability. It was damaging because 3i's prestigious shareholders might cease to provide the backing which the bond markets had assumed. We could no longer promise the ongoing shareholder commitment which had been so valuable in establishing its market reputation. A statement to the effect that some shareholders were considering reducing their holdings was made available to potential investors in 1986, but could not be used indefinitely, and it was not until 1991, six years after 3i's Board had put forward the proposal, that the shareholders finally agreed that the Company might be floated. During the whole of that time we felt that 3i was in limbo, and we could not justify asking investors to commit funds for ten years or more with such uncertainty surrounding its ownership.

We were fortunate to enter this period, during which no public issues of debt were made, very well-funded, and we set about generating cash in every possible way. We had in any case thought that 3i's debt was growing excessively in contrast to the risk profile of its assets, which included an increasing proportion of equity investments. So in 1986 we began a programme of aggressive asset sales, in all those areas where realization would not affect our customer relationships and jeopardize the fundamental long-term investment policy. The rise in stock-market values had increased the size of our quoted portfolio beyond a sensible level, and we began a three-year selling programme which raised some £300 million and added about half that amount to the Group's reserves. We also sold most of the investment properties and began to sell off the development portfolio, though the recession of the late 1980s overtook that process.

We were also fortunate that the £100 million which we realized from the sale of the 40 per cent holding in British Caledonian came in during that period, and all told, in the five years from 1985 to 1990, 3i's capital and reserves doubled while outstanding debt remained almost static. This halving of balance-sheet exposure took place while the rest of the corporate sector seemed intent on doing the opposite. We could not claim to have foreseen the severe recession which followed but we certainly entered it well prepared, with the hatches battened down and a strong balance sheet.

The borrowing problem of that period, which proved a blessing in disguise in forcing us to liquidate assets, was exacerbated by the fact that Moody's, the US rating agency, took it upon themselves, without our consent, to issue a rating for 3i's debt based on the yen bond issue we had made in late 1985. Because we had subsequently entered a period of uncertainty while the shareholders deliberated on what to do, it seemed a singularly inappropriate time for a rating to be issued. Despite all our protests Moody's went ahead, setting the rating at AA1, only a single step below the coveted AAA and a remarkable outcome for an institution whose portfolio contained a high proportion of risky and illiquid assets. We regarded this accolade as a poisoned chalice because many investors, especially the Japanese, would only take on assets with ratings of AA and above. At any time the shareholders might decide to float 3i or sell their holdings to less creditworthy investors, and we should face an inevitable downrating. We could not risk the damage to 3i's hard-won reputation that would ensue if investors who had bought an AA stock suddenly found it was only rated A.

So we decided to make no further bond issues until the shareholder question was resolved and the rating revised. In fact, Moody's did not wait for the resolution of the shareholding position, they found sufficient cause in the general UK economic decline and the provisions we had to make in 1990 to reduce the rating to AA2 and, shortly afterwards, to single A.

It was only then, after the rating had been brought down and shareholders had made public their intention to float, that 3i felt able to go back to the market. The voluntary abstention was worthwhile, for, thanks to another spectacular Warburg effort, a very successful issue of £100 million was made in late 1991, meeting an investor demand which seemed to ignore both the expected change in shareholdings and the downrating.

In the interim, thanks to the strong inflow of cash, we had survived without undue stress; but it had been necessary to raise two large, expensive, and uncomfortably short-dated bank facilities. These were symptomatic of the difficulties we faced in the late 1980s.

Margins

The interest rate charged on loans to customers has always reflected the market rate for funds of similar kind and maturity available to larger companies. Until 1959 ICFC was taking a considerable risk in offering fixed-rate money at a price related to the yield on quoted debenture stocks, which were the appropriate analogue for its own long-term loans. The cost of funds provided by its shareholders reflected short-term deposit rates which caused uncontrollable fluctuations in margins and consequently in the early years' profits. This problem was only overcome when ICFC was allowed to issue its own debenture stocks on the public market. Over the next ten years, lending rates were set in relation to those in the market where ICFC itself was issuing, and so bore a direct relationship to its own money cost.

In that period the margin risk was limited to one of timing. One £15 million debenture issue was normally enough for a year's net outflow on loan investment, but rates could not be fixed for a whole year in relation to ICFC's

actual money cost, so margins were set on the basis of the daily quotation for debenture yields in the *Financial Times*. Fortunately for ICFC, interest rates were following a rising pattern throughout the 1960s, so that funds raised in advance of need were usually on-lent on a cost basis which exceeded the actual cost of money, offsetting the short-term running loss which arose from their deposit in the market pending advance to customers.

After debenture issues ceased to be possible at the end of the 1960s, fund-raising became more complicated, and we found that our money costs were increasingly related to yields on government stocks—a relationship which was confirmed by the 1973 issue of £75 million sponsored by the Bank of England in the Gilt Market. From that point gilt-edged became effectively the only bench mark, and the main emphasis of my job was on trying to narrow and hold down that differential, for we had no choice but to offer customers terms which reflected our own money cost and showed an acceptable margin. Bearing in mind that compensation for risk was dealt with by taking equity, we were able to price fixed-rate loans at a fairly slender margin over money cost. When the spread of that cost over gilts was taken into account we were normally able to lend at an interest rate which was no more than two or three percentage points above gilt-edged stock. By careful management of 3i's credit, and by the appropriate timing of issues, we were able to establish a money cost which was generally no more than half of one per cent, or 50 basis points, above gilt-edged. Customers benefited from this narrow spread in paying about an additional two percentage points above that money cost. Not many investors, faced with the choice of earning 10 per cent on a gilt-edged stock and 12.5 per cent on a loan to a small private company, would choose the latter.

When 3i began making floating-rate loans the margin problem was less complicated, but we had correspondingly less room for manœuvre in managing our money cost; everything was related to LIBOR. We established our own short-term money cost at about LIBOR, occasionally having to go above it and often finding swap opportunities which would take us below it. There was no way we could pay less than the banks on a consistent basis, and so we were directly competing with them. It was possible to moderate money costs by intelligent mismatching at the short end of the market, but this could not provide more than part compensation for the cost of our treasury operation without taking unacceptable risks. So the price quoted by 3i for floating-rate loans was some rate above LIBOR. We were quite inflexible in 3i's treasury in computing these money costs, and investment controllers were discouraged from trying to undercut the banks because they were the main source of our short- and medium-term money and it was therefore virtually impossible to guarantee a money cost below LIBOR. 3i lost a substantial amount of floating-rate loan business to the banks, which had a normal money cost below the offered rate and were thus able to accept lower spreads over LIBOR. Where they would often lend in the half- to one-per cent range, 3i could rarely offer less than $1\frac{1}{4}$ per cent. Controllers had to find other ways of selling floating rate loans if they were to offset the banks' pricing advantage—the main device being the droplock loan, which gave customers the option to convert their floating rate into a fixed rate on prearranged terms.

The principle on which the treasury operated in fund-raising was that it must have funds continuously available to meet all demands made on it. This would have been easy enough if there had been no cost constraints; we could simply have bid up to whatever level was necessary to get in the funds. But our money cost always had to be competitive. Although other sources were not necessarily offering identical loan products, the threat of being undercut, particularly by the banks, was ever-present. It was an accepted fact of life that an offer of capital made by 3i had its own value as a vote of confidence in the prospects of the offeree, and could be paraded round the market to give other possible lenders necessary comfort. It was easy (or so it seemed) for a competitor to say 'If 3i will do it, so will we for half a per cent less'. So the treasury had to find all the money 3i needed at a competitive cost.

In the absence of any form of guarantee or cheap funds from government we had to rely entirely on skilful marketing of 3i's name as a borrower in both domestic and international capital markets in order to keep money costs down. In the domestic market, as I have shown, we were hindered by the over-whelming presence of government as a competing borrower, but in the inter-national markets the Bank of England's skilled management of UK government credit and the extreme rarity of its euro-issues—I can recall no more than three in the last twenty years—provided a kind of halo effect from which 3i benefited. As an unusual institution, close to the centre of the British economy, with a prestigious group of shareholders, including the Bank of England itself which was not in the habit of taking stakes in private companies, 3i was seen as an undoubted credit, despite the nature of its business. This per-ception, skilfully nurtured by Warburgs, gave us access to rare sources of pri-vate placements as well as bond markets in all the major currencies. None of our borrowing in the international markets, when translated into sterling, cost us more than 50 basis points above gilt-edged, and for most of the 1980s we were able to price fixed-rate loans at a margin over a money cost which was set by 3i's treasury at gilt plus half a per cent.

Does 3i's Funding Experience Prove Anything?

The debate between those who argue that British industry would have invested more if they could have found the capital and those who believe they invested inadequately because they had insufficient opportunities of making a satisfac-tory return will no doubt revive whenever the rate of British economic growth falls short of that achieved by others. At least since the end of the 1950s 3i's experience has been that whatever may be the reasons for a particular level of investment demand, the resources were always found to meet it. Domestic sources proved adequate until the end of the 1970s, when exchange controls were removed, finally giving British industry unfettered access to the world's capital markets, an occurrence of real significance whose importance has not been properly recognized. As exchange-control barriers have come down, investors and investees have had access to each other on a global basis, and cap-ital now flows across currency boundaries with great freedom, adding a new dimension to the debate about capital starvation. In the year before FFI's first eurobond issue the Chairman, Lord Seebohm, had commented critically in his Annual Statement on this continuing argument.

The controversy over the investment record of private industry continues unabated. A sharp fall in new manufacturing investment brought about by low profitability and lack of confidence is described by some as a strike by big business accompanied by the inevitable collectivist non-solutions. Observers outside this country are dismayed at the proposals coming forward to extend State Control and intervention of one kind or another over the already overburdened private sector. Proposals for the coercion of industrial investment, compelling firms to invest out of blocked profits or forcing private savings unwillingly into directions chosen by the planners, disregard the obvious liquidity of financial institutions and the remarkable resilience of the capital market which has, during our financial year, supplied well over £1 billion in the form of new equity capital for commerce and industry. The most disturbing aspect of all is the lack of effective arguments to counter these distorted views. From time to time a lone voice is heard explaining how profits and investment are interdependent and how together they determine an efficient distribution of resources. But there is no sustained exposé of how the neo-Luddites would reduce the wealth of the country irretrievably and make any rise in the standard of living impossible.

As recently as the 1992 election the Labour Party was arguing that British industry needed more investment, implying if not stating in so many words that access to external sources of money was all that was needed for industrial investment to surge ahead and thus create more jobs. It has been argued here that, with the exception of the period in the 1950s when credit controls limited the shareholders' ability to supply ICFC with capital, we have never been short of funds for viable investment projects. The international dimension which capital markets took on with the opening of the sterling market to foreign investors, and the subsequent abolition of exchange controls, allowed industrial companies access to virtually unlimited funds in all usable currencies and at a very competitive cost. They were no longer restricted to their own domestic sources of funds, but could go wherever the funds were cheapest and most appropriate for their needs.

For large public companies, direct access to the international markets was now possible in their own names. For smaller companies in the UK, 3i provided a bridge to these new sources of funds. It was of course equally possible, once exchange controls had been dismantled, for the UK investment institutions which had been ICFC's and FFI's principal source of funds to divert investments into their portfolios overseas. This had no effect on us, the more so because the competitive nature of the international markets gave them a cost advantage over the UK's domestic market, where institutional investors had been weaned on the continuous supply of government stock, with attractive yields, perfect credit, absolute liquidity, and a variety of maturities. This was what the expression 'crowding out' really meant: there was no absolute barrier for companies wanting to raise capital in the domestic UK market—money could be raised in the domestic market as we had shown, but its price had to take account of the government's advantages.

Nevertheless the accusations that British industry was being starved of funds continued into the 1980s, now on the grounds that the City institutions were moving their portfolios into competing economies. It was hard to see the justification for this argument from FFI's point of view, because we had become able to choose whether we went to the domestic market or borrowed from foreign investors. It was of no concern to us if domestic institutions preferred US corporate bonds to those issued by FFI. We were actually able to borrow more cheaply from the foreign investor, who was looking to supplement the return on investment by a currency gain. Since 1978 all FFI's and, subsequently, 3i's fixed-interest issues have been in the international capital markets.

The fact that these markets were centred on the City of London gave 3i a real advantage, because all the relevant banks had branches or subsidiaries in London. There was no need for us to travel the world meeting the legendary Belgian dentist, or his equivalent, Mrs Watanabe the Japanese housewife, the archetypes of the internationally orientated private investor. They could place their funds through their local banks in international bond issues managed or underwritten by those same banks' London offices.

For 3i, access to funds has usually depended on price, rather than availability of money, but there has always been a market-driven limit to the price we could afford to pay and still keep our profit-and-loss account in the black. Moreover, it would have been just as damaging to our reputation to have paid too much as it would if we had underpriced our issues.

This description of our funding efforts should make it clear that, since it has been free to raise its own funds, 3i has always been able to meet its commitments to provide long-term and permanent capital and has not had to hold back for lack of money. With the benefit of that experience it is difficult to accept an argument which attributes British industry's low investment levels simply to a shortage of money. The causes are more complicated and an attempt is made elsewhere in this book to get at the real issues.

NOTES

[1] See Ch. 1, p. 16.
[2] See Ch. 3, p. 53-66.
[3] See Ch. 5, p.123-7.

Chapter 11

Management Style and Strategy

The Piercy/Kinross Era: Creating the Ethos

ONE OF 3i'S MORE PROVOCATIVE advertisements claimed that we were 'more like businessmen than bankers'. This was true enough: the people who ran 3i were not bankers, and its staff were rarely recruited from the banks. Perhaps this fact was the only common thread, for the staff recruited over the first twenty-five years, at least, had all manner of business experience and were employed for their willingness and ability to assess commercial risk.

It was to be in the attitude to risk that its founding fathers would differentiate ICFC from the banks. Lord Piercy's vision was that of a major national institution, operating with the grain of government policy, although not financially dependent on the State, and supplementing the banks' short-term lending function by providing the private-company sector with all its capital needs. His close ties with the Labour Party, which first achieved unequivocal power a few weeks before ICFC's formation, gave him entry to government circles; and a number of the staff were active members of the Labour Party, including Ted Cole, an early industrial adviser and one of ICFC's great characters, who was a Labour Party organizer, and Chris Attlee, one of the first and most innovative of ICFC's investment controllers, who was a nephew of the Prime Minister. Nothing much came of the early links with government, although it may have had some value in protecting ICFC from the hostility of certain of its shareholders, but it took forty years to shake off the widespread impression that ICFC was some sort of quango.

A strong antidote to the sense of national purpose which Lord Piercy brought to ICFC was provided by the hard-headed commercialism of John Kinross; JBK was a legend in his own time in ICFC. Having been present at its opening in 1945 he remained connected, more or less closely, until only six months before his death at the age of 85 in 1989. His investment judgement was remarkable, and based essentially on an understanding of human nature which enabled him to make uncannily accurate assessments of people and their likely behaviour. He was proud of the fact that he had made his own fortune on the Stock Market by turning an initial investment of £10 into £7 million (the bulk of which he had handed over to a charitable trust), and it was undoubtedly his investment judgement which set the standard for ICFC. It would be difficult to overstate the beneficial effects of JBK's influence on ICFC's development over a period of more than forty years. He was the master at whose feet all the subsequent Chief Executives sat and sharpened their own investment skills.

The juxtaposition of Lord Piercy and JBK at the head of ICFC thus epitomized and to a great extent was responsible for its ambivalence; poised between City and government, strictly commercial in every transaction but encompassing a broad view of the national need for a source of private-company capital.

Neither was sympathetic to bureaucracy, and the organization they built round them was remarkable for its loose structure, the easy delegation of responsibility, and its ready acceptance by a team of individuals who seem to have been chosen for the quality of their minds rather than for any proven investment skills. Even when I joined in 1964, nearly twenty years after ICFC's formation, the atmosphere of freedom and informality was refreshing to a young recruit, and the opportunity to shape one's own job profile without interference was an attractive challenge. Such informality had its negative side, however, in particular in the lack of an organizational structure through which ambitious staff could hope to progress, and the total absence of any kind of salary policy. So my excitement at the prospect of working for such a stimulating organization was tempered by an opinion expressed over lunch in my first week that ICFC was 'a great place for a young man with no ambition and a private income'. But the lack of policy direction, other than that filtering down through the investment decisions of Cases Committee provided opportunities both for idiosyncratic behaviour and for innovative solutions to customers' problems. Investment staff found it possible to identify strongly with a customer's needs in the knowledge that any agreed financing scheme which emerged would have to pass the scrutiny of Cases Committee in order to ensure that it also suited ICFC's book.

Cases Committee: The Key to it All

It was apparent to all the staff that reputations were forged in the fire of Cases Committee by the submission of imaginative but commercial investment proposals. Although the loose structure and the open-door policy of the top management invited direct approaches by aspiring young controllers, it was clear that such ease of vertical access was not to be abused by personal lobbying but was made available for discussion of investment matters only. This approach allowed ICFC to develop as an enlightened organization, where individuals earned the respect of their peers by their professionalism and commitment. It also had the advantage of ensuring that no controller needed to go out on a limb in his negotiations with a potential customer because consultation was encouraged. The need for a close rapport with customers in order that appropriate financial packages could be put together was well understood, as was the consequent vulnerability of the controller to customer pressure for a favourable deal. He could always refer back for advice, and was expected to, but the investment proposal submitted to Cases Committee was his responsibility; it had to come with a clear commitment and firm recommendations. It was no use setting out the pros and cons and leaving the rest to Cases Committee. If its members felt sufficiently well informed on the facts, and were satisfied that the finance was structured to provide a reasonable deal for the customer and a satisfactory return for ICFC, it would accept the proposal and from that point it would become a corporate responsibility. If the investment subsequently went wrong there would be no witch hunt, although this would not prevent informal opinions being formed retrospectively about the soundness of a controller's judgement.

It was Lord Piercy and JBK who set up the Cases Committee system for investment decisions, at the same time establishing it not only as the vehicle for formulating investment policy but also as an informal mechanism for assessing the performance of the controllers and the various professionals, industrial advisers, and investigating accountants who were involved in the investment process. It is not surprising that, as the organization grew, the access provided to top management through Cases Committee came to be seen as the key to career success and, eventually, with the broadening of the range of activity and development of support services, as the creator of a two-tier organization. One group had direct access to management through the Cases Committee system, and those who did not tended to feel underprivileged by their relative remoteness.

Cases Committee lay at the heart of ICFC, and was arguably the key factor in its success at taking on the unpromising task laid down by its founders of providing support for the small business sector and developing it into the successful investment capital business it was to become—making a veritable silk purse from a sow's ear. Formally constituted as a Committee of the Board, it usually included not only the Chairman, Deputy Chairman, and General Manager, but other senior members of the management, all with direct experience of investment negotiation, and it has remained essentially unchanged to this day. Through a gradual process of delegation the Board assigned authority for investment decisions of increasing amounts, first to Cases Committee and subsequently to regional and local managers; but some final decision-making was always reserved to Cases Committee, with the very largest proposals going on to the Board. Despite the onerous task of case-reading this imposed on the top management for their twice weekly meetings—cases often numbered ten or more, all meticulously prepared—it was always regarded as essential for Cases Committee to see at least some of the proposals coming through.

Through its decisions the Committee could formulate and disseminate investment policy as part of an evolutionary process. Each proposal was related to an actual and current customer need, but the decision could take account not only of the changing market conditions reflected in the cases coming forward, but also of ICFC's own needs for an adequate and appropriate return on the capital it was asked to deploy. Investment policy was thus formulated not only as a sensitive response to the changing market but also as a means of monitoring the content of ICFC's own portfolio, both as to the nature of the investments, whether loans or shares, and in the mix of industries within the portfolio. From time to time it was felt necessary to increase the equity content to match the growth of shareholders' equity, or to change the portfolio weighting. Occasionally a series of individual decisions led to an excessive amount of capital being tied up in a particular sector; computer bureaux and property companies were notable examples of sectors where negligible risk inherent in individual companies was enhanced by the systemic risk of a particularly vulnerable sector. This was relatively unusual, because it was rare for companies of the size normally financed by ICFC to hold a dominant market position, but it was preferable to manage such changes through the decision-making process. To make pre-emptive policy declarations might lead to loss of attractive business or to the discovery, too late, that an industry which was in danger of oversupply was over-represented in the portfolio. This approach made it possible to invest even in declining industries when an outstanding management team was discovered, capable of increasing market share as the competitors pulled out or failed.

The chief virtue of the Cases Committee system lay in the reconciliation it provided between ICFC's interests and those of its customers; but it was by no means simply an arbitrator. Within the membership of Cases Committee lay a variety of individual experience which forced a consensus among the members on every decision, maintaining the integrity of the process and its quality standards over many years. As with all such bodies it was as fallible as the individuals who comprised its membership. Proposals could be written to take account of a particular member's prejudices, or submissions might be deferred if the likely composition of the Committee was thought unfavourable. But, seen from my uninvolved position, the checks and balances of Cases Committee seemed to result in decisions of consistently high quality.

Looked at from the standpoint of management it is clear that Cases Committee was always an integral element in the policy-making process. With no written policies laid down by the Board, investment policy was formulated through its decisions and disseminated through formal minutes recording each decision. As the only document of policy formation, Cases Committee minutes had wide circulation and were subject to minute analysis. They were the runes by which the organization was guided through the dangers and difficulties of commercial life. Only the decision itself was recorded in the minutes, with occasional touches on the tiller to indicate that a particular decision was not a precedent for others of a similar kind, or that the Committee had seen enough cases from a particular industry. But alongside this formal mechanism lay a subtle and sensitive informal channel of communication, the Cases Committee secretary. Because this was a Board Committee the secretarial service was normally provided by the Company Secretary or an assistant whose job was not only to record and distribute the minutes, but also to convey the sense of the meeting to the controllers. This job was, therefore seen as very important by the whole organization, and at one stage was allocated to promising young controllers for a six-month or one-year stint. Surprisingly, although those who did it realized the enormous value of sitting in on Cases Committee decisions, it was seen by most aspiring young controllers as a diversion from their career path which would leave them behind their colleagues in the promotion stakes. In at least one case it proved to be no impediment to promotion: Neil Cross, the first incumbent, later became a main Board director in charge of international operations. But the idea was dropped when volunteers ceased to put themselves forward.

With the growth of competition in the UK and the development of overseas offices the virtues of Cases Committee as a quality-control mechanism were to an extent offset by its practical disadvantages. Competitors in the 1980s, who knew the Cases Committee system, were able to exploit the delays which it caused by making conditional offers long before a decision could be produced by 3i, and were able to portray it as a creaking bureaucracy. The overriding need to control quality from the centre proved an irritant and caused delays which were unacceptable to many customers. Solving this problem was not easy without undermining the fundamental basis of 3i's success: its ability to make high quality judgements before committing capital.

Nevertheless, for many years Cases Committee worked well both as a forum for investment decisions and as a conduit for investment-policy transmission. New ideas for solving actual problems in the market-place were tested out on Cases Committee and, if approved, became adopted as policy. However, the success of this informal system depended on the small size of the organization, allowing everyone to know each other's strengths and weaknesses and encouraging an *esprit de corps* to develop. Geographical dispersal inevitably put

259

this desirable cohesiveness under strain, and it is perhaps surprising that the system survived for so long. In the 1960s the policy of opening offices close to the customers, establishing an area structure to manage them, and at the same time setting up separate industrial and legal departments, diluted the cohesion of a single organization operating under one roof. It was inevitable that, as the business grew, the enlightened informality of the first fifteen years or so must give way to a more formal structure. As management authority was delegated so local fiefdoms could be established to challenge the authority and omniscience of the centre.

Cases Committee probably helped to prolong that desirable cohesiveness. Whilst management responsibility was heavily delegated and local managers were encouraged to become significant members of the community in which they worked, they were given very little actual investment authority. Only gradually was it delegated to regional offices, by periodically raising local investment limits. In the early days controllers presented their cases in person and ran the gauntlet of the Committee's scepticism: an invaluable formative experience which geographical dispersal eventually rendered impractical. From the mid-1960s controllers were required to send their proposals to London, with the blessing of their branch or area managers.

There was scope here for misunderstanding by the Committee, based as they were in London and increasingly out of touch with the market. But its members, the Chairman, JBK, and Larry Tindale in particular, saw it as most important to see for themselves what was going on in the field, to meet customers, and, at the same time to provide moral support for their staff. There was great sympathy at the centre for the stresses and strains of a provincial controller's life, and it became usual for ICFC's top management to tour the country, visiting offices, meeting customers, and speaking at conferences organized to boost both the local team's morale and its image in the community.

At the same time there was the equally serious possibility of branch staff being suborned by would-be customers offering flattery and more tangible inducements to represent their case with sympathy, and to propose particularly favourable terms. The requirement to present their proposals to Cases Committee with its collection of wise and experienced investment practitioners who had seen it all before, was an important deterrent to local staff going native.

The Tindale Era: Regional Expansion

With the change of Chairman in 1964 and the retirement of Arthur English—the other joint General Manager whose concerns were mainly internal and particularly tax-related—Larry Tindale effectively took sole charge of the organization. In Lord Sherfield he had a Chairman who was much less directly involved than his predecessor, and gave his General Manager considerable freedom to shape the institution to his own ends. Larry was supported strongly by John Kinross, who had become Deputy Chairman, and they became close personal friends, but essentially it was now Larry's show and the management style changed dramatically. To those of us who grew up under his tutelage, Larry was the nearest thing to a genius we had ever met. His all-encompassing intelligence was awe-inspiring, and it was soon realized that every unsupported assertion would be challenged, every bright new idea would be tested against his own private plan of where ICFC was going. The intellectual rigour he brought to bear on all subjects was both stimulating and frightening. The clarity of his thinking and his almost total detachment took him rapidly to the essence of a problem, although for some his brutal outspokenness was intimidating.

It is doubtful whether under Lord Piercy and JBK there was any formal strategic direction. The first Chairman had set the pattern of opportunistic responses to market needs as they arose, provided they fitted his grand vision of ICFC as a major financial institution. To the extent that he had allowed ICFC to diversify it had been an eclectic choice. The Fuel and Power Scheme reflected his wish to work closely with government; Ship Mortgage was almost wholly outside the original ICFC remit but met a particular market need. On the other hand EDITH was a perfectly logical extension of its function, as was TDC, a response to the report of the Radcliffe Committee to which Lord Piercy gave evidence.

The practice of opportunistic response to market needs was continued under Larry and became effectively formal policy, but its emphasis was different. His strategic vision was of a highly focused institution, unequivocally commercial but providing support for the small business sector as a whole, not only in the provision of capital but in meeting the need for services which were not readily available to the smaller company. So TDC was taken under ICFC's full control; NUMAS (the Advisory Service of the National Union of Manufacturers) was bought in to provide tailor-made consultancy for small companies, whilst sale and leaseback of property was started *ab initio*, as were leasing and hire purchase of plant, corporate finance, and fund management. The extension of ICFC's remit to public companies, though logical at the smaller end, was not easy, because its shareholding position would have led to conflicts of interest between ICFC and the other shareholders; but two specialized investment trusts, LAIT and NBC, were formed for this purpose, ICFC providing the management and a substantial minority of the initial capital.

It was a feature of Larry's period as Chief Executive that the Company was run on a very thin administrative structure, with all senior managers reporting to him. It was only when Jon Foulds took over that the General Management team was broadened to spread responsibility for what had by then become a diversified business.

In the 1960s the strategy of focusing on the small company sector had as its main objective to stave off the ever-present threat of government intervention. If ICFC was not manifestly filling the small company gap the government would find it easier to justify setting up its own creature which, with its access to subsidized funds, would inevitably undermine ICFC's position. Larry had seen the need to distance ICFC from government in order to counter the general impression that it was a state-owned body, a misconception which seriously hampered the marketing of its major competitive advantage as a complementary source of capital to the banks. The owners of private businesses were fiercely independent and keen to keep the government out. They would have been happy to take subsidized money, but not to accept the strings which were invariably attached. In particular they did not want to give government departments access to their records. They feared a loss of confidentiality which could prejudice their competitive position. Many also thought accepting money from a Labour administration would open the door to the trade unions.

Larry's policy of diversifying into areas of activity which were relevant to ICFC's basic function of supporting the small business sector was thus narrowly justified in terms of keeping the government at arms length. It may also have had some effect in raising the entry threshold for private-sector competitors and thus at least delaying the growth of competition until the market was large enough to bear it. Such a defensive policy was justified so long as ICFC had all the resources it needed to meet demand, and was neither able nor willing to exploit its dominant market position. In practice pricing policy was generally market-related, and financial packages were tailored to the customers' ability to pay as well as to ICFC's own requirements. The customer was protected by ICFC's need to establish and maintain a long-term working partnership with him.

The weakness of the diversification policy lay mainly in the complex management and information structures which were necessary to control a range of widely differing businesses, and yet were not justified in terms of the financial benefits. It was all held together by Larry's own remarkable ability to understand the whole business and to carry all the relevant information in his head. His successor, Paul Hildesley, was left with a broadly based organization but without the management structure to control it. It was unfortunate that this organizational weakness coincided with the serious economic instability of the mid-1970s, precipitated by the property boom which was itself facilitated by the ready availability of cheap credit. ICFC had made the sensible decision to sell its City head office at the height of the boom, and the £15 million of cash and the reserves this generated provided valuable protection when the crash wiped out the assets of the property-development business which was the latest and most alien of ICFC's diversifications. This, together with the Stock Market collapse which eliminated all ICFC's accumulated capital profits, caused a grave crisis of confidence with the shareholders just at the time when ICFC's traditional role was being expanded with the purchase of FCI.

The Hildesley Era: Difficult Times

Paul Hildesley faced a trying time as the difficulties he inherited were compounded by further problems brought on by the serious economic recession of 1974–75. But he was strongly supported both by the new Chairman, Lord Seebohm, and by Larry, on his return from the DTI, as Deputy Chairman, in the face of criticism from within the Board, and doubts among the shareholders who were at the same time being asked to put up £25 million of new capital. Fortunately the financial position remained strong enough for the new FFI to go on raising funds without further assistance from the shareholders, and for the core business to go on expanding. But the coincidence of these events with the Roadships affair and the need to write off, within a year of its commitment, the whole £4.5 million which had been absorbed by underwriting BCal's purchase of British United Airways, left the business weakened in terms of its credibility with shareholders and markets.

Lord Seebohm, who had been on the Board for some years, was a distinguished and experienced banker who knew ICFC well enough to have acquired considerable respect for it, but he also had an uncomfortable baptism on taking over from Lord Sherfield in 1974. As he said in his 1975 statement:

I need not remind shareholders of the unprecedented difficulties that have struck all major financial institutions. We announced at half time the necessity for making special provisions against certain major investments of £4.4m. We also foreshadowed other provisions which might amount to another £18m, caused in part by the need (which arose from the publication of the Government's land proposals) [this referred to the Development Land Tax intended to tax windfall gains on property development] to write down the value of development sites in our subsidiary, Anglia Commercial Properties Limited, to current-use values and partly by the decline in market values of equities.

He commented on the general economic situation:

In today's conditions to look forward is fraught with difficulty. It seems that we must accept the imposition of harsh and unpleasant financial and social policies or willy nilly learn to live with a frightening rate of inflation. I believe that the choice cannot long be delayed in that if there is future procrastination the second will come about.

The rake's progress condemned so forcefully by Lord Seebohm in July 1975 continued for another year, culminating in the collapse of sterling, an inflation rate of 26 per cent, gilt yields over 16 per cent and the arrival of the IMF to sort things out. By mid-1977, when Paul retired after five years in a very hot seat, the situation had improved markedly. The integration of FCI had been completed and its rapid expansion initiated by Jon Foulds was under way, whilst ICFC's own position had stabilized with the recovery in the Stock Market, and its long period of dynamic growth under David Marlow had begun. Lord Seebohm's powerful influence with the Board and the shareholders had allowed the management breathing space to stabilize the property situation and set about the profitable completion of the development portfolio. We had been helped materially by the £1 billion fund, which the Governor of the Bank of England had put together to demonstrate the willingness of the City to finance industrial investment at a time of deep recession and the renewed threat of government intervention.

The Foulds Style: Collective Government

Jon Foulds took over as Chief Executive in 1977 at a time when the difficulties of the early 1970s had been resolved. The portfolio was sound, FCI had been successfully established, and ICFC had begun its long period of strong investment growth. However, he faced serious difficulties in controlling the disparate collection of businesses which had been grafted onto the original ICFC.

Whilst Jon had been trained in the ICFC tradition and was a disciple of Larry Tindale and John Kinross in investment matters, the management style he adopted was new. Paul Hildesley had effectively followed the Tindale method, carrying most of the responsibility for managing the increasingly unwieldy and diverse organization and delegating relatively little. The style adopted by Jon was more collegiate; he gathered round him a group of senior colleagues, to whom he delegated general management responsibilities. Although very experienced in ICFC's business, it was a young team.

David Marlow, the youngest at 42, and Jon's eventual successor, had joined in 1960, and his seventeen years' experience was almost entirely in the ICFC investment business which now became his responsibility. Nigel Olsen had joined in 1963 and also had long experience of ICFC business, but his growing understanding of larger company affairs prompted his appointment to take over Jon's responsibility for FCI's development, a task which required wholly different skills and experience from those of ICFC. Ivan Momtchiloff, a more recent arrival, but with valuable industrial experience, manfully took on the activities of TDC, leasing, property, and consultancy, all of them going through identity crises.

Finance and accounting were my responsibility, and the remaining aspects of administration were covered by Brian Mann, who had been Chief Legal Officer for many years and whose commercial acumen and dedication were greatly appreciated by his colleagues. The team lacked experience in general management and had no knowledge of the ways of corporate governance, though much had been learned at one remove from the customers, and those who had come from the eternally fascinating investment business found the distraction provided by Cases Committee, which they all quite properly continued to sit on, a tempting diversion from less exciting general management concerns: the formulation, modification, and reformulation of staff car policy was a particularly tedious example of the chores which became its daily business. It was difficult, as it is in any organization, to make the transition from line to general management; the skills and experience which come from many years at the coalface are not easily jettisoned, but seem remarkably irrelevant when the new function is the broader and more complex administration of a diverse organization.

Jon Foulds, who was intuitively commercial and always fascinated by investment matters, must have found it difficult to discipline himself and let go of the reins which had been held so tightly by his predecessors. But his consultative style allowed his colleagues great freedom, both in the management of their own parts of the business, and in the formulation of policy for the Group as a whole. By this means he intended to create a cohesive organization out of one which lacked organizational coherence. The activities of the constituent parts were so different and their financial significance covered such a wide spectrum that inevitably there was a sense of conflict between the old-established ICFC-based part of the Group and the newcomers. Despite the strains, general management worked well together under Jon's leadership, helped by mutual respect, his even-handed chairmanship of meetings, and the regular awaydays which forged a much closer spirit of mutual understanding than might otherwise have been the case.

Looking back on the period of ten years under Jon's leadership it seems remarkable that such a diverse organization could have held together for so long. It is a tribute to his determination to make it do so by treating all parts as far as possible equally. The preservation of unity was both helped and hindered by the great financial success which was achieved in the period 1977 to 1987, a time of very rapid investment growth and of substantial increases in both revenue and capital profits. The Group's overall success allowed the great disparities in performance to be overlooked, but it also caused inner tensions; it was almost entirely due to ICFC and concealed some very poor performances elsewhere. The shipping division, which had been built up in the 1960s and 1970s with few problems, found that weakening covenants and a serious over-supply of ships worldwide forced on it some £25 million of write-offs during the first half of the 1980s. 3i Ventures, which had begun its new life on the American pattern with two resounding successes—Rodime and LSI Logic—found itself unable to repeat them, and its returns relied more and more on hopeful projections rather than on actual realizations. The property division also found itself offsetting its profitable realizations with write-downs of underperforming developments which undermined the Group's revenue growth.

With the shift towards market-related remuneration packages, aimed primarily at helping to recruit into 3i Ventures and at the same time protecting ICFC from poaching by the rapidly growing venture capital market, the potential for schism increased. The level playing field could not be sustained if staff were to be rewarded by reference to external conditions in their various industries rather than, as previously, by a homogeneous set of valuations determined principally by job content.

Throughout the late 1970s and the 1980s this need to control and motivate what had become a diverse organization gave rise to increasing formality in organizational terms. We had always been gap-fillers, ready to respond to a market opportunity if it fell into a quite loosely defined range of compatible activities. Larry had narrowed down Lord Piercy's broad vision to the smaller company sector, but the acquisition of FCI then allowed the expansion of the large company side of the business, which had previously only been involved in shipping. The opportunistic management which preceded Jon had been able to justify each addition to the range of businesses on its own terms and by reference to the strategy of the time. The resulting Group encompassed small-company capital, large company financial engineering, shipbuilding, the leasing of plant, office equipment and agricultural machinery, property development and investment, management consultancy, fund management, and corporate finance; it had no real coherence.

At first the main strategic efforts during Jon's term as Chief Executive were concentrated on finding a role for FCI, trying to bring the performance of the peripheral parts of the Group up to scratch, and making sense of the varied collection of businesses he had inherited, rather than questioning their existence. The importing of alien skills and experience had never been very successful, but it was a risk which had to be taken to recruit an experienced property man, Peter Willcock, who could be entrusted with a task none of the team knew much about, that of rescuing the development portfolio and improving the return on the property investments. This was followed by the recruitment of Geoff Taylor, an Englishman who had worked in California, to breathe life into the moribund TDC, which although it had never lost much money had never made any either.

It was felt that FCI could be run by experienced ICFC people, Jon himself having managed its integration into the Group and developed its early investment strategy. There was thus a less serious culture clash here than in properties or TDC. Nigel Olsen, who took on General Management responsibility, was one of the most experienced ICFC operators and he was able to build a team which quickly adapted to the particular needs of the medium-sized quoted companies which were FCI's natural customers. New management was also imported into the corporate finance and fund management businesses where ICFC experience was inappropriate, and the organization became, during the late 1970s and early 1980s, a very loose collection of separate fiefdoms, each with its own culture, and many owing more to the outside experience of the managers than to the influence of the long ICFC tradition. Whilst the attempt to bring relevant expertise to bear across the Group was clearly justified, it inevitably exposed the very diverse nature of the businesses which had been collected together under the banner of FFI and the lack of commercial logic in the resulting Group.

Jon's consultative style led him quite soon to find out what the staff thought about this via a series of opinion surveys. At the same time we were having great difficulty in getting the outside world to understand what FFI was: ICFC's long-standing struggle to gain public awareness of what it did was only exacerbated by the existence of its new parent, FFI, and its sibling, FCI. It was difficult to maintain ICFC's posture as the supporter of the small business sector when FCI was doing highly publicized business with large companies. The public perception of FFI was even more confused; the name was similar to those of its subsidiaries and its existence did nothing for ICFC's campaign to distance itself from government. We felt obliged to advertise in the name of FFI, in order to explain how the different parts of the Group hung together, but it was not very effective.

In the public-bond market FFI soon became recognized as a major financial institution of undoubted credit standing, and its ownership by the Bank of England and the clearers was well understood; but its component parts on the asset side were known only in their own markets, and their relationship with each other and the fact that they were part of a powerful financial institution were not understood.

Jon explained his dilemma in a memorandum addressed to senior managers in 1981:

The diversity of the individual investment activities is reinforced by the absence of a strong unifying parent ... It was a deliberate choice not to promote FFI externally except as a fundraising vehicle—in order not to give the impression of losing interest in the small company sector. Internally it was felt that each activity should be free to develop its own identity as historically ICFC had done. But we need to re-examine the face presented to the world and strengthen the central identity of FFI. We ought to consider an entirely new name, which like Exxon or Kodak can be dressed up in different colours to suit different circumstances—and for this we shall need outside advice. The

Compounding the confusion: FFI's attempt to explain itself in an advertisement
DDB Needham

top company attracts little group loyalty and a semi-feudal structure of divisional and departmental barons exists who have a strong sense of exclusivity and tend to tread warily with each other.

Jon saw his task, therefore, as one of creating a coherent image of the whole organization which would add value to the parts rather than detract from their public perception. But it was of no use to manufacture a unifying image if the parts were indeed separate in everything they did. FFI might as well be a financial-services conglomerate, which, though possible, would not make use of the potential for cross-fertilization. Jon saw the possibility of synergy between most parts of his organization: Portfolio Management could manage pension funds for investment customers, Consultancy could have access to the whole ICFC portfolio to do work on improving customer performance, and thus the value of the Group's investments. Ventures could take on the difficult start-up cases, devoting more time and effort to them than ICFC could, and, as they matured, pass them on to be further managed and financed by ICFC. Corporate Finance could provide advice to portfolio companies wanting to sell out or buy other companies. Investment proposals coming through the ICFC offices with a heavy property content could make use of the property division's skills.

The Chief Executive's mission might be summarized as one of unifying FFI, not for its own sake but to enhance the total performance of the Group, so that the whole would be greater than the sum of its parts. Most of his ten years in the position were taken up with trying to fulfil this mission. It was not easy to see at the time, but with hindsight unification seems to have been a procrustean ambition, such was the variety of functions among the divisions, so diverse were the skills and experience of their management and, crucially, their cultures. Add in the enormous range of financial performance, in particular the almost total dominance of ICFC, and the task was virtually impossible, despite the enormous amounts of energy and money which were put into the unification attempt. It was the main internal justification for changing the parent's name, although at the same time it gave greater visibility, both to the Group and to its operating divisions: '3i Ventures', '3i Consultants', '3i Corporate Finance', even—after a strong rearguard action by ICFC—'3i Regions'.

When Jon gave way to David Marlow in 1987, having presided over and inspired the most remarkable period of growth in the Company's history, the strategy was already beginning imperceptibly to change from diversification to a gradual concentration on the core business. The leasing businesses of Highland and Hamilton had been sold some time before, in 1980 and 1981. They had been bought in only to preserve ICFC's investments in them, and were obviously out of step with the main Group. They were heavily labour-intensive, employing almost half the total Group staff, and very short-term in their orientation.

Otherwise there were no disposals until David Marlow became Chief Executive. But by 1985 external pressures had begun to make themselves felt. The shareholders' decision in that year to consider ways of disposing of all or part of their holdings forced upon us a reappraisal of the Group's direction. The effective independence of 3i, its lack of accountability, their own inability to control and direct it, the inadequacy of the information and the miserly dividends they received were all issues which had rumbled on since the formation of ICFC; but they had never previously considered selling their shares.

3i's management had contributed to the shareholders' new interest in their forty-year-old offspring by responding almost too effectively to the shareholders' growing demands for better information, and complaints about poor performance. In a series of detailed presentations which Jon Foulds and I gave to the general management of individual shareholding banks, the rapidly growing value of their investment was made apparent. In particular they were enabled to see beyond the meagre dividend yield to the considerable growth in the capital value of their investments which had been achieved by ploughing back the bulk of the revenue and capital profits. It was frustrating for them that they could effectively only bring into their own accounts the cash income they received by way of dividend. Most of them were sceptical of the additional share of 3i's profit which equity accounting allowed them to bring into their own revenue accounts, and none of them felt able to take account of the growth in capital values.

With the clearing banks becoming more vociferous in their demands for an exit route, the Bank of England adopted a strictly neutral position, saying it would not stand in the way of an agreed solution and would do what it could to facilitate an orderly disposal. The 3i Board's response to these demands was that, whilst it would prefer to preserve the *status quo* in the interests of the business and in particular the companies which had accepted 3i as a long-term partner, it could not object to the shareholders' perfectly reasonable wishes to unlock their holdings. But the preservation of the Company and its obligations to customers were more important than the wishes of any single shareholder; and we quickly put forward a proposal for the flotation of 3i as an investment trust. As we saw it, this was the only solution which could allow individual shareholders to make their own decisions as and when they wished, without jeopardizing the basic functions and essential independence of the company. Our proposal put forward in 1985 was not accepted until some six years later, and for the whole of that time the prospect of a change of ownership and the likelihood of flotation dominated the strategic thinking of Board and management.

So, for the first time since Larry's day, the long-established strategy of opportunistic gap-filling came seriously into question, and we began to review the fundamental policies and strategic direction of the Group. A planning round was instituted, with the object of setting a course which would be consistent with flotation in the event that shareholders decided to accept the Board's recommendation. Inevitably the planning process brought the separate activities of the Group under the spotlight; each had to justify its own existence, both in its own right, and as an integral part of 3i Group. It would be essential to retain no part of the Group whose place in it was not logically justified, and whose performance in its own field was not comparable with that of the core investment business. It would be unacceptable for the market perception of the business to be adversely affected by the presence of under-performing divisions.

Although the general strategic direction was set by Jon and agreed by the General Management team, planning was essentially bottom up, each division preparing its own plan and forecast performance, the whole being aggregated centrally before submission to the Board. If it had not been apparent before, this process made it clear to all how varied were the standards of performance existing across the Group. The overall results appearing in the published accounts had obscured some elements which were seriously below par and were dragging down the consolidated results, even though year after year new records were being achieved in investments, in balance sheet growth, and in realized capital profits.

David Marlow: Managing Rationalization

With a new Chairman, Sir John Cuckney, taking over from Lord Caldecote, and a new Chief Executive in David Marlow, 1987 was a turning-point. A record year, despite the Stock Market crash, it really saw the end of the high growth period and marked the beginning of a period of concentration. While the arguments with and among the shareholders continued, Board and management went on assuming that the only rational outcome would be flotation, and continued preparing the business for that event. At the same time other external influences came into play; the Financial Services Act and a new Banking Act imposed unaccustomed supervision on 3i's management, forcing us to adopt the Bank of England's model procedures and control mechanisms, including the establishment of an audit committee, and at the same time to accept supervision of investment activity by the Securities and Investments Board (SIB). Within the space of two or three years, the traditional informality, mutual reliance, and tolerance with which 3i had been run for forty years, arguably very successfully, were replaced by planning, targeting, compliance, recording, and accountability.

Inevitably the Board, which had been content for many years to allow the management free rein to pursue agreed objectives, had to become more directly involved. For the first time senior managers other than the Chief

Executive were appointed Group directors and the whole Board became involved in strategic planning, whilst committees of the Board were established to bring non-executives into such areas as remuneration policy, treasury operations, and audit. The ultimate responsibility of both executive and non-executive directors for all the actions taken on behalf of the business had become more explicit in the wake of the Guinness and Blue Arrow affairs, making necessary more specific delegation by the Board and formal accountability to it.

The management found itself having to justify all its actions, or at least have the records which would allow their subsequent justification. Fund-raising, which had been elevated to a remarkable pitch of efficiency, permitting major bond issues to be agreed and authorized within hours by consultation between Chairman, Chief Executive, and Finance Director, became subject to formal authorization by a treasury committee. It had once been possible to agree a major bond issue from a public telephone box on Fifth Avenue, such was the degree of mutual trust between the Board and the General Management; and as a result of this ability to make good decisions quickly, some breathtakingly efficient transactions had been completed in the very fast-moving international bond markets. Then an audit committee was formed which not only concerned itself with the Annual Accounts, but with matters of organization, control, and compliance with Bank of England and SIB regulations. It took a year to write up the Group's procedures manual so that it could be audited for the Bank of England, and its effectiveness monitored at tripartite meetings where the auditors reported to the Bank on the Group's systems in the presence of 3i management. All this entailed more formal relationships; policies had to be written down and communication formalized so that written justification could always be produced in the event of a disaster like Blue Arrow. The cost in top management time, and in fees, was enormous, but the benefits to 3i were limited.

At the same time David Marlow faced the problem of changing basic strategy to meet the needs of a quoted company, and reshaping the organization to carry it out. It was an inevitable consequence of building a diversified but at the same time unified Group, that an expensive administration system was needed to service it. Not only were vertical information flows essential for control, but a lateral communications network had to be created to enable the divisions to work effectively with each other. This implied not only a Group administration feeding consolidated information up to the management and the Board, but separate divisional information systems. These were either sub-contracted to the central administration, which was then accused of becoming too large, or they were carried out by back-up staff recruited into the divisions, risking wasteful and confusing duplication of effort and creating local systems which were incompatible with what came out of the centre.

Whilst the central systems worked quite well in terms of the production

3i Chief Executives clockwise from left Jon Foulds 1977–87, Paul Hildesley 1972–77, David Marlow 1987–92, Larry Tindale 1964–72

of accurate, timely, and mainly useful information for the management and the Board, the system for providing compatible local information and inter-divisional communication never worked effectively. This caused serious tensions between people whose corporate reputations and, significantly, remuneration packages were directly affected by the financial information coming out. It was a huge and complex problem, and it was tackled by the creation of a central

Meggitt

ONE OF 3i'S FASTEST GROWING and most innovatory investment techniques during the 1980s was the management buy-in (MBI). Like the management buy-out, the MBI backed a management team to take over the ownership and running of an existing enterprise, although in this case it meant supporting managers wishing to move into an established firm from outside, rather than take over the running of the company in which they were already employed.

3i became involved in the Meggitt MBI in November 1983, backing Ken Coates and Nigel McCorkell to take over what was at the time a small quoted machine tool distributor and metal basher. Coates, an engineer in his early fifties, had a successful career as managing director of an aerospace engineering company but was keen to branch out on his own. The opportunity arose to invest in Meggitt, which was basically sound but had suffered from trading problems and had been losing money for a number of years. Joined by McCorkell, an accountant, Coates approached 3i and a deal was swiftly arranged, taking only six weeks from start to finish. This investment gave 3i 19.9 per cent of the equity but, following an agreement on long-term plans for the development of the business, conferred management control on Coates and McCorkell.

Manufacturing for the civil and defence markets, the company grew rapidly, embarking on a series of acquisitions throughout the 1980s. By 1990, it was divided into four major divisions—aerospace, controls, electronics, and energy. Products range from bus ticket machines to aircraft instruments, from petrol pumps to explosives' detectors and operations have been extended into Europe and the United States. In 1991 3i confirmed its confidence in the long-term prospects of Meggitt by subscribing in full for its share of a £40 million rights issue. Total turnover now exceeds £300 million.

accounting system fed by the divisions and intended to be capable of disaggregation to supply divisional information as well as compatible Group figures. It inevitably took a long time; and while it was being developed the shape of the organization changed dramatically.

For forty years the Group had grown like 'Topsy', more and more peripheral activities being hung on the core business; always growing, never being rationalized. But once the annual corporate-planning cycle had got under way and strategy was reviewed annually, the agglomeration of disparate activities which was 3i in 1985 had begun to come into sharper focus. One by one the peripheral businesses were put to the test and asked how relevant they were to the business as a whole—would they improve or damage 3i's prospects as a public company? None of them could seriously be regarded as contenders, and over a period of some four years they were all, with the exception of the City Office, Corporate Finance, and Portfolio Management, closed down and their assets sold or incorporated in the portfolio of the investment business. There can be no question that the decision to revert to the core business was right, but David Marlow's task was infinitely depressing against a rapidly declining economic background and continuing uncertainty over what the shareholders wanted to do. Once this shrinking was under way the large and unwieldy central administration was no longer necessary. 3i had ceased to be a conglomerate and was reverting to the simple organization that ICFC had originally been, but much larger, more in the public eye.

Having lost one-third of its staff in the two years to 1991 it was difficult for 3i to retain the corporate spirit which had been established in the earlier days; but there were other and earlier causes for this problem. One was the difficulty in maintaining such a diverse conglomerate in the face of the overpowering ICFC ethic, with its combination of public virtue and commercial success. The equilibrium established under Jon's talented leadership was never stable: the peripheral activities should probably have been floated off as soon as they had proved, on strictly applied criteria, either worthless or inherently successful.

Overhanging these internal complications were the ongoing discussions with the shareholders over the future of their holdings. Their protracted nature and the uncertainty about the future of 3i which they caused, had a serious effect on staff morale. It also began to raise questions among the customers, many of whom were understandably concerned that 3i's substantial minority holdings in their capital which they had assumed to be permanent, might be up for sale. At the same time the management had to deal with an expanding overseas presence which created a new layer of administrative complexity. One of Jon Foulds's most significant achievements had been to give 3i an international dimension. A study carried out in 1980 by our own staff established a clear need for institutions like 3i in all the advanced economies. For a variety of reasons nothing like ICFC had been established elsewhere, but by the late 1970s the lack of a source of private-company capital was being noticed in a number of countries, particularly in France and Germany. In the United States the Small Business Administration (SBA) had failed to establish an institutional source of risk capital and the venture capital industry had emerged, using private capital for a very limited number of specialized business situations. No equivalent to ICFC had been set up to meet the needs of the rest of the American small business community, nor was there anything like it in Japan.

We concluded that the Macmillan gap was a global phenomenon and that it had only been effectively filled in the United Kingdom; consequently

"I DON'T NEED THIS AGGRAVATION!"

"HE DON'T NEED THIS AGGRAVATION!"

there seemed greater prospects for a worldwide network of 3i investment businesses based on the ICFC concept, than for the UK-based financial conglomerate which 3i had become. Whilst the strategic arguments for a significant presence in the three major developed economic regions of Europe, North America, and the Far East seemed sound enough, as with so many British ventures in the United States, 3i's own never justified the high hopes held out for it. Surprisingly, it was much easier to transplant the 3i culture into Continental Europe than into the United States. The most serious problem was that, however much effort was put into bringing the US business into the 3i fold, it remained determinedly separate, following the pattern of US venture capital businesses which were run by groups of individuals personally staked in each investment while the institutional partner took a back seat.

The American part of the business made a number of good investments in the early days, but was unable to improve on this through the mid-1980s as the industry generally turned down. The clearing banks' dislike of this diversion of their capital into a high-risk area was to some extent shared by 3i's non-executive directors, who were concerned particularly about the potential for litigation. Failure to build on the early successes, and the fear of the US becoming a black hole which could absorb unlimited capital, made it difficult to sustain the central strategy. Some presence in the United States seemed essential as a window on new technologies, but it became increasingly difficult to justify it in financial terms. However, it was not until the early 1990s that the decision to run American business down was taken and the global strategy shrank to a more manageable European scale. This was another case of inadequate infrastructure to manage a far-flung and potentially rebellious empire. It was only in the late 1980s that an international division was formed, and then only on a very limited scale; this imposed huge burdens on Neil Cross, the director concerned with directing 3i's presence across the globe.

The Internationalizing of Management Style and Strategic Direction

Looking back over forty-odd years of management styles, I see a remarkable consistency in the strategic direction of 3i in its various manifestations but great differences in the way it has been managed. Until the late 1980s the successive Chief Executives, with greater or lesser input from their Chairmen, set the general direction. Their main priority was always to put into the original ICFC business all the resources necessary to make it capable of meeting any level of demand for capital from the private company sector, without ever chasing market share for its own sake. Subject to this overriding need they were prepared to take any opportunity which presented itself and could be regarded as in some way related to, or supportive of, the main business.

Only on the arrival in 1987 of a more interventionist Chairman and a naturally cautious Chief Executive did this eclectic process cease and the strategy of focusing on the core investment function emerge, with the consequent examination of all the darkest recesses of the business and the closure of virtually all of the peripheral activities.

Management style was originally set by the partnership of Lord Piercy and John Kinross, which established the ICFC tradition of controlling with a light rein a team of talented, committed, and mutually supportive professionals, bound together by the doctrine of corporate responsibility for the consequences of investment decisions. This tradition was honoured by Larry Tindale who, with a less involved Chairman, brought to bear his own individualistic approach, running the whole organization and planning its direction with a minimum of delegation. The Tindale style was adopted more or less as it stood by Paul Hildesley, but radically altered by Jon Foulds's consultative style of collegiate governance. Throughout their terms the Board was a supportive group of non-executives who accepted the general direction of the business and, whatever their private concerns, fully backed the Chief Executive and his managers, whilst the Chairmen of the period, Lord Seebohm and Lord Caldecote, managed the Group's external relationships with tact and firmness.

The style changed again with the arrival of Sir John Cuckney as chairman and David Marlow as Chief Executive at a time when corporate governance was coming under increased surveillance. With the narrowing strategic focus involving both Board and shareholders, against a background of greater corporate accountability and renewed economic decline, the old ICFC traditions inevitably suffered a serious erosion, leaving Ewen Macpherson with a more compact organization but a major task in restoring its damaged morale and creating a new vision.

Whatever points successive Chief Executives might have scored for their strategic direction, the one egregious quality shared by all of them has been their investment judgement. Some spent the whole of their formative years in the branch system dealing with customers; all were involved in the decision-making process over many years as members of Cases Committee, seeing this as a crucial part of their job, whatever other pressures they might face. It was only by this method that they could set and monitor the continuously evolving investment policy which would make or break the business. The case load was an enormous burden to carry on top of the Chief Executive's normal responsibilities, but by continuing to be involved in Cases Committee they not only set investment policy, but they monitored and set the standard for quality in the preparation and presentation of cases and the commercial judgement reflected in the setting of terms. Stripped to essentials, 3i's business is about taking risks and being appropriately compensated. It is possible to argue that the continuous involvement of successive Chief Executives in investment decisions distracted their attention from the broader strategic picture; but there can be little doubt that it is the factor which has contributed most to the maintenance of 3i's successful financial record over so many years. It has been a considerable achievement to have combined this commercial success with an unshakeable commitment to serving the small business sector.

Chapter 12

Diversification: The Policy Ellipse

The Arguments for Diversification

AT ITS FOUNDATION ICFC had only one narrowly defined purpose: the provision of loan and share capital to businesses which had no access to the capital markets. Over the next thirty-five years, however, a range of other activities was grafted onto the original business, only for the whole apparatus to be dismantled in the late 1980s, leaving a specialized organization combining the original ICFC function with that of FCI.

3i was not alone, either in the diversification of the 1960s and 1970s or in the reversion to core activities of the late 1980s; both, as it happened, were fashionable things to do among the larger corporations. But having set up such a specialized business, and even that regarded by its founding shareholders as of doubtful relevance, we may ask how the management could justify moving into other fields, what were the financial consequences, and what caused the about-face which resulted in almost all the peripheral businesses being shed within a relatively short time?

For the first fifteen years of its life ICFC was concerned almost wholly with establishing its basic business. It was a slow, steady process of accumulating a portfolio of sound investments, all of which were expected to be on the books for a very long time. By 1960 they totalled only £38.6 million and it was another two years before total assets exceeded the shareholders' original commitment of £45 million.

In policy terms the diversification which followed ICFC's greater funding freedom had its justification in the need to promote, protect, and preserve its role in serving the small company sector. An example was its refusal to raise the lower investment limit of £5,000 as inflation made it increasingly unrealistic, justified by the concern that in such a politically sensitive area any vacuum left by ICFC might suck in subsidized government money. The same arguments could be applied to other non-investment aspects of the small business problem. ICFC needed to make the sector its own preserve, not to the exclusion of competitors altogether, but to ensure that competing would be expensive and thus deter the cut-throat pricing of fly-by-night operators. The same reasoning led to the conclusion that ICFC's role as champion of the small business sector should be enhanced by ensuring that all necessary services were available to it.

It can be argued that this policy of enlightened self-interest was successful because for many years ICFC occupied an unchallenged position in the supply of investment capital to private companies. Its dominance was sustained by a range of additional services tailored to the needs of the smaller business which other, less specialized, competitors would have found difficulty in matching. It was a good example of the market leader pushing up the entry price to discourage cut-price competition. It could equally well be argued, on the contrary, that it was not a sufficiently profitable market to attract serious competition and ICFC need not have bothered to erect such a complex system of entry barriers. Certainly they were not sufficient, when that perception changed in the early 1980s, to discourage a rash of competitors, all looking for the more profitable niches in the overall private company market. But perhaps it held the competition at bay longer than might otherwise have been possible. ICFC's greatest period of growth was in the decade after 1975, when it put in place a powerful marketing organization; by the time the competition had become a serious threat it had established a dominant position and the entry costs had been pushed much higher.

Estate Duties Investment Trust

The only significant diversion from strict adherence to the original brief during the first twenty years or so was to meet a need for estate duty provision. It seemed a natural extension of ICFC's function for it to buy a holding of shares in such situations, allowing estate duty liabilities to be met without draining the business of funds. For ICFC it had the advantage of bringing within its ambit a large number of private companies which would not normally be in need of new capital and were generally very profitable. The opposition of the clearing banks to this modest extension of ICFC's brief left it holding only a minority interest but providing all the management services for the new Estate Duties Investment Trust, or EDITH as it was always familiarly known. This was better than nothing from ICFC's point of view, because it met a real need among the family businesses which were ICFC's natural constituency and provided at the same time the access which it wanted. But during the whole of EDITH's thirty-year existence the clearing banks' initial refusal to allow ICFC direct access to the investments it identified and negotiated on behalf of EDITH remained difficult to understand. The amounts of capital required were very small and could have been comfortably provided from ICFC's annual profits, but the potential for gain was considerable. It seemed pointless to give away the bulk of this attractive business, a view which, for successive ICFC managements, was reinforced by the growing conflict between its own needs and those of EDITH as competition in the small company market intensified. The need to reconcile responsibility to its own shareholders with the fiduciary duty it owed to those of EDITH made it extremely difficult to manage equitably the necessary sharing of scarce investment opportunities. There were never enough to satisfy ICFC's needs, and it was particularly galling for its staff in the field to see attractive prospects they had unearthed and negotiated, often with great difficulty, being offered to EDITH rather than being kept wholly for ICFC.

EDITH nevertheless became a successful business in its own right. Its flotation as a specialized investment trust allowed other institutions to take a stake in the smaller company sector without the expense of doing so directly, with the risk more widely spread, and with a means of exit available through EDITH's own quoted shares. Because its Board refused to attempt a valuation of the unquoted investments which made up the bulk of EDITH's portfolio, they stood in at cost, with the alluring implication that there might be a crock of gold hidden beneath its balance sheet. In practice the potential gains were never realized to the extent implied by EDITH's market capitalization. Instead it became the stable, high-yielding trust it had set out to be, whose practice of trading voting rights for income gave it an unusually strong revenue stream, out of which it was able to maintain steady dividend growth. At the same time its capital profits allowed it to establish a tradition of annual bonus issues. The ingenious preferred ordinary shares coupled with high yielding preference shares provided an attractive income, while limiting the proportion of equity given up by the family shareholders and the degree of voting power ceded to EDITH. None of this prevented the market from taking a rosy view of EDITH's prospects, and for many years it enjoyed a consistently high rating, expressed in the relatively low discount to net assets of its market capitalization. It is an awkward feature of the investment trust sector that the Stock Market applies a discount to the value of a trust's assets which can range up to 40 per cent or sometimes even more. In most cases they hold quoted shares, and the size of the discount can be easily calculated by reference to the aggregated market value of their holdings. In EDITH's case the holdings were in private companies and so not capable of independent valuation; it would have required a subjective judgement about each case, consistently made from year to year, and EDITH's Board felt this would tend to be misleading. It was therefore left to the market to make its own calculation of the unrealized surpluses which lay in

"And to my son Edward, I leave £100,000 in taxes due."

The need to provide for Capital Transfer Tax can present the family company with many unwelcome problems. In some cases, the sale of shares required to meet tax liabilities can result in the transfer of control to outside interests.

But Estate Duties Investment Trust can help. EDITH will invest on a long term basis in minority shareholdings in soundly managed businesses, allowing major shareholders to provide for CTT, without any loss of control. We won't require a directorship, nor will we interfere in the day-to-day management of the company.

For further information please contact our offices in Aberdeen (Tel: 0224-53028), Edinburgh (Tel: 031-226 3885) and Glasgow (Tel: 041-221 4456). **EDITH**
Managed by ICFC.

EDITH Advertisement   *DDB Needham*

282

the portfolio. The same problem on a larger scale bedevilled the question of 3i's own flotation many years later.

The conflict of interest inherent in ICFC's management of EDITH intensified over time as competition in the small company sector grew and investment opportunities became more difficult to find. Although ICFC operated a policy of scrupulous impartiality in offering EDITH every opportunity which met its criteria, almost all were good investments which ICFC could have taken entirely for itself. The sharing of investments by ICFC and EDITH caused further difficulty in the after-care stage, when the two institutions' interests were not always identical; EDITH was often unable to put up new capital in the same form and to the same extent as ICFC, although it had the same rights and obligations as a shareholder.

The staff entrusted with the stewardship of EDITH thus faced a constant dilemma. They were employed by ICFC, to whom they owed a duty of loyalty, but they must represent the interests of EDITH's other shareholders in finding, negotiating, completing, and monitoring investments which, though suitable for EDITH, could equally well have been taken by ICFC. It took a particular kind of independent-minded individual to accept this conflict of loyalties, and the sucessive managers of EDITH all shared a distinctively idiosyncratic approach, guarding their territory with apparent disregard for their personal advancement in the organization at large. To their credit they were all prepared to stand up for EDITH's interests in the face of pressure from their peers. Peter Wreford, EDITH's first manager, was so independent-minded that he eventually went off to found Gresham Trust and build it into an effective competitor. He was followed as manager by James Turner, then Edgar Felstead and Roger Plant, all of whom were highly regarded both for their investment judgement and their integrity by the normally hypercritical ICFC staff who had to negotiate with them over the sharing of investments.

While EDITH was flourishing the position was containable, but its narrowly conceived function eventually led to difficulties. Opportunities for investment of the kind EDITH needed diminished, both because of increased competition and because the population of traditional businesses was declining as more were sold off or went public. Significant changes in managerial attitudes during the late 1970s and early 1980s meant less attachment to the perpetuation of family traditions and more concern with maximizing capital gains by floating or selling off businesses. At the same time EDITH's traditional investment media, particularly the preference share, became more risky as the profitability of its customers declined. Shares whose dividend and capital had been fully covered by steady earnings growth and ample retained profits became exposed when profits and assets cover shrank in the difficult conditions of the 1970s.

Whilst ICFC was able to adapt its investment products to the changing circumstances, accepting a reduced income where there was potential for capital gain, EDITH could not do so without fundamentally changing its purpose. As a result suitable investment opportunities became fewer; it also became apparent, as EDITH began to follow ICFC's example by valuing its investments, that there was no crock of gold hidden in the balance sheet. Disillusion set in and the share price suffered. In his Statement with 3i's Accounts for 1984 Lord Caldecote wrote a brief and unsentimental obituary, recording 3i's decision to bid for those shares in EDITH which it did not already own. 'The weight of new funds being brought to bear in the small company market had for some time made it difficult for us to find enough investments of the right kind for our associate EDITH and we felt it right to offer its shareholders the opportunity to realize their investment at a price which reflected the underlying value of the portfolio.'

EDITH had done a very valuable job in helping to preserve the independence of private businesses, but its function would have been better carried on by ICFC as a natural extension of its brief. The difficulty of finding enough opportunities to sustain both bodies as separate entities is a further illustration of the availability of more than adequate funds to meet the demand for investment capital among the smaller businesses, during the post-war period. If it is looked at as a diversification of ICFC's natural business it seems ironic that a perfectly logical extension of its function, employing all the same skills and having the same traditions of service to the smaller business, should have been undertaken only on a partial ownership basis. Other activities, less closely related and certainly less profitable, were adopted as wholly owned subsidiaries carrying the full faith, credit, and reputation of the parent company.

Finance Corporation for Industry

By 1973 ICFC had consolidated its position in the small business sector, and the acquisition of FCI, encouraged at that time by the Bank of England, provided the opportunity to extend the investment activity into companies of all sizes. Within a year the mid-1970s recession had set in and the stock market was struggling to meet corporate capital needs, even quite large companies having difficulty in raising capital. This extension of ICFC's function up the size scale could not properly be called a diversification, although the skills needed were different from those ICFC had developed in providing capital for private companies. But it was the most significant change in the whole history of 3i. The investment activity could now legitimately cross the quotation boundary and seek out financial opportunities among companies of any size. Owning FCI gave a flexibility which permitted entry into all the profitable investment areas which opened up in the 1980s.

Plant Purchase

A similar extension of the investment activity was the provision of industrial plant by way of hire purchase. Lumpy items of expenditure, like the purchase of a single machine tool, would not justify the expense of ICFC's typical long-term loan agreement; but nor were they easily financed by the consumer-orientated hire purchase companies. It was relatively simple for the manager of an ICFC regional office to authorize an advance on hire purchase terms for the purpose, because it was normal for large loans to be secured by an all-moneys debenture, that is a charge which caught any money owing by the customer at any time, including, therefore, amounts due under HP agreements. Hire pur-chase never accounted for much in money terms but it is noteworthy as the first loosening of the purse-strings by ICFC's central management. The devolution of authority to approve hire purchase transactions up to £5,000 in the mid-1960s was the first time local managers had any personal authority to approve a financial commitment, and it was greatly welcomed by the branch managers.

Plant Leasing

Hire purchase was joined in the mid-1960s by plant leasing when it was realized that with the advent of 100 per cent writing-down allowances many companies quickly accumulated more tax losses than could be absorbed by current profits. The object of such fiscal generosity was obviously to encourage and accelerate investment in new plant, but without sufficient profits to absorb the allowances their effect would be vitiated and the benefit deferred indefinitely. ICFC there-fore began offering to acquire plant on behalf of its customers and lease it to them at a fixed annual rent. This had advantages for the customers in spreading the cost over the useful life of the plant but it also gave them the benefit of the allowances which would otherwise have to be deferred until profits were avail-able to absorb them. Their value could be taken into account, effectively as income of the year the plant came into operation, in calculating the rental charge. ICFC was one of the leaders in this field, being one of the first to employ sophisticated evaluation techniques for the return on capital employed in leasing. Because the cash-flows were complicated and variable, the return on the capital invested could only be properly calculated by using discounted cash-flow techniques. These had hitherto been little-known in business, and with computers still in their infancy the calculations were difficult and time-consuming. But the concept of the time value of money suddenly achieved real significance in calculating the return on capital from variable cash-flows. The effective recovery of a sum equal to corporation tax on the whole cost of the plant within a year of its purchase had a dramatic effect on the true cost of the money, and enabled ICFC to offer correspondingly low rental rates on leased plant.

There was much political criticism of this practice of selling capital allowances, caused mainly by misunderstanding of its purpose. Industrial companies which used the new plant for production purposes, and were thus seen as virtuous, sold their tax allowances to financial institutions which in the eyes of their critics were parasites, existing only to make money out of manufacturing industry's efforts. By the 1980s, when leasing had become a highly specialized industry in its own right and its image tarnished by a number of well-publicized abuses, it was generally forgotten what a cheap and flexible source of finance it provided for manufacturing industry, and how effectively it enabled the value of 100 per cent first-year allowances to be realized. This acceleration of capital allowances, allowing the whole cost of plant to be written off against taxable profit in the first year, does not appear to have been copied elsewhere in the industrial world and was the envy of industrialists in other countries; but so low was the profitability of British industry that leasing was the only practical way of converting the fiscal incentive into cash. Even levels of capital expenditure which were low in international terms produced volumes of tax allowances which far exceeded corporate profitability and without leasing their incentive value would have been severely reduced.

When the 100 per cent writing-down allowance was finally abolished in 1984 the Chancellor of the Exchequer made the reasonable comment that their availability had undoubtedly raised the level of investment, but there were grounds for doubting the quality of what had been done. The existence of a whole industry set up to take advantage of excess capital allowances and the extension of their use to non-corporate bodies, and eventually foreign companies, no doubt also contributed to the Chancellor's decision to abolish these allowances and substitute a lower rate of corporation tax.

An example of diversification in the leasing field, which was more or less unplanned but at the time fitted into the general strategic direction of the business, was the addition in the mid-1970s of two very specialized leasing companies: Hamilton Leasing, providing 'small-ticket' items of office equipment, and Highland Leasing, which financed agricultural machinery. ICFC had provided substantial amounts of capital to both in the normal course of its business.

They were both very different from ICFC's own leasing subsidiary, financing their equipment purchases by means of bank loans, over terms of only one to three years; and because the individual items were so small in value their business was labour-intensive. For each of them the mid-1970s recession caused difficulties, with large-scale repossessions affecting their return flow and making their consortium of banks nervous. FFI therefore stepped in, repaid the bank loans, to the chagrin of some of the banks who would have quite liked to continue with the benefit of the new parent's guarantee, and took over the companies to protect its own investment. It had been accepted that their businesses resembled ICFC's own leasing operation to justify their treatment as associated companies, but the effect of their acquisition was dramatic. The Group's staff numbers doubled overnight and new investment figures went up significantly but, whereas ICFC's investments were permanent or very long-term, the new subsidiaries' leases were essentially short-term and needed bank funding. With such a short asset life their marketing activity was frantic—a treadmill which could never stop.

The cultural differences between these two businesses and ICFC put a disproportionate strain on the central management, administrative, and treasury functions. After five years we concluded that, profitable as they now were, they would be better under the wing of a bank rather than a long-term investment business, and they were sold in the early 1980s, Hamilton to Barclays and Highland to Lloyds. The main objective, to preserve and enhance the original investment, had been accomplished; but at the same time, and for the first time, the limitations of diversification had become apparent.

Shipowning

While it lasted leasing provided a smooth, efficient, and flexible method of helping industrial companies to minimize the cost of plant and spread it over the income-earning life. It was also accepted by government as a valid mechanism for financing the building of ships in British yards. ICFC had already extended its own activity into this area of perceived national need—saving the British shipbuilding industry from the threat of foreign competition—by joining in the establishment of Ship Mortgage Finance Company.

With the advent of the 1967 Shipbuilding Industry Act SMFC's usefulness as a straightforward long-term lender was diminished, and ICFC took on the task of administering the government's new scheme. The management of the scheme was entrusted to SMFC for a fee, thus enabling it to continue in existence. The attractions of leasing also persuaded the management of ICFC to become a shipowner, even though this hardly squared with the notion of supporting small business. Shipping was very specialized, and a separate marine department was established at ICFC's head office in the mid-1960s to administer both SMFC's loans and the new shipowning business, which was run for over twenty years alongside the administration of the government scheme.

Although shipping finance was so specialized it proved possible for at least some of the ICFC staff to make the transfer and achieve the necessary expertise in shipping finance together with the essential contacts. Peter Cox, who established the shipping department, became well-respected in the industry and left after three years or so to take up a senior post elsewhere. His successor, Stanley Warren, had been Company Secretary of ICFC. Bill Kirkpatrick, who took over on Stanley's retirement some years later, had spent his life with ICFC in investment and corporate finance. All of them displayed the versatility and adaptability which was one of the most attractive characteristics of ICFC's staff, bringing to bear in the building of a large shipping portfolio the same dedication and skill that they had shown in their previous, quite different positions.

To the extent that ICFC was earning profits, it was able to take on bareboat chartering to major ship-owners whose building programme had completely absorbed their own profits. With the advent of the government guarantee, all new ships built in British yards were eligible for the reduced interest rate in addition to the 100 per cent write-off in the first year. All this was factored into the charter hire, making leasing attractive for the ship-operators as well as for ICFC. Whether it was good for the British economy generally is another question; what the British government did to protect its own shipbuilding industry others could do for theirs. The outcome of this competition between governments was a growth in the world shipping fleet during the 1960s and 1970s which far exceeded the growth in demand. During the recession years of the early 1980s the industry suffered a bout of severe indigestion, ship values fell and a number of operators collapsed. Although 3i had done well out of ship-owning and chartering, these failures and the reduced valuations led to heavy write-downs of the shipping fleet.

This was a surprising outcome in some respects because the charter was protected both by the covenant of the operators, which were generally substantial, and by the residual value of the ship if the operator failed. It was in taking on business from foreign shipping companies, whose credentials were particularly difficult to establish, that trouble arose; in one extreme case a sovereign government refused to stand behind a national shipping company of which it was part-owner. The great bulk of the write-offs, totalling some £25 million over the five years to 1985, involved foreign operators who had built ships in British yards.

So, overall, despite the fact that the new ships taken onto the books of 3i deferred corporation tax for many years, it must be doubtful whether, after the write-offs, 3i made an acceptable return on all the capital and effort invested over twenty years.

Consultancy

The first move away from the pure investment business came in the purchase of an advisory service operated by the National Union of Manufacturers for its small business members. This was merged with a wholly owned subsidiary of ICFC and was called ICFC-NUMAS. The object of the acquisition was to develop its specialized consultancy services and make them available to all small businesses. It was a separately managed and staffed subsidiary throughout its life and was not in any way intended as a support service for ICFC's investment business. It was made clear at the outset that ICFC-NUMAS had to earn its own keep by charging fees at a level which would at least allow it to break even. It was particularly important for ICFC to preserve its non-interfering posture, which had proved so valuable in overcoming the natural resistance of owner-managers to a financial partner. Branches were therefore only allowed to offer an introduction to the consultancy if customers themselves felt the need for it; but they were not permitted to prescribe a dose of consultancy as a precondition of providing capital.

The idea was good because there was a shortage of small-scale consul-tancies; it was not economical for the large firms to send in one consultant for two or three weeks, which was all most of the smaller businesses needed or wanted. In many respects it worked well, providing consultancy advice on the right scale to solve specific problems, but the difficulty throughout its life lay in maintaining consistently high standards; the consultancy business could not be closely integrated with ICFC because it had to operate at arms' length. Many branch staff remained sceptical, fearing that one inadequate consultancy job might damage not only the carefully cultivated long-term relationship with a customer, but more widely, 3i's reputation in the local community.

So the consultancy always had an uphill, perhaps impossible, task in convincing 3i's own staff that it was safe to recommend its services to their cus-tomers. Despite the ready-made client list, therefore, the consultants had to do their own marketing, finding business where they could. Again in an ideal world this should have meant cross-fertilization from introductions by the con-sultants to the branches. This did happen, but not to any extent, and the main difficulty, which effectively kept the investment business and consultancy at arms' length, was the clash of cultures.

Throughout 3i's history the investment business had its own powerful culture, difficult to define but incorporating an odd mixture of idealism and professionalism, combined with a hard-nosed commercial outlook and a remarkable dedication to maintaining high standards of both corporate and personal commitment to the small business sector. It was inevitably difficult to graft on the wholly different culture of a consultancy business. Perhaps because consultancy involved short-term advice and management help, whereas the investment business involved the permanent or very long-term commitment of money, it was difficult for the consultants to match the high level of common standards across the organization achieved by ICFC. Working individually or in small groups out in the field, they were never able to establish effective standards of work and common procedures which could protect the business from those odd failures which the branch staff feared. It was always possible, therefore, for an ineffective operator to be let loose on a valued customer, not understanding the needs of the long-term relationship which had been painstakingly built up by a succession of like-minded controllers.

There is no doubt, from the unsolicited testimonials of clients, that very high standards of work were achieved by many of the consultants, but despite this the doubts of the investment staff were never fully overcome and the two cultures proved irreconcilable. The danger to the corporate good name of poor consultancy work was deemed too great to justify continuing a business whose financial contribution was, on balance, nil. Despite the large volume of good work done by the consultants they were never able to clear that most important hurdle.

Another factor influencing the eventual disbanding of the consultancy business, which had nothing to do with culture, was that by the late 1980s the gap in consultancy provision for small businesses which ICFC–NUMAS was intended to fill no longer existed. For some time the regional investment staff had been aware that the existence of an in-house consultancy business was affecting their ability to give patronage to the local accountancy firms who were a main source of new investments but for whom consultancy had become an important part of their own business. It was felt in the regional offices that 3i could create better relationships with the accountancy firms if it could introduce consultancy business to them. So the original reason for taking on the NUMAS consultancy was no longer valid, and consultancy had become an impediment to the development of the investment business, rather than a support for it. It was therefore agreed that there was no justification for it continuing to operate independently. There might be a case for bringing it under the control of the investment side if its work could be restricted to providing assistance to customers in direct support of 3i's investments. This was tried for a year or so, but in a period of cost constraint the reduced activity never seemed likely to cover its costs, and in 1991 it was finally wound up.

Corporate Finance

Another service to the smaller company which was not readily available in the 1960s was what is now known as corporate finance, the provision of assistance to companies in mergers, acquisitions, flotations, and capital-raising. As ICFC's customers grew it was inevitable that some would wish to go public, and as early as the 1950s it began in selected cases to act as an issuing house promoting their flotation. This appeared to cause few problems with the shareholders of ICFC, perhaps because no additional capital was needed; indeed, by

An early 1970s advertisement featuring personalities from various parts of ICFC.
DDB Needham

helping its customers to go public ICFC was creating an opportunity for divestment, providing the exit route which its shareholders had feared might not exist. It was also a field in which the banks themselves were not at that time involved. But this did not prevent protests from the merchant banks which were to some extent a source of business, although their interests generally lay in the funding requirements of major corporations. By restricting flotation to companies in which it held investments ICFC was able to contain this problem, and a number of successful issues were made in the 1950s and 1960s without the need for a specialist department.

However, in 1968 it was decided that the new interest among the corporate community in mergers and acquisitions justified a more proactive approach. A subsidiary, Industrial Mergers Limited, was therefore formed to offer a corporate advisory service for medium-sized companies generally and in particular those which, although quoted, were not of a size to interest the merchant banks. Although the market need was clear, this was another example of enlightened self-interest. ICFC was willing and able to provide capital for companies after their shares had been publicly quoted, and did not wish to be limited in the provision of capital only to unquoted companies. Quotation was a quite arbitrary dividing line and had little significance when it came to capital raising. There were many substantial private companies which would have had less trouble in raising funds than some of the smaller quoted companies. What mattered most was the company's market capitalization; below a certain level there would be inadequate liquidity in the secondary market to attract institutional investors. There were also cost problems in raising small amounts by a public issue. The expenses were not directly proportional to the amounts raised, containing a large fixed element of professional fees and advertising costs. A study carried out by ICFC's own corporate finance subsidiary showed a range of costs for issues, including its own, from 7 per cent to 25 per cent of the cash raised.

ICFC therefore saw its market for new capital provision extending into the smaller quoted companies: its funds should be available to all companies which had inadequate access to the capital markets. But dealing with quoted companies was far more complicated than ICFC's normal business of investing in private companies. There were many more interests involved, with potential for conflicts between ICFC and other investors and a need for public dissemination of information to ensure equality of treatment to all. It required a specialized approach incorporating all the expensive corporate finance skills of the merchant banks. In particular, if ICFC was to provide new capital for a quoted company it would need to be by way of a rights issue, giving all existing investors the right to subscribe and with ICFC underwriting the issue.

Merger activity also crossed the boundary between private and public companies. Public companies were buying private as well as other public com-

Logitech

LOGITECH BEGAN MODESTLY WHEN it was founded in 1965 by Bob Wilson, a professor in Glasgow University's electrical engineering department, to manufacture machines for polishing and shaping thin sections of rock, crystal, and ceramics. For the first few years the company struggled to become established in what was a very specialized and uncertain market. When TDC's John Wishart went to discuss finance with Wilson in 1971, he was ushered into a 6ft by 3ft cubicle in the corner of an old knitwear factory. As Wilson recalls, 'there were papers all over the floor, the floorboards were rotten . . . Looking back it was horrendous.' The company's turnover was £25,000 and its profit before tax £100.

Wilson had approached both TDC and an Edinburgh merchant bank, but chose the former, even though TDC had insisted on 'a largish slice'—35 per cent—of the equity. This was accompanied by a secured loan of £18,000, and was followed the next year by another loan of the same amount. Not unusually, these early years were a struggle for survival, the difficulties compounded by the development of what Wilson later described as an 'over ambitious' machine tool. In a limited and specialized market, much of which was overseas, it had been difficult to establish a price level which would sustain the company's growth plans and the crisis was only resolved when John Wishart suggested that the company had been underpricing its products. Following this suggestion Logitech instigated a 30 per cent increase, which customers accepted, and the company turned the corner.

In 1979 3i provided the funds which enabled Logitech to move to a custom-built factory at Old Kilpatrick on the Clyde and, later, made available more capital for the establishment of Logitech Inc. in order to achieve penetration of the American market. 3i also provided hire purchase facilities to buy new equipment when the company expanded its Old Kilpatrick site.

By 1988 when Bob Wilson decided to sell out, 3i's investment had increased to £187,000. A number of alternatives had been canvassed, including a USM listing and a management buy-out, but 3i Corporate Finance introduced a buyer, Stuers A/S based in Copenhagen, whose business was a natural fit with that of Logitech and could provide world-wide marketing and distribution for its products. The purchase price of £2.2 million gave 3i a profit of £753,000 on its equity cost of £1,725 but also provided Wilson with a satisfactory sale without jeopardizing the future of the business he had created.

panies and ICFC's own customers were frequently in need of advice in taking a decision to sell out and managing the sale process, which would include the issue of shares by the quoted purchaser and perhaps a combination of cash and quoted shares as consideration. In yet other cases two private companies might wish to merge and float the resulting enlarged company.

For these reasons Industrial Mergers found plenty of work in sponsoring mergers, acquisitions, and flotations. Its costs were amply covered by the fees earned, and it performed a valuable service to the medium-sized companies which were looking to expand by merger, having been thwarted by sluggish economic conditions in their attempts to expand by natural growth. It was a time when the 'urge to merge' was fashionable, and growth by acquisition was encouraged by government and the City alike. The more efficient use of assets made possible by merger seemed logical at a time when British industrial performance was manifestly lagging behind that of the EEC and Japan. Inevitably, however, the process led to excesses and the infamous 'asset-stripping' of the early 1970s, when some companies became so effective in selling off assets that they ended up with nothing but cash—which in some cases amounted to rather less than their outstanding debt.

At its best the process of acquisition led to the replacement of poor management by better, to more effective investment, and to a much higher growth rate for the businesses taken over. It was a perfectly legitimate business for ICFC to take up; it increased its public profile, gave it entry to the smaller quoted companies which had seen the value of merchant banking advice, enabled it to sponsor the flotation of a number of its own customers, and allowed it to provide useful help to those companies trying to decide whether to sell out or remain independent. But once again it faced conflicts of interest which were difficult to manage and could result in damage to its overriding long-term interests, particularly in cases where ICFC was already a substantial shareholder. As a holder of 30 or 40 per cent of a company's equity, ICFC would be particularly affected by any decision on the company's future; and yet as its financial adviser, even through a separate subsidiary, it had to be scrupulously fair to all parties involved. This was particularly so when Industrial Mergers, or later ICFC Corporate Finance, acted as issuing house for a company in which ICFC already held a large part of the equity. The effect of ICFC's subsidiary being the sponsor was to limit the parent company's ability to deal freely with its investment: clearly it must not adversely affect the share price and jeopardize the flotation by selling large amounts of stock into the market. It was necessary to accept obligations not to sell more than a predetermined amount in the flotation and to exercise restraint in the after-market, which would not have been so onerous if the subsidiary had not acted as sponsor—although there would clearly have been practical limitations on selling large holdings in any circumstances.

My own view was that the value of the fees earned by the corporate finance subsidiary never justified this unnatural constraint on ICFC's freedom to deal out of its large holdings. They should have been realized, as market opportunities arose, to provide funds for reinvestment. It was a two-edged sword in another sense, because the widespread publicity attaching to a public issue joined ICFC's name and reputation to that of the company being floated, and its sponsorship gave great comfort to the market. This was understandable, but of doubtful value to ICFC, because it implied a knowledge of the business which ICFC's hands-off policy could not in fact guarantee. Almost inevitably there came a time when an issue went wrong and the mud thrown up by a particularly messy collapse stuck to ICFC. Things were never the same again after the failure of Roadships, and the number of flotations fell away from that point, although the corporate finance subsidiary continued in the more limited role of adviser on mergers and acquisitions. The extension of its life was probably due to the acquisition of FCI in 1973 and the consequent need to have skills available for dealing with the more sophisticated public companies which thenceforth fell within the Group's normal funding capacity. It was of value too in the 1980s, with the emergence of more professional management teams moving from the larger corporations to the smaller companies, who needed the kind of advice merchant banks could provide but ICFC was not structured to give.

So 3i Corporate Finance has survived under its long-standing manager Neil Williamson, where most other peripheral activities disappeared, thanks mainly to the increased sophistication of the smaller business, the much greater activity in the complex fields of management buy-outs and buy-ins and the corporate finance skills which these companies now required. The survival may also be due to a much greater cultural affinity with the core business than had been possible for the consultants, despite the need for 'Chinese walls' to preserve the confidentiality of an advisory business operating inside an investment business.

Portfolio Management

Another fairly natural extension of the business, justified for the same reasons as corporate finance, was fund management. ICFC's own investments were, until the 1970s, almost entirely in unquoted companies; but inevitably some of these grew to a size where the owners felt justified in seeking a stock-market quotation. There was a variety of motives for flotation, most of which we thought did not justify the resulting public accountability. It was certainly not necessary for corporate capital-raising purposes, because ICFC could go on providing it; nor was it the principal way of raising cash for the shareholders: EDITH stood ready to buy. Some argued that being publicly quoted gave their

If I had been in charge what would I have done differently?
Fair question. For starters, I would have had this line
representing profits move up instead of down.

businesses better exposure and improved their credit standing. This was probably so when all was going well; but in a downturn poor results could not be concealed and damage limitation was more difficult than for a private company.

However, we did not stand in the way of flotation when it was the wish of the majority shareholders; it was, after all, the most appropriate mechanism for realizing our investment. But ICFC's holding was usually too large for us to sell out completely at the time of flotation and it was necessary to retain some proportion. We also felt, having supported the controlling shareholders over many years, that any disposal should be orderly, using the company's brokers if possible, and taking account of the majority holders' wishes. It would not be acceptable, for example, to sell out, without consultation, to a potentially hostile bidder.

All these complex considerations needed careful handling by experts in stock market operations and a degree of central management control. This was generally outside the experience of the local ICFC manager who had nursed the relationship up to the point of flotation. Furthermore, once the shares were quoted and thus potentially realizable, they became a source of new, or recycled, funds for ICFC's own investment programme.

It was logical, therefore, to bring the management of the quoted element of the portfolio into a central department staffed with specialists. As time went by the quoted portfolio grew to a size which would have justified specialist management in its own right: by the end of the 1980s it was worth as much as £500 million. But in the early 1970s when the portfolio management department was in its infancy it was relatively small; as I mentioned elsewhere, the stock market collapse of 1974 was sufficient to eliminate, temporarily as it turned out, the whole of the surplus which had accumulated to that point in the quoted portfolio.

As with some other activities which required different skills, it seemed sensible, having recruited the necessary specialists, to utilize their skills more fully and at the same time earn some external income which might cover their costs. Therefore, the portfolio management department took on not only their own portfolio, but also that of the company's pension fund, and the two quoted investment trusts specializing in smaller quoted companies, London Atlantic and North British Canadian. A small number of other pension funds and one more investment trust were brought in, and for some years the department was set targets for increasing the funds under management and covering its costs by the fees it could earn.

I was always sceptical of the prospects for success in this field. The competition among the merchant banks, stock brokers, clearing banks, and specialist fund managers became intense. Many had huge amounts of money under management and I could see no niche for us other than in the smaller company sector. Even there we faced serious competition, and although our investment trusts performed consistently well, the unit trust which we set up for the same purpose was an embarrassing flop. Fortunately the growth in our portfolio provided its own justification for limiting the expansion of fund management generally—which was as well, because the staff of the department showed none of the necessary aptitude for selling 3i's services in this field.

The department was set up by Roger Plant, who soon moved on to run EDITH, and for a number of years it was managed by John Evans, an experienced fund manager who built up a team of able managers before his untimely death from leukaemia. He and his successor John Davies, faced up to the formidable array of top management experts with remarkable aplomb. I felt some sympathy for them at the weekly investment committee when they regularly faced Larry Tindale, John Kinross, and Jon Foulds who all had considerable knowledge of the market and strong views about it.

The need for specialized management of the Group's portfolio was never seriously challenged, particularly during the 1980s when its value grew strongly and active culling became necessary. Combined with their failure to generate more fund-management business, which in the cut-throat conditions of the 1980s could hardly have been profitable, this probably saved the portfolio management subsidiary from closure.

However, it was never a comfortable bedfellow for the regional offices. Tensions inevitably arose when the Group's need to raise money by market sales conflicted with the local directors' ambitions for further investment business. But in principle we felt that a company's decision to go public changed the relationship fundamentally. It could be reconstituted on a more open basis with 3i becoming just one of a number of sources of capital and advice as the price of our new freedom to sell. In the more competitive era of the 1980s, as owners took advantage of the increasing numbers of venture capitalists to shop around, so 3i felt less obligation to hold onto its quoted shares. It was nevertheless essential to ensure that they were not sold without consultation, and regional offices were required to submit lists of the quoted holdings in their area, noting those where there was some constraint on selling. Over the last ten years or so the main cause of constraint became the possession of price-sensitive information. This was often acquired accidentally in the course of a routine company visit by regional staff, but could place a tiresome and often costly check on the central department's ability to sell freely. It became necessary to construct 'Chinese walls' between those managing the quoted portfolio and the rest of the organization. This problem would have become even greater had the management of external portfolios grown as planned, and it would have forced us to separate our own portfolio from the others. It was substantially resolved eventually by relinquishing the management of LAIT and NBC. I thought this would become necessary at some point if 3i were itself to become quoted as an investment trust; invidious comparisons would inevitably have been made between its own performance and that of the other trusts, and conflicts of interest similar to those with EDITH would have been unavoidable.

Properties

In the late 1960s the popularity of leasing led to the purchase of property as an investment asset, the new owner granting a leaseback to the former owner-occupier. For ICFC it seemed a sensible extension of the traditional long-term lending business because loans were normally secured by a charge on the industrial property occupied by the borrower, which in many cases was owned outright. For this purpose ICFC had relied on expert valuations by a team of specialized surveyors, whose principal concern was to determine how much might be realized in the event of foreclosure on a loan and sale of the property securing it. Forced-sale values tended to be very much lower than open-market values, with the consequence that a loan would normally only be fully secured for up to 60 to 65 per cent of the property's current value. Any excess would have to be provided on some other basis, in ICFC's case by a convertible loan or by subscription for equity, because over a twenty-year period the difference must be regarded as at risk.

Whilst for some owners retaining the equity in their own property was an article of faith, for others it seemed more attractive to realize its full value for use in the business rather than take a loan limited to only 60 per cent of value or, if they borrowed more, have to give up equity in the business as a whole. Sale and leaseback, as the transactions were known, thus became an acceptable alternative to a loan, because large amounts could be raised without watering down the equity, although the calculation of the alternative benefits and costs was very imprecise. The equity in the property would grow with property values which would almost certainly be at a different rate from the growth in value of the equity in the business, so the owners were taking a gamble, in selling the property rather than taking new equity, that they could make their business grow more rapidly than the property market. There was of course a third alternative—to limit the loan to the amount of security available and hope to get by on the smaller amounts or by increasing bank facilities. These were not easy decisions; but in offering sale and leaseback ICFC was providing a choice of financing options.

Although it seemed a natural enough extension of secured lending, it was in fact a significant diversification into a wholly new field, and it became apparent by the early 1970s that, like the quoted investments, the growing portfolio of investment properties needed specialized management; it was beyond the capacity of the branch staff, whose experience was mainly financial. It was difficult to find expert property managers because the prospect of looking after a portfolio of small industrial and warehouse properties was not likely to set a real property man's pulse racing; something more was needed to attract able candidates. The answer was to form a joint venture with a property developer in which ICFC had an investment. Although the property market was very strong when the joint venture was set up, its timing could hardly have been worse, particularly for the kind of small industrial estates which it was to build.

With hindsight, the activity was more speculative than it should have been, or indeed needed to be for ICFC's purposes, but the argument held that a stream of development opportunities was necessary to motivate management. What this meant in practice was that ICFC supplied substantial amounts of capital for Anglia's management to buy likely sites, some of which were in areas of white land not yet zoned for development. With the collapse of the property market in 1974, partly due to the incoming Labour government's proposal to tax windfall gains on development land, some of these purchases became virtually valueless. In the event heavy provisions were necessary, not only against the sites but also against completed and let properties.

This was perhaps the most significant example of the culture clash, at least in terms of its financial effect. Property operators tended to be individualistic and unused to working within a tightly organized corporate framework such as ICFC had developed to control its own organization. But there was no means of monitoring their performance without strict management controls from the centre. Perhaps most crucially, the ICFC senior management had no experience of the property world. With the addition of property development to the consultancy business, corporate finance, portfolio management, and leasing, it had become a diversified business, but the management structure to control this range of activities was not put into place until later in the 1970s.

With the collapse of the property market and heavy provisions in the 1974–5 accounts, it was decided to bring the property work in-house, and specialist staff were recruited under Peter Willcock, an experienced institutional property man, who was charged with unravelling the complex problems of the development portfolio. This was a sensible decision in the circumstances, for it gave better control over the funding of property and over the activity of its management; with the broadening of the general management team which followed Jon Fould's appointment, property came under the control of a general manager. In this new structure much good work was done to repair the damage, so that by the mid-1980s most of the properties had been developed and sold. It remained, nevertheless, a difficult activity to control, and never worked comfortably with the investment divisions. Although some properties were sold off at a profit, the writing down of developments continued through the early 1980s, with damaging consequences to the Group profit-and-loss account, and it became increasingly difficult to see the value of having such an alien business forming part of the 3i Group.

As a provider of investment capital 3i had acquired a considerable reputation and was the clear market leader, but the property activity had no parallel achievement to its name. This became an issue when the management began to consider the proposal to float 3i in 1985. The investment record fully justified flotation as an investment trust but, however property was viewed, it could not bear comparison with the best of the quoted property companies and its record would inevitably drag down the parent's rating in the market. It was also difficult to justify the commercial logic of retaining a property business which was tying up large amounts of capital at a time when the core investment activity was itself growing rapidly, producing superior returns, and needing increasing amounts of equity. The clearing bank shareholders, who had never seen the logic of the property activity, were in no mood to provide the additional capital when their own was under pressure. It seemed inevitable that it should give way to the needs of the core business.

First the bulk of the investment property portfolio was sold off in 1987 as a package, providing useful additional funds for investment in the core business. The property development business continued as a trading activity, for although it absorbed as much as £60 million at a time the capital involved was outstanding for only two or three years, unlike that invested in shares and loans. Nevertheless a Board-imposed limit of £50 million on the work in progress outstanding implied that this amount would be permanently in use. However, the sale of completed properties rarely seemed to happen on schedule, with the result that the ceiling on work in progress was frequently breached. It was never clear what return was being made on the property development business and write-downs continued even in the boom years of the mid-1980s, so it was not surprising when the decision was taken to cease new property developments altogether.

As with the other peripheral activities, it had filled a need in the small business sector, by providing premises of suitable size either individually or in groups on small industrial estates. In later years the property division was actively engaged in building science parks, again providing useful premises for embryonic and very small science-based businesses. There were, however, a number of occasions when it strayed into rather grander developments, of shopping centres in particular, which absorbed large amounts of capital for long periods and could hardly be justified as support for the small business sector. By the late 1980s it was clear that its profitability and reputation did not match those of the investment business, and, although it absorbed relatively little capital it would make no sense, if 3i became an investment trust, to have such a property business attached to it. It also absorbed large amounts of central management time and created serious complications for the Group's administration in maintaining effective management controls and information flows.

Thus the development portfolio was put on the market, but the timing of its sale was as unfortunate as that of its creation. The recession of the late 1980s overtook the negotiations and it was decided to work out the portfolio over a period of years.

3i Ventures and the Culture Clash

Technical Development Capital, or 3i Ventures as it became known, has been dealt with elsewhere, but is worth a mention here as an element in the diversification process, similar in many respects to the core business, but fundamentally different in cultural terms. It was an attempt to bring American venture capital techniques and skills to bear on the one area of investment which ICFC had never been able to do profitably, financing high-risk start-ups in areas of new technology. It satisfied a long-felt obligation to do this kind of business, since TDC itself was formed after the Radcliffe Report, and the formation of 3i

Ventures in 1979 was intended to put it onto a profitable basis. But as with the less closely related activities which were grafted onto the core investment business, it suffered from a serious clash of cultures. 3i Ventures was the most difficult of all the implants for the body corporate to accept.

Despite considerable efforts by successive Chief Executives and their general management teams it never proved possible to weld the whole organization into a homogeneous unit, with similar standards of behaviour, in relation to Group objectives, long-term relationships with owner-managers, staff and compensation issues, and all the myriad facets of corporate life. ICFC's standards of professionalism, integrity, commitment, and commercialism had been forged in the fires of those difficult first fifteen years. The founding fathers had passed on their standards to their young successors, and as the organization became larger it remained possible, through the training system and the management development programme, but particularly through the leadership of successive Chief Executives, to instil these qualities into each intake of recruits. It was this process which lay behind 3i's great success; the attention to detail and refusal to cut corners, the hard-nosed commercialism in project evaluation, were blended with a strongly developed idealism which permeated the whole of the investment and support staff. But it never proved possible to imbue the staff of the other activities with those same values. There were constant tensions, feelings on the part of investment staff that they were being let down by inadequate performance from the other parts of the business, whilst the other staff felt they were second-class citizens, excluded from the privileged élite of the investment operation.

Even at General Management level this cultural problem made itself felt, although efforts were made to bring the peripheral parts of the business into the centre of things and to moderate the power and influence of the old ICFC clan to which most of the General Management belonged. It had not escaped notice that the surest route to the top was through the branch system. Jon Foulds, David Marlow, Nigel Olsen, and I had all been branch managers in our time. The change of name emerged partly from this process of formalizing the diversification in recognition that 3i had become a multi-faceted business where all parts were of equal significance. These efforts might possibly have succeeded if the financial performance of the peripheral activities had been manifestly superior to that of the investment business, or even if they had held their own. But by the mid-1980s the investment business was out in front, generating ever-increasing amounts of new business and making exceptional returns on capital while the other businesses were achieving very little. Ships and properties were being written down, Ventures was unable to convert its early successes into a trend, the consultants were struggling to break even, and leasing had become virtually non-existent with the abolition of 100 per cent first-year allowances.

In fact the whole diversified organization was being carried in financial terms by one dominant division which, perhaps surprisingly, was the original business set up in 1945. Unlike many diversifications which led companies into new fields, 3i's core activity was going from strength to strength, forty years after its formation, whilst the newcomers had produced no new sources of profit. In truth it was not for this reason that the various peripheral businesses had been acquired or started, but we had nevertheless added management and administrative structures, made necessary by increasing regulatory demands and by the need for control. This greatly increased the cost of maintaining the whole organization, exacerbated the internecine rivalries, and worst of all, diverted the attention of top management from the strategic direction of the business. It was a serious dilemma: the General Management needed to maintain the cohesion of the widespread organization but at the same time had to concentrate scarce resources where they were best used. The rapid growth of the overseas businesses, with their heavy initial costs not matched by inflows, increased the capital demands and put further pressure on the revenue account at a time when the UK investment business was already supporting the whole range of unprofitable peripheral businesses and the organization needed to sustain them. For a business which had always had enough capital for any diversification or expansion it wanted to undertake, the new stringency created unfamiliar stresses between its constituent parts.

In the end it was the decision by 3i's shareholders to consider disposing of their holdings which concentrated our minds on resolving this growing problem. It was apparent that, whatever might be the internal needs for a cohesive organization, and whatever might be our hopes and expectations for the peripheral businesses, their performance so far would not stand up to the scrutiny of a wider investing public. 3i would have to make them profitable or abandon them, and it was apparent to me even in 1985 what the outcome would be if 3i were to be floated. Fortunately the core business was performing so well and had such a strong market position that it could stand alone without the support of any peripheral businesses; as we cleared the decks for flotation this fact became increasingly apparent and concentration on the core business in the UK and Europe eventually became the single strategic objective.

The reduction of a complex, diversified organization to a single simplified business was inevitably painful. It involved the closure over a period of four years of all the peripheral businesses except Corporate Finance and Portfolio Management, a commensurate reduction in the support services, and a severe slimming down of the central administration. What remained was little more than the combined businesses of FCI and ICFC with the significant addition of the overseas subsidiaries, established on the ICFC pattern. The diversification had been justifiable and the dismantling was also manifestly justified; but it would be surprising if in reducing the business to its core over such a short time

3i did not lose much of the idealism bequeathed to it by its founders and which had helped to make it unique.

Perhaps the main practical disadvantage of the diversification was the complex management structure it forced upon us, which could never be justified by the financial results. But a much more fundamental problem was the cultural divisions it brought with it. The differences in attitude to basic issues of corporate policy were never resolved, with consequent damage to the cohesiveness of the whole organization, to relationships, and to commitment. It was this concern which underlay the strategic decision to revert to the core business, rather than the purely financial arguments, which were powerful enough but not overwhelming.

I believe the diversification was justified, but the eventual dismantling of the excessively complex organization which resulted was also right, although perhaps it could have been done sooner; but it remains to be seen whether in 'sticking to the knitting' 3i will be able to recapture that powerful ethic of service and the relaxed professionalism which underlay the tough-minded commercialism of its early years and was the foundation of its success.

Investment Capital versus Venture Capital

ICFC's Real Purpose

THE FORMATION OF ICFC in 1945 came about by a peculiarly British process: a need had been identified by the Macmillan Committee, which we can now be certain was real, but at the time was not supported by evidence. So its perception by Macmillan—or probably by Keynes, the only member of the Committee with significant stock market experience—was more intuitive than based on fact, and the proposed solution was pragmatic rather than idealistic— a gap exists in the market mechanism, so an institution should be formed to fill it. There was no suggestion by Macmillan of public-sector intervention to compensate for market failure, rather the thought that an opportunity might exist for a commercially successful venture in the supply of capital to small businesses.

An unusual feature of Macmillan's proposal was its implication of a need shared by the whole small business sector: all companies below a certain size were denied access to long-term and permanent capital and thus had to rely entirely on their own retained profits to finance growth. This confident assertion met a cynical response from those who believed that any potentially profitable gap in a market would inevitably be filled without artificial prompting. The lack of hard evidence and the failure to unearth any by the few bodies which were set up in response to Macmillan's suggestion seemed, at least to the bankers who were asked to set up ICFC, sufficient proof that no gap existed.

So the formation of ICFC as Richard Coopey describes it was not the result of visionary drive on the part of its sponsors. Rather it was the result of political expediency, the banks having their arms twisted to participate in ICFC under the more or less explicit threat of government intervention.

Nevertheless, at its formation ICFC had a clearly defined function. The problem of capital provision to small business was of long standing whatever

*'I'm sorry, but you can't take it with you. If you'll just leave it
with me I'll see that it's put to good use.'*

the banks thought, and ICFC was the first serious attempt to solve it by institutional means, without public-sector assistance or subsidized credit. Its
particular characteristics were a long-term approach, a passive policy of
non-intervention, the need for an assured flow of income to compensate for a
necessary inability to influence the course of the customer's business and the
uncertainty of an exit from it.

These characteristics permitted the creation of a large and diverse
portfolio with an attractive spread of risk. ICFC was not concerned about the
nature of its customers' businesses but about their ability to manage them profitably, and as virtually all of them would have a very small market share it was
possible for good management to succeed even in declining industries. This
passive approach allowed owner-managers whose principal need was for managerial independence to operate without interference, but in the knowledge

306

that ICFC had a deep pocket and could provide fresh capital whenever it was justified. ICFC could be a significant shareholder but would always hold a minority of the capital and of the voting power. The majority shareholders were free to make their own decisions about divestment. They were under no pressure to float their companies or to sell out: their decision on such major issues would be supported by ICFC. This method has never varied, although alternatives were tested for special purposes, and it became apparent, particularly during the very competitive 1980s, that it has great merits, not least because it meets the needs of the great majority of owner-managers.

Although we can now see the logic of ICFC's formation and the manifest need for an institution to fill the gap at the bottom end of the capital market, it was a solution unique to the United Kingdom. The most obvious place to look to for a parallel is the United States, which has a similar financial system, with rigidly separated banking and capital markets. There were indeed attempts between the wars and even earlier at a state level, to establish capital funds for small businesses, but none lasted long and none enjoyed commercial success. A review of the small business sector in the United States, published in 1948[1] identified the same problems of finance as Macmillan had identified in the United Kingdom: there had been no successful institutional solutions to the chronic shortage of long-term and permanent capital for small businesses. 'The sector of small business financing that remains least cared for and in the long run has the most crucial implications for the American economy is the supply of more permanent or venture capital for small, independent enterprises.' The cost of raising funds on the capital market, for those large enough to do so, was prohibitive, and for most it was impossible to attract funds at all. The Securities and Exchange Commission (SEC) had published a study of capital-raising costs which, said Kaplan, 'confirms the general opinion that the established investment channels, on the record to date, hardly serve to float any substantial number of securities or to find individual investors for new independent enterprises or going concerns of moderate size that need outside capital for expansion'. He was able to quote other reliable sources in support of his view, and to draw parallels with the situation elsewhere, in particular that in the UK as described by Macmillan.

The American Answer: Venture Capital

Kaplan's own proposals for a system of local 'capital banks' similar in function to ICFC, were not taken up. Instead the small business lobby was able to persuade the Federal Government to step in where local efforts had failed and, remarkably for the home of free enterprise, to create a federally funded institution which would provide soft credits for small businesses. The Small Business

Administration became an enormous institution, operating right across the union, but its bureaucratic approach and its inability to take risks and thus to provide real capital made it relatively unpopular, particularly with the more successful small businesses, who saw it as subsidizing their inefficient competitors. In an attempt to remedy the lack of permanent capital the SBA sponsored in the 1960s some 2,700 privately owned Small Business Investment Companies (SBICs). Their function was to provide equity capital, but they benefited from low-interest credits of up to four times their share capital. The capital structure which this implies was extraordinary for a risk-taking body concentrating on low or zero yielding investments which were irredeemable. The temptation to take up cheap money was, however, irresistible, and much of it went for purposes which were barely justifiable. It soon became apparent that even the low rate of interest could not make a 4:1 gearing ratio produce a positive return for shareholders on equity investment alone; of those SBICs which were not wound up many moved into lending, usually on a subordinated basis, and the whole purpose of their foundation was negated.

A much more effective way of providing outside capital for growing companies was by small groups of individuals with industrial and financial experience, raising funds from wealthy investors who were looking for high rates of return and willing to accept high degrees of risk. The extraordinary success of American Research and Development (ARD), the investment business founded in 1946 by General George Doriot, through just one investment, Digital Equipment Corporation (DEC), fired the imagination of the nation and put venture capital on the map as a means of making very large amounts of money very quickly. ARD was set up specifically to identify opportunities for high-growth investment and to back them with both risk capital, provided mainly by wealthy individuals, and management help. Although ARD's other investments were moderately successful, with DEC General Doriot hit the jackpot. An investment of just under $77,000 becoming worth over $37 million at the point of DEC's flotation on the Stock Market some nine years later.

Specialist investment funds set up on the ARD pattern were concentrated in new businesses starting up with the benefit of new technology in high-growth industries. The object was to create a rapid growth of profits in the new company which could be sold on substantial multiples to the wider investing public by floating it within a few years of formation. This highly focused form of capital provision, which was termed venture capital, differed in several fundamental respects from the ICFC approach.

Venture capital was non-institutional; its managers were themselves entrepreneurial individuals whose object was to create wealth for themselves in the process of building up and selling off profitable businesses. It was structured, therefore, as partnerships of individuals with the suppliers of capital joining them as limited partners; and its *modus operandi* was a joint venture with the client company. The rewards, coming in capital realization rather than from income, would be shared by the participants *pro rata* to their interest, with the management team taking a share of the capital profit as their principal compensation. The management group would pick a small number of promising ventures in areas of business which were familiar to them, would join boards, and would become active in the management.

In all these respects venture capital differed from ICFC's way of doing things. ICFC was a passive investor; venture capital was active. ICFC was long-term; venture capital was short-term. Venture capital looked for capital profit; ICFC was also concerned with income. ICFC employed its own staff who were not allowed to join boards or become involved in management; venture capitalists were partners and closely involved. ICFC was a generalist with a specialized knowledge of finance; venture capital specialized in a small number of companies in high-growth industries. ICFC covered the whole spectrum of industry and its capital was available to all who could justify it; venture capital was limited to particular industries and within those restricted its interest to high-growth situations. ICFC was building up a long-term portfolio; venture capital restricted itself to a small portfolio to be disposed of by flotation, sale, or distribution *in specie* at the end of a predetermined period, usually not more than ten years. The venture capital approach is normally described as cherry-picking; only a very small number of promising businesses are selected for the venture capitalists' highly focused approach. The rejection rate is high and in the United States at least, it ignores the less exciting majority of small businesses whose capital needs have no external provider.

The returns from venture capital have been very variable as economic conditions and capital gains tax rates have shifted. It is unlikely that the enormous gain made by investors in ARD from the success of DEC has been repeated in more than a handful of cases, but the significance for ICFC is that there was a period in the early 1980s when venture capital investors made attractive returns; and it was during this time that its exponents in the United States began to look towards Europe and Japan for the kind of opportunities that had made rapid fortunes at home.

Venture Capital: UK Style—3i's Response

Its manifestation in the United Kingdom was essentially on American lines—opportunistic, small in scale though deploying large amounts of money, seeking exceptional capital gains from high growth businesses. The number of serious investors in the small-business field rose sharply with this influx. From perhaps a dozen serious competitors in the late 1970s the number of active participants rose to over 120 during the following decade, many of them modelled

British Caledonian

THE LARGEST SALE IN THE Group's history came in December 1987 when 3i sold its interest in British Caledonian Airways to British Airways for just over £100 million, marking the successful end of a long-term investment which had begun with the airline's foundation in the 1960s. 3i's involvement had, however, posed considerable difficulties during its lifetime.

The relationship with BCal began in 1967 when ICFC's Glasgow office provided development capital to Caledonian Airways, a company founded by Adam Thomson, which operated charter flights to North America, Europe, and the Near East. Later, in response to the Edwards Report, which was published in 1969 and recommended the establishment of a 'second force' in British aviation to compete with the nationalized carriers, BEA and BOAC, a merger was proposed between Thomson's company and British United Airways to form British Caledonian. ICFC was active in orchestrating this merger and jointly underwrote the finance required. There was, however, unanticipated scepticism about the need for a second airline and the equity proved difficult to place, even among the Scottish finance community to which John Kinross made widespread appeals on nationalistic grounds. As a result of this lack of interest, ICFC took rather more of the equity than originally envisaged and further support followed in the form of leasing and loan guarantees. In 1973 ICFC was obliged to help again by taking up two-thirds of a rights issue boosting its share of the company to just over 40 per cent.

ICFC staff, led by Paul Hildesley, spent considerable time on BCal, including work obtaining route approvals. It was hoped that business would improve following the 1975 Civil Aviation Review which extended the company's network and permitted diversification into general holiday business, including hotels.

The company had a strategic weakness, however, in that many of its routes had low traffic volumes or involved politically or economically unstable areas such as the Middle East, Africa, and South America. The important Nigerian routes, for example, were hit in the early 1970s by political turmoil and currency problems. Other African routes were similarly affected and oil industry problems in the Middle East further undermined profits, resulting in a highly geared balance sheet. By the mid-1970s ICFC's equity stake in BCal had risen to 47 per cent, but prospects looked so bleak that ICFC wrote off the investment, making a provision for a total loss of nearly £4½ million.

However, BCal still faced further capital requirements in order to maintain its existing network and 3i was becoming increasingly uncomfortable with its position as such a large shareholder, which had made it necessary to appoint its own deputy chairman, Larry Tindale to the Board. All this was difficult to reconcile with its hands-off approach to investment and BCal's chronic shortage of capital. Given its chequered history, 3i advised that an approach to the Stock Market was unlikely to be successful but the problem was resolved in 1987 when, following interest from a number of rival airlines, Larry Tindale masterminded an amalgamation with the now privatized British Airways. The Monopolies and Mergers Commission accepted that the competition policy, which the Edwards Report had hoped to foster had not been successful and gave the go ahead for the sale of BCal. BA's initial share for share offer, based largely on the potential value of the BCal routes but materially reduced in value by the intervening Stock Market collapse, was judged unacceptable by both the BCal Board and 3i, prompting a search for an alternative partner.

The strongest interest came from the Scandinavian carrier SAS which had an interest in creating a pan-European operation. Knowing that, if the bids were comparable, BCal's Board would want to go with SAS and that 3i would support the Board's decision, BA raised its bid substantially to £250 million.

This final outcome fully vindicated the time and money dedicated to one of 3i's longest, largest and most difficult investments, in producing a fully satisfactory result for both 3i and the company.

on the American style of venture capital. In some cases large institutions, including 3i's clearing bank shareholders, established their own in-house funds, allocating discrete amounts of their own capital to a small subsidiary set up for the purpose. In other cases merchant banks established managed funds which invited subscriptions from other institutions lacking the necessary skills. Some funds were set up very closely on the American model by groups of individuals with institutional backing. Others became more like 3i, but not many were prepared to incur the cost of investing in such small amounts or covering the whole range of small- and medium-sized business.

The growth of the British venture capital industry, though fuelled by the great success of American venture capital in the early 1980s, was also stimulated by 3i's own visible growth. But the number of 'high-tech start-ups', the staple diet of US venture capitalists, particularly on the West Coast, was limited in the United Kingdom and the competition for them led to a gross over-supply of funds. This in turn raised the price at which such investment deals could be done, and early results were not such as to encourage further concentration of money; performance was patchy and the venture capitalists were forced to look for other ways of using their investors' capital, so they moved into management buy-outs, specializing in the larger end of a fruitful form of business venture which ICFC had introduced into the United Kingdom in the late 1970s.

The BCal Jackpot 1987: Larry Tindale, Deputy Chairman of 3i with Sir Adam Thomson

The American version of the MBO, the 'leveraged buy-out', at its most extreme could hardly have been more different from 3i's business. Very large companies were bought by the use of huge quantities of debt issued in the so-called junk bond market during a period when the equity base of the American corporate sector was falling dramatically. Its replacement by progressively rising debt had a destabilizing effect and made the companies concerned vulnerable to a fall-off in economic activity. This duly happened, and the asset sales which had been counted on to reduce the initial debt burden became more difficult, leaving many companies unable to meet their massive interest obligations.

The extremes of scale did not cross the Atlantic but, as competition in this area also intensified, the terms on which MBO's were financed became more risky. 3i lost many MBO opportunities to the more adventurous competitors but was nevertheless drawn into the larger MBO market by the perceived need to be seen as a participator in these high-profile financings. It was felt that to retain market leadership required a visible presence in the larger transactions which were hardly typical of the classic 3i operation, so through the City Office we began both to participate in and to syndicate some of the very large MBOs. Although the need for visibility was accepted, some of us were not happy about the concentration of risk which large-scale MBOs required from 3i, particularly when it acted as syndicate leader. We felt more comfortable with the traditional ICFC spread—fifty investments of £1 million each seemed preferable to one of £50 million.

However, providing capital to facilitate changes of ownership was regarded in 3i as a normal extension of its business, and over a period of some ten years it financed about 1,000, almost all of them in companies of a size which would be its typical customers. The venture capitalists, on the other hand, still seeking a rapid exit after high initial growth, tended to concentrate on a small number of larger-scale buy-outs, following the fashion in the United States in support of management teams whose own ambition was the rapid flotation of their business. The ability to mobilize large amounts of investment capital and to create capital structures of dizzying complexity, with gearing rising towards infinity, was the essential characteristic of these transplants from the US venture capital 'industry'.

The seriousness of this competition for 3i lay more in its attraction for

SINCE PIONEERING THE ART OF MANAGEMENT BUY-OUTS, WE'VE *HELPED OVER 600 COMPANIES* START FROM A SOUND FINANCIAL BASE

1980s advertisement for 3i
DDB Needham

WHEN YOU'VE KISSED AS MANY FROGS AS WE HAVE, YOU GET GOOD AT SPOTTING PRINCES.

For over 45 years has been helping to transform British businesses by investing the capital they need to succeed. Over the years we have developed a very good eye for winners. First of all we get to know all we can about you and your plans. That way, when we decide to invest in you, we think you're going to make it. We know the qualities it takes to succeed, we know how to look beneath the superficial and beyond the short-term, and we know how a long-term approach can help you achieve success. An approach which, in our view, is the important difference between investment capital and venture capital.

As one of the world's leading investment capital companies, we have helped create a considerable number of successful businesses. Whatever your particular business opportunity – maybe you want to buy the company you work for, set up your own company or buy into another company – can help you make that change. We offer a wide range of investment capital solutions all based on years of experience and backed by considerable financial resources.

This means that once we've all agreed that you have it in you to become a prince, we are ready to give you the chance to prove that you can. If you'd like to see how investment capital could transform your business, just contact your local office.

Late 1980s advertisement for 3i

J. Walter Thompson

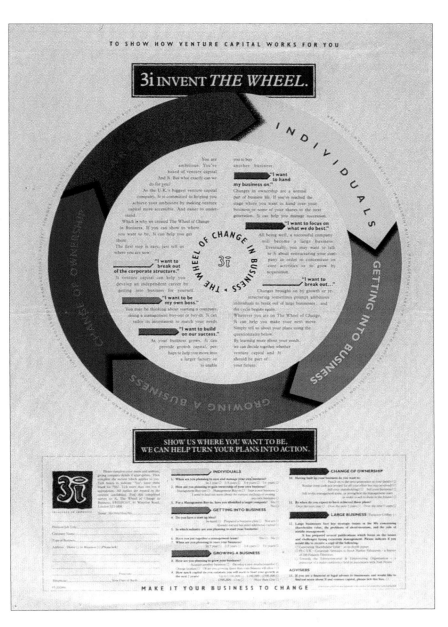

1980s coupon advertisement for 3i

Rapp Collins

1990s advertisement for 3i

J. Walter Thompson

Works of art acquired by 3i Group plc 1988–93

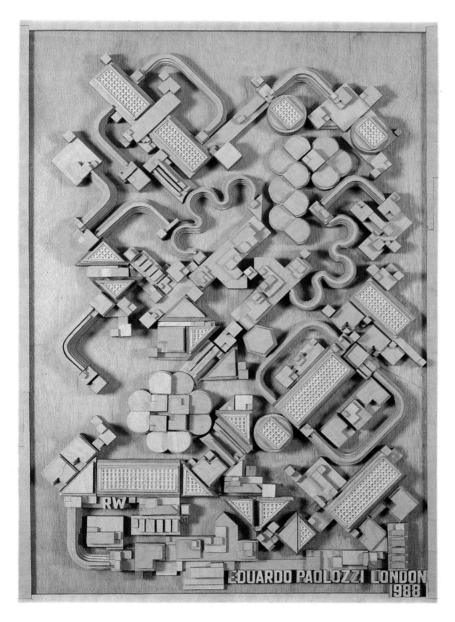

EDUARDO PAOLOZZI
Ponti 1988
Acquired by 3i Group plc

JOHN HUBBARD
Garden

183 × 182.9 cm, oil on canvas
Acquired by 3i Group plc 1991

BRIDGET RILEY
Midsummer

164.5 × 159 cm, oil on linen
Commissioned by 3i Group plc 1989

GILLIAN AYRES
Sikar I

63 × 63 cm, oil on canvas
Acquired by 3i Group plc 1993

GILLIAN AYRES
Sikar II

63 × 63 cm, oil on canvas
Acquired by 3i Group plc 1993

JOHN HOYLAND
Slow Dancer

101.6 × 76.2 cm, acrylic on canvas
Acquired by 3i Group plc 1990

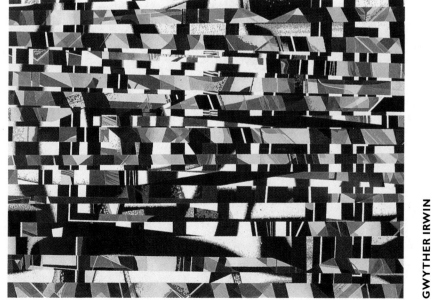

GWYTHER IRWIN
Superstructure

122 × 152 cm, watercolour on paper
Acquired by 3i Group plc 1992

some of our most able staff than in the business which it took. Much of the financing being done by the new competitors was on terms which would have been unacceptable to 3i. However, by poaching our staff they not only acquired expensive and rare skills, they took valuable knowledge of 3i's methods and were able to exploit its weaknesses—of which the principal one was a relative slowness of response.

3i's market share undoubtedly declined during the 1980s, at a time when its market was expanding rapidly. Much business which we had carefully investigated and would have been willing to do was lost to the competition, effectively reducing productivity. Thus, although venture capital is quite different from 3i's form of capital provision, which can be described as 'investment capital', much of what the venture capitalists were prepared to do in substitution for their preferred field of activity encroached on 3i's natural territory.

In response to the growth of competition we attempted initially to distinguish 3i in terms of size rather than product or business method. We joined the British Venture Capital Association in order to benefit from the general publicity generated for the 'industry' by that body and in order to have our own statistics included within those of the whole industry, thus demonstrating 3i's size and market leadership. As usual its business did not quite fit and its statistics produced uncomfortable distortions in the figures. We were virtually alone in providing straight loan capital which could hardly be described as venture capital, as opposed to subordinated debt which really ranked as equity. So attempts were made to extract those parts of 3i's figures which did not rank as 'pure' venture capital. An examination of 3i's own portfolio illustrates the problem: in the risk profiling carried out in order to determine how much of 3i's capital should be allocated to the various investment products, our own venture capital subsidiary was regarded as being at the extremity of the risk spectrum and needing 100 per cent equity backing. All the rest of the portfolio, some 95 per cent of the total, was able to carry some proportion of debt. The implication of this was that the risk element in our normal business was noticeably less than that of pure venture capital.

I thought the attempt to identify with the competition at that time was a mistake not only because the statistics did not fit, but because it was inconsistent with the attempt 3i was making at the same time to produce a distinctive image, by changing the name and developing an aggressive marketing strategy.

A more fundamental reaction to competition on our home ground was to begin dismantling the confusing, distracting, and unprofitable array of related businesses, in ship finance, property development and investment, and management consultancy. Between 1987 and 1991, when all these activities were closed down or were being run off, it became apparent that the association of 3i's name with venture capital was a mixed blessing, and was also giving misleading messages. Venture capital was by no means universally respected. The methods employed both in getting business and in managing the subsequent relationships were coming in for criticism; it was an aspect of 'short-termism'—the last accusation we wanted to hear levelled at 3i.

It thus became clear that for 3i to be known as a venture capital company was obscuring the particular qualities which had proved so valuable over the years. It was tempting to be associated with the publicity which was generated by the large MBOs on a scale which our own more modest investments never attracted. It was also thought important for our figures to be included in the statistics of the industry, because otherwise 3i, the biggest investor in the private company sector, could be ignored. But overall it was felt that the disadvantages of association with venture capital far outweighed these advantages, and we set about redefining the core business, which was becoming our only activity, in order to differentiate it from venture capital.

As the need to distinguish the traditional 'ICFC method' from American-style venture capital became apparent, so 3i's own involvement in venture capital, American-style, came into question. 3i had established its own venture capital business in the late 1970s in the United Kingdom as a development of Technical Development Capital and latterly in the early 1980s in the United States. It is interesting in this context that it was felt there should be scope for an ICFC-style investment or development capital business even in the United States; and almost from its start in 1981 the US operation had two separate parts—3i Ventures and 3i Development Capital. The extra risk inherent in venture capital—start-up investment in large quantities concentrated in particular industries—needed to generate quite exceptional returns over a long period to justify the allocation of scarce capital. Initially it did so with two enormously successful investments, Rodime in the UK and LSI Logic in the USA; but sustaining the record proved more difficult[2].

Internal Stresses for 3i: A Culture Gap

A more serious problem in some ways was how to manage the conflicts of interest which arose between 3i and its customers and between 3i's staff and their employer in venture capital situations. These normally required staff to be on the boards of customer companies and stand alongside their employer in the potential capital gains. It was expected by entrepreneurs who understood US venture capital practice that they would have direct management support from 3i staff appointed to their boards. Accustomed as we were to making a long-term commitment, including the provision of further capital, whenever it was justified, we felt that the presence of members of 3i's staff on boards would debar them from acting on any matter involving the customer's financial

Rodime

3i's INVESTMENT IN RODIME illustrates well the volatility of the 1980s high-technology investment boom. The company, founded in 1980 to manufacture computer disc drives, was established in Glenrothes—Scotland's 'silicon glen'—by a Scottish and American team which had gained experience working in the US computer giant Burroughs. 3i Ventures provided some £840,000 in the form of equity as part of a start-up package. Only two years later the company was floated on the over-the-counter market in New York, where its shares rapidly rose from the opening $8 to over $20, valuing 3i's holding at over $40 million. Expansion followed as Rodime established a lead in manufacturing 3.5 inch drives and extended manufacturing operations into the USA and Far East.

Despite its early technological edge Rodime could not be immune from competition and by the mid-1980s, the company, not yet five years old, was under pressure to develop new lines but suffered delays in releasing new products, and difficulties in patent enforcement. In 1989 a restructuring package became necessary in which 3i invested a further £2.8 million, becoming Rodime's largest shareholder with 25 per cent of the equity. Problems persisted however and in January 1991 manufacturing operations at Glenrothes were terminated. In August that year the other operating subsidiaries went into receivership or 'Chapter 11' in the USA with a holding company remaining to enforce patent settlements and trade on intellectual property rights.

It was possible to sell some 20 per cent of 3i's original holding in the two years after the New York flotation, realizing approximately £6.5 million and since 1992 further sales of shares in the holding company have realized £2.1 million.

In an interesting sequel to the Rodime story, 3i led an international syndicate of investors backing a 1992 start-up in Glenrothes, formed by six former Rodime employees. Calluna Technology, whose managing director Norman White was one of Rodime's founders, has been set up to manufacture credit card-sized disc drives for a new generation of palm-top computers.

requirements, because their duty to the company and that to their employer were in conflict, in addition to the complications caused by their personal interest in the success of the business. In the second and third rounds of financing which are common in venture capital, these conflicts became more acute. Problems of agreeing valuations for the new subscription of shares and the decision on whether to join in the further financing were difficult enough with other parties involved, but much more so with an interested staff member on the company's board.

There were concerns too that the presence of a major institution as a shareholder, rather than a group of individuals, particularly if it was represented on the board by a staff member and held a large, perhaps dominant stake in the equity, could lead to litigation in a particularly litigious country. Without exceptional, or even adequate, returns to justify these extra risks a 3i involvement in venture capital was unjustifiable. As returns from venture capital became more and more dependent on future hopes rather than current performance the invidious comparisons with the long-established investment capital business became inevitable. The venture capital successes of the early 1980s did not continue, whilst the main business in the UK went from strength to strength, producing returns which were good even by venture capital standards.

Inevitably there were strains within 3i as the performance gap between the two parts of the business widened. In order to compete with the US-based venture capitalists 3i Ventures in both countries had to recruit and reward in a similar way. The personal stake in investee companies demanded by staff recruited from the venture capital industry offered the prospect of capital gains in addition to their substantial salaries. It was hardly surprising that these arrangements caused unrest and envy among the other staff, who at that time had no prospect of personal capital gains; and 3i began to lose a number of experienced managers and controllers to competitors who were able to offer 'a slice of the action'.

Perhaps worse was the enormous cultural difference between the newly recruited Ventures staff and the ICFC staff, who were brought up in a strictly controlled and highly disciplined environment, hard-nosed and sharp-pencilled, and at the same time imbued with a sense of mission to the small-business sector as a whole. These were people with quite different backgrounds, imported from other venture capital businesses, accustomed to a more free-wheeling, less disciplined approach, using performance projections which were inevitably based on little hard fact, and direct, 'hands-on' involvement with individual investee companies.

Coexistence with Ventures inevitably led to expensive changes in the remuneration system for the rest of the organization with the object, both of providing matching benefits, and of discouraging important investment staff from leaving. So long as Ventures was producing the attractive returns shown by Rodime and LSI, its existence alongside the old ICFC was tenable, but as the returns fell and no further Rodimes appeared to boost the figures, the friction between the two parts became intolerable. But even if these internal strains could have been contained, the decision to distance 3i from venture capital with a redefinition of its main product as 'investment capital' made it inevitable that both the small venture capital subsidiary in the United Kingdom and the similar business in the United States should be discontinued.

The contemporary Japanese experience in adopting US-style venture capital as a model offers an interesting comparison. It seems odd that in a country where long-termism is a prime virtue the American pattern of venture capital should have been followed rather than the British one, the more so since 3i received a seemingly endless stream of Japanese delegations in the 1970s looking at its unique way of doing business. The experience of Japanese venture capitalists had been disastrous in the early years, despite the generally rapid growth of the Japanese economy and its stock market. The concentration on short-term gains, copied from the United States, limited the field for possible investment opportunities to those small companies which were growing rapidly and planning a flotation or 'initial public offering'. This constraint would at any time allow limited opportunities for investment, but in Japan the competition was ferocious, resulting in the inevitable overpricing of investment deals. In the rush for quick profits the opportunity for long-term capital provision of the 3i type was totally ignored. As 3i's success in the United Kingdom became more widely appreciated, to a great extent because we were becoming well known as a borrower among Japanese investment institutions, further sorties were made on behalf of would-be investors anxious to avoid repeating the disastrous mistakes of earlier ventures, and eager to join forces with an institution which appeared to have found a secret formula for success on lines which might be thought typically Japanese. During a visit to Tokyo we were flattered to be told

'Gentlemen, I like it. It's got "toaster" written all over it.'

317

by the largest Japanese venture capital group, which had studied 3i's success, that with hindsight they should have copied us rather than adopting the US venture capital method. Our response was eventually to enter into a joint venture with one of the few similar-minded long-term institutions, the Industrial Bank of Japan, to carry on traditional ICFC business. Whether this venture will succeed in transplanting 3i's special know-how into Japan and make an acceptable return it is too early to say, but there seems no reason why it should fail provided it adopts the rigorous appraisal and monitoring standards followed in the UK.

In general 3i has found its particular way of choosing, negotiating, monitoring, and realizing investments too difficult to implant through joint ventures, and has preferred to start up alone in other countries, training local nationals by secondment to the United Kingdom and sending out experienced investment managers to establish both the methodology and the quality standards which have been essential for success at home. Experience of operating in other countries indicates that the original ICFC formula was unique. As 3i subsidiaries have been established, first in France, then Germany, Spain, and Italy, so it has become apparent that nothing existed before quite like ICFC. But in the last few years there has been a substantial growth in venture capital US-style, and even some institutional competitors modelled on ICFC.

Venture Capital and Investment Capital: The Pros and Cons

Investment capital versus venture capital seems, in terms of 3i's experience, not to be a real contest. Investment capital, as defined by 3i in its advertising, is the full-scale substitute for the whole corporate capital market, permanently available to small companies of any size in any industry which are capable of growth. Venture capital is a specialized subset of investment capital, limiting itself consciously to high growth industries and companies within those industries which aim for a rapid progress to public flotation, and thus the prospect of a realization of the investment within a limited period. Venture capital concerns itself with a small number of short-term opportunities where massive amounts of capital can be concentrated in promising companies with a view to its extraction and redeployment in other opportunities after a fairly rapid realization, generally by way of flotation. Its motives, methods, expected returns, and time horizons are totally different and unsuited to the organized, long-term, institutional approach which 3i has adopted. For owner-managers whose objectives are similar to those of the venture capitalist there should be no problem. For those looking for long-term financial support which allows them to get on with the independent management of their business it is investment capital which is needed. This need is continuous and universal but, without the sharp focus or cherry-picking approach of the venture capitalist, it cannot be expected to produce the above-average investment returns for which some investors are looking, although in our experience it is possible to make sustained returns at a high level over long periods.

Venture capital misses out on one valuable feature of investment capital which possibly accounts for both the surprising success of what looks like a rather dull business and the very patchy record of venture capital. In all economies the number of private companies which are at any moment about to start a period of high growth will be limited, but it is on this small group of ripe cherries that all the venture capitalists concentrate. If the funds available for these limited opportunities are excessive, severe price competition must develop. Thus the number of good investments will be few and the entry price will be high. This is probably what happened in the mid-1980s when a few stunning successes like Rodime and LSI attracted enormous volumes of investment funds into the venture capital market. It is certainly one of the reasons for the disasters in the Japanese pre-IPO market. On these terms the chances of picking a winner and being able to invest in it at a sensible price must seem like a gamble with very long odds. Once this gamble has succeeded and the investment has been made there remains the problem of making it perform to the high standards necessary for an acceptable return—which for 3i Ventures was commonly in the range 50 to 60 per cent compound.

The investment capitalist, on the other hand, is not looking for major growth points—points of change, certainly, but all growing companies will have these from time to time—and the number of investment opportunities will be correspondingly greater. 3i has been able to make investments in between 600 and 1,000 of these companies per annum in recent years. However, not only are there more such investments to be made, but the amounts of money will tend to be smaller. The investment exposure is therefore smaller, both in terms of the capital value of the business being financed and in terms of portfolio spread.

So quite small amounts of capital can be committed on a passive basis by the investment capitalist and left to mature. If they are lost, the carrying cost will have been small because the investment was effectively dormant, but if growth does begin it is already in place when the venture capitalists come knocking on the customer's door. There are countless examples of such small investments becoming big successes, but the most interesting illustration of this phenomenon I know of is a company called Civil and Marine. In the 1960s ICFC acquired a 20 per cent stake in what was then a fledgling dredging business, being unwilling to finance two expensive dredgers for a virtually new business without some compensation for the risk. The 20 per cent stake cost £7,500 and was effectively forgotten about because it was too small to appear on the monitoring lists. But some twenty years later the company was sold for £100 million and 3i made a profit of nearly £20 million on its investment. The question to be asked in this case is, at what point in the twenty-year life of 3i's investment could a venture capitalist have negotiated a 20 per cent stake in this company? In effect ICFC had taken a permanent option on 20 per cent of the equity for £7,500. But it cannot be separated from the risk of the ship financing taken on at the same time and which effectively set the company on its way.

It would be interesting to compare the returns on capital of 3i and its venture capital competitors, but not enough facts are available about the competition. Our own experience has been that venture capital suffers from feast and famine. A very small number of investments will from time to time produce astonishing returns, like DEC for ARD, but the chances of one investor finding more than one or two winners must be remote, and the fact that one has been found does not guarantee others. It is very like gambling, despite the undoubted skill which goes into identifying and exploiting promising situations.

The investment capital method will never produce *overall* returns at the level of DEC. Although it is possible in individual cases to produce similar percentage returns, the spread of risks and the ongoing cost of establishing and monitoring a large portfolio indefinitely must hold down the overall returns. Nevertheless, the more modest return on investment capital can be maintained over very long periods. 3i's total compound return on capital over the ten years to 1990 was 20 per cent per annum after taking account of tax, not only on income and realized capital gains but on unrealized gains as well and after taking full account of losses and provisions.

The Macmillan Committee saw no reason why the institution it envisaged should not make reasonable commercial returns. ICFC was that institution, and it did make commercially acceptable returns, even though its business is different in fundamental respects from venture capital. Nor should we lose sight of the value which such an institution can bring to the economy as a whole. It has become apparent in recent years that at least one investment capital body is needed in every industrial economy to fill the gap which inevitably exists at the bottom end of the capital market, standing ready to provide long-term and permanent capital to all who can use it profitably. 3i's experience has proved that this can be done successfully with acceptable commercial returns. If such an institution is in place the needs of the private company sector as a whole will be met, and venture capital will provide a beneficial supplementary source of funds for special situations needing the concentrated application of money and management over brief periods which are inappropriate for the long-term investment capitalist.

NOTES

[1] A. P. H. Kaplan, *Small Business: Its Place and Problems* (McGraw Hill N.Y., 1948).
[2] See Case Studies: Rodime, Chapter 13; LSI Logic, Chapter 15.

Chapter 14

Defining the Business: 3i's Tax Case

The Big Issue: Trading or Investing

3i's BUSINESS HAS FEW analogues in the United Kingdom or elsewhere; indeed, it has been described by rating agents Moody's, who should know, as unique. I have discussed earlier some of the many innovations which lack of precedents forced upon us, but perhaps the most remarkable example arose in 1985 when, after forty years of being taxed as though ICFC were a trading company, we realized that its business for tax purposes was in fact 'investing', and the Group's tax status had to be completely rethought.

Before ICFC was formed there had been discussions between the shareholders and the Inland Revenue on how the new institution was to be taxed. It was by no means clear at that stage how it would operate, but it was agreed that it should be taxed on a trading basis rather than as an investment business, which would allow provisions and realized losses to be set against income in the year in which they arose; the shareholders were not sanguine about ICFC's prospects of success and were concerned that it might be paying tax on its income while suffering capital losses.

It seems unlikely that the concept of capital-market substitution, with its implications of long-term and permanent investment, had been thought through at that stage. As the shareholders' 'Announcement to the Public' seemed to imply, it was seen, by them at least, as an extension of banking business with the possibility of share subscription added on almost as an afterthought. But it was not as a long-term credit bank that ICFC operated. From the very beginning it set out to provide a package of different kinds of capital in any combination that the investee company, or 'customer', as they were always called,[1] might need. Whatever the amount asked for, it could be met by a cocktail of loans and shares appropriate to the existing capital structure of the business and the life and earning-power of the assets being acquired. At the extremes the capital could take the form of a pure loan or pure equity, and between those extremes could be any combination which fitted the customer's existing capital structure. For most of the companies seeking assistance from ICFC the investment they were going to make was very large in relation to their existing business, and the financing method would inevitably have a major impact on their balance sheets. However, the capital structure of every business would be unique, and it was to accommodate the great variety of structures that ICFC's founders devised the loan and share package.

From time to time the question did arise as to whether ICFC was being correctly taxed, but it never became an issue, and was ignored until the question of flotation arose. One reason for the lack of interest in the subject was the expectation, despite the shareholders' initial misgivings, that it would make little difference which way the Company was taxed. As a trading company it was allowed to take the tax credit for potential losses at the time specific provisions were made, rather than waiting until the loss actually crystallized, but paid tax on capital profits. As an investment company it would have paid tax on its profits realized from the sale of investments, but would have been unable to charge off losses until they were realized.

Flotation: The Issue Crystallizes

It was not until 1985, when the question of a disposal by some of the shareholders arose, that the whole question had to be addressed *ab initio*. The shareholders had reached agreement in February of that year on an instruction to Morgan Grenfell for advice 'as to possible ways and means of disposing in a way financially satisfactory to them, of a substantial part or the whole of their shareholdings in a manner that would endeavour to maintain the position and character of 3i as a provider of long-term finance to UK industry and commerce'.

The Board had no wish to stand in the way of a sale, although the banks' ownership had served the business well over forty years, allowing it to develop and maintain sound long-term policies which were consistent with its market-substitution role and gave great comfort to its customers. But they were concerned that the disposal should be managed in such a way that the 'position and character' of the business would indeed be maintained; control by one existing shareholder would not guarantee that, nor a sale to a third party; in the Board's view the best outcome for shareholders, as well as the Company, given the desire for disposal, would be flotation. This would allow those who wanted to leave an opportunity to sell, and would convert the holdings of those who stayed into a marketable security. The market price set by flotation could hardly be argued with and, as Warburgs suggested, if the banks were worried about that they could even offer their holdings to their own members.

We believed that 3i's long-term function could be most effectively protected from the day-to-day pressures of the Stock Market if it became an
investment trust. This was a form of company which was long-established, but
had fallen out of favour in recent years with the growth of unit trusts. The earliest investment trusts were formed in the nineteenth century to acquire and
hold long-term corporate debentures; their shares were generally held by individuals and provided a spread of risk together with professional portfolio management. They were an excellent mechanism for matching the small investor
with the market, able to deal more economically in substantial units of stock
and providing a reasonable liquidity for their investors. With the introduction
of capital-gains tax they were allowed to benefit from fiscal transparency, so
that any capital gains realized by the trust were exempt from capital-gains tax.
The price of this concession—though relieving their shareholders from being
taxed twice on the same profit could hardly be called a concession—was that
distributions of those capital profits by way of dividend was prohibited.
Furthermore, to qualify as an investment trust the company must distribute at
least 85 per cent of its income from investments.

Such a status could well have suited 3i earlier, but a further essential
qualification was that the company's shares must be listed. So it was only now,
when the shareholders had begun seriously to consider a means of disposal, that
the possibility arose. The advantages of investment trusts were familiar
through the management of EDITH which itself bought unquoted investments, and the two trusts which invested in small quoted companies, London
Atlantic Investment Trust and North British Canadian Investment Trust. But
for 3i itself the question had never arisen because a listing for its shares had not
been an option. Now that this possibility had arisen, investment trust status had
to be seriously explored because it seemed the most effective way of achieving
the necessary protection for 3i's position and character. The present ownership
arrangements would have been preferable, but the shareholders' wish to be
able to realize their investments was fully understood, and 3i was certainly big
enough to stand on its own feet. The management's main concern was that
pressure for short-term performance in the form of a high and growing dividend yield should not force the premature realization of assets; this would
undermine the support traditionally provided for young and growing companies which were normally unable to divert resources into dividend payments
in their formative years. Our concern was not entirely altruistic: it was from
these early-stage investments that the greatest capital gains had been garnered;
but they needed time to mature.

The prohibition on distributing capital profits would make investment
trust status a very suitable shelter for these long-term policies; there would be
no pressure to realize investments prematurely and the exemption from tax
would allow the whole of the capital gain, whenever it was realized, to be re-

CBarsotti

"SETTLE OUT OF COURT? WHERE'S THE FUN IN THAT?"

invested in new opportunities. But there were snags and one of them gave rise to a very large obstacle indeed. In order to become an investment trust a company had to be treated for tax purposes as an investment company. 3i Group itself was taxed as a trading company and its principal subsidiary, the original ICFC which held almost all the assets, had been taxed as a trading company since its inception forty years before.

Investment trust status, because of its particular tax privileges, is not readily granted by the Inland Revenue and trusts are normally specifically designed to conform with strict rules; for 3i to achieve the necessary preliminary qualification as an investment company would be difficult, given its long history.

The definition of an investment company (in S304(5) Income and Corporation Taxes Act 1970) is 'a company whose business consists wholly or mainly in the making of investments and the principal part of whose income is derived therefrom'. It is a remarkably simple definition, but the Revenue made it hard to qualify by effectively saying that all companies were assumed to be carrying on a trade unless they could prove that their sole activity was to make investments. As they put it in an initial exchange of letters, '[3i's] business is undoubtedly specialized but does not appear to us to have the character of an investment business which comprises the making and holding of investments'.

For an existing business taxed as a trader wishing to gain entry to investment status, one of the ramparts erected by the Revenue was the taxation of all the unrealized gains lying in its portfolio at the point of their transfer from trading status to investment. Several hundred million pounds of such gains had accumulated in the old ICFC portfolio over many years and would, of course, be taxed as and when realized, but if it changed its status by an appropriation from trading stock to investment the tax charge would be immediate. Calculations indicated that a bill of at least £150 million would result from this deemed disposal. It was a price which could not be justified in any circumstances, and the internal tax department began working on ways of getting round the problem.

Because ICFC, now known as 3i plc (a wholly owned subsidiary of 3i Group plc), had always been taxed as a trading company, it seemed unlikely that it could be converted into an investment company without this immediate tax charge on the deemed disposal of its assets. Solving this problem was the responsibility of 3i's taxation manager. Bernard Davies was another example of the versatility shown by many of the staff; recruited as chief accountant in the mid-1960s, he had converted himself into a highly respected tax expert and it was his original thinking which set us off on the track to investment trust status. Bernard devised a promising solution involving the transfer of 3i plc's assets into an existing investment company. It was, however, necessarily complicated and fraught with danger, for if the process was held to be a tax-avoidance device the transfer would itself give rise to the tax charge. The problem was therefore put to leading Tax Counsel Charles Beatty QC.

Re-examining the Business with the Help of Tax Counsel

We were surprised and delighted when Bernard returned with Mr Beatty's response that the complicated scheme put to him was unnecessary because in his opinion 3i plc was already carrying on an investment business and from the information before him it always had done. The brief to Mr Beatty was therefore revised and he was simply asked:

(1) Is 3i now carrying on an investment business and if so has it always done so?

(2) If the answers to the questions in (1) above are yes are there any circumstances in which the Inland Revenue could justify a tax charge on a deemed disposal of 3i's investment?

On the basis of the facts presented to him he was able to respond, 'It is my opinion in the light of the facts which I have outlined above that 3i has at all times been, and still is, an investor in relation to its subscriptions for shares . . . and loans, and not a dealer.' Consequently, 'the answer to the contention that trading stock had been appropriated to investment would be that 3i had made no alteration to its business and so no appropriation of trading stock to investment'.

In short, ICFC had been taxed on the wrong basis since 1945. If this opinion was confirmed there would be no deemed transfer of assets, no consequent tax charge, and 3i plc, established as an investment company, or another company formed for the purpose, could become an investment trust: there was no deemed appropriation on transfers between investment companies. The elegance of the argument was impressive and it was all the more attractive because it followed that there was no point during the whole life of the company when a change of status from trading to investment could be deemed to have occurred, and so no retrospective tax charge.

But how on earth, we wondered, could this argument be sold to the Inland Revenue? They would not easily accept that they had been taxing 3i plc wrongly since 1945, particularly as its status had never seriously been questioned. But the stakes were very high: investment trust status was essential if the integrity of the business was to be preserved after a flotation. It was also impossible to ignore the formal advice given by leading Tax Counsel and continue as though it had not happened. Moreover, the senior management of 3i, who had been with the business for up to thirty years, all felt intuitively that if it was a matter of fact rather than of law then the nature and continuity of the original ICFC business could be convincingly demonstrated. The General Management had all been involved in the decision-making process and knew that investment policy had never changed. A number of peripheral services had been added, mainly through subsidiary companies, but the share and loan package was what the business was all about, a point which was graphically demonstrated subsequently by the stripping-out of most of those services in the late 1980s to leave the core business as it had always been.

The Proposal to Float

It was therefore worth a fight to get this novel idea accepted and in consequence to be able to meet the shareholders' wishes by floating 3i as an investment trust. The Board, totally supportive as usual, accepted the force of these opinions and agreed with the management's proposal that flotation as an investment trust should be put to the shareholders as the company's response to their instruction to Morgan Grenfell. So a clear-cut recommendation to float the following year, after clearing the tax position, was submitted by the Board to the shareholders in the form of a set of proposals. There was no prevarication, even though a continuation of the *status quo* would have been preferable from the company's point of view. The proposal, dated 15 September 1985, said unequivocally:

In making the present recommendation the Board and management firmly believe that not only is it the best financial solution for the shareholders but the right one for 3i. Furthermore we see no alternative solution which will not materially jeopardize either the shareholders' financial interest or the maintenance of 3i's position and character. [This last opinion took account of the shareholders' own wishes, according to their brief to Morgan Grenfell.] We propose as follows:

1. We should be authorized to approach the Inland Revenue immediately for acceptance of our contention, supported by Counsel's unequivocal written opinion, that 3i is now and always has been carrying on an investment business through its subsidiary 3i plc.

2. When the Inland Revenue has accepted this view 3i should become an investment company and a listing be obtained for its shares in mid-July 1986, the company thereafter immediately becoming authorized as an investment trust. No public announcement should be made until the negotiations with the Inland Revenue are complete.

3. In the event of the Inland Revenue refusing to accept our view within the time necessary to permit a July listing, it should be deferred while the matter is pursued with the Special Commissioners and if necessary the Court.

4. Consideration should be given, subject to the shareholders' needs being satisfied, to raising up to £100m of additional capital in the issue.

The shareholders did not exactly jump at the idea of flotation; in fact it was not finally accepted for another six years. They were initially doubtful whether, even if Counsel's advice was correct, 3i would be able to persuade the Inland Revenue to reverse a practice hallowed by forty years' unquestioning acceptance. To counter this scepticism and to gain reassurance about the likelihood of winning, 3i took the precaution of seeking a second opinion from John Gardiner QC, another leading Tax Counsel. He concurred with Mr Beatty's view but offered only a 50 per cent chance of success in view of the history and the enormous burden of proof which that imposed on 3i. At the shareholders' request he considered the worst possible outcome if 3i were to fail in its appeal, but concluded that the only serious risk would be the loss of banking status for tax purposes. This had been granted as a concession some years previously, allowing 3i to receive and pay interest gross rather than under deduction of tax.

The shareholders' working party set up to consider 3i's proposal and Morgan Grenfell's recommendations invited Mr Beatty to repeat his opinion, which he did in September 1986, in conference held, unusually, at the Bank of England rather than in chambers. There was some concern that a change of status for 3i might result in a reassessment of the tax position of the shareholders' own subsidiaries, which to a greater or lesser extent were its competitors, and this continued to affect their attitude for some time to come. Mr Beatty confirmed his views on the likelihood of 3i succeeding and, while emphasizing the heavy onus of proof which inevitably lay on the Company, saw 'no obstacle in law to 3i's success which would depend on the weight of evidence in its favour. So far I see no reason to suppose that 3i would not succeed'.

Doubts continued to assail the shareholders as one window of opportunity for flotation followed another. The two leading Counsel so far consulted having been briefed by 3i, the shareholders felt it necessary to approach yet another leading Tax Counsel for an opinion, taking account of their own position. He agreed with the first two but also had doubts about an appeal succeeding in the unusual circumstances of 3i's case.

Eventually, in the absence of a consensus among the banks, 3i felt obliged to proceed with its case to the Special Commissioners, if only to clarify the proper treatment of tax in its own accounts. In the meantime, the existence of such strong advice from two leading Counsel could not be ignored and was incorporated by way of note to the accounts, together with a calculation of the effect of a change on the amount of tax payable. There were six years' tax computations still not agreed, although tax had been paid on account of the final liabilities, which meant that if the old ICFC's status were changed the tax would have to be recalculated back to 1980. This was difficult to do accurately because there were few precedents for such a change and some peculiar transitional effects would arise. For example, provisions which had been allowed before 1980 would stand, yet losses which actually arose after 1980 would also be allowed, so there would be double relief for those losses which had been previously provided for. On the other hand, tax payable on interest accrued before 1980 would be paid again on the same interest when it was received. It was all very odd, but on such calculations as 3i and the auditors were able to do the total effect of the change over the whole of the six open years netted down to an additional liability of about £10 million, tending to confirm the previous view that so long as the company was unquoted it did not matter much which way it was taxed. But of course it did matter in the context of a possible flotation and in any case the tax status must now be settled formally.

Arguing It Out with the Revenue

Two years after the Board's submission of its proposals the shareholders were still mulling over their response, so 3i decided it must settle the matter and entered into a dialogue with the Revenue, submitting Counsel's opinion in support of its case. The Inland Revenue were predictably dismissive of the arguments, although I thought their reasons for challenging the claim seemed illogical. They appeared mainly concerned to defend a set of established procedures which had served them well in limiting access to the valuable investment trust status. They clearly did not fully understand the nature of 3i's business and deployed arguments which applied to quite different situations. It was a good example of the difficulties which the unique character of 3i caused the official mind: it could not be conveniently pigeon-holed with any other category of business. They argued that it was providing a service by supplying finance, and that the acquisition of equity in private companies was ancillary to that service—a strange contention, since even in its very first year of existence 40 per cent of the amount committed by ICFC was in the form of share capital and it had always offered the package of share and loan capital, even though one or the other might not be needed in particular cases.

The Revenue argued that the making of investments was an entirely passive function, though I could find no statutory support for this view. It was acceptable for 'investment' to consist of simply buying and selling shares and other securities on the stock market, which could be done by a small central staff using brokers. If the would-be investor ceased to be passive and went out looking for investment opportunities, by establishing branch offices, advertising for business, and giving help and advice to those companies, that had all the trappings of a trade—the provision of a financial service. They argued:

The company conducts a well-established and well-organized business of providing financial services: it provides finance on a very large scale by way of loan and subscription for shares with loans forming the major part, to members of the public for their own businesses, as well as providing advice and a variety of other services; it actively markets its services and seeks out its customers, advertising its services in competition with other institutions; it seeks to make a profit from these activities.

The implication of this, it seemed to me, was that only secondary-market buying and selling could qualify as an investment business: therefore the acquisition of private-company securities which, by definition, had no market and had to be sought out by other means could not possibly be treated as investment. And yet the statutory definition of investment involved the carrying on of a business.

In our initial arguments I had commented:

You agreed that the company is not dealing—it could hardly be possible with the great bulk of our portfolio in the form of untradeable investments. But you appeared to confine your view of what constituted investment to the purchase of shares and debentures through the secondary market. The implication of this limitation seemed to be that you regard the tradeable nature of listed securities as more significant in determining investment than the untradeable nature of unlisted securities. Clearly a secondary market exists to facilitate selling so the logic of treating primary investment, without the ability to sell, as trading and purchasing in the secondary market as investing is difficult to follow.

Greggs plc

GREGGS PLC, BAKERS AND CONFECTIONERS, was founded in Newcastle during the 1930s by the father of the present chairman, Ian Gregg, who gave up his practice as a solicitor to take charge on his father's death.

3i's involvement began in 1974 with a £100,000 loan which enabled the company to buy the freehold of its head office. At that time it employed 600 staff and owned 60 retail shops in the Newcastle and Glasgow areas. The following year 3i purchased 15 per cent of the equity from family members and over the next few years provided leasing and hire purchase facilities.

In 1983, a major extension of the bakery was made possible by a further loan of £400,000 and the company's continuing expansion made feasible a quotation for its shares; the public issue in 1984 was 97 times over-subscribed.

3i made 7 per cent of its holding available to the market but kept the remainder as long-term holding. At the same time it provided guarantees for loan notes issued as consideration for an acquisition.

Yet another secured loan was advanced in 1986 for further expansion and 3i still retains 9.7 per cent of the equity. The company has continued to grow through careful expansion of its main business and shrewd acquisitions, announcing in 1994 pre-tax profits of £9 million whilst the number of shops has grown to 900 and staff employed to over 6,000.

The 3i view was that all businesses have characteristics in common and that the badges of trade, which had been established in the courts as determining whether individuals were carrying on a business at all, were largely irrelevant in deciding whether an acknowledged business was one of trading or one of investing. It seemed odd that the Revenue so narrowly defined investment as to limit it in practice to the buying and selling of quoted securities. Their logic must lead to the conclusion that there was no effective difference between investment in securities and dealing in securities, which was certainly a trading activity. The distinction, according to the Revenue, was a matter of frequency. They advised us not to draw too heavily on the experience of investment trusts because there was already some concern that a number of them had been buying and selling too frequently to justify their investment company status! In that case, we claimed triumphantly, then surely 3i plc's total inability to dispose of an investment once acquired must make it more like an investment business than trusts which held only marketable investments. The main reason for choosing to hold marketable rather than unmarketable investments must be in order to sell them.

They were not to be persuaded by the power of these arguments; with a long-established position to defend they were not prepared to acknowledge voluntarily that 3i plc might have been wrongly taxed for forty years; only a decision by the Special Commissioners would make them accept a change in status. The management for our part were prepared to put up a case, but realized that in the face of the Revenue's intransigence it could take up to two years to get a decision, and that might not be the end of it, even if the case were decided in favour of 3i, because the Revenue might choose to appeal. So the flotation timetable suggested to the shareholders would suffer further disruption. Some effort was put into reducing the period of uncertainty, because no action could be taken until this matter was settled, but despite approaches to the Board of Inland Revenue, the Bank of England, and Treasury ministers, nothing more than sympathy was gained, and we decided to go ahead with an appeal to the Special Commissioners. Although the tax case did not open until July 1989, nearly four years after the Board's formal proposal was submitted to shareholders, it was to be a further two years before the shareholders finally decided to float 3i.

Taking it to the Special Commissioners

The preparation and presentation of the case and its hearing were fascinating. Despite their title (the Special Commissioners for Income Tax) the Commissioners are not part of the Inland Revenue but an independent branch of the judiciary, and their procedure is similar to that of the courts, though less formal. Documentary evidence is required, supported by witnesses, to establish the facts; and it was encouraging for us to know that the judgement as to whether a company is carrying on an investment business is determined primarily by the facts.

It was particularly inconvenient that Bernard Davies's retirement occurred in the later stages of this process. He had been heavily involved from the beginning of the case and his knowledge of 3i's tax history was encyclopaedic. Fortunately, however, his successor, John Moore, had been understudying Bernard for some years and proved a fully competent substitute.

The 3i case put by Mr Gardiner when he opened on 17 July 1989 was simply that:

The Corporation [that is, 3i plc, the original ICFC] acquires assets for investment. Acquiring assets is not the provision of a service; if it was every investor, including those like EDITH—recognized investment companies—would be a trader . . . If anything I would say that the venture capital companies [accepted as investment companies] like 3i Ventures, are more hands-on; they are still investment businesses but, if anything, if one is taking a spectrum, they are closer to the edge of trade than the core business of the Corporation which is very long term, passive and hands-off . . . it is a contradiction in terms to suggest that the investment must become stock in trade of a trade in providing services. . . . Traders who buy and sell with a view to turning over at a profit have stock in trade turning over profit in the short term, but somebody who provides services does not have stock in trade. I do not have any stock in trade.

The Revenue's position was summarized in opening by their leading Counsel, Mr D. Milne, QC:

This unique company, 3i, falls to be treated like banks and insurance in relation to its investments, in that investments are all part and parcel of its centre core activity and that it is providing a financial service to the public at large, and that it is an integral part of that package that it would provide investments as well as loans.

Larry Tindale, who was the first witness for 3i, was able to describe the evolution of an investment policy devised initially by John Kinross which, despite remaining unrecorded, has stood the test of time. He said of JBK:

He had a natural ability to create an investment package which would give the Corporation what it needed—by which I mean a mix of running income to cover costs and capital appreciation—and what the customer company would need, by which I mean a sound balance sheet, adequate income cover to service its borrowings, and appropriate retentions for at least part of its expansion scheme.

No further explanation of policy had been necessary, said Larry,

because the business is and always has been to make investments by subscribing a mixture of loan capital and equity capital. We did not need to keep reminding the staff about this. We all knew the investment policy. The desire was not there because we have never wished to lay down rigid policies as to the exact form as opposed to the nature that an investment should take. We wish to remain flexible.

I think there is a good example of that. The way we develop new investments, we meet an actual practical application. Somebody works on it and suggests a method of investing in those circumstances. If it is good it stands up to examination, and the whole procedure of Cases Committee minutes and various things going round means that it becomes available as background knowledge throughout the Corporation.

As expected Counsel for the Inland Revenue made much of 3i's use of the word 'customer', which he claimed was unusual if the business was one simply of acquiring investments, and of the word 'investment'. He also pointed to self-conscious use of other expressions like 'investee companies' and 'transactions' as evidence that 3i now knew the danger of using expressions which could indicate a trading activity. But what emerged from his cross-examination of Larry was the distinction between the process of finding an investment and putting it on the books, which was a transaction, and 'assets acquired by this process', which were investments.

Q. Suddenly you are talking about transactions rather than investments. Is there any significance in that change of wording, or are they interchangeable?

A. I do not think they are interchangeable. To me the transaction is the thing which one is engaged in at the moment. It produces an investment, but I am not always literal in my use of words.

And again

Q. I noticed when you started giving evidence this morning you were talking about 'investee companies', but you soon relaxed back into 'customers' because that is a more natural word. One could perhaps use strained words if one were trying to put forward a particular impression, but investee company, really is rather difficult, is it not?

A. It is technically accurate but not one easy to enunciate.

Q. Exactly. I do not hold you any more to the use of the word customers than you can hold me or Moody's to the use of the word investment.

Another area which the Revenue regarded as evidence of trading was the syndication of large investments by the City Office. In cross-examining Jon Foulds, Counsel for the Revenue pointed out the claim which had appeared in a 3i City brochure that '3i combines experience, skill, imagination, and money to help companies bring about positive change' and 'at 3i we have always had a talent for developing imaginative solutions—most recently to the financing of larger syndicated management buy-outs . . . We are well-qualified to lead these larger syndicates since we can invest significant amounts of our own money as well as industrial and financial expertise'.

Q. Do you agree what you are doing is more than simply providing money?

A. What we are doing is what is necessary to create the investment opportunity for ourselves.

Q. One cannot be a pure investor in this sort of business, is that right?

A. I would say we were pure investors, but in order to make the investment you have to be willing to do other things, but the objective is to make the investment. Syndication is not a pure objective in itself.

In these answers Jon encapsulated the whole of 3i's argument, exposing the narrowness of the Revenue's approach to investment. Their argument that investment must only be a passive function could not apply to the acquisition of investments in private companies, particularly where it is primary investment, the subscription of new capital, as opposed to secondary investment, which involves the purchase of existing stock.

Counsel then asked Jon to compare what 3i was doing with what an investment trust might do.

Q. Supposing you were an investment trust, investing purely in quoted securities. You would obviously investigate carefully the track record of any quoted company you were planning to invest in, but you would not need to, then, perform any service for the company. You would simply make up your own mind whether the investment was worth investing, would you not?

A. That would depend on the objectives of the trust. Certain trusts do give themselves the objective of adding value.

Q. It is a fact of life that if you are putting money into this sort of company that 3i put money into you have to go about your affairs very differently from if you were simply investing in quoted companies. . . . You are having to perform a much greater service. Indeed you are having to perform a service in relation to those companies whereas if they had been quoted companies, you make an investment decision to buy the shares on the Stock Exchange.

A. You would always, if you were prudent, gather as much information as you can from whatever source. You would do your due diligence, but that would take a different form.

Q. I accept that. I think we agree with you. I should say that on the primary facts there does not seem to be much between us. It is the inference which is a matter of argument on which we are at variance.

Counsel for the Inland Revenue continued to pursue the argument that 3i provided more than money even through 3i plc, accepting that some services were supplied through separate companies within the 3i Group.

Q. Cutting out all those activities that are done by other subsidiaries, it is still a picture here of a very active business being carried on by 3i which is very much indeed removed from that of a pure investor.

A. I think we have to disagree about that.

Mr Gardiner called Bill Govett, a non-executive director of 3i Group, but also an experienced manager of investment trusts, to make an authoritative comparison between the activities of 3i and investment trusts. In the course of his evidence he was able to make the telling point that investment trusts had historically invested in loans as well as shares.

I would say, going back to the old days, investment trusts were large investors in loans and preference shares and more lately moved to equities and a mixture of both. It is quite interesting today, we are seeing investment trusts investing in all three packages again, straight loans, straight equity and preference and convertible loans. . . . 3i as a long-term investor, of course, shows remarkable similarities, in my view, with the aims of investment trusts.

He was also able to explain the need for 3i

to look very hard for these potential investments in the first place and then spend a great deal of time and effort in deciding whether they have the potential for what we are looking for as a satisfactory long term investment. . . . We in a sense are doing the same thing, whether it is at John Govett or at 3i, but perhaps the cost and effort of finding an unquoted investment is far greater than it is finding a satisfactory quoted investment.

The comparison with investment trusts moved into interesting territory when Mr Govett said:

Where I see much more similarity today is that the conventional investment trust is engaging much more in the type of 3i activity because the whole investment product today is changing. We are much more into the world of management buy-outs and leverage buy-outs than we have been previously used to.

He also answered effectively the Revenue's claim that 3i spent a remarkably large amount of money on promoting itself—its 'services', they would say.

Q. How would you compare your advertising budget with that of, say, an investment trust?

A. Our advertising budget, as such—well, investment trusts do not advertise very much because they are mainly investing in quoted securities, but of course, where they are investing in unquoted securities, and you have seen I think already a number of trusts which are, their advertising budgets would probably compare with 3i's.

These views were echoed by Richard Bunn of Hoare Govett, who confirmed that 'there is a sizeable number of investment trusts that do invest in part in unquoted'; and in respect of its active publicity:

In part through its advertising and regional network, but also by word-of-mouth recommendations the Corporation has been able to build its portfolio. Institutions which invest principally in listed securities do not face the same problems in finding their investments. However, all major investment institutions have sizeable organizations which operate in a fairly systematic way in the selection of their investments.

One of the unusual features of this case was that 3i's decision to proceed was taken in spite of earlier calculations that over the period of open assessments an additional £10 million tax liability would arise. This was confirmed in evidence by Howard Brown, the audit partner from Ernst & Young, who, once

Mr Beatty's original advice had been received, had insisted on showing the effect of a possible change in the published accounts. This was greatly to 3i's advantage; it demonstrated conclusively that the appeal had not been taken up in order to gain a tax advantage. In the 1988 Finance Act, investment companies were given substantial relief from tax on previous inflationary increases in asset values, which would be beneficial to 3i if the case was won; but it was

'So we're agreed. Honesty is the best policy. Okay. Let's label that Option A.'

not easy for Revenue Counsel to demonstrate that this fortuitous event was a reason for the appeal, since this manifestly was not the case. Nor did he attempt to challenge Howard Brown's opinion that 'the Supplementary Accounts of 3i Group plc support the view that the Group, and thus the Corporation as the principal subsidiary, is carrying on an investment business'. Howard Brown had explained that the historic cost accounts, which had always been the 'legal' accounts, would have been equally suitable for either a trading or an investment company, but the Supplementary Accounts which had started in 1985 showed a much more complete view of the total performance of the group and of 3i plc.

Another witness called by Mr Gardiner was Ernest Harbottle, who had both dealt frequently with 3i over many years and managed investment trusts. He went further than any other witness in his comparison of 3i with investment trusts in saying:

I have always regarded the Corporation as a special investor which has a special organization designed to pick and to manage long-term investments. By contrast most investment trusts and funds I have come across are essentially dealers. In my view a typical investment trust is essentially a securities trading organization. There is no share held by an investment trust which is not for sale and their criteria seem to be moving more and more to the short term.

Eyebrows were raised at this description of investment trusts which prompted Revenue Counsel to comment: 'no doubt those behind are taking notes rapidly.' It went further than anyone in 3i would have done but it was essentially making the fundamental point we had already made to the Revenue, that a secondary market exists for selling shares and by acquiring only quoted shares investment trusts would be putting themselves into a position to sell, with the connotations of dealing which that implies. 3i, by acquiring only unquoted shares, could never be accused of doing so with a view to dealing.

Sir David Scholey of Warburgs was brought in as an expert witness to set 3i's activity in the context of the financial system as a whole. He described a spectrum of institutions ranging from banks to investment trusts, and placed 3i squarely at the investment end of the spectrum—it had no resemblance to any kind of bank or finance company. This firmly contradicted the Revenue's view expressed in an earlier letter:

One is looking at a wide spectrum, there will be a substantial grey area in the middle, on the evidence at present before us we think that 3i falls well on the trading side of that spectrum.

The view of 3i's function given by Mr Harbottle and Sir David was strongly supported by Robin Angus of County NatWest Securities, an analyst specializing in investment trusts who was pleased to appear as a witness because he believed that 3i would be the archetypal investment trust. He was able to trace the history of investment trusts, describing the kind of assets they acquired and the methods they employed to find them:

I am familiar with the affairs of a number of investment trusts which invest in the unquoted sector. I am a director of one of these, Personal Assets Trust plc, and I am able to comment from experience. It is common for such investment trusts to be offered investments via a mix of loan and share capital. That suits the unlisted company raising the capital because it leaves the company with the correct level of gearing. It also suits the investment trust because it provides a running yield and equity to provide capital appreciation.

He made a useful comparison between the rate at which the portfolio of investment trusts is turned over with 3i's turnover, and contended, 'I would say that [3i] were very comfortably within the range that one would expect from a listed investment trust and indeed were at the low end of that range.'

Sir Kenneth Berrill, the Revenue's first expert witness, drew a different set of conclusions from making the same comparisons. He had, however, been under the misapprehension that 3i plc encompassed all the services provided in fact by other companies in the group. The same misunderstanding affected the evidence of a second expert witness, John Crosland of Robert Fleming, who thought the major distinguishing feature was 3i's portfolio of loans with no equity link. It was, he considered, untypical of an investment business, although as Mr Gardiner pointed out, Sir Kenneth Berrill had thought they were typical, and so also had Robin Angus and Bill Govett.

The Crown's case, after all the evidence had been taken, was that while acknowledging that 3i was a purveyor of capital to businesses which do not have access to the capital market, it was actually doing much more—relying heavily on Jon Foulds's description of it:

We are not just interested in lending money. Our business is the creation of wealth. . . . A man we are interested in is one who says I want a financial partner who can bring something else to the party besides money. . . . Having heard all the evidence we would describe 3i's business as the provision of a package of financial services to small- and medium-sized businesses in the UK, the core of that package being the provision of medium and long-term capital . . . the remainder being a variety of services supplied to customers as required.

3i was unlike an investment trust because it serviced its customers, whereas a trust services its shareholders. Other distinctions were:

(a) 3i's volume of business is generated by the amount of business it can attract. . . . The business of investment trusts is governed by their capital endowment.

(b) If 3i has lined up more business than it can fund out of dividends interest and equity realization, it goes out and borrows further funds. . . . Investment trusts rarely if ever borrow to any material effect.

(c) Investment trusts traditionally invest in quoted securities. That is a very different business from investing in unquoted securities.

But the most important point in relation to investment trusts, particularly those which have recently been set up to acquire equity in unquoted companies, is . . . that their tax status is not in question in this appeal. . . . It may or may not be that Mr Harbottle was right [in his description of trusts as essentially dealers].

The question of similarity to investment trusts had no bearing in this case, said Revenue Counsel. He nevertheless found it significant to compare what 3i did in some respects with investment trusts:

I do not say (the word 'customer') is conclusive, but it does seem that I have been unable to find the word 'customer' in anybody else's literature of the investment trusts.

He was able to draw heavily on the use of the specialized language used in describing 3i's commitment to its customers as evidence of a trading mentality. In fact most of the Revenue Counsel's winding-up address was concerned with 3i's public statements of what it did and why it did it—helping its customers rather than maximizing return for its shareholders. The whole *raison d'être* of the Corporation was described in the Chairman's statement in 1983:

Our principal objective continues to be the support of British business and I have no doubt that the development of our overseas activities will help us to do this more effectively.

We shall be devoting much effort to ensuring that the change in the structure of the Group, designed to give greater cohesion and co-operation between our various parts, is fully understood and contributes effectively to providing a better service to our customers.

The whole argument in the end was about what 3i plc did and the extent to which it provided services in addition to its core investment activity. The Revenue case was that 3i provided services in which its investments played an integral part. Our argument was that 3i made investments, and such services as it provided were peripheral to that main function.

In fact, said Revenue Counsel, 'the reward that 3i was getting for its services (of providing capital) was . . . partly the opportunity to share in the success of the company through profits or realization of equity'. Its service was the provision of capital, its reward was the return from that capital. He did not try to say how that was different from investment.

Mr Gardiner considered that the Revenue's arguments had not taken the case much further than their previous position. The arguments on law were wrong and those of fact were not based on the evidence the Commissioners had actually heard. The key to the case in a nutshell was that 'the holder of share and loan capital, held for the benefit of income, held long-term, no doubt in the hope of some realization in the future of a gain, such a holder is inevitably an investor, for the assets he holds are investments.'

The Revenue's case was not concerned with facts, which had been set out in the documents, but with description. The rewards which 3i received—interest, dividends, and capital profits—were not the rewards of a service but the reward of the capital it had invested.

A Critical Decision

It was some months before the Commissioners' Decision in Principle was known, but it was worth waiting for. They were quite clear that 3i was not a bank of any kind, even though it made loans, some of which were 'free-standing'. These were significantly different from those of banks, particularly in their term, and were seen as necessary to provide guaranteed income to meet its exceptionally high revenue outgoings, in particular salaries. They 'do not in our view evidence a difference of objective between the Corporation and the other companies with which Mr Crosland compared it'.

The 3i argument was that if marketable securities are '*prima facie* purchased and sold by way of investment and not by way of trade . . . that presumption must be stronger where the securities being unquoted are essentially unmarketable'. Such a presumption would not apply if 3i were a dealer in securities, which all agreed it was not, or if the investments were held for the purpose of a distinct trade, such as insurance or banking, 'but the circumstances required for the application of that principle are absent from the present case'.

Mr Gardiner had contended that 3i's business could be brought neither within the well-established interpretations of 'trade'—the provision of goods for reward—nor the provision of services for reward. Mr Milne had disagreed: 'The Corporation was trading because it provided financial services for reward'. The Commissioners noted that,

We are bound to say that Mr Milne was greatly assisted in that argument by the brochures which the Corporation distributes describing what it (and other parts of the group through it) can offer to what it has always referred to as its 'customers'.

But the Commissioners accepted that 3i's brochures were an exercise in marketing and that the Annual Reports which made similar claims were generally available. 'They are flavoured accordingly,' they said. However, they had been impressed by the evidence given not only by Larry and Jon but also by three senior managers who had been called to describe 3i's business and its pro-cedures—Brian Larcombe, John Platt, and David Wilson. To those who had been present at the hearing their oral evidence had been a model of clarity and their long-standing commitment to 3i was obvious. The Commissioners com-mented flatteringly but perceptively:

Having heard the evidence of a number of people who have worked in the Corporation in different capacities, we are left in no doubt that there is deeply ingrained in the Corporation an ethic of service, in a general sense, to small- and medium-sized busi-nesses. . . . But that is not the same as saying that it is in the business of providing services to particular concerns.

They regarded the argument that 3i looked for investments whilst con-ventional investment companies looked for funds as having nothing to say on the trading/investing issue. But they did accept that the publicity given to ser-vices was significant.

Corporate finance was regarded as too small to affect the view of the business as a whole. The giving of advice in a more general sense was 'bound up inextricably with the making or monitoring of investments and no fees are charged for it'. This was not the provision of financial services.

The key point in the Revenue's argument was that the provision of money, whether as a loan or a subscription for shares, was itself a financial ser-vice, the reward coming in any form. This distinguished 3i from conventional investment companies which bought shares. The Commissioners thought this distinction could apply to short-term finance, but not to loans which were so long in term that they must be seen as investments.

The Commissioners' distinction between short- and long-term was subtle but crucial to their decision, because if loans could be described as investments then it followed that shares must be similarly described:

Once the lending has gone long-term, so that the loan can be characterized as an invest-ment, the position is not the same. The acquisition of an asset is not the provision of ser-vices.

The loan is the price of the loan stock and the loan interest is not the 'reward' for the lending but the natural fruit of the investment purchased by the lending.

Apart from comparisons with building societies, which the Com-missioners did not accept, the final Revenue argument was that there was a con-siderable 'turnover' in the Corporation's assets, and that the proceeds of these sales were relied on substantially for funding its business:

Substantial 'turnover', is of course a well-known badge of trade, but its importance is a matter of degree. The Chief Executive's Review printed in the Group's 1985–86 accounts discloses that in that year, 7 of the companies in which we have invested joined the Unlisted Securities Market, making a total of 30 since the market opened five years ago. A further 9 obtained Stock Market quotations. The portfolio totals around 5,000 companies. The analysis of the portfolio demonstrates that listing and realizing are far from synonymous. We do not think we need to say more.

The conclusion was firm and unambiguous, reflecting the quality of the evidence and the conduct of the case:

We are therefore of the clear opinion that the Corporation does not trade: it is an investor.

NOTES

[1] No one has ever thought of a better one-word description, and readers will find the word used throughout this book as a term of 3i jargon.

Chapter 15

The International Dimension: A Global Macmillan Gap

Looking Abroad for Inspiration

ONE OF OUR PREOCCUPATIONS during the 1970s was the possibility of nationalization. With hindsight the risk was never very great, but the complaints about the City's preference for 'candy-floss' industries, the Billion Pound Fund,[1] and the general concern about British industry's lack of competitiveness, poor performance and, worse, its investment record, led inevitably to invidious comparisons with the rest of the EEC and Japan. Included in these concerns was a pervasive view that one, possibly the main, reason for Britain's relatively poor performance was shortage of capital on the right terms. We put some effort during this period into countering these charges and examining what was really happening elsewhere.

We were not helped by a research project carried out by Dr Yao-Su Hu of Hong Kong University, comparing FFI with its German and French counterparts.[2] He concluded that the ICFC part of FFI, though worthy enough ('a very well managed, efficient, and sound credit institution'), was far too small to have any significant impact, whereas the German and French institutions both played an important role in implementing a national industrial policy. 'There is a difference between a small, well-managed credit institution serving a well-defined market segment and large institutions designed as instruments of national policy.' We knew from our experience as a member of the Association of Long-Term Credit Institutions in the EEC, familiarly known as 'The Club', that FFI was indeed a minnow among the continental whales and much less significant than they were in national economic life.

Dr Hu's report had some influence on Labour Party thinking, stirring up renewed calls for government intervention in industrial financing; but the change of government in 1979 effectively put an end to this possibility. Nevertheless, the idea that British industry needed more investment and lacked adequate access to the necessary capital retained its currency in Labour Party thinking, emerging as policy in the 1992 manifesto commitment to set up a public-sector equivalent of 3i. Surprisingly, however, the Conservative government began to toy with its own idea of support for small companies, which finally emerged as the Loan Guarantee Scheme, though this was to be administered by the private sector.

Despite the change of government, therefore, we felt it worthwhile to illuminate the debate on state intervention by examining the experience of other countries and comparing it with our own. To gather the necessary information we despatched a number of our own staff, most of them experienced controllers but also all graduates, some with masters' degrees and even one or two with Ph.D.s, to produce reports on industrial financing in other countries. Using our existing links with The Club, among others, they were able to gain access to the necessary sources in government, industry, and the financial institutions.

Their reports produced a remarkably similar story across the industrialized world, which we summarized in an occasional paper entitled 'The Capital Structure of Industry in Europe', published in 1982. Much of the argument in this chapter derives from the survey, which made it clear that the response of the United Kingdom to the post-war need for industrial regeneration, including the formation of ICFC, was totally different from that of other countries. It confirmed Dr Hu's conclusion that the UK, like the United States, separated the private sector from the state, whereas most other countries adopted an 'integrationist' policy, the state, finance, and industry working in a close partnership.

From Richard Coopey's research it appears that it was the prospect of renewed unemployment in the aftermath of the Second World War which led to the formation of ICFC. It was a wholly pragmatic response to what was seen as a short-term problem; none of its founders gave it much chance of success and some expected it would be wound up after a few years when the post-war recovery was under way and the political pressure had eased. It was only incidentally that it was to be the capital-market substitute which Macmillan had envisaged.

Nowhere is there evidence that ICFC formed part of a grand strategy for the post-war regeneration of British industry which might have restored the country's position as a major economic power. FCI, itself intended to be nothing more than a lender of last resort, was the only other institutional response to the huge need for fresh industrial capital. Both new bodies were to be funded by the private sector, and it was not thought necessary to boost the availability

"MITCHELL, WE SHOULD BE MORE LIKE
THE JAPANESE."

of investment funds by introducing subsidized public money. Marshall Aid was used in other countries to provide an ongoing source of cheap capital for industrial regeneration, but no such facilities were made available to British industry, and little was done in practice to promote the restoration of the nation's industrial base. It was the memory of the 1930s' unemployment which was uppermost in policy-makers' minds, just as German thinking was dominated by the inflationary experiences of the 1920s.

So ICFC was created for the wrong reasons, probably at the wrong time, to do a job which few thought was needed. It is even more odd that, at a time when a Labour administration was coming into power for the first time with a substantial majority, bent on taking over the commanding heights of the economy and converting it from a market-driven to a centrally planned system, it should permit the creation in the private sector of an institution designed to compensate for market failure. The reason probably lies in the overwhelming importance attached to employment creation. It is clear that there was disagreement in Whitehall over the nature of the problem ICFC was to solve, notably between the Treasury and the Board of Trade, the latter fearing that a private-sector body would be too narrowly focused on short-term profits and unable or unwilling to take the necessary proactive stance.

The Foreign Response to Post-War Reconstruction

Other countries did not have the luxury of being able to make such a choice. The physical capital of both Germany and Japan had been destroyed, as had much of that in the occupied countries, and their financial resources had been consumed. They now needed enormous injections of new capital which could

Overseas Investments

IN THE LATE 1980s 3i REFOCUSED its overseas operations on Europe. Branches in France, Germany, Italy, and Spain were established or expanded in a bid to extend 3i investment methods into new markets. One of the first management buy-outs funded by 3i in Germany, in 1988, was Woma, a new company formed to acquire the controlling interest in Woma Apparatebau Wolfgang Maasberg and Co., a high-pressure pump manufacturer in Duisberg-Rheinhausen, from its American parent, Flow Inc. The proposal was introduced by a local consultant, Wolfgang Wistdorf, who had seen 3i's MBO advertisement, and by the managing director, Theo Sausen. 3i arranged a loan of DM 3.5 million and subscribed for 34 per cent of the equity in the new company.

3i later extended the MBO concept to Italy. A typical example is the Bergamo-based manufacturer, Nolan, introduced in 1992 by a local accountant Dr Lanfranchi, who was to become chairman of the new company. Nolan, which was the second largest manufacturer of helmets and optical products for motorcyclists—exporting a large proportion of production—was to be sold by the bank which held shares as security against lending to its larger parent group. 3i provided around £800,000 for the MBO using a combination of preferred ordinary shares and convertible bonds, with a maximum equity share of just over 40 per cent.

3i's investments in Spain include the purchase of equity in Carbonica de Navarra. This company, established over 40 years, produces, bottles and distributes a range of soft drinks including the well known 'Gaseosa', often used as a mixer with wine. In 1992 Jesus Oderiz, who jointly owned the company with his brother, Angel, wanted to retire and sell his 50 per cent share. 3i agreed to take a stake by paying £1.25 million for 42.5 per cent of the equity, leaving the company to be run by Angel Oderiz.

3i's first investments in continental Europe were made through its Paris office which opened in 1983. France is the largest of its continental European bases with over 160 investments made since 1983. Sofamor, for example, is a specialist company manufacturing metallic implants to correct spinal deformities and damage—an innovatory product reducing surgical risks and speeding patient recovery. Growth in the 1980s, especially in export markets and notably in the USA, led the company to seek investment partners in 1990. 3i led a syndicate that invested 46 million French Francs, taking a 21 per cent equity stake. In 1993 Sofamor merged with a US company, Danek, to form a group, quoted on the New York Stock Exchange, controlling around 40 per cent of the world market.

Outside Europe, 3i found a new market for its style of investment in Japan by taking a 40 per cent stake in 3iBJ—a joint venture with the Industrial Bank of Japan. 3iBJ made over sixty investments in its first four years of operation, including the first management buy-outs—highly unusual in the Japanese market, where venture capital is typically invested in large, relatively mature companies planning to become listed. Alphax Food Systems is an example of the MBO market which 3iBJ is seeking to expand. This computer software company started when the parent of Alphax, a real estate company, was trying to improve the performance of one of its peripheral operations, a restaurant. The software devised to improve management control was subsequently revised and extended and sold to over 3,000 restaurants in Japan. In January 1994 3iBJ constructed a loan/warrant bond package in support of a buy-out led by Alphax' president, Takamori Tamura, which took just 7 weeks from introduction to completion.

only be provided by the United States. It was appropriate in these circumstances that new institutional structures should be created by Governments to act as conduits for Marshall Aid and, as recovery began, to mobilize private savings for the priority needs of industrial investment. Capital markets were inactive and it was natural for the banks to resume their pre-war role as the main source of industrial capital. But in addition new institutions were set up or old ones regenerated to provide credit for longer periods than was possible for the deposit-taking banks. Because these long-term credit institutions were instruments of public policy, intended to follow and support national economic strategies, they were either wholly or mainly state-owned, their investment being state-directed or influenced by government representation on their boards.

In Germany for example, the chosen instrument was the Kreditanstalt für Wiederaufbau, which was, and remains, a central institution 80 per cent owned by the Federal Government and 20 per cent by the Länder, carrying out government policies in the provision of funds to German industry. With the benefit of a state guarantee of its credit, in addition to its access to Marshall Aid, it was able to raise large amounts of loan capital on favourable terms and redeploy it either directly or through other specialized institutions which accept the on-lending risk. KfW describes itself as 'a bank with functions of a politico-economic character' fulfilling its role 'in the public interest'.[3] Its domestic lending activity includes small- and medium-sized firms, regional development, sectoral restructuring, and environmental protection. In addition it finances exports and acts as the channel for federal government loans to developing countries.

In France the Credit National, only partly state-owned but heavily influenced by the government's power to nominate its president and some of its board, originally performed a similar but more limited role. Its lending, subsidized by the state, was mainly directed at the medium-sized company sector, but it now provides both loan and equity capital to companies of all types including 'financing operations on behalf of the French Government'.

Japan's answer to the problem was more complex, with a variety of Government-owned agencies, notably the Japan Development Bank (JDB) which was funded directly by the postal savings network used by government as a conduit for subsidy by allowing interest to be tax-free in the hands of its depositors. JDB and other government bodies worked in parallel with private-sector institutions, including the long-term credit banks whose special status entitled them to privileged access to the public-bond markets. This exclusive arrangement compensated the long-term banks for their inability to compete with the commercial banks in short-term lending. Special arrangements for small companies were catered for by a number of national and regional institutions, all with their own statutory constitutions. Even in the United States there was a federal response to the capital needs of small business, the Small Business Administration, set up to provide loans and guarantees to the small-business sector.

Only in Britain, it seems, was the problem of mobilizing capital for industrial regeneration seen to justify a mainly private sector solution. Elsewhere governments became heavily involved because the scale of the investment needed was too great for the banking system to handle. Against this global background, ICFC was an oddity, and the small scale on which it was set up, with strict limits on its scope, reflected its specialized private sector function. With FCI also restricted in what it could do, and neither having access to public funds, the scale of government-sponsored intervention in the provision of private industrial capital was tiny by comparison with that of other countries. This difference in scale and purpose, to which Dr Hu drew attention, is well-illustrated by the membership of The Club of EEC long-term credit institutions, which 3i joined in 1973 on the UK's accession to the EEC. With the exception of the Irish Industrial Credit Corporation, which was modelled on ICFC and operated on a similar scale, all the other member institutions are more important in national economic terms than 3i. It is significant that FCI and ICFC, which were conveniently merging at the time, were the only British institutions even remotely resembling those of the other EEC countries; but the resemblance was indeed remote. ICFC was an aggressive, commercially driven institution providing permanent capital as well as loans and wholly separate from government apart from the small Bank of England shareholding. The other members of The Club were all owned or effectively controlled by their national governments, with a prime objective of implementing national industrial policy. Profit was not a serious objective; in fact, many were rendered unable to make profits by being forced to take on lame-duck lending to satisfy their governments: financing a declining steel industry in Belgium, building a new steel works in the Mezzogiorno of Italy, or funding nuclear plants in France. Most were heavily involved in infrastructure finance, like the joint funding of a natural-gas pipeline system, which in the United Kingdom was wholly within the responsibility of government departments and the cost of which fell on the national budget. By the end of the 1980s this centralized restructuring role had generally ceased to be significant and in the face of increasing competition from commercial banks most had begun to seek a more market-orientated function. De Nationale Investeringsbank, the Dutch member, for example, was 'established in 1945 to finance post-war reconstruction' but 'has since developed into an industrial development bank'.

Our regular discussions with the other members of The Club tended to confirm Dr Hu's conclusion that it was this separation of the private sector from government and their mutual antipathy which differentiated the British way of economic management from that in the rest of Europe and Japan. Other countries seem to have developed an ambivalent institutional structure which allowed government to influence or even direct and guarantee investment without it being treated as public expenditure, or the funding for it included in the government's own borrowing. In the United Kingdom state support for industry has generally been channelled through government departments or, in the case of IRC and NEB, through its own statutory bodies. Although 3i has been involved in a small number of publicly funded initiatives, it has generally preferred to remain wholly independent, resisting the temptation to seek subsidies, guarantees, or cheap funds from government. This different, British way of doing things is well illustrated by a meeting of The Club in Tokyo when we were joined by the Japanese long-term credit banks at a symposium for what the hosts called 'policy-implementing financial institutions'. 3i was the only institution represented which was not involved in 'policy-implementing'.

In the British financial system the separation of government and the private sector is exemplified by the continuing mutual distrust of the City and Whitehall; but it is the City which provides the funds and other financial services for both private industry and government. 3i, born in the City but inspired by government, has always sat uncomfortably between the two, the awkward relationship symbolized by its physical location south of the Thames at Waterloo. But there should be no doubt that it is a private sector institution filling a private-sector need on purely commercial terms; it has needed no government funds, no guarantees, and no subsidies. What such an institution cannot do is to act as a substitute for a whole financial system, and its effectiveness in national economic terms should be judged accordingly.

Government Guarantees versus Equity: a New Debate

The continental European and Japanese systems, developed as they were from the structures created after the war, have been heavily orientated towards the provision of credit. The residual risks, which in the British and American financial systems were taken by the holders of equity, had to be taken by government because the capital infrastructure, and thus the value of equity, had been destroyed. Some have argued that this lack of equity gave European and Japanese industry no choice but to re-equip with modern plant, whereas British and American manufacturers still retained their capital base, reflected in usable but out-of-date plant, and were tempted to retain it rather than commit capital to a replacement programme. The story comes to mind of a small manufacturing customer of ICFC who, in the twenty years after the war ended, had not bought a single piece of new plant, although its annual general meetings were held at the Savoy and I was collected for visits in the chairman's Rolls-Royce. When they finally did spend £5,000 it was only to update a machine built in 1925 and it was both too little and too late to prevent the ultimate collapse.

Equity meant very little in continental Europe during the reconstruction years. The founders and owners of businesses had few resources of their own and depended on low-cost government credits for the whole of their early capital needs; Marshall Aid was initially lent out at an interest rate of 1 per cent in Germany. It was growth in profits and the ability to retain them in the business which, over a period, created the owners' equity and permitted a contribution from 'own funds' to their capital-expenditure programmes. The retained equity created by growing profitability and ample low-cost long-term debt provided the base capital and financial stability to underpin the post-war miracles of Germany and Japan and the former occupied countries. Steady growth and low inflation helped to ensure that what, in the stop-go economy of the UK, would have been suicidal levels of debt caused no serious problems. That is, until 1974, when the fivefold increase in oil prices brought a long period of uninterrupted growth to a halt and a new era of relative instability began.

From 1974 until 1979 world economic growth slowed down to a fraction of its former levels, but European businesses which had been accustomed to expanding continuously went on increasing their investment levels, despite the fact that profits and therefore the 'own funds' formerly used to fund capital expenditure had stopped growing, pushing them into increasing reliance on debt. By 1979, when world inflation took off and interest rates were raised to counter it, the debt burden had become intolerable. For those who had borrowed at variable rates the problem was theirs; where borrowings were at fixed rates the pain was borne by the banks who had not bothered to match their liabilities to their assets, assuming continuation of the positive-yield curve—

short-term rates lower than long-term rates—which had persisted for many years. Our survey found in 1981 that:

Government action has exacerbated the problems in Europe in two ways. In the first place, by subsidizing interest rates and offering soft loans of various kinds the authorities have encouraged and indeed obliged the banks to relax the normal commercial criteria which they would have applied to loan applications in the absence of government intervention. The result is over-lent banks and over-borrowed companies, to the detriment of business in the long run. Secondly, many continental governments have massively increased the level of borrowing by the public sector, helping to raise interest rates to much higher levels than were customary in the early 1970s and increasing the burden of any given quantity of debt incurred by the private sector.

In Britain, where business was encouraged to supplement 'own funds' or retained earnings with fresh equity, rather than taking on excessive amounts of debt, the crisis was bad enough. In countries where equity markets and institutional sources of equity were non-existent the difficulties were severe, with many corporate failures and hitherto powerful banks having to be bailed out.

The credit-based financial system, which had funded the remarkable post-war growth in many countries, was at this point found wanting; and it was the orthodox, market-based systems of the United States and Britain which proved the more effective protection against overwhelming financial disaster. 3i, which is a microcosm of the capital markets, began to be studied by delegations from other industrialized countries as a model for the institutional source of equity which was now seen to be needed. Our friends in The Club were intrigued by 3i, finding it difficult to understand in their cautious, 'bankerly' minds how a body which took such incredible risks in equity financing had not only stayed solvent but had made substantial profits over many years without ever needing government support.

The idea began to take root, notably in France and Germany, that corporate balance sheets needed a lower ratio of debt to base capital and that, in the absence of internal profit growth, equity would have to be provided by an external source. In France the *Loi Monory* of 1979 encouraged both investment by individuals in French equities and the creation of institutional sources of equity capital. A year earlier the Deutsche Bundesbank had called for German companies to strengthen their capital base by taking on new equity. Its monthly review of October 1978 sounded a warning, which is worth quoting at length:

Economic developments since the mid-sixties have appreciably weakened the capital base of German enterprises. This has beeen due to a variety of factors. To begin with (from 1968 onwards) the expansion of enterprises was so rapid that, even when profitability was good, firms were unable to keep the increase in their own funds in line with the growth of their fixed and current assets. This phase was not followed by one of balance-sheet consolidation (although this would have been desirable), not least because of the abrupt change in economic trends in the years after 1973. Moreover, even before 1973 enterprises' earnings had come under increasing pressure—despite the acceleration in the pace of price rises—owing to both higher labour costs and to the growing government share in overall income. Following the rapid increase in the cost of imported raw materials caused chiefly by the oil price hike in 1973, and following the adoption of the indispensable anti-inflation policy in Germany permitted by the transition to floating exchange rates, the pressure on enterprises' profit margins mounted further. Firms then tried to strengthen their financial base by cutting down their capital investment, but in general they only managed to ensure in this way that their own funds decreased no further relative to their balance sheet total. Increases in their own funds through issues of public and private limited company shares remained modest during those years (and the corporation tax reform that came into force at the beginning of 1977 has not so far significantly enhanced companies' activity in this field). Even a slight change for the better in enterprises' earnings in 1976 made no difference to the downward trend in the ratio of own funds to enterprises' overall financing. In fact, the capital base ought really to have been enlarged as a safeguard against risks, given the growing hazards facing enterprises as a result of the movements of costs, the sales and earnings prospects (particularly in the export field), the legal conditions to be met when establishing new industrial plant, etc.

Moving into Europe: An Equity Gap

Hitherto 3i had been wholly committed to the British Isles, the first sortie outside the United Kingdom having been to the Channel Islands, where offices were established by Larry Tindale and John Kinross in 1968. The £100 million invested over the next twenty-five years was significant in its local economic effect, but it had little impact on the funding required to meet our domestic needs, which remained fully adequate. Britain's accession to the EEC in 1973 had led to links with the central financial institutions in Luxembourg, but only to give access to cheaper funds than could be raised domestically; the European Investment Bank and the European Coal and Steel Community both provided lines of credit on favourable terms which were passed on to qualifying customers in the UK. But no move onto the Continent was made until nearly ten years after Britain's accession. There were enough problems at home for much of the 1970s, and there were no indications during the first few years of Britain's membership that the EEC might provide fertile ground for 3i's native-bred products. But the evidence provided by our survey, and the publication of concerns such as those quoted above, indicated a changing sentiment in continental Europe as the disadvantages of excessive indebtedness to both providers and users became apparent.

During the 1970s I had found it particularly difficult in dealing with the European Commission to get across the concept of risk and reward. EIB and ECSC were themselves unable to take risks with their publicly funded and guaranteed capital or their triple-A-rated debt, and they insisted that all on-lending of the funds borrowed from them should be fully secured. This severely limited the amount of money 3i could lend, so that in many cases where the mortgage security was inadequate we could not provide the full amount for which a customer qualified—50 per cent of the cost of capital expenditure. The normal response to this problem would have been to provide the excess from our own funds by way of convertible loan or equity subscription; but the Brussels bureaucracy suspected that we should be making excessive profits from the equity element on the back of their money. This was odd, because it was 3i who carried the risk of loss, but it typified the continentals' inability to understand equity risk. It took several years for this artificial restriction to be removed; by then the general need for external sources of equity had become more widely accepted.

It was clear from our 'Club' connections that we should have great difficulty in penetrating the market on the Continent for long-term debt; the institutional arrangements were comprehensive, and because it was through them that government support for industry was channelled, we should have no chance of competing on equal terms. But by 1979 it was clear that equity opportunities must exist in some countries at least. An investment in the newly formed French investment company, Siparex, showed us how the owners of private French businesses responded to the idea of taking on new equity. The foreign element among the owners of Siparex was put forward as a positive advantage, particularly to those smaller French businesses wishing to export and needing contacts overseas. At least in the Rhône-Alpes region, where Siparex was based, the idea of an equity partner seemed to be quite readily accepted by a significant number of controlling shareholders, and with the benefit of our own international survey we quite soon decided that France was the most promising country for our first foreign venture. There was no particular difficulty in persuading the shareholding banks that 3i should extend its remit to cover the EEC; it seemed logical enough, we were not relying on them to fund it, and the resources needed were in any case not great because the French business was started from scratch. This cautious approach was necessary because there were no suitable French partners to be bought or joined. It was a new field in France, and it seemed essential to impose 3i's own standards. Credit National, the obvious partner, was not yet interested in moving into equity, although it did so later and became a significant competitor through its Financière Saint-Dominique subsidiary.

What we did not know was how the owners of French businesses would react to giving up part of their equity to a foreign investor, although our indirect experience with Siparex had been encouraging; nor were we clear how best to recruit staff, train them in the 3i way of conducting business, and teach them the sophisticated financing techniques which had been developed over forty years. In the event neither proved as difficult as we had feared. There was official encouragement for our decision to open in Paris; a French managing director was recruited and quickly learned the essentials of the business. A

LSI Logic Inc

IN THE EARLY 1980S, FFI made a renewed effort, through TDC (later 3i Ventures), to invest in high technology companies. Part of this strategy meant looking to the USA for opportunities, particularly among the clusters of new industries springing up in Massachusetts and California. Under the guidance of Geoff Taylor, recruited as managing director in April 1980, TDC made a number of investments in computer-related manufacturing companies, including LSI Logic. Taylor had previous executive experience in this field, having worked for Dataproducts Corporation in the USA.

LSI Logic manufactured logic or gate arrays—silicon chips of standard design, but only partially completed at the first stage of manufacture and subsequently finished to the customer's specific requirement. The idea was introduced in the 1960s, but standardization was then the norm. In the 1980s, however, more customized, flexible applications were demanded and semi-'tailor-made' chips found an expanding market, ideal for smaller 'niche' producers. TDC first invested in LSI Logic in January 1981, providing $500,000 for a 5 per cent stake in the company. This was part of a total of $6 million raised from a number of leading venture capitalists in Britain and the USA. At the same time, in a move which reflected the new operating style of TDC, Geoff Taylor was appointed to the board of the company.

LSI Logic was floated on the New York over-the-counter market in 1983, at which point 3i's share was valued at £17 million, making it one of the most profitable investments of the 1980s. Since then the company has grown to become a Fortune 500 company with worldwide revenues of $750 million. 3i retains a small equity holding.

bilingual controller, who had proven UK experience and had been seconded to Siparex for a year, was attached to the Paris office to provide the technical know-how, but it was still thought essential for all investment proposals, though approved by the French board, to be vetted by Cases Committee in London.

The problem of setting sufficiently rigorous standards of appraisal and negotiating commercial terms in every case was to remain a difficulty, not only in France but in all the overseas territories. In addition to the control problem we had to ensure that the local team, with their own national loyalties, became committed 3i staff, marketing the Group's brand name and selling its standard products. There was always the possibility that the team, having established its own credibility, with the advantages of the 3i name and its financial muscle behind them, might go off on its own or join a rival organization. We had lost enough good staff to the British competition; how much more easily might we lose foreign staff not brought up in the ICFC tradition and working far from the centre of events.

The Paris office, however, flourished after a slow start; it proved possible to recruit high-calibre staff who had to spend some time working in the UK and going through its training scheme; and for a number of years we had a stable and committed team, who proved well able to find interesting investment opportunities. The pool of efficiently run medium-sized businesses seemed much larger than in Britain, an impression supported by the recent 3i research into the medium-sized company sector; and the competition, at least in the early days, was not great, permitting the 3i name to become well established. The fact of foreign ownership was generally welcomed as an opportunity to develop overseas business; the customers easily adopted the financial techniques imported from the UK and they seemed pleasantly surprised to find that 3i's non-interventionist attitude and its long-term approach to realization of investments were genuine. Although both local and foreign competition grew rapidly, the 3i name became well established, thanks to the thorough marketing programme supported by a reputation for taking on only first-class business.

The management in London were impressed by the high calibre of the French staff. In general they had both greater formal qualifications and a wider range of relevant experience than their British counterparts, who were generally recruited much younger, from business schools, the accountancy profession, or even directly from university with only a first degree.

The success of the French experiment encouraged us to start up in Germany. We had thought France would be difficult, but Germany promised to be a much harder nut to crack and we could not be sure the French success would be repeated. We foresaw in Germany powerful resistance from the banks, who had virtually monopolized the financing of German industry for over a hundred years and were much closer to their customers than in Britain, or, it seemed, France. They also had the reputation of being willing to take equity stakes in support of their banking business. This latter concern was probably a red herring: on the funding side I had frequent contact with the major German banks and found none where taking equity stakes was important. German bankers tended to complain, on the contrary, that their equity positions were the unwanted flotsam of previous lending disasters. Nevertheless it was clear that they had real influence over their corporate customers, and 3i's Frankfurt office, from its opening in 1985, found little co-operation from bankers in seeking out equity opportunities. Partly for this reason the German office was even slower than France in creating a portfolio, but there were other significant differences. Perhaps the most important was the fact that German companies were content with a return on capital which was lower than in France and even more so than in Britain. Where at that time we looked for 25 per cent return on the capital we invested in Britain, German companies rarely offered as much as 10 per cent. It was difficult to justify allocating our precious capital to the German business when we could expect higher returns in the UK.

The cause of 3i's eventual breakthrough in Germany was demographic. It became apparent in the late 1980s that, particularly in Germany but also to an extent in France, businessmen who had founded their businesses after the war and had remained sole owners were beginning to reach an age when they wanted to retire, or reduce their involvement. Very few had wanted to go public: less than 500 German companies were at that time quoted on the Frankfurt stock exchange. An opportunity was thus available for the first time in forty years for an institutional investor to prise open the tightly held ownership of many substantial and profitable businesses.

The departure of its founding managing director after only three years made little difference to the credibility of 3i's German office. With the two obvious markets now covered it was not difficult to justify offices in Spain and Italy, both of which were opened in 1990.

The United States: A Mature Market

At the same time as the European expansion was taking place 3i was being established in the United States. It was tempting to think we could succeed in the home of free enterprise, as a purveyor of equity capital, both by joining in the venture capital network which was flourishing on the West Coast, and by setting up the traditional ICFC business in New England. The strategic justification for a move into the United States was different from that for Europe. We saw the Continent as an extension of the home market where, despite the cultural and language difficulties, similar industrial and financial structures existed but where we had discovered a clear gap in the private company equity market. The United States was a long way away and a presence would be difficult to control; it was a huge and diverse market and, in those areas which looked promising to us, venture capital was already well established. But the US was the source of much technological innovation and we thought it essential to have first-hand knowledge of it through direct investment in fields such as electronics, in order to be better informed in our UK investment decisions, particularly those being made in our own Ventures division.

357

To achieve these objectives we had to get into the venture capital industry, and having recruited Geoff Taylor to convert TDC in the United Kingdom we asked him, with the guidance of Ivan Momtchiloff, to set up our own venture capital subsidiary in California. By this means 3i was able to join in the so-called 'deal stream', the flow of investment opportunities which circulated in the venture capital community; despite the competition, it was normal for deals to be shared among investors in order to spread the risk. At the same time Ivan set up in Boston a development capital business based on the ICFC model and run by an experienced British branch manager. In time venture capital and development capital businesses were established on both coasts, and 3i committed over $200 million to the whole US operation, which made us a major player in that highly fragmented market.

But there were good reasons why the market was so fragmented and the scale of our presence began to cause some concern. Unlike the European expansion, the American venture was never fully accepted by 3i's shareholders, and it gave rise to serious doubts on our own Board, especially among those directors who had first hand experience of the United States. Their fears were concentrated both on the amount of 3i's capital which might be sucked into that enormous market and on the potential for litigation. Following the US pattern, 3i was an active investor with board representation; but unlike the American fund managers we were known to have deep pockets, and we could hardly be 'limited partners' in our own venture capital business as were most American investors. Shareholders also expressed worries about the amount of top management time which would be needed to run the American operation, particularly if, as some of them had found, it did not run smoothly. These doubts had to be taken seriously, but it was some time before we established a fully staffed international division to provide the necessary UK management control.

If the American subsidiaries had made returns to justify these extra risks all would have been well but, apart from one real winner, LSI Logic, the performance never matched the remarkable returns being generated in the UK. We had entered the US market at a time in the early 1980s when venture capital was flourishing and returns were being made on 'high-tech' businesses like LSI Logic which were quite exceptional; but by the middle years of the decade returns began to falter at the same time as new funds began pouring into the market, attracted by the returns which had been made earlier. As the market for Initial Public Offerings (IPO) dried up, our own team found increasing difficulty in realizing investments, with the result that more capital had to be introduced each year to meet the continuing requirement for new investment. With very little income flowing in from dividends it was not possible to cover overheads out of revenue and, with the state of the IPO market allowing virtually no contribution from capital profits, the American performance became increasingly dependent on the valuations attributed to investments for which there was no market. Eventually, back in Waterloo Road, scepticism about the real value of the US portfolio took hold, and by the late 1980s we had decided to stop putting new money into the American business.

Moderating the Global Ambition

There was disagreement within 3i and on the Board over the need for closure; but two principal arguments prevailed. It was increasingly clear that we had little, if any, claim on the loyalties of the staff, who saw themselves as entrepreneurial venture capitalists rather than employees of 3i which, to them, was the passive supplier of funds, like the limited partners they were accustomed to. This dichotomy would have led to disaster sooner or later, but, perhaps more importantly, we realized that both human and financial capital were being spread too thinly, and the signs were that the US was going to need increasing amounts of both at a time when that economy was moving into its most serious and prolonged recession since the war. These concerns were exacerbated by the prospect of 3i's own flotation, in which an unsuccessful American venture could only be damaging; the stock market had seen enough failed US ventures dragging down British companies. So what had been briefly a global ambition—'world class in the 1990s' was one ambitious planning slogan—soon reverted to a European strategy, with the American operation confined to a small staff engaged in progressive realization of the portfolio. Latest forecasts indicate a compound return of 10 to 15 per cent.

Other elements of the global ambition were retained, but on a more realistic scale. Although the need for 3i's type of investment capital was real enough, our ability to deliver it to UK standards by remote control was limited. The presence in Japan was therefore restricted to a minority position in a joint venture with the Industrial Bank of Japan. A similar partnership with Westpac, later joined by Australian Mutual Provident (AMP), in Australia, although in itself adversely affected by prolonged recession, had worked well. Such arrangements imposed clear limits on 3i's obligation to provide both money and management, and the idea of exporting know-how rather than capital began to take hold, as the demands grew for new money in the United States and the financial constraints on European expansion became more apparent. By the early 1990s the international strategy had been refined to allow for the concentration of capital in the European Community and 'know-how' agreements elsewhere which would cover costs and provide some potential for capital profits if the venture succeeded. It was all part of the process of returning to the core business. In my pre-retirement assessment of these policies, written in March 1991 and entitled '3i: Back to its Roots' I summarized the future direction in the following terms:

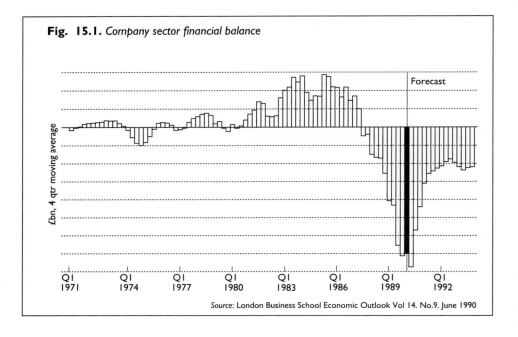

Fig. 15.1. *Company sector financial balance*

Source: London Business School Economic Outlook Vol 14. No.9. June 1990

3i's strategy for the 1990s, developed in response to the competitive pressures and the new opportunities of the 1980s, is to deploy its exceptional financial muscle in maintaining the unique brand of investment capital in a dominant position in the UK and establishing significant market positions elsewhere.

The 3i brand of investment capital is designed specifically to fill the Macmillan gap, which is a continuing phenomenon both in the UK and overseas, by making permanently available capital-market products to those companies which have no access to the capital markets.

In acting as a capital markets substitute 3i carries out a socially useful function in all the national capital markets where it chooses to operate. It will operate only in those markets, and make those investments, which offer an acceptable return to 3i.

The Foreign Experience: What Lessons for Britain?

3i's international experience will probably bring rewards over time for the one main reason that a source of base capital for private companies is needed in every industrialized country. 3i has proved it can be done profitably in the United Kingdom, which might be thought an unpromising place to start such a high-risk business: how much more profitable should it be in more prosperous countries, provided the control of quality can be ensured?

As 3i began to benefit from the less discriminatory atmosphere and to make investment decisions in France, Germany, and the United States on a basis which was comparable with that we had used in the UK, it began to be apparent that investment criteria in those countries varied considerably. It was particularly interesting to study Germany, whose rate of GNP growth had far outstripped that of Britain except for a few years in the mid-1980s. We were accustomed even in those halcyon days, a time of 3 per cent inflation, low interest rates and soaring profits, to look for a 25 per cent rate of return on investment. In the venture capital field 40 per cent was expected on average and as much as 60 per cent in individual cases. At that time government bonds yielded perhaps 10 per cent to 12 per cent so the risk premium we sought was substantial. The reason can only be that, in common with others making capital-investment decisions, we were not satisfied that growth would continue, because we were unconvinced that inflation had been brought under control. Expectations remained of a return to high inflation at some time during the life of the investment. Another reason for 3i's need for a high return on total capital was the relatively low gearing we could tolerate on equity investments. For most of ICFC's first thirty years its rule of thumb was that a customer's total debt should not exceed capital and reserves. Such a gearing ratio would provide reasonable protection from the erosion of profits by inflation and the periodic interest rate rises needed to protect sterling. This 50 per cent gearing would have been regarded as excessive by the stock market for comparable quoted companies. In 3i's own balance sheet, even as a financial institution a ratio of 1 : 1 was thought prudent; it would rarely exceed 2 : 1, or two-thirds of total capital in the form of debt and one in equity.

In contrast to 3i's situation, we found in our 1981 study that German companies had much higher gearing. Although this was said to be artificially increased by a more rapid rate of asset depreciation, that seemed to be offset by the inclusion in their capital of borrowings from their own pension funds, which we would not have regarded as permanent capital. Whatever may be the true comparison, it was the apparent 80 to 90 per cent debt levels in the capital of German companies which were a source of serious concern to the Bundesbank when it made its call for more base capital to be injected into the corporate sector. Although there were serious difficulties when short-term interest rates had subsequently to be raised sharply to correct a rise in inflation, the general record of German industry does not seem to indicate that this level of borrowing did any lasting harm. But it did allow a rate of return on the total capital in a project which was much lower than those we had to look for in Britain. This could account for the experience of 3i's German office in finding itself offered projects with rates of return of less than 10 per cent which were not acceptable on UK gearing ratios, but would provide a highly geared German company with a very acceptable return on its smaller equity base. There are naturally many more projects offering 10 per cent than 25 per cent, and they will generally be less risky, so it can be argued that the high gearing of

German companies is partly justified by the low risk and the large number of projects they can take on.

This may be one reason why total investment in Germany has been higher than in the UK, and it is likely that similar arguments can be applied to Japan, whose recovery was built on a similar base of long-term credit. From these arguments comes the tentative conclusion, which might justify further study, that it is the most efficient users of equity who achieve the best economic performance. Efficient use of base capital must imply being able to maintain high levels of gearing without excessive risk. British industry has faced such extreme risks in terms of volatile interest rates and unstable inflation that only very low levels of gearing have been justified. When, in the late 1980s, this cautious approach to debt was abandoned, exemplified by the ridiculous gearing levels of many highly publicized management buy-outs, corporate liquidity was allowed to fall, over a period of two years, from its highest ever level to its lowest ever level. Between 1986 and 1988 a £5 billion surplus of liquid assets had become a £25 billion deficit. There was no justification for this change of attitude to gearing levels, and there can be no doubt that it contributed materially to the exceptional severity of the recession which followed, as the government was forced yet again to drive interest rates up and rein in another bout of inflation.

This tendency to inflation at the slightest sign of an increase in demand is an unfortunate feature of the British economy which may not easily be eradicated. My own view is that its main cause is the chronic shortage of modern skills, brought about by an inadequate education system, leading inevitably in times of growing demand to a bidding process for such skills as are available and a consequent rise in the cost of labour, with no compensating increase in productivity. 3i itself was a victim of 'poaching' throughout the 1980s; we were known as the 'university of venture capital' because we alone put time and money into training staff. When demand for capital exploded the easiest and quickest way for a new venture capital fund to meet it was by bidding for staff from 3i. To do so they had to offer in many cases 50 per cent more than we were paying; but whether the individuals concerned produced 50 per cent more output after leaving 3i must be doubtful, though no doubt a few did. Whatever the truth may be in those cases, the inevitable result was that we had to raise our own salaries in order to stem the outflow of our highly trained staff, which at one point reached 25 per cent of the investment cadre in a single year. It seems that such poaching of skills in short supply is endemic in British industry.

It is not surprising, therefore, that the economy is so easily prone to inflation, with all the instability and uncertainty which it causes. In Germany and Japan careful economic management, in which the control of inflation has been a continuing national priority, has permitted a degree of economic stability which has been reinforced by nationally controlled wage rounds and an education and training system designed to produce ample supplies of highly skilled and adaptable workers. The result has been low inflation and interest rates which have rarely had to be raised to levels at which business activity is stifled. This allows industry to make long-term plans in the reasonable expectation of stable demand growth, and so investment has continued at a high level, producing continuous improvements in efficiency. The virtuous circle is reinforced by the availability of long-term credit at low fixed rates, permitting higher levels of borrowing for any given interest cost, and making the resulting gearing levels less risky than they would be in the United Kingdom. The circle is completed by the consequent ability of German and Japanese industry to take on a larger number of investment projects because they can accept lower returns on the total capital employed, the higher gearing pushing up the return on the equity element to acceptable levels.

Recently both the Japanese and German economies have begun to develop unaccustomed problems which have shattered the virtuous circles so painstakingly maintained over 45 years. In each case excessive debt has been the cause. First Japan's domestic economy began to flag, bringing down the grossly over-inflated equity and property values which had been propped up on unsustainable quantities of borrowed money. An outstanding example of the over-valuation of assets was the price/earnings multiple of 270, at which the newly privatized telecommunications monopoly, NTT, was capitalized; we had thought a twenty-year multiple of current earnings was dangerous in the UK. Then Germany began to take on the daunting task of bringing the East up to the productivity levels of Western Germany, at the same time exchanging currencies on a parity basis. The German problem is no doubt unique and will be solved at the expense of a recession, which would be less harmful in the long term than letting inflation take root, but it has been tackled by a sharp rise in interest rates producing a British-style halt in industrial confidence. With the high gearing levels prevalent in German industry, the effect of even a small unexpected rise in rates must be severe. In Japan the problem could be called the *reductio ad absurdum* of the theory expounded above; stratospheric levels of gearing encouraged the flow of debt-financed investment into speculative assets, forcing the Government into an inflationary stimulus of the economy in order to prevent a complete melt-down of asset values.

So perhaps the arguments laid out here will no longer apply in the post-recessionary world; but it remains plausible to blame the failure to maintain Britain's position in the world growth tables on that inability of governments to create the stable economic conditions, reflected particularly in interest rates and inflation, which would have permitted more long-term investment, funded more economically and more safely by larger amounts of debt. The availability of long-term fixed-interest debt and share capital of the kind provided by 3i and the capital market has, no doubt, protected part of the

UK corporate sector from even worse damage than might have occurred without it, but it has not provided effective compensation for the failure of successive governments to put industry's investment needs before their own electoral concerns. With such a need to protect long-term economic strategies from short-term electoral pressures, independent control over monetary policy seems indispensable. Only thus would confidence be restored in the long-term stability of prices and interest rates, allowing the safe use of larger quantities of debt and encouraging more, and lower-yielding, investment projects, thus in turn enhancing and securing the long-term rate of return on equity—that most precious and politically underrated financial commodity.

But perhaps the most important lesson to be drawn from this comparison of the British experience with that of other countries is that equity cannot be treated as a residual item. The more unstable the economic conditions, the larger the proportion of equity in corporate capital must be; and if, as in the cases cited by the Bundesbank in its 1978 Review, retained profits or 'own funds' are inadequate, then base capital should be supplemented from external sources. It is this essential purpose that, almost alone among the post-war financial institutions, 3i has fulfilled.

NOTES

[1]   See Ch. 10, p. 237.
[2]   Yao-su Hu, 'Industrial Banking and Special Credit Institutions: A Comparative Study', *Policy Studies Institute*, 632 (Oct. 1984).
[3]   Club Brochure, Sept. 1987.

Chapter 16

Doing Well by Doing Good

RECONCILING THE NATIONAL interest, embodied in its support of the small business sector with the commercial imperatives of making an adequate return for its shareholders, has been the ambition of 3i's management since its foundation. By the end of the 1980s that ambition had arguably come close to achievement.

This concluding essay considers, first, the financial performance of the 1980s, and then the broader question of 3i's contribution to the economy, finally asking whether it could, and should, have been encouraged to do more for British industry.

I Doing Well: Opportunity and Challenge in the Thatcher Years

The New Entrepreneurial Spirit: Small is Beautiful Again

Compared with the previous thirty-five years of its existence the 1980s were a period of momentous change for 3i. They can conveniently be called the Thatcher years, not only because they coincide more or less exactly with Margaret Thatcher's term as Prime Minister, but because her government's policies and the economic events which flowed from them had a powerful impact on 3i and its customers. It is difficult to recall that for most of the 1960s and 1970s the word 'profit' was politically unacceptable. Investment was encouraged in order to create jobs, rather than to create profit, and much of 3i's own public relations was concerned with its national role in support of small business. The object of making a reasonable long-term return for its shareholders, while always present in the minds of its management, was not emphasized publicly and indeed did not seem to preoccupy the banks, whose only stipulation in that respect was that they would like to see a progressive dividend policy. Another management objective not publicly discussed was to finance 3i's growth entirely by retained profits and borrowings. It was only during the Thatcher years that all these objectives were met.

Government policies since the war had been primarily concerned with maintaining and protecting high employment levels. As a result there had grown up an employee culture: the 'organization man' had settled into the comfortable protective atmosphere of the large corporation with its tax-efficient fringe benefits and generous pension scheme. There was no incentive to break out and face the risks of self-employment, particularly when any real success would be taxed at 83 per cent and even 98 per cent. This adverse risk-reward balance changed in the Thatcher years, with the breakdown of the old security of tenure, unemployment more than doubling from under 5 per cent in 1979 to 10 per cent in 1982, the crumbling of corporate cultures as the 'urge to merge' of the early 1970s gave way to the forced demergers of the 1980s, and the shift of taxes from direct to indirect. The result was a loosening of the ownership patterns of British industry and a marked increase in the number of owner-managers. They were a different breed of people from those 3i had been used to; private companies were usually tightly controlled by family shareholders and provided career opportunities for the sons and daughters of the owners but were often closed to outsiders. Occasionally exceptional entre-preneurs started up a business *ab initio*, but rarely were they the trained business managers, with specialist skills in marketing, finance, or production manage-ment, who peopled the large corporations. When those professional managers became entrepreneurs they brought a full range of business skills with them, particularly where a whole management team was involved in a buy-out. This gave the emergent business a much greater chance of success, but it also required a different approach from 3i, which itself had to become more adept at negotiation and more aggressive in its marketing. In a subtle way its rela-tionship with its customers was changing. Not only were the new breed of owner-managers more experienced and professional, but 3i's visible success was attracting competitors and it was forced to find new ways of bringing its wares to the attention of private companies.

Coping with Competition: A New Experience

The more active marketing approach, developed in the second half of the 1970s under David Marlow, arrived none too soon, for 3i now had to fight for busi-ness as it never had before. The new competitors took investments it would have wanted to make—as well as some it was happy to lose—but they also deprived 3i of some of its most able investment managers, lured away by the enticement of running their own show and of capital gains from a carried interest in their investments. The entrepreneurial revolution was beginning to have its own divisive effect on 3i, by showing its staff the enormous gains which were available to the new breed of owner-managers, but denied to the equally enterprising 3i staff. Their long tradition of loyalty to the small business ideal and the mutual support and respect which bound them together began to break down. At the same time the new venture capital industry began to encroach on 3i's territory, bringing with it American methods of remuneration more suited to the boutique, with its small group of individual venturers, than to institutions like 3i. The problems intensified when 3i's own venture capital subsidiary, 3i Ventures, adopted those same American methods of remuneration which allowed individuals an interest in their own investments as a major part of the package. In order to stem the flow of staff looking elsewhere for similar possibilities of capital gain 3i was forced to introduce its own incentive schemes. Although it could not go as far as the competitors it was able to offer a share-option scheme to senior managers, and share and bonus schemes to staff generally. All this was a far cry from the original simple, across-the-board system of remuneration, based on a combination of skill, responsibility, and merit, which had kept the organization unified and loyal, with its ultimate promise of an attractive pension.

It was fortunate that the introduction of those schemes coincided with the strongest period of profit and investment growth in 3i's history, which allowed substantial rewards to be paid and to a great extent kept the inter-departmental rivalries subdued. It was during this period, and partly as a result of 3i's manifest success, that a fundamental change took place in relations between the Company and its shareholders. The last rights issue of £25 million was made in 1974 and dividends, which had been relatively static throughout the 1960s and had fallen to nominal levels in the mid-1970s, only began to grow consistently after their resumption in 1978. Shareholders had become used to thinking of their return wholly in terms of the dividend they received, and it was only when the concept of total return was applied to the Group's results in the mid-1980s that they began to appreciate the potential value of their investment. That it had become significant was because 3i's long-term investment policy had at last begun to bear fruit in the form of substantial capital profits and real increases in the value of its portfolio. The growth in both realized and unrealized profits which continued until the last year of the decade, not only helped to fund an equally rapid rise in new investment but increased the banks' long-standing frustration at being locked into their holdings. For many years they had regarded it as an unattractive investment over which they had no control and which produced a poor return, measured solely by the amount of the dividend they received. That they were unable to bring into their balance sheets any part of the increased capital value made it irritating enough; once it became apparent that the locked chest contained real treasure in the form of a substantial asset value, the search began for the key to open it. So in 1984 the long process of discussion about how they could best realize this value was put in train; it was an argument which preoccupied the management and dominated relationships with the shareholders for the rest of the decade. The 1945 agreement had made it impossible for any single shareholding bank to dispose of its shares without the consent of all the others. This had been an effective deterrent to any attempt to break ranks, but now acted as an equally effective impediment to consensus. 3i's Board and management, however, although preferring to maintain the *status quo*, had no wish to obstruct a disposal; our overriding concern was for the preservation of 3i's special function, and in particular of its continued ability to honour long-term obligations as a passive investor in several thousand private businesses. It was fortunate that the rapid growth in the early years of the decade had, by 1985, made 3i strong enough to stand on its own feet, because the political atmosphere of that time was not sympathetic to the continued protection of a sheltered institution, however *pro bono publico* its function might be. At the same time, the informal influence which the Bank of England had exercised over the clearing banks was beginning to wane, whilst with its new statutory responsibility for the banking system it had become concerned about its own conflict of interests as both regulator and shareholder of 3i.

Girding Up to Ride the Entrepreneurial Wave

So the 1980s saw it emerge from the skirts of its parents and begin to look after its own interests. This was a curious process, because it had originally been formed as an act of self-denial by its shareholders in what they were then assured was the national interest; forty years later it had become a commercial success, with the public good taking a back seat. For us in 3i, its prime objective had always been to serve the small company sector: the national interest was subsumed in that objective and was never allowed to obscure the need for a commercial return. So the withdrawal of government sympathy, at the same time as 3i's shareholders began to talk of shedding their investment, was neither surprising nor disappointing to its Board and management. The Company was on its own and must fight its own battles.

The fact that 3i had proved capable of funding its own very rapid growth and of making a satisfactory return without assistance from anyone gave us the necessary confidence to take the initiative in proposing flotation and to adopt a dynamic strategy for its achievement. Out of the revised strategy came the decision to concentrate on the core business, whose success had continued undiminished. All the peripheral activities had been attached when the concept of serving the small business community was more important than the immediate return. As we have seen, none of the peripheral activities had managed to achieve comparable success, and it was almost inevitable that what had started the 1980s as a diverse financial conglomerate ended the decade stripped to its original form. It was a fine irony that it was the provider of capital to small businesses, given so little chance of success back in 1945, which had first survived, then thrived and finally become the dominant player in the exciting and fast growing venture capital market of the 1980s.

The restoration of the entrepreneurial spirit which spurred this growth was, in my opinion, a direct and lasting achievement of Thatcherism. Starting with the reduction of marginal tax rates from 83 per cent to 60 per cent, later further reduced to 40 per cent, the abolition of exchange controls, the encouragement of the profit motive, and individual self-reliance, there began in the 1980s a restoration of entrepreneurialism such as had not been seen probably since the nineteenth century. It had its pitfalls in moral terms—the encouragement of greed, the acquisition of wealth at any price and its flaunting in crude and offensive ways, and an outbreak of large-scale financial fraud. Commercially it led to the pursuit of growth for its own sake, beyond the ability of businesses to finance it from their own resources. Consequently, in the late

'Mr Berkolis, the leveraged buy out has gone through and your rum raisin cone is here.'

1980s, encouraged by an unnecessary loosening of monetary policy, an astonishing increase in the indebtedness of the corporate sector dragged it inexorably to disaster when inflation rose sharply and interest rates had to be increased to check it.[1]

For all its failings, the entrepreneurial revolution which began in the Thatcher years had one significant outcome—the creation of a class of self-reliant owner-managers, willing to take substantial financial risks as the price of running their own show and, in doing so, creating substantial capital gains for themselves and their shareholders. It was the reduction in burdensome taxation and the encouragement of the profit motive by government which created the inspiration for such people; the opportunity was provided by the recession of the early 1980s and the consequent dash for liquidity by the large corporations, releasing both people and assets onto the market-place; and it was the development of the appropriate financial techniques, where 3i played a crucial role, which made available the resources. By supplying the majority of the capital needed for a management buy-out, while remaining a minority shareholder, 3i helped many hundreds of managers to realize a dream by leaving their large corporate employers and owning their own business.

Emerging from the Shadows: Preparing for Flotation

A frequent complaint voiced by the shareholding banks in the early 1980s was that we were providing insufficient information, despite Annual Accounts which were unusually detailed, quarterly management accounts circulated among the shareholders, and half-yearly meetings between 3i's Chairman and the Chairmen of the shareholders, chaired by the Governor of the Bank of England, supported by meetings of Chief Executives again chaired by a director of the Bank of England. It was a problem of the relationship with shareholders that there was little continuity in the clearing banks' representation at those meetings, and consequently little understanding of the finer points of 3i's business. It was in an attempt to remedy this difficulty that Jon Foulds and I made our tour of the shareholders with a presentation which seemed to impress them with its demonstration of 3i's asset strength, ultra-conservative accounting policies, low gearing, and rapid portfolio growth. It is quite likely that they had not until then appreciated the potential of their investment in 3i. Shortly afterwards, an article in a Greenwells brokers' circular drew attention both to the financial plight of the Midland Bank, in the wake of the Crocker affair, and the value of their investment in 3i. This seemed to be the spark which ignited the tinder of the shareholders' frustration at such a poor cash return from so valuable an investment.

The change of name from FFI to 3i, which took place at about the same time, had nothing to do with this process but was concerned entirely with the effects of competition and the need for cohesion in the face of both external pressures and internal stresses. But its coincidence with the sudden prominence of shareholder interest in disposal led to the widespread assumption that decks were being cleared for flotation. In fact, the initial reaction of 3i's management was to resist the idea of flotation. The *status quo* had allowed us to develop a successful business out of taking the long-term view of investment and it was difficult to imagine an alternative ownership which would perpetuate that virtuous combination. But 3i's own higher profile, with its much-increased size, its changed name, its colourful advertising, and its aggressive public relations, together with the perceived need of some shareholders to strengthen their capital base, meant that the shareholder relationship could no longer be managed discreetly in the parlours of the Bank of England. By virtue of these events, the year 1985 marks a watershed in 3i's affairs. It was in February of that year that the shareholders agreed to look at ways of realizing their investments which, explicitly, would not jeopardize the Company's long-term business. It was in September that 3i's Board decided the only proper answer to the shareholders' wishes would be a public quotation of its shares, preferably with the banks retaining sufficient shares to prevent control passing into undesirable hands.

Although no decision was taken on this before the end of the decade the possibility of flotation affected the whole of 3i's strategic direction and, two years after the change of name, preparations began seriously to be made for an outcome which was seen by management as almost inevitable.

The most visible changes were in the Annual Accounts, the appeal to the Special Commissioners for Income Tax against 3i's trading status, and the progressive reversion to the core business of ICFC and FCI which, by the time the shareholders made their decision on flotation in late 1991, had all been accomplished. The successful appeal against trading company status which had been the basis of 3i plc's tax for over forty years, confirmed the investment treatment in the Accounts and prepared the ground for flotation as an investment trust. This was the form which the management firmly believed most appropriate for the basic investment business of 3i as a publicly quoted company, although it involved considerable restructuring and a complete reconsideration of the strategic direction which had prevailed since Larry Tindale became General Manager in 1964.

Advice from Warburgs made it plain that it would be difficult to sell to the investing public the idea of an investment trust which was effectively a financial conglomerate, including a venture capital operation in the United States, property development, management consultancy, and corporate finance, as well as shipping finance and plant leasing. It might have been possible to justify the logic of such a diverse collection of businesses if the strategic case could have been supported by a financial performance which enhanced that of the core business. Sadly, this was not so.

As 3i's strategic planning procedures began to isolate and analyse both the justification for, and the financial performance of, every part of the business, it became apparent that it was the remarkable success of the core 'ICFC/FCI' business which was sustaining the whole organization, but that the need to unify and derive synergy from the disparate elements had led to a complex and top-heavy management. So not only were the peripheral elements jeopardizing the excellent performance of the core business, but they were causing management problems out of all proportion to their contribution. Even the costly name-change might not have seemed necessary if the business had comprised only the original capital-market substitution role.

The 1980s also saw significant changes at the top of 3i. Lord Seebohm, who had steered the newly formed FFI through its early difficult years, had retired in 1979. Lord Caldecote, his successor as Chairman, was content to allow a competent management, under a very able Chief Executive, freedom to run the business within broad guidelines. He was rewarded by the most dramatic period of change and growth in the company's long life. Jon Foulds, who had become Chief Executive in 1977, successfully preserved the strong ethic of service to the small business community at the same time as recogniz-

THE ARBITRAGE BOYS ON THEIR WAY TO A BUYOUT AT O.K. CORRAL INDUSTRIES, INC.

ing, and taking strong action to meet, the competitive challenges which were sweeping in from the United States and emerging from 3i's own shareholders. He it was who almost single-handedly forced through the reappraisal of objectives and name change in 1983 which did so much to confirm 3i's conversion into a marketing organization. He also took the precaution of building around him a strong General Management team, including in particular David Marlow, his eventual successor. It was David who, starting in 1975, had developed the original ICFC's marketing ability to the point where it was well able to meet the threat to its market dominance which emerged in the 1980s.

Lord Caldecote and Jon Foulds presided over both the rapid growth of the early and mid-1980s and the increasingly complex shareholder relations, leaving behind them in 1987 a powerful institution well capable of looking after itself but with the ownership debate still undecided: it was to outlast two more Chairmen whilst the restructuring of 3i for its eventual flotation fell to David Marlow.

A Decade of High Performance

Strong growth continued for two more years after Sir John Cuckney took over as Chairman, net assets per share rising from £4 in 1987 to £5.50 in 1989. In his Statement for 1988–9 the Chairman pointed to the rising trend of interest rates as the first clouds on the economic horizon, and gave a warning that 'for heavily geared companies the recent rises in short-term interest rates will undoubtedly cause discomfort', and alluding to the value of 3i's historic lending methods 'it is in circumstances like these that the traditional virtues of fixed interest become apparent'. He drew attention to the fact that in the two years since he took over, 3i had invested £1.1 billion—a quarter of the whole amount invested since 1945.

Despite Sir John's warnings of inflationary pressures and interest rate rises there was no real indication of the collapse in confidence which was to come, and he began his concluding remarks: 'There are no signs that the regrettable but necessary increases in interest rates have had a serious effect on confidence.' His final comment was, with hindsight, too optimistic: 'This may yet happen, and I take a rather more cautious view of prospects than at this time last year, but I remain convinced that the corporate sector is better fitted than at any time in the past to weather a difficult period.' In fact the corporate sector as a whole was uniquely unfitted to weather a difficult period because it had embarked on a huge spending spree, financed substantially by debt and, despite Sir John's strictures, mainly at variable rates of interest. It was the beginning of a period of stagnation for 3i, after an uninterrupted run of growth in all aspects of the core business, which had lasted for the whole of the Thatcher years to that point. The growth in new investment continued for another year, reaching its all-time high point of £597 million in 1990; but the growing need for provisions held the balance sheet at its previous level with no increase in shareholders' funds, a reasonable achievement, perhaps, in the light of the deepening recession.

In one critical respect during that heady growth period, 3i heeded its own advice and so, despite its own extraordinary expansion, was able to survive the recession of the early 1990s with its business and its resources intact. Between 1985 and 1990, by realizing its portfolio of quoted investments at every practical opportunity and selling off other unwanted assets into strong markets, we were able to generate enough profit to double shareholders' funds and enough cash to finance the bulk of the enormous investment programme and yet at the same time to hold indebtedness close to 1985 levels.

At 31 March 1985 shareholders' funds were £499 million; by 1990 they had more than doubled to £1.192 billion, yet net borrowings rose over the same period by only £262 million to £1.3 billion. A ratio of debt to equity of 2.08 times had almost halved to 1.09 times; yet in those five years 3i had invested £2.4 billion. To have ended a period of spectacular investment growth with the strongest financial position in its history was a quite remarkable achievement.

It might be argued that any reasonably competent management should have achieved exceptional results during the 1980s, and particularly over the last five years of the decade. So some comparisons are in order, although it was always difficult to measure 3i's financial performance against that of others, because its shares were unquoted and there was no publicly available analysis of the results. But in February 1991 at our request and as part of the preparations for flotation, S. G. Warburg Securities prepared for us a 'Comparison of Financial Performance' in the form of a normal broker's circular.

They confirmed for us that over the five years to March 1990 3i's average Compound Rate of Total Return, that is net asset growth, fully diluted, plus dividend yield, was 20.6 per cent, increased to 21.4 per cent on adjustment for a number of special factors. This compared with 10.7 per cent for the investment trust sector as a whole, 13.5 per cent for banks, and 13.3 per cent for the All-Share Index.

However, extending the comparison back five years to cover the whole of the 1980s produced a slightly less good performance at 19.0 per cent (19.7 per cent adjusted), although the investment trust sector showed 16.4 per cent, banks 19.4 per cent, and the All-Share Index 18.8 per cent. Specific comparisons with Electra Investment Trust and Murray Ventures, both quoted trusts with a large portfolio of unquoted shares, showed a similar pattern: almost identical performance over ten years and a much superior showing by 3i in the last five years.

3i's underperformance in the first five years was almost certainly caused by the heavy provisions we had to make against property developments and ships, tending to confirm the view we had formed earlier that the peripheral activities were dragging down the Group's overall performance. But the comparisons may not be entirely valid, because 3i's policies on valuation and provisions were almost certainly different from those of the investment trusts. Our cautious valuation policy, which invariably threw up large annual surpluses on the sale of investments, giving rise to positive transfers to capital reserve, was regarded by Warburgs as the most conservative.

Despite these differences, the Warburg review makes it clear that 3i's performance during the Thatcher years stands up well to comparison with other financial institutions. There is certainly no indication that the interests of its shareholders were in any way compromised by its own continuing perception of its national role, which was well expressed by Sir John Cuckney in his 1990 Statement: '3i has maintained its great tradition of always being there in the market place, continuing to offer the range of investment products which has been developed over many years. I see this constancy in the availability of capital from 3i through all economic climates as one of the most important aspects of its unique character.'

For 3i the Thatcher years were the most fruitful of its long and distinguished history. Already in the early 1990s that period is being vilified as greedy, unstable, unsustainable, and retrograde in many respects. 3i's experience tells a different story: of a powerful, stable, consistent, and progressive performance in support of, and benefiting from, a revival in the nation's entrepreneurial spirit; and for its shareholders, at virtually no cost to themselves, an investment worth five times its value ten years earlier and showing a compound return of 20 per cent. It is difficult to believe that the 1990s recession has completely snuffed out that new spirit of enterprise, that 3i is not ideally placed to help restore it, or that its shareholders will in the end be dissatisfied with their return.

II Doing Good: 3i's Contribution to the Economy

A Catalyst for Growth

Britain's economic performance has been a cause for concern since well before the First World War; it was, indeed, the principal reason for the establishment of the Macmillan Committee, whose recommendations led directly, if belatedly, to ICFC's formation. Given its provenance and the central position it has occupied between government, City, and industry it is worth considering what contribution 3i has made to the national economic well-being.

Few would deny that 3i has been commercially successful in doing what it was asked to do, or that it has persevered single-mindedly in that function throughout the five post-war decades. It has clearly made a major contribution to the health and wealth of the small- and medium-sized company sector, providing many thousands of businesses with permanent and long-term capital which they could not have found elsewhere, and has given them scope to expand on a scale which would otherwise have been beyond their resources. Helping its customers to grow has itself been profitable, to such an extent that less than one-tenth of the £1.3 billion net worth shown by its balance sheet at March 1993 was financed from cash provided by its shareholders. Nor has it been a drain on public funds, enjoying no tax privileges, no government guarantees, and no subsidies. It has provided a national service at no cost to the taxpayer and a substantial return for its shareholders at minimal cost to them. I expect that for Larry Tindale, the architect of the modern 3i, that dual achievement would suffice as its major contribution to the British economy.

3i has been a catalyst for the expansion of the smaller company sector, recycling the profits made from the use of its funds in an ever-increasing portfolio of independently managed businesses. By combining the careful identification of good management and prudent mixes of debt and equity with patient and skilled monitoring of the ensuing investments, it has ensured that success has bred more success, with only a small part of its resources wasted on unprofitable investments. Even among the failures, where its initial commitment has been written off, it has funded phoenix-like resurgences by putting new money behind fresh management. This ability to make a silk purse out of a sow's ear by recycling worn-out companies is one of 3i's unsung achievements and an important element in its contribution to the economy.

It has sometimes faced criticism for not taking a more active role in the restructuring of industries, but has generally declined invitations to become involved in either public or private initiatives, otherwise than passively, in its function as a provider of capital. Experience indicates that this was right; such limited attempts as were made to restructure businesses by taking them into its ownership were almost wholly unsuccessful, occupying disproportionate amounts of time and absorbing large amounts of capital which could have been better used in its normal business. 3i was at its most efficient—and therefore arguably most useful in national terms—when deploying its own specialized skills in analysing business prospects, assessing management potential, constructing appropriate capital packages and, in the event of trouble, initiating and executing constructive ways out. Such skills were most effectively deployed through small teams of experts applying leverage in the form of large amounts of capital carefully focused where they could be most profitably used. In this way the failures, in judging people, business prospects, economic developments, were limited. It was normal for companies with great potential to be singled out for special encouragement, just like those most at risk of failure; but companies without such prospects for good or ill were not ignored, they also were monitored carefully. In these instances it was in order to identify points of major change in the corporate life-cycle: the loss of a key manager, the chance of acquiring a compatible business, a revolutionary new product, or a new market for existing products. This process is well illustrated in the 'Wheel of Change' (see colour plates), invented by 3i to portray the landmarks in the development of a business at which capital injections could be most effectively used.

It is in such ways that 3i has made its practical contribution to British economic life: dedicated to the support of the private company, but not blinded by idealistic notions; working for an acceptable long-term return, and indifferent to short-term setbacks. Such a combination of objectives cannot easily be measured in statistical terms but its success has demonstrated both at home and internationally what British business is capable of. The 11,800 businesses it has financed since 1945 have all felt the impact of its professionalism, and most of the owner-managers who have accepted its support have been able to rise to the challenge of putting 3i's precious capital to good use and in the process have built businesses which, it has been estimated, employed around one million people in 1991.

Those businesses where 3i has an equity involvement have prospered to the extent of providing realized capital gains over the last five years alone of £620 million, and surpluses yet to be realized of a further £700 million. This success, in a corner of the British economy once thought by many to be incapable of providing investors with a satisfactory return, has itself inspired others to mobilize increasing amounts of capital for investment in unquoted companies. 3i has not only been the paradigm for this new industry but, as a prime source of highly trained investment staff, has involuntarily assisted in its rapid establishment. Such has been the growth of the UK venture capital industry that after barely a decade it now deploys larger amounts of capital than all the rest of the EC countries combined.

3i's Experience: A Model for Others?

It can be further argued that capital-market substitution as practised by 3i was not only appropriate to the United Kingdom but could have been successful elsewhere. In other countries the normal institutional source of capital for private companies was the long-term credit bank. 3i's ability to take risks in the form of equity and to make compensating returns without any form of state support was unique among the national development capital institutions established after the war.

It was only after European economic growth came to a halt with the oil shock of 1973 that the deficiencies of credit-based financing came to be recognized and 3i's methods began to be studied seriously. They became the object of such admiration that finally, in the late 1970s, its example began to be followed with the formation of new equity-financing institutions in other countries, which had previously relied on credit, funded, guaranteed, and subsidized by government to achieve similar objectives.

But 3i was set up to operate in the United Kingdom and was unable to escape the limitations of Britain's generally uncompetitive performance. Only during the period in the 1950s when its own shareholders were unable to supply it with loan capital has it been short of money to invest. Even in the brief spells of rapid growth, funds available for investment have been more than adequate to meet demand. The reasons for the shortage of demand are obscure although a number of possible explanations have been put forward. The most likely seems to be the relative shortage of successful medium-sized companies of the kind which seem so numerous in France and Germany (where the Mittelstand is accepted as a major engine of national success). The 100 largest firms quoted on the Stock Exchange account for two-thirds of total market capitalization and 40 per cent of total manufacturing net output. The same concentration is not evident elsewhere, and it is significant that at the time of writing of the 500 largest European companies over 200 are British-based.

Despite the quality of the equivalent medium-sized British companies, well documented in recent 3i research, their numbers appear to be very limited. The lack of growth among the large population of smaller businesses, which could take them through into what 3i calls the 'superleague' of medium-sized companies, may be due to a number of factors. One, noted in the same 3i research, was unwillingness to accept an external shareholding as the price of expansion. It was indeed a common complaint among 3i staff that many customers preferred to limit their growth rather than 'give away equity'. Others decided to pursue their growth plans relying wholly on debt and were liable to be caught out by the next economic crisis. Some of this reluctance to accept external sources of equity capital seems, on the basis of 3i's research, to have declined; but over the post-war years, when profits growth, and consequently internally generated capital have been inadequate, it may have been a significant impediment to the growth of smaller businesses into that important 'middle company' league.

Other impediments have probably been the high cost of debt, generally more expensive than in competing countries, and the inadequate growth of the domestic market. 3i as a passive supplier of capital could have no role to play in stimulating demand by artificial means. To the extent that it was called on it was able to provide all the capital that was needed, but there was never any doubt, certainly in the period since 1959 when ICFC received its funding freedom, that it could have coped with a much larger demand, both in terms of the skilled human resources and of the funds available to it. 3i's staff were often frustrated at the shortage of investment opportunities caused by the unwillingness of potential customers to commit themselves to high growth strategies. During the 1980s there were encouraging signs that more sophisticated management was emerging, and it is to be hoped that despite or, perhaps, because of the recent difficulties, the trend will continue towards a UK business scene peopled by expanding companies, whose owners are prepared to accept institutional equity partners as the normal price of growth.

In the past the main causes of the periodic collapse of business confidence have been the rises in interest rates forced on governments by the behaviour of sterling or of inflation or—usually—both, and 3i's continuing policy has been to minimize the damage such volatility can cause by ensuring that its customers are adequately capitalized. Each application for investment funds is considered in the light of the customer's existing debt, and the package of loan and/or shares is designed to minimize the exposure to external shocks, of which the possibility of future rises in interest costs is the most important. This is dealt with in two ways; the first is to ensure that the proportion of debt in the package is no greater than can be comfortably serviced, the balance being made up by share capital which does not have the same contractual requirement to bear interest and be repaid. The second is as far as possible to provide loan money on a fixed-interest basis, giving a degree of certainty and making the company less prone to the shock of interest rate rises.

To the extent that 3i has succeeded in persuading its customers to adopt a conservative capital structure and to accept fixed interest debt it will have been a stabilizing force, helping its customers to ride out the recurrent economic storms which have bedevilled the UK economy. But the scale on which it has operated, even in recent years, was in my belief never large enough.

It could hardly have been otherwise so long as its function was to provide a market substitute for companies unable to raise capital through the Stock Exchange mechanism. While 3i provided capital for up to 1,000 companies a year, this translated into relatively small amounts in money terms. In 1987–8, for example, when 3i for the first time provided over £500 million to smaller companies, larger businesses, including privatized utilities, raised some £25 billion on the stock market.

Fixed Interest Debt: A Lost Cause in the UK?

Another constraint on 3i's growth was the enormous amount of medium-term lending done by the banks. From being providers of self-liquidating working capital facilities at the time ICFC was founded, the clearing banks have become substantial term lenders, mainly at variable rates, which allows them to finance their lending from short-term deposits. The sharp rise in inflation between 1973 and 1976 and the accompanying increases in interest rates, following the credit explosion of the early 1970s, effectively killed off the long-term fixed-interest market. The corporate sector abandoned it to the government and turned to the banks in the hope that interest rates would fall and make future funding possible at lower levels. In practice this never happened, and 3i found itself continually in competition with the banks for medium- and long-term lending at margins which it could not or would not match.

There can be little doubt that the practice of borrowing term money at variable interest rates exacerbated the financial difficulties of the corporate sector in the successive downturns of the mid-1970s, the early 1980s and, most spectacularly, the late 1980s and early 1990s. Because virtually the only tool of economic policy available to government in the short term is to raise and lower interest rates, it must be foolish for economic agents—individuals, companies, or government itself, to become excessively reliant on a form of capital whose cost is directly affected by those rates. This view has been supported by the Director General of the CBI in looking at ways of restoring the small company sector after the disaster of the 1990s recession. In August 1993, as the UK began to recover, he wrote in *The Times:*[2]

If one looks at the overall balance sheet of small firms in the UK, one can see that variable-rate overdraft facilities account for 58 per cent of total debt. This compares with 35 per cent in Italy and 14 per cent in Germany. By contrast, long-term loans make up 31 per cent of small company debts in Germany compared with 11 per cent in the UK. This makes British firms more vulnerable to short-term interest-rate fluctuations, and particularly vulnerable when—as was the case from 1990 to 1992—they experience high interest rates at a time of recession.'

3i's failure to stem the tide of variable-rate borrowing was inevitable, given the government's inability to stabilize inflation and the very high levels of long-term rates which resulted. Unsurprisingly, when gilt-edged yields were forced up to 16 per cent by the 26 per cent inflation rate of 1976 it became virtually impossible to persuade ICFC's customers that a borrowing cost of 18 to 20 per cent, even though it was still negative in real terms, was a viable alternative to variable-rate debt. It is nevertheless surprising that the appetite for fixed rate debt never seriously recovered, particularly when towards the end of the 1980s corporate indebtedness began to rise sharply to meet the demand for buy-outs and other forms of acquisition, as well as rapidly growing investment programmes. By 1989, as the London Business School chart reproduced on page 360 shows, corporate debt had reached record levels, the bulk of it undoubtedly in variable rate form.

By that time 3i's fixed-rate loans had become only a small proportion of

Travellers Fare

IN 1988, THE BRITISH RAIL PROPERTY BOARD made the decision to dispose of some of its non-railway activities, including Sealink and its hotel interests. As part of this process, Travellers Fare—the catering arm of the rail network, was put up for sale providing an opportunity for 3i to lead a management buy-out. Over the previous ten years, Travellers Fare had undergone significant reshaping in a bid, as 3i saw it, 'to free itself from the stereotype of the curly sandwich'. The sell-off involved 270 catering units located at 140 stations, many operating under recently established brand names, including 'Casey Jones' and 'The Upper Crust'. The on-board train catering business had earlier been sold to Trusthouse Forte.

3i was impressed by the management team proposing the Travellers Fare buy-out and convinced that further cost controls and better marketing would increase profitability. The appraisal of the original proposal shows that the investment decision rested heavily on personality assessment—noting, for example, that one key member of the team was 'a careful person, . . . whom the team trust', but that 'the MBO possibility had stirred him to look closely at the level of overheads which he had agreed had received less attention under BR'. 3i recommended that a new chairman be recruited from outside to help the team manage successfully the transition to private ownership.

The process of setting up the deal involved submitting a tender to BR, in competition with other, mostly trade buyers, establishing a syndicate of investors and working out details of an employee share option package. 3i led a successful bid, providing a mezzanine loan and taking a 17 per cent equity stake. The other equity partners were Charterhouse, CINVen, and Globe Investment Trust. On completion of the sale in December 1988 at a price of £12.5 million, David Bailey, a British Rail manager with 19 years experience, took over as managing director at the head of a group of ten ex-BR employees.

In November 1992, Travellers Fare was sold for over £31 million to the Compass Group, itself an earlier 3i-led buy-out and an under-bidder in the original Travellers Fare sale. 3i had become a leader in the field of syndicated deals in the mid-1980s and was central to the formation of Compass in 1987 when a management team bought out the contract catering arm of Grand Metropolitan. Sixteen potential backers were approached, of whom fifteen agreed to invest, in addition to 3i's own investment of £31.4 million. Compass went on to achieve a full stock market listing in December 1988.

total lending, and the corporate bond market, though more active than in the past, was providing only a small part of corporate capital needs. Much the greatest part was supplied by the banks.

Whilst 3i has employed what might be termed the classical funding technique and by doing so has avoided really serious losses, it is a cause for regret that this technique did not become embedded in UK financial practice. Although 3i was funded by the banks it was in no sense sponsored by them. Similarly government, though approving of what 3i was doing, did nothing to encourage or facilitate an extension of its activity onto a scale which could have had some impact on the corporate sector as a whole.

In contrast, the German government established a centrally funded institution to provide long-term fixed-interest debt, whilst Japan and most European countries set up similar bodies whose function was to tap the personal savings market by giving tax advantages to individuals. This, together with the State's guarantee of the institutions' debt, encouraged very large amounts of low-cost money to flow into the industrial development banks, whereas in the United Kingdom such preferential tax treatment as was given by government went to building-society depositors, benefiting home owners rather than industry. Even in the United States tax-free industrial-revenue bonds were issued for use in industrial investment; but in the United Kingdom a Conservative government would refuse to encourage further distortions in the already privileged savings market and Labour preferred to set up its own body which could intervene directly in industry.

ICFC was therefore left to plough its own furrow both by its shareholders and by the government, except in 1974 when the so-called 'Billion Pound Fund' was set up to allow lending by the then FFI on a large scale to industrial companies unable temporarily to raise capital through a weak Stock Exchange. But even this involved no government support, in the form of either guarantees or subsidies. The resulting interest cost was inadequate to compensate institutional investors for what they saw as FFI's extra risk as a private-sector body, despite the quality of its ownership. The £75 million of 5-year loan stock issued by the Bank of England on behalf of 3i offered an interest rate 1.5 percentage points higher than the government's own stock, but without a government guarantee this was seen as inadequate, and the stock quickly fell to a substantial discount, at one point yielding a full 3 percentage points more than government stock. It was a telling indictment of the attempt to impose less than full market terms without the compensation of subsidy or guarantee. 3i has never had privileged access to funds, as happened elsewhere, but the schemes which it administered on behalf of the European Coal and Steel Community and the European Investment Bank showed what might have been achieved here and was achieved elsewhere on the Continent; fixed-interest savings were channelled on subsidized terms into industrial investment, not through government but in parallel with it, benefiting from its guarantee, whilst in Japan and in the United States industry received an indirect subsidy in the form of below-market interest rates made possible by tax reliefs to the private investor. At times when short-term interest rates were being raised to counter inflation and protect currency parities, the effect of low-cost fixed-rate long-term money would have been to preserve business confidence and encourage continuing activity, particularly in capital investment programmes.

The fact that 3i was always able to raise enough money to meet demand, on normal commercial terms, cannot disguise the relatively minor impact which it had on the general level of activity as the only institutional source of long-term and permanent capital. It would have been possible, with the benefit of a government guarantee, to raise very large sums on the capital market without interfering with the government's own fundraising programme. Attaching an interest-rate subsidy of only a small amount in normal circumstances would have allowed companies to justify long-term fixed-interest bor-

IN PURSUIT OF EXCELLENCE

rowing rather than continuing dependence on variable-rate debt. It was a brave finance director who could recommend to his board that they should approve a 20-year borrowing at 12 per cent when short- and medium-term money could be had, at least temporarily, at two percentage points less. In such circumstances a 3 per cent subsidy would have made the fixed-interest borrowing irresistible, the resulting desirable stability in money cost protecting the business against future rises in short rates and inflationary pressures on costs.

It would have been possible, but not necessary, to limit such subsidies to funds borrowed for qualifying capital expenditure purposes. Their proper use could be monitored through the publication of audited sources and use of funds statements or, as with EIB and ECSC funds, leaving it to 3i to monitor retrospectively the application of the money to qualifying purposes. But the main effect would have been to stabilize balance sheets, reducing the dependence on short-term debt and fixing money costs at attractive levels, thus providing a known and bearable money cost over a long period. It might then hardly have mattered, except to an interventionist government, what the subsidized funds were actually used for; investment, encouraged by the very fact of the availability of fixed-rate money and its relatively low cost, would have allowed higher gearing and thus lower target rates of return, resulting in a higher level of aggregate investment and more efficient use of equity capital.

Such a plan would not have protected British industry against all aspects of economic mismanagement, nor against its own incompetence, but it would have increased investment volumes, helped to sustain business confidence through difficult periods, and lessened the impact of sudden policy reversals. Nor would it have been easy for 3i to reconcile its commercial stance, the willingness to accept financial risks, and its aggressive pursuit of long term profit, with the closer government links implied by guarantees and subsidies. In general it was happier operating at arms' length from government: it could not be cajoled, threatened, or bribed into investing in uncreditworthy projects to satisfy politicians, but such pressure could not have been avoided if government money had been involved. Furthermore, any calls on government to honour its guarantees would have been politically awkward. However the State guarantee needed to apply only to 3i's borrowing rather than to its lending, as was the case with EIB and ECSC, whose loans to 3i were repayable on set terms, whether or not the corresponding loans made by 3i were themselves repaid. In return for accepting such commercial risks 3i could take its usual compensation in the form of equity, the subsidy being passed straight through in a reduction of the borrower's interest costs.

Another benefit of a stable long-term debt structure is a reduction in the amount provided by the banks and the risks they carried. Long-term debt, repayable over 25 to 30 years, ranks as quasi-capital, providing backing not solely for bank overdrafts used for the traditional seasonal purposes, but also for the banks' medium-term variable-rate loans which, in moderation, have their uses. In times of economic difficulty the banks' exposure would have been more limited: the amount their customers could borrow would also be contractually limited by the terms of the long-term debt. Whilst in 3i's experience there was undoubtedly some chafing against such constraints, they forced businessmen to think about their financial needs more constructively and to justify their calls for increased facilities not only to a possibly over-eager bank but also to a sceptical long-term debenture holder. If, as a result, they had to raise more permanent capital, that was likely to be for the long-term good of the business.

3i itself was unwilling to put forward such revolutionary ideas and get tangled up with government. But looked at from a national point of view, despite its success on its own terms, which was admired and to some extent emulated abroad, the country lacked an integrated long-term economic policy which might accommodate an efficient large-scale capital-raising mechanism for industry without submitting it to uncommercial pressures. It could not have succeeded without strong political backing, but neither would it have worked effectively if it was subject to close policy direction.

An Alternative Model: 3i as an Instrument of Policy?

Left to its own devices as it generally was, and lacking the encouragement of its shareholders or strong political support from government, 3i has remained a gap filler in the existing financial market-place. The Macmillan gap clearly did exist, and remains a fact of economic life in all countries where capital markets exist for the benefit of private business. 3i brilliantly succeeded in assuming that basic role of capital-market substitution and making a profit at it, but it also possessed both the people with the skills necessary to operate on a much larger scale in the provision of industrial capital, and the necessary access to funds. Allowed to follow its own hard-nosed commercial principles, it could have applied them constructively to a broader role in the implementation of a long-term economic strategy where industrial investment was a key element.

It is easy to scoff at such ideas because it is almost inconceivable that a British government would have the nerve to avoid intervention or policy U-turns which would limit the effectiveness of a long-term institution such as 3i. But there can be no doubt that such institutions have played major roles in the development of the world's two most successful post-war economies, Germany and Japan.

With the opening up of global capital markets and the greater interdependence of the major economies the time for such local discriminatory policies aimed at creating or preserving international competitiveness may have gone. Nevertheless, the form of linkage which 3i had with EIB and ECSC

Derwent Valley Foods

DERWENT VALLEY FOODS IS A STORY of entrepreneurship, industrial regeneration, and the importance of regional economic ties. The company, now famous for its Phileas Fogg range of snacks, began life in 1982 when Roger McKechnie and three partners put together a start-up plan to manufacture premium-priced adult snack foods. McKechnie had previously worked for Procter and Gamble and Tudor Crisps, a division of Smiths. Based in the North East, McKechnie decided to branch out on his own when faced with the prospect of moving South to company head-office.

McKechnie's plan involved setting up a factory in Consett, a town symbolic of 1980s de-industrialization, having been devastated by the recent closure of the British Steel plant. The company received advice and limited financial support through Consett Development Agency and the Government's Enterprise Initiative, but it was difficult to find the rest of the necessary capital. McKechnie recalls that many of the venture capitalists he approached judged Derwent Valley to be 'a crummy food business with disaster written all over it.' Between them McKechnie and his partners managed to raise almost £50,000 of personal capital, which, even when added to the help from the Development Agency, was still far short of the estimated £500,000 needed to get under way.

3i offered an initial package, involving loans and equity representing 25 per cent of the capital, amounting to £235,000. The company was set up on a site once occupied by British Steel, and began the manufacture of a range of snacks aimed at the adult market. These included Mignons Morceaux, Tortilla Chips, and Shanghai Nuts. Central to the firm's strategy was the distinctive packaging of these snacks, using the global exploits of Jules Verne's Phileas Fogg. As McKechnie recalls, the firm could not afford large advertising budgets, 'we had to make the package be our ad'.

The company was helped by further rounds of funding by 3i totalling some £2.5 million as it launched a series of new products throughout the 1980s. By 1993 Derwent Valley had captured over one-third of the premium-priced adult snack market with sales exceeding £20 million a year, and employed over 300 people in Consett. During 1992, the directors decided that it was time to find a larger partner, with greater distribution power, to grow the company internationally much more quickly than they could on their own. They appointed 3i Corporate Finance to manage a competitive sale process, which culminated early in 1993 in an offer of £24 million from United Biscuits being accepted. With the sale 3i realized £6.5 million for its stake. The company continues to run as a division within United Biscuits, which has global ambitions for the Phileas Fogg brand. Roger McKechnie remains rooted in the local North East economy, and is using part of his capital gained from the takeover to help fund start-up businesses in the Consett area.

could enable national priorities to be met through mediation by highly rated international borrowers. Whatever may be the future course for such institutional providers of industrial capital there seems little doubt that the United Kingdom could have made more effective provision for financing industrial investment over the last forty years or so and in the process made business confidence less vulnerable to short-term economic shocks.

It can be argued that if 3i had been armed with the resources granted to its Continental counterparts it would have been even more successful than they were in channelling funds into industrial investment. The European and Japanese versions of 3i, the so-called long-term credit institutions, were all set up as extensions of the banking system, with a function limited to the supply of credit for periods which went beyond the term normally possible for commercial banks, dependent as these were on short-notice deposits. It was acknowledged that in the period of post-war reconstruction lack of base capital would make it necessary for businesses to depend excessively on credit for their capital investment programmes; the risk which this implied could only be accepted if government provided guarantees both for the institutions' own borrowing and for their lending. The result in virtually all of the post-war economies was a centralized vehicle for government industrial policy which took in money from the state or borrowed publicly with its guarantee and made loans to private businesses, again underwritten by the state. Marshall Plan funds, initially provided by the United States at very low interest rates, were an invaluable source of the subsidized credit which such institutions were able to deploy in financing industrial development.

The close links with government inevitably meant that these institutions were controlled and directed through supervisory boards containing State nominees and representatives of other powerful interest groups. Their establishment as extensions of the banking system also meant that their staff and lending policies were typically those of banks. With the credit risk being taken by government there was no requirement to assess commercial risk and take equity compensation for it.

3i's experience in risk assessment demonstrates that, even in an unstable economy, it is possible to provide large amounts of capital through a central institutional mechanism without government guarantees and with a satisfactory return to its own shareholders. Translating Continental experience into the UK, with the institution's fund-raising guaranteed by government and only the remotest chance of failure, much larger amounts of money could have been raised on the finest terms. But government would have been relieved of the more chancy and politically sensitive involvement in individual investments through 3i's ability to assess risk and make a commercial return by negotiating appropriate compensation in each case. The problems of providing direct government support to private businesses were well illustrated by the experience of the National Enterprise Board, set up by the Labour government in the 1970s to feed capital into needy industrial companies. Although NEB set out effectively to emulate 3i by taking minority equity positions in private companies it was unable to continue taking a hands-off view in the many cases where its customers got into difficulties. Public accountability for the funds it had invested forced it into both taking control of failing businesses and having to account for its losses to a sceptical parliament.

Leaving 3i in the private sector, but giving it access to a state guarantee of its borrowing and a subsidy for its lending, would have allowed it to apply its great skill in investment judgement and its deep knowledge of industrial problems in continuing to provide commercially justified support for viable businesses, but on a much larger scale than was actually possible, while passing the benefits of subsidy directly through to the end user.

Similar benefits could have been seen on the Continent if the long-term credit banks had been given 3i's commercial freedom and staffed with non-bankers. Whilst the State guarantee was probably necessary during the post-war recovery period, it became a hindrance when growth in the continental economies lost its momentum after 1973. The importance of the central institutions declined as the commercial banks began lending at medium and long term, and all the credit institutions suffered in the inflation of the early 1980s as a direct result of excessive amounts of lending and unsustainable corporate gearing levels. It is only in recent years that 3i's example has been followed by the creation of equity finance affiliates with the object of restoring the weakened capital base of their customers.

In summary, 3i has played a valuable role in providing capital for private businesses, much admired both here and abroad, but its economic impact has been limited by comparison with its continental and Japanese equivalents. This is a cause for regret because 3i's uniquely successful experience as a capital market substitute could have been the basis for a much more significant national strategy of encouraging and funding stable industrial growth. It would have been capable of operating on a much greater scale if it had had access to the resources made possible by a government guarantee and, as a channel for low-cost fixed-interest loans to finance industrial investment, it could have played a constructive role in stabilizing economic activity. But such wishful thinking should not be allowed to detract from 3i's remarkable success, first in accomplishing the thankless task assigned to it by its founders, and secondly in making a fully satisfactory return on their investment. Herein lies its true economic impact.

NOTES

[1] See Fig. 15.1, p. 360.
[2] Howard Davies, The Times, 23 Aug. 1993.

Postscript: 1991 to 1995

by Ewen Macpherson

THE STORY TOLD BY our authors ends in 1991 when Don Clarke retired as 3i's Finance Director and Richard Coopey began his research project under the aegis of the London School of Economics' Business History Unit. The story of the next four years can only be told by those of us who have steered 3i through a severe recession into the calmer waters of 1994 and the long-awaited flotation which was finally achieved on 18 July 1994. By the time this book is published 3i will have been in existence for half a century and publicly listed for nearly one year.

The present management team started working together in March, 1992 and consists of myself as Chief Executive, Brian Larcombe as Finance Director, Neil Cross as Director of International Investment, John Platt and

'Oh, and while you were out the recession ended.'

The team for flotation. From left to right Sir Max Williams, (Deputy Chairman), Ewen Macpherson (Chief Executive), Sir George Russell, (Chairman), Brian Larcombe (Finance Director)

Rupert Wiles as Directors of UK Investment, and Richard Summers as Director of Systems Administration and Control. We have been ably supported by Peter Brown as Company Secretary, who joined the team in 1994 following flotation with additional responsibilities for Group legal and compliance matters. It is interesting to observe that all members of the team, except one, began their careers with 3i in the years 1969–74.

The authors have described a unique institution which has contrived to satisfy the general demand of small- and medium-sized businesses for permanent and long-term capital without sacrificing the need to reward its shareholders' capital.

We were thus bequeathed a strong institution whose staff combined a dedication to the ideals of 3i's founders with a hard-nosed commercialism in their dealings with individual small- and medium-sized businesses. 3i had benefited, over the years, from the protective umbrella of its shareholders, which allowed it to develop long-term policies in the capital market substitution role for which they created it. It had been through a long phase of expansion and, towards the end of the 1980s and early 1990s, a short period of contraction which proved both painful and beneficial. The extreme and unforeseen depth of the recession forced on us one further round of cost cutting, which took place in the autumn of 1992, accompanied by some heavy provisions, before the resumption of growth for which the high quality portfolio and 3i's exceptionally strong balance sheet provided the launching pad.

3i is to some extent a bell-wether of the national economy as our quarterly customer survey, the 3i Enterprise Barometer, demonstrates. It was cheering to see the strength of the UK recovery in our pre-flotation results (year ending 31 March 1994). Our success is that of our investee companies—without them 3i is nothing and it is a tribute to the quality of their management that they have, soon after a damaging recession, produced the dividends and capital profits which have given 3i the highest ever total return on shareholders' funds.

That the 1993–4 outcome was so good can also be attributed to 3i's concentration on its core business of investment in the loan and share capital of private companies. The closure and disposal of the peripheral businesses, which had been accumulated over many years, was necessary because their financial performance had both dragged down that of the core business and diverted management attention.

The financial position which we as a management team inherited was adequate to see 3i through the recession and position it strongly for the recovery in demand in the UK, but it was not strong enough to allow expansion in five major economies at the same time: the USA, France, Germany, Italy, and Spain. It was for this reason, and because we were unable to write sufficiently attractive terms in the competitive and well-developed market in the USA, that we decided to run down our operations there releasing capital which could be used in the less developed markets in continental Europe.

In order to expand in continental Europe we felt we needed to ensure we had adequate capital and so we decided in 1992 to attempt to raise a fund from institutional investors which would be managed by us and invested alongside our own money. It was a significant achievement of 1993–94 that Neil Cross and his team were able to attract major institutional investors into partnerships with us raising ECU330m.

We also decided, for different reasons, to raise a fund in the UK to invest alongside 3i in larger management buy-outs. This was brought together in March 1994 by Rupert Wiles and his team. In this case, shortage of capital was not the problem. We were already market leaders in the field, but as such we passed out many deals to syndicate partners for which we got little return. By having our own fund we were better remunerated and became more efficient in the market-place. All of this is a far cry from the days when ICFC was forced, against its will, to establish EDITH as a separate fund. Opportunities then were few and ICFC's capital was more than adequate to meet the demand.

As so much has been written about the flotation over the years, I do not think it would be possible to conclude this book without a few words about what actually happened in the run up to the successful flotation exercise in the summer of 1994.

3i was emerging from the recession in 1993: the worst period for business activity was the autumn of 1992 at around the time the UK was leaving the ERM. Interest rate volatility and the consequent uncertainty did little for businessmen's confidence and their ability to make investment decisions. From December 1992 onwards there was a steady improvement in conditions, levels of activity, and company profitability.

Following this period, 3i's results began to improve. The cost of the autumn 1992 redundancies and office closures were carried in the Accounts for the year ending 31 March 1993. Management took various other steps to ensure that the net gearing ratio of the company started to fall and the revenue account to improve after a 3-year period of decline. By the autumn of 1993, it was clearly apparent that the numbers were moving in the right direction. In

'Happy days are here again. The shares you hold have split again. We plan to raise the dividend. Happy days are here again!'

September 1993, Sir George Russell, who had been on the Board for a year, became chairman and agreed that following publication of the Interim Results in December, it would be appropriate to visit all the shareholder Bank chairmen to present the company's position and set out the case for flotation. Our proposal was, in essence, that part only of the equity should be sold, in order to qualify for investment trust status with the benefits which that would bring.

These meetings which involved the Chairman, Brian Larcombe and myself, went well, and were followed by some weeks of negotiations so that by the end of February 1994 we were able to make an announcement that we intended to float the Company in the summer. We were to be sponsored by Barings, with brokers de Zoete and Bevan, NatWest Securities and James Capel. Slaughter and May were solicitors to the Company.

There then began one of the most intense periods of activity I have ever come across in my business career. I think this view was shared by several of my executive colleagues. Not only did enormous amounts of detailed technical work have to be done on changing the Memorandum and Articles, revising the share option scheme, revising the profit-sharing scheme, drafting the Prospectus and verifying every statement in it, but at the same time we had to prepare the statutory Annual Accounts which had to be included in the Prospectus. On top of all this we had to market the Company to the UK institutions and potential retail investors.

Educating the potential institutional investors about 3i was correctly identified as a major requirement of the marketing efforts. As a starting point in this process, a series of lunches and dinners was held at Waterloo Road during March 1994 at which Brian Larcombe and I explained how the business worked and provided some information about the finances of the company. These sessions were well attended and well received, and covered about sixty major institutional investors. Brian and I were supported at these sessions by several colleagues who helped deal with detailed questions, such as Neil Cross (International), Hugh Richards (UK Investment Activities), John Kirkpatrick (Industry Department), and Charles Richardson (Corporate Affairs). I had incidentally insisted that some members of the Executive Team should not be involved in flotation activities to ensure that some senior people remained available to deal with the day-to-day requirements of the business!

At the beginning of April, an extensive piece of brokers' research was launched by BZW. The next major hurdle was to launch the Pathfinder Prospectus, which, of course, had to be fully verified and approved by the Board and ran to 110 pages. This was achieved by the end of May.

Brian Larcombe and I then spent the next six weeks making between six and seven presentations a day to potential institutional investors. Morning and afternoon sessions were on a one-to-one basis, with a small group at lunch time. Questioning and general understanding of the company was varied, and it was quite clear that some people had read the Prospectus more carefully than others. In all, we spoke directly to about 160 institutions.

During this period, financial market conditions were volatile, with a general downward trend in the FTSE indices. Several companies, who aspired to flotation, pulled out of the exercise. We were determined to keep going and were fully supported in this by our shareholders.

When the day to price the shares arrived, market conditions could hardly have been more unfavourable. But, thanks to the excellent preparatory work by the brokers, led by de Zoete and Bevan, there was no problem in getting the placing and sub-underwriting together, and we were able to sign off the Prospectus on 21 June and launch it on 22 June, with the shares priced at 272p, a discount of $13^1/_2\%$ to 31 March net asset value.

Market conditions remained uncertain for virtually the whole of the offer period which meant that there was some disappointment that the retail offer was not more successful, being oversubscribed 1.1 times, and producing 75,000 shareholders for 3i. Earlier market research had suggested the number of 'Jeremy's' interested in buying shares might have been much higher.

The first day of dealings had been fixed for 18 July 1994, to coincide with the start of the Stock Exchange's new settlement arrangements, and from shortly before this date market conditions became distinctly more positive than they had been during the marketing and offer periods. The first day's dealings therefore took place at a reasonable premium to the offer price and closed at 293p which we were all very pleased about. Subsequently, the price strengthened considerably and broke through the 300p barrier a few days later. The unexpected consequence of this firm demand for 3i shares was that our market capitalization rose to a level which justified our inclusion in the list of FTSE-100 companies, and we were all delighted when this happened with effect from 19 September 1994.

Flotation is now providing an opportunity for both institutional and private investors to share in 3i's successful investment in the small- and medium-sized business sector. At one time a Cinderella sector, which the clearing banks entered in 1945 with the greatest reluctance, small- and medium-sized businesses have now been recognized for what they are, an important engine of economic growth with potential to achieve attractive capital gains for both owners and investors, and to become 'the companies of tomorrow'. The downside is the risk of failure, inevitable in businesses whose finances are constantly stretched as they strive for expansion in the good times and survival in the bad. Here it is that careful selection, skilled structuring of the financial arrangements and close monitoring can make the difference between speculative investment and the stable long-term growth fund which 3i is—and has been since 1945.

3i will enter its sixth decade firmly established as one of the UK's largest and most successful businesses with some 11,000 companies having benefited from its investment and at the same time contributed to its success. Most of these companies have been British but increasingly in future they could be from other countries in the European Union.

In all this success, the key has been the high quality of 3i's staff. To say this is not merely to pay lip-service to the employees' contribution. The ability to construct original financial proposals which reconcile investee companies' needs with our own, to negotiate terms and bring them to a successful conclusion, is critical to our success. To be able to monitor those inherently risky investments over long periods and bring 3i both income and capital profit from the majority is proof of an exceptionally able and dedicated group of people. This book has not dealt excessively with individuals, partly because it would be invidious to do so, but I hope enough will have been seen of the quality of the people who have worked for 3i and their ability to turn out performances of which the founders would have been proud. Long may they continue to do so.

"LET'S GO TO LUNCH."

Appendix I: Statistical Tables

Table A.1. *ICFC Ltd.: investment by size, by number (year ending September or March)*

	New approvals																Outstanding											
	Sept.[a] 1946		Sept. 1947		Sept. 1948		Sept. 1949		Mar.[b] 1950		Mar. 1951		Mar. 1952		Mar. 1953		Mar. 1954		Mar. 1955		Mar. 1956		Mar. 1957		Mar. 1958		Mar. 1959	
Size of investment	No.	%	No.	%	No.	%	No.	%	No.	%	No.	%	No.	%	No.	%	No.	%	No.	%	No.	%	No.	%	No.	%	No.	%
Up to £10,000	35	26	7	8	6	12	4	9	7	15	8	10	11	11	7	11	74	16	74	15	89	16	86	15	104	17	120	18
£10,001–£20,000	32	24	14	16	9	17	3	7	5	11	6	7	15	15	18	28	61	13	74	15	77	14	82	14	89	14	94	14
£20,001–£50,000	38	29	30	34	14	27	15	34	18	38	36	43	45	41	17	27	160	35	175	35	187	34	201	34	210	33	208	32
£50,001–£100,000	19	14	18	20	16	31	11	25	11	23	16	19	24	22	10	16	81	18	94	19	105	19	112	19	120	19	122	19
£100,001 and above	9	7	19	22	7	13	11	25	6	13	18	21	16	14	12	19	84	18	85	17	96	17	105	18	106	17	111	17
TOTAL	133		88		52		44		47		84		111		64		460		502		554		586		629		655	

[a] Cumulative total approved.
[b] NB Some double-counting with year to Sept. 1949.

Table A.2. *ICFC Ltd.: outstanding investment by size, by number (year ending March)*

Size of investment	1960		1961		1962		1963		1964		1965		1966		1967		1968		1969		1970		1971		1972		1973	
	No.	%	No.	%	No.	%	No.	%	No.	%	No.	%	No.	%	No.	%	No.	%	No.	%	No.	%	No.	%	No.	%	No.	%
Up to £10,000	105	16	113	16	138	17	144	17	162	17	198	19	236	19	345	23	386	23	425	23	476	23	494	22	479	21	493	21
£10,001–£20,000	119	18	116	17	128	16	150	17	154	16	161	15	208	17	255	17	302	18	326	18	406	20	435	19	456	20	451	19
£20,001–£50,000	188	28	195	28	242	30	261	30	285	30	315	29	331	27	397	26	419	25	490	26	517	25	576	26	597	26	596	26
£50,001–£100,000	128	19	136	20	153	19	162	19	166	17	178	17	208	17	241	16	289	17	306	16	338	16	372	17	364	16	371	16
£100,001 and above	120	18	134	19	145	18	152	17	185	19	216	20	–	–	–	–	–	–	–	–	–	–	–	–	–	–	–	–
£100,001–£150,000													103	8	–	–	–	–	–	–	–	–	–	–	–	–	–	–
£150,001–£200,000													69	6	–	–	–	–	–	–	–	–	–	–	–	–	–	–
£200,001 and above													80	6	–	–	–	–	–	–	–	–	–	–	–	–	–	–
£100,001–£200,000															180	12	186	11	198	11	211	10	209	9	226	10	238	10
£200,001–£300,000															60	4	64	4	68	4	70	3	82	4	91	4	85	4
£300,001 and above															36	2	42	2	47	3	59	3	70	3	–	–	–	–
£300,001–£500,000																									46	2	55	2
£500,001 and above																									35	2	47	2
	660		694		806		869		952		1,068		1,235		1,514		1,688		1,860		2,077		2,238		2,294		2,336	
Shipping subsidiary	–		–		–		–		–		–		–		6		8		12		60		59		54		43	
TOTAL	660		694		806		869		952		1,068		1,235		1,520		1,696		1,872		2,137		2,297		2,348		2,379	

Table A.3. *ICFC Ltd.: outstanding investment by size, by number (year ending March)*

Size of investment	1974 No.	%	1975 No.	%	1976 No.	%	1977 No.	%	1978 No.	%	1979 No.	%	1980 No.	%	1981 No.	%	1982 No.	%	1983 No.	%
Up to £10,000	506	21	502	22	n.a.	—	449	20	443	20	n.a.	—	n.a.	—	444	13	448	12	474	12
£10,001–£20,000	418	18	385	17	n.a.	—	325	15	333	15	n.a.	—	n.a.	—	482	14	513	14	453	12
£20,001–£50,000	592	25	551	24	n.a.	—	582	26	527	24	n.a.	—	n.a.	—	902	27	1,016	27	1,036	27
£50,001–£100,000	394	17	390	17	n.a.	—	356	16	372	17	n.a.	—	n.a.	—	621	18	722	19	786	20
£100,001–£200,000	257	11	275	12	n.a.	—	261	12	279	13	n.a.	—	n.a.	—	478	14	565	15	608	16
£200,001–£300,000	107	4	91	4	n.a.	—	91	4	107	5	n.a.	—	n.a.	—	179	5	198	5	194	5
£300,001–£500,000	52	2	67	3	n.a.	—	76	3	90	4	n.a.	—	n.a.	—	160	5	177	5	112	3
£500,001 and above	57	2	70	3	n.a.	—	61	3	55	2	n.a.	—	n.a.	—	134	4	158	4	237	6
TOTAL	2,383		2,331		n.a.		2,201		2,206		n.a.		n.a.		3,400		3,797		3,900	

Table A.4. *3i Group plc: outstanding investment by size, by number (year ending March)*

Size of investment	1984 No.	%	1985 No.	%	1986 No.	%	1987 No.	%	1988 No.	%	1989 No.	%	1990 No.	%	1991 No.	%	1992 No.	%	1993 No.	%
Up to £10,000	487	12	481	11	487	10	462	10	439	9	405	10	389	9	368	9	352	9	317	9
£10,001–£20,000	475	11	395	9	468	10	406	9	382	8	267	7	248	6	217	5	181	5	155	4
£20,001–£50,000	1,074	26	941	21	1,162	24	1,033	22	884	18	552	14	522	13	468	13	406	10	357	10
£50,001–£100,000	816	20	902	20	893	19	870	18	861	18	653	16	584	14	539	13	491	13	435	12
£100,001–£200,000	637	15	724	16	726	15	738	15	860	18	685	17	727	18	724	18	701	18	611	17
£200,001–£300,000	212	5	322	7	321	7	355	7	418	9	424	10	417	10	443	11	421	11	424	12
£300,001–£500,000	197	5	270	6	305	6	333	6	313	7	337	8	428	10	480	12	472	12	473	13
£500,001–£1,000,000	137	3	197	4	254	5	282	5	327	7	368	9	390	9	400	10	390	10	408	11
£1,000,001–£2,000,000	71	2	112	3	117	2	143	3	165	3	217	5	233	6	256	6	255	7	244	7
£2,000,001–£5,000,000	37	1	52	1	61	1	78	2	105	2	111	3	138	3	147	4	153	4	150	4
£5,000,001 and above	21	1	27	1	22	0	24	1	35	1	46	1	50	1	50	1	57	1	62	2
TOTAL	4,164		4,423		4,816		4,724		4,789		4,065		4,126		4,092		3,879		3,636	

Table A.5. ICFC Ltd.: investment by size, by amount; £000 (year ending September or March)

	New approvals																	Outstanding													
	Sept.[a] 1946		Sept. 1947		Sept. 1948		Sept. 1949		Mar.[b] 1950		Mar. 1951		Mar. 1952		Mar. 1953		Mar. 1954		Mar. 1955		Mar. 1956		Mar. 1957		Mar. 1958		Mar. 1959	
Size of investment	Amount	%	Amount	%	Amount	%	Amount	%	Amount	%	Amount	%	Amount	%	Amount	%	Amount	%	Amount	%	Amount	%	Amount	%	Amount	%	Amount	%
Up to £10,000	260	5	49	1	49	1	31	1	47	2	66	1	79	1	51	1	441	2	449	2	466	1	459	1	539	1	646	2
£10,001–£20,000	505	10	219	4	149	5	54	2	88	3	111	2	257	4	292	7	929	3	1,085	4	1,253	4	1,228	4	1,397	4	1,449	4
£20,001–£50,000	1,433	28	1,082	17	437	13	548	16	659	25	1,408	24	1,896	27	691	17	5,865	21	6,325	22	6,701	21	6,691	20	7,041	21	6,938	19
£50,001–£100,000	1,450	29	1,341	22	1,237	38	957	28	844	32	1,325	23	2,113	31	899	22	6,154	22	7,010	24	7,956	25	8,210	25	8,845	26	9,047	25
£100,001 and above	1,423	28	3,491	56	1,414	43	1,886	54	991	38	2,931	50	2,560	37	2,152	53	14,438	52	13,753	48	15,817	49	16,521	50	16,466	48	17,619	49
TOTAL	5,071		6,182		3,285		3,476		2,629		5,841		6,904		4,085		27,827		28,622		32,193		33,109		34,288		35,699	

[a] Cumulative total approved. [b] Some double-counting with year to Sept. 1949.

Table A.6. ICFC Ltd.: outstanding investment by size, by amount; £000 (year ending March)

	1960		1961		1962		1963		1964		1965		1966		1967		1968		1969		1970		1971		1972		1973	
Size of investment	Amount	%	Amount	%	Amount	%	Amount	%	Amount	%	Amount	%	Amount	%	Amount	%	Amount	%	Amount	%	Amount	%	Amount	%	Amount	%	Amount	%
Up to £10,000	588	2	686	2	897	2	1,221	2	1,221	2	1,059	2	1,292	2	1,698	2	2,134	2	2,223	2	2,250	2	2,402	2	2,789	2	2,737	1
£10,001–£20,000	1,810	5	1,767	4	1,930	4	2,232	4	2,284	4	2,345	4	2,988	4	3,511	4	4,318	4	4,461	4	5,629	4	6,037	4	7,120	4	6,870	4
£20,001–£50,000	6,355	17	6,638	16	8,341	18	8,828	17	9,375	16	10,428	16	11,180	14	13,088	14	13,948	14	15,669	14	16,391	13	18,512	13	20,509	12	19,977	11
£50,001–£100,000	9,292	24	9,617	23	10,901	23	11,568	23	11,869	21	12,510	19	14,531	19	17,303	19	20,488	20	21,446	19	23,726	19	26,392	18	27,166	16	27,074	15
£100,001 and above	20,321	53	23,384	56	24,904	53	27,129	53	32,760	57	40,084	60	—	—	—	—	—	—	—	—	—	—	—	—	—	—	—	—
£100,001–£150,000	—	—	—	—	—	—	—	—	—	—	—	—	12,215	16	13,182	14	—	—	—	—	—	—	—	—	—	—	—	—
£150,001–£200,000	—	—	—	—	—	—	—	—	—	—	—	—	11,360	14	11,715	13	—	—	—	—	—	—	—	—	—	—	—	—
£200,001 and above	—	—	—	—	—	—	—	—	—	—	—	—	24,935	32	30,839	34	—	—	—	—	—	—	—	—	—	—	—	—
£100,001–£200,000	—	—	—	—	—	—	—	—	—	—	—	—	—	—	—	—	25,253	25	27,310	25	28,920	23	28,399	19	32,283	19	33,605	18
£200,001–£300,000	—	—	—	—	—	—	—	—	—	—	—	—	—	—	—	—	14,568	14	15,548	14	16,639	13	19,940	14	22,294	13	20,744	11
£300,001 and above	—	—	—	—	—	—	—	—	—	—	—	—	—	—	—	—	20,780	20	24,194	22	31,795	25	45,686	31	—	—	—	—
£300,001–£500,000	—	—	—	—	—	—	—	—	—	—	—	—	—	—	—	—	—	—	—	—	—	—	—	—	17,919	11	20,728	11
£500,001 and above	—	—	—	—	—	—	—	—	—	—	—	—	—	—	—	—	—	—	—	—	—	—	—	—	40,280	24	53,606	29
	38,366		42,092		46,974		50,978		57,509		66,426		78,501		91,336		101,489		110,851		125,350		147,368		170,360		185,341	
Shipping subsidiary	—		—		—		—		—		—		—		—		7,853		14,239		26,762		30,546		34,587		36,763	
Sub-total	38,366		42,092		46,974		50,978		57,509		66,426		78,501		91,336		109,342		125,090		152,112		177,914		204,947		222,104	
Provision	—		—		—		—		—		—		—		—		—		—		—		—		-5,181		-4,950	
TOTAL	38,366		42,092		46,974		50,978		57,509		66,426		78,501		91,336		109,342		125,090		152,112		177,914		199,766		217,154	

Table A.7. ICFC Ltd.: outstanding investment by size, by amount; £000 (year ending March)

Size of investment	1974 Amount	%	1975 Amount	%	1976 Amount	%	1977 Amount	%	1978 Amount	%	1979 Amount	%	1980 Amount	%	1981 Amount	%	1982 Amount	%	1983 Amount	%
Up to £10,000	2,735	1	2,691	1	n.a.	–	2,435	1	2,319	1	n.a.	–	n.a.	–	2,265	1	2,305	1	2,498	1
£10,001–£20,000	6,191	3	5,727	3	n.a.	–	4,985	2	5,163	2	n.a.	–	n.a.	–	7,467	2	7,910	2	6,923	1
£20,001–£50,000	19,678	9	18,326	8	n.a.	–	20,042	9	18,054	8	n.a.	–	n.a.	–	31,439	8	36,147	8	36,431	8
£50,001–£100,000	28,524	14	28,107	12	n.a.	–	25,677	12	27,298	13	n.a.	–	n.a.	–	45,368	11	52,619	11	57,107	12
£100,001–£200,000	36,364	17	38,912	17	n.a.	–	37,288	18	39,547	18	n.a.	–	n.a.	–	68,740	17	79,721	17	85,712	18
£200,001–£300,000	26,214	13	22,312	10	n.a.	–	22,294	11	26,510	12	n.a.	–	n.a.	–	43,948	11	48,022	10	47,328	10
£300,001–£500,000	20,001	10	24,804	11	n.a.	–	29,489	14	35,253	16	n.a.	–	n.a.	–	64,067	16	69,907	15	39,692	8
£500,001 and above	70,000	33	84,055	37	n.a.	–	69,731	33	61,274	28	n.a.	–	n.a.	–	136,768	34	161,888	35	208,806	43
	209,707		224,934		n.a.		211,941		215,418		n.a.		n.a.		400,062		458,519		484,497	
Other assets	35,369		21,966		–		10,908		23,125		–		–		51,411		56,162		45,121	
TOTAL	245,076		246,900		n.a.		222,849		238,543		n.a.		n.a.		451,473		514,681		529,618	

401

Table A.8. 3i Group plc: outstanding investment by size, by amount; £000 (year ending March)

Size of investment	1984 Amount	%	1985 Amount	%	1986 Amount	%	1987 Amount	%	1988 Amount	%	1989 Amount	%	1990 Amount	%	1991 Amount	%	1992 Amount	%	1993 Amount	%
Up to £10,000	2,966	0	2,458	0	2,348	0	2,399	0	2,125	0	1,808	0	1,734	0	1,602	0	1,537	0	1,306	0
£10,001–£20,000	6,918	1	7,281	1	6,961	1	6,404	0	5,756	0	3,983	0	3,768	0	3,243	0	2,724	0	2,398	0
£20,001–£50,000	42,498	4	39,786	3	38,892	3	35,589	3	30,020	2	18,501	1	18,646	1	16,324	1	14,165	1	12,808	1
£50,001–£100,000	66,218	7	67,851	6	66,277	6	65,170	5	62,679	4	49,053	3	44,157	2	41,407	2	37,478	2	33,576	2
£100,001–£200,000	98,833	10	101,228	9	104,072	9	110,217	9	105,650	7	100,680	6	107,224	5	105,104	5	104,173	5	91,497	4
£200,001–£300,000	57,323	6	74,711	7	78,523	7	91,415	7	101,696	6	106,025	6	104,375	6	110,209	5	104,930	5	106,873	5
£300,001–£500,000	84,997	9	100,063	9	118,258	10	133,008	10	122,448	8	131,187	7	173,682	9	196,136	10	192,325	9	194,608	9
£500,001–£1,000,000	96,856	10	138,865	12	176,590	15	204,317	15	221,936	14	246,504	14	273,472	14	282,270	14	277,578	13	294,586	14
£1,000,001–£2,000,000	132,436	13	149,274	13	164,010	14	176,658	14	221,690	14	316,456	18	320,880	16	348,264	17	353,796	17	348,683	16
£2,000,001–£5,000,000	129,472	13	171,286	15	197,073	17	258,700	20	326,636	21	318,302	18	417,690	21	442,167	21	468,491	22	478,405	23
£5,000,001 and above	269,814	27	288,926	25	236,728	25	226,739	17	371,127	24	465,861	26	553,960	27	512,348	25	560,412	26	555,901	26
	988,331		*1,141,729*		*1,189,732*		*1,310,616*		*1,571,763*		*1,758,360*		*2,019,588*		*2,059,074*		*2,117,609*		*2,120,641*	
Other assets	416,366		462,053		498,623		400,799		326,189		357,786		328,547		317,304		350,173		307,600	
TOTAL	1,404,697		1,603,782		1,688,355		1,711,415		1,897,952		2,116,146		2,348,135		2,376,378		2,467,782		2,428,241	

Table A.9. ICFC Ltd.: investment by region £000 (year ending September or March)

| | Cumulative total approved | | | | | | | | Total outstanding | | | | | | | | | | | | | | | | | |
| | Sept. 1947 | | Sept. 1948 | | Sept. 1949 | | Mar.ª 1950 | | Mar. 1951 | | Mar. 1952 | | Mar. 1953 | | Mar. 1954 | | Mar. 1955 | | Mar 1956 | | Mar. 1957 | | Mar. 1958 | | Mar. 1959 | |
Region	Amount	%	Amount	%	Amount	%	Amount	%	Amount	%	Amount	%	Amount	%	Amount	%	Amount	%	Amount	%	Amount	%	Amount	%	Amount	%
Scotland	543	5	634	4	792	4	778	4	771	4	981	4	1,230	5	1,244	4	1,391	5	1,859	6	1,918	6	2,242	7	2,397	7
Northern (1946–50: NE)	991	9	961	6	970	5	1,042	5	779	4	750	3	877	3	903	3	932	3	843	3	696	2	589	2	504	1
East and West Ridings (1946–50: S.Yorks.)	1,154	10	1,707	11	2,237	11	2,236	11	2,364	11	2,650	11	2,742	10	2,980	11	2,533	9	2,770	9	2,733	8	2,943	9	2,901	8
North-Western	2,038	18	2,953	20	3,683	19	4,065	20	3,497	17	4,062	17	4,663	18	4,872	18	4,877	17	4,654	14	4,454	13	4,438	13	4,315	12
North-Midland (1946–50: East Midlands)	360	3	391	3	781	4	771	4	976	5	1,334	6	1,562	6	1,538	6	1,592	6	2,038	6	2,262	7	2,144	6	2,314	6
Midland (1946–50: West Midlands)	978	9	1,071	7	1,540	8	1,692	8	2,212	11	2,661	11	3,278	12	3,563	13	3,574	13	4,056	13	4,715	14	5,245	15	5,452	15
Wales	253	2	333	2	463	2	613	3	545	3	701	3	729	3	683	2	651	2	638	2	622	2	651	2	643	2
Eastern	1,175	10	1,372	9	1,834	9	1,952	9	1,884	9	839	4	861	3	843	3	558	2	639	2	602	2	740	2	805	2
London	2,863	25	4,174	28	5,487	28	5,752	28	5,981	30	8,460	36	8,968	34	9,619	35	10,650	37	12,240	38	12,637	38	12,899	38	13,753	39
Southern	250	2	498	3	598	3	599	3	386	2	469	2	602	2	679	2	775	3	1,345	4	1,453	4	1,399	4	1,432	4
South-Eastern	349	3	468	3	688	4	783	4	586	3	606	3	593	2	557	2	723	3	718	2	713	2	708	2	826	2
Western (1946–50: South-West)	283	3	306	2	330	2	327	2	271	1	176	1	181	1	346	1	366	1	393	1	304	1	290	1	357	1
TOTAL	11,237		14,868		19,403		20,610		20,252		23,689		26,286		27,827		28,622		32,193		33,109		34,288		35,699	

ª Some double-counting with year to Sept. 1949.

403

Table A.10. ICFC Ltd.: outstanding investment by region; £000 (year ending March)

Region	1960		1961		1962		1963		1964		1965		1966		1967		1968		1969		1970		1971		1972		1973	
	Amount	%	Amount	%	Amount	%	Amount	%	Amount	%	Amount	%	Amount	%	Amount	%	Amount	%	Amount	%	Amount	%	Amount	%	Amount	%	Amount	%
Scotland	2,734	7	2,909	7	3,080	7	4,015	8	5,505	10	6,469	10	8,200	10	9,663	11	10,457	10	11,505	10	12,518	10	16,469	11	18,318	11	17,912	10
Northern Ireland	–		–		–		–		–		–		–		–		225	0	234	0	297	0	266	0	317	0	322	0
Northern	707	2	820	2	843	2	860	2	1,084	2	1,214	2	1,507	2	1,924	2	2,006	2	2,010	2	2,504	2	2,895	2	3,106	2	3,582	2
East and West Ridings	3,028	8	3,443	8	3,772	8	4,315	8	5,228	9	6,577	10	6,973	9	8,158	9	9,102	9	10,137	9	12,005	10	14,006	10	13,408	8	15,870	9
North-West	4,192	11	4,414	10	4,573	10	4,513	9	4,911	9	5,734	9	6,242	8	7,571	8	8,060	8	8,977	8	9,872	8	11,725	8	15,731	9	20,415	11
North-Midlands	2,634	7	3,334	8	3,701	8	4,516	9	5,321	9	6,137	9	7,672	10	9,163	10	10,887	11	11,351	10	12,059	10	14,288	10	15,193	9	18,093	10
Midlands	6,179	16	6,797	16	7,344	16	7,110	14	7,183	12	7,972	12	9,385	12	10,601	12	11,249	11	12,602	11	15,217	12	16,566	11	18,383	11	19,607	11
Wales	778	2	844	2	1,021	2	952	2	873	2	1,012	2	1,570	2	1,728	2	2,153	2	2,338	2	2,477	2	2,933	2	3,619	2	4,409	2
East	1,073	3	863	2	1,194	3	1,448	3	1,666	3	1,901	3	2,569	3	3,396	4	4,275	4	4,201	4	5,032	4	6,768	5	7,709	5	10,118	6
London	14,129	37	15,078	36	16,845	36	17,911	35	20,078	35	23,250	35	26,910	34	29,587	32	31,688	31	34,160	31	37,414	30	43,215	30	52,752	31	51,203	28
Southern	1,554	4	1,753	4	1,974	4	2,142	4	2,020	4	2,031	3	2,568	3	3,101	3	3,660	4	4,190	4	4,739	4	5,191	4	6,799	4	7,787	4
South-East	1,041	3	1,291	3	1,589	3	1,839	4	1,696	3	1,970	3	2,019	3	2,875	3	3,262	3	4,352	4	4,671	4	5,836	4	6,450	4	7,312	4
West	317	1	546	1	1,038	2	1,357	3	1,944	3	2,159	3	2,886	4	3,569	4	4,465	4	4,787	4	5,433	4	5,843	4	6,859	4	6,758	4
	38,366		42,092		46,974		50,978		57,509		66,426		78,501		91,336		101,489		110,844		124,238		146,001		168,644		183,388	
Channel Islands	–		–		–		–		–		–		–		–		–		7		1,112		1,367		1,716		1,953	
	38,366		42,092		46,974		50,978		57,509		66,426		78,501		91,336		101,489		110,851		125,350		147,368		170,360		185,341	
Shipping subsidiary	–		–		–		–		–		–		–		–		7,853		14,239		26,762		30,546		34,587		36,763	
Sub-total	38,366		42,092		46,974		50,978		57,509		66,426		78,501		91,336		109,342		125,090		152,112		177,914		204,947		222,104	
Provision	–		–		–		–		–		–		–		–		–		–		–		–		-5,181		-4,950	
TOTAL	38,366		42,092		46,974		50,978		57,509		66,426		78,501		91,336		109,342		125,090		152,112		177,914		199,766		217,154	

Table A.11. *ICFC Ltd.: outstanding investment by region; £000 (year ending March)*

Region	1974		1975		1976		1977[a]		1978[b]		1979		1980		1981		1982		1983	
	Amount	%	Amount	%	Amount	%	Amount	%	Amount	%	Amount	%	Amount	%	Amount	%	Amount	%	Amount	%
Scotland	21,612	10	22,970	10	n.a.	–	21,382	10	23,294	10	n.a.	–	32,635	10	40,863	10	46,196	10	48,105	10
Northern Ireland	319	0	447	0	n.a.	–	n.a.	–	519	0	n.a.	–	554	0	515	0	908	0	1,571	0
North-East	24,612	12	24,487	11	n.a.	–	25,336	12	22,588	9	n.a.	–	35,172	10	40,804	10	47,069	10	51,149	11
North-West	22,097	11	22,366	10	n.a.	–	18,946	9	23,012	10	n.a.	–	26,099	8	28,494	7	30,370	7	31,553	7
East Midlands	16,438	8	18,341	8	n.a.	–	16,457	8	18,215	8	n.a.	–	27,295	8	30,562	8	33,349	7	34,958	7
West Midlands	22,044	11	24,009	11	n.a.	–	17,649	8	19,524	8	n.a.	–	28,158	8	35,753	9	41,848	9	41,122	8
Wales	4,428	2	4,948	2	n.a.	–	5,340	3	5,533	2	n.a.	–	9,865	3	10,864	3	13,927	3	16,873	3
East Anglia	11,715	6	11,691	5	n.a.	–	11,296	5	9,176	4	n.a.	–	12,599	4	16,009	4	16,762	4	15,910	3
Greater London	55,843	27	64,885	29	n.a.	–	58,169	27	58,320	24	n.a.	–	82,878	25	101,485	25	117,652	26	123,794	26
South-East	20,679	10	19,779	9	n.a.	–	23,615	11	37,770	16	n.a.	–	56,529	17	64,576	16	65,764	14	72,890	15
South-West	7,310	3	7,089	3	n.a.	–	7,583	4	13,348	6	n.a.	–	16,864	5	19,041	5	23,644	5	26,330	5
Total UK	207,097		221,012		n.a.		205,773		231,299		n.a.		328,648		388,966		437,489		464,255	
Channel Islands and Isle of Man	2,610	1	3,922	2	n.a.	–	6,168	3	6,569	3	n.a.	–	8,476	3	8,287	2	17,218	4	15,604	3
Overseas	n.a.	–	n.a.	–	n.a.	–	n.a.	–	675	0	n.a.	–	950	0	2,809	1	3,812	1	4,638	1
	209,707		224,934		n.a.		211,941		238,543		n.a.		338,074		400,062		458,519		484,497	
Other assets	35,369		21,996		n.a.		10,908		—		n.a.		40,235		51,411		56,162		45,121	
TOTAL	245,076		246,930		n.a.		222,849		238,543		n.a.		378,309		451,473		514,681		529,618	

[a] Investment by regional office recorded in this year, so figures placed in closest region.
[b] 'Other assets' included in geographical spread.

Table A.12. *3i Group plc: outstanding investment by region; £000 (year ending March)*

Region	1984 Amount	%	1985 Amount	%	1986 Amount	%	1987 Amount	%	1988 Amount	%	1989 Amount	%	1990 Amount	%	1991 Amount	%	1992 Amount	%	1993 Amount	%
Scotland	80,120	9	91,281	9	84,245	8	89,266	8	116,778	8	112,681	7	106,331	7	107,742	6	105,071	6	119,747	7
Northern Ireland	2,818	0	3,910	0	3,802	0	3,914	0	3,984	0	4,249	0	4,276	0	5,184	0	4,867	0	7,040	0
North-East	113,793	12	124,253	12	135,289	12	122,003	10	182,979	13	161,658	10	174,368	10	166,355	10	194,199	11	188,004	10
North-West	50,447	5	52,614	5	50,550	5	56,600	5	76,917	5	107,610	7	124,939	7	113,591	7	124,381	7	141,232	8
East Midlands	83,586	9	87,977	8	71,583	7	69,481	7	81,851	6	102,586	7	119,354	7	120,658	7	140,890	8	137,256	8
West Midlands	95,917	10	104,211	10	109,135	10	88,086	10	93,234	7	105,253	7	125,717	7	120,265	7	144,952	8	137,837	8
Wales	19,297	2	24,237	2	29,477	3	34,594	3	45,497	3	41,701	3	56,617	3	59,086	3	66,678	4	64,094	4
East Anglia	33,922	4	34,149	3	42,465	4	45,895	4	54,477	4	50,736	3	51,977	3	83,695	5	86,174	5	87,961	5
Greater London	233,471	25	267,848	26	286,770	26	336,571	26	407,319	29	471,140	30	575,759	32	542,551	31	513,892	28	479,430	27
South-East	144,538	16	170,444	16	196,872	18	256,297	22	282,220	20	317,109	20	350,469	20	313,176	18	344,029	19	333,235	19
South-West	63,064	7	76,685	7	73,007	7	59,655	5	75,956	5	95,412	6	100,213	6	109,551	6	106,601	6	104,125	6
Total UK	*920,973*		*1,037,609*		*1,083,195*		*1,162,362*		*1,421,212*		*1,570,135*		*1,790,020*		*1,741,854*		*1,831,734*		*1,799,961*	
Channel Islands and Isle of Man	18,627		24,709		30,091		48,403		36,867		39,710		51,993		53,510		46,031		37,800	
Overseas	48,731		79,411		76,446		99,851		113,684		148,515		177,665		263,710		239,844		282,880	
	988,331		*1,141,729*		*1,189,732*		*1,310,616*		*1,571,763*		*1,758,360*		*2,019,678*		*2,059,074*		*2,117,609*		*2,120,641*	
Other assets	416,366		462,053		498,623		400,799		326,189		357,786		328,547		317,304		350,173		307,600	
TOTAL	1,404,697		1,603,782		1,688,355		1,711,415		1,897,952		2,116,146		2,348,225		2,376,378		2,467,782		2,428,241	

Table A.13. *ICFC Ltd.: gross investment during year by region; £000 (year ending March)*

Region	1964 Amount	%	1965 Amount	%	1966 Amount	%	1967 Amount	%	1968 Amount	%	1969 Amount	%	1970 Amount	%	1971 Amount	%	1972 Amount	%	1973 Amount	%
Scotland	1,779	16	1,576	11	2,035	11	2,271	11	2,551	13	2,609	12	2,098	8	5,169	15	2,653	8	1,475	4
Northern Ireland	–	–	–	–	–	–	–	–	225	1	–	–	64	0	–	–	23	0	7	0
North	345	3	261	2	470	3	541	3	357	2	261	1	520	2	610	2	447	1	956	3
East and West Ridings	1,234	11	1,826	13	1,212	7	2,025	10	1,388	7	2,090	9	2,955	11	2,209	6	3,553	10	4,248	12
North-West	929	8	1,200	8	1,189	6	2,040	10	1,500	8	1,594	7	2,536	10	4,013	12	3,739	11	5,935	17
North Midlands	1,351	12	1,199	8	2,517	14	2,471	12	2,670	13	1,840	8	2,111	8	3,371	10	2,909	8	4,879	14
Midlands	620	5	1,300	9	2,331	13	2,010	10	1,507	8	3,349	15	3,435	13	2,930	8	2,525	7	2,952	8
Wales	43	0	239	2	646	4	318	2	508	3	427	2	461	2	704	2	780	2	1,178	3
East	297	3	414	3	848	5	1,028	5	1,139	6	1,032	5	1,197	5	2,475	7	1,762	5	1,377	4
London	3,682	33	5,325	37	5,107	28	5,361	26	5,386	27	5,867	26	7,531	28	9,296	27	12,406	36	8,316	24
South	99	1	322	2	707	4	802	4	952	5	1,140	5	1,110	4	767	2	1,828	5	1,585	5
South-East	222	2	317	2	347	2	1,245	6	520	3	1,203	5	1,026	4	1,765	5	1,139	3	1,213	3
West	697	6	433	3	975	5	889	4	1,150	6	799	4	1,449	5	1,193	3	1,175	3	941	3
Total UK	*11,298*		*14,412*		*18,384*		*21,001*		*19,853*		*22,211*		*26,493*		*34,502*		*34,939*		*35,062*	
Channel Islands											7		1,106		275		576		421	
	11,298		*14,412*		*18,384*		*21,001*		*19,853*		*22,218*		*27,599*		*34,777*		*35,515*		*35,483*	
Shipping subsidiary	–		1,333		2,023		5,465		785		8,946		5,187		7,885		8,649		9,003	
TOTAL	11,298		15,745		20,407		26,466		20,638		31,164		32,786		42,662		44,164		44,486	

Table A.14. *ICFC Ltd.: gross investment during year by region; £000 (year ending March)*

Region	1974 Amount	%	1975 Amount	%	1976 Amount	%	1977[a] Amount	%	1978[b] Amount	%	1979 Amount	%	1980 Amount	%	1981 Amount	%	1982 Amount	%	1983 Amount	%
Scotland	5,607	13	4,938	11	n.a.		4,503	17	5,913	9	n.a.	–	9,121	9	11,128	12	8,110	7	8,050	9
Northern Ireland	0	0	150	0	n.a.		n.a.	n.a.	0	0	n.a.	–	n.a.	n.a.	n.a.	n.a.	428	0	788	1
North-East	7,119	16	3,371	7	n.a.		878	3	5,282	8	n.a.	–	11,192	11	11,559	12	11,231	10	9,645	10
North-West	3,646	8	3,469	8	n.a.		2,942	11	8,191	12	n.a.	–	6,265	6	5,676	6	6,529	6	4,919	5
East Midlands	1,502	3	3,667	8	n.a.		1,899	7	3,967	6	n.a.	–	8,679	8	5,623	6	6,831	6	5,851	6
West Midlands	4,837	11	4,719	10	n.a.		1,802	7	4,351	6	n.a.	–	10,064	10	10,825	11	9,969	9	5,115	6
Wales	510	1	1,208	3	n.a.		1,186	4	973	1	n.a.	–	4,875	5	1,560	2	3,629	3	4,668	5
East Anglia	2,004	5	2,416	5	n.a.		2,000	7	5,087	7	n.a.	–	5,882	6	3,960	4	2,803	3	3,300	4
Greater London	12,192	28	15,232	34	n.a.		7,117	27	18,296	27	n.a.	–	23,995	23	23,461	25	28,362	26	20,491	22
South-East	4,079	9	3,379	8	n.a.		2,205	8	11,477	17	n.a.	–	15,954	15	13,375	14	18,327	17	18,328	20
South-West	965	2	951	2	n.a.		1,038	4	3,009	4	n.a.	–	5,625	5	4,914	5	6,293	6	6,405	7
Total UK	*42,461*		*43,500*		*n.a.*		*25,570*		*66,546*		*n.a.*		*101,652*		*92,081*		*102,512*		*87,560*	
Channel Islands and Isle of Man	695	2	1,549	3	n.a.		1,266	5	1,544	2	n.a.	–	2,859	3	2,363	2	5,551	5	1,667	2
Overseas	0	0	0	0	n.a.		0	0	0	0	n.a.	–	15	0	1,260	1	1,656	2	3,489	4
	43,156		*45,049*		*n.a.*		*26,836*		*68,090*		*n.a.*		*104,526*		*95,704*		*109,719*		*92,716*	
Other assets	2,095		6,212		n.a.		4,491		n.a.		n.a.		28,643		24,459		19,756		20,536	
TOTAL	45,251		51,261		n.a.		31,327		68,090		n.a.		133,169		120,163		129,475		113,252	

[a] Investment by regional office recorded in this year, so figures placed in closest region.
[b] 'Other assets' included in geographical spread.

Table A.15. *3i Group plc: gross investment during year by region; £000 (year ending March)*

Region	1984 Amount	%	1985 Amount	%	1986 Amount	%	1987 Amount	%	1988 Amount	%	1989 Amount	%	1990 Amount	%	1991 Amount	%	1992 Amount	%	1993 Amount	%
Scotland	8,106	5	21,995	10	17,604	7	24,016	9	21,099	5	21,413	5	26,223	6	21,261	8	22,074	6	33,440	13
Northern Ireland	826	0	1,468	1	192	0	1,263	0	475	0	330	0	370	0	1,260	0	673	0	3,568	1
North-East	11,280	6	20,038	9	34,568	15	18,759	7	88,818	20	34,934	8	38,627	8	30,996	11	46,729	14	26,626	10
North-West	6,427	4	10,668	5	9,596	4	13,224	5	12,992	3	33,319	8	31,666	7	12,270	5	43,241	13	26,088	10
East Midlands	13,950	8	13,804	6	11,787	5	12,850	5	28,613	6	26,617	6	51,340	11	20,801	8	33,597	10	13,955	5
West Midlands	20,814	12	16,030	7	16,013	7	15,624	6	29,182	6	29,802	7	24,999	5	16,941	6	40,205	12	13,216	5
Wales	2,696	2	7,205	3	7,725	3	8,123	3	19,565	4	15,518	4	15,912	3	11,659	4	11,416	3	8,288	3
East Anglia	7,177	4	4,261	2	14,030	6	9,086	3	15,485	3	12,083	3	22,406	5	9,119	3	11,766	3	17,661	7
Greater London	51,452	29	73,404	32	79,407	33	84,244	31	146,753	33	146,224	34	144,733	32	65,462	24	42,956	13	39,076	15
South-East	45,939	26	42,679	18	34,933	15	73,364	27	66,145	15	88,191	20	76,225	17	57,275	21	77,678	23	62,726	24
South-West	9,794	5	19,319	8	12,417	5	15,358	6	21,516	6	25,038	6	22,158	6	24,409	9	12,183	4	12,412	5
Total UK	*178,461*		*230,871*		*238,272*		*275,911*		*450,643*		*433,469*		*454,659*		*271,453*		*342,518*		*257,056*	
Channel Islands and Isle of Man	3,736		9,291		5,525		4,697		13,044		19,031		14,388		8,758		2,941		1,674	
Overseas	11,467		27,398		16,308		52,212		39,442		52,356		85,304		77,165		49,436		42,578	
	193,664		*267,560*		*260,105*		*332,820*		*503,129*		*504,856*		*554,351*		*357,376*		*394,895*		*301,308*	
Other assets	69,734		77,819		58,226		36,000		34,000		64,000		42,824		24,954		19,600		9,163	
TOTAL	263,398		345,379		318,331		368,820		537,129		568,856		597,175		382,330		414,495		310,471	

Table A.16. ICFC Ltd.: investment by industry, £000 (year ending September or March)

Industry	Cumulative total approved										Total outstanding																	
	Sept. 1946		Sept. 1947		Sept. 1948		Sept. 1949		Mar.ᵃ 1950		Mar. 1951		Mar. 1952		Mar. 1953		Mar. 1954		Mar. 1955		Mar 1956		Mar. 1957		Mar. 1958		Mar. 1959	
	Amount	%	Amount	%	Amount	%	Amount	%	Amount	%	Amount	%	Amount	%	Amount	%	Amount	%	Amount	%	Amount	%	Amount	%	Amount	%	Amount	%
Agriculture and forestry	129	3	5	0	185	1	185	1	185	1	328	2	321	2	377	1	341	1	314	1	286	1	265	1	252	1	239	1
Mining and quarrying	0	0	7	0	7	0	7	0	7	0	0	0	0	0	15	0	15	0	16	0	70	0	87	0	82	0	136	0
Metal manufacture	350	7	540	5	573	5	641	3	641	3	895	4	1,301	5	1,520	6	1,600	6	1,628	6	1,766	5	2,135	6	2,448	7	2,539	7
Chemicals and allied industries	218	4	821	7	1,281	9	1,563	8	1,729	8	1,836	9	1,799	8	2,477	9	2,599	9	2,473	9	1,630	5	1,680	5	1,613	5	1,624	5
Mechanical engineering	1,259	25	2,196	20	3,025	20	3,907	20	4,248	21	3,876	19	4,248	18	4,857	18	4,801	17	4,455	16	5,524	17	6,033	18	6,396	19	6,685	19
Electrical engineering	357	7	898	8	1,081	7	1,689	9	1,617	8	1,464	7	1,774	7	1,664	6	1,618	6	1,320	6	1,659	5	1,645	5	1,559	5	1,556	4
Vehicles and shipbuilding	461	9	781	7	942	7	1,296	7	1,295	6	1,281	6	833	4	1,199	4	1,496	5	1,498	5	1,606	5	1,554	5	1,560	5	1,532	4
Other metal goods	654	13	1,644	15	2,003	13	2,348	13	2,385	12	1,622	8	1,474	6	1,510	6	1,587	6	1,767	6	2,045	6	2,242	7	2,394	7	2,281	6
Food, drink, and tobacco	86	2	224	2	224	2	196	1	610	3	671	3	1,145	5	1,264	5	1,375	5	1,642	5	2,037	6	2,024	6	1,940	6	1,946	5
Textiles	260	5	795	7	1,132	7	1,535	8	1,807	8	1,873	9	2,873	12	3,330	13	3,836	13	3,711	14	3,855	12	3,602	11	3,491	10	3,227	9
Clothing, footwear and leather	213	4	324	3	400	3	503	3	678	3	820	4	1,162	5	1,110	5	1,061	4	1,232	4	1,472	4	1,418	4	1,426	4	1,435	4
Bricks, pottery, glass, etc.	361	7	525	5	581	5	1,153	4	1,174	6	779	4	817	4	675	3	701	3	759	3	955	3	963	3	890	3	875	2
Timber, furniture, etc.	20	0	58	1	107	1	150	1	686	3	562	3	674	3	765	3	604	3	625	2	678	2	655	2	688	2	658	2
Paper, printing, and publishing	185	4	355	3	492	3	695	3	692	4	737	4	731	3	812	3	950	3	1,429	3	1,857	5	1,876	6	1,972	6	2,069	6
Other manufacturing	190	4	580	5	721	5	817	5	892	4	977	4	1,122	5	1,243	5	1,415	5	1,443	5	1,413	5	1,396	4	1,407	4	1,475	4
Construction	57	1	146	1	191	1	580	3	602	3	459	3	804	2	890	3	991	3	1,068	3	1,194	4	1,258	4	1,459	4	1,701	5
Distribution	223	4	1,263	11	1,726	12	1,752	12	961	9	1,386	5	1,691	7	1,411	7	1,542	5	1,826	6	2,149	6	2,124	7	2,464	6	3,006	8
Hotel and catering	–	0	6	0	6	0	210	1	180	1	158	1	188	1	180	1	162	1	150	1	140	0	128	0	116	0	95	0
Transport and communication	8	0	8	0	163	1	63	0	108	0	384	2	438	2	545	2	507	2	476	2	738	2	740	2	799	2	902	3
Other services	40	1	61	1	28	0	113	1	113	1	144	1	294	1	442	1	626	2	790	2	1,119	2	1,284	3	1,332	4	1,718	5
TOTAL	5,071		11,237		14,868		19,403		20,610		20,252		23,689		26,286		27,827		28,622		32,193		33,109		34,288		35,699	

ᵃ Some double-counting with year to Sept. 1949.

410

Table A.17. ICFC Ltd.: outstanding investment by industry; £000 (year ending March)

Industry	1960		1961		1962		1963		1964		1965		1966		1967		1968		1969		1970		1971		1972		1973	
	Amount	%	Amount	%	Amount	%	Amount	%	Amount	%	Amount	%	Amount	%	Amount	%	Amount	%	Amount	%	Amount	%	Amount	%	Amount	%	Amount	%
Agriculture and forestry	563	1	562	1	518	1	505	1	478	1	358	1	325	0	543	1	548	1	713	1	875	1	1,119	1	1,193	1	1,082	1
Mining and quarrying	184	0	285	1	270	1	287	1	353	1	337	1	370	0	443	0	838	1	1,011	1	1,202	1	1,832	1	1,722	1	2,411	1
Metal manufacture	2,894	8	2,968	7	3,260	7	3,201	6	3,639	6	4,035	6	4,954	6	5,213	6	5,343	5	5,166	5	5,609	4	6,823	5	7,273	4	6,764	4
Chemicals and allied industries	1,401	4	1,511	4	1,537	3	1,612	3	1,614	3	1,656	2	1,700	2	2,099	2	2,351	2	2,580	2	3,036	2	3,348	2	3,417	2	3,295	2
Engineering and electrical goods of which:	8,868	23	9,405	22	9,544	20	9,939	19	11,153	19	15,029	23	16,981	22	19,567	21	22,352	22	25,216	23	28,518	23	33,438	23	39,013	23	43,085	23
Mechanical engineering	6,590		6,859		7,002		7,370		8,482		n.a.		n.a.		n.a.		n.a.		n.a.		n.a.		n.a.		n.a.		n.a.	
Electrical and electronic engineering	2,278		2,546		2,542		2,569		2,671		n.a.		n.a.		n.a.		n.a.		n.a.		n.a.		n.a.		n.a.		n.a.	
Vehicles and shipbuilding	1,423	4	1,350	3	1,399	3	1,316	3	1,282	2	1,415	2	1,973	3	2,286	3	2,913	3	2,653	2	3,722	3	4,084	3	3,644	2	3,357	2
Other metal goods	2,220	6	2,161	5	2,802	6	2,561	5	2,964	5	2,853	4	3,286	4	4,721	5	5,191	5	5,733	5	5,990	5	6,204	4	6,403	4	6,462	3
Food, drink, and tobacco	2,299	6	2,121	5	2,327	5	2,343	5	2,450	4	2,732	4	2,851	4	3,103	3	3,399	3	3,430	3	3,235	3	3,580	2	3,933	2	4,521	2
Textiles	3,148	8	3,235	8	3,280	7	3,613	7	4,370	8	4,513	7	5,028	6	5,607	6	6,046	6	6,546	6	7,199	6	7,595	5	8,972	5	9,658	5
Clothing, footwear, and leather	1,581	4	1,742	4	2,088	4	2,527	5	2,116	4	2,110	3	2,491	3	2,855	3	3,050	3	3,290	3	3,387	3	3,493	2	3,651	2	5,505	3
Bricks, pottery, glass, etc.	795	2	1,102	3	1,195	3	1,431	3	1,798	3	2,092	3	2,590	3	3,358	4	3,430	3	3,182	3	3,270	3	4,049	3	4,097	2	3,475	2
Timber, furniture, etc.	656	2	1,064	3	1,092	2	1,202	2	1,465	3	1,455	2	1,959	2	2,364	3	3,029	3	3,232	3	3,414	3	3,655	2	4,241	2	5,458	3
Paper, printing, and publishing	2,315	6	2,557	6	3,014	6	3,266	6	3,097	5	3,560	5	4,168	5	5,526	6	6,908	7	7,196	6	7,824	6	8,846	6	10,168	6	9,853	5
Other manufacturing	1,393	3	1,316	3	1,950	4	2,138	4	2,738	5	1,313	2	1,543	2	1,792	2	2,168	2	2,767	2	2,983	2	3,003	2	3,706	2	3,850	2
Construction	2,322	6	2,940	7	3,172	7	3,647	7	4,006	7	5,287	8	6,428	8	7,496	8	8,054	8	8,585	8	9,273	7	10,615	7	12,185	7	13,102	7
Distribution	3,273	9	3,805	9	4,700	10	5,698	11	6,343	11	7,955	12	9,661	12	11,462	13	13,298	13	15,417	14	18,042	14	19,061	13	20,000	12	22,113	12
Hotel and catering[a]	71	0	414	1	528	1	475	1	747	1	n.a.		n.a.		n.a.		n.a.		n.a.		2,401	2	2,735	2	3,636	2	5,396	3
Transport and communication	909	2	1,052	2	1,241	3	1,205	2	1,971	3	1,950	3	2,686	3	3,290	4	2,999	3	3,786	3	4,412	4	8,361	6	9,900	6	10,143	5
Other services	2,051	5	2,502	6	3,057	7	4,012	8	4,925	9	7,776	12	9,507	12	9,611	11	9,572	9	10,348	9	10,958	9	15,527	11	23,206	14	25,811	14
Sub-total	*38,366*		*42,092*		*46,974*		*50,978*		*57,509*		*66,426*		*78,501*		*91,336*		*101,489*		*110,851*		*125,350*		*147,368*		*170,360*		*185,341*	
Shipping subsidiary	0		0		0		0		0		0		0		0		7,853		14,239		26,762		30,546		34,587		36,763	
Sub-total	*38,366*		*42,092*		*46,974*		*50,978*		*57,509*		*66,426*		*78,501*		*91,336*		*109,342*		*125,090*		*152,112*		*177,914*		*204,947*		*222,104*	
Provision	0		0		0		0		0		0		0		0		0		0		0		0		-5,181		-4,950	
TOTAL	38,366		42,092		46,974		50,978		57,509		66,426		78,501		91,336		109,342		125,090		152,112		177,914		199,766		217,154	

a Separate breakdown not available for 1964–67 – included in 'Other services'.

Table A.18. *ICFC Ltd.: outstanding investment by industry; £000 (year ending March)*

Industry	1978[a] Amount	%	1979 Amount	%	1980 Amount	%	1981 Amount	%	1982[b] Amount	%	1983[b] Amount	%
Agriculture and forestry	1,777	1	n.a.	—	2,866	1	3,128	1	5,921	1	5,307	1
Energy and water	711	0	n.a.	—	1,209	0	1,199	0	2,021	0	1,378	0
Mining and quarrying	1,408	1	n.a.	—	2,153	1	2,271	1	2,568	1	2,799	1
Metal manufacture	6,408	3	n.a.	—	7,350	2	9,811	2	32,250	7	34,744	7
Chemicals and allied industries	5,445	2	n.a.	—	8,038	2	9,605	2	12,612	3	13,717	3
Engineering and electrical goods	38,009	16	n.a.	—	52,684	16	65,669	16	87,524	19	94,899	20
of which:												
Mechanical engineering	23,408				27,846		34,809		47,355		52,195	
Instrument engineering	3,353				7,806		8,943		11,666		11,451	
Electrical and electronic engineering	11,248				17,032		21,917		28,503		31,253	
Vehicles and shipbuilding	3,619	2	n.a.	—	5,829	2	5,456	1	8,681	2	9,784	2
Other metal goods	10,868	5	n.a.	—	15,312	5	19,100	5				
Food, drink, and tobacco	12,827	5	n.a.	—	12,740	4	15,051	4	16,591	4	17,057	4
Textiles	9,870	4	n.a.	—	10,148	3	10,163	3	10,465	2	10,810	2
Clothing, footwear, and leather	4,286	2	n.a.	—	10,006	3	10,014	3	9,953	2	10,527	2
Bricks, pottery, glass, etc.	5,764	2	n.a.	—	5,947	2	7,003	2				
Timber, furniture, etc.	7,832	3	n.a.	—	9,971	3	10,385	3	11,092	2	11,432	2
Paper, printing and publishing	12,429	5	n.a.	—	20,444	6	26,371	7	29,047	6	32,842	7
Other manufacturing	8,804	4	n.a.	—	11,470	3	15,327	4	19,464	4	19,364	4
Construction	13,730	6	n.a.	—	23,201	7	26,051	7	12,617	3	11,833	2
Distribution	36,067	15	n.a.	—	47,176	14	50,799	13	60,779	13	64,697	13
Hotel and catering	8,213	3	n.a.	—	15,413	5	21,801	5	29,688	6	32,588	7
Transport and communication	10,309	4	n.a.	—	18,073	5	20,700	5	12,863	3	10,580	2
Other services	40,167	17	n.a.	—	58,044	17	70,158	18	94,383	21	100,139	21
	238,543		n.a.		*338,074*		*400,062*		*458,519*		*484,497*	
Other assets	n.a.		n.a.		—		—		56,162		45,121	
TOTAL	238,543		n.a.		338,074		400,062		514,681		529,618	

[a] 'Other assets' included in industry spread.
[b] 'Other metal goods' included in 'Metal manufacture'; 'Bricks, pottery, glass, etc.' included in 'Chemicals and allied industries'.

Table A.19. 3i Group plc: outstanding investment by industry; £000 (year ending March)

Industry	1984 Amount	%	1985 Amount	%	1986 Amount	%	1987 Amount	%	1988 Amount	%	1989 Amount	%	1990 Amount	%	1991 Amount	%	1992 Amount	%	1993 Amount	%
Agriculture and forestry	4,680	0	5,317	0	5,879	0	8,502	1	10,404	1	11,086	1	10,660	1	10,006	0	10,451	0	11,213	1
Energy and water	18,675	2	28,899	3	24,504	2	21,258	2	20,066	2	27,888	2	22,740	1	23,095	1	27,065	1	33,745	2
Mining and quarrying	4,027	0	3,519	0	7,534	0	10,159	1	9,449	1	14,841	1	9,120	0	8,338	0	11,798	1	14,219	1
Metal and other mineral manufacture	86,187	9	85,929	8	78,378	7	85,890	7	131,759	8	101,763	6	108,366	5	75,712	4	67,486	3	78,745	4
Chemicals and allied industries	47,061	5	56,790	5	59,737	5	58,117	5	69,208	4	87,944	5	85,060	4	61,920	3	60,687	3	57,339	3
Mechanical engineering	85,844	9	84,152	7	88,188	7	81,591	7	114,171	7	118,892	7	116,692	6	171,814	8	210,949	10	189,499	9
Manufacture: office and data processing machines	12,247	1	15,110	1	14,913	1	20,180	2	25,627	2	24,449	1	30,027	1	32,453	2	23,815	1	18,563	1
Electrical and electronic engineering	44,298	4	50,195	4	78,974	7	106,467	8	93,294	6	108,910	6	92,950	5	106,041	5	93,963	4	87,786	4
Vehicles and transport manufacture	11,299	1	11,062	1	19,486	2	22,423	2	25,209	2	35,968	2	48,450	2	43,985	2	52,840	2	56,416	3
Instrument engineering	13,240	1	12,929	1	12,024	1	26,524	2	28,576	2	34,249	2	28,398	1	28,993	1	20,760	1	22,037	1
Food, drink, and tobacco	74,652	8	75,341	7	64,654	5	59,504	5	74,296	5	85,019	5	97,558	5	83,742	4	95,808	5	93,440	4
Textiles	17,023	2	17,228	2	20,951	2	19,304	1	25,944	2	33,041	2	36,743	2	34,594	2	31,388	1	30,415	1
Clothing and footwear	10,834	1	12,515	1	14,101	1	12,415	1	16,113	1	18,227	1	24,069	1	21,851	1	24,388	1	20,993	1
Timber and furniture	15,575	2	17,149	2	16,387	1	22,395	2	65,930	4	52,763	3	49,584	2	48,967	2	44,885	2	46,914	2
Paper, printing and publishing	40,197	4	45,129	4	55,429	5	64,193	5	58,926	4	117,549	7	120,931	6	100,801	5	111,788	5	125,063	6
Other manufacturing and repairs	85,767	9	101,665	9	82,713	7	52,199	4	49,710	3	55,769	3	68,820	3	84,739	4	82,851	4	82,122	4
Construction	30,619	3	36,910	3	33,711	3	40,190	3	49,653	3	46,258	3	40,355	2	55,244	2	49,017	2	59,657	3
Wholesale distribution	51,448	5	66,799	6	64,399	6	69,632	5	89,570	6	97,509	6	177,805	9	179,202	9	199,535	9	201,879	10
Retail distribution	48,562	5	72,551	6	62,868	5	75,598	6	84,605	5	109,469	6	186,906	9	180,328	9	187,772	9	204,093	10
Hotel and catering	74,553	8	85,434	7	72,043	6	78,641	6	129,826	8	124,802	7	121,175	6	144,129	7	133,656	6	125,297	6
Transport and communication	67,187	7	71,686	6	69,225	6	74,580	6	61,044	4	62,513	4	90,013	4	83,627	4	104,724	5	111,975	5
Financial and other business services	118,556	12	152,286	13	190,557	16	238,151	18	273,708	17	314,245	18	378,866	19	398,141	19	389,415	18	364,357	17
Health, education, and community services	14,242	1	16,505	1	19,935	2	34,515	3	34,923	2	37,135	2	39,438	2	47,118	2	48,901	2	52,934	2
Recreation and personal services	11,558	1	16,629	1	33,142	3	28,188	2	29,752	2	38,071	2	34,952	2	34,234	2	33,667	2	31,940	2
	988,331		*1,141,729*		*1,189,732*		*1,310,616*		*1,571,763*		*1,758,360*		*2,019,678*		*2,059,074*		*2,117,609*		*2,120,641*	
Other assets	416,366		462,053		498,623		400,799		326,189		357,786		328,547		317,304		350,173		307,600	
TOTAL	1,404,697		1,603,782		1,688,355		1,711,415		1,897,952		2,116,146		2,348,225		2,376,378		2,467,782		2,428,241	

Table A.20. ICFC Ltd.: gross investment during year by industry; £000 (year ending March)

Industry	1964 Amount	%	1965 Amount	%	1966 Amount	%	1967 Amount	%	1968 Amount	%	1969 Amount	%	1970 Amount	%	1971 Amount	%	1972 Amount	%	1973 Amount	%
Agriculture and forestry	23	0	31	0	45	0	245	1	35	0	133	1	207	1	303	1	161	0	22	0
Mining and quarrying	134	1	85	1	81	0	149	1	518	3	295	1	534	2	821	2	263	1	977	3
Metal manufacture	793	7	512	4	1,254	7	606	3	593	3	593	3	951	3	1,875	5	937	3	632	2
Chemicals and allied industries	90	1	272	2	532	3	568	3	461	2	429	2	710	3	855	2	301	1	266	1
Engineering and electrical goods	2,873	25	3,475	24	3,442	19	4,801	23	4,918	25	6,547	29	6,494	24	8,449	24	8,113	23	7,078	20
Vehicles and shipbuilding	237	2	369	3	516	3	807	4	717	4	294	1	1,344	5	312	1	939	3	189	1
Other metal goods	649	6	438	3	893	5	1,617	8	836	4	1,090	5	1,003	4	1,018	3	751	2	1,042	3
Food, drink, and tobacco	259	2	382	3	418	2	680	3	511	3	569	3	156	1	941	3	731	2	1,041	3
Textiles	876	8	703	5	1,077	6	1,020	5	947	5	1,198	5	1,474	5	1,003	3	1,601	5	2,072	6
Clothing, footwear, and leather	47	0	104	1	553	3	565	3	498	3	526	2	425	2	424	1	215	1	2,153	6
Bricks, pottery, glass, etc.	515	5	480	3	666	4	1,091	5	338	2	606	3	637	2	950	3	441	1	274	1
Timber, furniture, etc.	357	3	190	1	759	4	608	3	882	4	336	2	493	2	539	2	692	2	1,817	5
Paper, printing and publishing	256	2	796	6	1,025	6	1,788	9	1,745	9	1,009	5	1,377	5	1,636	5	1,957	6	644	2
Other manufacturing	230	2	425	3	569	3	659	3	495	2	887	4	572	2	568	2	1,189	3	539	2
Construction	518	5	1,560	11	1,983	11	1,551	7	1,295	7	1,714	8	1,693	6	2,194	6	3,115	9	2,764	8
Distribution	1,107	10	2,171	15	2,385	13	2,381	11	2,396	12	3,314	15	3,588	13	2,575	7	2,471	7	3,800	11
Hotel and catering[a]	n.a.	—	n.a.	—	n.a.	—	n.a.	—	454	2	355	2	366	1	593	2	1,218	3	1,654	5
Transport and communication	839	7	185	1	911	5	795	4	512	3	867	4	938	3	4,034	12	2,034	6	886	2
Other services	1,495	13	2,234	16	1,275	7	1,070	5	1,702	9	1,456	7	4,637	17	5,687	16	8,386	24	7,633	22
	11,298		*14,412*		*18,384*		*21,001*		*19,853*		*22,218*		*27,599*		*34,777*		*35,515*		*35,483*	
Shipping subsidiary	0		1,333		2,023		5,465		785		8,946		5,187		7,885		8,649		9,003	
TOTAL	11,298		15,745		20,407		26,466		20,638		31,164		32,786		42,662		44,164		44,486	

[a] Separate breakdown not available for 1964–67; included in 'Other services'.

Table A.21. *ICFC Ltd.: gross investment during year; £000 (year ending March)*

Industry	1974 Amount	%	1975 Amount	%	1976 Amount	%	1977ᵃ Amount	%	1978ᵃ Amount	%	1979 Amount	%	1980 Amount	%	1981 Amount	%	1982ᵇ Amount	%	1983ᵇ Amount	%
Agriculture and forestry	76	0	150	0	n.a.	n.a.	363	—	636	1	n.a.	—	1,034	1	393	0	917	1	696	1
Energy and water	0	0	0	0	n.a.	n.a.	7	0	254	0	n.a.	—	0	—	30	0	849	1	169	0
Mining and quarrying	46	0	214	0	n.a.	n.a.	194	—	279	0	n.a.	—	783	1	412	0	47	0	637	1
Metal manufacture	917	2	913	2	n.a.	n.a.	685	2	1,583	2	n.a.	—	2,349	2	2,528	3	6,724	6	5,952	6
Chemicals and allied industries	334	1	644	1	n.a.	n.a.	432	—	1,564	2	n.a.	—	3,153	3	2,165	2	3,664	3	2,108	2
Engineering and electrical goods	6,965	16	4,845	11	n.a.	n.a.	4,573	15	9,543	14	n.a.	—	16,603	16	16,250	17	22,942	21	17,388	19
of which:																				
Mechanical engineering	n.a.		n.a.		n.a.		2,782		5,569		n.a.		7,083		9,055		14,118		7,653	
Instrument engineering	n.a.		n.a.		n.a.		386		570		n.a.		3,176		2,171		1,581		1,283	
Electrical and electronic engineering	n.a.		n.a.		n.a.		1,405		3,404		n.a.		6,344		5,024		7,243		8,452	
Vehicles and shipbuilding	495	1	585	1	n.a.	n.a.	215	—	1,333	2	n.a.	—	2,013	2	1,069	1	2,428	2	961	1
Other metal goods	2,549	6	1,706	4	n.a.	n.a.	1,898	6	2,441	4	n.a.	—	4,681	4	5,043	5	6,695	6	2,298	2
Food, drink, and tobacco	1,818	4	2,939	7	n.a.	n.a.	1,585	5	5,186	8	n.a.	—	3,860	4	2,833	3	3,670	3	1,519	2
Textiles	3,623	8	2,256	5	n.a.	n.a.	1,809	6	1,344	2	n.a.	—	1,870	2	1,417	1	1,511	1	2,580	3
Clothing, footwear and leather	950	2	755	2	n.a.	n.a.	797	3	621	1	n.a.	—	2,536	2	1,474	2				
Bricks, pottery, glass, etc.	555	1	766	2	n.a.	n.a.	814	3	3,042	4	n.a.	—	2,780	3	1,709	2				
Timber, furniture, etc.	1,067	2	1,079	2	n.a.	n.a.	1,455	5	2,561	4	n.a.	—	1,911	2	1,874	2	1,427	1	2,532	3
Paper, printing and publishing	2,112	5	1,818	4	n.a.	n.a.	1,756	6	2,623	4	n.a.	—	9,020	9	7,416	8	5,410	5	6,551	7
Other manufacturing	1,082	3	980	2	n.a.	n.a.	1,805	6	3,072	5	n.a.	—	2,887	3	5,362	6	5,831	5	3,667	4
Construction	3,002	7	3,931	9	n.a.	n.a.	2,182	7	2,566	4	n.a.	—	9,741	9	5,728	6	2,168	2	1,681	2
Distribution	3,515	8	3,309	7	n.a.	n.a.	5,959	19	12,049	18	n.a.	—	14,186	14	9,247	10	14,179	13	12,451	13
Hotel and catering	1,701	4	1,466	3	n.a.	n.a.	400	—	2,020	3	n.a.	—	5,447	5	7,828	8	5,966	5	5,280	6
Transport and communication	3,265	8	2,489	6	n.a.	n.a.	1,333	4	3,830	6	n.a.	—	6,651	6	3,294	3	1,406	1	2,257	2
Other services	9,084	21	14,204	32	n.a.	n.a.	3,065	10	11,543	17	n.a.	—	13,021	12	19,632	21	23,885	22	23,989	26
	43,156		*45,049*		n.a.		*31,327*		*68,090*		n.a.		*104,526*		*95,704*		*109,719*		*92,716*	
Other assets	2,095		6,212		n.a.		—		—		n.a.		28,643		24,459		19,756		20,536	
TOTAL	45,251		51,261		n.a.		31,327		68,090		n.a.		133,169		120,163		129,475		113,252	

ᵃ 'Other assets' included in industry spread. ᵇ 'Other metal goods' included in 'Metal manufacture'; 'Bricks, pottery, glass, etc.', included in 'Chemicals and allied industries'.

Table A.22. 3i Group plc: gross investment during year by industry; £000 (year ending March)

Industry	1984 Amount	1984 %	1985 Amount	1985 %	1986 Amount	1986 %	1987 Amount	1987 %	1988 Amount	1988 %	1989 Amount	1989 %	1990 Amount	1990 %	1991 Amount	1991 %	1992 Amount	1992 %	1993 Amount	1993 %
Agriculture and forestry	859	0	1,608	1	1,000	0	3,672	1	1,355	0	4,446	1	1,136	1	1,027	0	1,585	0	1,794	1
Energy and water	7,595	4	11,309	4	4,244	2	1,014	0	3,846	1	13,606	3	3,536	1	728	0	7,565	2	8,474	3
Mining and quarrying	1,363	1	814	0	4,159	2	4,382	1	518	0	5,346	1	730	0	57	0	3,925	1	3,000	1
Metal and other mineral manufacture	5,373	3	11,692	3	15,889	6	10,189	3	49,436	10	9,689	2	35,014	6	12,723	4	12,617	3	4,914	2
Chemicals and allied industries	20,692	11	14,582	5	2,949	1	4,781	1	14,373	3	20,821	4	20,452	4	15,693	4	21,386	5	13,914	5
Mechanical engineering	12,740	7	14,706	5	18,178	7	12,967	4	34,784	7	27,426	5	23,160	5	40,215	11	43,997	11	20,893	7
Manufacture: office and data processing machines	5,475	3	3,953	1	3,784	1	5,174	2	12,264	2	8,634	2	14,282	3	2,559	1	3,709	1	3,579	1
Electrical and electronic engineering	18,013	9	18,982	7	30,851	10	33,380	10	17,605	3	20,748	4	25,374	5	15,121	4	18,666	5	11,551	4
Vehicles and transport manufacture	5,885	3	1,652	1	9,917	4	4,411	1	8,072	2	9,864	2	24,301	4	4,354	1	9,225	2	7,949	3
Instrument engineering	1,842	1	2,607	1	2,843	1	21,729	7	3,969	1	8,353	2	6,650	1	5,704	2	1,832	0	2,017	1
Food, drink, and tobacco	6,766	3	10,711	4	7,763	3	6,971	2	31,594	6	15,585	3	15,942	3	14,828	4	19,424	5	16,049	5
Textiles	2,833	1	2,297	1	5,164	2	1,402	0	7,449	1	10,915	2	8,214	1	3,973	1	2,064	1	2,637	1
Clothing and footwear	1,899	1	4,331	2	2,623	1	710	0	5,861	1	5,261	1	7,940	1	3,800	1	3,271	1	1,942	1
Timber and furniture	3,447	2	4,078	2	5,382	2	11,417	3	48,941	10	8,104	2	8,475	2	5,501	2	2,964	1	3,940	1
Paper, printing and publishing	6,419	3	11,829	4	12,004	5	12,812	4	16,852	3	68,447	14	16,366	3	10,159	3	27,522	7	26,512	9
Other manufacturing and repairs	4,557	2	15,783	6	7,248	3	15,742	5	20,922	4	13,547	3	11,514	2	23,256	7	15,882	4	13,858	5
Construction	2,216	1	13,242	5	11,684	4	8,834	3	14,917	3	10,997	2	9,279	2	22,346	6	12,035	3	13,736	5
Wholesale distribution	10,979	6	8,168	3	15,733	6	25,026	8	20,103	4	25,954	5	73,386	13	37,951	11	47,869	12	23,330	8
Retail distribution	13,813	7	16,645	6	10,583	4	23,491	7	27,402	5	42,614	8	101,275	18	19,784	6	34,557	9	34,850	12
Hotel and catering	18,749	10	20,783	8	10,123	4	10,692	3	64,078	13	33,606	7	17,132	3	29,630	8	10,607	3	6,416	2
Transport and communication	8,085	4	11,833	4	12,520	5	11,896	4	13,016	3	11,199	2	33,914	6	13,926	4	39,842	10	20,346	7
Financial and other business services	28,062	14	52,421	20	42,864	16	77,990	23	73,590	15	101,768	20	78,970	14	62,844	18	41,476	11	40,675	13
Health, education, and community services	2,911	2	4,838	2	5,025	2	17,830	5	7,822	2	7,994	2	8,433	2	4,799	1	8,626	2	16,251	5
Recreation and personal services	3,091	2	8,696	3	17,575	7	6,308	2	4,360	1	20,932	4	8,876	2	6,398	2	4,249	1	2,681	1
	193,664		267,560		260,105		332,820		503,129		505,856		554,351		357,376		394,895		301,308	
Other assets	69,734		77,819		58,226										24,954		19,600		9,163	
TOTAL	263,398		345,379		318,331		332,820		503,129		505,856		554,351		382,330		414,495		310,471	

Table A.23. *ICFC Ltd.: loans and shares outstanding; £000 (year ending September or March)*

	Sept. 1948 Amount	%	Sept. 1949 Amount	%	Mar. 1950 Amount	%	Mar. 1951 Amount	%	Mar. 1952 Amount	%	Mar. 1953 Amount	%	Mar. 1954 Amount	%	Mar. 1955 Amount	%	Mar. 1956 Amount	%	Mar. 1957 Amount	%	Mar. 1958 Amount	%	Mar. 1959 Amount	%
Loans – secured	3,873	55	5,410	57	5,604	56	7,341	62	9,287	64	10,785	65	10,764	65	10,709	64	11,967	64	12,466	65	13,975	68	15,124	70
Loans – unsecured	3,209	45	4,095	43	4,319	44	4,415	38	5,274	36	5,690	35	5,791	35	6,108	36	6,709	36	6,720	35	6,581	32	6,579	30
Total loans	7,082	66	9,505	63	9,923	63	11,756	58	14,561	61	16,476	63	16,555	59	16,817	59	18,676	58	19,186	58	20,557	60	21,703	61
Preference shares	2,888	27	4,232	28	4,477	29	6,722	33	7,286	33	7,801	30	8,530	31	9,389	33	10,561	33	10,813	33	10,547	31	10,546	30
Equity	801	7	1,333	9	1,268	8	1,775	9	1,842	9	2,010	8	2,741	10	2,417	8	2,957	9	3,110	9	3,185	9	3,450	10
TOTAL	10,771		15,070		15,668		20,252		23,689		26,286		27,827		28,622		32,193		33,109		34,288		35,699	

Table A.24. *ICFC Ltd.: loans and shares; £000 (year ending March)*

	1960 Amount	%	1961 Amount	%	1962 Amount	%	1963 Amount	%	1964 Amount	%	1965 Amount	%	1966 Amount	%	1967 Amount	%	1968 Amount	%	1969 Amount	%	1970 Amount	%	1971 Amount	%	1972 Amount	%	1973 Amount	%
Loans – secured	16,005	70	18,261	74	22,595	80	25,695	82	29,075	84	33,227	85	42,213	87	51,699	88	58,319	90	64,605	91	71,738	91	80,129	87	84,481	89	85,772	85
Loans – unsecured	6,878	30	6,559	26	5,598	20	5,519	18	5,733	16	5,709	15	6,414	13	7,185	12	6,276	10	6,008	9	6,939	9	11,497	13	10,344	11	15,450	15
Total loans	22,883	60	24,820	59	28,193	59	31,214	61	34,808	61	38,936	59	48,627	64	58,884	67	64,595	67	70,613	66	78,677	66	91,626	67	94,825	62	101,222	60
Preference shares	11,377	30	12,118	29	12,924	28	13,000	26	14,313	25	15,085	23	14,992	20	15,473	18	12,460	13	11,287	11	11,341	10	11,023	8	12,382	8	12,426	7
Equity	4,106	11	5,154	12	5,857	12	6,764	13	8,388	15	11,536	18	12,574	17	13,759	16	20,001	21	24,804	23	29,126	24	34,274	25	46,274	30	55,798	33
TOTAL	38,366		42,092		46,974		50,978		57,509		65,557		76,193		88,116		97,056		106,704		119,144		136,923		153,481		169,446	

Table A.25. Finance for Industry Ltd. — group accounts: loans and shares outstanding; £000 (year ending March)

	1974		1975		1976		1977		1978		1979		1980		1981		1982		1983	
	Amount	%	Amount	%	Amount	%	Amount	%	Amount	%	Amount	%	Amount	%	Amount	%	Amount	%	Amount	%
Loans – secured	121,976	69	131,678	71	189,253	63	254,356	67	297,275	68	291,110	67	355,086	68	416,417	71	460,795	72	500,444	74
Loans – unsecured	55,503	31	53,656	29	112,929	37	127,426	33	136,725	32	140,579	33	168,141	32	167,361	29	175,915	28	179,181	26
Total loans	177,479	71	185,334	77	302,182	85	381,782	86	434,000	87	431,689	86	523,227	86	583,778	86	636,710	86	679,625	85
Preference shares	12,486	5	11,378	5	11,091	3	9,286	2	13,109	3	15,524	3	19,200	3	23,264	3	27,055	4	30,766	4
Equity	59,106	24	43,195	18	42,032	12	53,056	12	52,217	10	57,580	11	68,956	11	71,374	11	75,901	10	89,604	11
TOTAL	249,071		239,907		355,305		444,124		499,326		504,793		611,383		678,416		739,666		799,995	

Table A.26. 3i Group plc: loans and shares outstanding; £000 (year ending March)

	1984		1985		1986		1987		1988		1989		1990	
	Amount	%	Amount	%	Amount	%	Amount	%	Amount	%	Amount	%	Amount	%
Loans – secured	518,782	71	556,832	68	547,553	67	581,131	68	674,198	71	762,181	73	829,747	74
Loans – unsecured	208,333	29	265,518	32	271,235	33	267,863	32	276,993	29	278,975	27	290,944	26
Total loans	727,115	79	822,350	77	818,788	73	848,994	69	951,191	65	1,041,156	62	1,120,691	61
Preference shares	39,408	4	51,431	5	68,719	6	86,756	7	126,624	9	190,769	11	243,866	13
Equity	152,233	17	191,393	18	229,775	21	299,397	24	394,664	27	445,945	27	487,773	26
TOTAL	918,756		1,065,174		1,117,282		1,235,147		1,472,479		1,677,870		1,852,330	

Table A.27. *ICFC Ltd.: capital structure; £000 (year ending September or March)*

	Sept. 1946		Sept. 1947		Sept. 1948		Sept. 1949		Mar. 1950		Mar. 1951		Mar. 1952		Mar 1953		Mar. 1954		Mar. 1955		Mar. 1956		Mar. 1957		Mar. 1958		Mar. 1959	
	Amount	%	Amount	%	Amount	%	Amount	%	Amount	%	Amount	%	Amount	%	Amount	%	Amount	%	Amount	%	Amount	%	Amount	%	Amount	%	Amount	%
Share capital	1,500	87	3,000	50	6,000	54	6,000	47	7,500	47	7,500	36	7,500	31	7,500	28	7,500	26	7,500	25	7,500	23	7,500	22	7,500	20	15,000	39
Retained profit/ revenue reserves	-29	-2	-145	-2	-113	-1	-54	0	181	1	542	3	854	3	1,107	4	1,367	5	1,870	6	2,450	7	2,994	9	3,431	9	3,950	10
Shareholders' loans	150	9	3,000	50	5,010	45	6,660	52	8,160	51	12,500	61	15,500	65	17,750	66	19,750	68	20,000	66	22,000	67	22,800	67	25,000	68	19,000	49
Current liabilities, provisions, minority interests, etc	100	6	109	2	127	1	236	2	161	1	83	0	168	1	403	2	415	1	710	2	811	2	713	2	822	2	780	2
TOTAL ASSETS	1,721		5,964		11,024		12,842		16,002		20,625		24,022		26,760		29,032		30,080		32,761		34,007		36,753		38,730	

Table A.28. *ICFC Ltd.: capital structure; £000 (year ending March)*

	1960		1961		1962		1963		1964		1965		1966		1967		1968		1969		1970		1971		1972		1973	
	Amount	%	Amount	%	Amount	%	Amount	%	Amount	%	Amount	%	Amount	%	Amount	%	Amount	%	Amount	%	Amount	%	Amount	%	Amount	%	Amount	%
Share capital	15,000	33	15,000	33	15,000	27	16,667	30	20,000	31	22,500	31	30,000	36	40,000	38	40,000	33	40,000	28	40,000	24	40,000	19	40,000	19	40,000	17
Share premium	0	0	0	0	0	0	833	1	2,500	4	0	0	3,750	4	0	0	0	0	0	0	0	0	0	0	0	0	0	0
Retained profits	4,155	9	4,744	10	6,147	11	6,910	12	7,461	12	8,423	12	8,981	11	8,451	8	9,841	8	10,612	7	11,527	7	11,837	6	13,657	6	22,785	10
Shareholders' loans	15,000	33	15,000	33	12,500	23	10,000	18	8,250	13	8,250	11	6,000	7	0	0	0	0	0	0	0	0	0	0	0	0	0	0
Debentures and other borrowings	10,000	22	10,000	22	20,000	36	20,000	36	24,300	38	30,000	41	30,000	36	45,000	43	60,000	49	70,000	49	81,082	48	94,633	45	124,869	59	127,083	55
Current liabilities, provisions, minority interests, etc.	1,051	2	1,135	2	1,413	3	1,508	3	1,566	2	3,119	4	5,470	6	12,333	12	11,578	10	23,009	16	35,624	21	66,127	31	33,283	16	41,386	18
TOTAL ASSETS	45,206		45,879		55,060		55,918		64,077		72,292		84,201		105,784		121,419		143,621		168,233		212,597		211,809		231,254	

Table A.29. *Finance for Industry Ltd.: consolidated capital structure; £000 (year ending March)*

	1974ª Amount	%	1975 Amount	%	1976 Amount	%	1977 Amount	%	1978 Amount	%	1979 Amount	%	1980 Amount	%	1981 Amount	%	1982 Amount	%	1983 Amount	%
Share capital	60,000	18	85,000	17	85,000	15	89,000	13	89,000	12	100,000	12	100,000	10	100,000	10	100,000	9	115,000	9
Share premium	13,280	4	13,030	3	13,030	2	13,030	2	13,030	2	2,030	0	2,030	0	2,030	0	2,030	0	36,530	3
Retained profit/revenue reserves	24,677	7	6,026	1	9,701	1	12,702	2	23,634	3	34,577	4	43,618	4	70,904	7	88,358	8	59,919	5
Debentures and other borrowings	213,711	65	354,854	72	436,868	76	561,220	79	562,107	77	646,333	75	734,959	75	781,237	75	880,299	78	998,806	78
Current liabilities, provisions, minority interests, etc.	18,738	6	32,603	7	33,170	6	35,640	6	44,995	6	73,941	9	93,839	10	93,483	9	64,130	6	71,905	6
TOTAL ASSETS	330,406		491,513		577,769		711,592		732,766		856,881		974,446		1,047,654		1,134,817		1,282,160	

ª First report and accounts of Finance for Industry Ltd.

Table A.30. *3i Group plc: consolidated capital structure; £000 (year end March); (historic cost basis)*

	1984 Amount	%	1985 Amount	%	1986 Amount	%	1987 Amount	%	1988 Amount	%	1989 Amount	%	1990 Amount	%
Share capital	115,000	8	115,000		115,154	6	115,340	6	115,537	5	232,273	10	232,728	9
Share premium	36,530	2	36,530	2	36,694	2	37,018	2	37,569	2	0	0	957	0
Retained profit/revenue reserves	87,002	6	105,261	6	125,179	7	170,441	9	288,545	14	286,705	12	349,897	14
Debentures and borrowings	1,158,625	78	1,368,680	79	1,476,333	79	1,488,565	76	1,478,309	69	1,579,038	69	1,725,630	68
Current liabilities, provisions, minority interests, etc.	88,432	6	99,903	6	123,327	6	135,641	7	215,963	7	201,805	9	237,550	9
TOTAL ASSETS	1,485,589		1,725,374		1,876,687		1,947,005		2,135,923		2,299,821		2,546,762	

Table A.31. *3i Group plc: capital structure; £000 (year ending March); (investment company basis)*

	1985 Amount	%	1986 Amount	%	1987 Amount	%	1988 Amount	%	1989 Amount	%	1990 Amount	%	1991 Amount	%	1992 Amount	%	1993 Amount	%	1994 Amount	%
Share capital	115,000	20	115,154	14	115,340	11	115,537	11	232,273	18	232,728	18	235,120	19	235,822	18	236,422	17	238,730	13
Share premium	36,530	6	36,694	5	37,018	3	37,569	3	0	0	957	0	1,984	0	2,318	0	2,966	0	3,499	0
Unrealized appreciation reserve	189,036	33	318,898	40	441,244	41	399,437	37	509,463	39	406,242	32	419,090	35	475,301	36	548,206	38	1,021,049	55
Investment realization profits reserve	39,023	7	58,473	7	103,525	10	241,671	22	237,821	18	350,418	27	334,732	28	282,024	22	261,716	18	294,972	16
Revenue reserve	118,997	21	128,386	16	139,406	13	159,361	15	187,838	14	196,692	15	201,149	17	272,715	21	280,990	20	292,381	16
Deferred tax on unrealized appreciation	81,016	14	136,670	17	237,592	22	123,046	11	153,037	12	95,575	7	22,299	2	35,032	3	98,493	7	12,632	1
(subtotal)	*579,602*		*794,275*		*1,074,125*		*1,076,621*		*1,320,432*		*1,282,612*		*1,214,374*		*1,303,212*		*1,428,793*		*1,863,263*	
Borrowing, deferred tax and minorities	1,125,168		1,135,988		1,115,309		1,087,089		1,230,906		1,333,982		1,138,561		1,272,941		1,227,095		970,396	
TOTAL ASSETS LESS CURRENT LIABILITIES	1,704,770		1,930,263		2,189,434		2,163,710		2,551,338		2,616,594		2,352,935		2,576,153		2,655,888		2,833,659	

Appendix II: Examples of Accounts

Table B.1. Inflation Accounting – Extracts from FFI's published Accounts
Group balance sheet, March 31 1982

1981 £ millions			1982 £ millions	
		Non-Monetary Liabilities		
	215.4	Capital and reserves		238.4
100.0		Issued share capital	100.0	
2.0		Share premium	2.0	
42.5		Revaluation reserve	48.0	
70.9		Retained surplus	88.4	
215.4			238.4	
24.9	24.9	Deferred tax on revaluation	26.3	26.3
240.3			264.7	
		Monetary Liabilities		
	781.2	Borrowings		880.3
		Fixed rate, medium and long term—		
488.6		financing fixed rate assets	477.2	
		Short term and medium term variable rate—financing		
204.0		variable rate and droplock loans	261.7	
88.6		Short term—financing money market assets	141.4	
781.2			880.3	
4.7	4.7	Current liabilities less assets	3.7	3.7
49.6	49.6	Deferred tax	55.4	55.4
835.5			939.4	
		Balance of non-monetary liabilities financing monetary		
22.1		assets—brought down	10.2	
857.6			949.6	
	1,075.8	Total non-monetary and monetary liabilities		1,204.1

1981 £ millions			notes	1982 £ millions
		Non-Monetary Assets		
	218.2	Equity shares and properties		254.5
97.1		Equity shares		109.0
56.3		Property		67.3
30.4		Development sites		37.4
34.4		Associated companies and LAIT		40.8
218.2			9	254.5
		Balance of non-monetary		
		liabilities financing monetary		
22.1		assets—carried down		10.2
240.3				264.7
		Monetary Assets		
	746.3	Investment assets		800.9
420.4		Fixed rate Loans and preference shares		426.1
35.2		Hire purchase receivable		16.5
120.1		Leased plant and ships under charter		137.0
575.7				579.6
204.0		Variable rate and droplock loans		261.7
779.7				841.3
33.4		Less provisions		40.4
746.3				800.9
111.3	111.3	Money market assets	148.7	148.7
857.6				949.6
	1,075.8	Total non-monetary and monetary assets		1,204.1

Table B.1 continued. Inflation Accounting – Extracts from FFI's published Accounts
Note on the accounts, 31 March 1982

9. Non-monetary assets

Non-monetary assets have been shown in the balance sheet at their inflation adjusted carrying value

	Historic cost carrying value £ millions	Current valuation £ millions	Inflation adjusted carrying value £ millions
Equity shares	79.7	213.5	109.0
Property	43.4	72.9	67.3
Development sites	30.9	45.3	37.4
Associated companies and LAIT	26.2	42.0	40.8
	180.2	373.7	254.5

The inflation adjusted carrying value of non-monetary assets is calculated by taking the lower of current valuation and adjusted cost. Current valuation is arrived at for these purposes by the following means:

a   property and development sites at professional valuation
b   listed equity investments at mid-market price
c   unlisted equity shares at a price based on the application to the latest reported earnings of price earnings ratios appropriate to similar listed investments, less a discount for non-marketability. Where the company's latest accounts show a loss the valuation is based on half the book amount of net tangible assets.
d   associated companies and LAIT are valued on the same basis as other equity investments.

Whilst the directors consider these methods appropriate for the purpose of preparing inflation accounts it should not be assumed that the assets so valued are currently realizable. Adjusted cost is calculated by indexing the cost by reference to the change in the RPI since the date of purchase or, where specific provision has been made, by indexing the historic cost carrying amount by reference to the change in the RPI since the date of the last provision.

Table B.2 Investment Company Accounting—Extract from the
Supplementary Accounts for 1985–86.

All amounts are in thousands of pounds

	1986	1985
Investment assets		
Equity shares	655,983	434,358
Associated companies & LAIT	36,382	32,015
Investment properties	81,382	79,194
Loans and preference shares	885,916	868,719
Finance lease receivables	220,794	231,090
	1,880,457	1,645,376
Fixed assets in use by the group	22,017	16,387
Trading assets less liabilities	27,789	43,007
	1,930,263	1,704,770
Net borrowings and deferred tax	1,135,988	1,125,168
	794,275	579,602
Capital and reserves		
Share capital	115,154	115,000
Share premium	36,694	36,530
Revenue reserve	128,386	118,997
Capital reserve	58,473	39,023
Revaluation reserve	318,898	189,036
	657,605	498,586
Deferred tax on revaluation	136,670	81,016
	794,275	579,602

Table B.3 Maturity patterns of Contractual Assets and Liabilities —
Extracts from Accounts for 1989–90

Maturity Analyses
a   Contractual maturities of fixed rate borrowings and assets the income from which is at
fixed rates—

All amounts are in thousands of pounds

| | | Repayment of borrowings | | | Net | Cumulative |
	Repayment of borrowings	Swaps	after swaps (note 5)	Capital inflows	inflow (outflow)	net inflow (outflow)
Year to 31 March 1992	177,287	(61,498)	115,789	103,816	(11,973)	(11,973)
1993	151,439	(99,553)	51,886	107,635	55,749	43,776
1994	138,053	(22,697)	115,356	121,182	5,826	49,602
1995	172,144	(75,083)	97,061	79,082	(17,979)	31,623
1996	68,019	15,000	83,019	82,054	(965)	30,658
1997	24,807		24,807	59,931	35,124	65,782
1998	9,301		9,301	59,509	50,208	115,990
1999	65,124	10,149	75,273	37,863	(37,410)	78,580
2000	43	115,000	115,043	29,969	(85,074)	(6,494)
2001	9,444		9,444	16,856	7,412	918
2002	5,000		5,000	11,622	6,622	7,540
2003	10,500		10,500	15,042	4,542	12,082
2004	22,460		22,460	13,844	(8,616)	3,466
2005			0	16,566	16,566	20,032
2006		10,000	10,000	12,993	2,993	23,025
2007		10,000	10,000	10,765	765	23,790
2008		10,000	10,000	9,664	(336)	23,454
2009			0	6,244	6,244	29,698
2010			0	4,497	4,497	34,195
2011 and after	1,149		1,149	32,256	31,107	65,302
	854,770	(88,682)	766,088	831,390	65,302	

Maturity Analyses continued

b Contractual maturities of variable rate borrowings and assets the income from which is at variable rates—

All amounts are in thousands of pounds

	Repayment of borrowings	Swaps	Repayment of borrowings after swaps (note 5)	Capital inflows	Net inflow (outflow)	Cumulative net inflow (outflow)
Year to 31 March 1992		61,498	61,498	51,434	(10,064)	(10,064)
1993	220,000	99,553	319,553	58,254	(261,299)	(271,363)
1994	817	22,697	23,514	58,966	35,452	(235,911)
1995	169,729	75,083	244,812	54,892	(189,920)	(425,831)
1996		(15,000)	(15,000)	53,090	68,090	(357,741)
1997			0	56,666	56,666	(301,075)
1998			0	47,914	47,914	(253,161)
1999		(10,149)	(10,149)	36,448	46,597	(206,564)
2000		(115,000)	(115,000)	80,848	195,848	(10,716)
2001	4,895		4,895	18,028	13,133	2,417
2002			0	14,738	14,738	17,155
2003			0	13,525	13,525	30,680
2004			0	12,832	12,832	43,512
2005			0	9,418	9,418	52,930
2006		(10,000)	(10,000)	4,088	14,088	67,018
2007		(10,000)	(10,000)	5,866	15,866	82,884
2008		(10,000)	(10,000)	10,547	20,547	103,431
2009			0	3,644	3,644	107,075
2010			0	1,218	1,218	108,293
2011 and after	434		434	11,509	11,075	119,368
	395,875	88,682	484,557	603,925	119,368	

Of the variable rate assets, loans totalling £396,810,817 incorporate an option giving the borrower the right for a period during the term of the loan to convert from a variable rate to a fixed rate if and when long term fixed interest rates decline to a level pre-selected by the borrower.

Borrowings include £360,422,000 which, when raised, was the subject of interest swap agreements under which counterparties have undertaken to pay amounts equal to the Group's fixed interest obligations in consideration of amounts payable by the Group equivalent to variable rates of interest.

Borrowings also include an amount of £155,000,000 which when raised was the subject of interest rate swap agreements under which counterparties have undertaken to pay amounts equal to the Group's variable interest obligations in consideration of amounts payable by the Group equivalent to fixed rates of interest.

In addition, the Company has entered into further swap agreements which effectively leave a net amount of £103,615,000 of variable rate borrowings converted to a fixed rate basis.

Appendix II: Examples of Accounts

Table B.4. Statistics 1945 to 1989 (£ million a January 1987 prices). This table, prepared to enable graphical illustrations to be displayed in the Annual Accounts, represents the only consistent series of corporate results ever prepared for 3i. The figures have been recast at 1987 prices and give some indication of the real performance over the greater part of 3i's life until 1989 when the series was discontinued.

Column key — Annual investment: a = Gross investment, b = Repayments & realizations. Portfolio: c = Net cost, d = Surplus on valuation, e = Assets at valuation (c+d), f = Cumulative gross investment. Profit: g = Profit before tax, h = Cumulative profit before tax. Cumulative reserves: i = Reserves, j = Accounts adjustments, k = Surplus on valuation (after tax), l = Capitalization of reserves, m = Total reserves (i+j+k+l), n = Capital subscribed, o = Net asset value (m+n).

Period	Year	a	b	c	d	e	f	g	h	i	j	k	l	m	n	o
Sept. (Year to Sept.)	1946	16.1		16.1		16.1	16.1		0.0	0.0				0.0	20.2	20.2
	1947	53.9		69.0		69.0	69.0		-1.3	0.0				0.0	37.6	37.6
	1948	62.7	-2.3	124.3		124.3	126.6		-1.2	-1.2				-1.2	69.7	68.5
6 mths to Mar.	1949	34.6	-9.2	148.9		148.9	160.5		0.0	-1.2				-1.2	69.3	68.1
Year to Mar.	1950	44.6	-13.4	175.1		175.1	199.6	-1.3	4.5	2.2				2.2	83.6	85.9
	1951	62.4	-13.8	214.8		214.8	251.9	1.2	10.6	5.3				5.3	79.4	84.7
	1952	51.8	-18.6	231.5		231.5	284.3	4.5	17.6	8.8				8.8	73.3	82.1
	1953	43.2	-18.8	247.1		247.1	316.7	6.4	24.4	10.3				10.3	70.5	80.8
	1954	34.5	-20.5	259.4		259.4	348.9	7.8	32.7	13.1				13.1	70.0	83.0
	1955	40.2	-32.9	261.2		261.2	381.8	8.4	43.8	17.4				17.4	68.5	85.9
	1956	57.8	-26.8	278.0		278.0	418.7	11.9	53.6	21.6				21.6	64.8	86.3
	1957	25.3	-17.7	279.0		279.0	434.2	12.1	63.2	25.3				25.3	63.2	88.5
	1958	27.7	-17.9	279.0		279.0	446.6	11.0	70.0	27.7				27.7	61.0	88.7
	1959	32.7	-21.6	285.1		285.1	471.2	8.9	79.9	31.9				31.9	119.8	151.7
	1960	52.7	-31.1	306.7		306.7	523.9	11.2	94.2	33.5				33.5	119.8	153.3
Consol.	1961	58.7	-18.0	341.3		341.3	572.2	14.4	108.0	47.0				47.0	117.4	164.4
	1962	69.1	-34.6	362.1		362.1	618.4	15.7	119.5	45.8				45.8	112.7	158.5
	1963	61.1	-31.3	380.6		380.6	660.0	15.8	132.4	50.2				50.2	127.4	177.6
	1964	80.5	-33.8	422.4		422.4	732.1	16.7	151.6	53.9				53.9	161.6	215.5
	1965	98.3	-29.5	472.7		472.7	798.4	20.8	165.6	59.8				59.8	154.6	214.4
	1966	134.5	-53.4	534.8		534.8	900.8	20.6	180.7	59.4				59.4	222.9	282.3
	1967	168.8	-56.7	628.8		628.8	1,039.0	21.8	199.4	54.1				54.1	254.8	309.0
	1968	126.3	-61.0	673.4		673.4	1,131.2	24.8	218.1	54.2				54.2	246.4	300.7
	1969	179.7	-88.1	725.4		725.4	1,244.3	25.3	230.8	61.5				61.5	231.9	293.4
	1970	179.2	-30.3	838.7		838.7	1,362.5	25.5	245.4	63.4				63.4	220.6	284.0
	1971	215.3	-84.6	901.4		901.4	1,467.4	25.9	248.8	59.8				59.8	202.7	262.5
	1972	207.7	-104.5	940.9		940.9	1,571.5	23.3	258.5	63.1				63.1	188.4	251.5
	1973	193.8	-118.0	945.9		945.9	1,647.1	30.1	269.1	99.3				99.3	174.2	273.5
FCI addition			-239.4	1,072.9		1,072.9	1,451.2		237.0	0.0				0.0	0.0	0.0
FFI Group	1974	208.7	-67.5	1,214.1	30.3	1,244.4	1,660.0	28.8	265.9	94.8		21.1		115.9	281.3	397.2
	1975	190.4	-84.9	1,107.6	21.5	1,129.2	1,560.6	-63.0	156.5	20.0		14.6		34.5	310.4	344.9
	1976	418.8	-101.2	1,231.8	67.2	1,299.0	1,706.8	19.6	148.7	25.4		46.0		71.4	256.2	327.6
	1977	279.9	-111.8	1,223.4	81.7	1,305.2	1,742.1	27.1	154.5	28.4		57.3		85.8	228.4	314.2
	1978	332.3	-192.1	1,261.6	138.3	1,399.9	1,929.1	45.2	186.8	48.4	15.4	96.9		160.7	209.4	370.1
	1979	452.0	-307.1	1,293.8	225.8	1,519.7	2,208.9	47.5	217.6	64.7	18.1	158.2		241.0	190.7	431.7
	1980	432.6	-200.1	1,312.9	189.8	1,502.7	2,277.1	45.0	226.7	68.1	24.5	132.8		225.4	159.2	384.6
	1981	366.8	-288.1	1,244.6	224.2	1,468.8	2,389.0	43.0	244.3	98.3	33.4	137.0		268.7	141.4	410.1
	1982	331.0	-226.4	1,232.5	235.9	1,468.4	2,495.9	35.4	256.8	111.1	27.8	148.4		287.2	128.1	415.3
	1983	312.9	-248.2	1,242.7	311.7	1,554.4	2,698.4	30.0	275.4	71.9	29.1	179.0	42.0	322.0	139.9	461.9
	1984	337.8	-192.2	1,326.3	365.5	1,691.9	2,901.7	43.4	305.1	99.3	49.7	204.4	39.9	393.4	132.9	526.3
	1985	371.4	-191.0	1,430.7	431.0	1,861.7	3,106.7	41.5	329.1	102.5	67.5	203.2	37.6	410.9	125.3	536.2
	1986	328.4	-209.8	1,491.1	545.4	2,036.5	3,308.9	47.7	363.4	129.2	63.7	329.0	36.1	557.9	120.5	678.5
	1987	365.7	-311.8	1,490.6	749.6	2,240.2	3,553.8	66.0	416.1	169.4	72.2	438.6	34.8	714.9	116.6	831.5
	1988	515.6	-372.5	1,583.5	617.5	2,201.0	3,949.9	217.9	620.0	277.1	108.1	383.7	33.6	802.5	113.4	915.9
	1989	517.4	-334.2	1,651.0	724.4	2,375.4	4,178.8	139.4	714.2	255.3	89.2	453.7	134.5	932.7	106.9	1,039.5

Appendix III:
Extracts from the public record of oral evidence to official committees

1. Committee on the Working of the Monetary System (Radcliffe Committee — August 1959, CMND 827)

Minutes of Evidence. Extracts from pages 881–886

Thursday, 15th January, 1959. The Lord Piercy, C.B.E., Chairman, Industrial and Commercial Finance Corporation Ltd., called and examined.

PROFESSOR A. K. CAIRNCROSS: *The Macmillan Committee thought that £200,000 was about the minimum for a public issue; that figure would currently be nearer £1mn.?*
PIERCY: One could still comfortably float an issue of £200,000 or £300,000 in the thirties; one could float issues of £50,000, and my General Manager, Mr Kinross, claims that he floated one or two of £30,000.

THE RT. HON THE LORD RADCLIFFE, C.B.E., CHAIRMAN: *But the main cause for this tendency is the fact that the big source of investment is the large institutions, and that they have specialised requirements of which marketability is an important one?*
PIERCY: Marketability is important; and of course the present-day race of investment managers know perfectly well what they are doing. It was rather the private investor who was attracted by these small issues. They had to be very attractive for my institution to take an interest.

CAIRNCROSS: *Do you draw any distinction when you speak of the small industrialist between the man who is simply expanding and continuing to do what he has been doing, and the man who has got on to something quite new and is assuming risks of a different character? Is the second type of man worse placed?*
PIERCY: The second type of man is very apt to be an inventor who has a notion or invention and then thinks that he ought to set up and manufacture and market it. Apart from his personal friends he would find it very difficult to get backing. A person like that who happens to be persuasive as well as ingenious can still often find someone in the City to back him for a few thousands; that is rather an odd feature of this business. But it will be more difficult for the second class of concern to raise money than any other class.

CAIRNCROSS: *The first class of man already in business and expecting to expand a successful business would be able to quote the profits he has been earning over the past few years and that would weigh a good deal with the various institutions you mentioned?*
PIERCY: A very great deal. When a financier sees no profit record, or only a short profit record, he thinks two or three times before he does anything about it; whereas if he sees a profit record going back some time and reasonably solid, that greatly encourages him.

CAIRNCROSS: *Would you say that most of these institutions, particularly investment trusts, would be likely to insist on a profit record before they made a loan or took an interest?*
PIERCY: Definitely. Investment trusts do not really like unquoted shares.

CAIRNCROSS: *Are there particular insurance companies interested in the finance of small firms?*
PIERCY: One or two: the United Kingdom Provident and, strangely enough, the Clerical, Medical and General had a department that did it. Since I.C.F.C. have been in existence we have been able to lay off a certain amount with various institutions. Of course they then do it on our backs, knowing that we have money in it and are looking after it.

CAIRNCROSS: *Has this possibility of laying off developed in the last ten years?*
PIERCY: Yes. We are rather inclined to lay of a bit of a larger proposition; on the whole that is not very favourable looked upon by some of our shareholders, but we do it.

CAIRNCROSS: ... *Do all the small businessmen who might come to I.C.F.C. know of its existence?*
PIERCY: I think that the small man is not familiar with the opportunities; and, although one might think that his auditor would be more familiar and able to tell him, that is not generally true either.

THE VISCOUNT HARCOURT: *How do most of your clients in the I.C.F.C. come to you? Are they brought to you by some adviser, such as their own accountant or bank manager?*
PIERCY: Mostly by auditors, firms of chartered accountants, though a good many come direct.

RADCLIFFE: *It is a constant interest with I.C.F.C. to get its services more widely known in the country?*
PIERCY: Yes. At the outset for many years we were shy of piling up expenses and the amount of advertising done was very little. Even today it is not large. We relied at the beginning very largely upon going about giving talks. I gave many addresses of that sort, and so did other people in the Corporation; we had a lot of notice in the Press, and accountants took a good deal of interest in us. But I think that we ought to have done more to make ourselves known, and we are stepping up our propaganda.

CAIRNCROSS: *Do you find substantial differences between different parts of the country in their resort to I.C.F.C. and the need for finance of this kind?*

PIERCY: Rather little gets through to us in Scotland because the bankers intercept most of it. We have no complaint on that, of course. Otherwise I do not know that I have any special comment to make. We have been extremely well established in Birmingham where we seem to take people's fancy. We find it very difficult in Manchester. It partly depends on personalities; we sent a man whom we thought very enterprising to Leicester, but he had no success; another man made great business there, and Leicester is by now a small Birmingham. It rather turns on the selling.

CAIRNCROSS: *You do not think that a good deal depends also on industrial structure? You were discussing the Glasgow area, for instance, which I gather is probably pretty well supplied because there are relatively few requirements whereas in Birmingham I should expect something different?*

PIERCY: I entirely agree. There is a great deal of small and moderate sized industry in Birmingham, and much less of that in Scotland, even in Glasgow and areas round about it. That is perfectly true.

PROFESSOR R. S. SAYERS: *The geographical spread of the banks and their financial connections with the small businessman would make them very natural points of contact, and you must have thought of the banks as being people who were very likely to bring a good deal of this business to you. Have they in fact done so?*

PIERCY: We started with precisely the thought you mention; I think the first literary work I did in the first week or two was to draw up a leaflet that I hoped the banks would send round. One or two did send it to a limited number of branches. We have always found the banks a little sticky about that sort of thing. I think myself that, if there had been a ready co-operation on the part of the banking system locally, we should have done a good deal more business than we did; but you must appreciate that the banks among themselves are of course intensely competitive, and it is always possible to think that we may be treading on the borders of banking business. At the very beginning in consultation with one of my most experienced City directors, Lord Blackford, we invented the formula that we would compete with everyone but not the banks. We have stuck to that, but it is difficult to get that over on the other side. The position of the banks is therefore a little ambivalent. We have a good deal of business put up to us through the banks in certain regions, not much in other regions. We have discovered with rather a shock lately that there are a great many branch managers and bankers of that sort who do not recognise the name of I.C.F.C. or know what it is that we do. We are now taking steps to remedy that. You may have noticed the new advertisement in *The Banker* last month. We are starting to carry our gospel to the practising banker.

RADCLIFFE: *You spoke just now of a certain ambivalence of the attitude of the banks*

*towards I.C.F.C. It was not quite clear as to what you attributed this ambivalence of atti-
tude to. You are the bankers' venture on the one hand; on the other they seem not very
anxious that you should develop to your full possible potentialities?*

PIERCY: It stems from two feelings. The main one is that, with or without justification, a great many bankers, including a number of general managers and even
in my experience chief general managers, believe that somehow or other I.C.F.C.
competes with them and from that point of view they rather dislike it. Coupled
with that I believe that it was with a certain reluctance the banking community in
the City undertook this project, that many of those at the beginning remained
believing that the whole thing was unnecessary and that it could not succeed. In
that kind of way there was always an attitude that I.C.F.C. was bit of a cuckoo in
the nest.

CAIRNCROSS: *May I put a point to you about the man who has an invention? From the
social point of view any innovations carried out either by small or large firms are particularly important to countries like ours, more important perhaps than expansion of a firm
doing what a larger firm may already be doing. You do not specifically single out this type
of individual in your paper, but you did agree either that he had perhaps greater difficulty
than most people in raising finance. Do you see anything that can be done for a man of that
type, who has perhaps suffered more than others from the extinction of private backers,
through I.C.F.C. or through other institutions? As I understand it an inventor would be
unlikely to want to part with the equity, and would want a loan. At the same time he
would have very little to offer by way of backing for the loan, and it would be necessary
therefore to offer money that was at considerable risk, on terms that assumed that it would
eventually be repaid. I do not suppose that your interest rates go very high; but do you feel
that there may be a place for loans to persons in this position at rates above the current
level?*

PIERCY: We have never done anything explicitly like that in I.C.F.C., because we
have been rather forced into the good business in recent years; but I have often
thought of it. At the present time we are taking on whatever we can see; a lot of
these small firms are starting up in the electronic field. We have backed a few
inventions, some on a large scale, some on a small scale, and I would hesitate to
say how it has come out on balance. We have burned our fingers on one or two
occasions.

CAIRNCROSS: *Would you, or other financial institutions, be disposed to make loans in
such circumstances if it were possible to lay off part of the risk with some central institution which would, for commission, accept the risks and stand part of any total loss that
resulted, and if at the same time that central institution had at its disposal the technical
advisory services to assist you in judging whether the invention were one with real
prospects or one not meriting further consideration?*

PIERCY: The N.R.D.C. answers that to a certain extent, although their emphasis
is on development. We are always on the look out for something we can do in col-

laboration with them. At one time we had a lot of discussions about printed circuits when they were much less well known than now. We never actually succeeded in finding one, but I think the idea is good. My impression is that the N.R.D.C. in past years has done it in some instances. There was a project for using isotopes, which they laid off among three or four institutions, of whom we were one.

CAIRNCROSS: *N.R.D.C. are only presumably interested in inventions in which they themselves possess the rights. I am speaking of private inventors who may be rather sensitive about parting with their rights. I would not have thought therefore that would necessarily be the best institution to which to recommend a private inventor to look for further assistance on finance?*
PIERCY: If some subsidiary organisation were set up under the D.S.I.R., staffed partly by them and partly by financial people, they could employ them in this way in backing a thing if there was suitable participation from the inventor and from other financiers. It would be worth gambling a million or half a million on that to see how it went.

MR W. E. JONES: *Suppose that you have applications for loan capital which greatly outstrip your capacity to meet those applications, though they may be good and very desirable loan applications; have you any policy in relation to the proportion of the amounts required that you will lend, say a tenth or half of the amount applied for? What sort of situation would be remaining to the small firm in consequence of what you are able to do? In other words, are there occasions when, because of the size of the problem and the limitation of funds, you are not able to fill the gap?*
PIERCY: On the broad point as you have stated it, yes. As regards these applications we cannot do, we are of course frequently slicing down applications. I was looking at one yesterday which began at £90,000 and is ending at £45,000. But that is a case of a project that can be rearranged. Broadly speaking we cannot do any good, as a rule, by providing one-tenth of the amount for a particular project. It is not good, if an extension to the factory costs £25,000, to offer £5,000. They would go to the banks for that sort of thing, not to us. What we have tried to do in the past is, when we have had a suitable proposition and our funds were tight, as they have been for some years, to put it in a form in which we can interest some insurance company to take a part of it. Sometimes we have been able to make suggestions which put it in another form and another context. We quite commonly say: 'if you make an issue to shareholders we will under-write it and find ourselves 30 or 40 per cent of it'. But we have had to pass by a good deal of business rather on the lines of taking the better and leaving the worse, which is not really very good practice.

MR G. WOODCOCK: *What is the spread of the rates you charge?*
PIERCY: At any given moment the difference between the highest and lowest rates we charge is hardly one per cent; more like a half.

CAIRNCROSS: *Is that a deliberate decision that you should not have a wide spread of rates?*
PIERCY: No. The policy is not to charge high rates. We are regulated very much by the rates of insurance companies; they are really the pace makers in all these rates on loans, particularly on property and things like that. We stick rather close to them. We go rather for the lower end of the market than the higher end as regards rates.

CAIRNCROSS: *Does it not mean that you take the rather better risks?*
PIERCY: It all depends. In the last few years our funds have been somewhat limited and we have had to take the better risks. Broadly we know that we have to accept a certain amount of risk that is not very good, and our shoulders are pretty broad, at any rate for smaller amounts from £5,000 to £25,000.

CAIRNCROSS: *It has been suggested that you are sometimes inhibited from higher rates be cause you feel it might give rise to criticism in Parliament or elsewhere?*
PIERCY: No. We have never really come under the attention of Parliament, certainly not in the matter of rates, or giving loans or not giving them.

CAIRNCROSS: *. . . You must find, I take it, that it is quite expensive to investigate some of these businesses in relation to the ultimate earnings you make on loans to them?*
PIERCY: Yes. Loans of £5,000, £10,000 and £15,000 cannot pay us, but they are part of our business and we do as many as we can.

CAIRNCROSS: *Do you in those cases recommend a borrower to make use of hire purchase, which presumably economises waste of this description?*
PIERCY: I cannot say we do, because we regard hire purchase as extremely expensive. In recent years we have sometimes contemplated placing loans upon an instalment basis rather like hire purchase, thinking that in a context like a development area it would be much better security, but basing it on low rates instead of high rates. On the other hand, we do not necessarily grab every business that comes along. We very often find ourselves steering businesses in other directions; but not very much towards hire purchase.

CAIRNCROSS: *Do you make a charge to the borrower for the cost of investigations?*
PIERCY: Not specifically. Originally we did not make any charges at all; now when the business is accepted we make a charge of about one per cent which covers everything except the borrower's own legal expenses.

SAYERS: *When you deliberately take on these small propositions, knowing that they cannot pay after taking into account the cost of investigation, the rationale of your decision, I suppose is that among them there will be some winners who will grow?*
PIERCY: I do not know that we are very consciously swayed by that, although it does sometimes turn out like that. It is rather a feeling that, if there is a need for money which they cannot raise conveniently elsewhere and there is a case for them having the money, then we ought to provide it. Of course, a loan from us of

£5,000 or £10,000 makes a concern happier and in turn enables them to get more facilities from the bank. So that in that way we are probably doing more than £5,000 worth of good in loaning £5,000.

SAYERS: *The loss you take on is it justified by the fact that you are preserving in good running order a concern that is socially worth preserving?*
PIERCY: Yes. Our criteria in social worthiness would be, on the one hand, whether it does show some capacity for making a reasonable profit, having regard to its circumstances, and secondly, whether it is a reasonably decent, well laid out show and the people running it are the sort of people who ought to get a chance of that kind. If I had a philosophy on the subject, it would be that lots of men can be socially extremely useful as leaders in a small company who would not find a comparably suitable niche in larger industries.

2. Expenditure Committee (Trade and Industry Sub-committee) Session 1970–71

Minutes of Evidence, Wednesday, 20th October 1971—House of Commons (320-xvi). Extracts from pages 368–377

Question from the Chairman of the Committee—Mr William Rodgers

Do you find no difficulty in following a middle course between the public interest, as you describe it, or your role as you believe it to be, and maximising the profitability of your investment?
LORD SHERFIELD: No, I do not think we do. We are conscious that we must perform both functions, but it does not cause us a great deal of difficulty?
MR L.V.D. TINDALE: I think the term 'maximising return on investment' is a very hard one, and we must also look at the period over which one is going to maximise return. If we were merely looking at a one-year or two-year time cycle, then I think one would run the Corporation on a different basis in certain areas than we have done in the past. If we take a very long-term view, I think we are satisfied that what we are doing is reconciling the two objectives.
SHERFIELD: We lend money for long periods, up to twenty years, and we tend as a matter of policy to stay with our customers and carry them along until hopefully they are ready for a flotation.

Questions from Mr Hughes

In paragraph 28 of document M.22 (a) you say 'T.D.C. takes no part in the day-to-day management of its customers' affairs but keeps a close watch on progress . . .'. In this Committee we are looking at how Government keeps a close watch on the money that it lends. Can I ask in some detail what you do in the way of keeping a watch, and what sanctions you can put on if, having kept a watch, you are not very happy with what you see?

SHERFIELD: Perhaps I could first of all say that I think the financing of innovation has certain special features. A number of the companies financed by T.D.C. are new companies. They may consist of two or three people. They may relate to one particular innovation. The company may not have much experience in marketing, and so on. So that particularly in the case of technological innovation, but also to some extent in other cases too, we keep in particularly close touch with the progress of the company. We do it either through our branches or, in the case of T.D.C., sometimes through the management of that company.

And, if necessary, as you say here, you may take the right to put a director in?
SHERFIELD: We may ask to appoint a director. We may detail one of our industrial advisers to be very close to the company and keep in contact with what they are doing on a week-to-week basis. In general, we have no settled procedure. We treat every company that we finance, or have relations with, separately. We finance them in various ways to suit their needs. We give them advice or not, as they may wish. But there are special situations in which we keep in particularly close touch.
MR TINDALE: We like to think that the greater part of our work is done by influence, and because we are proposing something which is a sensible course. We essentially deal with the smaller company. On both sides there is always the knowledge that if this company is going to go well or need assistance over a bad patch we are going to have to get together again. This operates as a very good lever on a management in the company to take account of what we are saying.

Can I turn to another paragraph in this paper, page 382, paragraph 35, Industrial Mergers Limited was set up in 1967. Did at any time the activities of this part of your operation come into conflict with, or run parallel to, I.R.C.'s?
SHERFIELD: During the period when I.R.C. was operating we kept in very close touch with them. There was never any question of conflict between the two organisations. Indeed, on more than one occasion I.R.C. passed over to us certain tasks, such as producing a rationalisation scheme for some section of industry, which they either thought we were better set up to do than they were or because it was rather too small for them to deal with. So throughout the whole period— and I think you can confirm this—we were in close touch with them, and we did collaborate in certain areas where it was desirable that we should do so.

Following from that, would the presence of public money in your hands inhibit your activities?
SHERFIELD: If it were desired that we should operate in any particular respect as an agent for the Government, I think we could handle the Government's money. I do not think it would inhibit our general operations.
MR TINDALE: That is an extremely complex question, of course. I agree with my Chairman's general hypothesis. On the other hand, I firmly believe myself in the need for competition in financing small companies because it is highly desirable

to keep the maximum number of judgement centres, essentially deciding whether the company is credit-worthy. Therefore anything which inhibits the number which can compete in this market is, to my mind, in the end undesirable for the market. If all the users had Government money, which essentially is subsidised money when viewed in commercial terms, then there would be no problem. But if one were to be preferred user, as BOTAC is the preferred user in development areas, it does create this problem of the number of judgement centres.

Question from Mr Morrison

Can I look at the same question from another viewpoint. Are there any fields for investment into which you would like to enter but which, for some reason you have been unable to do so, obviously because you have not been able to persuade someone to make use of your services? If the answer is 'Yes', it must follow to some extent that you are taking a longer view than a view which can be said to be rather more in the national interest, I would have thought?

SHERFIELD: I do not think there are many fields of investment in which we are not involved in one way or another.

MR TINDALE: Over the period of the credit squeeze, for example, we have had qualitative directives from the Bank of England, the net result of that has probably been that we are not as heavily involved in, let us say, commercial activities as we might have been if those directives had not been in existence.

SHERFIELD: But those directives representing public policy were directives which we could not ignore for whatever commercial reason; we naturally observed them.

Question from Mr Butler

Lord Sherfield, you say that you could handle public money, but why do you think it should be necessary to have any?

SHERFIELD: I myself am not advocating that we should have public money. All I was saying was that we should be able to handle it if we were so asked, but we are not seeking to be asked. If I might add one more point. As Mr Tindale has said there will be difficulties. I think we could overcome them, but there will be difficulties in developing public money, and we would, therefore, expect—at least, I would expect that the conditions on which it was to be deployed would be carefully defined in advance. In other words, we would need instructions. Just as the Bank of England gave instructions in terms of lending, so in any field in which we were asked to act we would need instructions. In other words, it should be clear what the policy was in relation to that particular money.

Questions from Mr Rodgers

Your table 3, dealing with financial facilities analysed by regions, seems to show a rela-

tively small proportion of your facilities deployed in the northern region, a very small proportion in Northern Ireland, and a small proportion, though less small relatively, in Wales. The view is taken that these parts of the country are most in need of industrial restructuring. As Mr Maxwell-Hyslop says, these are regions which are relatively less sophisticated in their access to funds. Do you make any particular efforts here, or do you concentrate your main effort in London and the South East and the Midlands which, between them absorb over 50 per cent of your resources?

SHERFIELD: We make an equal effort in every part of the United Kingdom through our branches. I am excluding Northern Ireland where we really operate in association with the Northern Ireland Development Corporation, with them, but in these areas in the north there are not all that number of our type of company. They are either very large industries, basic industries, or the investment is done under development area legislation.

You say you make an equal effort, you do not think in the public interest there is a case for unequal effort?

MR TINDALE: We do make an unequal effort, in fact. We have branches in Newcastle and in Cardiff, both of which by the standards of the other branches are less profitable, shall we put it that way. In fact, when we look at the northern area, although recently this has been very difficult because of economic circumstances, as we know in terms of population or anything else—pounds per head— we are slightly down in the total average but not all that down. We believe really it to be the result of the structure of industry, the heavy industries which would predominate. We did an analysis of this about six years ago in respect of Wales, and came up with the answer that our Welsh office was doing as much as we could expect, having regard to what the other areas of the country were doing. Also, the development area loans are a major factor. It is rather like Agricultural Mortgage. A good bit of what we would be doing in the non-development parts of the country is done by the development area loans.

Questions from Mr Barnett

You said before that you were a commercial organisation primarily. Why then do you make an unequal effort in the regions?

SHERFIELD: I think I said that we acted commercially but we were not unaware of the national interest considerations, and I think I also said in reply to an earlier question that it was not a great problem to us to take account of both these considerations, and at the same time produce a proper return to our shareholders.

It was Mr Tindale who said you made an unequal effort. I am not clear whether this was intended to mean at least partially altruistic rather than commercially?

MR TINDALE: I think we are in a grey area here. We put more resources into, let us, say, the northern area than a strict calculation of the investment that we have in there would justify taken commercially as a whole. We do so though in the belief, or shall we say the hope, that we will get the investment out of that effort to justify the return. You can never operate on an average right the way across the country, obviously. There will always be some which are better than others, but where the effort is justified.

If the Government were to say to you 'We would like you to invest in that industry or in that region and it may in the short and medium term not necessarily be as commercially viable as other projects which you would have in mind', would you consider this compatible with your function which you said was almost entirely commercial?

SHERFIELD: If there were a question, as clearly there would be, that we should lend at uncommercial or subsidised rates, then I think we would have to say that we would certainly do what the Government asked us to, but we would require the funds to enable us to deal with that type of operation.

It is generally more likely to be more complicated than that. It is not likely to be a matter of subsidy of a particular amount. It is more likely to be that the particular project may be the sort that you would not otherwise lend money to at all because of the degree of risk or the length of time by which you could hope to see a return. The point I am trying to get at is this. I thought I understood you to say earlier that your type of organisation is not suitable to mix with an organisation that was also involved with primarily the national interest, say like the I.R.C. or similar agency. Would that be summing up correctly what you said?

SHERFIELD: I was talking in general, but it could apply equally to I.C.F.C. I thought it was not for a corporation or a body to set themselves up as a judge of the national interest. They may, of course, be aware of considerations of national interest, but if we are asked to act in ways which involve subsidy, or in lending on uncommercial terms, then I think we should require—we or any other body—fairly precise indications of the criteria which we should apply, and also be provided with funds to meet that particular type of operation.

So this would, in effect, be a separate function. There would be two separate functions then, your commercial side and this side which is involved with the national interest?

SHERFIELD: Precisely, it would go in a separate department.

3. House of Commons Trade and Industry Committee— Competitiveness of UK Manufacturing Industry.

Minutes of Evidence, Wednesday 15th December 1993
(HC 41-iv) extracts from pages 358–364

Evidence given on behalf of 3i Group plc by John Platt, Executive Director (Regional Investment Activities) and John Kirkpatrick, Chief Industrial Adviser.

Questions from Chairman—Mr Richard Caborn

During the discussion with the previous witnesses from NatWest, they spoke about the cost of the small investment. Given that cost, how is it that 3i can deliver that which many other institutions cannot?

MR PLATT: That is a good question. Certainly providing risk capital in smallish amounts is an expensive exercise. The decision that 3i took some years ago was to set up a network of offices across the country. So we operate out of 17 offices outside head office. We try to do a volume of business. On that basis we can make the model work. What we cannot do is to provide, and it would be uncommercial, a lot of hands-on time commitment in support of the investment. So we have developed a model which basically is as a hands-off investor. We select the businesses which we think justify our support. We put the money in behind those businesses and then, subject to a limited amount of liaison and support, basically we have to leave the management team to run their own business. On that basis and by decentralising our activities across the country, we can make a commercial return.

Why cannot the City institutions do that?—They probably have a greater infrastructure and more branch offices than you have. Why cannot they do that?

MR PLATT: If they made the investment in the network, I guess they could do the same. One or two of our direct competitors have done that in a limited way. National Westminster's County Bank, for instance, has a network of six offices. In a sense they are following our model. But most venture capital institutions have tended to operate out of London and have focused themselves on a smaller number of situations, but have put in a more direct, closer involvement on time. They do more of a hands-on business.

Question from Mr J. Butterfill

Is it not true that one of the reasons why people are frightened of outside equity is that they think an external investor will be looking to the short-term and to realise gain quickly and that he will impose constraints on the way they run the business which they do not see in the long-term interests of the business? That is something that many entrepreneurs have expressed to me.

MR PLATT: I agree that part of the difficulty is a lack of understanding of what the alternatives mean—an understanding by a small business that allowing an institution to participate in its equity does not mean that they lose control of the business and so on. So there is an education to be carried out. Advisers and other bodies need to spread that word. What can we do about it? What we try to do is advertise ourselves quite widely. Through our regional network we spend a lot of time trying to contact businesses in the areas which we think would be suitable for venture capital and try to promote ourselves. But there is a preference by small businesses if they can get by on bank debt. That is a matter of education. That is where I think venture trusts may well play a good role in encouraging the greater use of outside equity. How acceptable it will be will depend on the conditions that the venture trusts attach to the money that they put in. One of the difficulties with the BES, when it was investing in trading businesses, was that the providers were looking for an exit after five years. That might not have suited the company's stance, but because the BES wanted its money back, they had to repay it. By contrast, we do not impose such an exit requirement on the business. We will put in our money and say we will exit as and when it suits the business cycle. We are not only hands-off in the sense that we do not want to sit on their board, but we do not require an exit.

Questions from Dr M. Clark

Could you tell us what rate of return 3i expect to get?
MR PLATT: It depends on the proposition and the risks that we perceive in that proposition. At one end of the scale we would provide long-term loans purely for the benefit of the margin on those loans, which might typically be 2 per cent to 3 per cent.

Above bank rate? Or 2 per cent to 3 per cent full stop?
MR PLATT: Above bank rate. We are not that altruistic. But that would be where a pure loan is provided, because we can see the loan being serviced and that would be secure. At the other end of the scale, if we were financing a start-up, where we are putting in risk money, we would be looking for some form of running return by way of interest or divided plus a stake in the business, which might typically be 25 per cent of the shares.

Could you quantify the rate of return that you might be looking for?
MR PLATT: For a start-up we would want to see ourselves with the potential of a return of over, say, 40 per cent.

Question from Mr J. Butterfill

Is that an IRR?
Mr Platt: IRR. Let me explain if I may how we get to that. That is not a running return that we would expect the company to service year on year. The only servicing that we could expect from the company year on year would be some yield by way of interest or dividend. The majority of that 40 per cent IRR would come from the uplift in the value of the shares when the business is ultimately sold. And the business is not itself having to service it. That return comes because the shares become valuable enough to provide our capital profit.

Questions from Dr M. Clark

Do these two extremes that you have mentioned—one at 2 per cent to 3 per cent above bank rate and the other at 40 per cent overall, in the way you have described—at times excluded manufacturing companies which feel that they cannot afford to participate at that rate of return?

MR PLATT: No, certainly not. My colleague might like to come in here a minute. But perhaps I could just say that as a business we do not try to pick sectors. Our policy to invest in any business which we believe has the management and the potential to be a worthwhile investment. So we do not pick sectors. As it happens about 50 per cent of the investment we make is in manufacturing. We like manufacturing. Manufacturing is suited to our long-term type of investment.

MR KIRKPATRICK: The sort of 40 per cent returns that my colleague mentioned is really at the top high-tech end. You have to appreciate that you will get some returns like that from a few to compensate for the ones that are going to fail—because some will fail. In fact we are a bit disappointed if some do not fail, because that means we are not taking enough risk. On the ones that are left we have to make enough to compensate for the ones that we thought would fly but through a variety of circumstances did not. On the manufacturing side, manufacturing industry tends to be in sectors that are that much more stable. But because of that they tend to be that much more forward-looking. So you are going for the long-term because the industry itself is not changing very rapidly. So you cannot, as with say electronics or bio-technology, be looking for a very quick uplift. Some manufacturing is actually going for a long slow haul and you have to go for that long slow haul with them.

Are the schemes you describe that your company offer typical of the venture capital sector?

MR PLATT: In general terms, yes. Where we are probably different from most of our competitors is that we will look at amounts probably smaller than some will. Many of them will have a minimum level of investment higher than our level. Some of them would not be interested in participating, for example, in start-ups whereas we will invest across the range of a company's life—start-up, expansion, change of ownership, rescue bid. A lot of them are more focused on the change of ownership area of the product. But in terms of how we structure it, we are not too concerned I suppose.

Questions from Mr R. Caborn

It is quite intriguing what you say about your model against the NatWest model where you are hands-off. How do you follow up your investment? How do you monitor that?

MR PLATT: We do it in a number of ways. We do obtain information from the business. One of the disciplines that we would impose would be to ask for regular information.

How regular?

MR PLATT: It would depend on the company. But certainly monthly for youngish businesses; less frequently perhaps for well established businesses. We would look for plans once a year and have review meetings with the business. The level of involvement will vary. At times of crisis, it becomes a daily involvement. When the business is going strongly, that involvement can become more detached. But obtaining information and disciplining the business to provide information is one way in which we can help. The other thing we would do is to reinforce the management by introducing non-executive directors. These are not individuals who are on our payroll typically—occasionally but very rarely—but individuals whom we think have substantial experience in a particular area which can add to the company's management. If we believe that the management team needs some strengthening, we would introduce a non-executive director.

Is that a relatively new innovation?
Mr PLATT: It is something that has grown in the past five years, yes. We now run a register of 200 to 300 people who we think have a lot to offer. We probably introduce about 80 a year to businesses in which we invest. They will be jobs from chairman through to non-executive director with a financial input or marketing bias.

Questions from Mr M. Clapham

Looking at your submission of 25th August, it appears that you have investments totalling £2.7 billion in some 3,700 firms across a wide manufacturing base. That indicates a great deal of experience. From your experience of dealing with manufacturing industry, would 3i say that there is a problem of short-termism? If so what are the characteristics? How might we start to get over short-termism?
Mr PLATT: We deliberately set out to be long term. We set out to be complementary to the clearing banks. So from the very early days we would not provide a loan of less than five years. Typically our loans would be over 15 to 20 years and the share capital. So we complement the banks in that sense. I am not conscious of short-termism as being so much of a problem among the providers of finance. I would say that there is a short-termism among the users of finance. As I said earlier, I think that a lot of smaller companies are reluctant to make the long-term commitment and will depend on short-term money when in fact they ought to take long-term money. That is an issue. We have recently done a comparative study on financing in European countries and the UK. We found that in Germany, for example, small businesses are more heavily borrowed than businesses in the UK, but they have a much greater proportion of long-term debt; whereas in the UK businesses have a much higher proportion of short-term debt. I do not think that this is just a problem on the supply side. It is a problem of demand. A smaller business wants to retain flexibility and is nervous about the long-term commitment.

From what you have said about 3i and the way that 3i looks at investment in the long-term, how would you go about assessing innovation before you make an investment in a company?

MR KIRKPATRICK: With great difficulty! You have to look basically at what the track record of the company has been to date and, as we mentioned before, how competent are the management in doing what they have done and how capable they are of growing with the business to do the innovation that they are talking about. Frankly, you have to do as much of verification on those innovative ideas as you possibly can and ensure that they have done it. Sometimes you would be right, hopefully in the vast majority of cases, and sometimes you would be wrong, but you must try to have fall-back situations all the time, especially if it is, say, a manufacturing company going for a blue sky development. The safer way is to ensure that if it goes wrong, in the worst case it will not destroy the business. So you will have a couple of tries at it. In my experience, certainly in start-ups, if the management team does not rewrite its business plan about three times in the first nine months there is something wrong. They do not normally get it right first time. You have to do it that way. It is not easy. It is a combination of a lot of objectivity and, frankly, a bit of subjectivity as well.

Question from Mr M. Bruce

I understand that. Do you feel that there is a role for you to help improve our industrial base? This inquiry is about the competitiveness of our manufacturing industry. One of the problems with this type of inquiry is that you get all the good examples. People come to tell you what good things they are doing. But in fact there are not enough people doing that. That seems to be the simple problem. Now that we have got more competitiveness, what role does an organisation like yours have to play? Clearly, you are an important player in the game.

MR PLATT: Clearly there are deficiencies which we have been commenting on. One of them at the moment is start-ups. I am not talking here about what is often thought to be the difficulty, that is the very small business. I am talking about the good size businesses, where it is quite difficult to find institutional start-up finance to come in alongside ourselves. In that sense there is an issue which needs addressing. I think that bodies such as the venture trusts, which have been mentioned, will go someway to helping them. In one of our earlier papers to a previous committee we mentioned a substantial start-up proposal with which we have been struggling for 18 months. That is an import substitution business which we would like to finance and we are finding it difficult to find partners. We can exert the influence we have as a market leader in our own industry to try to get other people in our industry to support these types of ventures and we certainly do so. The other area in which we have a role to play is an educational one of trying to persuade businesses about the benefits of long-term capital and sharing the risk. We work on that all the time. There is a big educational problem.

Question from Mr J. Butterfill

On the point of international comparisons, we have had conflicting evidence about the general quality of British management. For example, some people have said that it is not as good as elsewhere and has deficiencies; others have said that in their opinion it is at least as good as what they find in continental Europe. You have some experience in international markets. What assessment do you have of the general qualities of British management? What do you think are its strengths and weaknesses?

MR KIRKPATRICK: The best British management in my opinion is probably better than anybody else's. The reason for that is that they are if anything more flexible and have been more able to learn and pick up the good traits of all the other better management teams, whether they are Japanese, American or whatever. Where the UK management teams are still probably deficient is in the medium sector area, where they are still probably enthusiastic but lacking in information and knowledge of what they should be doing. That is gradually improving. It is improving a lot because, for example, of Nissan coming into the North-East and gradually improving their sub-contractors, or Marks and Spencer improving their sub-contractors. So it is gradually happening. If you ask me the direct question: is British management *in toto* better or worse than the Germans or French, I would say no, they are not worse. I would say that they are on a plane and in some cases a lot better. Where they are having to have a harder job than, say, the French or the Germans, is that they are taking a lot of their industrial companies from a very mature and established position and trying to make a lot of change. In Germany, you have people starting up immediately after the war with a relatively greenfield site and able to go. A lot of the UK companies have had to change from a very established and entrenched position. One of the best examples that we should be proud of is someone like Rover. Rover started off in the late 1970s and 1980s and now they are very very good. But it has taken a lot of hard work and a lot of very good management to get there. I certainly rate people like that very highly.

Abbreviations

AEA	Atomic Energy Authority
AMP	Australian Mutual Provident
ARD	American Research and Development
BES	Business Expansion Scheme
BIDC	Bankers Industrial Development Company
BIMBO	Buy-in management buy-out
BLEC	Business Loans and Equity Capital (Australia)
BOTAC	Board of Trade Advisory Committee
BVCA	British Venture Capital Association
CBI	Confederation of British Industry
CLCB	Committee of London Clearing Bankers
CEO	Chief Executive Officers' committee of the CLCB
CFI	Credit for Industry
CIC	Capital Issues Committee
CID	Charterhouse Industrial Development Company
CISCO	City Group for Smaller Companies
CMBOR	Centre for Management Buy-out Research at Nottingham University
CN	Credit National (France)
CPO	Convertible Preferred Ordinary Shares
CPWDF	Committee on Post-War Domestic Finance
CPWE	Committee on Post-War Employment
DATAC	Development Areas Treasury Advisory Committee
DDS	Deep Discounted Securities
DEC	Digital Equipment Corporation (USA)
ECSC	European Coal and Steel Community
EDITH	Estate Duties Investment Trust
EIB	European Investment Bank
ERM	Exchange Rate Mechanism
FCI	Finance Corporation for Industry
FFI	Finance for Industry
FFS	Finance for Shipping
GLC	Greater London Council

HP	Hire Purchase
ICFC	Industrial and Commercial Finance Corporation
IMC	Industrial Mortgage Corporation
IMF	International Monetary Fund
IPO	Initial Public Offerings
IRC	Industrial Reorganisation Corporation
JBK	John Blythe Kinross
JDB	Japan Development Bank
KfW	Kreditanstalt für Wiederaufbau (Germany)
LAIT	London Atlantic Investment Trust
LCC	London County Council
LIBOR	London Interbank Offered Rate
LSE	London School of Economics and Political Science
MBI	Management buy-in
MBO	Management buy-out
NBC	North British Canadian Investment Trust
NCT	National Chamber of Trade
NEB	National Enterprise Board
NIB	National Investment Board
NIESR	National Institute of Economic and Social Research
NP	National Provincial Bank
NRDC	National Research Development Corporation
NTT	Nippon Telegraph and Telephone Corporation (Japan)
NUMAS	National Union of Manufacturers Advisory Service
RE	Research Exploitation
RPI	Retail Price Index
SARA	Special Areas Reconstruction Association
SBA	Small Business Administration (USA)
SBIC	Small Business Investment Companies (USA)
SEC	Securities and Exchange Commission (USA)
SIB	Securities and Investments Board
SMFC	Ship Mortgage Finance Company
SMT	Securities Management Trust
TDC	Technical Development Capital
UDT	United Dominions Trust
USM	Unlisted Securities Market

Index